NEW PERSPECTIVES ON

XML

3rd Edition

COMPREHENSIVE

Patrick Carey
Sasha Vodnik

Australia • Brazil • Mexico • Singapore • United Kingdom • United States

New Perspectives on XML
3rd Edition, Comprehensive

Product Director: Kathleen McMahon

Senior Director of Development: Marah Bellegarde

Senior Product Manager: Jim Gish

Product Development Manager: Leigh Hefferon

Senior Content Developer: Kathy Finnegan

Marketing Director: Michele McTighe

Senior Marketing Manager: Eric La Scolla

Developmental Editor: Pam Conrad

Composition: GEX Publishing Services

Art Director: Marissa Falco

Text Designer: Althea Chen

Cover Designer: GEX Publishing Services

Cover Art: ©Tarek El Sombati/E+/Getty Images

Copyeditor: GEX Publishing Services

Proofreader: Vicki Zimmer

Indexer: Richard Carlson

For product information and technology assistance, contact us at
Cengage Learning Customer & Sales Support, 1-800-354-9706

For permission to use material from this text or product, submit all requests online at **www.cengage.com/permissions**
Further permissions questions can be emailed to
permissionrequest@cengage.com

Library of Congress Control Number: 2014952799
ISBN: 978-1-285-07582-2

Cengage Learning
20 Channel Center Street
Boston, MA 02210
USA

Cengage Learning is a leading provider of customized learning solutions with office locations around the globe, including Singapore, the United Kingdom, Australia, Mexico, Brazil, and Japan. Locate your local office at: **www.cengage.com/global**

Cengage Learning products are represented in Canada by Nelson Education, Ltd.

For your course and learning solutions, visit **www.cengage.com**

Purchase any of our products at your local college store or at our preferred online store **www.cengagebrain.com**

Some of the product names and company names used in this book have been used for identification purposes only and may be trademarks or registered trademarks of their respective manufacturers and sellers.

Microsoft and the Office logo are either registered trademarks or trademarks of Microsoft Corporation in the United States and/or other countries. Cengage Learning is an independent entity from the Microsoft Corporation, and not affiliated with Microsoft in any manner.

Disclaimer: Any fictional data related to persons or companies or URLs used throughout this book is intended for instructional purposes only. At the time this book was printed, any such data was fictional and not belonging to any real persons or companies.

ProSkills Icons © 2014 Cengage Learning.

Printed in the United States of America
Print Number: 01   Print Year: 2014

Preface

The New Perspectives Series' critical-thinking, problem-solving approach is the ideal way to prepare students to transcend point-and-click skills and take advantage of all that XML has to offer.

In developing the New Perspectives Series, our goal was to create books that give students the software concepts and practical skills they need to succeed beyond the classroom. We've updated our proven case-based pedagogy with more practical content to make learning skills more meaningful to students. With the New Perspectives Series, students understand *why* they are learning *what* they are learning, and are fully prepared to apply their skills to real-life situations.

About This Book

This book provides complete coverage of XML including the following:
- Using XSLT to transform XML data into HTML format
- Creating custom reports using XSLT 2.0 and XPath 2.0
- Designing database queries using XQuery

New for this edition!
- Each session begins with a Visual Overview, which includes colorful, enlarged figures with numerous callouts and key term definitions, giving students a comprehensive preview of the topics covered in the session, as well as a handy study guide.
- New ProSkills boxes provide guidance for how to use the software in real-world, professional situations, and related ProSkills exercises integrate the technology skills students learn with one or more of the following soft skills: decision making, problem solving, teamwork, verbal communication, and written communication.
- Important steps are highlighted in yellow with attached margin notes to help students pay close attention to completing the steps correctly and avoid time-consuming rework.

System Requirements

This book assumes that students have access to a current browser that supports the viewing of XML files and XML files transformed using XSLT. Current versions of the major browsers support these features of XML with the exception of Google Chrome, which does not support XML documents stored locally. The screenshots of web pages in this book were produced using Internet Explorer 10 running on Windows 7 Professional (64-bit) and Internet Explorer 11 running on Windows 8.1 (64-bit), unless otherwise noted. Students who intend to validate their XML documents in Tutorials 2 through 4 should have access to an XML validating parser, such as Exchanger XML Editor, or to an online validation service. Students who intend to transform XML documents using XSLT should have access to an XSLT processor such as Exchanger, XMLSpy or Saxon. The transformations performed in Tutorials 5 through 8 were done using Saxon-HE (home edition) available free for Java or .NET at http://saxon.sourceforge.net. Students who perform XQuery data queries in Tutorial 9 should have access to an XQuery processor. Such queries were performed in Tutorial 9 using Saxon-HE. Students who are using processors other than Saxon should consult their processor's documentation for specific installation and operation instructions.

www.cengage.com/series/newperspectives

The New Perspectives Approach

Context

Each tutorial begins with a problem presented in a "real-world" case that is meaningful to students. The case sets the scene to help students understand what they will do in the tutorial.

Hands-on Approach

Each tutorial is divided into manageable sessions that combine reading and hands-on, step-by-step work. Colorful screenshots help guide students through the steps. **Trouble?** tips anticipate common mistakes or problems to help students stay on track and continue with the tutorial.

VISUAL OVERVIEW

Visual Overviews

New for this edition! Each session begins with a Visual Overview, a new two-page spread that includes colorful, enlarged figures with numerous callouts and key term definitions, giving students a comprehensive preview of the topics covered in the session, as well as a handy study guide.

PROSKILLS

ProSkills Boxes and Exercises

New for this edition! ProSkills boxes provide guidance for how to use the software in real-world, professional situations, and related ProSkills exercises integrate the technology skills students learn with one or more of the following soft skills: decision making, problem solving, teamwork, verbal communication, and written communication.

KEY STEP

Key Steps

New for this edition! Important steps are highlighted in yellow with attached margin notes to help students pay close attention to completing the steps correctly and avoid time-consuming rework.

INSIGHT

InSight Boxes

InSight boxes offer expert advice and best practices to help students achieve a deeper understanding of the concepts behind the software features and skills.

TIP

Margin Tips

Margin Tips provide helpful hints and shortcuts for more efficient use of the software. The Tips appear in the margin at key points throughout each tutorial, giving students extra information when and where they need it.

REVIEW

APPLY

Assessment

Retention is a key component to learning. At the end of each session, a series of Quick Check questions helps students test their understanding of the material before moving on. Engaging end-of-tutorial Review Assignments and Case Problems have always been a hallmark feature of the New Perspectives Series. Colorful bars and brief descriptions accompany the exercises, making it easy to understand both the goal and level of challenge a particular assignment holds.

REFERENCE

GLOSSARY/INDEX

Reference

Within each tutorial, Reference boxes appear before a set of steps to provide a succinct summary and preview of how to perform a task. In addition, each book includes a combination Glossary/Index to promote easy reference of material.

Our Complete System of Instruction

Coverage To Meet Your Needs

Whether you're looking for just a small amount of coverage or enough to fill a semester-long class, we can provide you with a textbook that meets your needs.

- Brief books typically cover the essential skills in just 2 to 4 tutorials.
- Introductory books build and expand on those skills and contain an average of 5 to 8 tutorials.
- Comprehensive books are great for a full-semester class, and contain 9 to 12+ tutorials.

So if the book you're holding does not provide the right amount of coverage for you, there's probably another offering available. Go to our Web site or contact your Cengage Learning sales representative to find out what else we offer.

CourseCasts – Learning on the Go. Always available…always relevant.

Want to keep up with the latest technology trends relevant to you? Visit http://coursecasts.course.com to find a library of weekly updated podcasts, CourseCasts, and download them to your mp3 player.

Ken Baldauf, host of CourseCasts, is a faculty member of the Florida State University Computer Science Department where he is responsible for teaching technology classes to thousands of FSU students each year. Ken is an expert in the latest technology trends; he gathers and sorts through the most pertinent news and information for CourseCasts so your students can spend their time enjoying technology, rather than trying to figure it out. Open or close your lecture with a discussion based on the latest CourseCast.

Visit us at http://coursecasts.course.com to learn on the go!

Instructor Resources

We offer more than just a book. We have all the tools you need to enhance your lectures, check students' work, and generate exams in a new, easier-to-use and completely revised package. This book's Instructor's Manual, Cengage Learning Testing Powered by Cognero, PowerPoint presentations, data files, solution files, figure files, and a sample syllabus are all available on this text's Instructor Companion Site. Simply search for this text at login.cengage.com.

SAM: Skills Assessment Manager

Get your students workplace-ready with SAM, the premier proficiency-based assessment and training solution for Microsoft Office! SAM's active, hands-on environment helps students master computer skills and concepts that are essential to academic and career success.

Skill-based assessments, interactive trainings, business-centric projects, and comprehensive remediation engage students in mastering the latest Microsoft Office programs on their own, allowing instructors to spend class time teaching. SAM's efficient course setup and robust grading features provide faculty with consistency across sections. Fully interactive MindTap Readers integrate market-leading Cengage Learning content with SAM, creating a comprehensive online student learning environment.

www.cengage.com/series/newperspectives

Acknowledgments

I would like to thank the people who worked so hard to make this book possible. Special thanks to my developmental editor, Pam Conrad, for her excellent hard work and dedication in editing this text, and to my Content Developer, Kathy Finnegan, who has worked tirelessly in overseeing this project and made my task so much easier with her enthusiasm and good humor. Other people at Cengage Learning who deserve credit are Jim Gish, Senior Product Manager; Christian Kunciw, Manuscript Quality Assurance (MQA) Supervisor; and John Freitas, Serge Palladino, Danielle Shaw, and Susan Whalen, MQA testers.

Feedback is an important part of writing any book, and thanks go to the following reviewers for their helpful ideas and comments: David Doering, St. Louis Community College; Ravinder Kang, Highline Community College; Diana Kokoska, University of Maine at Augusta; Barbara Rader, University of Maryland; Sheryl Schoenacher, Farmingdale State College; Dave Sciuto, University of Massachusetts—Lowell; John Whitney, Fox Valley Technical College; and Dawn Wick, Southwestern Community College.

I want to thank my wife Joan for her support during this project and for my six children to whom this book is dedicated.
– Patrick Carey

Many thanks to everyone who helped in this revision. Pam Conrad, my sharp-eyed developmental editor, suggested improvements and asked a lot of important questions that helped me immeasurably in tightening up the material. The good advice of Kathy Finnegan, my Content Developer, kept me focused on the important aspects of the revision process, and she sweated a lot of the small stuff so I didn't have to. I'm also grateful to Jim Gish, the Senior Product Manager, for keeping the faith during the evolution of this revision. The staff at GEX Publishing Services made it all look amazing. And MQA testers Serge Palladino, Danielle Shaw, and Susan Whalen read everything through, completed all the steps, and gave smart feedback that removed many roadblocks for future users. Finally, thanks to my husband, Jason Bucy, for encouraging me to balance diving deep into XML with stepping away from the computer, getting outside, and enjoying the world with him.
– Sasha Vodnik

BRIEF CONTENTS

TABLE OF CONTENTS

XML

OBJECTIVES

Session 1.1
- Describe the history of XML and the uses of XML documents
- Understand XML vocabularies
- Define well-formed and valid XML documents, and describe the basic structure of an XML document
- Create an XML declaration
- Work with XML comments
- Work with XML parsers and understand how web browsers work with XML documents

Session 1.2
- Create XML elements and attributes
- Work with character and entity references
- Describe how XML handles parsed character data, character data, and white space
- Create an XML processing instruction to apply a style sheet to an XML document
- Declare a default namespace for an XML vocabulary and apply the namespace to an element

Creating an XML Document

Developing a Document for SJB Pet Boutique

Case | *SJB Pet Boutique*

SJB Pet Boutique in Delafield, Wisconsin, creates beautiful jewelry and clothing accessories "for pets and their humans." The boutique's top two best-selling items are holiday pet costumes, and matching pet collar and human necklace pendants.

During the past year, the boutique has received more requests for custom work. The owners would like to further develop this aspect of their business by making it available on the SJB Pet Boutique website. Patricia Dean manages the boutique's website. She has been investigating using Extensible Markup Language to organize information about the boutique's product line and the custom work offered. **Extensible Markup Language (XML)** is a markup language that can be extended and modified to match the needs of the document author and the data being recorded. XML has some advantages in presenting structured content such as descriptions of available customizations. Data stored in an XML document can be integrated with the boutique's website. Through the use of style sheets, Patricia can present XML data in a way that would be attractive to potential customers.

The boutique's website already takes advantage of many of the latest web standards, including HTML5 and CSS. Patricia would like to gradually incorporate XML into the website and increase the use of style sheets. As a first step, she has asked for your help in creating a document that will display a small part of the boutique's inventory using XML.

STARTING DATA FILES

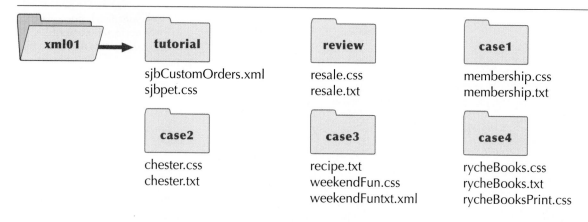

xml01 → tutorial

tutorial
sjbCustomOrders.xml
sjbpet.css

review
resale.css
resale.txt

case1
membership.css
membership.txt

case2
chester.css
chester.txt

case3
recipe.txt
weekendFun.css
weekendFuntxt.xml

case4
rycheBooks.css
rycheBooks.txt
rycheBooksPrint.css

Session 1.1 Visual Overview:

The **prolog** contains the XML declaration, optional comment lines, optional processing instructions, and an optional document type declaration.

The XML **declaration** indicates that the document is written in XML and specifies the version of XML used.

The **encoding** attribute identifies the character set used in the document.

The standalone attribute indicates whether the document contains any references to external files.

Comments in the prolog provide additional information about what a document will be used for and how it was created.

```
<?xml version="1.0" encoding="UTF-8" standalone="yes" ?>
<!--
    This document contains data on SJB Pet Boutique
    holiday specials

    Filename: sjbpet.xml
    Author:   Patricia Dean
    Date:     9/18/2017
-->
<products>
    <product>
        <productName>Dog Shirt Gift Basket</productName>
        <manufacturer>SJB Pet Boutique</manufacturer>
        <description>Something for every day of the week</description>
        <price>35.99</price>
        <price>26.79</price>
        <productItems>1200, 1201, 1202, 1203, 1204, 1205, 1206</productItems>
    </product>
</products>
<!-- generated by the finance department -->
```

The **document body** contains the document content in a hierarchical tree structure.

Found after the document body, the optional **epilog** contains any final comment lines and processing instructions.

DTDs schemas

Document Type Definitions (DTDs) and **schemas** are rules that specifically control what code and content a document may include.

XML Overview

A **well-formed document** has no syntax errors and satisfies the general specifications for XML code defined by the World Wide Web Consortium (W3C).

An **XML parser** or **XML processor** interprets a document's code and verifies that it satisfies the W3C specifications.

XML parser

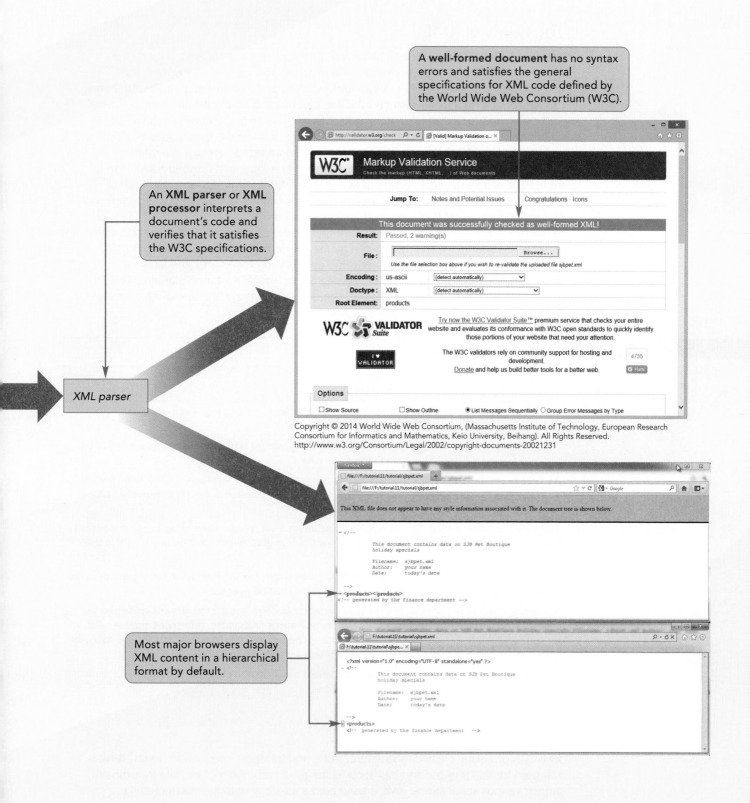

Most major browsers display XML content in a hierarchical format by default.

Introducing XML

The following short history lesson may help you better understand how XML fits in with today's technologies.

The Roots of XML

XML has its roots in **Standard Generalized Markup Language (SGML)**, a language introduced in the 1980s that describes the structure and content of any machine-readable information. SGML is device-independent and system-independent. In theory, this means that documents written in SGML can be used on almost any type of device under almost any type of operating system. SGML has been the chosen vehicle for creating structured documents in businesses and government organizations of all sizes.

Even though SGML provides tools to manage enormous projects, it is a difficult language to learn and to apply because of its power, scope, and flexibility. XML can be thought of as a lightweight version of SGML. Like SGML, XML is a language used to create vocabularies for other markup languages, but it does not have SGML's complexity and expansiveness. XML is a markup language that is extensible, so it can be modified to match the needs of the document author and the data being recorded. The standards for XML are developed and maintained by the **World Wide Web Consortium (W3C)**, an organization created in 1994 to develop common protocols and standards for sharing information on the World Wide Web. When the W3C started planning XML, it established a number of design goals for the language. The syntax rules of XML are easy to learn and easy to use, as shown in Figure 1-1.

| Figure 1-1 | Highlights of XML syntax rules |

Syntax Rule	Application
Every XML element must have a closing tag.	Every element must have a closing tag. A self-closing tag is permitted.
XML tags are case sensitive.	Opening and closing tags (or start and end tags) must be written with the same case.
XML elements must be properly nested.	All elements can have child (sub) elements. Child elements must be in pairs and be correctly nested within their respective parent element.
Every XML document must have a root element.	Every XML document must contain a single tag pair that defines the root element. All other elements must be nested within the root element.
XML elements can have attributes in name-value pairs.	Each attribute name within the same element can occur only once. Each attribute value must be quoted.
Some characters have a special meaning in XML.	The use of certain characters is restricted. If these characters are needed, entity references or character references may be used. References always begin with the character "&" (which is specially reserved) and end with the character ";".
XML allows for comments.	Comments cannot occur prior to the XML Declaration. Comments cannot be nested.

XML Today

XML was originally created to structure, store, and transport information. Today, XML is still used for that purpose and has become the most common tool for data transmission among various applications. XML is used across a variety of industries, including accounting, banking, human resources, medical records, information technology, and insurance. Generally, it is used in all major websites, including major web services.

XML with Software Applications and Languages

Currently, many software applications such as Microsoft Excel and Microsoft Word, and server languages such as Java, .NET, Perl, and PHP, can read and create XML files. As of the 2007 releases of Microsoft Office and OpenOffice, users can exchange data among Office applications and enterprise systems using XML and file compression technologies. Not only are the documents universally accessible, but the use of XML also reduces the risk of damaged files. Figure 1-2 shows Microsoft Excel's built-in mechanism for importing an XML file into an Excel spreadsheet.

| Figure 1-2 | Importing XML data into Microsoft Excel |

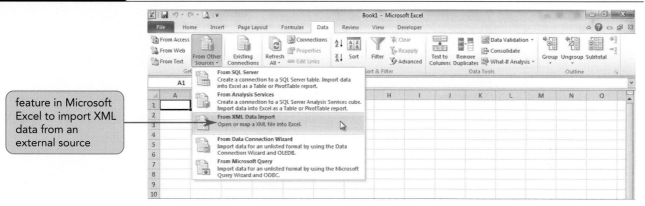

feature in Microsoft Excel to import XML data from an external source

XML and Databases

Databases store data, and XML is widely used for data interchange. All major databases, including Microsoft Access, Oracle, and MySQL, can read and create XML files. The fact that XML isn't platform-dependent gives the language flexibility as technologies change.

XML and relational databases are tightly woven together in most web applications. However, the two use distinctly different models to structure data. The relational model used by relational databases is based on two-dimensional tables, which have no hierarchy and no significant order. By contrast, XML is based on hierarchical trees in which order is significant. In the relational model, neither hierarchy nor sequence may be used to model information. In XML, hierarchy and sequence are the main methods used to represent information. This is one of the more fundamental differences between the two models, but there are more.

On web pages, XML is very useful because the structure of XML closely matches the structure used to display the same information in HTML. Both HTML and XML use tags in similar ways, often creating distinctly hierarchical structures to present data to users. Most of the data for web pages comes from relational databases and it must be converted to appropriate XML hierarchies for use in web pages. For these reasons, it makes more sense to see XML as a tool that works in conjunction with databases, rather than as a competitor to them. Major databases support easy-to-use integration with XML. For instance, Figure 1-3 shows how Access has incorporated easy XML importing and exporting of data.

| Figure 1-3 | Importing XML-formatted data into Access |

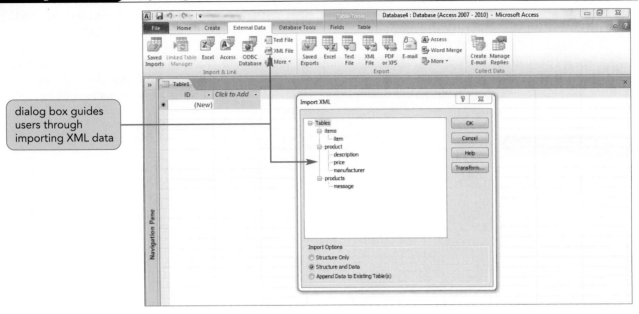

dialog box guides users through importing XML data

XML and Mobile Development

It is highly doubtful that when members of the W3C got together to discuss XML, they even considered mobile device development and the importance that XML would play in this area. In fact, mobile device platforms such as Google's Android and Apple's iOS use XML in a variety of ways.

In iOS, Apple has built in the ability to import and export data classes in XML format. This makes it very easy to transfer information via XML. A popular use of XML in the iPhone is in a preference list or property list—commonly abbreviated as p-list—to organize data into named properties and lists of values, as shown in Figure 1-4.

| Figure 1-4 | iOS p-list file written in XML |

```
<?xml version="1.0" encoding="UTF-8"?>
<!DOCTYPE plist PUBLIC "-//Apple Computer//DTD PLIST 1.0//EN"
        "http://www.apple.com/DTDs/PropertyList-1.0.dtd">
<plist version="1.0">
    <dict>
        <key>Accessories</key>
        <string>Collar Tag</string>
        <key>Shirt</key>
        <string>Week Day</string>
        <key>Bowls</key>
        <string>Ceramic 2 Holder</string>
    </dict>
</plist>
```

Android uses XML for screen layout and for working with data. Android provides a straightforward XML vocabulary for laying out content on the screen, allowing creation of XML layouts for different screen orientations, different device screen sizes, and different languages. Declaring an Android layout in XML makes it easier to visualize the structure of a user interface. Figure 1-5 shows an example of how Android uses XML to lay out the screen.

Figure 1-5	Android layout definitions written in XML

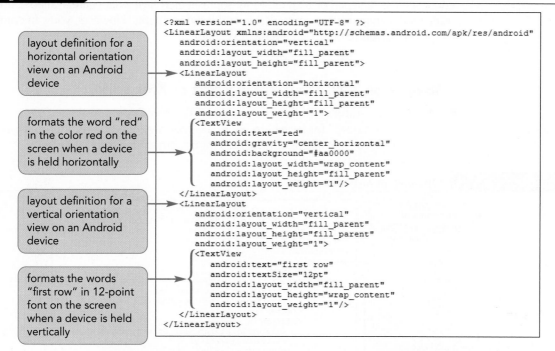

layout definition for a horizontal orientation view on an Android device

formats the word "red" in the color red on the screen when a device is held horizontally

layout definition for a vertical orientation view on an Android device

formats the words "first row" in 12-point font on the screen when a device is held vertically

```
<?xml version="1.0" encoding="UTF-8" ?>
<LinearLayout xmlns:android="http://schemas.android.com/apk/res/android"
    android:orientation="vertical"
    android:layout_width="fill_parent"
    android:layout_height="fill_parent">
  <LinearLayout
      android:orientation="horizontal"
      android:layout_width="fill_parent"
      android:layout_height="fill_parent"
      android:layout_weight="1">
    <TextView
        android:text="red"
        android:gravity="center_horizontal"
        android:background="#aa0000"
        android:layout_width="wrap_content"
        android:layout_height="fill_parent"
        android:layout_weight="1"/>
  </LinearLayout>
  <LinearLayout
      android:orientation="vertical"
      android:layout_width="fill_parent"
      android:layout_height="fill_parent"
      android:layout_weight="1">
    <TextView
        android:text="first row"
        android:textSize="12pt"
        android:layout_width="fill_parent"
        android:layout_height="wrap_content"
        android:layout_weight="1"/>
  </LinearLayout>
</LinearLayout>
```

Creating an XML Vocabulary

HTML is an SGML application and is the foundation of web development. Like SGML, XML can be used to create **XML applications** or **vocabularies**, which are markup languages tailored to contain specific pieces of information. If Patricia wanted to create a vocabulary for the items in the SJB Pet Boutique product catalog, she might use XML to store the product information in the following format:

```
<productName>Dog Shirt Gift Basket</productName>
<manufacturer>SJB Pet Boutique</manufacturer>
<description>Something for every day of the week
</description>
<price currency="USD">$35.99</price>
<price currency="EUR">€26.79</price>
<productItems>1200, 1201, 1202, 1203, 1204, 1204, 1205, 1206
</productItems>
```

You'll explore the structure and syntax of this document further in the next session, but you can already infer a lot about the type of information this document contains even without knowing much about XML. You can quickly see that this file contains data on a product named "Dog Shirt Gift Basket," including its manufacturer, its description, its two selling prices, and the product numbers of the items it includes.

The `productName`, `manufacturer`, `description`, `price`, and `productItems` elements in this example do not come from any particular XML specification; rather, they are custom elements that Patricia might create specifically for one of the SJB Pet Boutique documents.

Patricia could create additional elements describing things such as the product number, the seller name, and the quantity on hand. In this way, Patricia could create her own XML vocabulary that deals specifically with product, manufacturer, and inventory data.

You'll start your work for Patricia by examining an XML document and comparing the similarities between HTML and XML documents.

Like HTML documents, XML documents can be created and viewed with a basic text editor such as Notepad or TextEdit. More sophisticated XML editors are available, and using them can make it easier to design and test documents. However, you can complete the project in this tutorial with a basic text editor.

To open an XML document in a text or XML editor:

▶ **1.** In a text editor or XML editor, open **sjbCustomOrders.xml** from the xml01 ▶ tutorial folder where your data files are located. Figure 1-6 shows the contents of the sjbCustomOrders.xml document for the first order.

Figure 1-6   Opening an XML document

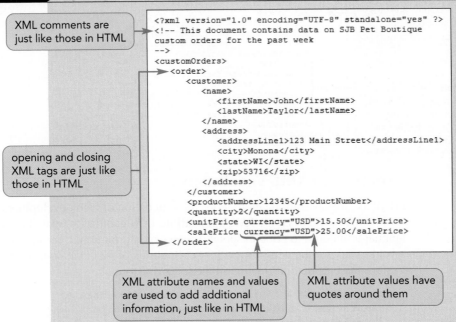

XML comments are just like those in HTML

opening and closing XML tags are just like those in HTML

XML attribute names and values are used to add additional information, just like in HTML

XML attribute values have quotes around them

```
<?xml version="1.0" encoding="UTF-8" standalone="yes" ?>
<!-- This document contains data on SJB Pet Boutique
custom orders for the past week
-->
<customOrders>
    <order>
        <customer>
            <name>
                <firstName>John</firstName>
                <lastName>Taylor</lastName>
            </name>
            <address>
                <addressLine1>123 Main Street</addressLine1>
                <city>Monona</city>
                <state>WI</state>
                <zip>53716</zip>
            </address>
        </customer>
        <productNumber>12345</productNumber>
        <quantity>2</quantity>
        <unitPrice currency="USD">15.50</unitPrice>
        <salePrice currency="USD">25.00</salePrice>
    </order>
```

▶ **2.** Examine the code, noting the similarities between an XML document and an HTML document, such as comments and opening and closing tags. You'll explore each aspect of an XML document's structure in the next session.

▶ **3.** Close the file.

Standard XML Vocabularies

If Patricia wanted to share the vocabulary that she uses for SJB Pet Boutique with other companies, she might use a standard vocabulary that is accepted throughout the industry. You can think of a **standard vocabulary** as a set of XML tags for a particular industry or business function. As XML has grown in popularity, standard vocabularies continue to be developed across a wide range of disciplines.

For example, chemists need to describe chemical structures containing hundreds of atoms bonded to other atoms and molecules. To meet this need, an XML vocabulary called **Chemical Markup Language (CML)** was developed, which codes molecular information. Figure 1-7 shows an example of a CML document used to store information on the ammonia molecule.

Figure 1-7   **Ammonia molecule described using CML**

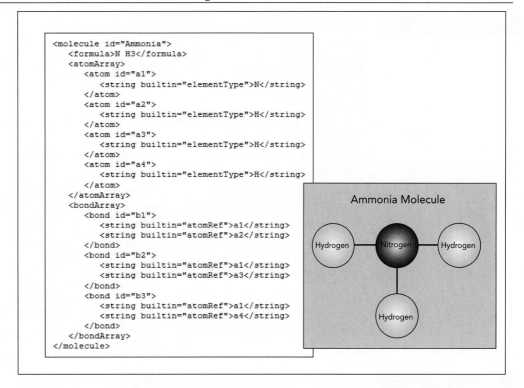

```
<molecule id="Ammonia">
    <formula>N H3</formula>
    <atomArray>
        <atom id="a1">
            <string builtin="elementType">N</string>
        </atom>
        <atom id="a2">
            <string builtin="elementType">H</string>
        </atom>
        <atom id="a3">
            <string builtin="elementType">H</string>
        </atom>
        <atom id="a4">
            <string builtin="elementType">H</string>
        </atom>
    </atomArray>
    <bondArray>
        <bond id="b1">
            <string builtin="atomRef">a1</string>
            <string builtin="atomRef">a2</string>
        </bond>
        <bond id="b2">
            <string builtin="atomRef">a1</string>
            <string builtin="atomRef">a3</string>
        </bond>
        <bond id="b3">
            <string builtin="atomRef">a1</string>
            <string builtin="atomRef">a4</string>
        </bond>
    </bondArray>
</molecule>
```

One of the more important XML vocabularies on the Internet is **Really Simple Syndication (RSS)**, which is the language used for distributing news articles or any content that changes on a regular basis. Subscribers to an RSS feed can receive periodic updates using a software program called a **feed reader** or an **aggregator**. Most current browsers contain some type of built-in feed reader to allow users to retrieve and view feeds from within the browser window. Most RSS feeds contain just links, headlines, or brief synopses of new information. Because an RSS file is written in XML, the RSS code follows the conventions of all XML documents. Figure 1-8 shows a segment of an RSS document.

Figure 1-8   **RSS document**

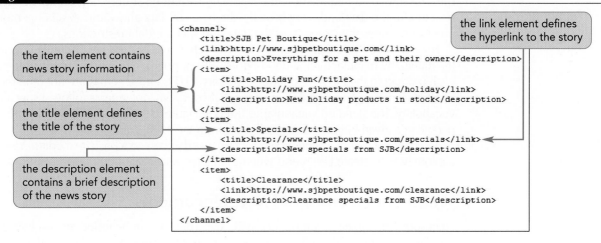

the item element contains news story information

the title element defines the title of the story

the description element contains a brief description of the news story

the link element defines the hyperlink to the story

```
<channel>
    <title>SJB Pet Boutique</title>
    <link>http://www.sjbpetboutique.com</link>
    <description>Everything for a pet and their owner</description>
    <item>
        <title>Holiday Fun</title>
        <link>http://www.sjbpetboutique.com/holiday</link>
        <description>New holiday products in stock</description>
    </item>
    <item>
        <title>Specials</title>
        <link>http://www.sjbpetboutique.com/specials</link>
        <description>New specials from SJB</description>
    </item>
    <item>
        <title>Clearance</title>
        <link>http://www.sjbpetboutique.com/clearance</link>
        <description>Clearance specials from SJB</description>
    </item>
</channel>
```

Figure 1-9 lists a few of the many vocabularies that have been developed using XML.

Figure 1-9	XML vocabularies

XML Vocabulary	Description
Bioinformatic Sequence Markup Language (BSML)	Coding of bioinformatic data
Extensible Hypertext Markup Language (XHTML)	HTML written as an XML application
Mathematical Markup Language (MathML)	Presentation and evaluation of mathematical equations and operations
Music Markup Language (MML)	Display and organization of music notation and lyrics
Weather Observation Definition Format (OMF)	Distribution of weather observation reports, forecasts, and advisories
Really Simple Syndication (RSS)	Distribution of news headlines and syndicated columns
Synchronized Multimedia Integration Language (SMIL)	Editing of interactive audiovisual presentations involving streaming audio, video, text, and any other media type
Voice Extensible Markup Language (VoiceXML)	Creation of audio dialogues that feature synthesized speech, digitized audio, and speech recognition
Wireless Markup Language (WML)	Coding of information for smaller-screened devices, such as PDAs and cell phones

TIP

You can learn more about several standard XML vocabularies at the W3C site, www.w3.org/XML/.

One of the more important XML vocabularies is **XHTML (Extensible Hypertext Markup Language)**, which is a reformulation of HTML as an XML application. You'll examine some properties of XHTML as you learn more about XML in the upcoming tutorials. Don't worry if you find all of these acronyms and languages a bit overwhelming.

DTDs and Schemas

For different users to share a vocabulary effectively, rules must be developed that specifically control what code and content a document from that vocabulary might contain. This is done by attaching either a Document Type Definition (DTD) or a schema to the XML document containing the data. Both DTDs and schemas contain rules for how data in a document vocabulary should be structured. A DTD defines the structure of the data and, very broadly, the types of data allowable. A schema more precisely defines the structure of the data and specific data restrictions.

For example, Patricia can create a DTD or schema to require her documents to list the name, the manufacturer, a description, a list of prices, and a list of product items for each product in the SJB Pet Boutique inventory. DTDs and schemas are not required, but they can be quite helpful in ensuring that your XML documents follow a specific vocabulary. The standard vocabularies listed in Figure 1-9 all have DTDs to ensure that people in a given industry or area all work from the same guidelines.

To create a DTD or a schema, you simply need access to a basic text editor. You'll explore how to create DTDs and schemas in later tutorials.

Well-Formed and Valid XML Documents

To ensure a document's compliance with XML rules, it can be tested against two standards—whether it's well formed, and whether it's valid. A well-formed document contains no syntax errors and satisfies the general specifications for XML code as laid out by the W3C. At a minimum, an XML document must be well formed or it will not be readable by programs that process XML code.

If an XML document is part of a vocabulary with a defined DTD or schema, it also must be tested to ensure that it satisfies the rules of that vocabulary. A well-formed XML document that satisfies the rules of a DTD or schema is said to be a **valid document**. In this tutorial, you'll look only at the basic syntax rules of XML to create well-formed documents. You'll learn how to test documents for validity in later tutorials.

PROSKILLS

Problem Solving: Designing for Efficiency and Effectiveness

Although XML can do many different things, it is used most effectively to communicate data. In this respect, XML and databases go hand-in-hand—XML communicates data, and databases store data. XML delivers structured information in a generic format that's independent of how that information is used. As a result, the data does not rely on any particular programming language or software. XML developers have the freedom to work with a wide range of applications, devices, and complementary languages. A much larger benefit to the structural and logical markup is the ability to reuse portions of the information easily in any context where the information is structurally valid. Because XML focuses on communicating the data, the overall structure is simple and easy to design and maintain. This approach allows for a high level of efficiency and effectiveness, which in the long term reduces the amount of time and money spent on development and maintenance.

Creating an XML Document

Now that you're familiar with the history and theory of XML, you're ready to create your first XML document.

The Structure of an XML Document

An XML document consists of three parts—the prolog, the document body, and the epilog. The prolog includes the following parts:

- **XML declaration**: indicates that the document is written in the XML language
- **Processing instructions** (optional): provide additional instructions to be run by programs that read the XML document
- **Comment lines** (optional): provide additional information about the document contents
- **Document type declaration (DTD)** (optional): provides information about the rules used in the XML document's vocabulary

Figure 1-10 illustrates the structure of a prolog.

Figure 1-10	Structure of a prolog

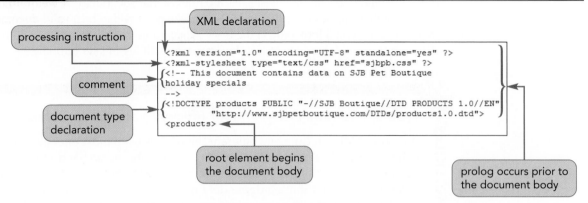

The document body, found immediately after the prolog, contains the document's content in a hierarchical tree structure. Following the document body is an optional epilog, which contains any final comments or processing instructions.

The XML Declaration

The XML declaration is the first part of the prolog as well as the first line in an XML document. It signals to the program reading the file that the document is written in XML, and it provides information about how that code is to be interpreted by the program. The syntax of the XML declaration is

```
<?xml version="version number" encoding="encoding type"
       standalone="yes|no" ?>
```

where *version number* is the version of the XML specification being used in the document and *encoding type* identifies the character set used in the document. The default version value is 1.0. Although you can also specify a version value of 1.1, only a few programs support XML 1.1. With the growth of the web, XML 1.1 was implemented to allow almost any Unicode character to be used in object names. **Unicode** is a computing industry standard for the consistent encoding, representation, and handling of text expressed in most of the world's written languages. Unicode can be implemented using different character encodings; the most commonly used encodings are UTF-8 and UTF-16. Aside from forward compatibility with the Unicode standard in XML 1.1, there is not much difference between the 1.0 and 1.1 specifications, and most programmers still use the default version, 1.0. If you include the `standalone` or `encoding` attribute, you must include the `version` attribute.

Because different languages use different character sets, the `encoding` attribute allows XML to be used across a range of written languages. The default encoding scheme is UTF-8, which includes the characters used in almost all widely used written languages. However, a number of encoding schemes predate UTF-8, and some are still in use. If your XML document is intended for use with a system that uses a different encoding scheme, you might need to specify the scheme. For example, setting the `encoding` value to `ISO-8859-1` tells a program reading the document that characters from the ISO-8859-1 (Latin-1) character set are being used in the document. The ISO-8859-1 character set has largely been replaced by UTF-8, but some systems and applications still use ISO-8859-1 encoding.

Finally, the `standalone` attribute indicates whether the document contains any references to external files. A standalone value of `yes` indicates that the document is self-contained, and a value of `no` indicates that the document requires additional information from external documents. The default value is `no`.

REFERENCE

Creating an XML Declaration

- To create an XML declaration, enter the code

    ```
    <?xml ?>
    ```

    in the first line of an XML document.
- To specify a version of XML to use, enter the code

    ```
    version="version number"
    ```

    after the opening `<?xml` tag, where *version number* is either 1.0 or 1.1.
- To specify a character encoding, enter the code

    ```
    encoding="encoding type"
    ```

    after the `version` attribute-value pair, where *encoding type* identifies the character set used in the document.
- To indicate whether the document is a standalone document, enter the code

    ```
    standalone="yes|no"
    ```

    after the `encoding` attribute-value pair, where the value **yes** or **no** indicates whether access to external files will be needed when processing the document.

Therefore, a sample XML declaration might appear as follows:

```
<?xml version="1.0" encoding="ISO-8859-1" standalone="yes" ?>
```

This declaration indicates that the XML version is 1.0, the ISO-8859-1 encoding scheme is being used, and the document is self-contained. If you instead entered the XML declaration

```
<?xml version="1.0" ?>
```

a processor would apply the default UTF-8 encoding scheme and the default `standalone` value of no.

Because XML is case sensitive, you cannot change the code to uppercase letters. The following code would generate an error because it is entered in uppercase.

Not well-formed code:

```
<?XML VERSION="1.0" ENCODING="ISO-8859-1" STANDALONE="YES" ?>
```

You also must ensure the quotation marks are included around the values in a declaration. The following XML declaration would result in an error because it is missing the quotation marks around the `version`, `encoding`, and `standalone` attribute values.

Not well-formed code:

```
<?xml version=1.0 encoding=ISO-8859-1 standalone=yes ?>
```

The optional attributes for the XML declaration cannot be switched around. The following code would result in an error because the `standalone` attribute must come after the `encoding` attribute.

Not well-formed code:

```
<?xml version="1.0" standalone="yes" encoding="ISO-8859-1" ?>
```

The following statements are samples of well-formed options for coding an XML declaration:

Well-formed code:

```
<?xml version="1.0" standalone="yes" ?>
<?xml version="1.1" standalone="no" ?>
<?xml version="1.0" encoding="UTF-8" ?>
<?xml version="1.1" encoding="UTF-8" ?>
```

Now that you've learned how to structure an XML declaration, you'll begin creating your first XML document by writing the prolog for an XML document to be used by SJB Pet Boutique.

To create the basic structure of an XML document:

1. Use your text editor to open a blank document.

Be sure to include both question marks; otherwise, browsers will not recognize the declaration statement.

2. Type the following line of code into your document:

   ```
   <?xml version="1.0" encoding="UTF-8" standalone="yes" ?>
   ```

3. Press the **Enter** key, and then compare your code to Figure 1-11.

Figure 1-11   Adding the XML declaration

```
<?xml version="1.0" encoding="UTF-8" standalone="yes" ?>
```

XML declaration must have both
opening <? and closing ?> tags

4. Save your document as **sjbpet.xml** in the xml01 ▸ tutorial folder.

   Trouble? Some editors, such as Notepad, automatically assign the .txt extension to text files. To specify the .xml extension in Notepad, type sjbpet. xml in the File name box, click All Files from the Save as type list box, and then click the Save button. If you're using a different text editor, consult that program's documentation.

Inserting Comments

Patricia wants you to include information in the document about its purpose and contents. Comments are one way of doing this. They can appear anywhere in the prolog after the XML declaration. Comments in the prolog provide additional information about what the document will be used for and how it was created. Generally speaking, comments are ignored by programs reading the document and do not affect the document's contents or structure.

To insert a comment in an XML document, enter

```
<!-- comment -->
```

where *comment* is the text of the comment. Comments cannot be placed before the XML declaration and cannot be embedded within tags or other comments. You should avoid using the two dashes (--) anywhere in a comment except at the beginning and the end. If you have a comment that will occupy more than one line, you can continue the comment on as many lines as you need. All text after <!-- is considered a comment until the close of the comment tag, which is signaled by the two dashes. Anything within comments is effectively invisible, so only code outside of the comments needs to be valid and well formed.

You'll add comments to the sjbpet.xml file describing its contents and purpose.

To insert an XML comment:

1. In the sjbpet.xml file, enter the following comment lines directly below the XML declaration, pressing the **Enter** key after each line, replacing the text *your name* and *today's date* with your name and the current date, respectively, and indenting as shown:

```
<!--
    This document contains data on SJB Pet Boutique
    holiday specials

    Filename: sjbpet.xml
    Author:   your name
    Date:     today's date
-->
```

Figure 1-12 shows the new comment in the document.

Figure 1-12	Adding a comment to the XML document

comment must begin after the XML declaration

multi-line comment describing the document

```
<?xml version="1.0" encoding="UTF-8" standalone="yes" ?>
<!--
    This document contains data on SJB Pet Boutique
    holiday specials

    Filename: sjbpet.xml
    Author:   Patricia Dean
    Date:     9/18/2017
-->
```

2. Directly below the comment closing tag, add the following code:

```
<products>
    <!-- document body content -->
</products>
```

This code serves as a placeholder for the document body.

Trouble? Some XML editors automatically add the closing HTML tag after you type the starting tag. Be sure to type the element content before the closing tag.

3. Add a comment to the document's epilog by placing the following text directly below the closing </products> tag:

```
<!-- generated by the finance department -->
```

Figure 1-13 shows the new placeholder and comment tags in the document.

Figure 1-13	Adding a comment to the epilog

```
<?xml version="1.0" encoding="UTF-8" standalone="yes" ?>
<!--
    This document contains data on SJB Pet Boutique
    holiday specials

    Filename: sjbpet.xml
    Author:   Patricia Dean
    Date:     9/18/2017
-->
<products>
    <!-- document body content -->
</products>
<!-- generated by the finance department -->
```

a placeholder for the document body

the epilog is found after the closing tag of the document body and is a single-line comment in this example

4. Save your changes to the sjbpet.xml document.

Patricia is pleased that you've created a basic XML document so quickly. Next, you'll add the content.

Commenting an XML Document

Although a developer should easily be able to read and understand the code of an XML document, it's good practice to include comments in a document's prolog. Typically, these comments summarize the contents of the XML data. If there's anything special about the original creation of the XML document, that information should be included as well.

Some businesses have very specific standards for how comments should be coded within a document. These rules might even dictate where opening and closing tags for a comment are coded. For example, you might encounter coding standards that require single-line and multi-line comments to have the opening tag, comments, and closing tag on separate lines, as in the following code:

```
<!--
     single-line comment or multi-line comment
-->
```

Likewise, you might see coding standards that allow a single-line comment to have the opening and closing tags on the same line, as follows:

```
<!-- single-line comment -->
```

Processing an XML Document

Now that you've created the very basic content for Patricia's pet store document, you can work with browsers to display that content.

XML Parsers

A program that reads and interprets an XML document is called an XML processor or XML parser, or simply a **processor** or **parser**. A parser has several functions. First, a parser interprets a document's code and verifies that it satisfies all the XML specifications for document structure and syntax. XML parsers are strict. If even one tag is omitted or one lowercase character should be uppercase, a parser reports an error and rejects the document. This might seem excessive, but that rigidity was built into XML to eliminate viewers' ability to interpret how the code is displayed—much like HTML gives web browsers wide discretion in interpreting markup code. A second function of a parser is to interpret PCDATA in a document and resolve any character or entity references found within the document. Finally, an XML document might contain processing instructions that tell a parser exactly how the document should be read and interpreted. A third job of a parser is to interpret these instructions and carry them out. Figure 1-14 illustrates the parsing process from document creation to final presentation.

Figure 1-14	XML parsing process

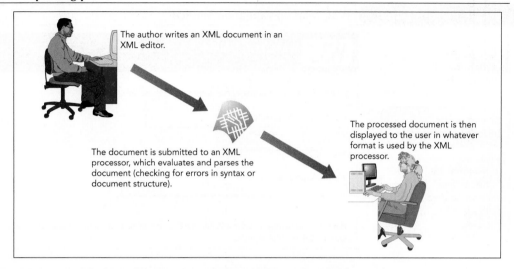

The author writes an XML document in an XML editor.

The document is submitted to an XML processor, which evaluates and parses the document (checking for errors in syntax or document structure).

The processed document is then displayed to the user in whatever format is used by the XML processor.

TIP

Because XML, by definition, includes no predefined elements, browsers can't apply default styles to elements as they do to HTML content; instead, they default to showing the document's tree structure.

The current versions of all major web browsers include an XML parser of some type. When an XML document is submitted to a browser, the XML parser built into the browser first checks for syntax errors. If it finds none, the browser then displays the contents of the document. Older browsers might display only the data content; newer browsers display both the data and the document's tree structure. Current versions of Internet Explorer, Chrome, and Firefox display XML documents in an expandable/collapsible outline format that allows users to hide nested elements. This is supported by a built-in extensible style sheet, which you'll learn more about in later tutorials. The various parts of a document might be color coded within the browser, making the document easier to read and interpret. Opera displays raw XML that is not expandable/collapsible, but is color coded. Safari parses the XML; in order to view the raw XML in Safari, you must select the View Source command.

You're ready to test whether the sjbpet.xml document is well formed. To test for well-formedness, you'll use an XML parser to compare the XML document against the rules established by the W3C. The web has many excellent sources for parsers that check for well-formedness, including websites to which you can upload an XML document. Several editors check XML code for well-formedness as well.

NOTE: The following steps instruct you to upload your document to validator.w3.org to check Patricia's sjbpet.xml document for well-formedness. If you don't have Internet access and you're using an XML editor, consult that program's documentation and follow those steps to check your document for well-formedness.

To check the sjbpet.xml file for well-formedness:

1. In your web browser, open **validator.w3.org**, and then click the **Validate by File Upload** tab. The W3C Markup Validation Service page opens, as shown in Figure 1-15.

Figure 1-15	W3C Markup Validation Service

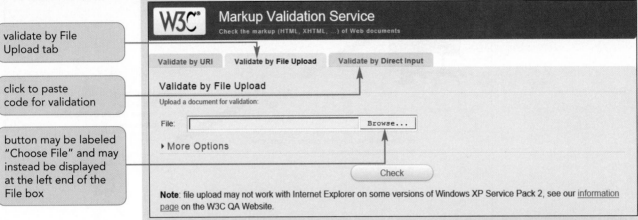

validate by File Upload tab

click to paste code for validation

button may be labeled "Choose File" and may instead be displayed at the left end of the File box

Copyright © 2014 World Wide Web Consortium, (Massachusetts Institute of Technology, European Research Consortium for Informatics and Mathematics, Keio University, Beihang). All Rights Reserved. http://www.w3.org/Consortium/Legal/2002/copyright-documents-20021231

2. Click the **Browse** or **Choose File** button, in the dialog box that opens navigate to your **xml01 ▸ tutorial** folder, click **sjbpet.xml** in the file list, and then click **Open**.

   Trouble? If the file list does not display the .xml extension at the end of the filename, select the file named sjbpet with a type of XML File.

3. Click the **Check** button. The file you selected is uploaded, and then the validation service displays your validation results, as shown in Figure 1-16.

Figure 1-16	Results of check for well-formedness

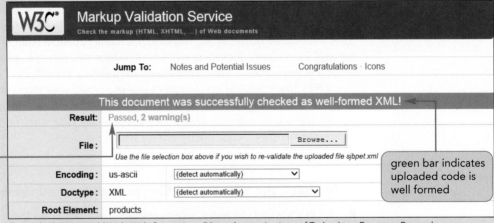

warnings are detailed at the bottom of the page and do not affect the well-formedness of the document

green bar indicates uploaded code is well formed

Copyright © 2014 World Wide Web Consortium, (Massachusetts Institute of Technology, European Research Consortium for Informatics and Mathematics, Keio University, Beihang). All Rights Reserved. http://www.w3.org/Consortium/Legal/2002/copyright-documents-20021231

Trouble? If the results page shows a red bar and indicates that the document was not found to be well-formed XML, check your XML code against the sjbpet.xml code shown in Figure 1-13. Your code must match exactly, including the use of uppercase and lowercase letters. Fix any discrepancies, be sure to save your changes, and then repeat Steps 1-3.

Most web browsers also function as XML parsers. To see how Patricia's basic document is displayed, you'll open it now in your browser.

To view the sjbpet.xml file in your browser:

1. Open the **sjbpet.xml** document in your web browser. Different browsers display XML content differently. Figure 1-17 shows the contents of the file as it appears in current versions of Firefox, Internet Explorer, and Chrome at the time this book was published. In Safari, the window is blank because the browser displays only the content of an XML document, and your document is currently empty.

| Figure 1-17 | Displaying the sjbpet.xml document in Firefox, Internet Explorer, and Chrome |

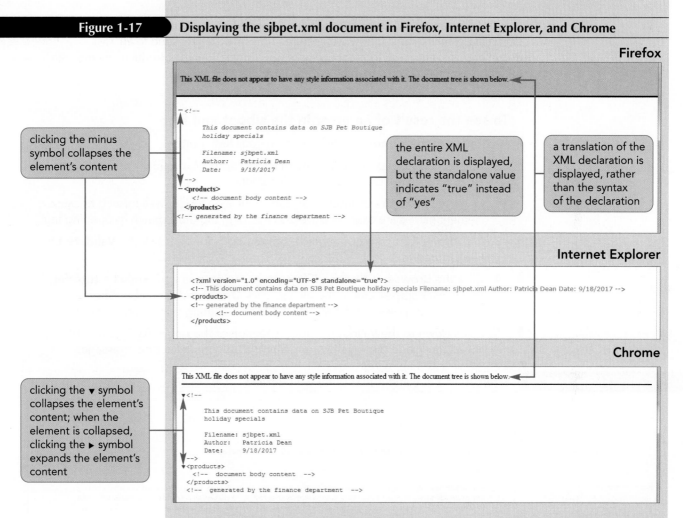

Trouble? If Internet Explorer displays a yellow information bar, click the bar, select Allow Blocked Content, and then click Yes in the Security Warning dialog box to fully display the file.

Trouble? If the sjbpet.xml file opened in another application instead of your browser, XML documents are probably associated with that application on your system. To instead open an XML document in your browser, locate the file in your file manager, right-click the filename, point to Open with, and then click the name of your browser in the list of available programs.

Trouble? In Windows 8, Internet Explorer may not be configured to open XML files stored locally. If you're using Windows 8, you may need to use a different browser, such as Firefox or Chrome, to complete the steps in this tutorial.

> **2.** If you are running a browser that displays the contents of the document in outline form, click the **minus (–)** or the **down-pointing triangle (▼)** in front of the `<products>` tag. The browser collapses the comment nested within the `products` element.

> **3.** Click the **plus (+)** or the **right-pointing triangle (▶)** in front of the `<products>` tag. The browser expands the comment nested within the `products` element.

Because the XML file is well formed, the browser has no trouble rendering the document content. Patricia now wants to see how browsers respond to an XML document that is not well formed. She asks you to intentionally introduce an error into the sjbpet.xml file to verify that the error is flagged by the browser.

To see the result of an error in the sjbpet.xml file:

> **1.** Return to the **sjbpet.xml** document in your XML editor.

> **2.** Change the second to the last line of the file from `</products>` to `</PRODUCTS>` and then save the changes to your document.
>
>   Once you make this change, your document is no longer well formed because element names are case sensitive and a closing tag must match its opening tag.

> **3.** In your web browser, open **validator.w3.org**, and then click the **Validate by File Upload** tab.

> **4.** Click the **Browse** or **Choose File** button, navigate to your **xml01 ▸ tutorial** folder, click **sjbpet.xml** in the file list, click **Open**, and then click **Check**. The page now displays a red bar near the top, indicating that errors were found.

> **5.** Scroll down to the Validation Output section of the page. As Figure 1-18 shows, the page displays two errors and a third informational message.

Figure 1-18	**Errors from a document that is not well formed**

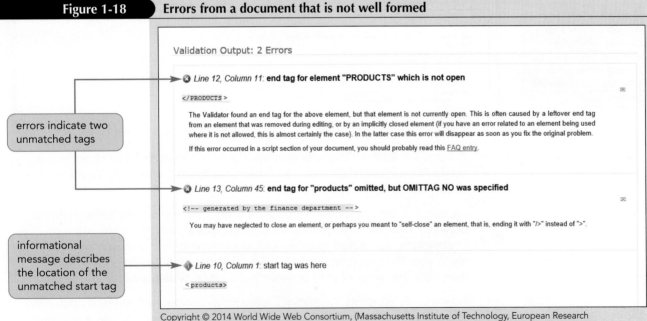

errors indicate two unmatched tags

informational message describes the location of the unmatched start tag

> **6.** Refresh or reload the **sjbpet.xml** document in your web browser. Figure 1-19 shows the contents of the file as it appears in Firefox, Chrome, and Safari.

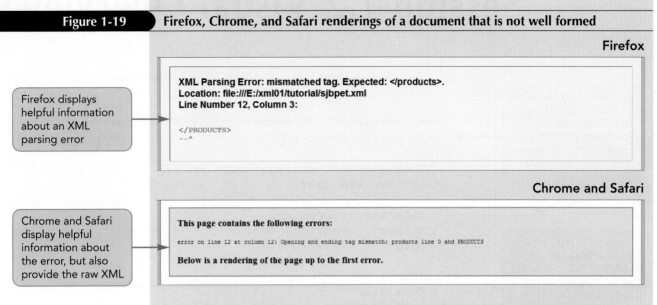

Figure 1-19   **Firefox, Chrome, and Safari renderings of a document that is not well formed**

Firefox

Firefox displays helpful information about an XML parsing error

> **XML Parsing Error: mismatched tag. Expected: </products>.**
> **Location: file:///E:/xml01/tutorial/sjbpet.xml**
> **Line Number 12, Column 3:**
>
> </PRODUCTS>
> --^

Chrome and Safari

Chrome and Safari display helpful information about the error, but also provide the raw XML

> **This page contains the following errors:**
>
> error on line 12 at column 12: Opening and ending tag mismatch: products line 0 and PRODUCTS
>
> **Below is a rendering of the page up to the first error.**

Trouble? Recent versions of Internet Explorer handle case-sensitivity of XML and CSS differently from all other browsers and show a blank window. To display the error message in Internet Explorer, press the F12 key to open the developer tools if they are not open at the bottom of the window, click Browser Mode on the Developer Tools menu bar, and then click Internet Explorer 8. The error message should now appear.

▶ 7. Return to your XML editor and then replace </PRODUCTS> with </products>. This returns the code to its original, well-formed state.

▶ 8. Save your changes to the document, repeat Steps 3 and 4, and then verify that the error message is replaced with an indication that the document is well formed.

▶ 9. Refresh or reload the **sjbpet.xml** document in your web browser, and then verify that the browser displays the document contents without any errors.

You have created a well-formed XML document containing a prolog, the shell for the document body, and an epilog. In the next session, you'll focus your attention on adding the contents of the document body.

Session 1.1 Quick Check

REVIEW

1. Define the term "extensible." How does the concept of extensibility relate to XML?
2. Name three limitations of HTML that led to the development of XML.
3. What is an XML vocabulary? Provide an example of an XML vocabulary.
4. What are the three parts of an XML document?
5. Provide an XML declaration that specifies that the document supports XML version 1.0, uses the ISO-8859-1 encoding scheme, and does not require information from other documents.
6. Write the XML code that creates a comment with the text "Data extracted from the sjbpetboutique.com database".
7. What is an XML parser?
8. What happens if you attempt to open an XML document in an XML parser when that document contains syntax errors?

Session 1.2 Visual Overview:

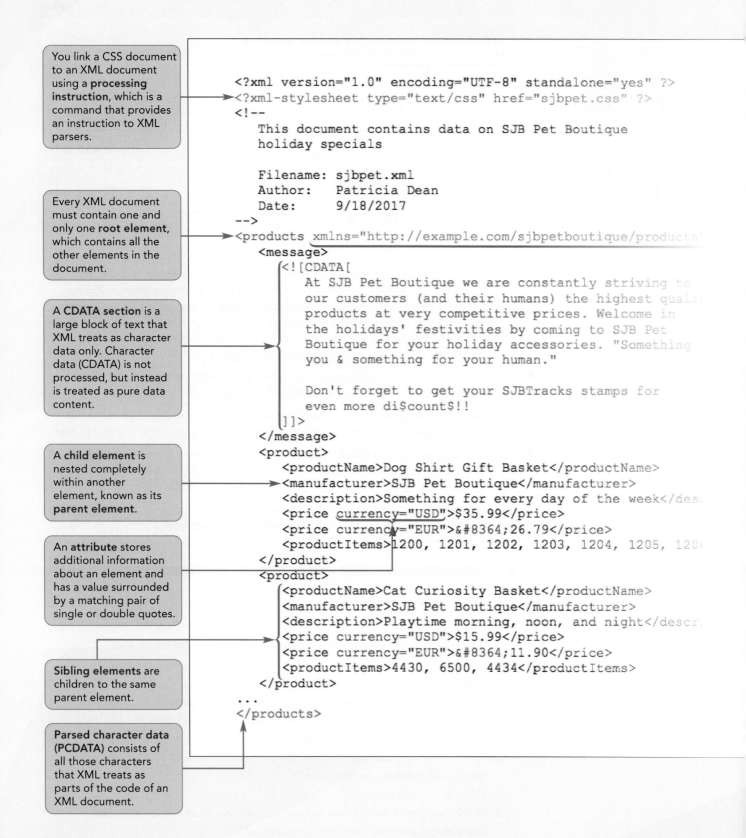

You link a CSS document to an XML document using a **processing instruction**, which is a command that provides an instruction to XML parsers.

Every XML document must contain one and only one **root element**, which contains all the other elements in the document.

A **CDATA section** is a large block of text that XML treats as character data only. Character data (CDATA) is not processed, but instead is treated as pure data content.

A **child element** is nested completely within another element, known as its **parent element**.

An **attribute** stores additional information about an element and has a value surrounded by a matching pair of single or double quotes.

Sibling elements are children to the same parent element.

Parsed character data (PCDATA) consists of all those characters that XML treats as parts of the code of an XML document.

```xml
<?xml version="1.0" encoding="UTF-8" standalone="yes" ?>
<?xml-stylesheet type="text/css" href="sjbpet.css" ?>
<!--
    This document contains data on SJB Pet Boutique
    holiday specials

    Filename: sjbpet.xml
    Author:   Patricia Dean
    Date:     9/18/2017
-->
<products xmlns="http://example.com/sjbpetboutique/product
    <message>
        <![CDATA[
        At SJB Pet Boutique we are constantly striving to
        our customers (and their humans) the highest qual
        products at very competitive prices. Welcome in
        the holidays' festivities by coming to SJB Pet
        Boutique for your holiday accessories. "Something
        you & something for your human."

        Don't forget to get your SJBTracks stamps for
        even more di$count$!!
        ]]>
    </message>
    <product>
        <productName>Dog Shirt Gift Basket</productName>
        <manufacturer>SJB Pet Boutique</manufacturer>
        <description>Something for every day of the week</des
        <price currency="USD">$35.99</price>
        <price currency="EUR">&#8364;26.79</price>
        <productItems>1200, 1201, 1202, 1203, 1204, 1205, 120
    </product>
    <product>
        <productName>Cat Curiosity Basket</productName>
        <manufacturer>SJB Pet Boutique</manufacturer>
        <description>Playtime morning, noon, and night</descr
        <price currency="USD">$15.99</price>
        <price currency="EUR">&#8364;11.90</price>
        <productItems>4430, 6500, 4434</productItems>
    </product>
    ...
</products>
```

Structuring an XML Document

A **Uniform Resource Identifier (URI)** is a text string that uniquely identifies a resource; one version of a URI is the **Uniform Resource Locator (URL)**, which is used to identify the location of a resource on the web, and the other is a **Uniform Resource Name (URN)**, which provides a persistent name for a resource, independent of that resource's location.

A **namespace** is a defined collection of element and attribute names.

Character references in XML work the same as character references in HTML.

```
0" encoding="UTF-8" standalone="yes" ?>
ype="text/css" href="sjbpet.css" ?>

ontains data on SJB Pet Boutique
ls

et.xml
icia Dean
/2017

ttp://example.com/sjbpetboutique/products">

t Boutique we are constantly striving to give
mers (and their humans) the highest quality
at very competitive prices. Welcome in
ays' festivities by coming to SJB Pet
for your holiday accessories. "Something for
thing for your human."

get to get your SJBTracks stamps for
e di$count$!!

e>Dog Shirt Gift Basket</productName>
er>SJB Pet Boutique</manufacturer>
n>Something for every day of the week</description>
ncy="USD">$35.99</price>
ncy="EUR">&#8364;26.79</price>
ms>1200, 1201, 1202, 1203, 1204, 1205, 1206</productItems>

e>Cat Curiosity Basket</productName>
er>SJB Pet Boutique</manufacturer>
n>Playtime morning, noon, and night</description>
ncy="USD">$15.99</price>
ncy="EUR">&#8364;11.90</price>
ms>4430, 6500, 4434</productItems>
```

Working with Elements

The document body in an XML document is made up of elements that contain data to be stored in the document. **Elements** are the basic building blocks of XML files. An element can have text content and child element content. The content is stored between an **opening tag** and a **closing tag**, just as in HTML. The syntax of an XML element with text content is

```
<element>content</element>
```

where `element` is the name given to the element and `content` represents the text content of the element. The opening tag is `<element>`, and `</element>` is the closing tag. Element names usually are selected by XML authors to describe element contents. Element names might be established already if an author is using a particular XML vocabulary, such as VoiceXML. As you saw in the last session, Patricia can store the name of a manufacturer using the following line of code:

```
<manufacturer>SJB Pet Boutique</manufacturer>
```

There are a few important points to remember about XML elements:

- Element names are case sensitive, which means that, for example, `itemnumber`, `itemNumber`, and `ItemNumber` are unique elements.
- Element names must begin with a letter or the underscore character (_) and may not contain blank spaces. Thus, you cannot name an element `Item Number`, but you can name it `Item_Number`.
- Element names cannot begin with the string *xml* because that group of characters is reserved for special XML commands.
- The name in an element's closing tag must exactly match the name in the opening tag.
- Element names can be used more than once, so the element names can mean different things at different points in the hierarchy of an XML document.

The following element text would result in an error because the opening tag is capitalized and the closing tag is not, meaning that they are not recognized as the opening and closing tags for the same element.

Not well-formed code:

```
<MANUFACTURER>SJB Pet Boutique</manufacturer>
```

REFERENCE

Creating XML Elements

- To create an XML element, use the syntax

```
<element>content</element>
```

where `element` is the name given to the element, `content` represents the text content of the element, `<element>` is the opening tag, and `</element>` is the closing tag.
- To create an empty XML element with a single tag, use the following syntax:

```
<element />
```

- To create an empty XML element with a pair of tags, use the syntax

```
<element></element>
```

Empty Elements

Not all elements contain content. An **open element** or **empty element** is an element with no content. White space, such as multiple spaces or a tab, is not considered content. An empty element tag usually is entered using a **one-sided tag** that obeys the syntax

```
<element />
```

where `element` is the name of the empty element. Alternatively, you can enter an empty element as a two-sided tag with no content, as follows:

```
<element></element>
```

Most programmers prefer the one-sided tag syntax to avoid confusion with two-sided tags, which normally have content.

All of the following are examples of empty elements:

```
<sample1 />
<sample2></sample2>
<sample3>   </sample3>
<sample4>

</sample4>
```

Empty XML elements are similar to HTML's collection of empty elements, such as the `<br />` tag for line breaks or the `<img />` tag for inline graphics.

If empty elements have no content, why use them in an XML document? One reason is to mark certain sections of the document for programs reading it. For example, Patricia might use an empty element to distinguish one group of products from another. Empty elements can also contain attributes that can be used to store information. Finally, empty elements can be used to reference external documents containing non-textual data in much the same way that the HTML `<img />` tag is used to reference image files.

Nesting Elements

In addition to text content, elements also can contain other elements. An element contained within another element is said to be a **nested** element. For instance, in the following example, multiple elements are nested within the `product` element:

```
<product>
    <productName>Dog Shirt Gift Basket</productName>
    <manufacturer>SJB Pet Boutique</manufacturer>
    <description>Something for every day of the week</description>
    <price>35.99</price>
    <price>26.79</price>
    <productItems>1200, 1201, 1202, 1203, 1204, 1205, 1206
    </productItems>
</product>
```

Like HTML, XML uses familial names to refer to the hierarchical relationships between elements. A nested element is a child element of the element in which it is nested— its parent element. Elements that are side-by-side in a document's hierarchy are sibling elements. In the example in Figure 1-20, the `productName`, `manufacturer`, `description`, `price`, and `productItems` elements are siblings to each other, and each of these elements is also a child of the `product` element.

Figure 1-20 **Parent, child, and sibling elements**

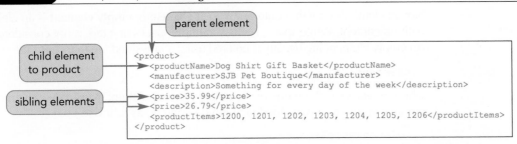

A common syntax error in creating an XML document is improperly nesting one element within another. Just as in XHTML, XML does not allow the opening and closing tags of parent and child elements to overlap. For this reason, the following XML code is not considered well formed because the `productName` element does not completely enclose the `manufacturer` element.

Not well-formed code:

```
<productName>Dog Shirt Gift Basket<manufacturer>SJB Pet Boutique
</productName></manufacturer>
```

To make the code well formed, the closing `</productName>` tag should be moved after the `</manufacturer>` tag to prevent any overlap of the element tags, as follows:

Well-formed code:

```
<productName>Dog Shirt Gift Basket<manufacturer>SJB Pet Boutique
</manufacturer></productName>
```

This syntax is correct because both `manufacturer` tags are within the opening and closing tags of the parent `productName` element.

The Element Hierarchy

The familial relationship of parent, child, and sibling extends throughout the entire document body. All elements in the body are children of a single element called the root element or **document element**. Figure 1-21 shows a sample XML document with its hierarchy represented in a tree diagram. The root element in this document is the `products` element. Note that the XML declaration and comments are not included in the tree structure of the document body.

Figure 1-21   **Code for an XML document along with its corresponding tree diagram**

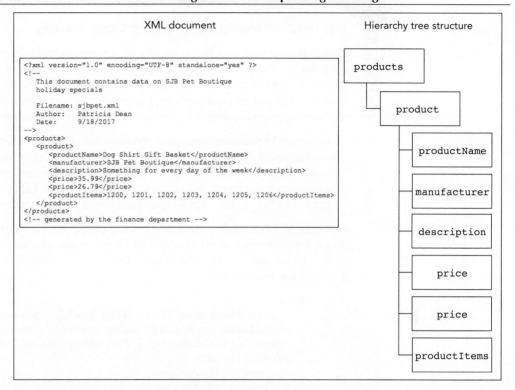

An XML document must include a root element to be considered well formed. The following document code is not well formed because it lacks a single root element containing all other elements in the document body.

Not well-formed code:

```
<?xml version="1.0" encoding="UTF-8" standalone="yes" ?>
<!--
   This document contains data on SJB Pet Boutique
   holiday specials
-->
<productName>Dog Shirt Gift Basket</productName>
<manufacturer>SJB Pet Boutique</manufacturer>
<description>Something for every day of the week</description>
<price>35.99</price>
<price>26.79</price>
<productItems>1200, 1201, 1202, 1203, 1204, 1205, 1206
</productItems>
```

PROSKILLS

Written Communication: Writing Code Visually

Including comments in a file is one way of communicating information about the file contents to other developers. The way you visually arrange your code is another way to communicate with other developers. Technically, child and sibling elements do not have to be coded on separate lines; parsers do not care. Thus, the following code, while challenging to understand at a glance, is considered well formed:

```
<product><productName>Dog Shirt Gift Basket</productName>
<manufacturer>SJB Pet Boutique</manufacturer><description>
Something for every day of the week</description><price>35.99
</price><price>26.79</price><productItems>1200, 1201, 1202,
1203, 1204, 1205, 1206</productItems></product>
```

However, by indenting the code and placing siblings on their own lines, you can visually reveal the hierarchy relationships and add a dimension of visual communication to your code. The following code is the same as the previous example, but now line breaks and indents have been added:

```
<product>
    <productName>Dog Shirt Gift Basket</productName>
    <manufacturer>SJB Pet Boutique</manufacturer>
    <description>Something for every day of the week
    </description>
    <price>35.99</price>
    <price>26.79</price>
    <productItems>1200, 1201, 1202, 1203, 1204, 1205, 1206
    </productItems>
</product>
```

Although the elements are coded exactly the same in both instances, a programmer would spend a lot more time identifying the parent, child, and sibling relationships in the first coding sample. By including simple line breaks and tabs in your documents, you can communicate the structure of your document in a way that complements written comments.

Charting the Element Hierarchy

A quick way to view the overall structure of a document body is to chart the elements in a tree structure like the one shown in Figure 1-21. This can become confusing, however, when a single element has several children of the same type. For example, the product element in Figure 1-21 contains two price elements within it. Other product descriptions might have differing numbers of price elements using this layout. It would be useful to have a general tree diagram that indicates whether a particular child element can occur zero times, once, or several times within a parent. Figure 1-22 displays the shorthand code you will see in the tree diagrams in this and subsequent tutorials to indicate the general structure of the document body.

Figure 1-22	Charting the number of child elements

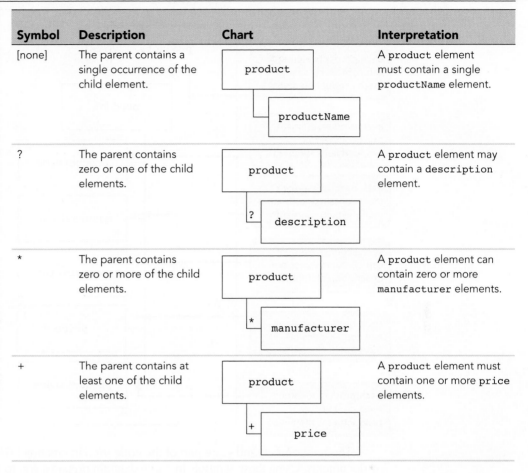

Symbol	Description	Chart	Interpretation
[none]	The parent contains a single occurrence of the child element.	product └ productName	A product element must contain a single productName element.
?	The parent contains zero or one of the child elements.	product ?└ description	A product element may contain a description element.
*	The parent contains zero or more of the child elements.	product *└ manufacturer	A product element can contain zero or more manufacturer elements.
+	The parent contains at least one of the child elements.	product +└ price	A product element must contain one or more price elements.

Figure 1-23 shows how these symbols apply to the structure of the XML document you will create for SJB Pet Boutique.

Figure 1-23   **Charting the sjbpet.xml document**

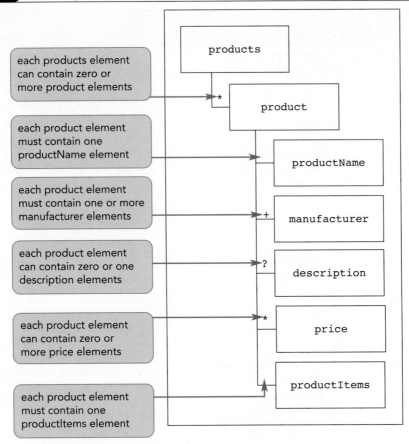

The symbols ?, *, and + are part of the code used in creating DTDs to validate XML documents. Using these symbols in a tree diagram prepares you to learn more about DTDs later on.

Writing the Document Body

Now that you've reviewed some of the aspects of XML elements, you're ready to use them in an XML document. You've already started creating the sjbpet.xml document, which will describe the SJB Pet Boutique's holiday specials. Patricia would like you to add information on the products shown in Figure 1-24 to this document. Patricia has indicated that no current XML vocabulary exists that meets her data requirements. Because you'll create your own XML vocabulary for this document, you'll use descriptive element names for all of the element items.

| Figure 1-24 | Product descriptions for the SJB Pet Boutique holiday specials |

Product Name	Manufacturer	Description	Price	Product Items
Dog Shirt Gift Basket	SJB Pet Boutique	Something for every day of the week	35.99 26.79	1200, 1201, 1202, 1203, 1204, 1205, 1206
Cat Curiosity Basket	SJB Pet Boutique	Playtime morning, noon, and night	15.99 11.90	4430, 6500, 4434
Piggy Snuggle Basket	ACME		17.50 13.03	3230, 3232
Dog Snuggle Basket	ACME		14.25 10.61	3230, 3232, 3250

The products element will be the root element of the document. The productName, manufacturer, description, price, and productItems elements all will be children of a parent product element for each item.

To add the products to the XML document:

1. If you took a break after the previous session, make sure the **sjbpet.xml** document is open in your editor.

2. Delete the code `<!-- document body content -->` from the document. You'll replace it with the actual document body content.

3. Between the opening and closing `<products>` tags, insert the following code, pressing the **Enter** key at the end of each line and indenting as shown:

```
<product>
    <productName>Dog Shirt Gift Basket</productName>
    <manufacturer>SJB Pet Boutique</manufacturer>
    <description>Something for every day of the week
    </description>
    <price>35.99</price>
    <price>26.79</price>
    <productItems>1200, 1201, 1202, 1203, 1204, 1205, 1206
    </productItems>
</product>
<product>
    <productName>Cat Curiosity Basket</productName>
    <manufacturer>SJB Pet Boutique</manufacturer>
    <description>Playtime morning, noon, and night
    </description>
    <price>15.99</price>
    <price>11.90</price>
    <productItems>4430, 6500, 4434</productItems>
</product>
<product>
    <productName>Piggy Snuggle Basket</productName>
    <manufacturer>ACME</manufacturer>
    <price>17.50</price>
    <price>13.03</price>
    <productItems>3230, 3232</productItems>
</product>
```

```
<product>
    <productName>Dog Snuggle Basket</productName>
    <manufacturer>ACME</manufacturer>
    <price>14.25</price>
    <price>10.61</price>
    <productItems>3230, 3232, 3250</productItems>
</product>
```

Figure 1-25 shows the code for the products added to the document.

Figure 1-25   **Adding elements to the XML document body**

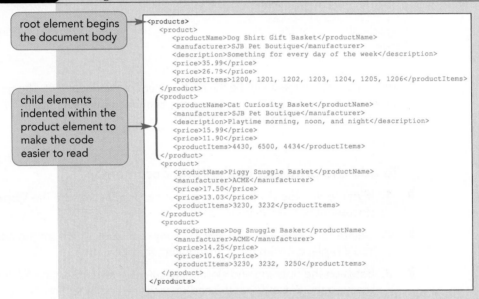

root element begins the document body

child elements indented within the product element to make the code easier to read

```
<products>
    <product>
        <productName>Dog Shirt Gift Basket</productName>
        <manufacturer>SJB Pet Boutique</manufacturer>
        <description>Something for every day of the week</description>
        <price>35.99</price>
        <price>26.79</price>
        <productItems>1200, 1201, 1202, 1203, 1204, 1205, 1206</productItems>
    </product>
    <product>
        <productName>Cat Curiosity Basket</productName>
        <manufacturer>SJB Pet Boutique</manufacturer>
        <description>Playtime morning, noon, and night</description>
        <price>15.99</price>
        <price>11.90</price>
        <productItems>4430, 6500, 4434</productItems>
    </product>
    <product>
        <productName>Piggy Snuggle Basket</productName>
        <manufacturer>ACME</manufacturer>
        <price>17.50</price>
        <price>13.03</price>
        <productItems>3230, 3232</productItems>
    </product>
    <product>
        <productName>Dog Snuggle Basket</productName>
        <manufacturer>ACME</manufacturer>
        <price>14.25</price>
        <price>10.61</price>
        <productItems>3230, 3232, 3250</productItems>
    </product>
</products>
```

4. Save your changes to the **sjbpet.xml** document, and then use your editor or **validator.w3.org** to check your document for well-formedness.

   Trouble? If your document is no longer well formed, check each line of code associated with an error message against the code in Step 3 and fix any errors. Save your work and, if necessary, repeat until the document is well formed.

You've finished adding the product elements and their child elements. Next, you'll add attributes to the sjbpet.xml document.

Working with Attributes

Every element in an XML document can contain one or more attributes. An attribute describes a feature or characteristic of an element. The syntax for adding an attribute to an element is

```
<element attribute="value"> ... </element>
```

where *attribute* is the attribute's name and *value* is the attribute's value. In the case of a one-sided element tag, the syntax is as follows:

```
<element attribute="value" />
```

Attribute values are text strings. Therefore, an attribute value always must be enclosed within either single or double quotes. For example, if Patricia wants to include the currency as an attribute of the price element, she could enter the following code:

```
<price currency="USD">35.99</price>
```

Alternatively, she could instead use single quotes, as follows:

```
<price currency='USD'>35.99</price>
```

Because they're considered text strings, attribute values may contain spaces and almost any character other than the less than (<) and greater than (>) symbols. You can choose any name for an attribute as long as it meets the following rules:

- An attribute name must begin with a letter or an underscore (_).
- Spaces are not allowed in attribute names.
- Like an element name, an attribute name should not begin with the text string *xml*.

An attribute name can appear only once within an element. Like all other aspects of XML, attribute names are case sensitive, and incorrect case is a common syntax error found in attributes. An attribute named `Currency` is considered distinct from an attribute named `currency`, so it's important to be consistent in your case when naming attributes.

REFERENCE

Adding an Attribute to an Element

- To add an attribute to an element, use the syntax

  `<element attribute="value"> … </element>`

  where *element* is the name given to the element, *attribute* is the attribute's name, and *value* is the attribute's value.
- To add an attribute to a single-sided tag, use the syntax

  `<element attribute="value" />`
- To specify multiple attributes for a single element, use the syntax

  `<element attribute1="value1" attribute2="value2" …> … </element>`

  where *attribute1* is the first attribute's name, *value1* is the first attribute's value, *attribute2* is the second attribute's name, *value2* is the second attribute's value, and so on. Each attribute is separated by a space.

Most of SJB Pet Boutique's business is in the U.S., but the company also has a sizable customer base in Ireland. For this reason, the XML document includes the prices for each item both in the U.S. dollar and in Ireland's currency, the euro. Patricia would like to specify the currency as an attribute of each `price` element instead of as a separate element. She wants to use the abbreviation USD for prices in U.S. dollars and EUR for prices in euros. Figure 1-26 shows the currency for each `price` element in the sjbpet.xml document.

Figure 1-26 **Currency values for price elements**

Product Name	Price	Currency
Dog Shirt Gift Basket	35.99	USD
	26.79	EUR
Cat Curiosity Basket	15.99	USD
	11.90	EUR
Piggy Snuggle Basket	17.50	USD
	13.03	EUR
Dog Snuggle Basket	14.25	USD
	10.61	EUR

You'll modify the sjbpet.xml document to include a `currency` attribute with the proper value for each `price` element.

To add the `currency` attribute to each `price` element:

1. Return to the **sjbpet.xml** document in your editor.

2. Locate the first `price` element for the first product, which has a value of 35.99.

3. Directly before the > in the `price` element's opening tag, insert a space and then type **currency="USD"**.

4. Repeat Steps 2 and 3 to add `currency` attributes to the remaining `price` elements, using the values found in Figure 1-26. Figure 1-27 shows the updated code.

Figure 1-27	Number attributes added to document body

```
<products>
   <product>
      <productName>Dog Shirt Gift Basket</productName>
      <manufacturer>SJB Pet Boutique</manufacturer>
      <description>Something for every day of the week</description>
      <price currency="USD">35.99</price>
      <price currency="EUR">26.79</price>
      <productItems>1200, 1201, 1202, 1203, 1204, 1205, 1206</productItems>
   </product>
   <product>
      <productName>Cat Curiosity Basket</productName>
      <manufacturer>SJB Pet Boutique</manufacturer>
      <description>Playtime morning, noon, and night</description>
      <price currency="USD">15.99</price>
      <price currency="EUR">11.90</price>
      <productItems>4430, 6500, 4434</productItems>
   </product>
   <product>
      <productName>Piggy Snuggle Basket</productName>
      <manufacturer>ACME</manufacturer>
      <price currency="USD">17.50</price>
      <price currency="EUR">13.03</price>
      <productItems>3230, 3232</productItems>
   </product>
   <product>
      <productName>Dog Snuggle Basket</productName>
      <manufacturer>ACME</manufacturer>
      <price currency="USD">14.25</price>
      <price currency="EUR">10.61</price>
      <productItems>3230, 3232, 3250</productItems>
   </product>
</products>
```

attribute name and value are defined in the opening tag of each element

5. Save the changes to your document.

Elements vs. Attributes

It's not always clear when to use an attribute value rather than inserting a new element. For example, the following code provides currency information about each `price` element using an attribute:

```
<price currency="USD">35.99</price>
<price currency="EUR">26.79</price>
```

However, you could instead insert the currency information for each `price` element as a sibling element using the following format:

```
<price>35.99</price>
<currency>USD</currency>
<price>26.79</price>
<currency>EUR</currency>
```

Either style is acceptable. Some developers argue that attributes never should be used because they increase a document's complexity. Their rationale is that when information is placed as an element rather than as an attribute within an element, it's more easily accessible by programs reading a document.

A general rule of thumb is that if all of the XML tags and their attributes were removed from a document, the remaining text should comprise the document's content or information. In this scenario, if an attribute value is something you want displayed, it really should be placed in an element, as in the second example above. However, if an attribute is not necessary in order to understand the document content, you can safely keep it as an attribute placed within an element, as in the first example above.

Another rule of thumb is that attributes should be used to describe data, but should not contain data themselves. However, this can be a difficult distinction to make in most cases.

So which should you use? Different developers have different preferences, and there's no right answer. However, when you're in doubt, it's probably safest to use an element.

Using Character and Entity References

Next, Patricia would like you to make sure that the symbols for the item prices display in browsers. Figure 1-28 displays the prices of the four products with the corresponding currency symbols.

| Figure 1-28 | Product prices |

Product	U.S. Price	Ireland Price
Dog Shirt Gift Basket	$35.99	€26.79
Cat Curiosity Basket	$15.99	€11.90
Piggy Snuggle Basket	$17.50	€13.03
Dog Snuggle Basket	$14.25	€10.61

To insert characters such as the € symbol, which is not available on a standard U.S. keyboard, you use a **numeric character reference**, also known simply as a **character reference**. The syntax for a character reference is

```
&#nnn;
```

where *nnn* is a character number from the ISO/IEC character set. The **ISO/IEC character set** is an international numbering system for referencing characters from virtually any language. Character references in XML work the same as character references in HTML.

TIP

Unicode can be used in conjunction with entity references to display specific characters or symbols.

Because it can be difficult to remember the character numbers for different symbols, some symbols also can be identified using a **character entity reference**—also known simply as an **entity reference**—using the syntax

&*entity*;

where *entity* is the name assigned to the symbol.

Make sure to start every character or entity reference with an ampersand (&) and end with a semicolon (;). Figure 1-29 lists a few of the commonly used character and entity references.

Figure 1-29 | **Character and entity references**

Symbol	Character Reference	Entity Reference	Description
>	&#62;	&gt;	Greater than
<	&#60;	&lt;	Less than
'	&#27;	&apos;	Apostrophe (single quote)
"	&#22;	&quot;	Double quote
&	&#38;	&amp;	Ampersand
©	&#169;	&copy;	Copyright
®	&#174;	&reg;	Registered trademark
™	&#153;		Trademark
°	&#176;		Degree
£	&#163;		Pound
€	&#8364;	&euro;	Euro
¥	&#165;	&yen;	Yen

Notice that not all symbols have both character and entity references.

REFERENCE

Inserting Character and Entity References

- To insert a character reference into an XML document, use

  &#*nnn*;

  where *nnn* is a character reference number from the ISO/IEC character set.
- To insert an entity reference, use

  &*entity*;

  where *entity* is a recognized entity name.

A common mistake made in XML documents is to forget that XML processors interpret the ampersand symbol (&) as the start of a character reference and not as a character. Often, XML validators catch such mistakes. For example, the following code results in an error message because the ampersand symbol is not followed by a recognized character reference number or entity name.

Not well-formed code:

```
<manufacturer>Hills & Barton</manufacturer>
```

To avoid this error, you need to use the `&#38;` character reference or the `&amp;` entity reference in place of the ampersand symbol, as follows:

Well-formed code:

```
<manufacturer>Hills &amp; Barton</manufacturer>
```

Character references are sometimes used to store the text of HTML code within an XML element. For example, to store the HTML tag `<img src="sjblogo.jpg" />` in an element named `htmlCode`, you need to use character references `&#60;` and `&#62;` to reference the < and > symbols contained in the HTML tag. The following code accomplishes this:

```
<htmlCode>&#60;img src="sjblogo.jpg" /&#62;</htmlCode>
```

The following code would not give the same result.

Not well-formed code:

```
<htmlCode><img src="sjblogo.jpg" /></htmlCode>
```

When encountering this code, an XML processor would attempt to interpret `<img src="sjblogo.jpg" />` as an empty element within the document and not as the content of the `htmlCode` element.

The character reference for the € symbol is `&#8364;`. You'll use this character reference now to add Ireland's currency symbol to the second `price` element for each product. You'll also use the keyboard to add the $ symbol to the first price element for each product.

To insert the dollar symbol and the euro character reference into the `price` elements:

1. Return to the **sjbpet.xml** document in your text editor.

2. Within the first `product` element, click after the opening tag for the first `price` element, and then type the **$** character.

3. Within the first `product` element, click after the opening tag for the second `price` element, and then type **€**.

4. Repeat Steps 2 and 3 for each of the remaining three `product` elements, as shown in Figure 1-30. You should insert both the $ character and the character reference a total of four times within the document.

TIP

After typing the first occurrence of the character reference, you can copy the reference to the Clipboard and then paste it in the other three locations to minimize typing errors.

Figure 1-30 **$ and euro symbol character reference inserted**

```
<products>
    <product>
        <productName>Dog Shirt Gift Basket</productName>
        <manufacturer>SJB Pet Boutique</manufacturer>
        <description>Something for every day of the week</description>
        <price currency="USD">$35.99</price>
        <price currency="EUR">&#8364;26.79</price>
        <productItems>1200, 1201, 1202, 1203, 1204, 1205, 1206</productItems>
    </product>
    <product>
        <productName>Cat Curiosity Basket</productName>
        <manufacturer>SJB Pet Boutique</manufacturer>
        <description>Playtime morning, noon, and night</description>
        <price currency="USD">$15.99</price>
        <price currency="EUR">&#8364;11.90</price>
        <productItems>4430, 6500, 4434</productItems>
    </product>
    <product>
        <productName>Piggy Snuggle Basket</productName>
        <manufacturer>ACME</manufacturer>
        <price currency="USD">$17.50</price>
        <price currency="EUR">&#8364;13.03</price>
        <productItems>3230, 3232</productItems>
    </product>
    <product>
        <productName>Dog Snuggle Basket</productName>
        <manufacturer>ACME</manufacturer>
        <price currency="USD">$14.25</price>
        <price currency="EUR">&#8364;10.61</price>
        <productItems>3230, 3232, 3250</productItems>
    </product>
</products>
```

character reference starts with & and ends with ;

5. Save your changes to the document.

6. If necessary, start your web browser and then open the **sjbpet.xml** document. As Figure 1-31 shows, each occurrence of the € character reference is converted into a € symbol.

Figure 1-31 **€ symbol rendered in browser**

```
− <products>
   − <product>
        <productName>Dog Shirt Gift Basket</productName>
        <manufacturer>SJB Pet Boutique</manufacturer>
        <description>Something for every day of the week</description>
        <price currency="USD">$35.99</price>
        <price currency="EUR">€26.79</price>
        <productItems>1200, 1201, 1202, 1203, 1204, 1205, 1206</productItems>
     </product>
   − <product>
        <productName>Cat Curiosity Basket</productName>
        <manufacturer>SJB Pet Boutique</manufacturer>
        <description>Playtime morning, noon, and night</description>
        <price currency="USD">$15.99</price>
        <price currency="EUR">€11.90</price>
        <productItems>4430, 6500, 4434</productItems>
     </product>
   − <product>
        <productName>Piggy Snuggle Basket</productName>
        <manufacturer>ACME</manufacturer>
        <price currency="USD">$17.50</price>
        <price currency="EUR">€13.03</price>
        <productItems>3230, 3232</productItems>
     </product>
   − <product>
        <productName>Dog Snuggle Basket</productName>
        <manufacturer>ACME</manufacturer>
        <price currency="USD">$14.25</price>
        <price currency="EUR">€10.61</price>
        <productItems>3230, 3232, 3250</productItems>
     </product>
  </products>
```

browser replaces each occurrence of € with € symbol

Understanding Text Characters and White Space

As you've seen from working on the sjbpet.xml document, XML documents consist only of text characters. However, text characters fall into three categories—parsed character data, character data, and white space. In order to appreciate how programs like browsers interpret XML documents, it's important to understand the distinctions among these categories.

Parsed Character Data

Parsed character data (PCDATA) consists of all those characters that XML treats as parts of the code of an XML document. This includes characters found in the following:

- the XML declaration
- the opening and closing tags of an element
- empty element tags
- character or entity references
- comments

Parsed character data also can be found in other XML features that you'll learn about in later tutorials, such as processing instructions and document type declarations.

The presence of PCDATA can cause unexpected errors to occur within a document. XML treats any element content as potential PCDATA because elements may contain other elements. This means that symbols such as &, <, or >, which are all used in creating markup tags or entity references, are extracted and the appropriate content is used in your program. For example, the following line would result in an error because the greater than symbol (>) in the temperature value would be viewed as the end of a markup tag.

Not well-formed code:

```
<temperature> > 98.6 degrees</temperature>
```

Because the greater than symbol does not have any accompanying markup tag characters, the document would be rejected for being not well formed. To correct this error, you would have to replace the greater than symbol with either the character reference > or the entity reference >. The correct temperature value would then be entered as follows:

Well-formed code:

```
<temperature>&gt;98.6 degrees</temperature>
```

If you instead wanted to display the above line without it being parsed, you would code it as follows:

```
&lt;temperature&gt; &gt;98.6 degrees&lt;/temperature&gt;
```

Character Data

After you account for parsed character data, the remaining symbols constitute a document's actual contents, known as **character data**. Character data is not processed, but instead is treated as pure data content. One purpose of character and entity references is to convert PCDATA into character data. For example, when the program reading an XML document encounters the entity reference >, it converts it to the corresponding character data symbol >.

White Space

The third type of character that an XML document can contain is white space. **White space** refers to nonprintable characters such as spaces (created by pressing the spacebar), new line characters (created by pressing the Enter key), or tab characters (created by pressing the Tab key). Processors reading an XML document must determine whether white space represents actual content or is used to make the code more readable. For example, the code you've entered in the SJB Pet Boutique document is indented to make it more readable to users. However, this does not have any impact on how the XML document's contents or structure are interpreted.

HTML applies **white space stripping**, in which consecutive occurrences of white space are treated as a single space. White space stripping allows HTML authors to format a document's code to be readable without affecting the document's appearance in browsers. As a result of white space stripping, the HTML code

```
<p>This is a
    paragraph.</p>
```

is treated the same as

```
<p>This is a paragraph.</p>
```

White space is treated slightly differently in XML. Technically, no white space stripping occurs for element content, which means that the content of the XML element

```
<paragraph>This is    a
        paragraph.</paragraph>
```

is interpreted as

```
This is    a
        paragraph.
```

This preserves both the new line character and all of the blank spaces.

However, the majority of browsers today transform XML code into HTML, and in the process apply white space stripping to element content. Thus, in browsers such as Internet Explorer, Firefox, or Chrome, the contents of the above XML element would be displayed as

```
This is a paragraph.
```

When white space appears in places other than element content, XML treats it in the following manner:

- White space is ignored when it is the only character data between element tags; this allows XML authors to format their documents to be readable without affecting the content or structure.
- White space is ignored within a document's prolog and epilog, and within any element tags.
- White space within an attribute value is treated as part of the attribute value.

In summary, white space in an XML document is generally ignored unless it is part of the document's data.

> **TIP**
>
> Not all browsers parse white space in the same way, so be sure to preview your documents in a variety of browsers.

Creating a CDATA Section

Sometimes an XML document needs to store significant blocks of text containing the < and > symbols. For example, what if you wanted to place all of the text from this tutorial into an XML document? If there were only a few < and > symbols, it might not be too much work to replace them all with `&#60;` and `&#62;` character references, or with `&lt;` and `&gt;` entity references. However, given the volume of text in this tutorial, it would be cumbersome to replace all of the < and > symbols with the associated character or entity references, and the code itself would be difficult to read.

As an alternative to using character references, you can place text into a CDATA section. A CDATA section is a block of text that XML treats as character data only. The syntax for creating a CDATA section is

```
<![CDATA [
    character data
]]>
```

A CDATA section may contain most markup characters, such as <, >, and &. In a CDATA section, these characters are interpreted by XML parsers or XML editors as text rather than as markup commands. A CDATA section

- may be placed anywhere within a document.
- cannot be nested within other CDATA sections.
- cannot be empty.

The only sequence of symbols that may not occur within a CDATA section is]] because this is the marker ending a CDATA section.

The following example shows an element named htmlCode containing a CDATA section used to store several HTML tags:

```
<htmlCode>
    <![CDATA[
        <h1>SJB Pet Boutique</h1>
        <h2>Fashion for Pets and Their Humans</h2>
    ]]>
</htmlCode>
```

The text in this example is treated by XML as character data, not PCDATA. Therefore, a processor would not read the <h1> and <h2> character strings as element tags. You might find it useful to place any large block of text within a CDATA section to protect yourself from inadvertently inserting a character such as the ampersand symbol that would be misinterpreted by an XML processor.

Patricia would like you to insert a message element into the sjbpet.xml document that describes the purpose and contents of the document. You'll use a CDATA section for this task.

To create a CDATA section:

▶ 1. Return to the **sjbpet.xml** document in your XML editor.

▶ 2. Insert a blank line below the opening <products> tag, and then enter the following code, pressing **Enter** at the end of each line:

```
<message>
  <![CDATA[
        At SJB Pet Boutique we are constantly striving to give
        our customers (and their humans) the highest quality
        products at very competitive prices. Welcome in
        the holidays' festivities by coming to SJB Pet
        Boutique for your holiday accessories. "Something for
        you & something for your human."

        Don't forget to get your SJBTracks stamps for
        even more di$count$!!
  ]]>
</message>
```

Figure 1-32 shows the code for the CDATA section in the document.

Figure 1-32   **Adding a CDATA section**

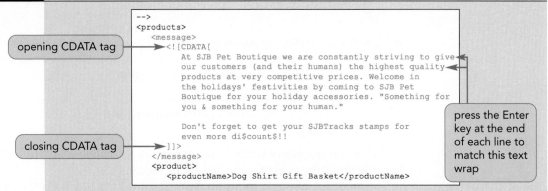

3. Save the changes to your document.

4. Verify that your document is well formed, and correct any errors if necessary.

Trouble? If your code is not well formed, check your XML code against the sjbpet.xml code shown in Figure 1-32. Your newly added code should match exactly, including the use of uppercase and lowercase letters. Fix any discrepancies, be sure to save your changes, and then verify that your document is well formed.

You've completed your work to create Patricia's XML document. Next, you'll display the document in a web browser.

CDATA Cans and Cannots

New authors of XML documents often mistakenly use CDATA to protect data from being treated as ordinary character data during processing. Character data is character data, regardless of whether it is expressed via a CDATA section or ordinary markup. CDATA blocks can be very useful as long as you keep a few CDATA rules in mind.

You *can* use CDATA blocks when you want to include large blocks of special characters as character data. This saves the time it would take to replace characters with their corresponding entity references. However, keep in mind the size of the CDATA sections. If you serve XML files through a web service, you must ensure that client applications can handle potentially large data transfers without timing out or blocking their user interfaces. You also should make sure your server can accept large upstream transfers from clients sending XML data. Sending large blocks of data from the browser in this manner can be error-prone and tends to lock up valuable resources on the server and the client. You also should keep in mind that many users may be using mobile platforms, and there may be implications with attempting such large data transfers.

You *cannot* expect to keep markup untouched just because it looks as though it would be securely concealed inside a CDATA section. New programmers often assume that they can hide JavaScript or HTML markup by putting it inside a CDATA section. The content is still there, but it's treated as text.

You *cannot* use XML comments in a CDATA section. The literal text of the comment tags and comment text, such as `<!-- December special events -->`, is passed directly to the application or screen.

You *cannot* nest a CDATA section inside another CDATA section. While processing the XML document, the nested section end marker `]]>` is encountered before the real section end, which can cause a parser to assume that the nested section marker is the end of your CDATA section. This might cause a parser error when it subsequently hits the real section end.

CDATA has its own special rules. If you master them, CDATA can be a very powerful tool for your XML documents.

To see how Patricia's document is displayed with all of the added content, you'll open it in your web browser.

To view the sjbpet.xml file in your browser:

▶ **1.** In your web browser, refresh or reload the **sjbpet.xml** document.

▶ **2.** Locate the `message` element. Because different browsers display XML content differently, in the CDATA section, the CDATA tags and white space might or might not be shown in a given browser. Figure 1-33 shows the contents of the file as it appears in Firefox, Chrome, and Internet Explorer. Safari and Opera display CDATA sections in a way similar to Chrome.

Figure 1-33	Displaying the sjbpet.xml document in Firefox, Chrome, and Internet Explorer

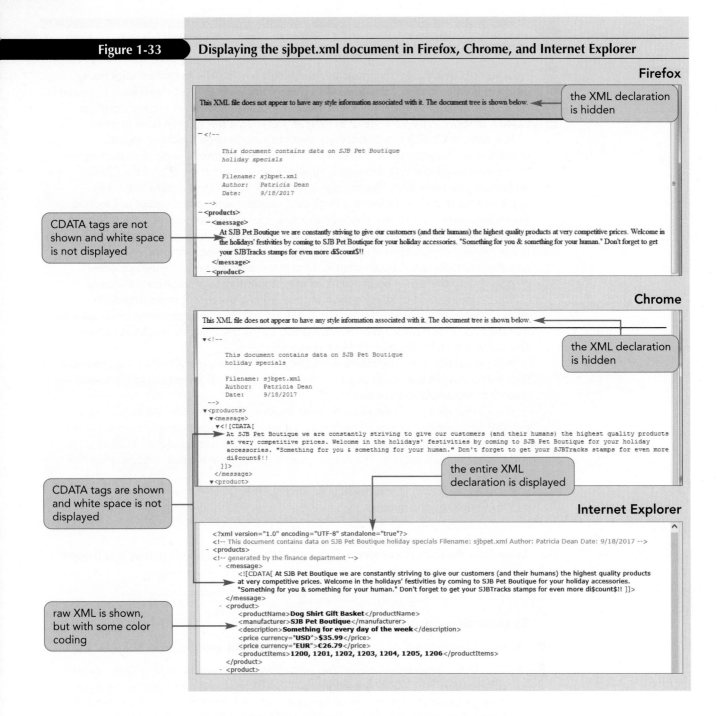

Formatting XML Data with CSS

Patricia appreciates your work on the XML document. She would like to share this type of information with other users and place it on the web. However, she does not want to display the contents in the default hierarchical format shown in Figure 1-33. She would instead like to have the data formatted in a visually attractive way.

In contrast to HTML documents, XML documents do not include any information about *how* they should be rendered. Rendering is determined solely by the parser processing the document. As seen previously, different browsers render XML differently when an XML document does not indicate how its data is to be formatted or displayed. If you want to have control over the document's appearance, you have to physically link the document to a style sheet. The XML document and the style sheet are then combined by an XML parser to render a single formatted document, as shown in Figure 1-34.

| Figure 1-34 | Combining an XML document and a style sheet |

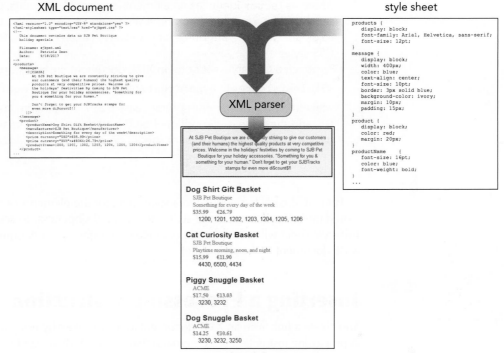

Applying a Style to an Element

Cascading Style Sheets (CSS), the style sheet language developed for use with HTML on the web, also can be used with the elements in any XML document. CSS styles are applied to an XML element using the style declaration

```
selector {
   attribute1: value1;
   attribute2: value2;
   ...
}
```

where *selector* identifies an element (or a set of elements with each element separated by a comma) from the XML document; *attribute1*, *attribute2*, and so on are CSS style attributes; and *value1*, *value2*, and so forth are values of the CSS styles. For example, the following style declaration displays the text of the `author` element in a red boldface type:

```
author {
   color: red;
   font-weight: bold;
}
```

REFERENCE

Creating and Attaching a Style to an Element in an XML Document

- To create a style rule for an element, use the syntax

```
selector {
    attribute1: value1;
    attribute2: value2;
    …
}
```

where `selector` identifies an element (or a set of elements, with each element separated by a comma) from the XML document; `attribute1`, `attribute2`, and so on are CSS style attributes; and `value1`, `value2`, and so forth are values of the CSS styles.

- To attach a CSS style sheet to an XML document, insert the processing instruction

```
<?xml-stylesheet type="text/css" href="url" media="type" ?>
```

within the XML document's prolog, where `url` is the name and location of the CSS file, and the value of the optional `media` attribute describes the type of output device to which the style sheet should be applied. If no `media` value is specified, a default value of `all` is used.

Patricia already has generated a style sheet for the elements of the sjbpet.xml file and stored the styles in an external style sheet named sjbpet.css. To see how the styles in this style sheet will affect the appearance of the sjbpet.xml document, you must link the XML document to the style sheet.

Inserting a Processing Instruction

You create a link from an XML document to a style sheet by using a processing instruction. A processing instruction is a command that tells an XML parser how to process the document. Processing instructions have the general form

```
<?target instruction ?>
```

where `target` identifies the program (or object) to which the processing instruction is directed and `instruction` is information that the document passes on to the parser for processing. Usually the instruction takes the form of attributes and attribute values. For example, the basic processing instruction to link the contents of an XML document to a style sheet is

```
<?xml-stylesheet type="style" href="url" media="type" ?>
```

where `style` is the type of style sheet the XML processor will be accessing, `url` is the name and location of the style sheet, and `type` is the type of output device to which the style sheet is to be applied. In this example, `xml-stylesheet` is the processing instruction's target, and the other items within the tag are processing instructions that identify the type, location, and output media for the style sheet. For a style sheet, the value of the `type` attribute should be `text/css`. The most commonly used `media` types are `screen` and `print`. If no `media` value is specified, a default value of `all` is used. The following example applies a style sheet called main.css to all output devices:

```
<?xml-stylesheet type="text/css" href="main.css" media="all" ?>
```

The same processing instruction for all output devices could be coded as follows:

```
<?xml-stylesheet type="text/css" href="main.css" ?>
```

Multiple processing instructions can exist within the same XML document for different media types. The following example shows two processing instructions being included within the same document:

```
<?xml-stylesheet type="text/css" href="main.css" media="screen" ?>
<?xml-stylesheet type="text/css" href="myPrint.css"
                 media="print" ?>
```

If you prefer to avoid using the media attribute, the @media and @import rules for CSS can be used instead. The following example uses the screen media type and the print media type within the same CSS file:

```
@media screen {
   product {
      font-size:   12pt;
   }
}
@media print {
   product {
      font-size:   10pt;
   }
}
```

The above CSS applies a 12-point font size to the product element if the information is displayed on a screen, but applies a 10-point font size to the product element if the information is sent to a printer.

You'll add a processing instruction to the sjbpet.xml file to access the styles in the sjbpet.css file.

To link the sjbpet.xml file to the sjbpet.css style sheet:

1. Return to the **sjbpet.xml** document in your text editor.

2. Below the XML declaration in the prolog, insert the following processing instruction, making sure not to include a space after the first question mark, and also making sure to include a space before the final question mark:

    ```
    <?xml-stylesheet type="text/css" href="sjbpet.css" ?>
    ```

    Figure 1-35 shows the link to the style sheet in the document.

Figure 1-35 | **Inserting the processing instruction**

processing instruction
for connecting to the
sjbpet.css style sheet

```
<?xml version="1.0" encoding="UTF-8" standalone="yes" ?>
<?xml-stylesheet type="text/css" href="sjbpet.css" ?>
<!--
    This document contains data on SJB Pet Boutique
    holiday specials

    Filename: sjbpet.xml
    Author:   Patricia Dean
    Date:     9/18/2017
-->
```

3. Save the changes to your document.

4. Refresh or reload the **sjbpet.xml** document in your web browser. Figure 1-36 shows the sjbpet.xml file in a browser with the sjbpet.css style sheet applied to the file's contents. The browser uses the specified style sheet in place of its default styles.

Figure 1-36 **The sjbpet.xml document with style sheet applied**

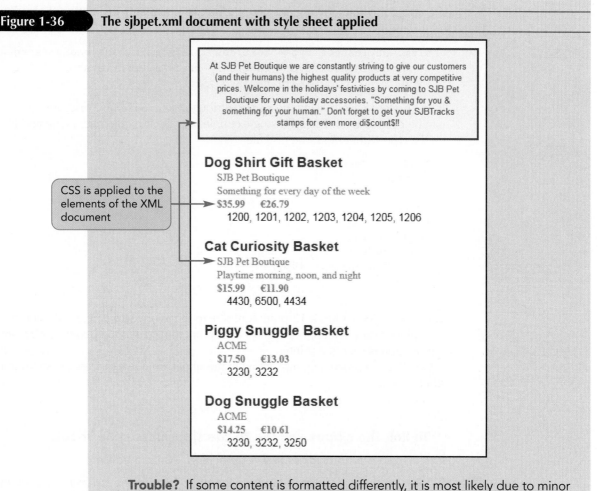

CSS is applied to the elements of the XML document

Trouble? If some content is formatted differently, it is most likely due to minor rendering differences among browsers and will not cause a problem.

INSIGHT

Creating Style Sheets for XML with XSL

CSS is only one way of applying a style to the contents of an XML document. Another way is to use **Extensible Stylesheet Language (XSL)**, which is a style sheet language developed specifically for XML. XSL is actually an XML vocabulary, so any XSL style sheet must follow the rules of well-formed XML. XSL works by transforming the contents of an XML document into another document format. For example, an XSL style sheet can be used to transform the contents of an XML document into an HTML file that can be displayed in any web browser. In addition, the HTML code generated by an XSL style sheet could itself be linked to a CSS file.

XSL is not limited to generating HTML code; an XML document instead could be transformed into another XML document.

Web browsers often use internal XSL style sheets to display XML documents. The outline form of Patricia's document shown in Figure 1-33 is actually the XML document as transformed by the XSL style sheet built into each browser's XML parser. This style sheet is used by the browser unless a different style sheet is specified by a processing instruction in the XML document.

You've finished creating the XML vocabulary for the holiday specials products at SJB Pet Boutique. Patricia anticipates creating future documents that combine elements from this vocabulary with elements from other XML vocabularies. She'd like you to ensure that you'll be able to distinguish elements in one vocabulary from elements in another vocabulary. XML enables you to do this using namespaces.

Working with Namespaces

A namespace is a defined collection of element and attribute names. For example, the collection of element and attribute names from Patricia's products vocabulary could define a single namespace. Applying a namespace to an XML document involves two steps:

1. Declare the namespace.
2. Identify the elements and attributes within the document that belong to that namespace.

Declaring a Namespace

To declare a namespace for an element within an XML document, you add an attribute within the opening tag for the element using the syntax

```
<element xmlns:prefix="uri"> ... </element>
```

where *element* is the element in which the namespace is declared, *prefix* is a string of characters that you'll add to element and attribute names to associate them with the declared namespace, and *uri* is a Uniform Resource Identifier (URI)—a text string that uniquely identifies a resource. In this case, the URI is the declared namespace. For example, the following code declares a namespace with the URI *http://example.com/sjbpetboutique/products* and associates that URI with the prefix prd within the products element:

```
<products xmlns:prd="http://example.com/sjbpetboutique/products">
...
</products>
```

The number of namespace attributes that can be declared within an element is unlimited. In addition, a namespace that has been declared within an element can be applied to any descendant of the element. Some XML authors add all namespace declarations to a document's root element so that each namespace is available to all elements within the document.

Applying a Default Namespace

You can declare a **default namespace** by omitting the prefix in the namespace declaration. Any descendant element or attribute is then considered part of this namespace unless a different namespace is declared within one of the child elements. The syntax to create a default namespace is

```
<element xmlns="uri"> ... </element>
```

For instance, to define the http://example.com/sjbpetboutique/products namespace as the default namespace for all elements in the document, you could use the following root element:

```
<products xmlns="http://example.com/sjbpetboutique/products">
```

In this case, all elements in the document, including the products element, are considered part of the http://example.com/sjbpetboutique/products namespace.

REFERENCE

Declaring a Namespace

- To declare a namespace for an element within an XML document, add the `xmlns:prefix` attribute to the opening tag of the element using the syntax

  `<element xmlns:prefix="uri"> ... </element>`

  where *element* is the element in which the namespace is declared, *prefix* is the namespace prefix, and *uri* is the URI of the namespace.
- To declare a default namespace, add the `xmlns` attribute without specifying a prefix, as follows:

  `<element xmlns="uri"> ... </element>`

The advantage of default namespaces is that they make the code easier to read and write because you do not have to add the namespace prefix to each element. The disadvantage, however, is that an element's namespace is not readily apparent from the code. Still, many compound documents use a default namespace that covers most of the elements in the document, and assign namespace prefixes to elements from other XML vocabularies. A **compound document** is an XML document composed of elements from other vocabularies or schemas. For example, you may combine elements from HTML and XML vocabularies. You'll learn how to work with compound documents in future tutorials.

INSIGHT

Understanding URIs

The URI used in namespaces looks like a web address used to create a link to a website; however, that is not its purpose. The purpose of a URI is simply to provide a unique string of characters that identify a resource.

One version of a URI is the Uniform Resource Locator (URL), which is used to identify the location of a resource (such as a web page) on the web. There is a good reason to also use URLs as a basis for identifying namespaces. If an XML vocabulary is made widely available, the namespace associated with that vocabulary must be unique. URLs serve as a built-in mechanism on the web for generating unique addresses. For example, assume that the home page of Patricia's company, SJB Pet Boutique, has the web address

`http://example.com/sjbpetboutique`

This address provides customers with a unique location to access all of SJB Pet Boutique's online products. To ensure the uniqueness of any namespaces associated with the vocabularies developed for SJB Pet Boutique documents, it makes sense to use the SJB Pet Boutique web address as a foundation. Note that although a URI doesn't actually need to point to a real site on the web, it's often helpful to place documentation at the site identified by a URI so users can go there to learn more about the XML vocabulary being referenced.

The use of URLs is widely accepted in declaring namespaces, but you can use almost any unique string identifier, such as SJBPetBoutiqueProductNS or P2205X300x. The main requirement is that a URI is unique so that it is not confused with the URIs of other namespaces.

Patricia wants you to declare a default namespace for the products vocabulary. You'll declare the namespace in the root element of the sjbpet.xml file. The URI for the namespace is *http://example.com/sjbpetboutique/products*. This URI does not point to an actual site on the web, but it does provide a unique URI for the namespace.

To declare a default namespace:

▶ **1.** Return to the **sjbpet.xml** file in your text editor.

▶ **2.** Within the opening `<products>` tag, insert the following default namespace declaration:

```
xmlns="http://example.com/sjbpetboutique/products"
```

Figure 1-37 shows the default namespace declaration in the document.

Figure 1-37 **The sjbpet.xml document with default namespace applied**

```
<?xml version="1.0" encoding="UTF-8" standalone="yes" ?>
<?xml-stylesheet type="text/css" href="sjbpet.css" ?>
<!--
    This document contains data on SJB Pet Boutique
    holiday specials

    Filename: sjbpet.xml
    Author:   Patricia Dean
    Date:     9/18/2017
-->
<products xmlns="http://example.com/sjbpetboutique/products">
    <message>
```

default namespace added to the root element

▶ **3.** Press **Ctrl+S** to save your work.

▶ **4.** Reload or refresh **sjbpet.xml** in your web browser. If you're using any major browser, the web page should look unchanged from Figure 1-36.

Trouble? If your browser reports a syntax error, return to the sjbpet.xml file in your text editor, ensure that the namespace is within the opening tag of the root element, save any changes, and then repeat Step 4.

Patricia is very happy with the work you've done. She'll show your work to the other members of her web team, and if they need more XML documents created in the future, they'll get back to you.

REVIEW

Session 1.2 Quick Check

1. What is the error in the following code?

```
<Title>Grilled Steak</title>
```

2. What is the root element?

3. What are sibling elements?

4. What is parsed character data?

5. Name three ways to insert the ampersand (&) symbol into the contents of an XML document without it being treated as parsed character data.

6. What is a CDATA section?

7. What is a processing instruction?

8. What code links an XML document to a style sheet file named standard.css?

9. What is a namespace?

10. What attribute would you add to a document's root element to declare a default namespace with the URI *http://ns.doc.book*?

Review Assignments

Data Files needed for the Review Assignments: resale.css, resale.txt

Patricia would like you to create another document for the SJB Pet Boutique resale business. She has provided you with a text file that she'd like you to convert to XML. Figure 1-38 outlines the structure of the final document that she wants you to create.

Figure 1-38   **The SJB Pet Boutique resale tree hierarchy**

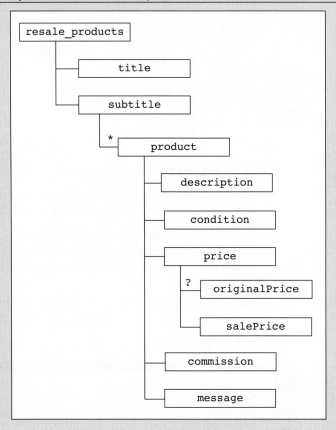

Patricia also would like the final document displayed using the provided *resale.css* style sheet, as shown in Figure 1-39.

Figure 1-39	The resale.xml document in the browser

Resale Products
Latest Offerings

8" Hamster Travel Cage
Good
- $35
- $15
- 15%

Dog and Cat Doorstop
Excellent
- $70
- $20
- 10%

Puppy Dog Rhinestone Collar
Excellent
- $25
- $10
- 15%

30" Kitty Travel Cage
New
- $40
- $35
- 20%

Interested in resale? The SJB Pet Boutique will publish for resale select items purchased at our store that you or your owner have outgrown. All sales are "as-is" condition. A commission is charged for listing the item for resale. If your resale item is sold and you purchase a new item at our store using the money from the sale of the item, you can save 50% off our commission price! ☺

Complete the following:

1. Using your text editor, open the **resale.txt** file located in the xml01 ► review folder included with your Data Files.
2. Save the document as **resale.xml**.
3. Create a prolog at the top of the document indicating that this is an XML document using the UTF-8 encoding scheme, and that it is a standalone document.
4. Create processing instructions to link the *resale.xml* document to the **resale.css** style sheet.
5. On a new line below the XML declaration, insert a comment containing the text
   SJB Pet Boutique resale products, latest offerings

   Filename: resale.xml
   Author: *your name*
   Date: *today's date*
   where *your name* is your first and last names, and *today's date* is the current date.
6. Enclose the document body content in a root element named **resale_products**.
7. Mark the text *Resale Products* with an element named **title**.
8. Mark the text *Latest Offerings* with an element named **subtitle**.
9. There are four new resale products. Create an element named **product**, which will contain all of the information about each product within a single product element.
10. Each **product** element should now contain five detail lines about each product, as shown in Figure 1-39.
11. Mark the first line of each product with an element named **description**, which contains a description of the product.

12. Mark the second line of each product with an element named **condition**, which contains data regarding the condition of the product.

13. Mark the third line of each product with an element named **originalPrice**, which will contain data regarding the original price of the product.

14. Mark the fourth line of each product with an element named **salePrice**, which will contain data regarding the resale price of the product.

15. Mark the fifth line of each product with an element named **commission**, which will contain data regarding the commission percentage to be earned on the sale.

16. Create a parent element named **price** for the child elements originalPrice and salePrice.

17. At the bottom of the document is a message to clients who are interested in resale. Enclose this message in a CDATA section and place the CDATA section within an element named **message**.

18. Patricia wants a smiley face (☺) to be displayed at the end of the contents of the message element. Delete the colon and closing parenthesis (**:)**) at the end of the message text. Outside the CDATA section but within the **message** element, add the character reference **☺**. (Note: The reference must be outside the CDATA section in order for parsers to translate it.)

19. Within the opening **<resale_products>** tag, insert a default namespace declaration to place all elements in the **http://example.com/sjbpetboutique/resale** namespace.

20. Save your changes to the resale.xml document.

21. Open the **resale.xml** document in your web browser. Compare the results to Figure 1-39. If your output does not match the expected output, correct any errors and refresh your browser to verify changes.

Case Problem 1

Data Files needed for this Case Problem: membership.css, membership.txt

MSN Baseball Fan Club   The MSN Baseball Fan Club is an online fan club based in Madison, Wisconsin. Anyone can be a member of the club; the only prerequisite is that the person is a fan of Madison baseball. Members have voted to add to the current website a page to display each club member's blog entries. The club wants the output displayed with a style sheet, which one of the members has provided. Figure 1-40 outlines the structure of the document you will create.

APPLY

| Figure 1-40 | Baseball membership tree hierarchy of combined documents |

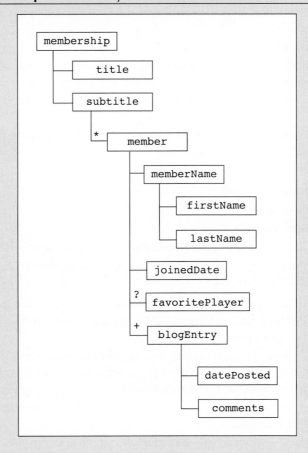

Figure 1-41 shows the document displayed with a style sheet.

| Figure 1-41 | The membership.xml document displayed using the membership.css style sheet |

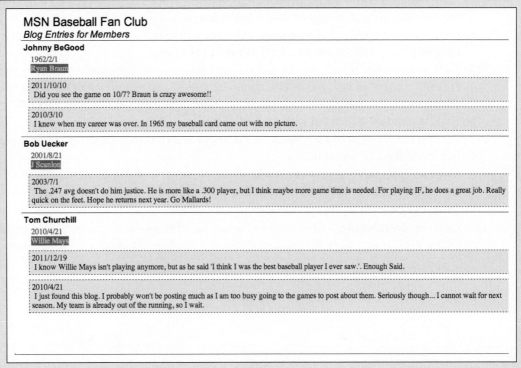

Complete the following:

1. Using your text editor, open the **membership.txt** file located in the xml01 ▶ case1 folder included with your Data Files.
2. Save the document as **membership.xml**.
3. Create a prolog at the top of the *membership.xml* document indicating that this is an XML document using the UTF-8 encoding scheme, and that it is a standalone document.
4. Create a processing instruction to link the *membership.xml* document to the **membership.css** style sheet.
5. Directly below the XML declaration, insert a comment containing the text
   MSN Baseball Fan Club Blog Entries

   Filename: membership.xml
   Author: *your name*
   Date: *today's date*
   where *your name* is your first and last names, and *today's date* is the current date.
6. Enclose the document body content in a root element named `membership`.
7. Enclose the text *MSN Baseball Fan Club* in an element named `title`.
8. Enclose the text *Blog Entries for Members* in an element named `subtitle`.
9. Three members have had data collected for the document. Enclose the information about each member within an element named `member`.

   Each `member` element should contain four detail lines about the member, as shown in Figure 1-41, prior to adding the blog content. Be sure the `member` element encloses all information about a member, including his blog entry(ies).
10. Mark the first line of each `member` element, which contains the member's first name, with an element named `firstName`.
11. Mark the second line of each `member` element, which contains the member's last name, with an element named `lastName`.
12. For each member, create a parent element named `memberName` that contains `firstName` and `lastName` as child elements.
13. Mark the third line of each member's information, which contains the date the member joined the fan club, with an element named `joinedDate`.
14. Mark the fourth line of each member's information, which contains the name of the member's favorite player, with an element named `favoritePlayer`.
15. Each member has at least one blog entry, which contains a date and a comment as shown in Figure 1-41. Enclose each date and comment within a `blogEntry` element. You may need to add more than one `blogEntry` element for a member who has multiple blog entries.
16. Enclose the date associated with each blog entry in a `datePosted` element.
17. Enclose the contents of each `comments` element in a CDATA section, with the `<comments>` tags outside of the CDATA section.
18. Insert a namespace declaration to add all the elements in the document body to the **http://example.com/msnmembball/membership** namespace.
19. Save your changes to the membership.xml document.
20. Open the **membership.xml** document in your web browser and compare the output to Figure 1-41. If necessary, correct any errors and re-verify the output in the browser.

Case Problem 2

Data Files needed for this Case Problem: chester.css, chester.txt

Chester's Restaurant   Chester's Restaurant is located in the quaint town of Hartland, Minnesota. Jasmine Pup, the owner and operator, wants to display the recently revamped breakfast menu on the web. She wants you to apply an existing style sheet to the document so the menu is nicely formatted on the web. She has saved the menu information to a text file and needs you to convert the document to XML. Figure 1-42 outlines the structure of the document you will create.

| Figure 1-42 | Chester's breakfast menu tree hierarchy |

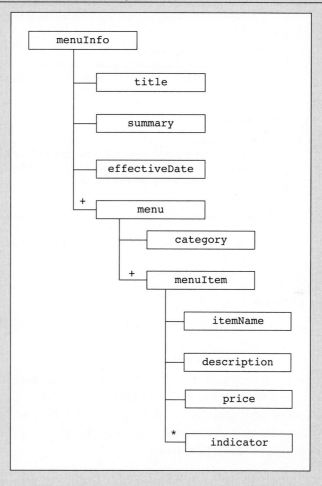

Figure 1-43 shows the document displayed with a style sheet.

Figure 1-43   **The chester.xml document displayed using the chester.css style sheet**

Chester's Breakfast Menu

If you've been craving an authentic homestyle country breakfast, look no further than Chester's! We've got your breakfast favorites served up just the way you like them!!

03/12/2016

Traditional Favorites

- **Rise n' Shine**
  Two Eggs* cooked to order with Grits, Gravy and Homemade Buttermilk Biscuits along with real Butter and the best fresh jam available. Served with your choice of Fresh Fruit or Hashbrown Casserole and Smoked Sausage Patties, Turkey Sausage Patties or Thick-Sliced Bacon.
  7.95

- **Fresh Mornin' Sampler**
  Low-Fat Vanilla Yogurt and Seasonal Fruit topped with our Honey Granola mix of Almonds and Dried Fruit. Served with a Wild Maine Blueberry Muffin or an Apple Bran Muffin.
  6.95 ♥ ♦ ♠

Lite and Quick

- **Oatmeal Breakfast**
  Our Oatmeal is served warm with your choice of Fried Apples, Pecans, Raisins, Fresh Sliced Bananas or 100% Pure Natural Syrup. Also, served with your choice of Apple Bran Muffin or Wild Maine Blueberry Muffin. Available all day.
  6.95 ♥ ♦ ♠

- **Chester's Meat Platter**
  Country Ham, Pork Chops or Steak* grilled to order, Three Eggs* cooked to order served with Cottage Cheese, Smoked Sausage Patties, Turkey Sausage Patties or Thick-Sliced Bacon.
  12.95 ♨

Complete the following:

1. Using your text editor, open the **chester.txt** file located in the xml01 ▸ case2 folder included with your Data Files.
2. Save the document as **chester.xml**.
3. Create a prolog at the top of the document indicating that this is an XML document using the UTF-8 encoding scheme, and that it is a standalone document.
4. Create a processing instruction to link the *chester.xml* document to the **chester.css** style sheet.
5. Directly below the XML declaration, insert a comment containing the text

    Chester's Restaurant Breakfast Menu

Filename:	**chester.xml**
Author:	*your name*
Date:	*today's date*

    where *your name* is your first and last names, and *today's date* is the current date.
6. Enclose the document body content in a root element named **menuInfo**.
7. Enclose the text *Chester's Breakfast Menu* in an element named **title**.
8. Enclose the three lines of text beginning with *If you've been craving* in an element named **summary**. Enclose the content for each **summary** element in a CDATA section.
9. Enclose the date found after the text *Effective thru* in an element named **effectiveDate**.
10. Add an attribute called **text** to the **effectiveDate** element with a value of **Effective thru**.

11. The menu information is divided into two categories. Add the first opening tag for the parent element called **menu** to the document on the line before the text *Traditional Favorites*. Add the closing tag for the first **menu** element and the opening tag for the second **menu** element on the line before the text *Lite and Quick*. Add the closing tag for the second **menu** element on the last line of the document.

12. Each menu category contains a description to be marked with a **category** element. Mark the text *Traditional Favorites* in the first **menu** element with a **category** element, and then mark the text *Lite and Quick* in the second **menu** element with another **category** element.

13. Each menu category also contains one or more child **menu** items and their associated information. On the next line below each **category** element, add a parent element named **menuItem**. Create element tags for each of the following child elements and place them within each **menuItem** parent element:

    a. Mark the first line of each menu category with an element named **itemName**, which will contain the name of the item on the menu. Be sure to place this element within the **menuItem** parent element.

    b. Mark the second piece of information for each menu category with an element named **description**, which will give a detailed description of what the menu item consists of. There may be several lines for the description. The content of the **description** element should be enclosed within a CDATA section. Be sure to place this element within the **menuItem** parent element.

    c. Mark the third piece of information for each menu category with an element named **price**, which will indicate the purchase price of the item. Be sure to place this element within the **menuItem** parent element.

    d. Mark the fourth piece of information for each menu category with an element named **indicator**, which contains optional text indicators that flag the menu item under one or more of the following subcategories:

       - ♥ *Heart Healthy*: character reference ♥
       - ♦ *Low Sodium*: character reference ♦
       - ♠ *Vegan*: character reference ♠
       - ♨ *Low Carb*: character reference ♨

       Because each menu item could fall under none or several categories, the number of indicator elements will vary. If a menu item includes an **indicator** element, use the appropriate character reference to display the symbol for the indicator instead of displaying the text description. Be sure to place this element within the **menuItem** parent element.

    e. Because others might not be familiar with the character references, include a single-line comment containing the text description for each character reference after the closing tag for each **indicator** element.

    f. If there are more **menuItem** elements, repeat Steps 13a–13e.

14. Add the namespace **http://example.com/chestershartland/menu** to the opening tag of the root element.

15. Save your changes to the **chester.xml** document.

16. Open the **chester.xml** document in your web browser and compare the output to Figure 1-43. If necessary, correct any errors and then re-verify the output in the browser.

Case Problem 3

Data Files needed for this Case Problem: recipe.txt, weekendFun.css, weekendFuntxt.xml

Weekend Fun Snacks   Cleo Coal is creating a website called *Weekend Fun Snacks*. The site will list her picks of the best and easiest recipes for kids to cook on the weekend (or anytime). Cleo has been entering recipe information into an XML document. However, she has run into some problems and has come to you for help. Cleo would like your help with cleaning up her XML document so it displays in a browser with her style sheet. Once you've corrected the XML document, she also would like you to add a new recipe to the document. Figure 1-44 displays a preview of the document's contents when all corrections are made and the new recipe is added.

Figure 1-44   **The corrected weekendFun.xml document**

Complete the following:

1. Using your text editor, open the **weekendFuntxt.xml** file located in the xml01 ▸ case3 folder included with your Data Files, and then save the document as **weekendFun.xml**.
2. Use http://validator.w3.org to identify the first error in the code.

⊕ **EXPLORE** 3. Using the error information reported, locate and correct the first error.

4. Save the modifications to **weekendFun.xml** and then check it again for well-formedness.

5. If the parser reports another error, repeat Steps 3 and 4 until all errors are corrected. The following are some errors to look for:
   - misspelled element names
   - missing quotes
   - misplaced closing tags
   - missing closing tags
   - invalid namespace

6. Save the modifications to **weekendFun.xml**.

7. Open the document in your browser.

8. Verify that the style sheet has been applied. If not, edit and reload the document in the web browser.

⊕ **EXPLORE** 9. Modify the prolog at the top of the document to indicate that the document uses the UTF-8 encoding scheme, and that it is a standalone document.

⊕ **EXPLORE** 10. Copy and paste the content from the recipe.txt document into the weekendFun.xml document as a new recipe. Using the existing recipe vocabulary as your guide, modify the newly added recipe data to use the vocabulary for the data.

11. Save the modifications to **weekendFun.xml**.

12. Reload the document in the browser.

13. Verify that all of the information for the new recipe is included, as shown in Figure 1-44.

⊕ **EXPLORE** 14. Draw the tree structure for the contents of the *weekendFun.xml* document. Each document can have many recipes, an optional description, at least one ingredient, an optional measurement, and at least one direction. Each other element occurs one time.

Case Problem 4

CREATE

Data Files needed for this Case Problem: rycheBooks.css, rycheBooks.txt, rycheBooksPrint.css

Ryche Books   David Ryche is the owner and operator of Ryche Books, which is an online bookstore that specializes in hard-to-find books. He often receives phone calls regarding his current stock of books and he would like this information available to his customers at his website. He has created a text file that contains data about his current inventory of books. He would like your help with converting his text file to an XML document and then displaying that information in a web browser. Figure 1-45 gives a preview of the document's contents in a browser.

Figure 1-45 **The browser output for the rycheBooks.xml document**

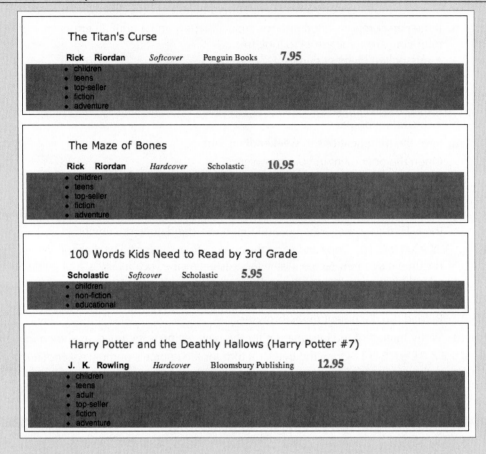

Figure 1-46 shows a print preview of the document's contents.

Figure 1-46 **The print preview output for the rycheBooks.xml document**

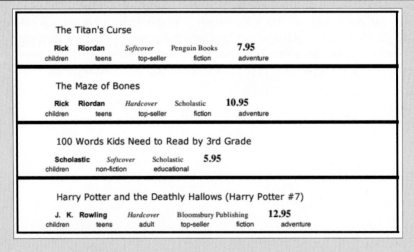

Complete the following:

1. Using your text editor, open the **rycheBooks.txt** file, which is located in the xml01 ▸ case4 folder included with your Data Files.

2. Save the document as **rycheBooks.xml**.

3. At the top of the document, add code indicating that this is an XML document using the UTF-8 encoding scheme, and that it is a standalone document.

4. Create processing instructions to link the XML document to the **rycheBooks.css** style sheet for screen media, and to the **rycheBooksPrint.css** style sheet for print media.

5. Within the document's prolog, include the filename, your name, today's date, and the purpose of the document in a comment.

6. Mark up the contents of the document using the following specifications:
   - The root element of the document should be named **books**.
   - The **books** element should contain multiple occurrences of a child element named **book**.
   - Each **book** element should have a single attribute named **ISBN** containing the International Standard Book Number (ISBN) of the book. (Note: The ISBN begins with the letter I, which is followed by several numeric digits.)
   - Each **book** element should have six child elements: **title**, **author**, **type**, **publisher**, **sellPrice**, and **categories**.
     - The **title** element should contain the book's title.
     - The **author** element should contain three child elements: **firstName**, **middleName**, and **lastName**. Each author name should be divided accordingly and stored in these elements. (Note: If the author is a business name such as *Scholastic*, it will not have all three child elements.)
     - The **type** element should contain the book's cover type: **hardcover** or **softcover**.
     - The **publisher** element should contain the name of the book's publisher.
     - The **sellPrice** element should contain the book's selling price.
     - The **categories** element should contain at least one child element called **category**. A book may have multiple **category** elements.

7. Add a default namespace for the books vocabulary using an appropriate URI.

8. Save your changes to the **rycheBooks.xml** document.

9. Open the **rycheBooks.xml** document in your web browser and compare the output to Figure 1-45.

10. If your web browser reports any syntax errors, locate and correct each error using the information from the web browser. Save any modifications to **rycheBooks.xml** and reload the document in your browser.

11. Verify that the style sheet is also properly applied to print media. To verify the print media style sheet, use the print preview feature of your browser and compare the output to Figure 1-46. If necessary, correct any errors and re-verify the output in the browser.

TUTORIAL 2

OBJECTIVES

Session 2.1
- Review the principles of data validation
- Create a DOCTYPE
- Declare XML elements and define their content
- Define the structure of child elements

Session 2.2
- Declare attributes
- Set rules for attribute content
- Define optional and required attributes
- Validate an XML document

Session 2.3
- Place internal and external content in an entity
- Create entity references
- Understand how to store code in parameter entities
- Create comments in a DTD
- Understand how to create conditional sections
- Understand how to create entities for non-character data
- Understand how to validate standard vocabularies

Validating Documents with DTDs

Creating a Document Type Definition for Map Finds For You

Case | Map Finds For You

Benjamin Mapps works at Map Finds For You, an online store that sells mass-produced and custom map products. Map Finds For You sells more than 1000 map products ranging from maps of the present-day world to detailed historical maps. Some are available in both paper and electronic formats. Part of Benjamin's job at Map Finds For You is to record information about the store's customers, including the individual orders they place.

Benjamin is starting to use XML to record this information, and he has created a sample XML document containing information on customers and their orders. Benjamin knows that his document needs to be well formed, following the XML syntax rules exactly, but he also wants the document to follow certain rules regarding content. For example, data on each customer must include the customer's name, phone number, and address. Each customer order must contain a complete list of the items purchased and include the date the order was placed. You will create an XML document for Benjamin that adheres to both the rules of XML and the rules Benjamin has set up for the document's content and structure.

Note: To complete this tutorial, you need access to a recent version of a major browser, such as Internet Explorer, Firefox, or Chrome, as well as an XML parser capable of validating an XML document based on a DTD.

STARTING DATA FILES

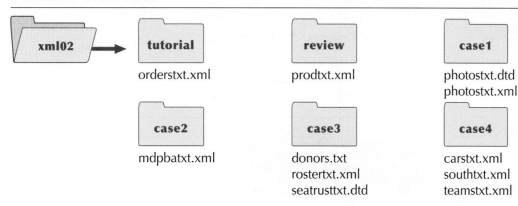

xml02 → **tutorial**
orderstxt.xml

review
prodtxt.xml

case1
photostxt.dtd
photostxt.xml

case2
mdpbatxt.xml

case3
donors.txt
rostertxt.xml
seatrusttxt.dtd

case4
carstxt.xml
southtxt.xml
teamstxt.xml

Session 2.1 Visual Overview:

The name of the root element follows the word DOCTYPE and must match the root element of the document.

The DOCTYPE, or document type declaration, must be added to the document prolog after the XML declaration and before the document's root element.

The declaration statements for an internal DTD are included within opening and closing brackets.

The closing > for the DOCTYPE must be placed after the closing].

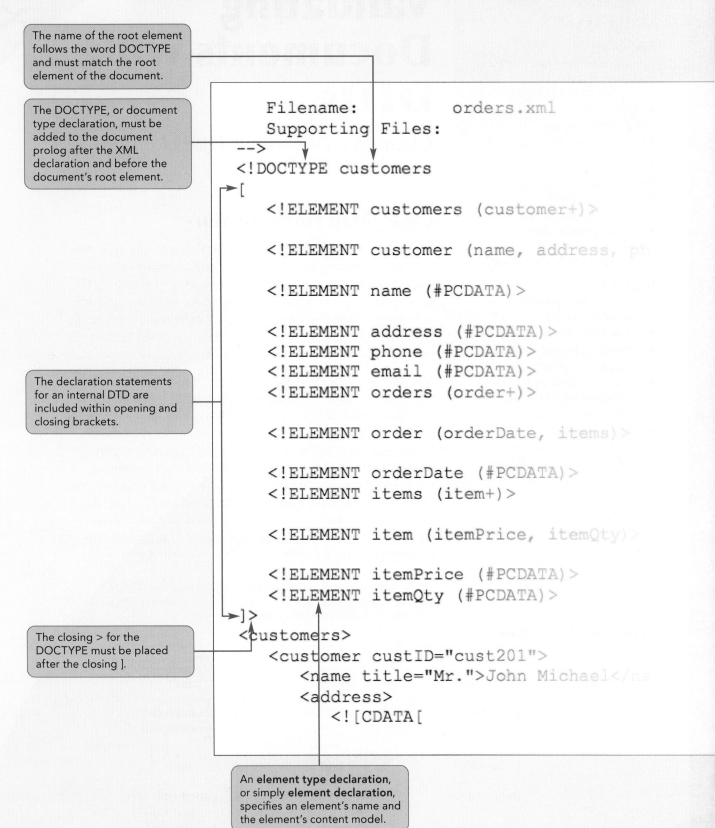

```
    Filename:         orders.xml
    Supporting Files:
-->
<!DOCTYPE customers
[
    <!ELEMENT customers (customer+)>

    <!ELEMENT customer (name, address, ph

    <!ELEMENT name (#PCDATA)>

    <!ELEMENT address (#PCDATA)>
    <!ELEMENT phone (#PCDATA)>
    <!ELEMENT email (#PCDATA)>
    <!ELEMENT orders (order+)>

    <!ELEMENT order (orderDate, items)

    <!ELEMENT orderDate (#PCDATA)>
    <!ELEMENT items (item+)>

    <!ELEMENT item (itemPrice, itemQty)

    <!ELEMENT itemPrice (#PCDATA)>
    <!ELEMENT itemQty (#PCDATA)>
]>
<customers>
    <customer custID="cust201">
        <name title="Mr.">John Michael</n
        <address>
            <![CDATA[
```

An **element type declaration**, or simply **element declaration**, specifies an element's name and the element's content model.

The Structure of a DTD

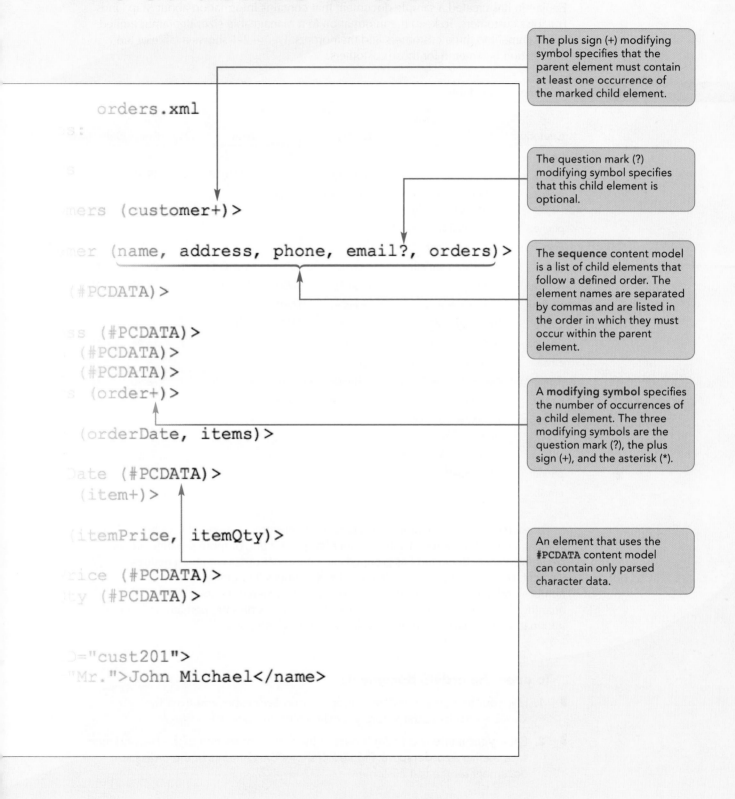

The plus sign (+) modifying symbol specifies that the parent element must contain at least one occurrence of the marked child element.

The question mark (?) modifying symbol specifies that this child element is optional.

The **sequence** content model is a list of child elements that follow a defined order. The element names are separated by commas and are listed in the order in which they must occur within the parent element.

A **modifying symbol** specifies the number of occurrences of a child element. The three modifying symbols are the question mark (?), the plus sign (+), and the asterisk (*).

An element that uses the **#PCDATA** content model can contain only parsed character data.

Creating a Valid Document

Benjamin has created a sample document that contains information about Map Finds For You's customers. To keep the information to a manageable size, Benjamin limited the document to three customers and their orders. Figure 2-1 shows a table of the information he entered for those customers.

| Figure 2-1 | Customer orders table |

Customer		Orders		Item	Qty	Price	Sale Item
name:	Mr. John Michael	orderID:	or1089	WM100PL	1	39.95	N
custID:	cust201	orderBy:	cust201	WM101P	2	19.90	Y
address:	41 West Plankton Avenue	orderDate:	8/11/2017				
	Orlando, FL 32820						
phone:	(407) 555-3476						
email:	jk@example.net						
name:	Mr. Dean Abernath	orderID:	or1021	WM100PL	1	29.95	N
custID:	cust202	orderBy:	cust202	WM105L	1	19.95	N
address:	200 Bear Avenue	orderDate:	8/1/2017				
	Front Royal, VA 22630	orderID:	or1122	H115E	2	24.90	Y
phone:	(540) 555-1788	orderBy:	cust202	H115F	1	14.95	N
email:	dabernath@example.com	orderDate:	10/1/2017				
name:	Riverfront High School	orderID:	or1120	WM140P	2	78.90	N
custID:	cust203	orderBy:	cust203				
address:	1950 West Magnolia Drive	orderDate:	9/15/2017				
	River Falls, WI 54022						
phone:	(715) 555-4022						
email:							

For each customer, Benjamin has recorded the customer's name, ID, address, phone number, and email address. Each customer has placed one or more separate orders. For convenience, Benjamin has grouped each customer order within an `orders` element. For each order, Benjamin recorded the order's ID number, customer ID number, and date. Finally, for each item ordered, he entered the item number, the quantity, the price of the item, and whether the item was on sale. Benjamin placed this information in an XML document, which you will open now.

To open the orders document:

1. Use your text editor or XML editor to open **orderstxt.xml** from the xml02 ▸ tutorial folder where your data files are located.

2. Enter **your name** and **today's date** in the comment section of the file, and then save the file as **orders.xml**. Figure 2-2 shows the contents of the orders.xml document for the first customer.

| Figure 2-2 | **First customer in the orders.xml document** |

```xml
<customer custID="cust201">
    <name title="Mr.">John Michael</name>
    <address>
        <![CDATA[
        41 West Plankton Avenue
        Orlando, FL  32820
        ]]>
    </address>
    <phone>(407) 555-3476</phone>
    <email>jk@example.net</email>
    <orders>
        <order orderID="or1089" orderBy="cust201">
            <orderDate>8/11/2017</orderDate>
            <items>
                <item itemNumber="WM100PL">
                    <itemPrice saleItem="N">39.95</itemPrice>
                    <itemQty>1</itemQty>
                </item>
                <item itemNumber="WM101P">
                    <itemPrice saleItem="Y">19.90</itemPrice>
                    <itemQty>2</itemQty>
                </item>
            </items>
        </order>
    </orders>
</customer>
```

Trouble? You can complete the steps in this tutorial in any code editor or basic text editor. An XML editor such as Exchanger XML Editor can verify that your code is both well formed and valid. Many free general-purpose code editors, such as Notepad++ and Komodo Edit, can check that your code is well formed, and you can upload the code to an online service like http://validator.w3.org to confirm that the code is valid.

3. Compare the elements and attributes entered in the document with the table shown in Figure 2-1, noticing whether each piece of data is coded as an element or an attribute.

4. If you're using Exchanger XML Editor, click **XML** on the menu bar, and then click **Check Well-formedness**. This setting ensures that you don't see validation errors until your document is ready for validation.

Some elements in Benjamin's document, such as the `name` and `phone` elements, should appear only once for each customer, while other elements, such as the `order` and `item` elements, can appear multiple times. The `email` element is optional: Two customers have email addresses and one customer does not. The `itemPrice` and `itemQty` elements each appear once per `item` element.

Benjamin created the diagram shown in Figure 2-3 to better illustrate the structure of the elements and attributes in his document. Recall that the + symbol in front of an element indicates that at least one child element must be present in the document, and the ? symbol indicates the presence of zero children or one child. Benjamin's diagram shows that the `customers`, `orders`, and `items` elements must have at least one `customer`, `order`, or `item` child, respectively, and that the `email` element is optional. Benjamin also indicated the presence of element attributes in blue below the relevant element names. An attribute name in square brackets ([ ]) is optional; all other attributes are required.

Figure 2-3	**Structure of the orders.xml document**

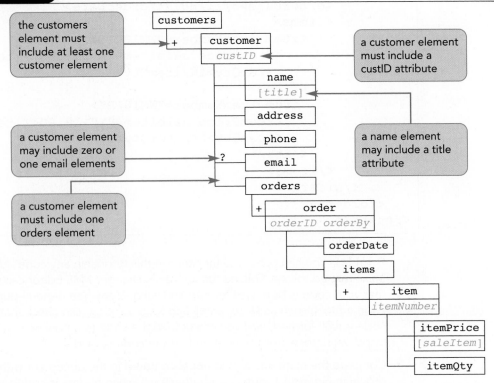

To keep accurate and manageable records, Benjamin must maintain this structure in his document. He wants to ensure that the customer information includes the address and phone number for each customer, the items each customer ordered, and the date each order was placed. In XML terms, this means that the document must be not only well formed, but also valid.

Declaring a DTD

One way to create a valid document is to design a document type definition, or DTD, for the document. Recall that a DTD is a collection of rules that define the content and structure of an XML document. Used in conjunction with an XML parser that supports data validation, a DTD can:

- Ensure that all required elements are present in the document.
- Prevent undefined elements from being used in the document.
- Enforce a specific data structure on document content.
- Specify the use of element attributes and define their permissible values.
- Define default values for attributes.
- Describe how parsers should access non-XML or nontextual content.

A DTD is attached to an XML document by using a statement called a **document type declaration**, which is more simply referred to as a **DOCTYPE**. The DOCTYPE must be added to the document prolog after the XML declaration and before the document's root element. The purpose of the DOCTYPE is to either specify the rules of the DTD or provide information to the parser about where those rules are located. Each XML document can have only one DOCTYPE.

Because DTDs can be placed either within an XML document or in an external file, you can divide a DOCTYPE into two parts—an internal subset and an external subset. A DOCTYPE can include either or both of these parts. The **internal subset** contains the rules and declarations of the DTD placed directly into the document, using the form

```
<!DOCTYPE root
[
    statements
]>
```

where *root* is the name of the document's root element and *statements* represents the declarations and rules of the DTD.

For example, the root element of the orders.xml document is customers, so a DOCTYPE in the orders.xml document has to specify `customers` as the value for the *root* parameter, as follows:

```
<!DOCTYPE customers
[
    statements
]>
```

TIP

The root value in a DOCTYPE must exactly match the name of the XML document's root element; otherwise, parsers will reject the document as invalid.

When the DTD is located in an external file, the DOCTYPE includes an **external subset** that indicates the location of the file. Locations can be defined using either a system identifier or a public identifier. With a **system identifier**, you specify the location of the DTD file. A DOCTYPE using a system identifier has the form

```
<!DOCTYPE root SYSTEM "uri">
```

where *root* is again the document's root element and *uri* is the URI of the external file. For example, if Benjamin placed the DTD for the orders.xml document in an external file named rules.dtd, he could access it using the following DOCTYPE:

```
<!DOCTYPE customers SYSTEM "rules.dtd">
```

Understanding URIs

The URI used in DOCTYPEs looks like a web address used to create a link to a website; however, that is not its purpose. The purpose of a URI is simply to provide a unique string of characters that identifies a resource.

One version of a URI is the Uniform Resource Locator (URL), which is used to identify the location of a resource (such as a web page) on the web—for instance, *http://www.example.com*. One reason to use URLs as a basis for identifying DTDs is that URLs serve as a built-in mechanism on the web for generating unique addresses. If an XML vocabulary is made widely available, the DTD associated with that vocabulary needs to be unique. So, to ensure the uniqueness of any DTDs associated with the vocabularies developed for documents used by a specific company, it makes sense to use the company's web address as a foundation. Note that, although a URI doesn't actually need to point to a real site on the web, it is often helpful to place documentation at the site identified by the URI so users can go there to learn more about the XML vocabulary being referenced.

The use of URLs in declaring DTDs is widely accepted, but you can use almost any unique string identifier, such as MapFindsForYouModelNS or WM140PL. The main requirement is that a URI is unique so that it is not confused with the URIs of other DTDs.

When an XML vocabulary becomes widely used, developers seek to make the DTD easily accessible. This is done by creating a name for the DTD; this name is called a **public identifier** or a **formal public identifier**. The public identifier, which is optional, provides XML parsers with information about the DTD, including the owner or author of the DTD and the language in which the DTD is written. The syntax of a DOCTYPE that has only an external subset and involves a public identifier is

```
<!DOCTYPE root PUBLIC "id" "uri">
```

where *root* is the document's root element, *id* is the public identifier, and *uri* is the system location of the DTD. The system location is included in case the XML parser cannot process the document solely based on the information provided by the public identifier. In one sense, the public identifier acts like the namespace URI because it doesn't specify a physical location for the DTD; instead, it provides the DTD with a unique name that can be recognized by an XML parser. For example, XHTML documents that conform strictly to version 1.0 standards employ the following DOCTYPE:

```
<!DOCTYPE html PUBLIC "-//W3C//DTD XHTML 1.0 Strict//EN"
          "http://www.w3.org/TR/xhtml1/DTD/xhtml1-strict.dtd">
```

The public identifier is -//W3C//DTD XHTML 1.0 Strict//EN, a string of characters that XML parsers recognize as the identifier for the XHTML strict DTD. An XML parser that recognizes this public identifier can use it to try to retrieve the DTD associated with the XML vocabulary used in the document. If the parser cannot retrieve the DTD based on the public identifier, it can access it from the system location provided by the *uri* value, which is http://www.w3.org/TR/xhtml1/ DTD/xhtml1-strict.dtd. As you can see, the system location acts as a backup to the public identifier. Most standard XML vocabularies such as XHTML and RSS have public identifiers. However, a customized XML vocabulary such as the one Benjamin created for Map Finds For You may not have a public identifier.

PROSKILLS

Written Communication: Interpreting Public Identifiers

A public identifier is simply a public name given to a DTD that an XML parser can use to process and validate the document. The parser can use the public identifier to find the latest version of the DTD on the Internet. Each public identifier name has the structure

```
standard//owner//description//language
```

where *standard* indicates whether the DTD is a recognized standard, *owner* is the owner or developer of the DTD, *description* is a description of the XML vocabulary for which the DTD is developed, and *language* is a two-letter abbreviation of the language employed by the DTD. For example, the identifier for the XHTML 1.0 Strict vocabulary

```
-//W3C//DTD XHTML 1.0 Strict//EN
```

can be interpreted in the following manner:

- The initial – character tells the parser that the DTD is not a recognized standard. DTDs that are approved ISO (Internal Organization for Standardization) standards begin with the string ISO, whereas DTDs that are approved non-ISO standards begin with the + symbol.
- The next part of the id, `W3C`, indicates that this DTD is owned and developed by the W3C (World Wide web Consortium).
- The description content, `DTD XHTML 1.0 Strict`, specifies that this standard is used for the XHTML 1.0 Strict vocabulary.
- Finally, the closing `EN` characters indicate that the DTD is written in English.

If an XML parser has an internal catalog for working with public identifiers, it can use the information contained in the public identifier to work with the DTD. However, parsers are not required to work with public identifiers, so you should always include system locations for your public DTDs to support parsers that do not work with public identifiers.

When writing code, you might create DOCTYPEs with both internal and external subsets. A DTD that is shared among many different XML documents would be placed within an external file, whereas rules or declarations specific to an individual XML document would be placed within the internal subset. A DOCTYPE that combines both internal and external subsets and references a system identifier has the following form:

```
<!DOCTYPE root SYSTEM "uri"
[
    declarations
]>
```

If the DTD has a public identifier, then the DOCTYPE has the following form:

```
<!DOCTYPE root PUBLIC "id" "uri"
[
    declarations
]>
```

When a DOCTYPE contains both an internal and an external subset, the internal subset takes precedence over the external subset when conflict arises between the two. This is useful when an external subset is shared among several documents. The external subset would define some basic rules for all of the documents, and the internal subset would define rules that are specific to each document, as illustrated in Figure 2-4.

| Figure 2-4 | Internal and external DTDs |

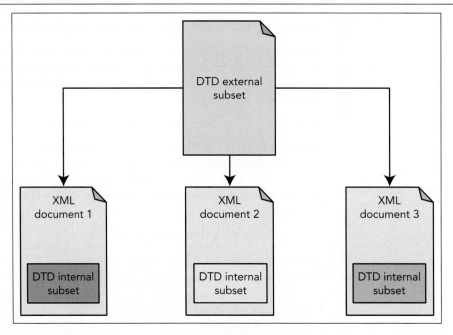

In this way, internal and external DTDs work in the same manner as embedded and external style sheets. An XML environment composed of several documents and vocabularies might use both internal and external DTDs.

Declaring a DTD

- To declare an internal DTD subset, use the DOCTYPE

```
<!DOCTYPE root
[
    declarations
]>
```

where *root* is the name of the document's root element and *declarations* represents the statements that constitute the DTD.
- To declare an external DTD subset with a system location, use the DOCTYPE

```
<!DOCTYPE root SYSTEM "uri">
```

where *uri* is the URI of the external DTD file.
- To declare an external DTD subset with a public location, use the DOCTYPE

```
<!DOCTYPE root PUBLIC "id" "uri">
```

where *id* is the public identifier of the DTD.

Writing the Document Type Declaration

Benjamin wants you to place the DTD directly in his XML document so he can easily compare the DTD to the document content. You'll start by inserting a blank DOCTYPE into the orders.xml file.

To insert a DOCTYPE into the orders.xml document:

The DOCTYPE must be located within the prolog, which is before the document body.

1. Directly above the opening `<customers>` tag, insert the following DOCTYPE:

```
<!DOCTYPE customers
[

]>
```

Figure 2-5 shows the updated document.

Figure 2-5	**Blank DOCTYPE inserted**

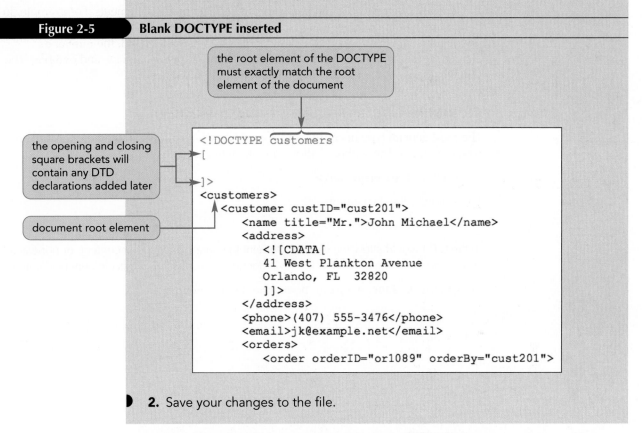

the root element of the DOCTYPE must exactly match the root element of the document

the opening and closing square brackets will contain any DTD declarations added later

document root element

```
<!DOCTYPE customers
[
]>
<customers>
   <customer custID="cust201">
      <name title="Mr.">John Michael</name>
      <address>
         <![CDATA[
         41 West Plankton Avenue
         Orlando, FL  32820
         ]]>
      </address>
      <phone>(407) 555-3476</phone>
      <email>jk@example.net</email>
      <orders>
         <order orderID="or1089" orderBy="cust201">
```

2. Save your changes to the file.

Now that you've added a DOCTYPE to Benjamin's document, you can begin adding statements to the DTD to define the structure and content of his XML vocabulary.

Declaring Document Elements

In a valid document, every element must be declared in the DTD. An element type declaration, or element declaration, specifies an element's name and indicates what content the element can contain. It can even specify the order in which elements appear in the document. The syntax of an element declaration is

TIP

Element declarations must begin with <!ELEMENT in all uppercase letters, and not <!Element or <!element.

`<!ELEMENT element content-model>`

where *element* is the name of the element and *content-model* specifies what type of content the element contains. The element name is case sensitive, so if the element name is VENDORS, it must be entered as VENDORS (not Vendors or vendors) in the element declaration. Remember that element names cannot contain any spaces or reserved symbols such as < or >. The *content-model* value can be one of three specific keywords (`ANY`, `EMPTY`, `#PCDATA`), or one of two content descriptions (sequence, `#PCDATA` with sequence), as follows:

- **`ANY`**: The element can store any type of content or no content at all.
- **`EMPTY`**: The element cannot store any content.
- **`#PCDATA`**: The element can contain only parsed character data.
- **Sequence**: The element can contain only child elements.
- **`#PCDATA` with sequence**: The element can store both parsed character data and child elements.

Generally, elements contain parsed character data or child elements. For example, in Benjamin's document, the `phone` element contains a text string that stores a customer's phone number, which is parsed character data. On the other hand, the `customer` element contains five child elements (`name`, `address`, `phone`, `email`, and `orders`). The following sections explore the five content types in more detail.

Elements Containing Any Type of Content

The most general type of content model is ANY, which allows an element to store any type of content. The syntax to allow any element content is

```
<!ELEMENT element ANY>
```

For example, the declaration

```
<!ELEMENT vendor ANY>
```

in the DTD would allow the `vendor` element to contain any type of content, or none at all. Any of the following content in the XML document would satisfy this element declaration:

```
<vendor>V12300 Mapping Down the Road</vendor>
```

or

```
<vendor />
```

or

```
<vendor>
    <number>PLBK70</number>
    <name>Mapping Down the Road</name>
</vendor>
```

Allowing an element to contain any type of content has little value in document validation. After all, the idea behind validation is to enforce a particular set of rules on elements and their content; allowing any content defeats the purpose of these rules.

Empty Elements

The EMPTY content model is reserved for elements that store no content. The syntax for an empty element declaration is

```
<!ELEMENT element EMPTY>
```

The element declaration

```
<!ELEMENT shelf EMPTY>
```

would require the `shelf` element to be entered as an empty element, as follows:

```
<shelf />
```

Including content in an element that uses the EMPTY content model would cause XML parsers to reject the document as invalid.

Elements Containing Parsed Character Data

Recall that parsed character data, or PCDATA, is text that is parsed by a parser. The #PCDATA content model value is reserved for elements that can store parsed character data, which are declared as follows:

```
<!ELEMENT element (#PCDATA)>
```

For example, the declaration

```
<!ELEMENT name (#PCDATA)>
```

permits the following element in an XML document:

```
<name>John Michael</name>
```

An element declaration employing the #PCDATA content model value does not allow for child elements. As a result, the name element

Not valid code:

```
<name>
    <first>John</first>
    <last>Michael</last>
</name>
```

is not considered valid because child elements are not considered parsed character data.

REFERENCE

Specifying Types of Element Content

- To declare an element that may contain any type of content, insert the declaration

  ```
  <!ELEMENT element ANY>
  ```

  where element is the element name.
- To declare an empty element containing no content whatsoever, use the following declaration:

  ```
  <!ELEMENT element EMPTY>
  ```

- To declare an element that may contain only parsed character data, use the following declaration:

  ```
  <!ELEMENT element (#PCDATA)>
  ```

The name, address, phone, email, orderDate, itemPrice, and itemQty elements in the orders.xml document contain only parsed character data. You'll add declarations for these elements to the DTD.

To declare elements containing parsed character data in the orders.xml document:

1. Within the DOCTYPE, insert the following element declarations:

```
<!ELEMENT name (#PCDATA)>
<!ELEMENT address (#PCDATA)>
<!ELEMENT phone (#PCDATA)>
<!ELEMENT email (#PCDATA)>
<!ELEMENT orderDate (#PCDATA)>
<!ELEMENT itemPrice (#PCDATA)>
<!ELEMENT itemQty (#PCDATA)>
```

Figure 2-6 shows the updated DOCTYPE.

Figure 2-6 **Element declarations**

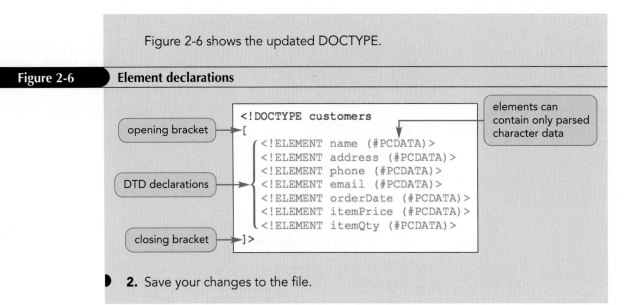

2. Save your changes to the file.

Working with Child Elements

Next, you'll consider how to declare an element that contains only child elements. The syntax for such a declaration is

```
<!ELEMENT element (children)>
```

where *element* is the parent element and *children* is a listing of its child elements. The simplest form for the listing consists of a single child element associated with a parent. For example, the declaration

```
<!ELEMENT customer (phone)>
```

indicates that the `customer` element can contain only a single child element named `phone`. The following code would be invalid under this element declaration because the customer element contains two child elements—`name` and `phone`:

```
<customer>
    <name>John Michael</name>
    <phone>(407) 555-3476</phone>
</customer>
```

For content that involves multiple child elements, you can specify the elements in a sequence or you can specify a choice of elements.

Specifying an Element Sequence

A sequence is a list of elements that follow a defined order. The syntax to specify child elements in a sequence is

```
<!ELEMENT element (child1, child2, ...)>
```

where *child1*, *child2*, etc., represents the sequence of child elements within the parent. The order of the child elements in an XML document must match the order defined in the element declaration. For example, the following element declaration defines a sequence of three child elements for each `customer` element:

```
<!ELEMENT customer (name, phone, email)>
```

Under this declaration, the following code is valid:

```
<customer>
   <name>John Michael</name>
   <phone>(407) 555-3476</phone>
   <email>jk@example.net</email>
</customer>
```

However, even though the elements and their contents are identical in the following code, the code is not valid because the sequence doesn't match the defined order:

```
<customer>
   <name>John Michael</name>
   <email>jk@example.net</email>
   <phone>(407) 555-3476</phone>
</customer>
```

Specifying an Element Choice

Rather than defining a sequence of child elements, the element declaration can define a choice of possible elements. The syntax used to specify an element choice is

```
<!ELEMENT element (child1 | child2 | ...)>
```

where *child1*, *child2*, etc., are the possible child elements of the parent. For example, the following declaration allows the `customer` element to contain either the `name` or the `company` element:

```
<!ELEMENT customer (name | company)>
```

Based on this declaration, either of the following code samples is valid:

```
<customer>
   <name>John Michael</name>
</customer>
```
or
```
<customer>
   <company>Mapping Down the Road</company>
</customer>
```

However, under this declaration, a `customer` element cannot include both the `name` and `company` elements because the choice model allows only one of the child elements listed.

An element declaration can combine both a sequence and a choice of child elements. For example, the following declaration limits the `customer` element to three child elements, the first of which is either the `name` or the `company` element, followed by the `phone` and then the `email` element:

```
<!ELEMENT customer ((name | company), phone, email)>
```

Under this declaration, both of the following code samples are valid:

```
<customer>
   <name>Lea Ziegler</name>
   <phone>(813)555-8931</phone>
   <email>LZiegler@example.net</email>
</customer>
```
or
```
<customer>
   <company>VTech Productions</company>
   <phone>(813)555-8931</phone>
   <email>LZiegler@example.net</email>
</customer>
```

However, a `customer` element that does not start with either a `name` element or a `company` element followed by the `phone` and `email` elements would be invalid.

Specifying Child Elements

- To specify the sequence of child elements, use the declaration

  `<!ELEMENT element (child1, child2, ...)>`

  where `child1, child2, ...` is the order in which the child elements must appear within the parent element.
- To allow for a choice of child elements, use the declaration

  `<!ELEMENT element (child1 | child2 | ...)>`

  where `child1, child2, ...` are the possible children of the parent element.
- To combine a choice and a sequence of child elements in the same declaration, specify the choice elements within an additional set of parentheses, in the appropriate place within the sequence, as in the following code:

  `<!ELEMENT element ((child1 | child2 | ...), child3, child4, ...)>`

Modifying Symbols

So far, all the content models you have seen assume that each child element occurs once within its parent. If you need to specify duplicates of the same element, you could repeat the element name in the list. For example, the following element declaration indicates that the `customer` element must contain two `phone` elements:

```
<!ELEMENT customer (phone, phone)>
```

However, it's rare that you specify the exact number of duplicate elements. Instead, DTDs use more general numbering with a modifying symbol that specifies the number of occurrences of each element. The three modifying symbols are the question mark (?), the plus sign (+), and the asterisk (*). These are the same symbols you saw when creating a tree diagram for an XML document. As before, the ? symbol indicates that an element occurs zero times or one time, the + symbol indicates that an element occurs at least once, and the * symbol indicates that an element occurs zero times or more. There are no other modifying symbols. If you want to specify an exact number of child elements, such as the two `phone` elements discussed above, you must repeat the element name the appropriate number of times.

In the orders.xml document, the `customers` element must contain at least one element named `customer`. The element declaration for this is

```
<!ELEMENT customers (customer+)>
```

As this code demonstrates, a modifying symbol is placed directly after the element it modifies. You can also include modifying symbols in element sequences. For example, in Benjamin's document, each `customer` element contains the `name`, `address`, `phone`, and `email` elements, but the `email` element is optional, occurring either zero times or one time. The element declaration for this is

```
<!ELEMENT customer (name, address, phone, email?)>
```

The three modifying symbols can also modify entire element sequences or choices. You do this by placing the character immediately following the closing parenthesis of the sequence or choice. For example, the declaration

```
<!ELEMENT order (orderDate, items)+>
```

indicates that the child element sequence (`orderDate, items`) can be repeated one or more times within each `order` element. Of course, each time the sequence is repeated, the `orderDate` element must appear first, followed by the `items` element.

When applied to a choice model, the modifying symbols allow for multiple combinations of each child element. The declaration

```
<!ELEMENT customer (name | company)+>
```

allows any of the following lists of child elements:

```
name
company
name, company
name, name, company
name, company, company, name
```

The only requirement is that the combined total of `name` and `company` elements be greater than zero.

REFERENCE

Applying Modifying Symbols

- To specify that an element can appear zero times or one time, use

  item?

  in the element declaration in the DTD, where *item* is an element name or a sequence or choice of elements.
- To specify one or more occurrences of an item, use

  item+
- To specify zero or more occurrences of an item, use

  *item**

Now that you've seen how to specify the occurrences of child elements, you'll add these declarations to the DTD for Benjamin's document. The declarations can be entered in any order, but you'll insert the declarations in the order in which the elements appear in the document. You'll also insert blank lines between groups of declarations to make the code easier to read.

To declare the child elements:

▶ **1.** In the DTD of the orders.xml file, on the line below the opening bracket, insert the following element declaration, followed by a blank line:

```
<!ELEMENT customers (customer+)>
```

This declaration specifies that the root `customers` element must contain at least one `customer` element.

▶ **2.** Above the `name` declaration, insert the following declaration followed by a blank line:

```
<!ELEMENT customer (name, address, phone, email?, orders)>
```

This declaration specifies that a `customer` element must contain, in order, a `name` element, an `address` element, and a `phone` element; it may then contain an `email` element; and then it must contain an `orders` element.

▶ **3.** Below the declaration for the `email` element, insert the following declaration:

```
<!ELEMENT orders (order+)>
```

This declaration specifies that an `orders` element must contain at least one `order` element.

▶ **4.** Below the `orders` declaration, insert a blank line followed by the following declaration:

`<!ELEMENT order (orderDate, items)>`

This declaration specifies that each `order` element must contain an `orderDate` element and an `items` element.

▶ **5.** Below the `orderDate` declaration, insert the following declaration:

`<!ELEMENT items (item+)>`

This declaration specifies that each `items` element must contain at least one `item` element.

▶ **6.** Below the `items` declaration, insert a blank line followed by the following declaration:

`<!ELEMENT item (itemPrice, itemQty)>`

This declaration specifies that the `item` element must contain the `itemPrice` and `itemQty` elements.

▶ **7.** Add a blank line after the `name` declaration, the `order` declaration, and the `item` declaration. Figure 2-7 shows the completed element declarations in the DTD.

Figure 2-7	Declarations for the child elements

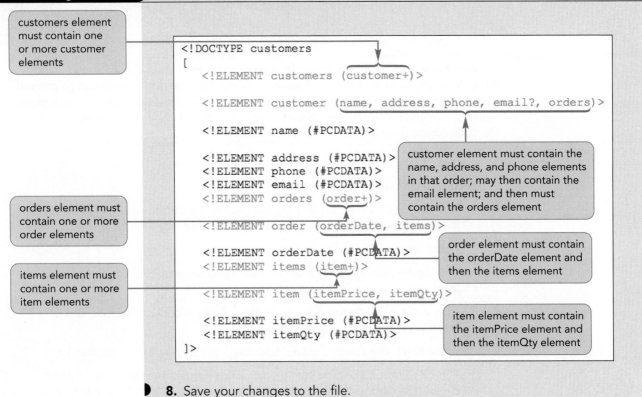

customers element must contain one or more customer elements

```
<!DOCTYPE customers
[
    <!ELEMENT customers (customer+)>

    <!ELEMENT customer (name, address, phone, email?, orders)>

    <!ELEMENT name (#PCDATA)>

    <!ELEMENT address (#PCDATA)>
    <!ELEMENT phone (#PCDATA)>
    <!ELEMENT email (#PCDATA)>
    <!ELEMENT orders (order+)>

    <!ELEMENT order (orderDate, items)>

    <!ELEMENT orderDate (#PCDATA)>
    <!ELEMENT items (item+)>

    <!ELEMENT item (itemPrice, itemQty)>

    <!ELEMENT itemPrice (#PCDATA)>
    <!ELEMENT itemQty (#PCDATA)>
]>
```

customer element must contain the name, address, and phone elements in that order; may then contain the email element; and then must contain the orders element

orders element must contain one or more order elements

order element must contain the orderDate element and then the items element

items element must contain one or more item elements

item element must contain the itemPrice element and then the itemQty element

▶ **8.** Save your changes to the file.

To see how these element declarations represent the structure of the document, compare Figure 2-7 with the tree diagram shown earlier in Figure 2-3.

INSIGHT

DTDs and Mixed Content

An XML element is not limited to either parsed character data or child elements. If an element contains both, its content is known as **mixed content**. For example, the `title` element in the following code contains both the text of the title and a collection of `subtitle` elements:

```
<title>The Adventures of Sherlock Holmes
    <subtitle>The Sign of Four</subtitle>
    <subtitle>by Sir Arthur Conan Doyle</subtitle>
</title>
```

To declare mixed content in a DTD, you use the following declaration:

```
<!ELEMENT element (#PCDATA | child1 | child2 | ...)*>
```

This declaration applies the * modifying symbol to a choice of parsed character data or child elements. Because the * symbol is used with a choice list, the element can contain any number of occurrences of child elements or text strings of parsed character data, or it can contain no content at all. For example, the declaration

```
<!ELEMENT title (#PCDATA | subtitle)*>
<!ELEMENT subtitle (#PCDATA)>
```

allows the `title` element to contain any number of text strings of parsed character data interspersed by `subtitle` elements. The `subtitle` elements themselves can contain only parsed character data.

Because they are very flexible, elements with mixed content do not add much defined structure to a document. You can specify only the names of the child elements, and you cannot constrain the order in which those child elements appear or control the number of occurrences for each element. An element might contain only text or it might contain any number of child elements in any order. For this reason, it is best to avoid working with mixed content if you want a tightly structured document.

At this point you've defined a structure for the elements in the orders.xml file. You will declare the attributes associated with those elements in the next session.

REVIEW

Session 2.1 Quick Check

1. What code would you enter to connect an XML document with the root element `Inventory` to a DTD stored in the file books.dtd?
2. What declaration would you enter to allow the `book` element to contain any content?
3. What declaration would you enter to specify that the `video` element is empty?
4. What declaration would you enter to indicate that the `book` element can contain only parsed character data?
5. What declaration would you enter to indicate that the `book` element can contain only a single child element named `author`?
6. What declaration would you enter to indicate that the `book` element can contain one or more child elements named `author`?
7. What declaration would you enter to allow the `part` element to contain a sequence that begins with a choice of the `partNum` or `partName` child elements, followed by child elements named `description` and then `price`?

Session 2.2 Visual Overview:

An **attribute-list declaration**, or simply **attribute declaration**, lists the names of all the attributes associated with a specific element. It also specifies the data type of each attribute, indicates whether each attribute is required or optional, and provides a default value for each attribute, if necessary.

The second term in an attribute-list declaration specifies the name of the element to which the attribute applies.

The third term in an attribute-list declaration specifies the name of the attribute.

The fourth term in an attribute-list declaration specifies the data type of the attribute.

```
<!DOCTYPE customers
[
    <!ELEMENT customers (customer+)>

    <!ELEMENT customer (name, address, phone, ema
    <!ATTLIST customer custID ID #REQUIRED>

    <!ELEMENT name (#PCDATA)>
    <!ATTLIST name title (Mr. | Mrs. | Ms.) #IMPL

    <!ELEMENT address (#PCDATA)>
    <!ELEMENT phone (#PCDATA)>
    <!ELEMENT email (#PCDATA)>
    <!ELEMENT orders (order+)>

    <!ELEMENT order (orderDate, items)>
    <!ATTLIST order orderID ID #REQUIRED>
    <!ATTLIST order orderBy IDREF #REQUIRED>

    <!ELEMENT orderDate (#PCDATA)>
    <!ELEMENT items (item+)>

    <!ELEMENT item (itemPrice, itemQty)>
    <!ATTLIST item itemNumber CDATA #REQUIRED>

    <!ELEMENT itemPrice (#PCDATA)>
    <!ATTLIST itemPrice saleItem (Y | N) "N">
    <!ELEMENT itemQty (#PCDATA)>
]>
```

Defining Attributes within a DTD

The fifth term in an attribute-list declaration indicates whether the attribute is required or optional.

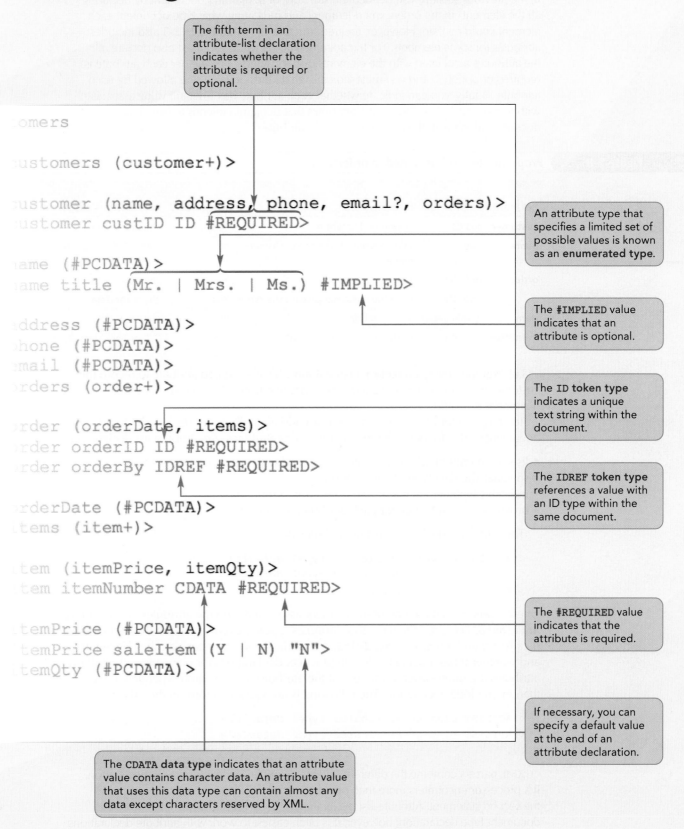

```
omers

ustomers (customer+)>

ustomer (name, address, phone, email?, orders)>
ustomer custID ID #REQUIRED>

ame (#PCDATA)>
ame title (Mr. | Mrs. | Ms.) #IMPLIED>

ddress (#PCDATA)>
hone (#PCDATA)>
mail (#PCDATA)>
rders (order+)>

rder (orderDate, items)>
rder orderID ID #REQUIRED>
rder orderBy IDREF #REQUIRED>

rderDate (#PCDATA)>
tems (item+)>

tem (itemPrice, itemQty)>
tem itemNumber CDATA #REQUIRED>

temPrice (#PCDATA)>
temPrice saleItem (Y | N) "N">
temQty (#PCDATA)>
```

An attribute type that specifies a limited set of possible values is known as an **enumerated type**.

The **#IMPLIED** value indicates that an attribute is optional.

The **ID token type** indicates a unique text string within the document.

The **IDREF token type** references a value with an ID type within the same document.

The **#REQUIRED** value indicates that the attribute is required.

If necessary, you can specify a default value at the end of an attribute declaration.

The **CDATA data type** indicates that an attribute value contains character data. An attribute value that uses this data type can contain almost any data except characters reserved by XML.

Declaring Attributes

In the previous session, you defined the structure of Benjamin's document by declaring all the elements in the orders.xml document and indicating what type of content each element could contain. However, the tree structure shown in Figure 2-3 also includes attributes for some elements. For the document to be valid, you must also declare all the attributes associated with the elements. You must indicate whether each attribute is required or optional, and you must indicate what kinds of values are allowed for each attribute. Finally, you can indicate whether each attribute has a default value associated with it. Figure 2-8 describes all the attributes that Benjamin intends to use in the orders.xml document along with the properties of each attribute.

Figure 2-8 **Properties of attributes used in orders.xml**

Element	Attribute	Description	Required?	Allowable Values
customer	custID	customer ID number	Yes	character data
name	title	title associated with the customer's name	No	"Mr.", "Mrs.", or "Ms."
order	orderID	order ID number	Yes	character data
	orderBy	ID of the customer placing the order	Yes	character data
item	itemNumber	item number	Yes	character data
itemPrice	saleItem	whether item price is a sale price	No	"Y" or "N" (default)

For example, every `customer` element must have a `custID` attribute to record the customer ID value. If a `custID` attribute is omitted from a `customer` element, the document is invalid.

To enforce attribute properties, you must add an attribute-list declaration to the document's DTD for each element that includes attributes. An attribute-list declaration:

- lists the names of all the attributes associated with a specific element
- specifies the data type of each attribute
- indicates whether each attribute is required or optional
- provides a default value for each attribute, if necessary

The syntax for declaring a list of attributes is

```
<!ATTLIST element attribute1 type1 default1
                  attribute2 type2 default2
          ... >
```

where *element* is the name of the element associated with the attributes; *attribute1*, *attribute2*, etc., are the names of attributes; *type1*, *type2*, etc., are the attributes' data types; and *default1*, *default2*, etc., indicate whether each attribute is required and whether it has a default value. In practice, declarations for elements with multiple attributes are often easier to interpret if the attributes are declared separately rather than in one long declaration. The following is an equivalent form in the DTD:

```
<!ATTLIST element attribute1 type1 default1>
<!ATTLIST element attribute2 type2 default2>
...
```

XML parsers combine the different statements into a single attribute-list declaration. If a processor encounters more than one declaration for the same attribute, it ignores the second statement. Attribute-list declarations can be located anywhere within the document type declaration; however, it is often easiest to work with attribute declarations that are located adjacent to the declaration for the element with which they are associated.

Declaring Attributes in a DTD

- To declare a list of attributes associated with an element, enter the declaration

```
<!ATTLIST element attribute1 type1 default1
                  attribute2 type2 default2
                  ...>
```

  or

```
<!ATTLIST element attribute1 type1 default1>
<!ATTLIST element attribute2 type2 default2>
```
  ...

  where *element* is the element associated with the attributes; *attribute1*, *attribute2*, etc., are the names of attributes; *type1*, *type2*, etc., are the attributes' data types; and *default1*, *default2*, etc., indicate whether each attribute is required and whether it has a default value.

- To indicate that an attribute contains character data, use

  attribute CDATA

  where *attribute* is the name of the attribute.

- To constrain an attribute value to a list of possible values, use

  attribute (*value1* | *value2* | *value3* | ...)

  where *value1*, *value2*, etc., are allowed values for the attribute.

- To indicate that an attribute contains ID values, use

  attribute ID

- To indicate that an attribute contains a white space–separated list of ID values, use

  attribute IDS

- To indicate that an attribute contains a reference to an ID value, use

  attribute IDREF

- To indicate that an attribute contains a white space–separated list of references to ID values, use

  attribute IDREFS

- To constrain an attribute to an XML name containing only letters, numbers, and the punctuation symbols underscore (_), hyphen (-), period (.), and colon (:), but no white space, use

  attribute NMTOKEN

- To constrain an attribute to a white space–separated list of XML names, use

  attribute NMTOKENS

As a first step in adding attributes to the DTD for the orders.xml document, you will declare the names of the attributes and the elements with which they are associated in the document.

Note: Because you are not yet going to include the data type and default values for the attributes, these attribute declarations are incomplete and would be rejected by any XML parser. You'll fix this later in this session.

To declare the attributes in the orders.xml document:

▶ **1.** If you took a break after the previous session, make sure the orders.xml file is open in your editor.

▶ **2.** Insert a new line below the `customer` element declaration, enter the following declaration, and then insert a new line:

`<!ATTLIST customer custID>`

This declaration indicates that the `customer` element can contain an attribute named `custID`.

▶ **3.** Insert a new line below the declaration for the `name` element, enter the following declaration, and then insert a new line:

`<!ATTLIST name title>`

This declaration indicates that the `name` element can contain a `title` attribute.

▶ **4.** On the blank line below the declaration for the `order` element, insert the following two declarations on new lines, and then insert a new line:

`<!ATTLIST order orderID>`
`<!ATTLIST order orderBy>`

These declarations indicate that the `order` element can contain attributes named `orderID` and `orderBy`.

▶ **5.** On the blank line below the declaration for the `item` element, enter the following attribute declaration, and then insert a blank line:

`<!ATTLIST item itemNumber>`

This declaration indicates that the `item` element can contain an attribute named `itemNumber`.

▶ **6.** Insert a blank line below the declaration for the `itemPrice` element, and then enter the following declaration:

`<!ATTLIST itemPrice saleItem>`

This declaration indicates that the `itemPrice` element can contain an attribute named `saleItem`. Figure 2-9 shows the revised code including the attribute-list declarations.

| Figure 2-9 | Declarations for the attribute names |

> you can place an attribute-list declaration anywhere within the DOCTYPE, but placing it after the relevant element declaration helps organize your code

```
<!DOCTYPE customers
[
    <!ELEMENT customers (customer+)>

    <!ELEMENT customer (name, address, phone, email?, orders)>
    <!ATTLIST customer custID>

    <!ELEMENT name (#PCDATA)>
    <!ATTLIST name title>

    <!ELEMENT address (#PCDATA)>
    <!ELEMENT phone (#PCDATA)>
    <!ELEMENT email (#PCDATA)>
    <!ELEMENT orders (order+)>

    <!ELEMENT order (orderDate, items)>
    <!ATTLIST order orderID>
    <!ATTLIST order orderBy>

    <!ELEMENT orderDate (#PCDATA)>
    <!ELEMENT items (item+)>

    <!ELEMENT item (itemPrice, itemQty)>
    <!ATTLIST item itemNumber>

    <!ELEMENT itemPrice (#PCDATA)>
    <!ATTLIST itemPrice saleItem>
    <!ELEMENT itemQty (#PCDATA)>
]>
```

7. Save your changes to the file.

Trouble? When you save changes, your XML editor may indicate that the document contains an error and is no longer well formed. This is because the attribute-list declarations you entered are not yet complete. You'll fix this error by completing the declarations in the steps that follow.

Working with Attribute Types

The next step in defining these attributes is to specify the type of data each attribute can contain. Attribute values can consist only of character data, but you can control the format of those characters. Figure 2-10 lists the different data types that DTDs support for attribute values. Each data type gives you a varying degree of control over an attribute's content. You will investigate each of these types in greater detail, starting with character data.

Figure 2-10	Attribute types

Attribute Value	Description
CDATA	Any character data except characters reserved by XML
enumerated list	A list of possible attribute values
ID	A unique text string
IDREF	A reference to an ID value
IDREFS	A list of ID values separated by white space
ENTITY	A reference to an external unparsed entity
ENTITIES	A list of entities separated by white space
NMTOKEN	An accepted XML name
NMTOKENS	A list of XML names separated by white space
NOTATION	The name of a notation defined in the DTD

Character Data

Attribute values specified as character data (CDATA) can contain almost any data except characters reserved by XML for other purposes, such as <, >, and &. To declare an attribute value as character data, you add the CDATA data type to the attribute declaration with the syntax

TIP

You'll learn more about default attribute values later in this tutorial.

```
<!ATTLIST element attribute CDATA default>
```

where the optional term *default* specifies a default value. For example, the item number of each item in Benjamin's document is expressed in character data. To indicate this in the DTD, you would add the CDATA attribute type to the declaration for the itemNumber attribute as follows:

```
<!ATTLIST item itemNumber CDATA>
```

Any of the following attribute values are allowed under this declaration because they all contain character data:

```
<item itemNumber="340-978"> ... </item>
<item itemNumber="WMPro"> ... </item>
<item itemNumber="WM101PL"> ... </item>
```

In Benjamin's document, the attribute itemNumber contains character data. You'll add this information to its attribute declaration.

To specify that the itemNumber attribute contains character data:

1. In the orders.xml file, within the attribute-list declaration for itemNumber, just before the closing >, type a **space**, and then type CDATA as shown in Figure 2-11.

Figure 2-11	Character data type added to the attribute-list declaration

```
<!ELEMENT orderDate (#PCDATA)>
<!ELEMENT items (item+)>

<!ELEMENT item (itemPrice, itemQty)>
<!ATTLIST item itemNumber CDATA>

<!ELEMENT itemPrice (#PCDATA)>
<!ATTLIST itemPrice saleItem>
<!ELEMENT itemQty (#PCDATA)>
]>
```

specifies that attribute values are composed of character data

▶ **2.** Save your changes to the file.

Even though you may work with attribute values that will use only numbers as data, it's not possible to declare that an attribute's values must contain only a certain type of characters, such as integers or numbers. To indicate that an attribute value must be an integer or a number, you use schemas—a topic you will study in a later tutorial.

Enumerated Types

The CDATA data type allows for almost any string of characters, but in some cases you want to restrict an attribute to a set of possible values. For example, Benjamin uses the `title` attribute to indicate the title by which a customer chooses to be addressed. He needs to restrict the `title` attribute to values of "Mr.", "Mrs.", or "Ms." An attribute type that specifies a limited set of possible values is known as an enumerated type. The general form of an attribute declaration that uses an enumerated type is

```
<!ATTLIST element attribute (value1 | value2 | value3 | ...)
          default >
```

where `value1`, `value2`, etc., are allowed values for the specified attribute. To limit the value of the `title` attribute to "Mr." or "Mrs." or "Ms.", Benjamin can include an enumerated type, as in the following declaration:

```
<!ATTLIST name title (Mr. | Mrs. | Ms.)>
```

Under this declaration, any `title` attribute whose value is not "Mr.", "Mrs.", or "Ms." causes parsers to reject the document as invalid. You'll add this enumerated type to the DTD along with an enumerated type to specify the enumerated values for the `title` attribute of the `name` element.

To declare enumerated data types for the two `title` attributes:

▶ **1.** Within the `title` attribute declaration for the `name` element, just before the closing >, type a **space** and then type **(Mr. | Mrs. | Ms.)**.

▶ **2.** Within the `saleItem` attribute declaration for the `itemPrice` element, just before the closing >, type a **space** and then type **(Y | N)**. Figure 2-12 shows the revised DTD.

Figure 2-12 ▶   **Attributes with enumerated data types**

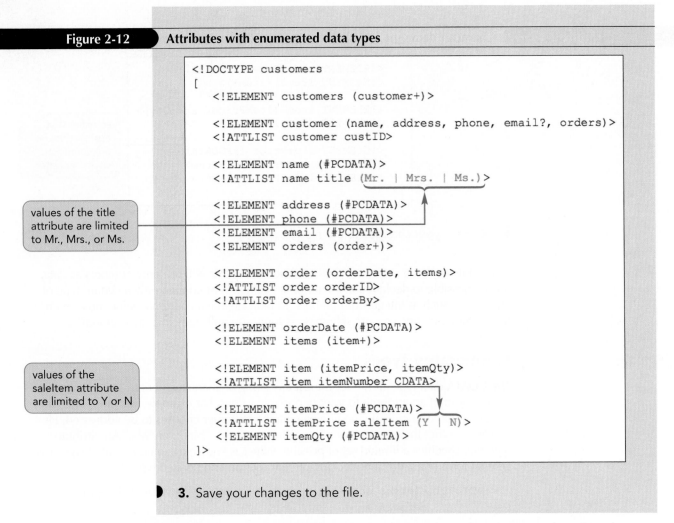

```
<!DOCTYPE customers
[
   <!ELEMENT customers (customer+)>

   <!ELEMENT customer (name, address, phone, email?, orders)>
   <!ATTLIST customer custID>

   <!ELEMENT name (#PCDATA)>
   <!ATTLIST name title (Mr. | Mrs. | Ms.)>

   <!ELEMENT address (#PCDATA)>
   <!ELEMENT phone (#PCDATA)>
   <!ELEMENT email (#PCDATA)>
   <!ELEMENT orders (order+)>

   <!ELEMENT order (orderDate, items)>
   <!ATTLIST order orderID>
   <!ATTLIST order orderBy>

   <!ELEMENT orderDate (#PCDATA)>
   <!ELEMENT items (item+)>

   <!ELEMENT item (itemPrice, itemQty)>
   <!ATTLIST item itemNumber CDATA>

   <!ELEMENT itemPrice (#PCDATA)>
   <!ATTLIST itemPrice saleItem (Y | N)>
   <!ELEMENT itemQty (#PCDATA)>
]>
```

values of the title attribute are limited to Mr., Mrs., or Ms.

values of the saleItem attribute are limited to Y or N

▶ **3.** Save your changes to the file.

Another type of enumerated type is a notation. A **notation** associates the value of an attribute with a `<!NOTATION>` declaration that is inserted elsewhere in the DTD. Notations are used when an attribute value refers to a file containing nontextual data, such as a graphic image or a video clip. You will learn more about notations and how to work with nontextual data in the next session.

Tokenized Types

Tokenized types are character strings that follow certain specified rules for format and content; these rules are known as **tokens**. DTDs support four kinds of tokens—ID, ID reference, name token, and entity.

An **ID token** is used when an attribute value must be unique within a document. In Benjamin's document, the `customer` element contains the `custID` attribute, which stores a unique ID for each customer. To prevent users from entering the same `custID` value for different customers, Benjamin can define the attribute type for the `custID` attribute as follows:

```
<!ATTLIST customer custID ID>
```

Under this declaration, the following elements are valid:

```
<customer custID="cust201"> ... </customer>
<customer custID="cust202"> ... </customer>
```

However, the following elements occurring in the same document would not be valid because the same custID value is used more than once:

```
<customer custID="cust201"> ... </customer>
<customer custID="cust201"> ... </customer>
```

When an ID value is declared in a document, other attribute values can reference it using the IDREF token. An attribute declared using the **IDREF token** must have a value equal to the value of an ID attribute located somewhere in the same document. This enables an XML document to contain cross-references between one element and another.

For example, the order element in Benjamin's document has an attribute named orderBy, which contains the ID of the customer who placed the order. Assuming the custID value of the customer element is defined using the ID token, Benjamin can ensure that the orderBy value refers to an actual customer by using the following declaration:

```
<!ATTLIST order orderBy IDREF>
```

When an XML parser encounters this attribute, it searches the XML document for an ID value that matches the value of the orderBy attribute. If one of the attribute values doesn't have a matching ID value in the document, the parser rejects the document as invalid. However, you cannot specify that an XML parser limit its search to only particular elements or attributes. Any attribute that has been declared by the data type ID is a candidate for an ID reference.

An attribute can contain multiple IDs and ID references in a list, with entries separated by white space. For example, Benjamin might list all the orders made by a certain customer as an attribute of the customer element as in the following sample code:

```
<customer orders="or1089 or1021 or1122">
   ...
   <order orderID="or1089"> ... </order>
   <order orderID="or1021"> ... </order>
   <order orderID="or1122"> ... </order>
   ...
</customer>
```

Each ID listed in the orders attribute must match an ID value located elsewhere in the document. If one does not, Benjamin would want the document to be declared invalid.

To declare that an attribute contains a list of IDs, you apply the IDS attribute type to the attribute declaration as follows:

```
<!ATTLIST element attribute IDS default>
```

To declare that an attribute contains a list of ID references, you use the IDREFS attribute type as follows:

```
<!ATTLIST element attribute IDREFS default>
```

For the code sample above, to indicate that the orders attribute contains a list of ID references and to indicate that the orderID attribute contains IDs, you would enter the following attribute declarations in the DTD:

```
<!ATTLIST customer orders IDREFS>
<!ATTLIST order orderID ID>
```

As with the IDREF token, all of the IDs listed in an IDREFS token must be found in an ID attribute located somewhere in the file; otherwise, parsers will reject the document as invalid. However, nothing in the attribute declaration defines in which attributes the referenced ID will be located. So, although the orders attribute defined above must reference an ID value, it is not required to find that ID value only in the order attribute.

TIP

Because an ID must be a valid XML name, it cannot begin with a number. Commonly used identifiers such as Social Security numbers must be prefaced with one or more alphabetical characters, such as SS123-45-6789.

In Benjamin's document, the `custID` and `orderID` attributes contain ID values, while the `orderBy` attribute contains a reference to the customer ID. You'll declare the `custID` and `orderID` attributes as `ID` data types, and the `orderBy` attribute as an `IDREF` data type.

To declare attributes as IDs and ID references:

1. Within the `custID` attribute declaration, before the closing >, type a **space** and then type `ID`. This ensures that each `custID` value in the document is unique.

2. Repeat Step 1 for the `orderID` attribute declaration.

3. Within the `orderBy` attribute declaration, before the closing >, type a **space** and then type `IDREF`. This ensures that each `orderBy` value references an ID value somewhere in the document. See Figure 2-13.

Figure 2-13 **Attribute IDs and IDREF added**

each custID value must be unique in the document

each orderID value must be unique in the document

each value of the orderBy attribute must match an ID value somewhere in the document

```
<!DOCTYPE customers
[
    <!ELEMENT customers (customer+)>

    <!ELEMENT customer (name, address, phone, email?, orders)>
    <!ATTLIST customer custID ID>

    <!ELEMENT name (#PCDATA)>
    <!ATTLIST name title (Mr. | Mrs. | Ms.)>

    <!ELEMENT address (#PCDATA)>
    <!ELEMENT phone (#PCDATA)>
    <!ELEMENT email (#PCDATA)>
    <!ELEMENT orders (order+)>

    <!ELEMENT order (orderDate, items)>
    <!ATTLIST order orderID ID>
    <!ATTLIST order orderBy IDREF>

    <!ELEMENT orderDate (#PCDATA)>
    <!ELEMENT items (item+)>

    <!ELEMENT item (itemPrice, itemQty)>
    <!ATTLIST item itemNumber CDATA>

    <!ELEMENT itemPrice (#PCDATA)>
    <!ATTLIST itemPrice saleItem (Y | N)>
    <!ELEMENT itemQty (#PCDATA)>
]>
```

4. Save your changes to the file.

The **NMTOKEN**, or name token, data type is used with character data whose values must meet almost all the qualifications for valid XML names. NMTOKEN data types can contain letters and numbers, as well as the underscore (_), hyphen (-), period (.), and colon (:) symbols, but not white space characters such as blank spaces or line returns. However, while an XML name can start only with a letter or an underscore, an NMTOKEN data type can begin with any valid XML character.

The limits on the NMTOKEN data type make name tokens less flexible than character data, which can contain white space characters. If Benjamin wants to make sure that an attribute value is always a valid XML name, he can use the NMTOKEN type instead of the CDATA type. For instance, he could use an NMTOKEN data type for an attribute whose value would always be a date stored in ISO date format (such as 2017-05-20). Specifying this data type would exclude obviously erroneous data, including anything with a string or a date separated by slashes (which are disallowed characters in an XML name).

When an attribute contains more than one name token, you define the attribute using the **NMTOKENS** data type and separate the name tokens in the list with blank spaces.

Working with Attribute Defaults

The final part of an attribute declaration is the attribute default, which defines whether an attribute value is required, optional, assigned a default, or fixed. Figure 2-14 shows the entry in the attribute-list declaration for each of these four possibilities.

Figure 2-14	Attribute defaults

Attribute Default	Description
#REQUIRED	The attribute must appear with every occurrence of the element.
#IMPLIED	The attribute is optional.
"default"	The attribute is optional. If an attribute value is not specified, a validating XML parser will supply the default value.
#FIXED "default"	The attribute is optional. If an attribute value is specified, it must match the default value.

Figure 2-8 showed how Benjamin outlined the properties for the attributes in the orders.xml document. Based on this outline, a customer ID value is required for every customer. To indicate this in the DTD, you would add the #REQUIRED value to the attribute declaration, as follows:

```
<!ATTLIST customer custID ID #REQUIRED>
```

On the other hand, Benjamin does not always record whether a customer wants to be addressed as Mr., Mrs., or Ms., so you would add the #IMPLIED value to the title attribute to indicate that this attribute is optional. The following shows the complete attribute declaration for the title attribute:

```
<!ATTLIST name title (Mr. | Mrs. | Ms.) #IMPLIED>
```

Based on this declaration, if an XML parser encounters a name element without a title attribute, it doesn't invalidate the document but it assumes a blank value for the attribute instead.

Another attribute from Benjamin's document is the saleItem attribute, which indicates whether the itemPrice value is a sale price. The saleItem attribute is optional; however, unlike the title attribute, which gets a blank value if omitted, Benjamin wants XML parsers to assume a value of N if no value is specified for the saleItem attribute. The complete attribute declaration for the saleItem attribute is

```
<!ATTLIST itemPrice saleItem (Y | N) "N">
```

The last type of attribute default is #FIXED default, which fixes the attribute to the value specified by default. If you omit a #FIXED attribute from the corresponding element, an XML parser supplies the default value. If you include the attribute, the attribute value must equal default or the document is invalid.

TIP

If you specify a default value for an attribute, omit #REQUIRED and #IMPLIED from the attribute declaration so parsers don't reject the DTD.

REFERENCE

Specifying an Attribute Default

- For an attribute that must appear with every occurrence of the element, insert the attribute default

  `#REQUIRED`

  within the attribute declaration.
- For an optional attribute, insert

  `#IMPLIED`
- For an optional attribute that has a value of *default* when omitted, insert

  `"default"`
- For an optional attribute that must be fixed to the value *default*, insert

  `#FIXED "default"`

Now that you've seen how to work with attribute defaults, you'll complete the attribute declarations by adding the default specifications.

To specify attribute defaults in the orders.xml document:

1. Within the `custID` attribute-list declaration, before the closing >, type a **space** and then type **#REQUIRED**. This indicates that this is a required attribute.

2. Repeat Step 1 for the `orderID`, `orderBy`, and `itemNumber` attribute-list declarations.

3. Within the `title` attribute-list declaration, before the closing >, type a **space** and then type **#IMPLIED**. This indicates that `title` is an optional attribute.

4. Within the `saleItem` attribute-list declaration, before the closing >, type a **space** and then type **"N"**. This indicates that this is the default value of the attribute if no attribute value is entered in the document. Figure 2-15 shows the final form of all of the attribute declarations in the DTD.

Figure 2-15   **Attribute defaults**

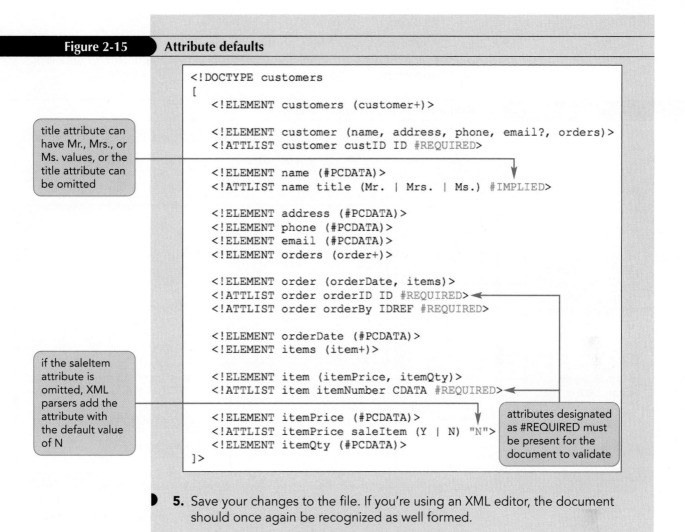

title attribute can have Mr., Mrs., or Ms. values, or the title attribute can be omitted

```
<!DOCTYPE customers
[
    <!ELEMENT customers (customer+)>

    <!ELEMENT customer (name, address, phone, email?, orders)>
    <!ATTLIST customer custID ID #REQUIRED>

    <!ELEMENT name (#PCDATA)>
    <!ATTLIST name title (Mr. | Mrs. | Ms.) #IMPLIED>

    <!ELEMENT address (#PCDATA)>
    <!ELEMENT phone (#PCDATA)>
    <!ELEMENT email (#PCDATA)>
    <!ELEMENT orders (order+)>

    <!ELEMENT order (orderDate, items)>
    <!ATTLIST order orderID ID #REQUIRED>
    <!ATTLIST order orderBy IDREF #REQUIRED>

    <!ELEMENT orderDate (#PCDATA)>
    <!ELEMENT items (item+)>

    <!ELEMENT item (itemPrice, itemQty)>
    <!ATTLIST item itemNumber CDATA #REQUIRED>

    <!ELEMENT itemPrice (#PCDATA)>
    <!ATTLIST itemPrice saleItem (Y | N) "N">
    <!ELEMENT itemQty (#PCDATA)>
]>
```

if the saleItem attribute is omitted, XML parsers add the attribute with the default value of N

attributes designated as #REQUIRED must be present for the document to validate

5. Save your changes to the file. If you're using an XML editor, the document should once again be recognized as well formed.

Validating an XML Document

You are ready to test whether the orders.xml document is valid under the rules Benjamin has specified. To test for validity, an XML parser must be able to compare the XML document with the rules established in the DTD. The web has many excellent sources for validating parsers, including websites in which you can upload an XML document for free to have it validated against an internal or external DTD. Several editors provide XML validation as well.

The following steps describe how to use Exchanger XML Editor to validate Benjamin's orders.xml document.

To validate the orders.xml file:

1. If necessary, use Exchanger XML Editor to open the **orders.xml** file.

Trouble? If you don't have access to Exchanger XML Editor, you can upload your document to http://validator.w3.org, just as you would an HTML document, to validate its content against the DTD. As long as the document is found to be valid, you can ignore any warnings generated.

2. On the menu bar, click **XML** and then on the submenu click **Validate**. As shown in Figure 2-16, the Errors tab reports that the orders.xml file is a valid document.

Figure 2-16	**Validation results in Exchanger XML Editor**

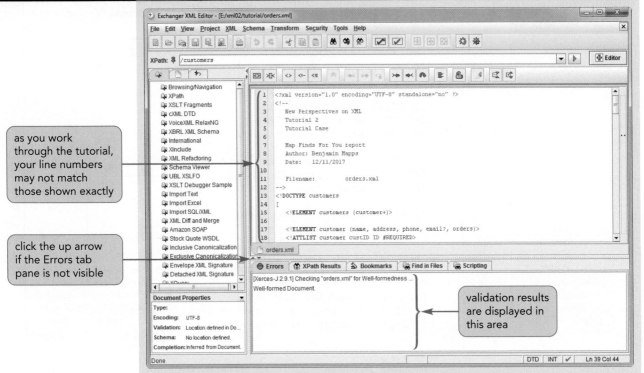

as you work through the tutorial, your line numbers may not match those shown exactly

click the up arrow if the Errors tab pane is not visible

validation results are displayed in this area

Trouble? If the Errors tab isn't visible, click the small up arrow in the lower-left corner of the pane displaying the document code.

Trouble? If a validation error is reported in the Errors tab, there is an error in the DTD code. Check your DTD code against the orders.xml code shown in Figure 2-15. Your code should match exactly, including the use of uppercase and lowercase letters. Fix any discrepancies, be sure to save your changes, revalidate, and then reexamine the Errors tab for validation information.

3. If necessary, save your changes to the file.

TIP

You can also press F7 (Windows) or fn+F7 (Mac) to validate a document in Exchanger XML Editor.

Although the file is valid, it is a good learning experience to place a few intentional errors in your XML code to see how validation errors are discovered and reported. You'll add the following errors to your document:

- Include an element not listed in the DTD.
- Include an attribute not listed in the DTD.
- Provide a value for an attribute declared as an ID reference that does not reference any ID value in the document.

Each of these errors should cause the document to be rejected by your XML parser as invalid.

To add intentional errors to the orders.xml file:

1. Return to the **orders.xml** file in your editor.

2. Scroll down to the first customer, John Michael, and then, directly below the `phone` element, insert a blank line and type the following new `cell` element:

   `<cell>(603) 555-1221</cell>`

   XML parsers will flag this as an error because the element is not declared in the DTD.

3. Scroll down to the first `order` element, with the `orderID` value or1089, click just before the closing >, insert a **space**, and then type the following new attribute:

   `orderType="online"`

   XML parsers will flag this as an error because the attribute is not declared in the DTD.

4. Within the same `order` element, change the value of the `orderBy` attribute from cust201 to **cust210**. Because no ID attribute entered into this document has the value cust210, the XML parser will flag this as an error. Figure 2-17 highlights the new and revised code in the document.

| Figure 2-17 | Intentional errors added to the orders.xml file |

```
<customers>
   <customer custID="cust201">
       <name title="Mr.">John Michael</name>
       <address>
           <![CDATA[
           41 West Plankton Avenue
           Orlando, FL  32820
           ]]>
       </address>
       <phone>(407) 555-3476</phone>
       <cell>(603) 555-1221</cell>
       <email>jk@example.net</email>
       <orders>
           <order orderID="or1089" orderBy="cust210" orderType="online">
               <orderDate>8/11/2017</orderDate>
               <items>
```

cell element has not been declared in the DTD as an element or as a child of customer

cust210 attribute value does not match any ID listed in the document

orderType attribute has not been declared in the DTD

5. Save your changes to the file.

Next, you'll again validate the orders.xml file to test whether an XML parser catches the errors and reports them. You added three intentional errors, but it is not unusual for one error to generate more than one error message. Therefore, it is a good idea to revalidate a document after correcting each error.

To validate the revised orders.xml file:

1. On the menu bar, click **XML**, and then on the submenu, click **Validate**. The parser reports two errors due to the addition of the cell element. First, the parser is expecting an element named cell to be defined. Additionally, because cell was not listed as a child element for the customer element in the DTD, another error message regarding the customer content type not matching is generated. Because of these errors and the additional errors generated from the other changes, the orders.xml file is rejected. See Figure 2-18.

Figure 2-18	Validation errors due to an invalid document

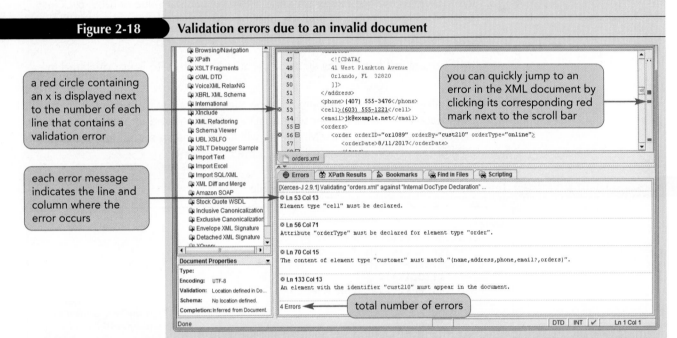

a red circle containing an x is displayed next to the number of each line that contains a validation error

each error message indicates the line and column where the error occurs

you can quickly jump to an error in the XML document by clicking its corresponding red mark next to the scroll bar

total number of errors

Trouble? If the validation errors are not appearing, check your code against Figure 2-18 and be sure they match exactly, save the file again to ensure that the errors you added are saved, and then re-validate the document.

Note that in Exchanger XML Editor, a red circle containing an x is displayed next to the number of each line that contains a validation error. In addition, you can quickly jump to an error in the XML document by clicking its corresponding red mark next to the scroll bar.

2. In the orders.xml code, remove the cell element that you entered in the previous set of steps, and then save your changes to the file.

3. Press **F7** (Windows) or **fn+F7** (Mac) to validate the file again, and then, if necessary, scroll down the error listing. Two errors have been eliminated. Now the first error being identified involves the undeclared attribute orderType. See Figure 2-19.

Figure 2-19	Reduced list of errors

undeclared cell element removed from between these two elements

validation error due to an invalid attribute

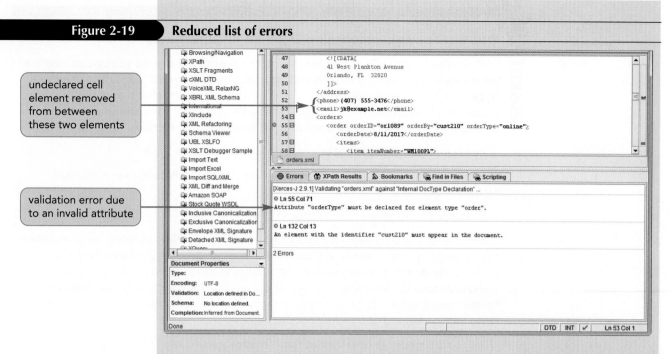

▶ **4.** Remove the orderType attribute and its attribute value from the first order element, and then save your changes to the file.

▶ **5.** Press **F7** (Windows) or **fn+F7** (Mac) to validate the file again, and then, if necessary, scroll down the error listing. Another error has been eliminated. As Figure 2-20 shows, the validator finds only one remaining error in the document: The cust210 value does not reference any ID value found in the document.

Figure 2-20	Final validation error

undeclared orderType attribute removed

validation error due to a missing ID value

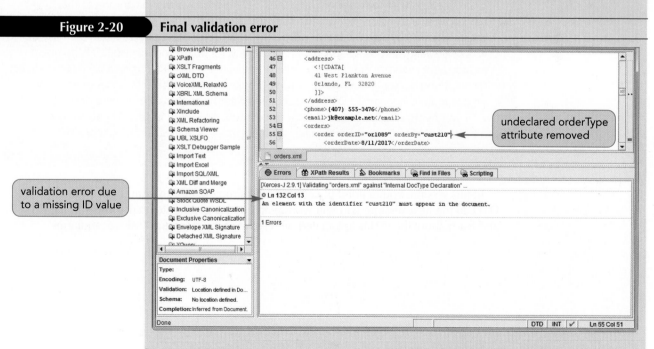

▶ **6.** Change the orderBy attribute value for the first order element from cust210 back to **cust201**, and then save your changes to the file.

▶ **7.** Press **F7** (Windows) or **fn+F7** (Mac) to validate the file again, and then verify that the validator reports no errors in the orders.xml file.

PROSKILLS

Problem Solving: Reconciling DTDs and Namespaces

One drawback with DTDs is that they are not namespace-aware, so you cannot create a set of validation rules for elements and attributes belonging to a particular namespace. To get around this limitation, you can work with namespace prefixes, applying a validation rule to an element's qualified name. For example, if the `phone` element is placed in the customers namespace using the `cu` namespace prefix

```
<cu:phone>(407) 555-3476</cu:phone>
```

then the element declaration in the DTD would need to include the same element name qualification:

```
<!ELEMENT cu:phone (#PCDATA)>
```

In essence, the DTD treats a qualified name as the complete element name including the namespace prefix, colon, and local name. It doesn't recognize the namespace prefix as significant. Any namespace declarations in a document must also be included in the DTD for a document to be valid. This is usually done using a `FIXED` data type for the namespace's URI. For example, if the root element in a document declares the customers namespace using the attribute value

```
<cu:customers xmlns:cu="http://example.com/mapfindsforyou/
customers">
```

then the DTD should include the following attribute declaration:

```
<!ATTLIST cu:customers xmlns:cu CDATA #FIXED "http://example.com/
mapfindsforyou/customers">
```

The drawback to mixing namespaces and DTDs is that you must know the namespace prefix used in an XML document, and the DTD must be written to conform to that namespace. This makes it difficult to perform validation on a wide variety of documents that might employ any number of possible namespace prefixes. In addition, there is no way of knowing what namespace a prefix in the DTD points to because DTDs do not include a mechanism for matching a prefix to a namespace URI. It is also difficult to validate a compound document using standard vocabularies such as XHTML because you cannot easily modify the standard DTDs to accommodate the namespaces in your document.

If you need to validate compound documents that employ several namespaces, a better solution is to use schemas, which are validation tools that do support namespaces.

In this session, you defined the content and structure of Benjamin's document in a DTD. In the next session, you will work with entities and nontextual content in the DTD and learn about the DTDs associated with some of the standard XML vocabularies.

REVIEW

Session 2.2 Quick Check

1. What attribute declaration creates an optional `title` attribute within the `book` element and specifies text string content for the `title` attribute?
2. A `play` element has a required attribute named `type`, which can have one of four possible values—`Romance`, `Tragedy`, `History`, and `Comedy`. Provide the appropriate attribute declaration for the `type` attribute.
3. What is the main difference between an attribute with the CDATA type and one with the NMTOKEN type?
4. A `book` element has a required ID attribute named `ISBN`. Provide the appropriate attribute declaration for the `ISBN` attribute.
5. An `author` element has an optional attribute named `booksBy`, which contains a white space–separated list of ISBNs for the books the author has written. If `ISBN` is an ID attribute for another element in the document, what declaration would you use for the `booksBy` attribute?
6. A `book` element has an optional attribute named `inStock` that can have the value `yes` or `no`. The default value is `yes`. What is the declaration for the `inStock` attribute?

Session 2.3 Visual Overview:

A comment within a DTD uses the same syntax as in XML and XHTML code.

When naming an entity, follow the same guidelines as for naming an XML element.

The value of an entity is contained within quotation marks.

DTD code

```
<!DOCTYPE customers
[
    <!-- Item code descriptions inserted as general entities -->
    <!ENTITY WM100PL "World map outlining countries and capitals; poster-size, laminated paper">
    <!ENTITY WM101P "World map outlining countries and capitals; poster-size, paper">
    <!ENTITY WM105L "World map outlining countries and populations; laminated paper">
    <!ENTITY WM140P "World map focusing on land and water features; paper roll">
    <!ENTITY H115E "United States hiking map including elevations; electronic">
    <!ENTITY H115F "United States hiking map including elevations; folded paper">

    <!ELEMENT customers (customer+)>

    <!ELEMENT customer (name, address, phone, email?, orders)>
    <!ATTLIST customer custID ID #REQUIRED>
```

Entities that are used within an XML document are known as **general entities**. An entity whose content is found within the DTD is known as an **internal entity**, and a **parsed entity** references text that can be readily interpreted by an application reading the XML document.

XML code

```
<customers>
    <customer custID="cust201">
        <name title="Mr.">John Michael</name>
        <address>
            <![CDATA[
            41 West Plankton Avenue
            Orlando, FL  32820
            ]]>
        </address>
        <phone>(407) 555-3476</phone>
        <cell>(603) 555-1221</cell>
        <email>jk@example.net</email>
        <orders>
            <order orderID="or1089" orderBy="cust210" orderType="online">
                <orderDate>8/11/2017</orderDate>
                <items>
                    <item itemNumber="WM100PL">
                        <desc>&WM100PL;</desc>
                        <itemPrice saleItem="N">39.95</itemPrice>
                        <itemQty>1</itemQty>
                    </item>
                    <item itemNumber="WM101P">
                        <desc>&WM101P;</desc>
                        <itemPrice saleItem="Y">19.90</itemPrice>
                        <itemQty>2</itemQty>
                    </item>
                </items>
            </order>
        </orders>
    </customer>
```

An entity reference starts with an ampersand (&) and ends with a semicolon (;).

Entities and Comments in a DTD

> An entity reference is replaced by its value when an XML document is parsed.

Parsed XML document

```
<?xml version="1.0" encoding="UTF-8"?>
<!-- New Perspectives on XML Tutorial 2 Tutorial Case Map Finds For You report Author: Benjamin Mapps Date:
12/11/2017 Filename: orders.xml -->
<!DOCTYPE customers>
- <customers>
   - <customer custID="cust201">
         <name title="Mr.">John Michael</name>
      - <address>
            <![CDATA[ 41 West Plankton Avenue Orlando, FL 32820 ]]>
         </address>
         <phone>(407) 555-3476</phone>
         <email>jk@example.net</email>
      - <orders>
         - <order orderBy="cust201" orderID="or1089">
               <orderDate>8/11/2017</orderDate>
            - <items>
               - <item itemNumber="WM100PL">
                     <desc>World map outlining countries and capitals; poster-size, laminated paper</desc>
                     <itemPrice saleItem="N">39.95</itemPrice>
                     <itemQty>1</itemQty>
                  </item>
               - <item itemNumber="WM101P">
                     <desc>World map outlining countries and capitals; poster-size, paper</desc>
                     <itemPrice saleItem="Y">19.90</itemPrice>
                     <itemQty>2</itemQty>
                  </item>
               </items>
            </order>
         </orders>
      </customer>
```

Introducing Entities

In the orders.xml document, Benjamin inserted item numbers for the different items ordered by customers. For example, the first customer in the file, Mr. John Michael, ordered two items with the item codes WM100PL and WM101P. Each of these item numbers is associated with a longer text description of the product. Figure 2-21 shows the item code and item description for each of the items in the orders.xml file.

Figure 2-21	Item codes and descriptions

Item Codes	Description
WM100PL	World map outlining countries and capitals; poster-size, laminated paper
WM101P	World map outlining countries and capitals; poster-size, paper
WM105L	World map outlining countries and populations; laminated paper
WM140P	World map focusing on land and water features; paper roll
H115E	United States hiking map including elevations; electronic
H115F	United States hiking map including elevations; folded paper

Benjamin wants some way to include the longer text descriptions of these items in his document without having to enter them into each order, which might result in some typographical errors. You can do this with entities. You have already worked with entities to insert special character strings into an XML document. XML supports the following five built-in entities:

- `&amp;` for the & character
- `&lt;` for the < character
- `&gt;` for the > character
- `&apos;` for the ' character
- `&quot;` for the " character

When an XML parser encounters one of these entities, it can display the corresponding character symbol. With a DTD, you can create a customized set of entities corresponding to text strings such as Benjamin's product descriptions, files, or nontextual content that you want referenced by the XML document. When an XML parser encounters one of your customized entities, it will also be able to display the corresponding character text.

Working with General Entities

TIP

For a long text string that will be repeated throughout an XML document, avoid data entry errors by placing the text string in its own entity.

To create a customized entity, you add it to the document's DTD. An entity is classified based on three factors—where it will be applied, where its content is located, and what type of content it references. Entities that are used within an XML document are known as general entities. Another type of entity, a **parameter entity**, is used within a DTD. You will work with parameter entities later in this session.

Entities can reference content found either in an external file or within the DTD itself. An entity that references content found in an external file is called an **external entity**, whereas an entity whose content is found within the DTD is known as an internal entity.

Finally, the content referenced by an entity can be either parsed or unparsed. A parsed entity references text that can be readily interpreted, or parsed, by an application reading the XML document. Parsed entities are used when text is repeated often, and can reference characters, words, phrases, paragraphs, or entire documents. The only requirement is that the text be well formed. An entity that references content that either is nontextual or cannot be interpreted by an XML parser is an **unparsed entity**. One example of an unparsed entity is an entity that references a graphic image file.

Different types of entities are declared slightly differently based on the above three factors. For Benjamin's product codes, you'll declare general parsed internal entities.

Creating Parsed Entities

To create a parsed internal entity, you add the entity declaration

```
<!ENTITY entity "value">
```

to the DTD, where *entity* is the name assigned to the entity and *value* is the text string associated with the entity. The entity name follows the same rules that apply to all XML names: It can have no blank spaces and must begin with either a letter or an underscore. The entity value itself must be well-formed XML text. This can be a simple text string or it can be well-formed XML code. For example, to store the product description for the product with the item code WM100PL, you would add the following entity to the document's DTD:

```
<!ENTITY WM100PL "World map outlining countries and capitals;
poster-size, laminated paper">
```

You can add markup tags to any entity declaration by including them in the entity value, as follows:

```
<!ENTITY WM100PL "<desc>World map outlining countries and capitals;
poster-size, laminated paper</desc>">
```

Any text is allowed to be used for an entity's value as long as it corresponds to well-formed XML. Thus, a document containing the following entity declaration would not be well formed because the declaration lacks the closing `</desc>` tag in the entity's value:

Not well-formed code:

```
<!ENTITY WM100PL "<desc>World map outlining countries and capitals;
poster-size, laminated paper">
```

Entity values must be well formed without reference to other entities or document content. You couldn't, for example, place the closing `</desc>` tag in another entity declaration or within the XML document itself. Although tags within entity references are allowed, this is not a recommended practice.

For longer text strings that would not easily fit within the value of an entity declaration, you can place the content in an external file. To create a parsed entity that references content from an external file using a system identifier, such as a filename or URI, you use the declaration

```
<!ENTITY entity SYSTEM "uri">
```

where *entity* is again the entity's name, SYSTEM indicates the content is located in an external file, and *uri* is the URI of the external file containing the entity's content. For instance, the following entity declaration references the content of the description.xml file:

```
<!ENTITY WM100PL SYSTEM "description.xml">
```

The description.xml file must contain well-formed XML content. However, it should not contain an XML declaration. Because an XML document can contain only one XML declaration, placing a second one in a document via an external entity results in an error.

An external entity can also reference content from an external file using a public identifier with the declaration

```
<!ENTITY entity PUBLIC "id" "uri">
```

where PUBLIC indicates the content is located in a public location, *id* is the public identifier, and *uri* is the system location of the external file (included in case an XML parser doesn't recognize the public identifier). An entity declaration referencing a public location might look like the following:

```
<!ENTITY WM100PL PUBLIC "-//MFY// WM100PL INFO" "description.xml">
```

In this case, the public identifier `-//MFY// WM100PL INFO` is used by an XML parser to load the external content corresponding to the `WM100PL` entity. If that identifier is not recognized, the parser falls back to the system location of the description.xml file. In this way, external entities behave like DOCTYPEs that reference external DTDs from either public or system locations.

Declaring and Referencing Parsed Entities

- To declare a parsed internal entity, use the declaration

  ```
  <!ENTITY entity "value">
  ```

  where *entity* is the entity's name and *value* is the entity's value.
- To declare a parsed external entity from a system location, use the declaration

  ```
  <!ENTITY entity SYSTEM "uri">
  ```

  where *uri* is the URI of the external file containing the entity value.
- To declare a parsed external entity from a public location, use the declaration

  ```
  <!ENTITY entity PUBLIC "id" "uri">
  ```

  where *id* is the public identifier for the external file.
- To reference a general entity within an XML document, enter

  ```
  &entity;
  ```

  where *entity* is the entity name declared in the DTD associated with the XML document.

Referencing a General Entity

After a general entity is declared in a DTD, it can be referenced anywhere within the body of the XML document. The syntax for referencing a general entity is the same as for referencing one of the five built-in XML entities, namely

```
&entity;
```

where *entity* is the entity's name as declared in the DTD. For example, if the `WM100PL` entity is declared in the DTD as

```
<!ENTITY WM100PL "World map outlining countries and capitals;
poster-size, laminated paper">
```

you could reference the entity's value in the XML document within a `desc` element as follows:

```
<desc>&WM100PL;</desc>
```

Any XML parser encountering this entity reference would be able to expand the entity into its referenced value, resulting in the following parsed code:

```
<desc>World map outlining countries and capitals; poster-size,
laminated paper</desc>
```

The fact that the entity's value is expanded into the code of the XML document is one reason why entity values must correspond to well-formed XML code. Because of the way entities are parsed, you cannot include the & symbol as part of an entity's value.

XML parsers interpret the & symbol as a reference to another entity and attempt to resolve the reference. If you need to include the & symbol, you should use the built-in entity reference `&amp;`. You also cannot use the % symbol in an entity's value because, as you'll learn later in this session, this is the symbol used for inserting parameter entities.

At the time of this writing, none of the major browsers support the use of external entities in combination with DTDs. These browsers use a built-in XML parser that does not support resolution of external entities. The reason is that if an entity declaration is placed in a file on a remote web server, the XML parser must establish a TCP/IP connection with the remote file, which might not always be possible. The major browsers consider such a connection to be a potential security risk. Thus, to ensure that an XML document can be properly read and rendered, browsers require entities to be part of the internal DTD.

Next, you'll declare parsed entities for all the product codes in the orders.xml document. You'll place the declarations within the internal DTD. You'll also add a declaration to the DTD for the desc element, which will contain the entities within the document code.

To create the entity declarations in an internal DTD:

1. If you took a break after the previous session, make sure the **orders.xml** file is open in your text editor.

2. Add the following entity declarations below the opening square bracket in the DOCTYPE declaration statement:

```
<!ENTITY WM100PL "World map outlining countries and capitals;
        poster-size, laminated paper">
<!ENTITY WM101P "World map outlining countries and capitals;
        poster-size, paper">
<!ENTITY WM105L "World map outlining countries and populations;
        laminated paper">
<!ENTITY WM140P "World map focusing on land and water features;
        paper roll">
<!ENTITY H115E "United States hiking map including elevations;
        electronic">
<!ENTITY H115F "United States hiking map including elevations;
        folded paper">
```

Figure 2-22 shows the updated DOCTYPE.

Figure 2-22	Creating general entities

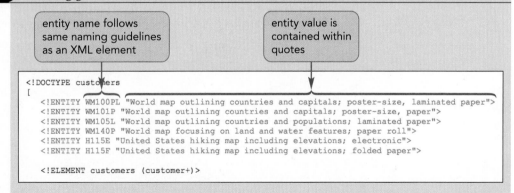

3. Scroll down to the element definition for the item element, place the insertion point after the opening parenthesis for the list of child elements and before the itemPrice element name, and then type **desc** followed by a comma and a space.

4. Insert a blank line before the `itemPrice` element definition, and then type the following new element definition on the blank line you just created:

```
<!ELEMENT desc (#PCDATA)>
```

Figure 2-23 shows the updated code in the DTD.

Figure 2-23 **Adding a new element to the DTD**

new desc element specified as a child of the item element

new desc element added

```
<!ELEMENT items (item+)>

<!ELEMENT item (desc, itemPrice, itemQty)>
<!ATTLIST item itemNumber CDATA #REQUIRED>

<!ELEMENT desc (#PCDATA)>
<!ELEMENT itemPrice (#PCDATA)>
<!ATTLIST itemPrice saleItem (Y | N) "N">
<!ELEMENT itemQty (#PCDATA)>
]>
```

5. Save the **orders.xml** file.

Now that you've defined the entities, you'll insert entity references to Benjamin's item description codes in the body of the XML document.

To add entity references:

1. Scroll down to the `customer` element for the first customer, John Michael, and then directly below the opening tag for the first `item` element, enter the following new `desc` element:

```
<desc>&WM100PL;</desc>
```

Notice that the entity reference is the value of the `itemNumber` attribute for the preceding `item` element, with & at the start and ; at the end.

2. Directly below the opening tag for the second `item` element for John Michael, add the following new `desc` element:

```
<desc>&WM101P;</desc>
```

Figure 2-24 shows the revised code for John Michael's orders.

Figure 2-24	Revised order information for John Michael

```
<customer custID="cust201">
    <name title="Mr.">John Michael</name>
    <address>
        <![CDATA[
        41 West Plankton Avenue
        Orlando, FL  32820
        ]]>
    </address>
    <phone>(407) 555-3476</phone>
    <cell>(603) 555-1221</cell>
    <email>jk@example.net</email>
    <orders>
        <order orderID="or1089" orderBy="cust210" orderType="online">
            <orderDate>8/11/2017</orderDate>
            <items>
                <item itemNumber="WM100PL">
                    <desc>&WM100PL;</desc>
                    <itemPrice saleItem="N">39.95</itemPrice>
                    <itemQty>1</itemQty>
                </item>
                <item itemNumber="WM101P">
                    <desc>&WM101P;</desc>
                    <itemPrice saleItem="Y">19.90</itemPrice>
                    <itemQty>2</itemQty>
                </item>
            </items>
        </order>
    </orders>
</customer>
```

desc element containing the general entity reference for the item description

general entity reference begins with an ampersand and ends with a semicolon

Be sure to include an ampersand (&) at the start of each entity reference and a semicolon (;) at the end of each one; otherwise, parsers will not correctly interpret them as entity references.

3. Insert a desc child element within each of the four item elements for Dean Abernath, each containing an ampersand (&) followed by the value of the itemNumber attribute for the preceding item element and then a semicolon (;), as shown in Figure 2-25.

| Figure 2-25 | Revised order information for Dean Abernath |

```
<email>dabernath@example.net</email>
<orders>
   <order orderID="or1021" orderBy="cust202">
      <orderDate>8/1/2017</orderDate>
      <items>
         <item itemNumber="WM100PL">
            <desc>&WM100PL;</desc>
            <itemPrice>29.95</itemPrice>
            <itemQty>1</itemQty>
         </item>
         <item itemNumber="WM105L">
            <desc>&WM105L;</desc>
            <itemPrice>19.95</itemPrice>
            <itemQty>1</itemQty>
         </item>
      </items>
   </order>
   <order orderID="or1122" orderBy="cust202">
      <orderDate>10/1/2017</orderDate>
      <items>
         <item itemNumber="H115E">
            <desc>&H115E;</desc>
            <itemPrice saleItem="Y">24.90</itemPrice>
            <itemQty>2</itemQty>
         </item>
         <item itemNumber="H115F">
            <desc>&H115F;</desc>
            <itemPrice saleItem="N">14.95</itemPrice>
            <itemQty>1</itemQty>
         </item>
      </items>
   </order>
</orders>
```

> **4.** Repeat Step 3 for the one remaining `item` element for the last customer, Riverfront High School. Figure 2-26 shows the revised code for the Riverfront High School order.

| Figure 2-26 | Revised order information for Riverfront High School |

```
<phone>(715) 555-4022</phone>
<orders>
   <order orderID="or1120" orderBy="cust203">
      <orderDate>9/15/2017</orderDate>
      <items>
         <item itemNumber="WM140P">
            <desc>&WM140P;</desc>
            <itemPrice>78.90</itemPrice>
            <itemQty>2</itemQty>
         </item>
      </items>
   </order>
</orders>
```

> **5.** Save the **orders.xml** file.

Now that you've added the entity references to Benjamin's document, you can verify that their values are resolved in your web browser.

> **6.** Open **orders.xml** in a web browser. When viewed in a browser that uses an outline format for XML files, the values of all seven product codes are displayed. Figure 2-27 shows the document in Internet Explorer.

| Figure 2-27 | The orders.xml file displayed in a browser |

```
<?xml version="1.0" encoding="UTF-8"?>
<!-- New Perspectives on XML Tutorial 2 Tutorial Case Map Finds For You report Author: Benjamin Mapps Date:
12/11/2017 Filename: orders.xml -->
<!DOCTYPE customers>
- <customers>
    - <customer custID="cust201">
        <name title="Mr.">John Michael</name>
      - <address>
            <![CDATA[ 41 West Plankton Avenue Orlando, FL 32820 ]]>
        </address>
        <phone>(407) 555-3476</phone>
        <email>jk@example.net</email>
      - <orders>
          - <order orderBy="cust201" orderID="or1089">
                <orderDate>8/11/2017</orderDate>
              - <items>
                  - <item itemNumber="WM100PL">
                        <desc>World map outlining countries and capitals; poster-size, laminated paper</desc>
                        <itemPrice saleItem="N">39.95</itemPrice>
                        <itemQty>1</itemQty>
                    </item>
                  - <item itemNumber="WM101P">
                        <desc>World map outlining countries and capitals; poster-size, paper</desc>
                        <itemPrice saleItem="Y">19.90</itemPrice>
                        <itemQty>2</itemQty>
                    </item>
                </items>
            </order>
        </orders>
    </customer>
```

parser translation of the &WM100PL; entity reference you entered in the desc element

Trouble? If your browser displays a warning message about the content of your file, click the necessary button(s) to allow the content to be parsed and displayed. Some browsers treat XML files with suspicion for computer security reasons; but because you created this file, you don't need to be concerned about opening it.

So far, you've placed all your entity declarations internally within the orders.xml document. However, you can also externally link declarations rather than defining them internally. There are two methods for linking to external declarations—revising the DOCTYPE to link to an external DTD file and using a parameter entity.

Working with Parameter Entities

Just as you use a general entity when you want to insert content into an XML document, you use a **parameter entity** when you want to insert content into the DTD itself. You can use parameter entities to break a DTD into smaller chunks, or **modules**, that are placed in different files. Imagine a team of programmers working on a DTD for a large XML vocabulary such as XHTML, containing hundreds of elements and attributes. Rather than placing all the declarations within a single file, individual programmers could work on sections suited to their expertise. Then a project coordinator could use parameter entities to reference the different sections in the main DTD. Parameter entities also enable XML programmers to reuse large blocks of DTD code, which saves them from retyping the same code multiple times.

The declaration to create a parameter entity is similar to the declaration for a general entity, with the syntax

```
<!ENTITY % entity "value">
```

where *entity* is the name of the parameter entity and *value* is the text referenced by the parameter entity. Like general entities, parameter entities can also reference external content in either system or public locations. The declarations for external parameter entities are

```
<!ENTITY % entity SYSTEM "uri">
```

and

```
<!ENTITY % entity PUBLIC "id" "uri">
```

where *id* is a public identifier for the parameter entity and *uri* is the location of the external file containing DTD content.

For example, the following code shows an internal parameter entity for a collection of elements and attributes:

```
<!ENTITY % books
    "<!ELEMENT Book (Title, Author)>
     <!ATTLIST Book Pages CDATA #REQUIRED>
     <!ELEMENT Title (#PCDATA)>
     <!ELEMENT Author (#PCDATA)>"
>
```

If you instead placed the elements and attributes referenced in the previous code in an external DTD file named books.dtd, you could use an external parameter entity to access the content of that document as follows:

```
<!ENTITY % books SYSTEM "books.dtd">
```

After a parameter has been declared, you can reference it within the DTD using the statement

```
%entity;
```

where *entity* is the name assigned to the parameter entity. Parameter entity references can be placed only where a declaration would regularly occur, such as within an internal or external DTD. You *cannot* insert a parameter entity reference within the element content of an XML document. For example, to reference the **books** parameter entity described above, you would enter the following line into the DTD:

```
%books;
```

Figure 2-28 shows how parameter entities can be used to combine DTDs from multiple files into a single (virtual) DTD.

TIP

Note that when declaring a parameter entity, you include a space after the %; but when referencing a parameter entity, there is no space between the % and the entity name.

Figure 2-28   **Creating a combined DTD using parameter entities**

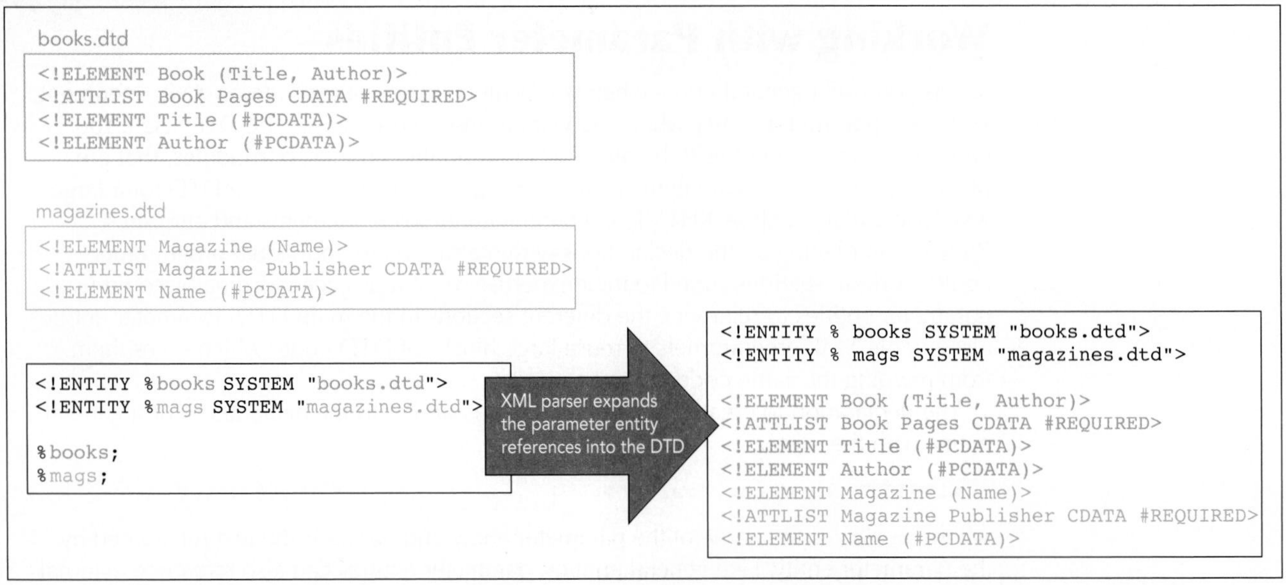

In the figure, two parameter entities—`%books;` and `%mags;`—are used to combine the contents of books.dtd and magazines.dtd into a master document.

Declaring and Referencing Parameter Entities

- To declare an internal parameter entity, add the line

  `<!ENTITY % entity "value">`

  to the DTD, where `entity` is the entity name and `value` is the entity value.
- To declare an external parameter entity for a system location, use

  `<!ENTITY % entity SYSTEM "uri">`

  where `uri` is the location of the external file containing DTD content.
- To declare an external parameter entity for a public location, use

  `<!ENTITY % entity PUBLIC "id" "uri">`

  where `id` is the public identifier.
- To reference a parameter entity, add the statement

  `%entity;`

  to the DTD, where `entity` is the name of the parameter entity.

Inserting Comments into a DTD

Benjamin is pleased with your work on creating the DTD for the sample XML document. However, he is concerned that the code in the DTD might be confusing to other programmers. He suggests that you add a comment. Comments in a DTD follow the same syntax as comments in XML. The specific form of a DTD comment is

```
<!-- comment -->
```

where `comment` is the text of the DTD comment. White space is ignored within a comment, so you can spread comment text over several lines without affecting DTD code.

Teamwork: Documenting Shared Code with Comments

When you're working on a large project with other developers to create a DTD, including comments in your code is important to help other team members quickly understand the code you've written. You can use comments to indicate changes you've made to existing code, to flag code that may need future changes, and simply to document what you've done and when. Although a DTD doesn't require comments, using them to document your work can make you a more valuable team member and increase your group's efficiency.

You'll add a comment now to the orders.xml DTD to summarize its content.

To add a comment to the DTD:

1. Return to the **orders.xml** file in your text editor.

▶ **2.** Within the DTD, after the opening bracket and above the first general entity (for the WM100PL item code), insert a blank line, and then enter the following comment:

```
<!-- Item code descriptions inserted as general entities -->
```

Figure 2-29 shows the final form of the DTD for the orders.xml file.

Figure 2-29 ▶ **DTD comment added**

```
<!DOCTYPE customers
[

   <!-- Item code descriptions inserted as general entities -->
   <!ENTITY WM100PL "World map outlining countries and capitals; poster-size, laminated paper">
   <!ENTITY WM101P "World map outlining countries and capitals; poster-size, paper">
   <!ENTITY WM105L "World map outlining countries and populations; laminated paper">
   <!ENTITY WM140P "World map focusing on land and water features; paper roll">
   <!ENTITY H115E "United States hiking map including elevations; electronic">
   <!ENTITY H115F "United States hiking map including elevations; folded paper">

   <!ELEMENT customers (customer+)>
```

▶ **3.** Save your changes to the **orders.xml** file, and then close the file.

Creating Conditional Sections

When you're creating a new DTD, it can be useful to try out different combinations of declarations. You can do this by using a **conditional section**, which is a section of the DTD that is processed only in certain situations. The syntax for creating a conditional section is

```
<![keyword[
   declarations
]]>
```

where *keyword* is either INCLUDE (for a section of declarations that you want parsers to interpret) or IGNORE (for the declarations that you want parsers to pass over). For example, the following code creates two sections of declarations—one for the Magazine element and its child elements, and another for the Book element and its child elements—and instructs parsers to ignore the Magazine-related elements and interpret the Book-related elements:

```
<![IGNORE[
   <!ELEMENT Magazine (Name)>
   <!ATTLIST Magazine Publisher CDATA #REQUIRED>
   <!ELEMENT Name (#PCDATA)>
]]>

<![INCLUDE[
   <!ELEMENT Book (Title, Author)>
   <!ATTLIST Book Pages CDATA #REQUIRED>
   <!ELEMENT Title (#PCDATA)>
   <!ELEMENT Author (#PCDATA)>
]]>
```

An XML parser processing this DTD would run the declarations related to the Book element, but would ignore the declarations related to the Magazine element. As you experiment with a DTD's structure, you can enable a section by changing its keyword from IGNORE to INCLUDE.

One effective way of creating IGNORE sections is to create a parameter entity that defines whether those sections should be included, and to use the value of the entity as the keyword for the conditional sections. For example, the following UseFullDTD entity has a value of IGNORE, which causes the conditional section that follows it to be ignored by XML parsers:

```
<!ENTITY % UseFullDTD "IGNORE">

<![ %UseFullDTD; [
   <!ELEMENT Magazine (Name)>
   <!ATTLIST Magazine Publisher CDATA #REQUIRED>
   <!ELEMENT Name (#PCDATA)>
]]>
```

By changing the value of UseFullDTD from IGNORE to INCLUDE, you can add any conditional section that uses this entity reference to the document's DTD. This enables you to switch multiple sections in the DTD on and off by editing a single line in the file, which is most useful when several conditional sections are scattered throughout a long DTD. Rather than locating and changing each conditional section, you can switch the sections on and off by changing the parameter entity's value.

Conditional sections can be applied only to external DTDs. Both sets of code samples above that illustrate conditional sections would need to be located in external files, rather than in the internal subset of a DTD. Although they may be useful in other contexts, you cannot apply them to the DTD in Benjamin's document because it uses only an internal DTD.

Working with Unparsed Data

So far in this session, you've created entities for character data. For a DTD to validate either binary data, such as images or video clips, or character data that is not well formed, you need to work with unparsed entities. Because an XML parser cannot work with these types of data directly, a DTD must include instructions for how to treat an unparsed entity.

The first step is to declare a **notation**, which identifies the data type of the unparsed data. A notation must supply a name for the data type and provide clues about how applications should handle the data. Notations must reference external content (because that content must contain nontextual data that is, by definition, not well formed) and you must specify an external location. One option is to use a system location, which you specify with the code

```
<!NOTATION notation SYSTEM "uri">
```

where *notation* is the notation's name and *uri* is a system location that gives the XML parser clues about how the data should be handled. The other option is to specify a public location, using the declaration

```
<!NOTATION notation PUBLIC "id" "uri">
```

where *id* is a public identifier recognized by XML parsers. The URI for the resource can either refer to a program that can work with the unparsed data or specify the actual data type. For example, if Benjamin wanted to include references in the orders.xml document to graphic image files stored in the PNG format, he could enter the following notation in the document's DTD:

```
<!NOTATION png SYSTEM "paint.exe">
```

Because an XML parser doesn't know how to handle graphic data, this notation associates the paint.exe program with the png data type. If you don't want to specify a particular program, you could instead indicate the data type using its MIME type value with the following notation:

```
<!NOTATION png SYSTEM "image/png">
```

In this case, an XML parser associates the png notation with the image/png data type as long as the operating system already knows how to handle PNG files. After a notation is declared, you can create an unparsed entity that references specific items that use that notation. The syntax to declare an unparsed entity is

```
<!ENTITY entity SYSTEM "uri" NDATA notation>
```

where entity is the name of the entity referencing the notation, uri is the URI of the unparsed data, and notation is the name of the notation that defines the data type for the XML parser. Again, you can also provide a public location for the unparsed data if an XML parser supports it, using the following form:

```
<!ENTITY entity PUBLIC "id" "uri" NDATA notation>
```

For example, the following declaration creates an unparsed entity named WM100PLIMG that references the graphic image file WM100PL.png:

```
<!ENTITY WM100PLIMG SYSTEM "WM100PL.png" NDATA png>
```

This declaration references the png notation created above to provide the data type.

After you create an entity to reference unparsed data, that entity can be associated with attribute values by using the ENTITY data type in each attribute declaration. If Benjamin wanted to add an image attribute to every item element in the orders.xml document, he could insert the following attribute declaration in the DTD:

```
<!ATTLIST item image ENTITY #REQUIRED>
```

With this declaration added, Benjamin could then add the image attribute to the XML document, using the WM100PLIMG entity as the attribute's value, as follows:

```
<item image="&WM100PLIMG;">
```

TIP

As an alternative to notations, you can place a URL that lists a resource for nontextual content in an element or attribute, and then allow your application to work with that element or attribute value directly.

It's important to understand precisely what this code does and does not accomplish. It tells XML parsers what kind of data is represented by the WM100PLIMG entity, and it provides clues about how to interpret the data stored in the WM100PL.png file—but it does not tell parsers anything else. Whether an application reading the XML document opens another application to display the image file depends solely on the program itself. Remember that the purpose of XML is to create structured documents, but not necessarily to tell programs how to render the data in a document. If a validating XML parser reads the <item> tag described above, it probably wouldn't try to read the graphic image file, but it might check to see whether the file is in the expected location. By doing so, the parser would confirm that the document is complete in its content and in all its references to unparsed data.

Current web browsers do not support mechanisms for validating and rendering unparsed data declared in the DTDs of XML documents, so you will not add this feature to the orders.xml file.

Declaring an Unparsed Entity

- To declare an unparsed entity, first declare a notation for the data type used in the entity, using the syntax

  `<!NOTATION notation SYSTEM "uri">`

  where *notation* is the name of the notation and *uri* is a system location that defines the data type or a program that can work with the data type.
- To specify a public location for the notation, use the declaration

  `<!NOTATION notation PUBLIC "id" "uri">`

  where *id* is a public identifier for the data type associated with the notation.
- To associate a notation with an unparsed entity, use the declaration

  `<!ENTITY entity SYSTEM "uri" NDATA notation>`

  where *entity* is the name of the entity, *uri* is the system location of a file containing the unparsed data, and *notation* is the name of the notation that defines the data type.
- For a public location of the unparsed entity, use the following declaration:

  `<!ENTITY entity PUBLIC "id" "uri" NDATA notation>`

Validating Standard Vocabularies

All of your work in this tutorial involved the custom XML vocabulary developed by Benjamin for orders submitted to Map Finds For You. Most of the standard XML vocabularies in popular use are associated with existing DTDs. To validate a document used with a standard vocabulary, you usually must access an external DTD located on a web server or rely upon a DTD built into your XML parser. Figure 2-30 lists the DOCTYPEs for some popular XML vocabularies.

Figure 2-30   **DOCTYPEs for standard vocabularies**

Vocabulary	DOCTYPE
XHTML 1.0 Strict	`<!DOCTYPE html PUBLIC "-//W3C//DTD XHTML 1.0 Strict//EN" "http://www.w3.org/TR/xhtml1/DTD/xhtml1-strict.dtd">`
XHTML 1.0 Transitional	`<!DOCTYPE html PUBLIC "-//W3C//DTD XHTML 1.0 Transitional// EN" "http://www.w3.org/TR/xhtml1/DTD/xhtml1-transitional.dtd">`
XHTML 1.1	`<!DOCTYPE html PUBLIC "-//W3C//DTD XHTML 1.1//EN" "http://www.w3.org/TR/xhtml11/DTD/xhtml11.dtd">`
MathML 1.01	`<!DOCTYPE math SYSTEM "http://www.w3.org/Math/DTD/mathml1mathml.dtd">`
MathML 2.0	`<!DOCTYPE math PUBLIC "-//W3C//DTD MathML 2.0//EN" "http://www.w3.org/Math/DTD/mathml2/mathml2.dtd">`
SVG 1.1 Basic	`<!DOCTYPE svg PUBLIC "-//W3C//DTD SVG 1.1 Basic//EN" "http://www.w3.org/Graphics/SVG/1.1/DTD/svg11-basic.dtd">`
SVG 1.1 Full	`<!DOCTYPE svg PUBLIC "-//W3C//DTD SVG 1.1//EN" "http://www.w3.org/Graphics/SVG/1.1/DTD/svg11.dtd">`
SMIL 1.0	`<!DOCTYPE smil PUBLIC "-//W3C//DTD SMIL 1.0//EN" "http://www.w3.org/TR/REC-smil/SMIL10.dtd">`
SMIL 2.0	`<!DOCTYPE SMIL PUBLIC "-//W3C//DTD SMIL 2.0//EN" "http://www.w3.org/TR/REC-smil/2000/SMIL20.dtd">`
VoiceXML 2.1	`<!DOCTYPE vxml PUBLIC "-//W3C//DTD VOICEXML 2.1//EN" "http://www.w3.org/TR/voicesml21/vxml.dtd">`

For example, to validate an XHTML document against the XHTML 1.0 Strict standard, you would add the following code to the document header:

```
<?xml version="1.0" encoding="UTF-8" standalone="no" ?>
<!DOCTYPE html PUBLIC "-//W3C//DTD XHTML 1.0 Strict//EN"
   "http://www.w3.org/TR/xhtml1/DTD/xhtml1-strict.dtd">
```

The W3C provides an online validator at http://validator.w3.org that you can use to validate HTML, XHTML, MathML, SVG, and other XML vocabularies. The validator works with files placed on the web or uploaded via a web form.

The DTDs of most standard vocabularies are available online for inspection. Studying the DTDs of other XML vocabularies is a great way to learn how to design your own. Figure 2-31 shows the part of the DTD for XHTML 1.0 that sets the syntax rules for the br (line break) element.

| Figure 2-31 | XHTML 1.0 Strict DTD for the br element |

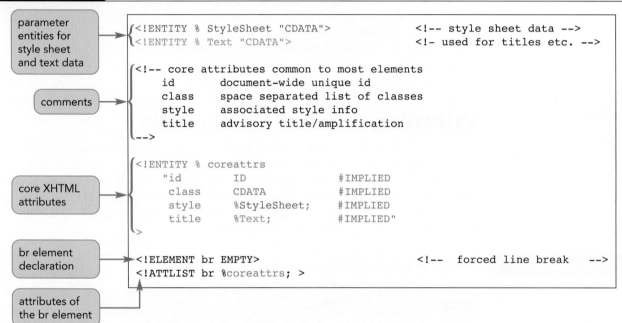

This DTD includes substantial use of parameter entities to allow the same set of attributes to be shared among the many elements of XHTML. For example, the coreattrs parameter entity contains a list of core attributes used by most XHTML elements. The StyleSheet and Text parameter entities contain code that sets the data types for style sheets and title attributes, respectively. From the DTD, you can quickly see that the four core attributes of XHTML are the id, class, style, and title attributes. You can also see that although they are available to almost all elements in the XHTML language, they are not required attributes. The specifications for the br element are fairly simple. Other elements of the XHTML language have more complicated rules, but all are based on the principles discussed in this tutorial.

Advantages and Disadvantages of DTDs

DTDs are the common standard for validating XML documents, but they do have some serious limitations. Because a DTD is not written in the XML language, XML parsers must support the syntax and language requirements needed to interpret DTD code. DTDs are also limited in the data types they support. For example, you cannot specify that the value of an element or an attribute be limited only to integers or to text strings entered in a specific format; nor can you specify the structure of a document beyond a general description of the number or choice of child elements. Finally, DTDs do not support namespaces and thus are of limited value in compound documents.

However, DTDs are a recognized and long-supported standard. Therefore, you should have little problem finding parsers and applications to validate your XML documents based on DTDs. DTDs also support entities, providing a mechanism for referencing nontextual content from your XML files.

If the limitations of DTDs are a severe hindrance to validating your XML documents, another standard—schemas—provides support for an extended list of data types and can be easily adapted to compound documents involving several namespaces.

You've completed your work on Benjamin's document. He will use the DTD you developed to ensure that any new data added to the orders.xml document conforms to the standards you established.

Session 2.3 Quick Check

1. What is the difference between a general entity and a parameter entity?
2. What is the difference between a parsed entity and an unparsed entity?
3. What declaration stores the text string `<Title>Hamlet</Title>` as a general entity named `Play`? What command references this entity in a document?
4. What declaration stores the contents of the plays.xml file as a general entity named `Plays`?
5. What code stores the contents of the plays.dtd file as a parameter entity named `Works`?
6. What is a notation?
7. How do you reference the image file shakespeare.gif in an unparsed entity named `Portrait`? Assume that this entity is using a notation named `GIF`.

PRACTICE

Review Assignments

Data File needed for the Review Assignments: prodtxt.xml

Benjamin needs your help with a document that lists some of Map Finds For You's map products. Figure 2-32 shows the tree structure of Benjamin's XML document.

Figure 2-32   **Structure of the products document**

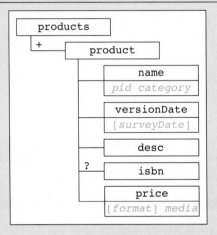

The document contains a root element named `products` with one or more occurrences of the `product` element containing information on map products. The `product` element contains five child elements—`name`, `versionDate`, `desc`, an optional `isbn`, and `price`. The `name` element stores the name of the product and supports two attributes—`pid`, the ID number of the product; and `category`, the type of product (`historical`, `state`, or `parks`). The `versionDate` element also supports an optional `surveyDate` attribute that indicates the date of the map survey, if known. The `desc` element stores a description of the product. The optional `isbn` element stores the ISBN for the product. The `price` element stores the name of the product and supports two attributes—`format`, the format of the product (`flat` or `raised`) with a default of `flat`; and `media`, the media type of the product (`paper` or `electronic`).

For this document, Benjamin wants to enforce a document structure to ensure that information recorded in the document is valid. Therefore, your task will be to create the DTD for the document.

Complete the following:

1. Using your text editor, open the **prodtxt.xml** file from the xml02 ▶ review folder provided with your Data Files, enter *your name* and *today's date* in the comment section of the file, and then save the file as **products.xml**.

2. In the products.xml file, insert an internal DTD for the root element **products** directly after the comment section and before the opening `<products>` tag.

3. Within the internal DTD, declare the following items:

    a. The **products** element, containing at least one occurrence of the child element **product**

    b. The **product** element, containing five child elements in the sequence `name`, `versionDate`, `desc`, an optional `isbn`, and `price`

    c. The **name**, **versionDate**, **desc**, **isbn**, and **price** elements, each containing parsed character data

4. Add the following attribute declarations to the product file:

    a. For the **name** element, a required **pid** attribute as an ID

    b. For the **name** element, a required **category** attribute equal to **historical**, **state**, or **parks**

c. For the `versionDate` element, an optional **surveyDate** attribute containing the date of the survey

d. For the `price` element, an optional **format** attribute equal to either **flat** or **raised**, with a default of **flat**

e. For the `price` element, a required **media** attribute equal to either **paper** or **electronic**

5. On the same line as the `format` attribute definition, insert a comment containing the text **format default is flat**.

6. Save your changes to the products.xml file, and then use Exchanger XML Editor or another XML tool to verify that the document is well formed.

7. Validate the document. If necessary, correct errors one at a time and revalidate until the document is valid.

Case Problem 1

Data Files needed for this Case Problem: photostxt.dtd, photostxt.xml

Note: To complete this case problem, you need an XML parser capable of validating an XML document based on an external DTD file, such as Exchanger XML Editor.

The Our Lady of Bergen Historical Society   Sharon Strattan is an archivist at the Our Lady of Bergen Historical Society in Bergenfield, New Jersey. The historical society is exploring how to transfer its listings to XML format, and Sharon has begun by creating a sample document of the society's extensive collection of photos. A schematic of the vocabulary she's developing is shown in Figure 2-33.

Figure 2-33   **Structure of the photos document**

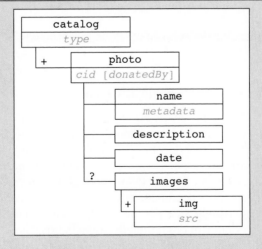

The vocabulary Sharon designed has a root element named `catalog` containing one or more `photo` elements. Each `photo` element contains the name of the photo, a description, the estimated date the photo was taken, and, in some cases, a list of image files containing scans of the original photo. Sharon also added attributes to indicate the type of collection the photos come from, the collection ID for each photo, who donated the photo, a list of keywords (metadata) associated with the photo, and the source of any image file. You'll assist Sharon by creating a DTD based on her XML vocabulary, and then you'll use the DTD to validate her sample document.

Complete the following:

1. Using your text editor, open **photostxt.dtd** and **photostxt.xml** from the xml02 ▸ case1 folder provided with your Data Files, enter *your name* and *today's date* in the comment section of each file, and then save the files as **photos.dtd** and **photos.xml**, respectively.

2. In the photos.dtd file, declare the following elements:

    a. The **catalog** element, containing one or more **photo** elements

    b. The **photo** element, containing the following sequence of child elements—name, description, date, and (optionally) images

    c. The **name**, **description**, and **date** elements, containing only parsed character data

    d. The **images** element, containing one or more **img** elements

    e. The **img** element, containing empty content

3. Declare the following attributes in the DTD:

    a. The **type** attribute, a required attribute of the **catalog** element, containing a valid XML name (*Hint*: Use the NMTOKEN data type.)

    b. The **cid** attribute, a required ID attribute of the **photo** element

    c. The **donatedBy** attribute, an optional attribute of the **photo** element, containing character data

    d. The **metadata** attribute, a required attribute of the **name** element, containing a list of valid XML names (*Hint*: Use the NMTOKENS data type.)

    e. The **src** attribute, a required attribute of the **img** element, containing character data

4. Save your changes to the photos.dtd file.

5. In the photos.xml file, directly after the comment section, insert a DOCTYPE that references the system location photos.dtd.

6. Save your changes to the photos.xml file.

7. Verify that the photos.xml file is well formed, and then validate it. Revalidate after correcting each error in the code, if necessary, until the document passes validation. (*Hint*: Because this document uses an external DTD, you must correct any validation errors related to the DTD in the photos.dtd file.) Note that you cannot use http://validator.w3.org to validate an XML file against a nonpublic external DTD file, so you must use a program such as Exchanger to validate this file.

Case Problem 2

APPLY

Data File needed for this Case Problem: mdpbatxt.xml

Midwest Developmental Pipe Band Association   Jacob St. John works as a coordinator for the Midwest Developmental Pipe Band Association (MDPBA), and is responsible for coordinating competitions for the MDPBA's many developmental pipe bands in the midwestern United States. A pipe band is a musical group consisting of pipe players and drummers. Pipe bands are traditional in Great Britain, as well as in other parts of the world that have received British cultural influence. Part of Jacob's job is to maintain a document that lists competition entries for each pipe band. Jacob has asked for your help in creating XML documents that maintain a consistent document structure. He has created a sample document describing five pipe bands. The document lists the competition program for each pipe band. Each program includes exactly two events in which each band plays one or more tunes. One event type is a March, Strathspey, & Reel (MSR). The other event type is a Medley event. Figure 2-34 shows a tree diagram for the vocabulary.

Figure 2-34   **Structure of the mdpba document**

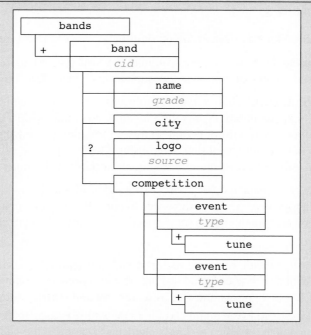

The document also contains an optional `logo` element that stores information about graphic files of the pipe band logos. Any DTD you create for this document also must work with the unparsed data contained in these graphic files.

Complete the following:

1. Using your text editor, open **mdpbatxt.xml** from the xml02 ▸ case2 folder provided with your Data Files, enter ***your name*** and ***today's date*** in the comment section of the file, and then save the file as **mdpba.xml**.

2. Review the contents of the mdpba.xml file. Directly after the comment section, insert a DOCTYPE that includes DTD statements for the following elements:

   a. The **bands** element, containing at least one occurrence of the child element `band`

   b. The **band** element, containing child elements in the sequence `name`, `city`, `logo` (optional), and `competition`

   c. The **name** and **city** elements, containing parsed character data

   d. The **logo** element as an empty element

   e. The **competition** element, containing exactly two child elements named `event`

   f. The **event** element, containing at least one occurrence of the child element `tune`

   g. The **tune** element, containing parsed character data

3. Declare the following required attributes in the DTD:

   a. The **band** element should contain a single required attribute named **cid** containing an ID value.

   b. The **name** element should contain a required attribute named **grade** with values limited to **1**, **2**, **3**, **4**, **5**, **juvenile**, and **novice**.

   c. The **logo** element should contain a required entity attribute named **source**.

   d. The **event** element should contain a required attribute named **type** with values limited to **MSR** or **Medley**.

4. Declare a notation named **JPG** with a system location equal to **image/jpg**.

5. Create two unparsed entities within the internal subset to the DTD. Each entity should reference the **JPG** notation. The first entity should be named **celtic** and reference the celtic.jpg file. The second entity should be named **badger** and reference the badger.jpg file.

6. Save your changes to the mdpba.xml file.

7. Verify that the document is well formed and then validate it.

CREATE

Case Problem 3

Data Files needed for this Case Problem: donors.txt, rostertxt.xml, seatrusttxt.dtd

Note: To complete this case problem, you need an XML parser capable of validating an XML document based on an external DTD file, such as Exchanger XML Editor.

The Save Exotic Animals Trust Sienna Woo is the donor coordinator for the Save Exotic Animals Trust (SEA Trust), a charitable organization located in central Florida. One of her responsibilities is to maintain a membership list of people in the community who have donated to SEA Trust. Donors can belong to one of four categories—Friendship, Patron, Sponsor, or Founder. The categories assist Sienna in marketing SEA Trust's fundraising goals and in developing strategies to reach those goals.

Currently, most of the data that Sienna has compiled resides in text files. To make the fundraising campaign strategies more effective, she wants to convert this data into an XML document and ensure that the resulting document follows some specific guidelines. You will create the XML document for her.

Complete the following:

1. Using your text editor, open the **rostertxt.xml** and **seatrusttxt.dtd** files from the xml02 ▸ case3 folder provided with your Data Files, insert *your name* and *today's date* in the comment section of each file, and then save the files as **roster.xml** and **seatrust.dtd**, respectively.

2. Add the data stored in the **donors.txt** file in the xml02 ▸ case3 folder to the roster.xml file as the document content, and then add XML elements to structure the data in the roster.xml file as follows: (*Note*: You should ignore any validation or well-formedness errors flagged by your editor until the document is finished.)

   a. A root element named **roster** should contain several **donor** elements.

   b. Each **donor** element should contain the following child elements, which should appear no more than once within the **donor** element, except as noted—name, **address**, **phone** (one or more), **email** (optional), **donation**, **method**, and **effectiveDate**.

   c. The **phone** element should contain an attribute named **type** that identifies the phone type—**home**, **work**, or **cell**. This should be a required attribute for each **phone** element.

   d. The **donor** element should contain an attribute named **level** that identifies the donor level—**friendship**, **patron**, **sponsor**, or **founder**. This should be a required attribute for each **donor** element.

3. In the seatrust.dtd file, create a DTD based on the structure you created in the roster.xml file. Save and close the seatrust.dtd file.

4. Apply your DTD to the contents of the roster.xml file. Save your changes to the roster.xml file.

5. Verify that the roster.xml file is well formed and valid.

CHALLENGE

Case Problem 4

Data Files needed for this Case Problem: carstxt.xml, southtxt.xml, teamstxt.xml

South Racing Danika Francis tracks team cars for South Racing's racing teams. As part of her job, she has created several XML vocabularies dealing with team series and the cars available to race in them. She wants to create a compound document combining information from the teams and cars vocabularies. She also wants to validate any data entered into her documents, and she asks you to develop a DTD. Because she is creating compound documents that combine elements from the teams and cars namespaces, she needs the DTD to work with namespaces. Figure 2-35 shows the tree structure of the compound document.

Figure 2-35   **Structure of the compound document**

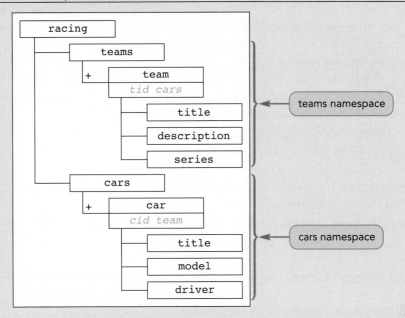

Danika wants you to create a master XML document containing a DTD for the teams and cars namespaces, and then use entities to read the information from different XML documents into the master compound document. Figure 2-36 shows a schematic of the file relationships in Danika's proposed project.

Figure 2-36   **File relationships for the compound document**

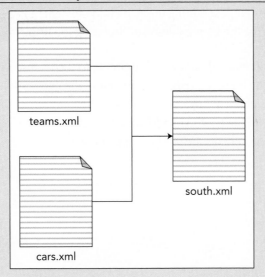

Complete the following:

1. Using your text editor, open the **carstxt.xml**, **southtxt.xml**, and **teamstxt.xml** files from the xml02 ▶ case4 folder, enter *your name* and *today's date* in the comment section of each file, and then save the files as **cars.xml**, **south.xml**, and **teams.xml**, respectively.

2. In the teams.xml file, place all the elements in the namespace **http://example.com/southracing/ teams** with the namespace prefix **t**. Save your changes to the file.

3. In the cars.xml file, place all the elements in the namespace **http://example.com/southracing/ cars** with the namespace prefix **c**. Save your changes to the file.

⊕ **EXPLORE** 4. In the south.xml file, insert an internal DTD subset with the following element declarations (making sure to include the namespace prefix **t** with all of the element names):

　　a. The `teams` element, containing at least one child element named `team`

　　b. The `team` element, containing the following sequence of child elements: `title`, `description`, and `series`

　　c. The `title`, `description`, and `series` elements, containing parsed character data

⊕ **EXPLORE** 5. Add an attribute declaration to the `teams` element to declare the **http://example.com/southracing/teams** namespace as a fixed value.

　6. Add the following attribute declarations to the `team` element:

　　a. An ID attribute named `tid`

　　b. An attribute named `cars`, containing a list of ID references

⊕ **EXPLORE** 7. Add the following element declarations (making sure all element references include the **c** namespace prefix):

　　a. The `cars` element, containing at least one child element named `car`

　　b. The `car` element, containing the following sequence of child elements: `title`, `model`, and `driver`

　　c. The `title`, `model`, and `driver` elements, containing parsed character data

⊕ **EXPLORE** 8. Add an attribute declaration to the `cars` element to declare the **http://example.com/southracing/cars** namespace as a fixed value.

　9. Add the following attribute declarations to the `car` element:

　　a. An ID attribute named `cid`

　　b. A `team` attribute containing a list of ID references

　10. Add the root element `racing` to the document belonging to the default namespace **http://example.com/southracing**.

⊕ **EXPLORE** 11. In the internal DTD subset, add the following declarations:

　　a. The `racing` element, containing the two child elements `t:teams` and `c:cars`

　　b. A fixed attribute of the `racing` element declaring the **http://example.com/southracing** namespace

　　c. An external entity named `teamsList` pointing to the teams.xml file

　　d. An external entity named `carsList` pointing to the cars.xml file

　12. Within the `racing` element, insert references to the `teamsList` and `carsList` entities.

　13. Save your changes to the south.xml file, and then close it.

　14. Verify that all the documents are well formed and valid.

TUTORIAL **3**

OBJECTIVES

Session 3.1
- Compare schemas and DTDs
- Explore different schema vocabularies
- Declare simple type elements and attributes
- Declare complex type elements
- Apply a schema to an instance document

Session 3.2
- Work with XML Schema data types
- Derive new data types for text strings, numeric values, and dates
- Create data types for patterned data using regular expressions

Validating Documents with Schemas

Creating a Schema for the ATC School of Information Technology

Case | *ATC School of Information Technology*

Sabrina Lincoln is an academic advisor for the School of Information Technology at Austin Technical College (ATC) in Austin, Utah, where she advises students in the information technology programs. Sabrina wants to use XML to create structured documents containing information on the different programs and the students enrolled in those programs. Eventually, the XML documents can be used as a data resource for the center's intranet, enabling faculty advisors to view program and student data online.

Accuracy is important to ATC, and Sabrina needs to know that the data she enters is error free. In particular, she must be able to confirm that the student data in her XML documents matches the criteria for the programs. Sabrina also needs to create documents from the various XML vocabularies she's created. For example, she may need to create a document that combines student information with information on the programs themselves.

DTDs cannot fulfill Sabrina's needs because DTDs have a limited range of data types and provide no way to deal with numeric data. Also, DTDs and namespaces do not mix well. However, schemas can work with a wide range of data types and do a better job of supporting namespaces than DTDs. In this tutorial, you'll develop schemas for the XML document that Sabrina has created.

STARTING DATA FILES

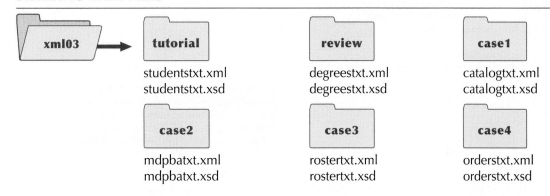

xml03 → tutorial
studentstxt.xml
studentstxt.xsd

review
degreestxt.xml
degreestxt.xsd

case1
catalogtxt.xml
catalogtxt.xsd

case2
mdpbatxt.xml
mdpbatxt.xsd

case3
rostertxt.xml
rostertxt.xsd

case4
orderstxt.xml
orderstxt.xsd

Session 3.1 Visual Overview:

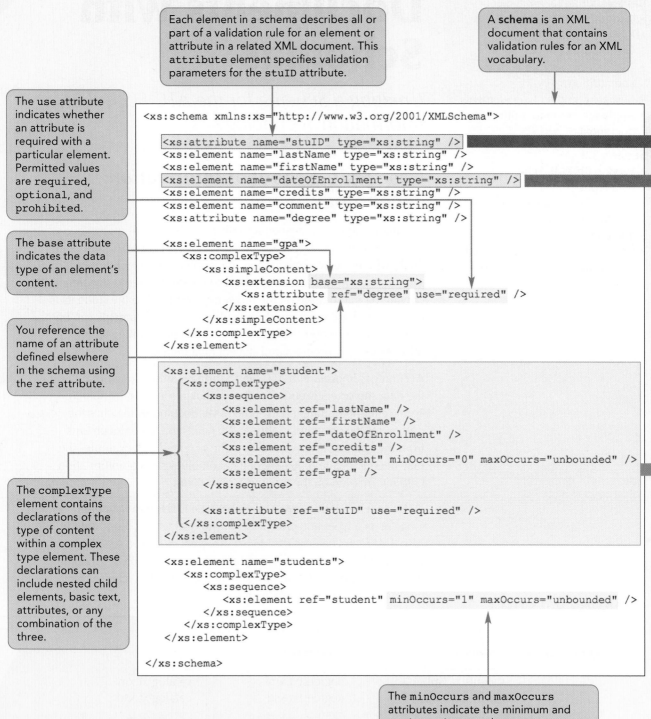

Each element in a schema describes all or part of a validation rule for an element or attribute in a related XML document. This `attribute` element specifies validation parameters for the `stuID` attribute.

A **schema** is an XML document that contains validation rules for an XML vocabulary.

The use attribute indicates whether an attribute is required with a particular element. Permitted values are required, optional, and prohibited.

The base attribute indicates the data type of an element's content.

You reference the name of an attribute defined elsewhere in the schema using the ref attribute.

The `complexType` element contains declarations of the type of content within a complex type element. These declarations can include nested child elements, basic text, attributes, or any combination of the three.

```
<xs:schema xmlns:xs="http://www.w3.org/2001/XMLSchema">

    <xs:attribute name="stuID" type="xs:string" />
    <xs:element name="lastName" type="xs:string" />
    <xs:element name="firstName" type="xs:string" />
    <xs:element name="dateOfEnrollment" type="xs:string" />
    <xs:element name="credits" type="xs:string" />
    <xs:element name="comment" type="xs:string" />
    <xs:attribute name="degree" type="xs:string" />

    <xs:element name="gpa">
        <xs:complexType>
            <xs:simpleContent>
                <xs:extension base="xs:string">
                    <xs:attribute ref="degree" use="required" />
                </xs:extension>
            </xs:simpleContent>
        </xs:complexType>
    </xs:element>

    <xs:element name="student">
        <xs:complexType>
            <xs:sequence>
                <xs:element ref="lastName" />
                <xs:element ref="firstName" />
                <xs:element ref="dateOfEnrollment" />
                <xs:element ref="credits" />
                <xs:element ref="comment" minOccurs="0" maxOccurs="unbounded" />
                <xs:element ref="gpa" />
            </xs:sequence>

            <xs:attribute ref="stuID" use="required" />
        </xs:complexType>
    </xs:element>

    <xs:element name="students">
        <xs:complexType>
            <xs:sequence>
                <xs:element ref="student" minOccurs="1" maxOccurs="unbounded" />
            </xs:sequence>
        </xs:complexType>
    </xs:element>

</xs:schema>
```

The `minOccurs` and `maxOccurs` attributes indicate the minimum and maximum times an element can occur, respectively. If either attribute is omitted, a default value of 1 is assumed.

Structure of a Basic Schema

An XML document to which a schema is applied is known as an **instance document** because it represents a specific instance of the rules defined in the schema.

```xml
<students xmlns:xsi="http://www.w3.org/2001/XMLSchema-instance"
        xsi:noNamespaceSchemaLocation="students.xsd">
   <student stuID="SI890-041-02">
      <lastName>Berstein</lastName>
      <firstName>Cynthia</firstName>
      <dateOfEnrollment>2017-05-22</dateOfEnrollment>
      <credits>12</credits>
      <gpa degree="MP">3.81</gpa>
   </student>

   <student stuID="SI771-121-10">
      <lastName>Boothe</lastName>
      <firstName>Jennifer</firstName>
      <dateOfEnrollment>2017-11-24</dateOfEnrollment>
      <credits>38</credits>
      <comment>Applied for summer studies internship</comment>
      <gpa degree="WPA">3.14</gpa>
   </student>

   <student stuID="SI815-741-03">
      <lastName>Bowen</lastName>
      <firstName>Kristi</firstName>
      <dateOfEnrollment>2017-04-25</dateOfEnrollment>
      <credits>19</credits>
      <gpa degree="MP">3.88</gpa>
   </student>

   <student stuID="SI701-891-05">
      <lastName>Sanchez</lastName>
      <firstName>Rosario</firstName>
      <dateOfEnrollment>2017-08-14</dateOfEnrollment>
      <credits>14</credits>
      <comment>Applied for student tutor</comment>
      <comment>Applied for Women in IT Scholarship</comment>
      <gpa degree="WPA">3.89</gpa>
   </student>

   <student stuID="SI805-891-08">
      <lastName>Russeon</lastName>
      <firstName>Alison</firstName>
      <dateOfEnrollment>2017-09-14</dateOfEnrollment>
      <credits>15</credits>
      <gpa degree="WPA">2.76</gpa>
   </student>
</students>
```

A **simple type** contains a single value such as the value of an attribute or the textual content of an element. The dateOfEnrollment element is a simple type because it includes only textual content.

A **complex type** contains two or more values or elements placed within a defined structure. The student element is a complex type because it contains an attribute as well as multiple child elements.

Introducing XML Schema

You and Sabrina meet at the School of Information Technology to discuss her work for Austin Technical College. She has brought along a file named students.xml, which contains a list of students accepted into programs within the school. You'll open this file now.

To open the students.xml document:

▶ **1.** Use your text editor to open **studentstxt.xml** from the xml03 ▶ tutorial folder provided with your Data Files, enter **your name** and **today's date** in the comment section, and then save the file as **students.xml**.

▶ **2.** Examine the contents of the document, paying close attention to the order of the elements and the values of the elements and attributes.

Figure 3-1 shows the tree structure of the XML vocabulary used in the document. For each `student` element in the document, Sabrina inserted the attribute `stuID`. The attribute contains the student's assigned student number. In addition, Sabrina has collected each student's last and first names, date of enrollment, credits, and GPA. Each `student` element can also contain multiple `comment` elements for any additional information that an advisor wants to add.

| Figure 3-1 | Structure of the students vocabulary |

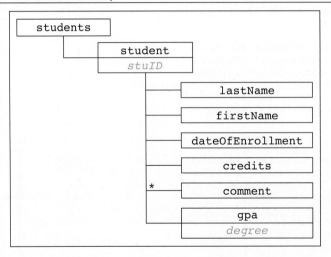

The students.xml file contains information on a few students in the information technology programs, but eventually it will contain more entries. As more students are added, Sabrina wants the document to require that the data for each student meet eligibility guidelines for the specified program of study. For example, students' GPAs must be at least 2.0 on a 4.0 scale, and every student must have a valid student ID number. For the initial faculty advising rollout, students must be enrolled in either the Mobile Programmer or Web Programmer/Analyst programs. Your task is to set up a validation system for this document.

The Limits of DTDs

DTDs are commonly used for validation largely because of XML's origins as an offshoot of SGML. SGML originally was designed for text-based documents, such as reports and technical manuals. As long as data content is limited to simple text, DTDs work well for validation. However, as XML began to be used for a wider range of document content, developers needed an alternative to DTDs.

One complaint about DTDs is their lack of data types. For example, Sabrina can declare a `gpa` element in the DTD, but she cannot specify that the `gpa` element may contain only numbers or that those numbers must fall within a specified range of values. Likewise, she can declare a `dateOfEnrollment` element, but a DTD cannot require that element to contain only dates. DTDs simply do not provide the control over data that Sabrina requires. DTDs also do not recognize namespaces, so they are not well suited to compound documents in which content from several vocabularies needs to be validated. This is a concern for Sabrina because her job at the ATC will involve developing several XML vocabularies that often will be combined into a single document.

Finally, DTDs employ a syntax called **Extended Backus–Naur Form (EBNF)**, which is different from the syntax used for XML. This means that a document's author must be able to work not only with the syntax of XML, but with EBNF as well. For developers who want to work with only one language, this could be a concern.

Because of XML's extensibility, you can instead use XML itself to document the structure and content of other XML documents. This is the idea behind schemas.

Schemas and DTDs

A schema is an XML document that contains validation rules for an XML vocabulary. When applied to a specific XML file, the document to be validated is called the instance document because it represents a specific instance of the rules defined in the schema. Schemas have several advantages over DTDs. XML parsers need to understand only XML, so all the tools used to create an instance document can also be applied to designing the schema. Schemas also support more data types, including data types for numbers and dates as well as custom data types for special needs. Additionally, schemas are more flexible than DTDs in dealing with elements that contain both child elements and text content, and they provide support for namespaces, making it easier to validate compound documents. Figure 3-2 summarizes some of the most significant differences between schemas and DTDs.

| Figure 3-2 | Comparison of schemas and DTDs |

Feature	Schemas	DTDs
Document language	XML	Extended Backus Naur Form (EBNF)
Standards	multiple standards	one standard
Supported data types	44 (19 primitive + 25 derived)	10
Customized data types	yes	no
Mixed content	easy to develop	difficult to develop
Namespaces	completely supported	only namespace prefixes are supported
Entities	no	yes

If schemas are so useful, why do you need DTDs? First, DTDs represent an older standard for XML documents and are more widely supported. DTDs are simpler to create and maintain than schemas because the language itself is easier to work with. This is partly due to the fact that DTDs are more limited than schemas. Thus, DTDs are easier to set up for basic documents that don't require much validation. Figure 3-3 compares a simple DTD to its equivalent basic schema.

Figure 3-3 **Comparison of simple DTD and simple schema**

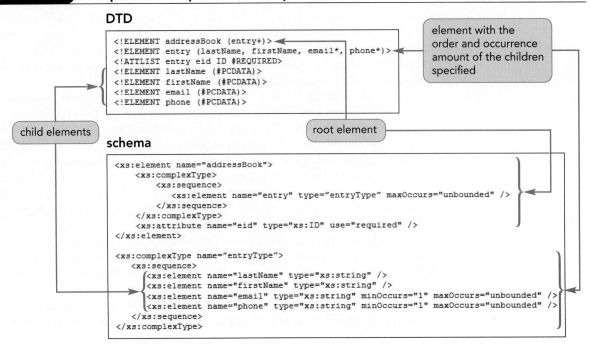

DTD

```
<!ELEMENT addressBook (entry+)>
<!ELEMENT entry (lastName, firstName, email*, phone*)>
<!ATTLIST entry eid ID #REQUIRED>
<!ELEMENT lastName (#PCDATA)>
<!ELEMENT firstName (#PCDATA)>
<!ELEMENT email (#PCDATA)>
<!ELEMENT phone (#PCDATA)>
```

element with the order and occurrence amount of the children specified

child elements

root element

schema

```
<xs:element name="addressBook">
    <xs:complexType>
        <xs:sequence>
            <xs:element name="entry" type="entryType" maxOccurs="unbounded" />
        </xs:sequence>
    </xs:complexType>
    <xs:attribute name="eid" type="xs:ID" use="required" />
</xs:element>

<xs:complexType name="entryType">
    <xs:sequence>
        <xs:element name="lastName" type="xs:string" />
        <xs:element name="firstName" type="xs:string" />
        <xs:element name="email" type="xs:string" minOccurs="1" maxOccurs="unbounded" />
        <xs:element name="phone" type="xs:string" minOccurs="1" maxOccurs="unbounded" />
    </xs:sequence>
</xs:complexType>
```

Schema Vocabularies

Unlike DTDs, a single standard doesn't exist for schemas. Instead, several schema vocabularies have been created to serve the needs of different XML developers. Because schemas are written in XML, a **schema vocabulary** is simply an XML vocabulary created for the purpose of describing schema content. Figure 3-4 describes some schema vocabularies.

Figure 3-4	Schema vocabularies

Schema	Description
XML Schema	The most widely used schema standard, XML Schema is developed and maintained by the W3C, and is designed to handle a broad range of document structures. It is also referred to as XSD.
Document Definition Markup Language (DDML)	One of the original schema languages, DDML (originally known as XSchema) was created to replicate all DTD functionality in a schema. DDML does not support any data types beyond what could be found in DTDs.
XML Data	One of the original schema languages, XML Data was developed by Microsoft to replace DTDs.
XML Data Reduced (XDR)	XDR is a subset of the XML Data schema, and was primarily used prior to the release of XML Schema.
Regular Language description for XML (RELAX)	A simple alternative to the W3C's XML Schema standard, RELAX provides much of the same functionality as DTDs, with additional support for namespaces and data types. RELAX does not support entities or notations.
Tree Regular Expressions for XML (TREX)	A TREX schema specifies a pattern for an XML document's structure and content, and thus identifies a class of XML documents that match the pattern. TREX has been merged with RELAX into RELAX NG.
RELAX NG (Regular Language for XML Next Generation)	RELAX NG is the current version of RELAX, combining the features of RELAX and TREX.
Schematron	The Schematron schema represents documents using a tree pattern, allowing support for document structures that might be difficult to represent in traditional schema languages.

Support for a particular schema depends solely on the XML parser being used for validation. Before applying any of the schemas listed in Figure 3-4, you must verify the level of support offered by your application for that particular schema. XML Schema, developed by the W3C in March 2001, is the most widely adopted schema standard. Although this tutorial focuses primarily on XML Schema, many of the concepts involved with XML Schema can be applied to the other schema vocabularies.

Starting a Schema File

A DTD can be placed within an instance document or within an external file. A schema, however, is always placed in an external file. XML Schema filenames end with the *.xsd* file extension. Sabrina has created a blank XML Schema file for you to work on. You'll open her file now.

To start work on the XML Schema file:

1. Use your text editor to open **studentstxt.xsd** from the xml03 ▶ tutorial folder, and then enter *your name* and *today's date* in the comment section.

   Trouble? If you open the file in an XML editor, such as Exchanger, you may see an error message indicating that the document is not well formed and contains a premature end of file. In later steps, after you add your first validation rule to this file, the error should be resolved. For now, there's no need to worry about it.

2. Save the file as **students.xsd**.

The root element in any XML Schema document is the `schema` element. For a parser to recognize that a document is written in the XML Schema vocabulary, the `schema` element must include a declaration for the XML Schema namespace using the URI *http://www.w3.org/2001/XMLSchema*. The general structure of an XML Schema file is

```
<?xml version="1.0" ?>
<schema xmlns="http://www.w3.org/2001/XMLSchema">
   content
</schema>
```

where *content* is the list of elements and attributes that define the rules of the instance document. By convention, the namespace prefix `xsd` or `xs` is assigned to the XML Schema namespace to identify elements and attributes that belong to the XML Schema vocabulary. Keeping well-defined namespaces in an XML Schema document becomes very important when you start creating schemas for compound documents involving several namespaces. Therefore, the usual form of an XML Schema document is

```
<?xml version="1.0" ?>
<xs:schema xmlns:xs="http://www.w3.org/2001/XMLSchema">
   content
</xs:schema>
```

This tutorial assumes a namespace prefix of `xs` when discussing the elements and attributes of the XML Schema language. However, you can choose to use a different prefix in your own XML Schema documents. You can also set XML Schema as the document's default namespace, which eliminates the need for a prefix. The only requirement is that you be consistent in the use of a namespace prefix.

REFERENCE

Creating a Schema

- To create an XML Schema document, insert the structure

```
<?xml version="1.0" ?>
<schema xmlns="http://www.w3.org/2001/XMLSchema">
   content
</schema>
```

in the file, where *content* consists of the XML Schema elements and attributes used in defining the rules for the instance document.
- To apply a namespace prefix (customarily `xs` or `xsd`) to the elements and attributes of the XML Schema vocabulary, use the following structure:

```
<xs:schema xmlns:xs="http://www.w3.org/2001/XMLSchema">
   content
</xs:schema>
```

You'll add the root `schema` element to the students.xsd file now, using the `xs` namespace prefix to place it in the XML Schema namespace.

To insert the `schema` element in the students.xsd file:

1. Directly below the comment section, insert the following code:

```
<xs:schema xmlns:xs="http://www.w3.org/2001/XMLSchema">
</xs:schema>
```

Figure 3-5 shows the `schema` element in the students.xsd file.

Figure 3-5 | XML Schema root element

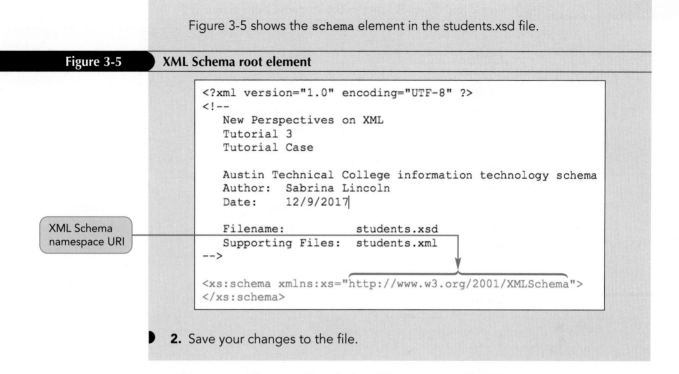

```
<?xml version="1.0" encoding="UTF-8" ?>
<!--
    New Perspectives on XML
    Tutorial 3
    Tutorial Case

    Austin Technical College information technology schema
    Author:   Sabrina Lincoln
    Date:     12/9/2017

    Filename:           students.xsd
    Supporting Files:   students.xml
-->

<xs:schema xmlns:xs="http://www.w3.org/2001/XMLSchema">
</xs:schema>
```

XML Schema namespace URI

2. Save your changes to the file.

Understanding Simple and Complex Types

XML Schema supports two types of content—simple and complex. A simple type contains only text and no nested elements. Examples of simple types include all attributes, as well as elements with only textual content. A complex type contains two or more values or elements placed within a defined structure. Examples of complex types include an empty element that contains an attribute, and an element that contains child elements. Figure 3-6 shows examples of both simple and complex types.

Figure 3-6 | Simple and complex types

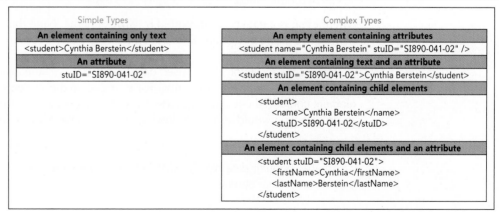

Simple Types	Complex Types
An element containing only text	**An empty element containing attributes**
`<student>Cynthia Berstein</student>`	`<student name="Cynthia Berstein" stuID="SI890-041-02" />`
An attribute	**An element containing text and an attribute**
`stuID="SI890-041-02"`	`<student stuID="SI890-041-02">Cynthia Berstein</student>`
	An element containing child elements

	`<student>`
	`<name>Cynthia Berstein</name>`
	`<stuID>SI890-041-02</stuID>`
	`</student>`

	An element containing child elements and an attribute

	`<student stuID="SI890-041-02">`
	`<firstName>Cynthia</firstName>`
	`<lastName>Berstein</lastName>`
	`</student>`

The students.xml file contains several examples of simple and complex types, which are listed in Figure 3-7. Note that all attributes in the document are, by default, simple types. The `students`, `student`, and `gpa` elements are complex types because they contain either nested child elements or attributes. The `lastName`, `firstName`, `dateOfEnrollment`, `credits`, and `comment` elements are all simple types because each contains only element text.

Figure 3-7	Simple and complex types in the students.xml document

Item	Contains	Content Type
students	nested child elements	complex
student	nested child elements	complex
stuID	an attribute value	simple
lastName	element text	simple
firstName	element text	simple
dateOfEnrollment	element text	simple
credits	element text	simple
comment	element text	simple
gpa	an attribute	complex
degree	an attribute value	simple

The distinction between simple and complex types is important in XML Schema because the code to define a simple type differs greatly from the code to define a complex type. You'll start writing the schema for Sabrina's document by defining all of the simple types found in the students.xml file.

Defining a Simple Type Element

An element in the instance document containing only text and no attributes or child elements is defined in XML Schema using the `<xs:element>` tag

```
<xs:element name="name" type="type" />
```

where `name` is the name of the element in the instance document and `type` is the type of data stored in the element. The data type can be one of XML Schema's built-in data types, or it can be a data type defined by the schema author. If you use a built-in data type, you must indicate that it belongs to the XML Schema namespace because it is a feature of the XML Schema language. Therefore, the code to use a built-in data type is

```
<xs:element name="name" type="xs:type" />
```

where `type` is a data type supported by XML Schema. Note that if you use a different namespace prefix or declare XML Schema as the default namespace for the document, the prefix will be different.

Perhaps the most commonly used data type in XML Schema is `string`, which allows an element to contain any text string. For example, in the students.xml file, the `lastName` element contains the text of the student's last name. To indicate that this element contains string data, you would add the following element to the XML Schema file:

```
<xs:element name="lastName" type="xs:string" />
```

Another popular data type in XML Schema is `decimal`, which allows an element to contain a decimal number.

Defining a Simple Type Element

• To define a simple type element, enter

```
<xs:element name="name" type="type" />
```

where *name* is the element name in the instance document and *type* is the data type.
• To use a data type built into the XML Schema language, place *type* in the XML Schema namespace as follows:

```
<xs:element name="name" type="xs:type" />
```

For now, you'll define the data type of each simple type element as a simple text string. You'll revise these declarations in the next session, when you examine the wide variety of data types supported by XML Schema as well as learn how to define your own data types.

To declare the simple type elements:

1. Within the schema root element, insert the following simple type elements, making sure to match the case:

```
<xs:element name="lastName" type="xs:string" />
<xs:element name="firstName" type="xs:string" />
<xs:element name="dateOfEnrollment" type="xs:string" />
<xs:element name="credits" type="xs:string" />
<xs:element name="comment" type="xs:string" />
```

Figure 3-8 shows the inserted simple type elements.

Figure 3-8   **Elements defined as simple types**

```
<xs:schema xmlns:xs="http://www.w3.org/2001/XMLSchema">
    <xs:element name="lastName" type="xs:string" />
    <xs:element name="firstName" type="xs:string" />
    <xs:element name="dateOfEnrollment" type="xs:string" />
    <xs:element name="credits" type="xs:string" />
    <xs:element name="comment" type="xs:string" />
</xs:schema>
```

simple type elements

element contains only a simple text string

2. Save your changes to the file.

Defining an Attribute

The other simple type content found in Sabrina's document consists of attribute values. To define an attribute in XML Schema, you use the `<xs:attribute>` tag

```
<xs:attribute name="name" type="type" default="default"
              fixed="fixed" />
```

where *name* is the name of the attribute, *type* is the data type, *default* is the attribute's default value, and *fixed* is a fixed value for the attribute. The *default* and *fixed* attributes are optional. You use the *default* attribute to specify a default attribute value, which is applied when no attribute value is entered in the instance document; you use the *fixed* attribute to fix an attribute to a specific value.

Attributes use the same collection of data types that simple type elements do. For example, the following code defines the `degree` attribute and indicates that it contains a text string with a default value of WPA:

```
<xs:attribute name="degree" type="xs:string" default="WPA" />
```

REFERENCE

Defining an Attribute

- To define an attribute, use the syntax

```
<xs:attribute name="name" type="type" default="default"
             fixed="fixed" />
```

where *name* is the attribute name in the instance document, *type* is the data type of the attribute, *default* specifies a default value for the attribute when no attribute value is entered in the instance document, and *fixed* fixes the attribute to a specific value. The *default* and *fixed* values are optional.

- For data types that are part of the XML Schema vocabulary, place *type* in the XML Schema namespace, as follows:

```
<xs:attribute name="name" type="xs:type" default="default"
             fixed="fixed" />
```

The students.xml file uses two attributes—`stuID` and `degree`. Neither of these attributes has a default value or a fixed value. You'll add the attribute declarations to the schema file below the element declarations you just created.

To define the attributes used in the students.xml file:

1. Add the following attribute definition on a new line above the first element definition:

```
<xs:attribute name="stuID" type="xs:string" />
```

As in a DTD, the declarations in a schema can be placed in any order. However, you can make your code easier to understand by keeping your declarations organized. Because the second attribute you'll declare occurs near the end of the XML code for each record, you'll place it below the other declarations.

2. Add the following attribute definition on a new line below the last element definition:

```
<xs:attribute name="degree" type="xs:string" />
```

Your completed code should match Figure 3-9.

| Figure 3-9 | Attributes defined as simple types |

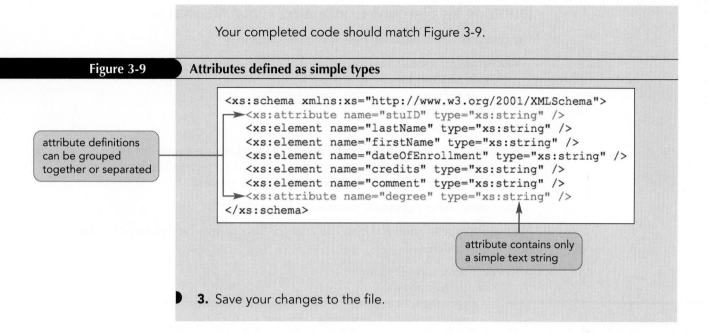

attribute definitions can be grouped together or separated

```
<xs:schema xmlns:xs="http://www.w3.org/2001/XMLSchema">
  <xs:attribute name="stuID" type="xs:string" />
  <xs:element name="lastName" type="xs:string" />
  <xs:element name="firstName" type="xs:string" />
  <xs:element name="dateOfEnrollment" type="xs:string" />
  <xs:element name="credits" type="xs:string" />
  <xs:element name="comment" type="xs:string" />
  <xs:attribute name="degree" type="xs:string" />
</xs:schema>
```

attribute contains only a simple text string

3. Save your changes to the file.

Defining a Complex Type Element

The two attributes you defined are not yet associated with any elements in Sabrina's document. To create those associations, you must first define the element containing each attribute. Because those elements contain attributes, they are considered complex type elements. The basic structure for defining a complex type element with XML Schema is

```
<xs:element name="name">
   <xs:complexType>
      declarations
   </xs:complexType>
</xs:element>
```

where *name* is the name of the element and *declarations* represents declarations of the type of content within the element. This content could include nested child elements, basic text, attributes, or any combination of the three. As shown in Figure 3-6, the following four complex type elements usually appear in an instance document:

- An empty element containing only attributes
- An element containing text content and attributes but no child elements
- An element containing child elements but no attributes
- An element containing both child elements and attributes

XML Schema uses a different code structure for each of these four possibilities. You'll start by looking at the definition for an empty element that contains one or more attributes.

Defining an Element Containing Only Attributes

The code to define the attributes of an empty element is

```
<xs:element name="name">
   <xs:complexType>
      attributes
   </xs:complexType>
</xs:element>
```

where *name* is the name of the empty element in the instance document and *attributes* is the set of simple type elements that define the attributes associated with the empty element. For example, the empty **student** element

```
<student name="Cynthia Berstein" gpa="3.81"/>
```

has two attributes—name and gpa. The code for this complex type element has the following structure:

```
<xs:element name="student">
   <xs:complexType>
      <xs:attribute name="name" type="xs:string" />
      <xs:attribute name="gpa" type="xs:decimal" />
   </xs:complexType>
</xs:element>
```

The order of the attribute declarations is unimportant. XML Schema allows attributes to be entered in any order within a complex type element.

Defining an Element Containing Attributes and Basic Text

If an element in the instance document contains attributes and text content but no child elements, the structure that declares the element and the attributes takes a different form. In these cases, the definition needs to indicate that the element contains simple content and a collection of one or more attributes. The structure of the element definition is

```
<xs:element name="name">
   <xs:complexType>
      <xs:simpleContent>
         <xs:extension base="type">
            attributes
         </xs:extension>
      </xs:simpleContent>
   </xs:complexType>
</xs:element>
```

where *type* is the data type of the element's content (or xs:*type* if the data type is part of the XML Schema vocabulary) and *attributes* represents a list of the attributes associated with the element. The purpose of the **simpleContent** element in this code is to indicate that the element contains only text and no nested child elements. The **<xs:extension>** tag is used to extend this definition to include the list of attributes. The **simpleContent** and **extension** elements are important tools used by XML Schema to derive new data types and to define complex content. For the students.xml document, you'll use them to define the **gpa** element, which is a complex type element that contains a text value and is associated with an attribute. The following is a sample of the type of content stored in this element:

```
<gpa degree="WPA">3.81</gpa>
```

The following code defines this element and associates it with the `degree` attribute:

```
<xs:element name="gpa">
   <xs:complexType>
      <xs:simpleContent>
         <xs:extension base="xs:string">
            <xs:attribute name="degree" type="xs:string" />
         </xs:extension>
      </xs:simpleContent>
   </xs:complexType>
</xs:element>
```

In this code, the `base` attribute in the `<xs:extension>` element sets the data type for the `gpa` element. At this point, you're assuming that the `gpa` element contains a text string. This code also sets the data type of the `degree` attribute to `xs:string`, indicating that it contains a text string.

Referencing an Element or Attribute Definition

You've already defined the `degree` attribute in the students.xsd file. You could revise the code to nest that attribute definition within the definition of the `gpa` element. However, XML Schema allows for a great deal of flexibility in writing complex types.

Rather than repeating that earlier attribute declaration within the `gpa` element, you can create a reference to it. The code to create a reference to an element definition is

```
<xs:element ref="elemName" />
```

where *elemName* is the name used in the element definition. Likewise, the code to create a reference to an attribute definition is

```
<xs:attribute ref="attName" />
```

where *attName* is the name used in the attribute definition. The following code defines the `degree` attribute and then references the definition from within the `gpa` element:

```
<xs:attribute name="degree" type="xs:string" />

<xs:element name="gpa">
   <xs:complexType>
      <xs:simpleContent>
         <xs:extension base="xs:string">
            <xs:attribute ref="degree" />
         </xs:extension>
      </xs:simpleContent>
   </xs:complexType>
</xs:element>
```

TIP

To repeat an attribute or element definition, simplify the schema by defining the attribute or element once, and then reference that definition wherever it is used.

REFERENCE

Defining a Complex Type Element

- To define an empty element containing one or more attributes, use

```
<xs:element name="name">
   <xs:complexType>
      attributes
   </xs:complexType>
</xs:element>
```

where *name* is the element name and *attributes* represents a list of attributes associated with the element.

- To define an element containing text content and one or more attributes, use

```
<xs:element name="name">
   <xs:complexType>
      <xs:simpleContent>
         <xs:extension base="type">
            attributes
         </xs:extension>
      </xs:simpleContent>
   </xs:complexType>
</xs:element>
```

where *type* is the data type of the text content of the element.

- To define an element containing only nested child elements, use

```
<xs:element name="name">
   <xs:complexType>
      <xs:compositor>
         elements
      </xs:compositor>
   </xs:complexType>
</xs:element>
```

where *elements* is a list of the child elements, and *compositor* is sequence, choice, or all.

- To define an element containing both attributes and nested child elements, use

```
<xs:element name="name">
   <xs:complexType>
      <xs:compositor>
         elements
      </xs:compositor>
         attributes
   </xs:complexType>
</xs:element>
```

You'll add the definition of the gpa element to the students.xsd file now.

To define the gpa element:

1. In the students.xsd file, below the declaration for the degree attribute, add the following complex type declaration:

```
<xs:element name="gpa">
   <xs:complexType>
      <xs:simpleContent>
         <xs:extension base="xs:string">
            <xs:attribute ref="degree" />
         </xs:extension>
      </xs:simpleContent>
   </xs:complexType>
</xs:element>
```

Figure 3-10 shows the complex type declaration inserted in the schema element.

Figure 3-10	Complex type element containing text and an attribute

```
<xs:schema xmlns:xs="http://www.w3.org/2001/XMLSchema">

   <xs:attribute name="stuID" type="xs:string" />
   <xs:element name="lastName" type="xs:string" />
   <xs:element name="firstName" type="xs:string" />
   <xs:element name="dateOfEnrollment" type="xs:string" />
   <xs:element name="credits" type="xs:string" />
   <xs:element name="comment" type="xs:string" />
   <xs:attribute name="degree" type="xs:string" />

   <xs:element name="gpa">
      <xs:complexType>
         <xs:simpleContent>
            <xs:extension base="xs:string">
               <xs:attribute ref="degree" />
            </xs:extension>
         </xs:simpleContent>
      </xs:complexType>
   </xs:element>

</xs:schema>
```

ref attribute value uses name defined for the degree attribute

the text content of the gpa element is a simple text string

2. Save your changes to the file.

Defining an Element with Nested Children

Next, you'll examine complex elements that contain nested child elements but no attributes or text. To define this type of complex element, you use the structure

```
<xs:element name="name">
   <xs:complexType>
      <xs:compositor>
         elements
      </xs:compositor>
   </xs:complexType>
</xs:element>
```

where *name* is the name of the element, *compositor* is a value that defines how the child elements appear in the document, and *elements* is a list of the nested child elements. You can choose any of the following compositors to define how the child elements display in the document:

- **sequence**—requires the child elements to appear in the order listed in the schema
- **choice**—allows any *one* of the child elements listed to appear in the instance document
- **all**—allows any of the child elements to appear in any order in the instance document; however, each may appear only once, or not at all

For example, the following code assigns four child elements—street, city, state, and country—to the address element:

```
<xs:element name="address">
   <xs:complexType>
      <xs:sequence>
         <xs:element name="street" type="xs:string" />
         <xs:element name="city" type="xs:string" />
         <xs:element name="state" type="xs:string" />
         <xs:element name="country" type="xs:string" />
      </xs:sequence>
   </xs:complexType>
</xs:element>
```

Because the definition uses the sequence compositor, the document is invalid if the address element doesn't contain all the listed child elements in the order specified.

The following definition allows the sponsor element to contain an element named parent or an element named guardian:

```
<xs:element name="sponsor">
   <xs:complexType>
      <xs:choice>
         <xs:element name="parent" type="xs:string" />
         <xs:element name="guardian" type="xs:string" />
      </xs:choice>
   </xs:complexType>
</xs:element>
```

Because the definition uses the choice compositor, the sponsor element can contain either element, but not both.

Finally, the following definition uses the all compositor to allow the Family element to contain elements named Father and/or Mother:

```
<xs:element name="Family">
   <xs:complexType>
      <xs:all>
         <xs:element name="Father" type="xs:string" />
         <xs:element name="Mother" type="xs:string" />
      </xs:all>
   </xs:complexType>
</xs:element>
```

It is also acceptable for the Family element to contain neither a Father nor a Mother element.

TIP

A complex element can contain only one `all` compositor; you cannot combine the `all` compositor with the `choice` or `sequence` compositor.

The `choice` and `sequence` compositors can be nested and combined. For example, the following definition uses two `choice` compositors nested within a `sequence` compositor to require the `Account` element to contain either the `Person` or the `Company` element followed by either the `Cash` or the `Credit` element:

```
<xs:element name="Account">
   <xs:complexType>
      <xs:sequence>
         <xs:choice>
             <xs:element name="Person" type="xs:string" />
             <xs:element name="Company" type="xs:string" />
         </xs:choice>
         <xs:choice>
             <xs:element name="Cash" type="xs:string" />
             <xs:element name="Credit" type="xs:string" />
         </xs:choice>
      </xs:sequence>
   </xs:complexType>
</xs:element>
```

Defining an Element Containing Nested Elements and Attributes

The next complex element you'll consider is an element containing both child elements and attributes. To define an element with this kind of content, you use the structure

```
<xs:element name="name">
   <xs:complexType>
      <xs:compositor>
          elements
      </xs:compositor>
      attributes
   </xs:complexType>
</xs:element>
```

where *name* is the name of the element; *compositor* is either `sequence`, `choice`, or `all`; *elements* represents a list of child elements nested within the element; and *attributes* represents a list of attribute definitions associated with the element. This is the same structure used for elements containing nested children except that a list of attributes is included. For example, the `student` element from Sabrina's students.xml file contains two attributes (`stuID` and `degree`) and six child elements (`lastName`, `firstName`, `dateOfEnrollment`, `comment`, `credits`, and `gpa`). Because you've already defined the content for the `stuID` attribute and the six child elements, you can insert references to those earlier definitions in the code, as follows:

```
<xs:element name="student">
   <xs:complexType>
      <xs:sequence>
         <xs:element ref="lastName" />
         <xs:element ref="firstName" />
         <xs:element ref="dateOfEnrollment" />
         <xs:element ref="credits" />
         <xs:element ref="comment" />
         <xs:element ref="gpa" />
      </xs:sequence>
```

```
            <xs:attribute ref="stuID" />
      </xs:complexType>
</xs:element>
```

You'll add this definition of the student element to the students.xsd file now.

To define the student element in the students.xsd file:

1. Below the definition of the gpa element, insert the following code:

```
<xs:element name="student">
    <xs:complexType>
        <xs:sequence>
            <xs:element ref="lastName" />
            <xs:element ref="firstName" />
            <xs:element ref="dateOfEnrollment" />
            <xs:element ref="credits" />
            <xs:element ref="comment" />
            <xs:element ref="gpa" />
        </xs:sequence>

        <xs:attribute ref="stuID" />
    </xs:complexType>
</xs:element>
```

Figure 3-11 shows the code for the student element in the students.xsd file.

Figure 3-11 **Element containing both child elements and attributes**

```
<xs:element name="gpa">
    <xs:complexType>
        <xs:simpleContent>
            <xs:extension base="xs:string">
                <xs:attribute ref="degree" />
            </xs:extension>                   ┌─────────────────────┐
        </xs:simpleContent>                   │ sequence indicates  │
    </xs:complexType>                         │ that the contained  │
</xs:element>                                 │ elements must be in │
                                              │ the specified order │
<xs:element name="student">                  └─────────────────────┘
    <xs:complexType>
        <xs:sequence>◄──────────────────────────┘
            <xs:element ref="lastName" />
            <xs:element ref="firstName" />
            <xs:element ref="dateOfEnrollment" />
            <xs:element ref="credits" />
            <xs:element ref="comment" />
            <xs:element ref="gpa" />
        </xs:sequence>

        <xs:attribute ref="stuID" />
    </xs:complexType>
</xs:element>
```

child elements of the student element

2. Save your changes to the file.

The only element from the students.xml file you haven't yet declared is the root students element. This element has no attributes but does contain the student element as a child. The definition of this element references the definition of the student element that you created earlier:

```
<xs:element name="students">
   <xs:complexType>
      <xs:sequence>
         <xs:element ref="student" />
      </xs:sequence>
   </xs:complexType>
</xs:element>
```

You'll add this definition to the file now.

To define the students element in the students.xsd file:

1. Below the definition of the student element, insert the following code:

```
<xs:element name="students">
   <xs:complexType>
      <xs:sequence>
         <xs:element ref="student" />
      </xs:sequence>
   </xs:complexType>
</xs:element>
```

Figure 3-12 shows the code for the students element in the students.xsd file.

Figure 3-12 **Element containing only a child element**

```
<xs:element name="student">
    <xs:complexType>
        <xs:sequence>
            <xs:element ref="lastName" />
            <xs:element ref="firstName" />
            <xs:element ref="dateOfEnrollment" />
            <xs:element ref="credits" />
            <xs:element ref="comment" />
            <xs:element ref="gpa" />
        </xs:sequence>

        <xs:attribute ref="stuID" />
    </xs:complexType>
</xs:element>

<xs:element name="students">
    <xs:complexType>
        <xs:sequence>
            <xs:element ref="student" />
        </xs:sequence>
    </xs:complexType>
</xs:element>
```

the only child element of the root students element is the student element

2. Save your changes to the file.

INSIGHT

Specifying Mixed Content

One limitation of using DTDs is their inability to define mixed content. An element is said to have **mixed content** when it contains both a text string and child elements. You can specify the child elements with a DTD, but you cannot constrain their order or number. XML Schema gives you more control over mixed content. To specify that an element contains both text and child elements, you add the `mixed` attribute to the `<complexType>` tag. When the `mixed` attribute is set to the value `true`, XML Schema assumes that the element contains both text and child elements. The structure of the child elements can then be defined with the conventional method. For example, assume you were working on a document containing the following XML content:

```
<summary>
    Student <firstName>Cynthia</firstName>
    <lastName>Berstein</lastName> is enrolled in an IT
    degree program and has completed <credits>12</credits>
    credits since 01/01/2017.
</summary>
```

You could declare the `summary` element for this document in a schema file using the following complex type:

```
<element name="summary">
    <complexType mixed="true">
        <sequence>
            <element name="firstName" type="string" />
            <element name="lastName" type="string" />
            <element name="credits" type="string" />
        </sequence>
    </complexType>
</element>
```

In an element with mixed content, XML Schema allows text content to appear before, between, and after any child element.

At this point, you have defined all of the simple and complex types in Sabrina's document. Next, you'll refine your schema by adding code that defines exactly how these simple and complex types are used and what kind of data they can contain.

Indicating Required Attributes

An attribute may or may not be required with a particular element. To indicate whether an attribute is required, the `use` attribute can be added to the statement that assigns the attribute to an element. The general syntax of the `use` attribute is

```
<xs:element name="name">
    <xs:complexType>
        element content
        <xs:attribute properties use="use" />
    </xs:complexType>
</xs:element>
```

where *use* is one of the following three values:

- `required`—The attribute must always appear with the element.
- `optional`—The use of the attribute is optional with the element.
- `prohibited`—The attribute cannot be used with the element.

For example, in Sabrina's document, the degree attribute is required with every gpa element. To force the instance document to follow this rule, you add the use attribute to the definition of the degree attribute, as follows:

```
<xs:attribute name="degree" type="xs:string" use="required" />
```

If you neglect to add the use attribute to an element declaration, XML parsers assume that the attribute is optional. The use attribute is applied only when assigning an attribute to a specific element from the instance document. After all, an attribute might be required for one element and optional for another.

The two attributes in Sabrina's document—stuID and degree—are both required for the document to be valid. You will indicate this in the schema by specifying the use of each attribute.

To indicate required attributes in the students.xsd file:

1. Within the code that defines the gpa element, locate the xs:attribute tag for the degree attribute, and then add the code **use="required"** to the tag. This code indicates that the degree attribute is required for the gpa element.

2. Within the code that defines the student element, locate the xs:attribute tag for the stuID attribute, and then add the code **use="required"** to the tag. This code indicates that the stuID attribute is required for the student element. Figure 3-13 highlights the revised code in the schema.

| Figure 3-13 | Attributes designated as required |

```
<xs:element name="gpa">
    <xs:complexType>
        <xs:simpleContent>
            <xs:extension base="xs:string">
                <xs:attribute ref="degree" use="required" />
            </xs:extension>
        </xs:simpleContent>
    </xs:complexType>
</xs:element>
```

the gpa element requires the use of the degree attribute

```
<xs:element name="student">
    <xs:complexType>
        <xs:sequence>
            <xs:element ref="lastName" />
            <xs:element ref="firstName" />
            <xs:element ref="dateOfEnrollment" />
            <xs:element ref="credits" />
            <xs:element ref="comment" />
            <xs:element ref="gpa" />
        </xs:sequence>

        <xs:attribute ref="stuID" use="required" />
    </xs:complexType>
</xs:element>
```

the student element requires the use of the stuID attribute

3. Save your changes to the file.

Specifying the Number of Child Elements

The previous code samples assumed that each element in the list appeared once and only once. This is not always the case. For example, Sabrina's document contains information on one or more students, so you need to allow for one or more `student` elements. To specify the number of times an element appears in the instance document, you can apply the `minOccurs` and `maxOccurs` attributes to the element definition, using the syntax

```
<xs:element name="name" type="type" minOccurs="value"
        maxOccurs="value" />
```

where the value of the `minOccurs` attribute defines the minimum number of times the element can occur, and the value of the `maxOccurs` attribute defines the maximum number of times the element can occur. For example, the following element declaration specifies that the `student` element must appear at least once and may appear no more than three times in the instance document:

```
<xs:element name="student" type="xs:string" minOccurs="1"
        maxOccurs="3" />
```

TIP

A minOccurs value of 0 with a maxOccurs value of unbounded is equivalent to the * character in a DTD. Likewise, values of 1 and unbounded are equivalent to the + character, and values of 0 and 1 are equivalent to the ? character.

Any time the `minOccurs` attribute is set to 0, an element is optional. The `maxOccurs` attribute can be any positive value, or it can have a value of `unbounded` for unlimited occurrences of the element. If a value is specified for the `minOccurs` attribute but the `maxOccurs` attribute is missing, the value of the `maxOccurs` attribute is assumed to be equal to the value of the `minOccurs` attribute. Finally, if both the `minOccurs` attribute and the `maxOccurs` attribute are missing, the element is assumed to occur only once.

The `student` element occurs one or more times in Sabrina's document, and the `comment` element occurs zero or more times. All the other elements occur only once. You'll add the appropriate `minOccurs` and `maxOccurs` values to the schema now for the `student` and `comment` elements.

Be sure to add the `minOccurs` and `maxOccurs` attributes to the `comment` element reference within the definition for the `student` element, and *not* within the definition of the `comment` element at the start of the schema.

To set the occurrences of the `student` and `comment` elements in the students.xsd file:

1. In the students.xsd file, within the code that defines the `student` element, locate the `xs:element` tag that references the `comment` element, and then add the code `minOccurs="0" maxOccurs="unbounded"` to the tag. This code allows for zero or more occurrences of the `comment` element.

2. Within the code that defines the `students` element, locate the `xs:element` tag that references the `student` element and then add the code `minOccurs="1" maxOccurs="unbounded"` to the tag. This code allows for one or more occurrences of the `student` element. Figure 3-14 highlights the new code in the schema.

Figure 3-14	The minOccurs and maxOccurs values

```
<xs:schema xmlns:xs="http://www.w3.org/2001/XMLSchema">

    <xs:attribute name="stuID" type="xs:string" />
    <xs:element name="lastName" type="xs:string" />
    <xs:element name="firstName" type="xs:string" />
    <xs:element name="dateOfEnrollment" type="xs:string" />
    <xs:element name="credits" type="xs:string" />
    <xs:element name="comment" type="xs:string" />
    <xs:attribute name="degree" type="xs:string" />

    <xs:element name="gpa">
        <xs:complexType>
            <xs:simpleContent>
                <xs:extension base="xs:string">
                    <xs:attribute ref="degree" use="required" />
                </xs:extension>
            </xs:simpleContent>
        </xs:complexType>
    </xs:element>

    <xs:element name="student">
        <xs:complexType>
            <xs:sequence>
                <xs:element ref="lastName" />
                <xs:element ref="firstName" />
                <xs:element ref="dateOfEnrollment" />
                <xs:element ref="credits" />
                <xs:element ref="comment" minOccurs="0" maxOccurs="unbounded" />
                <xs:element ref="gpa" />
            </xs:sequence>

            <xs:attribute ref="stuID" use="required" />
        </xs:complexType>
    </xs:element>

    <xs:element name="students">
        <xs:complexType>
            <xs:sequence>
                <xs:element ref="student" minOccurs="1" maxOccurs="unbounded" />
            </xs:sequence>
        </xs:complexType>
    </xs:element>

</xs:schema>
```

the comment element can occur any number of times, or not at all, within the student element

the student element must occur one or more times within the students element

▶ **3.** Save your changes to the file.

Validating a Schema Document

You're ready to test whether the students.xsd document validates. The web has many excellent sources for validating parsers including websites such as the W3C's, where you can upload or paste schema code to have it validated. Several editors provide schema validation as well.

The following steps use Exchanger XML Editor to validate Sabrina's students.xsd document.

To validate the students.xsd file:

1. If necessary, open **students.xsd** in Exchanger XML Editor.

2. Click **Schema** on the Menu bar, and then click **Validate XML Schema**. As shown in Figure 3-15, the error console reports that the students.xsd file is valid.

| Figure 3-15 | XML Schema validation |

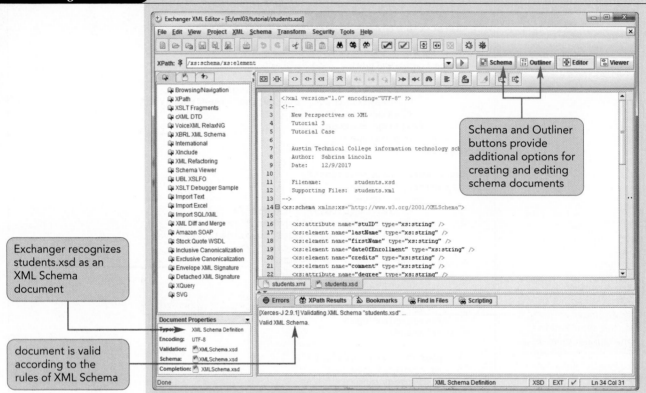

Exchanger recognizes students.xsd as an XML Schema document

document is valid according to the rules of XML Schema

Trouble? If a validation error is reported in the Errors tab, there is an error in the schema. Check your schema code against the students.xsd code shown in Figure 3-14. Your code should match exactly, including the use of uppercase and lowercase letters. Fix any discrepancies, be sure to save your changes, validate the schema again, and then reexamine the Errors tab for validation information.

Trouble? If your Exchanger XML Editor window doesn't match the one shown in Figure 3-15, close students.xsd and reopen it.

Now that you've confirmed that your schema is valid, you can apply it to your XML document.

Applying a Schema to an Instance Document

To attach a schema to an instance document, you declare the XML Schema instance namespace in the instance document, and then you specify the location of the schema file. To declare the XML Schema instance namespace, you add the following attribute to the root element of the instance document:

```
xmlns:xsi="http://www.w3.org/2001/XMLSchema-instance"
```

Although the prefix xsi is commonly used for the XML Schema Instance namespace, you can specify a different prefix in your documents.

You add a second attribute to the root element to specify the location of the schema file. The attribute you use depends on whether the instance document is associated with a namespace. If the document is not associated with a namespace, you add the attribute

```
xsi:noNamespaceSchemaLocation="schema"
```

to the root element, where *schema* is the location and name of the schema file. Note that the attribute requires the xsi namespace prefix because the attribute itself is from the XML Schema Instance namespace.

PROSKILLS

Teamwork: Working with Multiple Schema Documents

Especially on a large project involving multiple programmers, it can be useful to create multiple schema documents rather than a single large schema document. You can use the xs:include element within an XML Schema document to include the contents of another schema document. For instance, a project might break up into two teams—one creating customer.xsd, a schema for customer content, and another creating products.xsd, a schema for order information. To validate against the contents of both of these schemas, you would create a master schema file for your project and add the following two lines of code to it:

```
<xs:include schemaLocation="customer.xsd" />
<xs:include schemaLocation="products.xsd" />
```

Using the xs:include element enables you to validate instance documents against the validation rules defined in multiple XML Schema documents.

Sabrina has not yet placed the contents of her students.xml document in a namespace, so you'll add the following attribute to the root students element:

```
xsi:noNamespaceSchemaLocation="students.xsd"
```

To apply the students.xsd schema to the students.xml document:

▶ **1.** Return to the **students.xml** file in your editor.

▶ **2.** Within the opening tag for the students element, add the following attributes:

```
xmlns:xsi="http://www.w3.org/2001/XMLSchema-instance"
xsi:noNamespaceSchemaLocation="students.xsd"
```

Figure 3-16 shows the namespace attributes inserted in the root element.

Figure 3-16 | **Schema applied to a document without a namespace**

XML Schema
instance namespace

name of the
schema document

```
<students xmlns:xsi="http://www.w3.org/2001/XMLSchema-instance"
          xsi:noNamespaceSchemaLocation="students.xsd">
   <student stuID="SI890-041-02">
      <lastName>Berstein</lastName>
      <firstName>Cynthia</firstName>
      <dateOfEnrollment>2017-05-22</dateOfEnrollment>
      <credits>12</credits>
      <gpa degree="MP">3.81</gpa>
   </student>
</students>
```

▶ **3.** Save your changes to the file.

Now that you've applied your schema to Sabrina's instance document, you can validate the document against the rules defined in the students.xsd file. To validate the document, you use an XML parser. Although the following steps use the validator within Exchanger XML Editor, you can also validate using one of the free or commercial XML validating parsers available on the web.

To validate the students.xml document:

▶ **1.** If necessary, open **students.xml** in Exchanger XML Editor.

▶ **2.** Click the **Viewer** button in the upper-right corner of the window.

▶ **3.** Click **XML** on the menu bar, and then click **Validate**. As shown in Figure 3-17, the error console reports that the students.xml file is a valid document.

Figure 3-17 | **Validation results for the students.xml file**

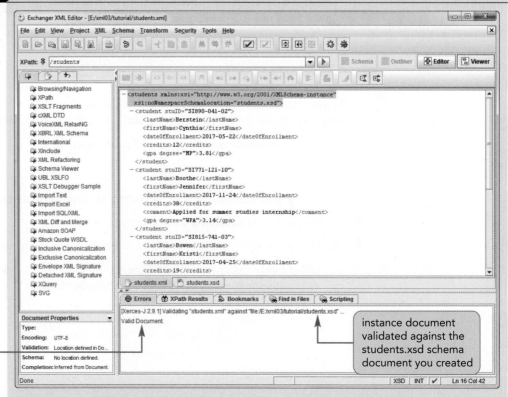

the contents of the
instance document
conform to the
rules of the schema

instance document
validated against the
students.xsd schema
document you created

Trouble? If a validation error is reported in the Errors tab and your schema validated successfully in the earlier steps, then there is an error in the namespace attributes you entered in the instance document. Check your students.xml code against the namespace attributes shown in Figure 3-16. Your code should match exactly, including the use of uppercase and lowercase letters. Fix any discrepancies, save your changes, and then revalidate.

Sabrina suggests that you add an intentional error to the students.xml file to confirm that the document is rejected as invalid. To do this, you'll add a second `credits` element to the first student's data. Because the schema you wrote permits only one `credits` element per student, this should result in an invalid document.

To add an error to the students.xml file:

▸ **1.** Return to the **students.xml** file in Exchanger XML Editor, and then click the **Editor** button in the upper-right corner.

▸ **2.** Within the `student` element containing information on Cynthia Berstein, add the following code:

```
<credits>14</credits>
```

Figure 3-18 shows the erroneous element added to the students.xml file.

Figure 3-18	Second credits element added to the students.xml file

```
<students xmlns:xsi="http://www.w3.org/2001/XMLSchema-instance"
          xsi:noNamespaceSchemaLocation="students.xsd">
   <student stuID="SI890-041-02">
      <lastName>Berstein</lastName>
      <firstName>Cynthia</firstName>
      <dateOfEnrollment>2017-05-22</dateOfEnrollment>
      <credits>12</credits>
      <credits>14</credits>
      <gpa degree="MP">3.81</gpa>
   </student>
```

a second credits element is not valid according to the schema

▸ **3.** Save your changes to the file.

▸ **4.** Click **XML** on the Menu bar, and then click **Validate**. The document is rejected as invalid due to the extra `credits` element. See Figure 3-19.

Figure 3-19 **Validation error**

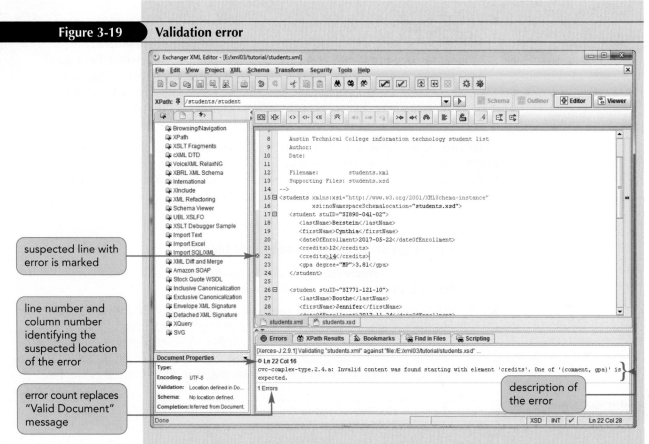

suspected line with error is marked

line number and column number identifying the suspected location of the error

error count replaces "Valid Document" message

description of the error

5. If necessary, click on the error message on the Errors tab to scroll the code in the editor to display the line containing the error. A red circle containing a white x marks the line containing the error.

6. Delete the line `<credits>14</credits>` and then save your changes to the file.

7. Click **XML** on the Menu bar, and then click **Validate**. The error console once again reports that the students.xml file is a valid document.

Sabrina is pleased with the initial work you've done on designing a schema for the students.xml document. In the next session, you'll implement additional validation rules that Sabrina would like applied to her document as you learn about data types.

Session 3.1 Quick Check

REVIEW

1. What is a schema? What is an instance document?
2. How do schemas differ from DTDs?
3. What is a simple type? What is a complex type?
4. How do you declare a simple type element named `Address` that contains string data?
5. How do you declare a complex type element named `Address` that contains, in order, the child elements `Apartment` (optional), `City`, `State`, and `Zip`? (Assume that the `Apartment`, `City`, `State`, and `Zip` elements are simple type elements containing text strings.)
6. The `Book` element contains simple text and a `Title` attribute. What code would you enter into a schema file to define this complex type element?
7. What code would you enter into a schema to create a reference to an attribute named `studentID`?
8. What attributes would you add to the root element of an instance document to attach it to a schema file named schema1.xsd? Assume that no namespace has been assigned to the schema file, and that you're using the XML Schema vocabulary.

Session 3.2 Visual Overview:

The string data type is a **built-in data type**, which is part of the XML Schema language. The string data type is an example of a **primitive data type** (also called a **base type**), which is a subgroup of built-in data types that are not defined in terms of other types.

The siType data type is a **user-derived data type**, which is a data type defined by a schema's author.

A regular expression is a text string that defines a character pattern.

A **pattern** is a constraining facet that limits data to a general pattern.

```xml
<?xml version="1.0" encoding="UTF-8" ?>
<xs:schema xmlns:xs="http://www.w3.org/2001/XMLSchema">

    <xs:attribute name="stuID" type="siType" />
    <xs:element name="lastName" type="xs:string" />
    <xs:element name="firstName" type="xs:string" />
    <xs:element name="dateOfEnrollment" type="xs:date" />
    <xs:element name="credits" type="creditsType" />
    <xs:element name="comment" type="xs:string" />
    <xs:attribute name="degree" type="degreeType" />

    <xs:simpleType name="siType">
        <xs:restriction base="xs:ID">
            <xs:pattern value="SI\d{3}-\d{3}-\d{2}" />
        </xs:restriction>
    </xs:simpleType>

    <xs:element name="gpa">
        <xs:complexType>
            <xs:simpleContent>
                <xs:extension base="gpaType">
                    <xs:attribute ref="degree" use="required" />
                </xs:extension>
            </xs:simpleContent>
        </xs:complexType>
    </xs:element>
```

A **character type** is a representation of a specific type of character. For instance, \d is the character type for a single digit.

Validating with Data Types

The integer data type is an example of a **derived data type**, which is one of 25 built-in data types that are developed from one of the base types.

minInclusive is a constraining facet that constrains the data to be greater than a minimum value. A **constraining facet** is a restriction placed on the facets of a preexisting data type.

maxInclusive is a constraining facet that constrains the data to be greater than or equal to a minimum value.

A **restricted data type** is a type of derived data type in which a restriction is placed on the facets of a preexisting data type. This code defines the degreeType data type by restricting the string data type to a list of values.

enumeration is a constraining facet that constrains data to a specified list of values.

```
<xs:simpleType name="creditsType">
    <xs:restriction base="xs:integer">
        <xs:minInclusive value="1" />
    </xs:restriction>
</xs:simpleType>

<xs:simpleType name="gpaType">
    <xs:restriction base="xs:decimal">
        <xs:minExclusive value="0" />
        <xs:maxInclusive value="4" />
    </xs:restriction>
</xs:simpleType>

<xs:simpleType name="degreeType">
    <xs:restriction base="xs:string">
        <xs:enumeration value="MP" />
        <xs:enumeration value="WPA" />
    </xs:restriction>
</xs:simpleType>
```

Validating with Built-In Data Types

The schema you designed for the students.xml document uses the `string` data type for all element and attribute content, which allows users to enter any text string into those items. Sabrina wants to ensure that dates are entered in the proper form, that only positive integers are entered for the student credits, and that the student IDs follow a prescribed pattern. You can do all of these using additional data types supported by XML Schema.

XML Schema supports two general categories of data types—built-in and user-derived. A built-in data type is part of the XML Schema language. A user-derived data type is a data type defined by a schema's author. You'll begin your work with data types by exploring the built-in data types in XML Schema.

XML Schema divides its built-in data types into two classes—primitive and derived. A primitive data type, also called a base type, is one of 19 fundamental data types that are not defined in terms of other types. A **derived data type** is one of 25 data types that are developed from one of the base types. Figure 3-20 provides a schematic diagram of all 44 built-in data types.

TIP

All built-in data types are part of the XML Schema vocabulary and must be placed in the XML Schema namespace.

Figure 3-20 XML Schema built-in data types

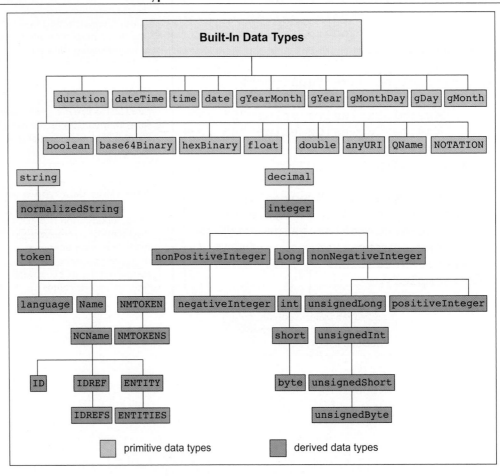

Derived data types share many of the same characteristics as the primitive data types from which they are derived, but incorporate one or two additional restrictions or modifications. To see how this is done, you'll examine the string data types.

String Data Types

In the previous session, you used only the primitive `string` data type, allowing almost any text string in the elements and attributes of Sabrina's document. The `string` data type is the most general of XML Schema's built-in data types. For that reason, it is not very useful if you need to exert more control over element and attribute values in an instance document. XML Schema provides several derived data types that enable you to restrict text strings. Figure 3-21 describes some of these data types.

| Figure 3-21 | Some data types derived from string |

Data Type	Description
xs:string	A text string containing all legal characters from the ISO/IEC character set, including all white space characters
xs:normalizedString	A text string in which all white space characters are replaced with blank spaces
xs:token	A text string in which adjoining blank spaces are replaced with a single blank space, and opening and closing spaces are removed
xs:NMTOKEN	A text string containing valid XML names with no white space
xs:NMTOKENS	A list of NMTOKEN data values separated by white space
xs: Name	A text string similar to the NMTOKEN data type except that names must begin with a letter or the colon (:) or hyphen (-) character
xs:NCName	A "noncolonized name," derived from the **Name** data type but restricting the use of colons anywhere in the name
xs:ID	A unique ID name found nowhere else in the instance document
xs:IDREF	A reference to an ID value found in the instance document
xs:IDREFS	A list of ID references separated by white space
xs:ENTITY	A value matching an unparsed entity defined in a DTD
xs:ENTITIES	A list of entity values matching unparsed entities defined in a DTD

Some of the data types in the list should be familiar from your work with DTDs. For example, the ID data type allows text strings containing unique ID values, and the IDREF and IDREFS data types allow only text strings that contain references to ID values located in the instance document.

REFERENCE

Applying Built-In XML Schema Data Types

- For any string content, use the data type `xs:string`.
- For an ID value, use `xs:ID`.
- For a reference to an ID value, use `xs:IDREF`.
- For a decimal value, use `xs:decimal`.
- For an integer value, use `xs:integer`.
- For a positive integer, use `xs:positiveInteger`.
- For a date in the format *yyyy-mm-dd*, use `xs:date`.
- For a time in the format *hh:mm:ss*, use `xs:time`.

Each student in Sabrina's document has a `stuID` attribute that uniquely identifies the student. You'll apply the ID data type to this attribute now.

To apply the ID data type:

▶ **1.** If you took a break after the previous session, make sure the **students.xml** and **students.xsd** files are open in your editor.

▶ **2.** Within the students.xsd file, locate the definition for the stuID attribute.

▶ **3.** Change the type value from **xs:string** to **xs:ID**. Just like the string data type, the ID data type is built into XML Schema, so you identify it using the xs namespace prefix. Figure 3-22 shows the updated type value.

| Figure 3-22 | ID data type applied |

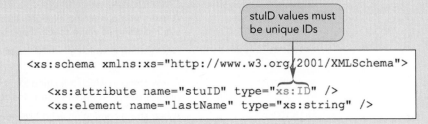

stuID values must be unique IDs

```
<xs:schema xmlns:xs="http://www.w3.org/2001/XMLSchema">

    <xs:attribute name="stuID" type="xs:ID" />
    <xs:element name="lastName" type="xs:string" />
```

▶ **4.** Save your changes to the **students.xsd** file.

Numeric Data Types

Unlike DTDs, schemas that use XML Schema support numeric data types. Most numeric data types are derived from four primitive data types—decimal, float, double, and boolean. Figure 3-23 describes these and some other XML Schema numeric data types.

| Figure 3-23 | Numeric data types |

Data Type	Description
xs:decimal	A decimal number in which the decimal separator is always a dot (.) with a leading + or - character allowed; no nonnumeric characters are allowed, nor is exponential notation
xs:integer	An integer
xs:nonPositiveInteger	An integer less than or equal to zero
xs:negativeInteger	An integer less than zero
xs:nonNegativeInteger	An integer greater than or equal to zero
xs:positiveInteger	An integer greater than zero
xs:float	A floating point number allowing decimal values and values in scientific notation; infinite values can be represented by -INF and INF; nonnumeric values can be represented by NaN
xs:double	A double precision floating point number
xs:boolean	A Boolean value that has the value true, false, 0, or 1

Sabrina's XML document includes the total credits for each of the students in the information technology programs. She wants you to validate that all the values she entered for the `credits` element are positive integers. Sabrina also entered a numeric score for each student's GPA. The GPA values range from 0 to 4. She wants you to change the data type for the `gpa` element to `decimal`. Because `gpa` is a complex type element containing text and attributes, you'll add the data type to the `base` attribute in the `simpleContent` element. You'll make these changes to your schema document now.

To apply the `positiveInteger` and `decimal` data types:

▶ **1.** Within the **students.xsd** file, locate the `xs:element` tag for the `credits` element and then change the value of the `type` attribute from `xs:string` to `xs:positiveInteger`.

▶ **2.** Within the code to define the `gpa` element, locate the opening `xs:extension` tag and then change the value of the `base` attribute from `xs:string` to `xs:decimal`. Figure 3-24 shows the revised code.

Figure 3-24	positiveInteger and decimal data types applied

```
<xs:schema xmlns:xs="http://www.w3.org/2001/XMLSchema">

    <xs:attribute name="stuID" type="xs:ID" />
    <xs:element name="lastName" type="xs:string" />
    <xs:element name="firstName" type="xs:string" />
    <xs:element name="dateOfEnrollment" type="xs:string" />
    <xs:element name="credits" type="xs:positiveInteger" />
    <xs:element name="comment" type="xs:string" />
    <xs:attribute name="degree" type="xs:string" />

    <xs:element name="gpa">
        <xs:complexType>
            <xs:simpleContent>
                <xs:extension base="xs:decimal">
                    <xs:attribute ref="degree" use="required" />
                </xs:extension>
            </xs:simpleContent>
        </xs:complexType>
    </xs:element>
```

values for the gpa element are limited to decimal values

values for the credits element are limited to positive integers

▶ **3.** Save your changes to the **students.xsd** file.

Data Types for Dates and Times

TIP

To support date strings such as 1/8/2017 or Jan. 8, 2017, you must create your own date type or use a date type library created by another XML developer.

XML Schema provides several data types for dates, times, and durations. However, XML Schema does not allow for any flexibility in the date and time formats it uses. For instance, date values containing a month, day, and year must be entered in the format

`yyyy-mm-dd`

where *yyyy* is the four-digit year value, *mm* is the two-digit month value, and *dd* is the two-digit day value. Month values range from 01 to 12, and day values range from 01 to 31 (depending on the month). The date value

2017-01-08

would be valid under XML Schema, but the date value

2017-1-8

would not be valid because its month and day values are not two-digit integers.
Times in XML Schema must be entered using 24-hour (or military) time. The format is

hh:*mm*:*ss*

where *hh* is the hour value ranging from 00 to 23, and *mm* and *ss* are the minutes
and seconds values, respectively, ranging from 00 to 59. No data type exists in XML
Schema for expressing time in the 12-hour AM/PM format. In the `time` data type, each
time value (hours, minutes, and seconds) must be specified. Thus, the time value

15:45

would be invalid because it does not specify a value for seconds. Figure 3-25
summarizes the different data types supported by XML Schema for dates and times.

Figure 3-25	Date and time data types

Data Type	Description
`xs:dateTime`	A date and time entered in the format *yyyy-mm-ddThh:mm:ss* where *yyyy* is the four-digit year, *mm* is the two-digit month, *dd* is the two-digit day, *T* is the time zone, *hh* is the two-digit hour, *mm* is the two-digit minute, and *ss* is the two-digit second
`xs:date`	A date entered in the format *yyyy-mm-dd*
`xs:time`	A time entered in the format *hh:mm:ss*
`xs:gYearMonthDay`	A date based on the Gregorian calendar entered in the format *yyyy-mm-dd* (equivalent to `xs:date`)
`xs:gYearMonth`	A date entered in the format *yyyy-mm* (no day is specified)
`xs:gYear`	A year entered in the format *yyyy*
`xs:gMonthDay`	A month and day entered in the format *--mm-dd*
`xs:gMonth`	A month entered in the format *--mm*
`xs:gDay`	A day entered in the format *---dd*
`xs:duration`	A time duration entered in the format *PyYmMdDhHmMsS* where *y, m, d, h, m,* and *s* are the duration values in years, months, days, hours, minutes, and seconds, respectively; an optional negative sign is also permitted to indicate a negative time duration

Sabrina recorded each student's date of enrollment in her XML document using the
`dateOfEnrollment` element. You'll apply the `date` data type to values of this element
to confirm that she entered all the date values correctly.

To apply the `date` data type:

▶ 1. Within the **students.xsd** file, locate the `xs:element` tag for the
`dateOfEnrollment` element, and then change the data type from `xs:string`
to **xs:date**, as shown in Figure 3-26.

Figure 3-26   date data type applied

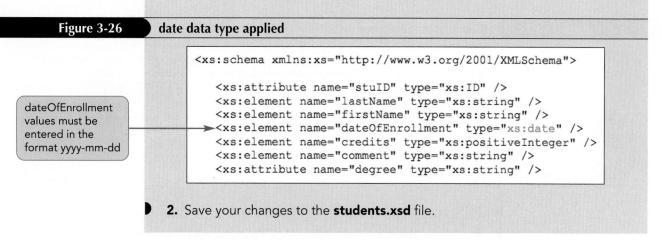

dateOfEnrollment values must be entered in the format yyyy-mm-dd

```
<xs:schema xmlns:xs="http://www.w3.org/2001/XMLSchema">

    <xs:attribute name="stuID" type="xs:ID" />
    <xs:element name="lastName" type="xs:string" />
    <xs:element name="firstName" type="xs:string" />
    <xs:element name="dateOfEnrollment" type="xs:date" />
    <xs:element name="credits" type="xs:positiveInteger" />
    <xs:element name="comment" type="xs:string" />
    <xs:attribute name="degree" type="xs:string" />
```

▶ **2.** Save your changes to the **students.xsd** file.

Now that you've added more specific data types to the students.xsd file, you'll validate the contents of the students.xml file to verify that Sabrina's data matches the rules of the schema.

To validate the students.xml file:

▶ **1.** In your XML editor, switch to the **students.xml** file and then click the **Viewer** button in the upper-right corner of the window.

▶ **2.** On the Menu bar, click **XML** and then click **Validate**. The document validates successfully against the schema.

Sabrina suggests that you add a few errors to the students.xml file to confirm that the modifications you just made to the schema work as expected. The schema you wrote allows only integer values for `credits` element, and allows only decimal values for the gpa element. In addition, date values for the `dateOfEnrollment` must follow a strict pattern. You'll modify the `credits`, `gpa`, and `dateOfEnrollment` values for the first student's data so they don't satisfy these criteria; if the schema works as intended, these changes should result in an invalid document.

To add errors to the students.xml file:

▶ **1.** Return to the **students.xml** file in your XML editor, and then click the **Editor** button in the upper-right corner of the window.

▶ **2.** Within the `student` element for Cynthia Berstein, in the `credits` element value, add a **space** after the number 12 and then type the word **credits**. With the additional characters, the value is no longer an integer.

▶ **3.** Within the `gpa` element for the same student, delete the element value 3.81. The empty value does not match the element's `decimal` data type.

▶ **4.** Within the `dateOfEnrollment` element for the same student, delete the leading 0 from the month value so the date reads **2017-5-22**. The date no longer matches the *yyyy-mm-dd* pattern for the `date` data type. Figure 3-27 shows the revised data for the first student in the document.

| Figure 3-27 | Three errors introduced into instance document |

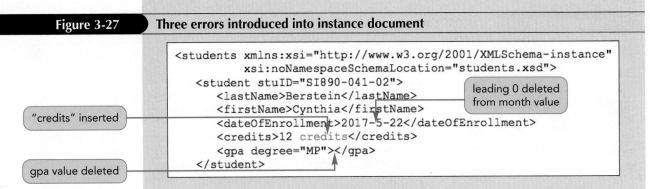

"credits" inserted

gpa value deleted

leading 0 deleted from month value

```
<students xmlns:xsi="http://www.w3.org/2001/XMLSchema-instance"
          xsi:noNamespaceSchemaLocation="students.xsd">
   <student stuID="SI890-041-02">
      <lastName>Berstein</lastName>
      <firstName>Cynthia</firstName>
      <dateOfEnrollment>2017-5-22</dateOfEnrollment>
      <credits>12 credits</credits>
      <gpa degree="MP"></gpa>
   </student>
```

▶ **5.** Save your changes to the **students.xml** file.

▶ **6.** On the Menu bar, click **XML**, click **Validate**, and then scroll through the list of errors on the Errors tab. The document is rejected with errors found due to the `credits`, `gpa`, and `dateOfEnrollment` element values you edited no longer matching the schema definitions.

▶ **7.** In the `credits` element for the first record, delete the space and the word "credits" that you entered so the value is once again 12; in the `gpa` element for the first record, enter the value **3.81**; in the `dateOfEnrollment` element, change the value to read **2017-05-22**; and then save your changes to the file.

▶ **8.** Revalidate the document and confirm that it passes the validation test.

▶ **9.** Save your changes to the **students.xml** file.

Deriving Customized Data Types

In addition to the built-in data types you're using, you also need to create some new data types to fully validate Sabrina's document. Sabrina has provided the following additional rules for the elements and attributes in her document:

- The value of the `credits` element must be at least 1.
- The `gpa` value must fall between 0 and 4.
- The value of the `degree` attribute must be either MP or WPA. (The value MP stands for Mobile Programmer, and the value WPA stands for Web Programmer/Analyst.)

Although XML Schema has no built-in data types for these rules, you can use it to derive—or build—your own data types. The code to derive a new data type is

```
<xs:simpleType name="name">
   rules
</xs:simpleType>
```

where *name* is the name of the user-defined data type and *rules* is the list of statements that define the properties of that data type. This structure is also known as a named simple type because it defines simple type content under a name provided by the schema author. You can also create a simple type without a name, which is known as an **anonymous simple type**. The code for an anonymous simple type is easier to create. However, one advantage of creating a named simple type is that you can reference that simple type elsewhere in your schema using the simple type name.

Each new data type must be derived from a preexisting data type found in either XML Schema or a user-defined vocabulary. The following three components are involved in deriving any new data type:

- **value space**—The set of values that correspond to the data type. For example, the value space for a `positiveInteger` data type includes the numbers 1, 2, 3, etc., but not 0, negative integers, fractions, or text strings.
- **lexical space**—The set of textual representations of the value space. For example, a value supported by the `floating` data type, such as 42, can be represented in several ways, including 42, 42.0, or 4.2E01.
- **facets**—The properties that distinguish one data type from another. Facets can include such properties as text string length or a range of allowable values. For example, a facet that distinguishes the `integer` data type from the `positiveInteger` data type is the fact that positive integers are constrained to the realm of positive numbers.

New data types are created by manipulating the properties of these three components. You can do this by:

1. Creating a list based on preexisting data types
2. Creating a union of one or more of the preexisting data types
3. Restricting the values of a preexisting data type

PROSKILLS

Problem Solving: Reusing Code with Named Model Groups and Named Attribute Groups

Named types are not the only structures you can create to be reused in your schemas. Another structure is a named model group. As the name suggests, a **named model group** is a collection, or group, of elements. The syntax for creating a model group is

```
<xs:group name="name">
    elements
</xs:group>
```

where *name* is the name of the model group and *elements* is a collection of element declarations. Model groups are useful when a document contains element declarations or code that you want to repeat throughout the schema.

Like elements, attributes can be grouped into collections called **named attribute groups**. This is particularly useful for attributes that you want to use with several different elements in a schema. The syntax for a named attribute group is

```
<xs:attributeGroup name="name">
    attributes
</xs:attributeGroup>
```

where *name* is the name of the attribute group and *attributes* is a collection of attributes assigned to the group.

You'll start by examining how to create a list data type.

Deriving a List Data Type

A **list data type** is a list of values separated by white space, in which each item in the list is derived from an established data type. You already have seen a couple of examples of list data types found in XML Schema, including the `xs:ENTITIES` and `xs:IDREFS` lists. In these cases, the list data types are derived from XML Schema's `xs:ENTITY` and `xs:IDREF` data types. The syntax for deriving a customized list data type is

```
<xs:simpleType name="name">
   <xs:list itemType="type" />
</xs:simpleType>
```

where *name* is the name assigned to the list data type and *type* is the data type from which each item in the list is derived. For example, Austin Technical College might decide to include a student's GPA for each semester along with the student's overall GPA. An element containing the GPA information by semester might appear as follows:

```
<semGPA>3.81 3.92 3.3 3.2</semGPA>
```

To create a data type for this information, you could define the following named simple type:

```
<xs:simpleType name="semList">
   <xs:list itemType="xs:decimal" />
</xs:simpleType>
```

In this case, you have a data type named `semList` that contains a list of decimal values. To apply this new data type to the `semGPA` element, you would reference the data type in the definition as follows:

```
<xs:element name="semGPA" type="semList" />
```

Notice that the type value does not have the `xs` namespace prefix because `semList` is not part of the XML Schema vocabulary; it is a named simple type created by the schema author.

Deriving a Union Data Type

A **union data type** is based on the value and/or lexical spaces from two or more preexisting data types. Each base data type is known as a **member data type**. The syntax for deriving a union data type is

```
<xs:simpleType name="name">
   <xs:union memberTypes="type1 type2 type3 ..." />
</xs:simpleType>
```

where *type1*, *type2*, *type3*, etc., are the member types that constitute the union. XML Schema also allows unions to be created from nested simple types. The syntax is

```
<xs:simpleType name="name">
   <xs:union>
      <xs:simpleType>
         rules1
      </xs:simpleType>
      <xs:simpleType>
         rules2
      </xs:simpleType>
      ...
   </xs:union>
</xs:simpleType>
```

where *rules1*, *rules2*, etc., are rules for creating different user-derived data types. For example, when collecting data on semester GPA values, Sabrina might want to specify the type of semester GPA, such as `program`, `genEd`, or `all`. As a result of this variety, the `semGPA` element might look as follows:

```
<semGPA>3.81 program 3.92 all 3.3 genEd 3.2 all</semGPA>
```

To validate this element, which contains a mixture of numeric and descriptive measures, she could create the following derived data type:

```
<xs:simpleType name="semType">
   <xs:union memberTypes="xs:decimal xs:Name" />
</xs:simpleType>
```

Based on this simple type definition, a parser will accept any value as long as it is either a decimal value or a text string of the `Name` data type. Next, Sabrina would use this data type to derive a list type based on the following union data type:

```
<xs:simpleType name="semList">
   <xs:list itemType="semType" />
</xs:simpleType>
```

This list data type would allow the `semGPA` element to contain a list consisting of either decimal values or XML names.

Deriving a Restricted Data Type

The final kind of derived data type is a restricted data type, in which a restriction is placed on the facets of a preexisting data type, such as an `integer` data type that is constrained to fall within a range of values. XML Schema provides 12 constraining facets that can be used to derive new data types; these facets are described in Figure 3-28.

| Figure 3-28 | Constraining facets |

Facet	Description
enumeration	Constrains the data to a specified list of values
length	Specifies the length of the data in characters (for text strings) or items (for lists)
maxLength	Specifies the maximum length of the data in characters (for text strings) or items (for lists)
minLength	Specifies the minimum length of the data in characters (for text strings) or items (for lists)
pattern	Constrains the lexical space of the data to follow a specific character pattern
whiteSpace	Controls the use of blanks in the lexical space of the data; the `whiteSpace` facet has three values—`preserve` (preserve all white space), `replace` (replace all tabs, carriage returns, and line feed characters with blank spaces), and `collapse` (collapse all consecutive occurrences of white space to a single blank space, and remove any leading or trailing white space)
maxExclusive	Constrains the data to be less than a maximum value
maxInclusive	Constrains the data to be less than or equal to a maximum value
minExclusive	Constrains the data to be greater than a minimum value
minInclusive	Constrains the data to be greater than or equal to a minimum value
fractionDigits	Specifies the maximum number of decimal places to the right of the decimal point in the data value
totalDigits	Specifies the maximum number of digits in the data value

Constraining facets are applied to a base type using the structure

```
<xs:simpleType name="name">
   <xs:restriction base="type">
      <xs:facet1 value="value1" />
      <xs:facet2 value="value2" />
      ...
   </xs:restriction>
</xs:simpleType>
```

where *type* is the data type on which the restricted data type is based; *facet1*, *facet2*, etc., are constraining facets; and *value1*, value2, etc., are values for the constraining facets. In Sabrina's document, each student's total credits must be at least 1. You could create a restricted data type using the `minInclusive` facet to restrict the `credits` value to at least 1, as in the following code:

```
<xs:simpleType name="creditsType">
   <xs:restriction base="xs:integer">
      <xs:minInclusive value="1" />
   </xs:restriction>
</xs:simpleType>
```

When applied to the `credits` element, this data type would require each `credits` value to be an integer with a minimum value of 1.

INSIGHT

Constraining Facets vs Form Validation

Like form validation in HTML, constraining facets in an XML schema let you place limits on the allowable values for data in your document. However, while you can use HTML validation to prompt users to correct information they've entered, an XML parser uses a schema to decide whether or not an entire document is valid, and rejects the whole document if it does not adhere to all the rules of the schema, including the constraining facets for specific elements. In short, HTML form validation is a tool to ensure valid collection of data from users, while constraining facets in an XML schema generally serve only as a check on data that has already been collected.

You'll add the `creditsType` data type to the schema and apply it to the `credits` element next.

REFERENCE

Deriving Customized and Patterned Data Types

- To derive a list data type, use

```
<xs:simpleType name="name">
   <xs:list itemType="type" />
</xs:simpleType>
```

where *name* is the name of the custom data type and *type* is the data type on which it is based.

- To derive a union data type, use

```
<xs:simpleType name="name">
   <xs:union memberTypes="type1 type2 type3 ..." />
</xs:simpleType>
```

where *type1*, *type2*, *type3*, etc., are the member types that constitute the union and upon which the custom data type is based. Alternatively, you can use the nested form

```
<xs:simpleType name="name">
   <xs:union>
      <xs:simpleType>
         rules1
      </xs:simpleType>
      <xs:simpleType>
         rules2
      </xs:simpleType>
      ...
   </xs:union>
</xs:simpleType>
```

where *rules1*, *rules2*, etc., are the rules that define the different data types in the union.

- To derive a data type by restricting the values of a preexisting data type, use

```
<xs:simpleType name="name">
   <xs:restriction base="type">
      <xs:facet1 value="value1" />
      <xs:facet2 value="value2" />
      ...
   </xs:restriction>
</xs:simpleType>
```

where *facet1*, *facet2*, etc., are constraining facets; and *value1*, *value2*, etc., are values for the constraining facets.

- To derive a data type based on a regular expression pattern, use

```
<xs:simpleType name="name">
   <xs:restriction base="type">
      <xs:pattern value="regex" />
   </xs:restriction>
</xs:simpleType>
```

where *name* is the name of the derived data type, *type* is a preexisting data type on which the derived type is based, and *regex* is a regular expression defining the pattern of characters in the data.

To create the `creditsType` data type:

1. Return to the **students.xsd** file in your editor.

2. Below the declaration for the gpa element, insert the following code to constrain the credits element to at least 1:

```
<xs:simpleType name="creditsType">
    <xs:restriction base="xs:integer">
        <xs:minInclusive value="1" />
    </xs:restriction>
</xs:simpleType>
```

Be sure to enter the data type as creditsType without a prefix, and *not* as xs:creditsType because the data type is user-defined.

3. In the xs:element tag for the credits element, change the value of the type attribute from xs:positiveInteger to **creditsType**. You do *not* include the xs namespace prefix when referencing the data type because creditsType is not part of the XML Schema vocabulary. Figure 3-29 shows the revised code in the schema.

Figure 3-29	The creditsType data type

credits values must follow the rules of the creditsType simple type

```
<xs:schema xmlns:xs="http://www.w3.org/2001/XMLSchema">

    <xs:attribute name="stuID" type="xs:ID" />
    <xs:element name="lastName" type="xs:string" />
    <xs:element name="firstName" type="xs:string" />
    <xs:element name="dateOfEnrollment" type="xs:date" />
    <xs:element name="credits" type="creditsType" />
    <xs:element name="comment" type="xs:string" />
    <xs:attribute name="degree" type="xs:string" />

    <xs:element name="gpa">
        <xs:complexType>
            <xs:simpleContent>
                <xs:extension base="xs:decimal">
                    <xs:attribute ref="degree" use="required" />
                </xs:extension>
            </xs:simpleContent>
        </xs:complexType>
    </xs:element>

    <xs:simpleType name="creditsType">
        <xs:restriction base="xs:integer">
            <xs:minInclusive value="1" />
        </xs:restriction>
    </xs:simpleType>
```

restricted data type with a constraining facet that limits values to integers greater than or equal to 1

4. Save your changes to the **students.xsd** file.

Facets can also be used to define lower and upper ranges for data. In Sabrina's data, GPA values range from 0 to 4, with 0 excluded and 4 included as possible values. You'll create a data type for this interval now using the minExclusive and maxInclusive facets. You'll set the value of the minExclusive facet to 0, and set the value of the maxInclusive facet to 4. You'll name the data type gpaType and apply it to the gpa element.

To derive the `gpaType` data type in the students.xsd file:

▶ **1.** Below the code for the `creditsType` simple type, insert the following code:

```
<xs:simpleType name="gpaType">
   <xs:restriction base="xs:decimal">
      <xs:minExclusive value="0" />
      <xs:maxInclusive value="4" />
   </xs:restriction>
</xs:simpleType>
```

This code specifies decimal values greater than 0 and less than or equal to 4.

▶ **2.** Within the code that defines the `gpa` element, locate the opening `xs:extension` tag and then change the value of the `base` attribute from `xs:decimal` to **gpaType**. Do *not* include the `xs` namespace prefix when referencing the data type. See Figure 3-30.

Figure 3-30   **The gpaType data type**

gpa values must follow the rules of the gpaType simple type

```
<xs:element name="gpa">
   <xs:complexType>
      <xs:simpleContent>
         <xs:extension base="gpaType">
            <xs:attribute ref="degree" use="required" />
         </xs:extension>
      </xs:simpleContent>
   </xs:complexType>
</xs:element>

<xs:simpleType name="creditsType">
   <xs:restriction base="xs:integer">
      <xs:minInclusive value="1" />
   </xs:restriction>
</xs:simpleType>

<xs:simpleType name="gpaType">
   <xs:restriction base="xs:decimal">
      <xs:minExclusive value="0" />
      <xs:maxInclusive value="4" />
   </xs:restriction>
</xs:simpleType>
```

restricted data type with a constraining facet that limits values to integers greater than 0, and up to and including 4

▶ **3.** Save your changes to the file.

Sabrina wants values of the `degree` attribute to be limited to either `MP` or `WPA`. When permitted content belongs to a set of specific values rather than a range, you can create a list of possible values using the `enumeration` element. The following simple type creates the restriction that Sabrina needs:

```
<xs:simpleType name="degreeType">
   <xs:restriction base="xs:string">
      <xs:enumeration value="MP" />
      <xs:enumeration value="WPA" />
   </xs:restriction>
</xs:simpleType>
```

You'll create this enumerated data type now and apply it to the schema.

To create the `degreeType` data type in the students.xsd file:

▶ **1.** Below the code that defines the `gpaType` simple type, insert the following code:

```
<xs:simpleType name="degreeType">
   <xs:restriction base="xs:string">
      <xs:enumeration value="MP" />
      <xs:enumeration value="WPA" />
   </xs:restriction>
</xs:simpleType>
```

▶ **2.** Within the `xs:attribute` element for the `degree` attribute, change the value of the `type` attribute from `xs:string` to **degreeType**. Do *not* include the `xs` namespace prefix when referencing the data type. Figure 3-31 highlights the revised code.

Figure 3-31	The degreeType data type

```
<xs:schema xmlns:xs="http://www.w3.org/2001/XMLSchema">

   <xs:attribute name="stuID" type="xs:ID" />
   <xs:element name="lastName" type="xs:string" />
   <xs:element name="firstName" type="xs:string" />
   <xs:element name="dateOfEnrollment" type="xs:date" />
   <xs:element name="credits" type="creditsType" />
   <xs:element name="comment" type="xs:string" />
   <xs:attribute name="degree" type="degreeType" />

   ...

   <xs:simpleType name="gpaType">
      <xs:restriction base="xs:decimal">
         <xs:minExclusive value="0" />
         <xs:maxInclusive value="4" />
      </xs:restriction>
   </xs:simpleType>

   <xs:simpleType name="degreeType">
      <xs:restriction base="xs:string">
         <xs:enumeration value="MP" />
         <xs:enumeration value="WPA" />
      </xs:restriction>
   </xs:simpleType>
```

degree values must follow the rules of the degreeType simple type

the degreeType data type limits values to "MP" and "WPA"

▶ **3.** Save your changes to the **students.xsd** file.

Before editing your schema further, you'll validate revisions to the schema and then revalidate it after introducing errors in the students.xml file and verifying that a parser flags the errors in validation.

To validate revisions to the schema, introduce errors into the students.xml file, and then test the validation rules for the schema file:

▶ **1.** Return to the **students.xml** file in Exchanger XML editor, and then, if necessary, click the **Viewer** button.

▶ **2.** Validate your document and confirm that it validates successfully.

Trouble? If any validation errors are listed on the Errors tab, return to the students.xsd document and be sure your code matches the code shown in Figures 3-29 through 3-31 exactly. Make changes as needed, save your document, and then return to students.xml and revalidate the document until it passes.

▶ **3.** Click the **Editor** button in the upper-right corner.

▶ **4.** Locate the `student` element for Cynthia Berstein, and then in the `gpa` element, change the value of the `degree` attribute to **MPA**. The data for the first `student` element in the document should match Figure 3-32.

Figure 3-32	Invalid degree value

```
<students xmlns:xsi="http://www.w3.org/2001/XMLSchema-instance"
          xsi:noNamespaceSchemaLocation="students.xsd">
   <student stuID="SI890-041-02">
      <lastName>Berstein</lastName>
      <firstName>Cynthia</firstName>
      <dateOfEnrollment>2017-05-22</dateOfEnrollment>
      <credits>12</credits>
      <gpa degree="MPA">3.81</gpa>
   </student>
```

content changed to invalid value to introduce an error

▶ **5.** Save your changes to the file.

▶ **6.** On the Menu bar, click **XML**, click **Validate**, and then review the error descriptions displayed on the Errors tab. The document is rejected and the parser reports errors because the value of the attribute `degree` for the element gpa does not match the schema definitions.

▶ **7.** In the gpa element for the first record, change the value of the `degree` attribute back to **MP**, and then save your changes to the file.

▶ **8.** Revalidate the document and confirm that it passes.

Deriving Data Types Using Regular Expressions

Sabrina has one final restriction to place on data values stored in her student records: Each student's student ID must be entered in the form SI###-###-##, where # is a digit from 0 to 9.

This rule involves the representation of the values, so you need to create a restriction based on the lexical space. One way of doing this is through a regular expression.

Introducing Regular Expressions

A regular expression is a text string that defines a character pattern. Regular expressions can be created to define patterns for many types of data, including phone numbers, postal address codes, and e-mail addresses—and, in the case of Sabrina's document, student IDs. To apply a regular expression in a data type, you create the simple type

```
<xs:simpleType name="name">
    <xs:restriction base="type">
        <xs:pattern value="regex" />
    </xs:restriction>
</xs:simpleType>
```

where *regex* is a regular expression pattern.

The most basic pattern specifies the characters that must appear in valid data. For instance, the following regular expression requires that the value of the data type be the text string *ABC*:

```
<xs:pattern value="ABC" />
```

Any other combination of letters, including the use of lowercase letters, would be invalid.

Instead of a pattern involving specific characters, though, you usually want a more general pattern involving character types, which are representations of different kinds of characters. The general form of a character type is

```
\char
```

where *char* represents a specific character type. Character types can include digits, word characters (any uppercase or lowercase letter, any digit, or the underscore character (_)), boundaries around words, and white space characters. Figure 3-33 describes the code for representing each of these character types.

Figure 3-33	Regular expression character types

Character Type	Description
\d	A digit from 0 to 9
\D	A non-digit character
\w	A word character (an upper- or lowercase letter, a digit, or an underscore (_))
\W	A non-word character
\b	A boundary around a word (a text string of word characters)
\B	The absence of a boundary around a word
\s	A white space character (a blank space, tab, new line, carriage return, or form feed)
\S	A non-white space character
.	Any character

TIP

In a regular expression, the opposite of a character type is indicated by a capital letter. So while \d represents a single digit, \D represents any character that is not a digit.

For example, the character type for a single digit is \d. To create a regular expression representing three digits, you would apply the following pattern:

```
<xs:pattern value="\d\d\d" />
```

Any text string that contains three digits would match this pattern. Thus, the text strings 012 and 921 would both match this pattern, but 1,020 and 54 would not.

For more general patterns, characters can also be grouped into lists called **character sets** that specify exactly what characters or ranges of characters are allowed in the pattern.

The syntax of a character set is

`[chars]`

where *chars* is the set of characters in the character set. For example, the pattern

```
<xs:pattern value="[dog]" />
```

matches any of the characters d, o, or g. Because characters can be sorted alphabetically or numerically, a character set can also be created for a range of characters using the general syntax

`[char1-charN]`

where *char1* is the first character in the range and *charN* is the last character in the range. To create a range of lowercase letters, you would use the following pattern:

```
<xs:pattern value="[a-z]" />
```

Any lowercase letter would be matched by this pattern. You can also match numeric ranges. The following pattern matches any digit from 1 to 5:

```
<xs:pattern value="[1-5]" />
```

Figure 3-34 lists many of the common character sets used in regular expressions.

Figure 3-34   **Common regular expression character sets**

Character Set	Description
`[chars]`	Match any character in the *chars* list
`[^chars]`	Do not match any character in *chars*
`[char1-charN]`	Match any character in the range *char1* through *charN*
`[^char1-charN]`	Do not match any character in the range *char1* through *charN*
`[a-z]`	Match any lowercase letter
`[A-Z]`	Match any uppercase letter
`[a-zA-Z]`	Match any letter
`[0-9]`	Match any digit from 0 to 9
`[0-9a-zA-Z]`	Match any digit or letter

The regular expressions you've looked at so far have involved individual characters. To specify the number of occurrences for a particular character or group of characters, a **quantifier** can be appended to a character type or set. Figure 3-35 lists the different quantifiers used in regular expressions. Some of these quantifiers should be familiar from your work with DTDs.

Figure 3-35   **Regular expression quantifiers**

Quantifier	Description
`*`	Repeat 0 or more times
`?`	Repeat 0 times or 1 time
`+`	Repeat 1 or more times
`{n}`	Repeat exactly *n* times
`{n,}`	Repeat at least *n* times
`{n,m}`	Repeat at least *n* times but no more than *m* times

TIP

On the web, you can find libraries of predefined regular expression patterns that can be applied to common text strings such as phone numbers, postal codes, credit card numbers, and Social Security numbers.

As you saw earlier, to specify a pattern of three consecutive digits, you can use the following regular expression:

```
\d\d\d
```

Alternatively, you can employ the quantifier {3} using the pattern

```
<xs:pattern value="\d{3}" />
```

which also defines a pattern of three digits. Likewise, to validate a string of uppercase characters of any length, you can use the * quantifier, as follows:

```
<xs:pattern value="[A-Z]*" />
```

Similarly, the following pattern uses the quantifier {0,10} to allow for a text string of uppercase letters from 0 to 10 characters long:

```
<xs:pattern value="[A-Z]{0,10}" />
```

Applying a Regular Expression

You have only scratched the surface of what regular expressions can do. The topic of regular expressions could fill an entire tutorial by itself. However, you have covered enough to be able to implement Sabrina's request that all student ID strings be in the format SI###-###-##, where # is a digit from 0 to 9. The pattern for this expression is

```
<xs:pattern value="SI\d{3}-\d{3}-\d{2}" />
```

where the character type \d represents a single digit, and the quantifiers {3} and {2} indicate that the digits must be in groups of three and two, respectively. Note that the characters SI at the start of the pattern must be matched literally, including capitalization; thus, a student ID value of Si448-996-22 would not match the pattern because the i isn't capitalized. You'll create a data type named siType now based on this pattern.

To derive the siType data type based on a regular expression:

1. Return to the **students.xsd** file in your editor, and then directly below the declaration for the degree attribute, insert the following code:

```
<xs:simpleType name="siType">
   <xs:restriction base="xs:ID">
      <xs:pattern value="SI\d{3}-\d{3}-\d{2}" />
   </xs:restriction>
</xs:simpleType>
```

   The base data type is xs:ID, indicating that this custom data type will be derived from unique ID values in the document.

2. Within the declaration of the stuID attribute, change the value of the type attribute from xs:ID to **siType**. Do *not* include the xs namespace prefix when referencing the data type.

   Figure 3-36 shows the revised code for the schema file.

Figure 3-36   **Declaring and applying the siType data type**

stuID values must follow the rules of the siType simple type

values must be unique IDs of the form SI###-###-##, where # is a digit

```
<xs:schema xmlns:xs="http://www.w3.org/2001/XMLSchema">

    <xs:attribute name="stuID" type="siType" />
    <xs:element name="lastName" type="xs:string" />
    <xs:element name="firstName" type="xs:string" />
    <xs:element name="dateOfEnrollment" type="xs:date" />
    <xs:element name="credits" type="creditsType" />
    <xs:element name="comment" type="xs:string" />
    <xs:attribute name="degree" type="degreeType" />

    <xs:simpleType name="siType">
      <xs:restriction base="xs:ID">
        <xs:pattern value="SI\d{3}-\d{3}-\d{2}" />
      </xs:restriction>
    </xs:simpleType>
</xs:schema>
```

▶ **3.** Save your changes to the **students.xsd** file.

Next, you'll validate Sabrina's document to ensure that all the student IDs match the pattern you defined.

To validate the student IDs:

▶ **1.** Return to the **students.xml** file in your XML editor, and then verify that you are in Editor view.

▶ **2.** Within the record for Cynthia Berstein, change the capital letters SI in the stuID value to the lowercase letters **si** so it reads si890-041-02. This value doesn't meet the validation criteria for the siType data type because the first two letters are lowercase. See Figure 3-37.

Figure 3-37   **Invalid stuID value**

first two letters of value changed to lowercase

```
<students xmlns:xsi="http://www.w3.org/2001/XMLSchema-instance"
        xsi:noNamespaceSchemaLocation="students.xsd">
   <student stuID="si890-041-02">
      <lastName>Berstein</lastName>
      <firstName>Cynthia</firstName>
      <dateOfEnrollment>2017-05-22</dateOfEnrollment>
      <credits>12</credits>
      <gpa degree="MP">3.81</gpa>
   </student>
```

▶ **3.** Save your changes to the file.

▶ **4.** On the Menu bar, click **XML**, click **Validate**, and then examine the contents of the Errors tab. The document is rejected with errors found because the value of the attribute stuID for the element student no longer matches the schema definitions.

▶ **5.** Change the stuID value for Cynthia Berstein back to **SI890-041-02**, and then save your changes to the file.

▶ **6.** Revalidate the document and confirm that it passes the validation test.

INSIGHT

Deriving Data Types and Inheritance

You can use XML Schema to create a library of new data types, and you can use each new data type you create as the base for creating yet another type. For example, you could start with a data type for integer values, use that to define a new data type for positive integers, use that to define a data type for positive integers between 1 and 100, and so forth. Note that unless you are creating a list or a union, every new type represents a restriction of one or more facets in a preexisting type.

In some cases, you might want to fix a facet so that any new data types based upon it cannot modify it. For example, if Sabrina defined the `credits` data type to have a maximum value of 130, she might want to prevent any data types based on `credits` from being able to change that maximum value. She could do so by applying the `fixed` attribute to the `maxInclusive` facet as follows:

```
<xs:maxInclusive value="130" fixed="true" />
```

As a result of this attribute, any data type based on the `credits` type would have its maximum value set at 130. Because fixing a facet makes a data type library less flexible, it should be used only in situations where changing the facet value would dramatically alter the original meaning of the data type.

You can also use XML Schema to prevent any new data types from being created from an existing data type. This is done using the `final` attribute

```
<xs:simpleType name="name" final="derivation">
   . . .
</xs:simpleType>
```

where *name* is the name of the new data type and *derivation* indicates which methods of creating new data types are prohibited (`list`, `union`, `restriction`, or `all`). For example, the following code defines the `credits` data type and prohibits it from being used in deriving a new data type through a union or a list:

```
<xs:simpleType name="credits" final="union list">
   . . .
</xs:simpleType>
```

When the `final` attribute is omitted or set to an empty text string, XML Schema allows for any kind of derivations of the original type.

Sabrina is pleased with the work you have done on creating a schema for the document describing the students enrolled in the information technology programs at Austin Technical College.

Session 3.2 Quick Check

1. Enter a definition for an element named Height containing only decimal data.
2. Enter the attribute definition for the productIDs attribute containing a list of ID references.
3. Define a data type named applicationDates that contains a list of dates.
4. Define a data type named Status that contains either a decimal or a text string.
5. Define a data type named Party that is limited to one of the following— Democrat, Republican, or Independent.
6. Define a data type named Percentage that is limited to decimal values falling between 0 and 1 (inclusive).
7. Define a data type named SocSecurity that contains a text string matching the pattern ###-##-####, where # is a digit from 0 to 9.

Note: *In the Review Assignments and Case Problems, some XML documents include intentional errors. Part of your job is to find and correct those errors using validation reports from the schemas you create.*

Review Assignments

Data Files needed for the Review Assignments: degreestxt.xml, degreestxt.xsd

Each department at Austin Technical College must maintain information on the associate's degrees it offers; each associate's degree must be approved by a college authority. Sabrina has created an XML vocabulary containing information about the different degrees offered by the Information Technology department. She wants you to create a schema to validate the degree information. Figure 3-38 shows the structures of the degrees vocabulary that you'll create.

Figure 3-38   The degrees vocabulary structure

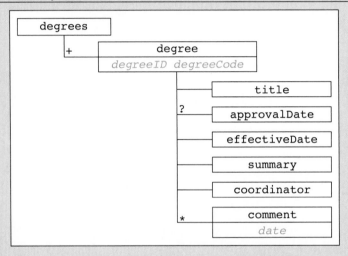

A description of the elements and attributes used in the degrees vocabulary is shown in Figure 3-39.

Figure 3-39   The degrees vocabulary

Element or Attribute	Description
degrees	The root element
degree	The collection of information about a degree
degreeID	The ID number of the degree with the format IT##-###-###, where # is a digit
degreeCode	The in-house code for the degree (MP, SP, or WPA)
title	The title of the degree
approvalDate	The date the degree was approved by the college authority
effectiveDate	The date the degree curriculum becomes effective
summary	The descriptive summary of the degree
coordinator	The currently assigned degree coordinator
comment	A comment regarding the degree
date	The date of the comment

Sabrina already created a document containing a list of degrees currently offered by the Information Technology department. She wants the document validated based on a schema you create.

Complete the following:

1. Using your XML editor, open the **degreestxt.xml** and **degreestxt.xsd** files from the xml03 ▶ review folder, enter *your name* and *today's date* in the comment section of each file, and then save the files as **degrees.xml** and **degrees.xsd**, respectively.

2. In the degrees.xsd file, add the root schema element to the document and declare the XML Schema namespace using the **xs** prefix, and then save your work.

3. In the degrees.xml file, attach the schema file **degrees.xsd** to this instance document, indicating that the schema and instance document do not belong to any namespace, and then save your work.

4. In the degrees.xsd file, create the following named simple types:
   a. **idType**, based on the **ID** data type and restricted to the regular expression pattern IT\d{2}-\d{3}-\d{3}
   b. **codeType**, based on the **string** data type and restricted to the following values—MP, SP, WPA

5. Declare the **degrees** element containing the child element **degree**.

6. Declare the **degree** element containing the following sequence of nested child elements— **title**, **approvalDate**, **effectiveDate**, **summary**, **coordinator**, and **comment**. Set the following properties for the nested elements:
   a. All of the child elements should contain string data except the **approvalDate** and **effectiveDate** elements, which contain dates. The **degree** element should also support two required attributes—**degreeID** and **degreeCode**. The **degreeID** attribute contains **idType** data, while the **degreeCode** attribute contains **codeType** data.
   b. The **degree** element must occur at least once, but its upper limit is unbounded. The **approvalDate** element is optional. The **comment** element is optional, and it may occur multiple times. All other elements are assumed to occur only once.
   c. Each **comment** element requires a **date** attribute of the **date** data type.

7. Save your changes to the degrees.xsd file, and then validate the schema document. Correct any errors you find.

8. Validate the degrees.xml file against the schema document you created. Correct any validation errors you discover in the instance document.

Case Problem 1

Data Files needed for this Case Problem: catalogtxt.xml, catalogtxt.xsd

The Our Lady of Bergen Historical Society   Sharon Strattan is an archivist at the Our Lady of Bergen Historical Society in Bergenfield, New Jersey. The historical society is exploring how to transfer its listings to XML format, and Sharon has begun by creating a sample document of the society's extensive collection of photos. As part of this process, she's asked for your help in developing the schema that will be used to validate the XML documents. She has created a sample document to work on. Eventually, your work will be used in a much larger system. The structure of the sample document is shown in Figure 3-40.

APPLY

Figure 3-40 **The catalog vocabulary structure**

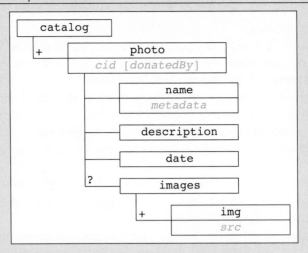

Figure 3-41 describes the elements and attributes in this sample document as well as the rules that govern the data that can be entered into a valid document.

Figure 3-41 **The catalog vocabulary**

Element or Attribute	Description
catalog	The root element
photo	The collection of information about a photo
cid	The ID number of the catalog with the format c####, where # is a digit
donatedBy	The name of the donor
name	The name of the photo
metadata	The metadata for the photo
description	The description of the photo
date	The approximate date of the photo
images	The collection of img elements
img	The element that references the image file
src	The source file containing the image; must end with .jpg

Your job will be to express this document structure and set of rules in terms of the XML Schema language, and then to validate Sharon's document based on the schema you create.

Complete the following:

1. Using your XML editor, open the **catalogtxt.xml** and **catalogtxt.xsd** files from the xml03 ▶ case1 folder, enter *your name* and *today's date* in the comment section of each file, and then save the files as **catalog.xml** and **catalog.xsd**, respectively.

2. Go to the catalog.xsd file in your text editor. Add the root schema element to the document and declare the XML Schema namespace using the **xs** prefix.

3. Attach the schema file **catalog.xsd** to the instance document, indicating that the schema and instance document do not belong to any namespace.

4. Create the following named simple types:

    a. **cidType**, based on the ID data type and restricted to the regular expression pattern c\d{4}

    b. **srcType**, based on the string data type and restricted to the regular expression pattern [a-zA-Z0-9]+.jpg

5. Declare the **catalog** element containing the child element photo. The photo element must occur at least once, but its upper limit is unbounded.

6. Declare the **photo** element containing the following sequence of nested child elements—name, description, date, and images. Set the following properties for the nested elements:

    a. All of the child elements should contain string data. The name element should also support the metadata attribute.

    b. The cid attribute is required. The donatedBy attribute is optional.

7. Declare the **img** element. It has no content and contains a required attribute, src.

8. Declare the following attributes and elements:

    a. The attribute **metadata** must have the string data type.

    b. The attribute **cid** must have the cidType data type.

    c. The attribute **src** must have the srcType data type.

    d. The attribute **donatedBy** must have the string data type.

    e. The element **description** must have the string data type.

    f. The element **date** must have the string data type.

9. Save your changes to the catalog.xsd file, and then validate the schema. Continue to correct any validation errors you discover until the schema validates.

10. Validate the catalog.xml file against the schema. Continue to correct any validation errors you discover until the instance document validates.

Case Problem 2

Data Files needed for this Case Problem: mdpbatxt.xml, mdpbatxt.xsd

Midwest Developmental Pipe Band Association   Jacob St. John works as a coordinator for the Midwest Developmental Pipe Band Association (MDPBA) and is responsible for coordinating competitions for the MDPBA's many developmental pipe bands in the Midwest. Part of Jacob's job is to maintain a document that lists competition entries for each pipe band. As part of this process, he's asked for your help with developing the schema that will be used to validate the XML documents. He has created a sample document to work on. The structure of the sample document is shown in Figure 3-42.

APPLY

Figure 3-42   The bands vocabulary structure

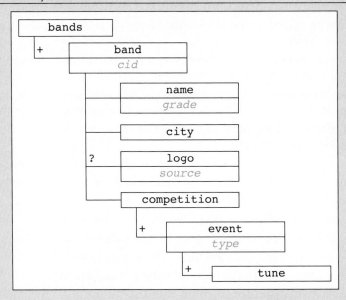

Figure 3-43 describes the elements and attributes in this sample document as well as the rules that govern the data that can be entered into a valid document.

Figure 3-43   The bands vocabulary

Element or Attribute	Description
bands	The root element
band	The collection of information about a band
cid	The ID number of the band with the format c####, where # is a digit
name	The name of the band
grade	The grade level at which the band is competing (juvenile, novice, 1, 2, 3, or 4)
city	The home city of the band
logo	The logo image
source	The source file containing the logo image
competition	The collection of information about a competition
event	The collection of information about an event
type	The type of event entered (MSR or Medley)
tune	The name of a tune

Your job will be to express this document structure and set of rules in terms of the XML Schema language, and then to validate Jacob's document based on the schema you create.

Complete the following:

1. Using your XML editor, open the **mdpbatxt.xml** and **mdpbatxt.xsd** files from the xml03 ▸ case2 folder, enter *your name* and *today's date* in the comment section of each file, and then save the files as **mdpba.xml** and **mdpba.xsd**, respectively.

2. Go to the mdpba.xsd file in your text editor. Add the root schema element to the document and declare the XML Schema namespace using the **xs** prefix.

3. Attach the schema file **mdpba.xsd** to the instance document, indicating that the schema and instance document do not belong to any namespace.

4. Create the following named simple types:

   a. **gradeType**, based on the `string` data type and limited to the enumerated values `novice`, `juvenile`, 1, 2, 3, and 4

   b. **eType**, based on the `string` data type and limited to the enumerated values `MSR` and `Medley`

   c. **cidType**, based on the `ID` data type and restricted to the regular expression pattern `c\d{4}`

   d. **srcType**, based on the `string` data type and restricted to the regular expression pattern `[a-zA-Z0-9]+.png`

5. Declare the **bands** element containing the child element `band`. The `band` element must occur at least once, but its upper limit is unbounded.

6. Declare the **band** element containing the following sequence of nested child elements—`name`, `city`, `logo`, and `competition`. Set the following properties for the nested elements:

   a. All of the child elements should contain string data. The `name` element should also support the required `grade` attribute.

   b. The `logo` element is optional.

   c. The `band` element must contain the `cid` attribute.

7. Declare the **logo** element, which has no content and contains the required attribute `source`.

8. Declare the **competition** element containing the child element `event`. The `event` element must occur at least once, but its upper limit is unbounded.

9. Declare the **event** element containing the child element `tune`. The `tune` element must occur at least once, but its upper limit is unbounded. The `event` element is required.

10. Declare the following attributes and elements:

    a. The attribute `grade`, which uses the `gradeType` data type

    b. The attribute `type`, which uses the `eType` data type

    c. The attribute `cid`, which uses the `cidType` data type

    d. The attribute `source`, which uses the `srcType` data type

    e. The element `city`, which uses the `string` data type

    f. The element `tune`, which uses the `string` data type

11. Save your changes to the mdpba.xsd file, and then validate the schema. Continue to correct any validation errors you discover until the schema validates.

12. Validate the mdpba.xml file against the schema. Continue to correct any validation errors you discover until the instance document validates.

Case Problem 3

Data Files needed for this Case Problem: rostertxt.xml, rostertxt.xsd

The Save Exotic Animals Trust Sienna Woo is the donor coordinator for the Save Exotic Animals Trust (SEA Trust), a charitable organization located in central Florida. One of her responsibilities is to maintain a membership list of people in the community who have donated to SEA Trust. A donor can belong to one of four categories—friendship, patron, sponsor, or founder. A donor's phone number can be classified in one of three categories—home, cell, or work. Each donor's preferred method of contact can be one of three methods—Phone, Personal, or Mail. Sienna has asked for your help with developing a schema to validate the sample XML document that she created. The structure of the sample document is shown in Figure 3-44.

CREATE

Figure 3-44   **The roster vocabulary structure**

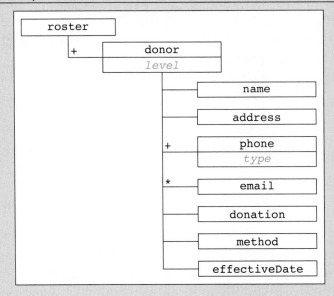

Your job will be to express this document structure in terms of the XML Schema language, and then to validate Sienna's document against the schema you create.

Complete the following:

1. Using your text editor, open the **rostertxt.xml** and **rostertxt.xsd** files from the xml03 ▸ case3 folder, enter *your name* and *today's date* in the comment section of each file, and then save the files as **roster.xml** and **roster.xsd**, respectively.

2. Go to the roster.xsd file in your text editor. Add the root schema element to the document and declare the XML Schema namespace using the **xs** prefix.

3. Attach the schema file **roster.xsd** to the instance document, indicating that the schema and instance document do not belong to any namespace.

4. Create the following named simple types:

   a. **pType**, based on the **string** data type and limited to the enumerated values **home**, **cell**, and **work**

   b. **methodType**, based on the **string** data type and limited to the enumerated values **Phone**, **Personal**, and **Mail**

   c. **levelType**, based on the **string** data type and limited to the enumerated values **founder**, **sponsor**, **patron**, and **friendship**

   d. **phoneType**, based on the **string** data type consisting of 14 characters—the first character should be a left opening parenthesis, followed by three digits from 0 to 9, followed by a right closing parenthesis, followed by a space, followed by three digits from 0 to 9, followed by a hyphen, and then four digits from 0 to 9 (*Hint*: Opening and closing parentheses are special characters in creating regular expressions. To include one of these characters in your expression, enter a backslash before it.)

5. Declare the **roster** element containing the child element listed in the vocabulary structure. The child element must occur at least once but its upper limit is unbounded.

   a. Declare the **donor** element containing the sequence of nested child elements shown in the vocabulary structure. Set properties for the minimum and/or maximum occurrences of the **donor**, **phone**, and **email** elements as illustrated in the vocabulary structure. Specify that the **donor** element must contain the required **level** attribute.

   b. Declare the **phone** element, containing the required attribute **type**.

6. Declare the following attributes and elements:
   a. The attribute `type`, which uses the `pType` data type
   b. The attribute `level`, which uses the `levelType` data type
   c. The element `name`, which uses the `string` data type
   d. The element `address`, which uses the `string` data type
   e. The element `email`, which uses the `string` data type
   f. The element `donation`, which uses the `decimal` data type
   g. The element `effectiveDate`, which uses the `date` data type
   h. The element `method`, which uses the `methodType` data type
7. Save your changes to the roster.xsd file, and then validate the schema. Continue to correct any validation errors you discover until the schema validates.
8. Validate the roster.xml file against the schema. In response to any validation errors, correct relevant values in the roster.xml document to match the schema rules. Continue to correct any validation errors you discover until the instance document validates.

Case Problem 4

Data Files needed for this Case Problem: orderstxt.xml, orderstxt.xsd

Map Finds For You   Benjamin Mapps is working on an XML document to hold data regarding customers who have placed orders with his store, Map Finds For You. Figure 3-45 shows the structure of the vocabulary employed by the document.

Figure 3-45	The customers vocabulary structure

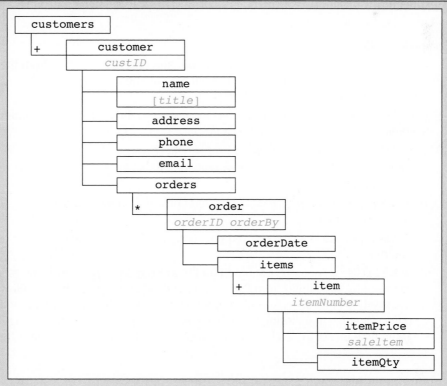

A description of the elements and attributes used for customer data is shown in Figure 3-46.

Figure 3-46   **The customers vocabulary**

Element or Attribute	Description
customers	The root element
customer	The collection of information about a customer
custID	The ID number of the customer with the format cust###, where # is a digit
name	The name of the customer
title	The title for the customer (Mr., Ms., or Mrs.)
address	The address for the customer
phone	The phone number for the customer
email	The email address for the customer
orders	The collection of information on orders
order	The collection of information on an individual order
orderID	The ID number of the order with the format or###, where # is a digit
orderBy	The ID number of the customer who placed the order
orderDate	The date the order was placed
items	The collection of information on items
item	The collection of information on a specific item
itemNumber	The item number of the item ordered
itemPrice	The price paid for the item
saleItem	Whether the itemPrice was a sale price (Y or N)
itemQty	The quantity of the item ordered

Benjamin needs your help with creating a schema that will validate the data he has already entered and will enter in the future.

Complete the following:

1. Using your text editor, open the **orderstxt.xml** and **orderstxt.xsd** files from the xml03 ► case4 folder, enter *your name* and *today's date* in the comment section of each file, and then save the files as **orders.xml** and **orders.xsd**, respectively.

2. Go to the orders.xsd file in your text editor and insert the root schema element. Declare the XML Schema namespace with **xs** as the namespace prefix.

✦ **EXPLORE** 3. Create the following simple data types:

   a. **idType**, based on the ID data type and consisting of the characters **cust** followed by three digits from 0 to 9

   b. **cidType**, based on the ID data type and consisting of the characters "or" followed by four digits from 0 to 9

   c. **titleType**, based on the string data type and limited to the enumerated values Mr., Ms., and Mrs.

   ✦ **EXPLORE** d. **phoneType**, based on the string data type consisting of a left parenthesis followed by three digits from 0 to 9, followed by a right parenthesis, followed by a space, followed by three digits from 0 to 9, followed by a hyphen, and then four more digits 0 to 9 (*Hint*: Opening and closing parentheses are special characters in creating regular expressions. To include one of these characters in your expression, enter a backslash before it.)

    e. **qtyType**, based on the integer data type and allowing only numbers with a value of 1 or more

    f. **saleType**, based on the string data type and limited to the values Y and N

4. Declare the **customers** complex element type, and then nest the customer element within it. The customer element must occur at least once, but its upper limit is unbounded.

⊕ **EXPLORE** 5. Set the data types of the elements and attributes of the customer element as follows:

    a. The child elements must occur in the sequence name, address, phone, email, orders. The name, address, and email elements use the string data type. The phone element uses the phoneType data type. The email element can occur once or not at all.

    b. The **name** element is a complex type element and uses a data type of string. The name attribute also contains an optional **title** attribute.

    c. The **orders** element is a complex type element and contains at least one **order** element.

    d. Declare an attribute named **custID**. The custID attribute is required and contains **idType** data.

⊕ **EXPLORE** 6. Set the data types of the elements and attributes of the order element as follows:

    a. The child elements must occur in the sequence orderDate, items. The orderDate element uses the date data type.

    b. The order element also contains required orderID and orderBy attributes containing cidType and IDREF data types, respectively.

    c. The items element is a complex type element and contains at least one item element.

⊕ **EXPLORE** 7. Set the data types of the elements and attributes of the item element as follows:

    a. The child elements must occur in the sequence itemPrice, itemQty. The itemPrice and itemQty elements use the decimal and qtyType data types, respectively.

    b. The item element also contains a required itemNumber attribute that uses the string data type.

    c. The itemPrice element is a complex type element and contains an attribute, saleItem, which uses the saleType data type and has a default value of N.

8. Save your changes to the orders.xsd file, and then validate the schema. Continue to correct any validation errors you discover until the schema validates.

9. Validate the orders.xml file against the schema. In response to any validation errors, correct relevant values in the orders.xml document to match the schema rules. Continue to correct any validation errors you discover until the instance document validates.

TUTORIAL **4**

OBJECTIVES

Session 4.1
- Explore the Flat Catalog schema design
- Explore the Russian Doll schema design
- Explore the Venetian Blind schema design

Session 4.2
- Attach a schema to a namespace
- Apply a namespace to an instance document
- Import one schema file into another
- Reference objects from other schemas

Session 4.3
- Declare a default namespace in a style sheet
- Specify qualified elements by default in a schema
- Integrate a schema and a style sheet with an instance document

Working with Advanced Schemas

Creating Advanced Schemas for Higher Ed Test Prep

Case | *Higher Ed Test Prep*

Gabby Phelps is an exam study coordinator at Higher Ed Test Prep, an Internet-based company that prepares students for academic exams such as the PSAT, ACT, SAT, and GRE. Gabby wants to use XML to create structured documents containing information about the different exams that she oversees and about the students who are studying for those exams.

Accuracy is important for Higher Ed, so Gabby is using a schema to make sure that the data she enters is error free. Although she has already created a basic schema document, she would like to explore some different schema designs. Gabby also needs to create compound documents from the various XML vocabularies she's created.

STARTING DATA FILES

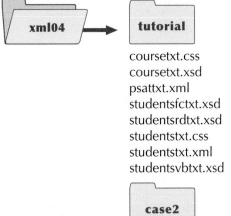

xml04 → **tutorial**

coursetxt.css
coursetxt.xsd
psattxt.xml
studentsfctxt.xsd
studentsrdtxt.xsd
studentstxt.css
studentstxt.xml
studentsvbtxt.xsd

review

coursetxt.css
coursetxt.xsd
psattxt.xml
sessionstxt.css
sessionstxt.xml
sessionstxt.xsd

case1

sitemapPS.xml
sitemapVS.xml
sitemapWFS.xml
sitestxt.xml
sitestxt.xsd

case2

menutxt.css
menutxt.xml
recipetxt.css
recipetxt.xml

case3

atclectxt.xml
ituneselem.txt

case4

carstxt.css
carstxt.xml
teamstxt.css
teamstxt.xml

Session 4.1 Visual Overview:

In a **Flat Catalog design**—sometimes referred to as a **Salami Slice design**—all element and attribute definitions have global scope.

A **Russian Doll design** has only one global element with everything else nested inside of it, much like Russian dolls nest one inside another.

```xml
<xs:schema xmlns:xs="http://www.w3.org/2001/XMLSchema">

    <xs:element name="students">
        <xs:complexType>
            <xs:sequence>
                <xs:element ref="student" minOccurs="1" maxOccurs="unbounded" />
            </xs:sequence>
        </xs:complexType>
    </xs:element>

    <xs:element name="student">
        <xs:complexType>
            <xs:sequence>
                <xs:element ref="lastName" />
                <xs:element ref="firstName" />
                <xs:element ref="examDate" />
                <xs:element ref="pretest" />
                <xs:element ref="score" minOccurs="0" maxOccurs="unbounded" />
            </xs:sequence>
            <xs:attribute ref="stuID" use="required" />
            <xs:attribute ref="courseID" use="required" />
        </xs:complexType>
    </xs:element>

    <xs:element name="lastName" type="xs:string" />
    <xs:element name="firstName" type="xs:string" />
    <xs:element name="examDate" type="xs:date" />
    <xs:element name="score" type="pretestType" />
    <xs:element name="pretest">
        <xs:complexType>
            <xs:simpleContent>
                <xs:extension base="pretestType">
                    <xs:attribute ref="level" use="required" />
                </xs:extension>
            </xs:simpleContent>
        </xs:complexType>
    </xs:element>

    <xs:simpleType name="pretestType">
        <xs:restriction base="xs:decimal">
            <xs:minExclusive value="0" />
            <xs:maxExclusive value="80" />
        </xs:restriction>
    </xs:simpleType>

    <xs:attribute name="stuID">
        <xs:simpleType>
            <xs:restriction base="xs:ID">
                <xs:pattern value="I\d{4}-\d{3}" />
            </xs:restriction>
        </xs:simpleType>
    </xs:attribute>

    <xs:attribute name="courseID">
        <xs:simpleType>
            <xs:restriction base="xs:string">
                <xs:pattern value="[A-Z]{4}-\d{3}-\d" />
            </xs:restriction>
        </xs:simpleType>
    </xs:attribute>

    <xs:attribute name="level">
        <xs:simpleType>
            <xs:restriction base="xs:string">
                <xs:enumeration value="L" />
                <xs:enumeration value="M" />
                <xs:enumeration value="H" />
            </xs:restriction>
        </xs:simpleType>
    </xs:attribute>

</xs:schema>
```

```xml
<xs:schema xmlns:xs="http://www.w3.org/2001/XMLSchema">

    <xs:element name="students">
        <xs:complexType>
            <xs:sequence>
                <xs:element name="student" minOccurs="1" maxOccurs="unbou
                    <xs:complexType>
                        <xs:sequence>
                            <xs:element name="lastName" type="xs:string" />
                            <xs:element name="firstName" type="xs:string" />
                            <xs:element name="examDate" type="xs:date" />
                            <xs:element name="pretest">
                                <xs:complexType>
                                    <xs:simpleContent>
                                        <xs:extension base="pretestType">
                                            <xs:attribute name="level" use="requ
                                                <xs:simpleType>
                                                    <xs:restriction base="xs:strin
                                                        <xs:enumeration value="L" /
                                                        <xs:enumeration value="M" /
                                                        <xs:enumeration value="H" /
                                                    </xs:restriction>
                                                </xs:simpleType>
                                            </xs:attribute>
                                        </xs:extension>
                                    </xs:simpleContent>
                                </xs:complexType>
                            </xs:element>
                            <xs:element name="score" type="pretestType" minO
                        </xs:sequence>
                        <xs:attribute name="stuID" use="required">
                            <xs:simpleType>
                                <xs:restriction base="xs:ID">
                                    <xs:pattern value="I\d{4}-\d{3}" />
                                </xs:restriction>
                            </xs:simpleType>
                        </xs:attribute>
                        <xs:attribute name="courseID" use="required">
                            <xs:simpleType>
                                <xs:restriction base="xs:string">
                                    <xs:pattern value="[A-Z]{4}-\d{3}-\d" />
                                </xs:restriction>
                            </xs:simpleType>
                        </xs:attribute>
                    </xs:complexType>
                </xs:element>
            </xs:sequence>
        </xs:complexType>
    </xs:element>
    <xs:simpleType name="pretestType">
        <xs:restriction base="xs:decimal">
            <xs:minExclusive value="0" />
            <xs:maxExclusive value="80" />
        </xs:restriction>
    </xs:simpleType>
</xs:schema>
```

An object with **global scope** is a direct child of the root schema element and can be referenced throughout the schema document. Each code block shaded purple in this Visual Overview has global scope.

Russian Doll designs have very few if any global scope declarations. This declaration is the only one other than the root element with global scope in this Russian Doll design schema.

Schema Design Comparisons

> An object with **local scope** can only be referenced within the object in which it is defined. This code block, shaded green, is the only code with local scope in these schema designs.

> A **Venetian Blind design** creates named types and references those types within a single global element.

```
">
maxOccurs="unbounded">

="xs:string" />
e="xs:string" />
="xs:date" />

testType">
level" use="required">

n base="xs:string">
tion value="L" />
tion value="M" />
tion value="H" />
on>

pretestType" minOccurs="0" maxOccurs="unbounded" />

uired">

-\d{3}" />

required">

ing">
}-\d{3}-\d />
```

```xml
<xsi:schema xmlns:xsi="http://www.w3.org/2001/XMLSchema">

    <xsi:element name="students">
        <xsi:complexType>
            <xsi:sequence>
                <xsi:element name="student" type="sType" minOccurs="1" maxOccurs="unbounded" />
            </xsi:sequence>
        </xsi:complexType>
    </xsi:element>

    <xsi:complexType name="sType">
        <xsi:group ref="childElements" />
        <xsi:attributeGroup ref="studentAtt" />
    </xsi:complexType>

    <xsi:group name="childElements">
        <xsi:sequence>
            <xsi:element name="lastName" type="xsi:string" />
            <xsi:element name="firstName" type="xsi:string" />
            <xsi:element name="examDate" type="xsi:date" />
            <xsi:element name="pretest" type="pretestComplex" />
            <xsi:element name="score" type="pretestType" minOccurs="0" maxOccurs="unbounded" />
        </xsi:sequence>
    </xsi:group>

    <xsi:attributeGroup name="studentAtt">
        <xsi:attribute name="stuID" type="idType" />
        <xsi:attribute name="courseID" type="courseType" />
    </xsi:attributeGroup>

    <xsi:complexType name="pretestComplex">
        <xsi:simpleContent>
            <xsi:extension base="pretestType">
                <xsi:attribute name="level" type="levelType" use="required" />
            </xsi:extension>
        </xsi:simpleContent>
    </xsi:complexType>

    <xsi:simpleType name="pretestType">
        <xsi:restriction base="xsi:decimal">
            <xsi:minExclusive value="0" />
            <xsi:maxExclusive value="80" />
        </xsi:restriction>
    </xsi:simpleType>

    <xsi:simpleType name="idType">
        <xsi:restriction base="xsi:ID">
            <xsi:pattern value="I\d{4}-\d{3}" />
        </xsi:restriction>
    </xsi:simpleType>

    <xsi:simpleType name="courseType">
        <xsi:restriction base="xsi:string">
            <xsi:pattern value="[A-Z]{4}-\d{3}-\d" />
        </xsi:restriction>
    </xsi:simpleType>

    <xsi:simpleType name="levelType">
        <xsi:restriction base="xsi:string">
            <xsi:enumeration value="L" />
            <xsi:enumeration value="M" />
            <xsi:enumeration value="H" />
        </xsi:restriction>
    </xsi:simpleType>

</xsi:schema>
```

> A Russian Doll design is often compact, but the multiple levels of nested elements can be confusing and can make it more difficult to debug; it also means the nested element and attribute declarations cannot be reused elsewhere in the schema because they are made locally.

> Globally defined complexTypes, simpleTypes, element groups, and attribute groups are used in a Venetian Blind design rather than globally defined elements and attributes. The only exception is the root element global definition.

Designing a Schema

You and Gabby meet to discuss the needs of Higher Ed Test Prep. She has provided you with students.xml, which is a file that contains a list of students enrolled in the PSAT Mathematics Course. She has also created three different versions of a schema for the students vocabulary and would like your help with choosing the most appropriate schema design for the needs of Higher Ed Test Prep.

There are many different ways to design a schema. The building blocks of any schema are the XML elements that define the structure; these are known collectively as objects. You can create objects such as named complex types and then reuse them through the schema file, or you can nest one complex type inside of another. The way you design the layout of your schema file can impact how that schema is interpreted and applied to the instance document.

One important issue in schema design is determining the scope of the different objects declared within the schema. XML Schema recognizes two types of scope—global and local. Objects with global scope are direct children of the root schema element and can be referenced throughout the schema document. One advantage of creating objects with global scope is that you can reuse code several times in the same schema file without having to rewrite it. Objects with local scope can be referenced only within the object in which they are defined. It can be an advantage to keep all definitions confined to a local scope rather than referencing them throughout a long document—especially in a large and sprawling schema file—to avoid having to keep track of a large set of global objects. This distinction between global and local scope leads to three basic schema designs—Flat Catalog, Russian Doll, and Venetian Blind.

Flat Catalog Design

In a Flat Catalog design—sometimes referred to as a Salami Slice design—all element and attribute definitions have global scope. Every element and attribute definition is a direct child of the root schema element and thus has been defined globally. The developer can then use references to the set of global objects to build the schema.

You'll open Gabby's students.xml file and the Flat Catalog version of the schema for the students vocabulary to explore what a schema that uses this design looks like.

To explore and apply the Flat Catalog version of the schema:

▶ 1. In your XML editor, open the **studentstxt.xml** and **studentsfctxt.xsd** files from the xml04 ▶ tutorial folder provided with your data files.

▶ 2. Within the comment section of each file, enter *your name* and *today's date*, and then save the files as **students.xml** and **studentsfc.xsd**, respectively. The studentsfc.xsd file is a Flat Catalog version of the schema for the students vocabulary.

▶ 3. Review the contents of the studentsfc.xsd document. As shown in Figure 4-1, all elements and attributes have global scope because they are all direct children of the root schema element.

Figure 4-1	Schema for students vocabulary using Flat Catalog design

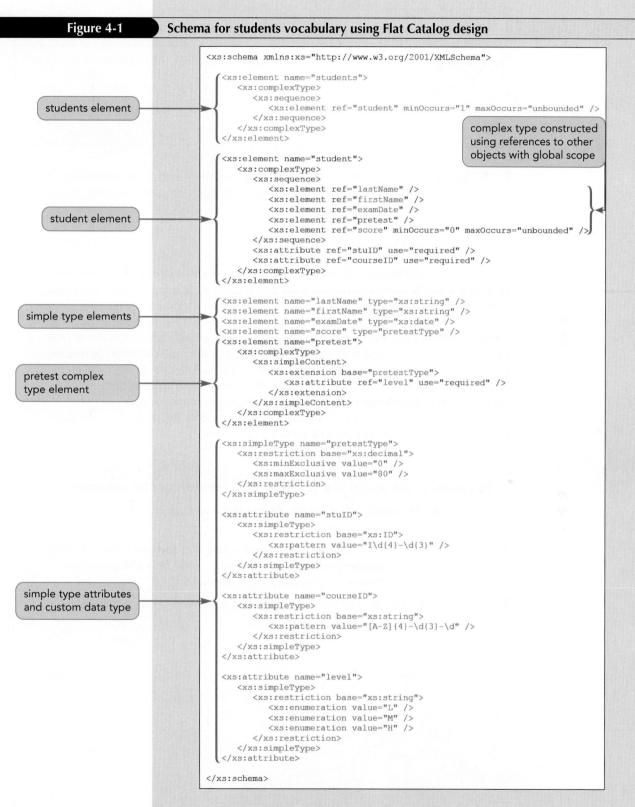

students element

student element

simple type elements

pretest complex type element

simple type attributes and custom data type

complex type constructed using references to other objects with global scope

```xml
<xs:schema xmlns:xs="http://www.w3.org/2001/XMLSchema">

<xs:element name="students">
    <xs:complexType>
        <xs:sequence>
            <xs:element ref="student" minOccurs="1" maxOccurs="unbounded" />
        </xs:sequence>
    </xs:complexType>
</xs:element>

<xs:element name="student">
    <xs:complexType>
        <xs:sequence>
            <xs:element ref="lastName" />
            <xs:element ref="firstName" />
            <xs:element ref="examDate" />
            <xs:element ref="pretest" />
            <xs:element ref="score" minOccurs="0" maxOccurs="unbounded" />
        </xs:sequence>
        <xs:attribute ref="stuID" use="required" />
        <xs:attribute ref="courseID" use="required" />
    </xs:complexType>
</xs:element>

<xs:element name="lastName" type="xs:string" />
<xs:element name="firstName" type="xs:string" />
<xs:element name="examDate" type="xs:date" />
<xs:element name="score" type="pretestType" />
<xs:element name="pretest">
    <xs:complexType>
        <xs:simpleContent>
            <xs:extension base="pretestType">
                <xs:attribute ref="level" use="required" />
            </xs:extension>
        </xs:simpleContent>
    </xs:complexType>
</xs:element>

<xs:simpleType name="pretestType">
    <xs:restriction base="xs:decimal">
        <xs:minExclusive value="0" />
        <xs:maxExclusive value="80" />
    </xs:restriction>
</xs:simpleType>

<xs:attribute name="stuID">
    <xs:simpleType>
        <xs:restriction base="xs:ID">
            <xs:pattern value="I\d{4}-\d{3}" />
        </xs:restriction>
    </xs:simpleType>
</xs:attribute>

<xs:attribute name="courseID">
    <xs:simpleType>
        <xs:restriction base="xs:string">
            <xs:pattern value="[A-Z]{4}-\d{3}-\d" />
        </xs:restriction>
    </xs:simpleType>
</xs:attribute>

<xs:attribute name="level">
    <xs:simpleType>
        <xs:restriction base="xs:string">
            <xs:enumeration value="L" />
            <xs:enumeration value="M" />
            <xs:enumeration value="H" />
        </xs:restriction>
    </xs:simpleType>
</xs:attribute>

</xs:schema>
```

4. In the **students.xml** document, within the opening <students> tag, add the attribute **xsi:noNamespaceSchemaLocation="studentsfc.xsd"** on its own line, as shown in Figure 4-2. This attribute links the students.xml instance document to the studentsfc.xsd schema file.

| Figure 4-2 | The students.xml document modified to use studentsfc.xsd schema |

```
<students xmlns:xsi="http://www.w3.org/2001/XMLSchema-instance"
          xsi:noNamespaceSchemaLocation="studentsfc.xsd">
    <student stuID="I8900-041" courseID="PSAT-080-5">
```

name of the Flat Catalog schema document

5. Save your changes to the **students.xml** document and then validate it. The document validates successfully against the studentsfc.xsd schema.

Russian Doll Design

A Russian Doll design has only one global element with everything else nested inside of it, much like Russian Matryoshka dolls nest one inside another. Russian Doll designs mimic the nesting structure of the elements in an instance document. The root element of the instance document becomes the top element declaration in the schema. All child elements within the root element are similarly nested in the schema. A Russian Doll design is much more compact than a Flat Catalog, but the multiple levels of nested elements can be confusing and can make it more difficult to debug. Also, the element and attribute declarations cannot be reused elsewhere in the schema because aside from the single root element, all object declarations are made locally.

You'll explore the Russian Doll version of the schema for the students vocabulary now and apply it to the students.xml instance document.

To explore and apply the Russian Doll version of the schema:

1. In your XML editor, open the **studentsrdtxt.xsd** file from the xml04 ▸ tutorial folder provided with your data files.

2. Within the comment section, enter **your name** and **today's date**, and then save the file as **studentsrd.xsd**. The studentsrd.xsd file is a Russian Doll version of the schema for the students vocabulary.

3. Review the contents of the studentsrd.xsd document, as shown in Figure 4-3.

| Figure 4-3 | Schema for students vocabulary using Russian Doll design |

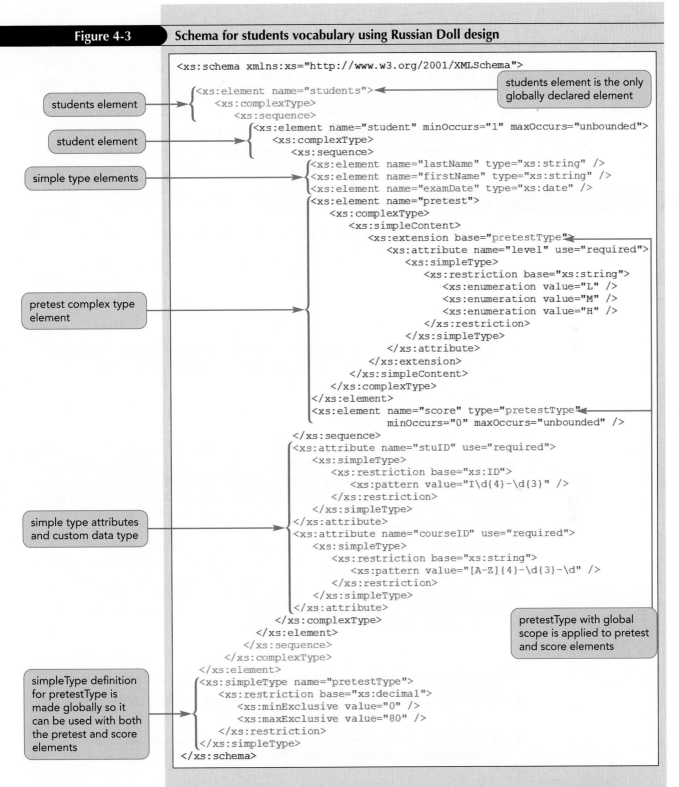

students element is the only globally declared element

students element

student element

simple type elements

pretest complex type element

simple type attributes and custom data type

pretestType with global scope is applied to pretest and score elements

simpleType definition for pretestType is made globally so it can be used with both the pretest and score elements

```
<xs:schema xmlns:xs="http://www.w3.org/2001/XMLSchema">
  <xs:element name="students">
    <xs:complexType>
      <xs:sequence>
        <xs:element name="student" minOccurs="1" maxOccurs="unbounded">
          <xs:complexType>
            <xs:sequence>
              <xs:element name="lastName" type="xs:string" />
              <xs:element name="firstName" type="xs:string" />
              <xs:element name="examDate" type="xs:date" />
              <xs:element name="pretest">
                <xs:complexType>
                  <xs:simpleContent>
                    <xs:extension base="pretestType">
                      <xs:attribute name="level" use="required">
                        <xs:simpleType>
                          <xs:restriction base="xs:string">
                            <xs:enumeration value="L" />
                            <xs:enumeration value="M" />
                            <xs:enumeration value="H" />
                          </xs:restriction>
                        </xs:simpleType>
                      </xs:attribute>
                    </xs:extension>
                  </xs:simpleContent>
                </xs:complexType>
              </xs:element>
              <xs:element name="score" type="pretestType"
                          minOccurs="0" maxOccurs="unbounded" />
            </xs:sequence>
            <xs:attribute name="stuID" use="required">
              <xs:simpleType>
                <xs:restriction base="xs:ID">
                  <xs:pattern value="I\d{4}-\d{3}" />
                </xs:restriction>
              </xs:simpleType>
            </xs:attribute>
            <xs:attribute name="courseID" use="required">
              <xs:simpleType>
                <xs:restriction base="xs:string">
                  <xs:pattern value="[A-Z]{4}-\d{3}-\d" />
                </xs:restriction>
              </xs:simpleType>
            </xs:attribute>
          </xs:complexType>
        </xs:element>
      </xs:sequence>
    </xs:complexType>
  </xs:element>
  <xs:simpleType name="pretestType">
    <xs:restriction base="xs:decimal">
      <xs:minExclusive value="0" />
      <xs:maxExclusive value="80" />
    </xs:restriction>
  </xs:simpleType>
</xs:schema>
```

As Figure 4-3 shows, the only element declaration with global scope is for the students element; all other elements and attributes are declared locally, nested inside of the students element. Also notice that the definition for the pretestType simple type is global because it is defined outside the nested part of the design. This allows the `pretestType` type to be reused in both the `pretest` and `score` elements. Because you can't set both a restriction and an extension to the same element definition, the only way to define the minimum and maximum values for the `pretest` element is by using a globally defined `simpleType` element. This is one area where strictly adhering to the Russian Doll design can be impractical.

▶ **4.** Return to the **students.xml** document, and then change the `xsi:noNamespaceSchemaLocation` value from studentsfc.xsd to **studentsrd.xsd** as shown in Figure 4-4.

Figure 4-4 ▶ **The students.xml document modified to use the studentsrd.xsd schema**

```
<students xmlns:xsi="http://www.w3.org/2001/XMLSchema-instance"
        xsi:noNamespaceSchemaLocation="studentsrd.xsd">
    <student stuID="I8900-041" courseID="PSAT-080-5">
```

name of the Russian Doll schema document

▶ **5.** Save your changes to the **students.xml** document and then validate it. The document validates successfully against the studentsrd.xsd schema.

Venetian Blind Design

A Venetian Blind design is similar to a Flat Catalog except that instead of declaring objects globally, it creates named types, named element groups, and named attribute groups and references those types within a single global element. A Venetian Blind design represents a compromise between Flat Catalogs and Russian Dolls. Although the various element and attribute groups and named types are declared globally (and can be reused throughout the schema), the declarations for the elements and attributes for the instance document are local and nested within element and attribute groups. The XML Schema `group` element is used to assign a name to a list of references to elements or attributes, and then the named group is referenced elsewhere using the `ref` attribute. Only the root element from the instance document—in this case, the `students` element—is defined globally.

You'll explore the Venetian Blind version of the schema for the students vocabulary now and apply it to the students.xml instance document.

To explore and apply the Venetian Blind version of the schema:

▶ **1.** In your XML editor, open the **studentsvbtxt.xsd** file from the xml04 ▶ tutorial folder provided with your data files.

▶ **2.** Within the comment section, enter *your name* and *today's date*, and then save the file as **studentsvb.xsd**. The studentsvb.xsd file is a Venetian Blind version of the schema for the students vocabulary.

▶ **3.** Review the contents of the studentsvb.xsd document, noting the use of named types, element groups, and attribute groups, as shown in Figure 4-5.

| Figure 4-5 | Schema for students vocabulary using Venetian Blind design |

students element
is the only globally
declared element

sType complex type

childElements group

studentAtt group

pretestComplex
complex type

pretestType custom
type definition

idType, courseType,
and levelType simple
types

student complex type is based
on the sType named type

sType named type references
the childElements element
group and the studentAtt
attribute group

```xml
<xsi:schema xmlns:xsi="http://www.w3.org/2001/XMLSchema">

  <xsi:element name="students">
    <xsi:complexType>
      <xsi:sequence>
        <xsi:element name="student" type="sType" minOccurs="1" maxOccurs="unbounded" />
      </xsi:sequence>
    </xsi:complexType>
  </xsi:element>

  <xsi:complexType name="sType">
    <xsi:group ref="childElements" />
    <xsi:attributeGroup ref="studentAtt" />
  </xsi:complexType>

  <xsi:group name="childElements">
    <xsi:sequence>
      <xsi:element name="lastName" type="xsi:string" />
      <xsi:element name="firstName" type="xsi:string" />
      <xsi:element name="examDate" type="xsi:date" />
      <xsi:element name="pretest" type="pretestComplex" />
      <xsi:element name="score" type="pretestType" minOccurs="0" maxOccurs="unbounded" />
    </xsi:sequence>
  </xsi:group>

  <xsi:attributeGroup name="studentAtt">
    <xsi:attribute name="stuID" type="idType" />
    <xsi:attribute name="courseID" type="courseType" />
  </xsi:attributeGroup>

  <xsi:complexType name="pretestComplex">
    <xsi:simpleContent>
      <xsi:extension base="pretestType">
        <xsi:attribute name="level" type="levelType" use="required" />
      </xsi:extension>
    </xsi:simpleContent>
  </xsi:complexType>

  <xsi:simpleType name="pretestType">
    <xsi:restriction base="xsi:decimal">
      <xsi:minExclusive value="0" />
      <xsi:maxExclusive value="80" />
    </xsi:restriction>
  </xsi:simpleType>

  <xsi:simpleType name="idType">
    <xsi:restriction base="xsi:ID">
      <xsi:pattern value="I\d{4}-\d{3}" />
    </xsi:restriction>
  </xsi:simpleType>

  <xsi:simpleType name="courseType">
    <xsi:restriction base="xsi:string">
      <xsi:pattern value="[A-Z]{4}-\d{3}-\d" />
    </xsi:restriction>
  </xsi:simpleType>

  <xsi:simpleType name="levelType">
    <xsi:restriction base="xsi:string">
      <xsi:enumeration value="L" />
      <xsi:enumeration value="M" />
      <xsi:enumeration value="H" />
    </xsi:restriction>
  </xsi:simpleType>

</xsi:schema>
```

In this layout, the only globally declared element is the students element. All other elements and attributes are placed within element or attribute groups or, in the case of the pretest element's level attribute, within a named complex type.

4. Return to the **students.xml** document, and then change the xsi:noNamespaceSchemaLocation value from studentsrd.xsd to **studentsvb.xsd** as shown in Figure 4-6.

| Figure 4-6 | The students.xml document modified to use the studentsvb.xsd schema |

```
<students xmlns:xsi="http://www.w3.org/2001/XMLSchema-instance"
          xsi:noNamespaceSchemaLocation="studentsvb.xsd">
   <student stuID="I8900-041" courseID="PSAT-080-5">
```

name of the Venetian
Blind schema document

5. Save your changes to the **students.xml** document and then validate it. The document validates successfully against the studentsvb.xsd schema.

PROSKILLS

Decision Making: Deciding Which Schema Design to Use

Which schema layout you use depends on several factors. If a schema contains several lines of code that need to be repeated, you probably should use a Flat Catalog or Venetian Blind design. If you are interested in a compact schema that mirrors the structure of the instance document, you should use a Russian Doll design.

Figure 4-7 summarizes some of the differences among the three schema designs.

| Figure 4-7 | Comparison of schema designs |

Feature	Flat Catalog (Salami Slice)	Russian Doll	Venetian Blind
Global and local declarations	All declarations are global.	The schema contains one single global element; all other declarations are local.	The schema contains one single global element; all other declarations are local.
Nesting of elements	Element declarations are not nested.	Element declarations are nested within a single global element.	Element declarations are nested within a single global element referencing named complex types, element groups, and attribute groups.
Reusability	Element declarations can be reused throughout the schema.	Element declarations can only be used once.	Named complex types, element groups, and attribute groups can be reused throughout the schema.
Interaction with namespaces	If a namespace is attached to the schema, all elements need to be qualified in the instance document.	If a namespace is attached to the schema, only the root element needs to be qualified in the instance document.	If a namespace is attached to the schema, only the root element needs to be qualified in the instance document.

Rather than using the original Flat Catalog design for the schema file, Gabby wants you to continue to work with the Venetian Blind design. She likes the fact that the Venetian Blind layout maintains the flexibility of a Flat Catalog while providing a structure similar to the contents of her instance document. She has also heard that using a Venetian Blind design will make it easier to apply a namespace to the schema and instance document, which you'll explore in the next session.

INSIGHT

The Garden of Eden Schema Design

In addition to the Flat Catalog, Russian Doll, and Venetian Blind layouts, other standardized schema designs exist. One of these, known as the Garden of Eden design, combines the Flat Catalog approach of declaring all elements globally with the Venetian Blind practice of declaring type definitions globally. Although this results in a schema in which all parts are easily reusable, its main trade-off is that it requires more code than either of the designs on which it is based.

REVIEW

Session 4.1 Quick Check

1. List and define the two types of scope for objects in a schema.
2. Name one advantage of each type of scope.
3. What is a Flat Catalog design and how does it differ from a Russian Doll design?
4. What is another name for the Flat Catalog design?
5. What is a Venetian Blind design, and how does it differ from the Flat Catalog and Russian Doll designs?

Session 4.2 Visual Overview:

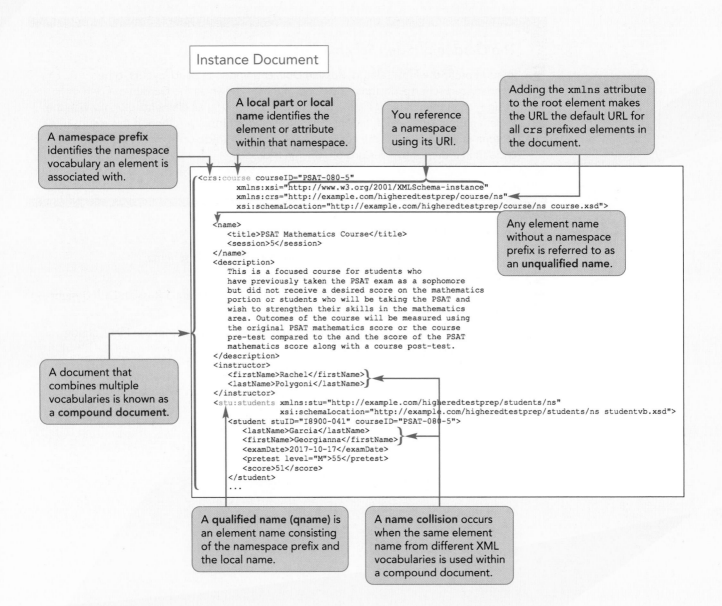

Instance Document

A **namespace prefix** identifies the namespace vocabulary an element is associated with.

A **local part** or **local name** identifies the element or attribute within that namespace.

You reference a namespace using its URI.

Adding the `xmlns` attribute to the root element makes the URL the default URL for all `crs` prefixed elements in the document.

```
<crs:course courseID="PSAT-080-5"
       xmlns:xsi="http://www.w3.org/2001/XMLSchema-instance"
       xmlns:crs="http://example.com/higheredtestprep/course/ns"
       xsi:schemaLocation="http://example.com/higheredtestprep/course/ns course.xsd">
  <name>
      <title>PSAT Mathematics Course</title>
      <session>5</session>
  </name>
  <description>
      This is a focused course for students who
      have previously taken the PSAT exam as a sophomore
      but did not receive a desired score on the mathematics
      portion or students who will be taking the PSAT and
      wish to strengthen their skills in the mathematics
      area. Outcomes of the course will be measured using
      the original PSAT mathematics score or the course
      pre-test compared to the and the score of the PSAT
      mathematics score along with a course post-test.
  </description>
  <instructor>
      <firstName>Rachel</firstName>
      <lastName>Polygoni</lastName>
  </instructor>
  <stu:students xmlns:stu="http://example.com/higheredtestprep/students/ns"
                xsi:schemaLocation="http://example.com/higheredtestprep/students/ns studentvb.xsd">
      <student stuID="I8900-041" courseID="PSAT-080-5">
          <lastName>Garcia</lastName>
          <firstName>Georgianna</firstName>
          <examDate>2017-10-17</examDate>
          <pretest level="M">55</pretest>
          <score>51</score>
      </student>
  ...
```

Any element name without a namespace prefix is referred to as an **unqualified name.**

A document that combines multiple vocabularies is known as a **compound document.**

A **qualified name (qname)** is an element name consisting of the namespace prefix and the local name.

A **name collision** occurs when the same element name from different XML vocabularies is used within a compound document.

A Compound Document

> The **import** element combines schemas when the schemas come from different namespaces.

Main Schema Document

```
<xs:schema xmlns:xs="http://www.w3.org/2001/XMLSchema"
           xmlns="http://example.com/higheredtestprep/course/ns"
           targetNamespace="http://example.com/higheredtestprep/course/ns"
           xmlns:stu="http://example.com/higheredtestprep/students/ns">

    <xs:import namespace="http://example.com/higheredtestprep/students/ns"
               schemaLocation="studentsvb.xsd" />
    <xs:element name="course">
        <xs:complexType>
            <xs:sequence>
                <xs:element name="name">
                    <xs:complexType>
                        <xs:sequence>
                            <xs:element name="title" type="xs:string" />
                            <xs:element name="session" type="xs:string" />
                        </xs:sequence>
                    </xs:complexType>
                </xs:element>
                <xs:element name="description" type="xs:string" />
                <xs:element name="instructor">
                    <xs:complexType>
                        <xs:sequence>
                            <xs:element name="firstName" type="xs:string" />
                            <xs:element name="lastName" type="xs:string" />
                        </xs:sequence>
                    </xs:complexType>
                </xs:element>
                <xs:element ref="stu:students" />
            </xs:sequence>
            <xs:attribute name="courseID" type="xs:ID" />
        </xs:complexType>
    </xs:element>

</xs:schema>
```

> The **ref** attribute is used to reference an object from an imported schema.

Imported Schema Document

```
<xsi:schema xmlns:xsi="http://www.w3.org/2001/XMLSchema"
            xmlns="http://example.com/higheredtestprep/students/ns"
            targetNamespace="http://example.com/higheredtestprep/students/ns">

    <xsi:element name="students">
        <xsi:complexType>
            <xsi:sequence>
                <xsi:element name="student" type="sType" minOccurs="1" maxOccurs="unbounded" />
            </xsi:sequence>
        </xsi:complexType>
    </xsi:element>

    <xsi:complexType name="sType">
        <xsi:group ref="childElements" />
        <xsi:attributeGroup ref="studentAtt" />
    </xsi:complexType>

    <xsi:group name="childElements">
        <xsi:sequence>
            <xsi:element name="lastName" type="xsi:string" />
            <xsi:element name="firstName" type="xsi:string" />
            <xsi:element name="examDate" type="xsi:date" />
            <xsi:element name="pretest" type="pretestComplex" />
            <xsi:element name="score" type="pretestType" minOccurs="0" maxOccurs="unbounded" />
        </xsi:sequence>
    </xsi:group>

    ...
```

Combining XML Vocabularies

Gabby has been working on a second XML vocabulary—one that documents the features of the different exam courses run by Higher Ed Test Prep. The structure of the course vocabulary is shown in Figure 4-8.

Figure 4-8 | **Structure of the course vocabulary**

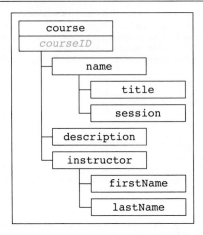

So far, the course vocabulary contains only basic information about each exam course: It records the course ID, name, title, session, and description of the course, and the first and last names of the course's instructor. As Gabby develops additional XML documents using this vocabulary, she will add more elements and attributes to it. Gabby already has created a schema file and an instance document based on this vocabulary. You will open both of those now.

To view the schema file and instance document for the course vocabulary:

1. Use your XML editor to open the **coursetxt.xsd** file from the xml04 ▸ tutorial folder, enter *your name* and *today's date* in the comment section, and then save the file as **course.xsd**.

2. Review the contents and structure of the course schema shown in Figure 4-9. This schema uses a Russian Doll design, with course being the only element declared globally in the file.

| Figure 4-9 | Schema for the course vocabulary |

```
<xs:schema xmlns:xs="http://www.w3.org/2001/XMLSchema">
   <xs:element name="course">
      <xs:complexType>
         <xs:sequence>
            <xs:element name="name">
               <xs:complexType>
                  <xs:sequence>
                     <xs:element name="title" type="xs:string" />
                     <xs:element name="session" type="xs:string" />
                  </xs:sequence>
               </xs:complexType>
            </xs:element>
            <xs:element name="description" type="xs:string" />
            <xs:element name="instructor">
               <xs:complexType>
                  <xs:sequence>
                     <xs:element name="firstName" type="xs:string" />
                     <xs:element name="lastName" type="xs:string" />
                  </xs:sequence>
               </xs:complexType>
            </xs:element>
         </xs:sequence>
         <xs:attribute name="courseID" type="xs:ID" />
      </xs:complexType>
   </xs:element>
</xs:schema>
```

course is the only element with global scope

Russian Doll design

3. Use your XML editor to open the **psattxt.xml** file from the xml04 ▸ tutorial folder, enter *your name* and *today's date* in the comment section, and then save the file as **psat.xml**. The psat.xml file contains basic information on a course that helps students improve their PSAT mathematics scores.

Gabby wants to combine the information about the PSAT Mathematics Course and the list of students enrolled in that course in a single compound document. A **compound document** is a document that combines elements from multiple vocabularies. Figure 4-10 shows a schematic diagram of the document Gabby wants to create, involving elements and attributes from both the course and students vocabularies.

Figure 4-10   **Structure of the compound document**

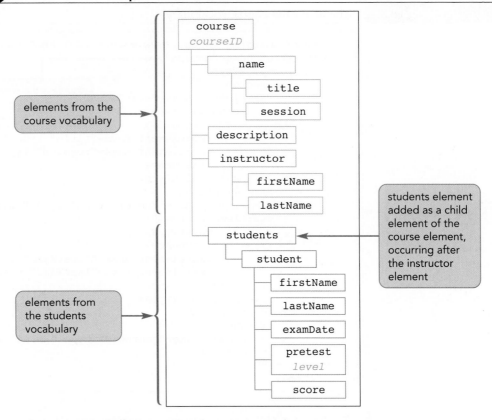

Creating a Compound Document

Gabby wants you to work with her XML files to create a sample compound document that she can use as a model for future projects. You'll start by combining the elements from the students and course vocabularies, storing the result in a new file named psatstudents.xml. You'll create this compound document now.

To create the psatstudents.xml compound document:

1. If necessary, return to the **psat.xml** file in your XML editor, and then save a copy of the file with the name **psatstudents.xml**.

2. In the comment section, change the filename to **psatstudents.xml**; in the supporting files list, add the filenames **course.css**, **students.css**, and **studentsvb.xsd**; and then save your changes.

Be sure to scroll down and copy all the student information in the students.xml file including the closing </students> tag, rather than stopping at one of the </student> tags.

3. Return to the **students.xml** file, and then copy the contents of the opening <students> tag through the closing </students> tag to the Clipboard.

4. Return to the **psatstudents.xml** file in your XML editor, and then insert the copied students.xml contents below the closing </instructor> tag.

5. In the opening `<students>` tag, delete both attributes and their values. The `xmlns` attribute declares the XML Schema instance namespace; however, it's unnecessary because the namespace is already declared in the `course` element, which encloses all the contents of this document. In addition, because you'll be using namespaces in this compound document, the `noNamespaceSchemaLocation` is no longer relevant. Figure 4-11 shows the compound document containing elements from both the course and students vocabularies.

Figure 4-11	Compound document showing information on first and last students

XML schema instance namespace attribute

duplicate attributes are deleted from the opening students tag

students element and contents copied from the students.xml document

```
<course courseID="PSAT-080-5"
        xmlns:xsi="http://www.w3.org/2001/XMLSchema-instance"
        xsi:noNamespaceSchemaLocation="course.xsd">

   <name>
      <title>PSAT Mathematics Course</title>
      <session>5</session>
   </name>
   <description>
      This is a focused course for students who
      have previously taken the PSAT exam as a sophomore
      but did not receive a desired score on the mathematics
      portion or students who will be taking the PSAT and
      wish to strengthen their skills in the mathematics
      area. Outcomes of the course will be measured using
      the original PSAT mathematics score or the course
      pre-test compared to the and the score of the PSAT
      mathematics score along with a course post-test.
   </description>
   <instructor>
      <firstName>Rachel</firstName>
      <lastName>Polygoni</lastName>
   </instructor>
<students>
   <student stuID="I8900-041" courseID="PSAT-080-5">
      <lastName>Garcia</lastName>
      <firstName>Georgianna</firstName>
      <examDate>2017-10-17</examDate>
      <pretest level="M">55</pretest>
      <score>51</score>
   </student>

   <student stuID="I8154-741" courseID="PSAT-080-5">
      <lastName>Browne</lastName>
      <firstName>Brenda</firstName>
      <examDate>2017-10-22</examDate>
      <pretest level="L">30</pretest>
   </student>

</students>
</course>
```

6. Save your changes to the **psatstudents.xml** file.

Notice that after combining the two vocabularies, some elements have the same names: Both the `instructor` and `student` elements contain child elements named `lastName` and `firstName`, as illustrated in Figure 4-12. Gabby would like you to investigate whether this is a problem.

| **Figure 4-12** | **Name collision in a compound document** |

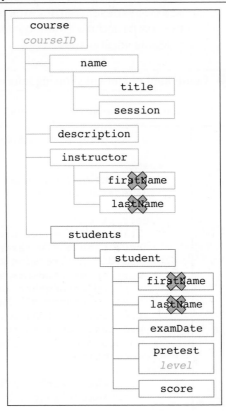

Understanding Name Collision

The duplication of these element names is an example of name collision, which occurs when the same element name from different XML vocabularies is used within a compound document. Higher Ed Test Prep could have been more careful in choosing element names to prevent name collisions among different vocabularies. However, name collisions are often unavoidable. After all, one benefit of XML vocabularies is the ability to use simple element names to describe data. Creating complex element names to avoid name collisions eliminates this benefit. Moreover, there are other XML vocabularies such as XHTML over which Gabby has no control. XHTML element names such as `title` and `address` are certain to be found in thousands of XML vocabularies.

Gabby could also avoid combining elements from different vocabularies in the same document to prevent name collisions; however, this would make XML a poor information tool. Instead, Gabby can use namespaces to distinguish elements in one vocabulary from elements in another vocabulary.

Working with Namespaces in an Instance Document

A namespace is a defined collection of element and attribute names. For example, the collection of element and attribute names from Gabby's courses vocabulary could make up a single namespace. Likewise, the element and attribute names from the students vocabulary could constitute a different namespace. Applying a namespace to an XML document involves two steps:

1. Declare the namespace.
2. Identify the elements and attributes within the document that belong to that namespace.

First, you will review how to declare a namespace.

Declaring and Applying a Namespace to a Document

To declare and apply a namespace to a document, you add the attributes

```
xmlns="uri"
xsi:schemaLocation="uri schema"
```

to an element in the document, where *uri* is the URI of the namespace and *schema* is the location and name of the schema file. For example, the following code declares a namespace with the URI http://example.com/higheredtestprep/course/ns within the course element and applies the schema file course.xsd to the document:

```
<course courseID="PSAT-080-5"
        xmlns="http://example.com/higheredtestprep/course/ns"
        xsi:schemaLocation="http://example.com/higheredtestprep/
        course/ns course.xsd">
...
</course>
```

The number of namespace attributes that can be declared within an element is unlimited.

REFERENCE

Declaring and Applying a Namespace in an Instance Document

- To declare a namespace, add the attribute

  `xmlns:prefix="uri"`

  to an element in the document, where *prefix* is the namespace prefix and *uri* is the URI of the namespace.
- To apply a schema file to a namespace you've declared, add the attribute

  `xsi:schemaLocation="uri schema"`

  where *schema* is the location and name of the schema file.
- To apply a namespace to an element, add the namespace prefix

  `<prefix:element> ... </prefix:element>`

  to the element's opening and closing tags, where *prefix* is the namespace prefix and *element* is the local part of the qualified element name. If no prefix is specified, the element is assumed to be part of the default namespace.
- To apply a namespace to an attribute, add the namespace prefix

  `<element prefix:attribute="value"> ... </element>`

  to the attribute name, where *attribute* is the attribute name. By default, an attribute is part of the namespace of its containing element.

Gabby wants you to create namespaces for the course and students vocabularies. You will declare each namespace in the root element of the content to which it applies; for the course vocabulary, this is the `course` element, and for the students vocabulary, this is the `students` element. The URIs for the two namespaces will be

http://example.com/higheredtestprep/course/ns
http://example.com/higheredtestprep/students/ns

These URIs do not point to actual sites on the web, but they do provide unique URIs for the two namespaces.

To declare the course and students namespaces:

1. If necessary, return to the **psatstudents.xml** file in your XML editor.

2. Within the opening `<course>` tag, delete the code `xsi:noNamespaceSchemaLocation="course.xsd"`, and then add the following code to declare the course namespace and specify the location of the schema file:

   ```
   xmlns="http://example.com/higheredtestprep/course/ns"
   xsi:schemaLocation="http://example.com/higheredtestprep/course/
   ns course.xsd"
   ```

3. Within the opening `<students>` tag, add the following code to declare the students namespace and specify the schema location:

   ```
   xmlns="http://example.com/higheredtestprep/students/ns"
   xsi:schemaLocation="http://example.com/higheredtestprep/
   students/ns studentsvb.xsd"
   ```

   Compare your namespace declarations to those in Figure 4-13.

Figure 4-13	Declaring namespaces within a compound document

```
<course courseID="PSAT-080-5"
        xmlns:xsi="http://www.w3.org/2001/XMLSchema-instance"
        xmlns="http://example.com/higheredtestprep/course/ns"
        xsi:schemaLocation="http://example.com/higheredtestprep/course/ns course.xsd">

    <name>
        <title>PSAT Mathematics Course</title>
        <session>5</session>
    </name>
    <description>
        This is a focused course for students who
        have previously taken the PSAT exam as a sophomore
        but did not receive a desired score on the mathematics
        portion or students who will be taking the PSAT and
        wish to strengthen their skills in the mathematics
        area. Outcomes of the course will be measured using
        the original PSAT mathematics score compared to a
        course post-test, or a course pre-test compared to the
        subsequent PSAT mathematics score.
    </description>
    <instructor>
        <firstName>Rachel</firstName>
        <lastName>Polygoni</lastName>
    </instructor>
    <students xmlns="http://example.com/higheredtestprep/students/ns"
              xsi:schemaLocation="http://example.com/higheredtestprep/students/ns studentsvb.xsd">
        <student stuID="I8900-041" courseID="PSAT-080-5">
```

course namespace declaration

location of schema file for the course vocabulary

students namespace declaration

location of schema file for the students vocabulary

4. Save the changes to **psatstudents.xml**.

Applying a Namespace to an Element

In an instance document containing elements from more than one namespace, after you declare the namespaces, you must indicate which elements in the document belong to each namespace. This process involves two steps:

1. Associate the namespace declaration with a prefix.
2. Add the prefix to the tags for each element in the namespace.

To apply an XML namespace to an element, you qualify the element's name. A qualified name, or qname, is an element name consisting of two parts—the namespace prefix that identifies the namespace, and the local part or local name that identifies the element or attribute within that namespace. The general form for applying a qualified name to a two-sided tag is

```
<prefix:element> ... </prefix:element>
```

where *prefix* is the namespace prefix and *element* is the local part. An element name without such a prefix is referred to as an unqualified name. You worked with qualified names previously when specifying elements from the XML Schema vocabulary in a schema file, using the `xs:` or `xsi:` prefix.

Namespaces have a scope associated with them. The scope of a namespace declaration declaring a prefix extends from the beginning of the opening tag to the end of the corresponding closing tag. The namespace declared in a parent element is connected with—or bound to—the defined prefix for that element as well as for all of its child elements. This is true unless the given prefix in the parent is overridden in a child element that has been assigned a different namespace. Some XML authors add all namespace declarations to the document's root element so that the namespace is available to all elements within the document. The association between the namespace and the prefix declared in an element does not apply to the siblings of that element.

A single namespace prefix can be declared as an attribute of an element, as shown in this example:

```
<crs:course courseID="PSAT-080-5"
    xmlns:crs="http://example.com/higheredtestprep/course/ns">
  <name>
     <title>PSAT Mathematics Course</title>
     <session>5</crs:session>
  </name>
  ...
</crs:course>
...
```

The opening `<course>` tag includes both the namespace prefix and the `xmlns` attribute to declare the namespace. This indicates that the course element itself is part of the namespace that it declares.

INSIGHT

Qualified and Unqualified Names

The use of qnames in elements and attributes is controversial because it creates a dependency between the content of the document and its markup. However, in its official position, the W3C doesn't discourage this practice. The syntax for default namespaces was designed for convenience, but they tend to cause more confusion than they're worth. The confusion typically stems from the fact that elements and attributes are treated differently, and it's not immediately apparent that nested elements are being assigned the default namespace identifier. Nevertheless, in the end, choosing between prefixes and default namespaces is mostly a matter of style except when attributes come into play.

In XML Schema, any element or attribute with global scope must be entered as a qualified name (i.e., with a namespace prefix). The reason is that elements and attributes with global scope are attached to the schema's target namespace, while elements and attributes declared locally are not. In the instance document, this is reflected by qualifying those global elements or attributes.

This fact may affect your choice of schema designs. In a Flat Catalog, all elements and attributes are declared globally, so each element and attribute must be qualified in the instance document. Because Venetian Blind and Russian Doll designs have a single global element, only the root element must be qualified in the instance document.

In the psatstudents.xml document, you'll use the `crs` prefix for elements from the course namespace and the `stu` prefix for elements from the students namespace. You will apply each namespace to the parent element that belongs to that namespace. There is no need to assign attributes to namespaces, so you will not add prefixes to attributes in the psatstudents.xml file.

To apply the courses and students namespaces:

1. Verify that the **psatstudents.xml** file is the active file in your XML editor.

2. In the opening `<course>` tag, add the prefix **:crs** to the `xmlns` attribute that declares the course namespace so the attribute reads as follows:

   `xmlns:crs="http://example.com/higheredtestprep/course/ns"`

   This associates the `crs` prefix with the course namespace.

3. In the opening `<students>` tag, add the prefix :**stu** to the `xmlns` attribute that declares the students namespace so the attribute reads as follows:

   `xmlns:stu="http://example.com/higheredtestprep/students/ns"`

   This associates the `stu` prefix with the students namespace.

> Add the crs: prefix to the closing tag as well as to the opening tag.

4. In the opening `<course>` tag, insert the **crs:** prefix just before the word `course`, and then repeat for the closing `<course>` tag.

   Adding the `crs` prefix to the opening and closing `<course>` tags specifies that the `course` element is part of the course namespace.

5. In the opening `<students>` tag, insert the **stu:** prefix just before the word `students`, and then repeat for the closing `</students>` tag. Figure 4-14 shows the updated code.

Figure 4-14 | **Declaring namespaces within a compound document**

```
<crs:course courseID="PSAT-080-5"
        xmlns:xsi="http://www.w3.org/2001/XMLSchema-instance"
        xmlns:crs="http://example.com/higheredtestprep/course/ns"
        xsi:schemaLocation="http://example.com/higheredtestprep/course/ns course.xsd">

    <name>
        <title>PSAT Mathematics Course</title>
        <session>5</session>
    </name>
    <description>
        This is a focused course for students who
        have previously taken the PSAT exam as a sophomore
        but did not receive a desired score on the mathematics
        portion or students who will be taking the PSAT and
        wish to strengthen their skills in the mathematics
        area. Outcomes of the course will be measured using
        the original PSAT mathematics score or the course
        pre-test compared to the and the score of the PSAT
        mathematics score along with a course post-test.
    </description>
    <instructor>
        <firstName>Rachel</firstName>
        <lastName>Polygoni</lastName>
    </instructor>
<stu:students xmlns:stu="http://example.com/higheredtestprep/students/ns"
              xsi:schemaLocation="http://example.com/higheredtestprep/students/ns studentvb.xsd">
    <student stuID="I8900-041" courseID="PSAT-080-5">
        <lastName>Garcia</lastName>
        <firstName>Georgianna</firstName>
        <examDate>2017-10-17</examDate>
        <pretest level="M">55</pretest>
        <score>51</score>
    </student>


    <student stuID="I8154-741" courseID="PSAT-080-5">
        <lastName>Browne</lastName>
        <firstName>Brenda</firstName>
        <examDate>2017-10-22</examDate>
        <pretest level="L">30</pretest>
    </student>
</stu:students>
</crs:course>
```

prefixes associated with namespaces

prefixes applied to opening and closing tags of root elements

TIP

By switching from the Flat Catalog to the Venetian Blind layout, you avoided having to change every element and attribute name in the instance document into a qualified name.

You don't have to qualify any of the child elements and attributes of the course element because none of them were declared globally in the course.xsd schema file. Only the course element was defined globally, which is why it is the only element that requires a qualified name. The same is true for the students element.

▶ **6.** Save your changes to the **psatstudents.xml** file.

Working with Attributes

Like an element name, an attribute can be qualified by adding a namespace prefix. The syntax to qualify an attribute is

```
<element prefix:attribute="value"> ... </element>
```

where *prefix* is the namespace prefix and *attribute* is the attribute name. For example, the following code uses the crs: prefix to assign both the course element and the courseID attribute to the same course namespace:

```
<crs:course crs:courseID="PSAT-080-5"
    xmlns:xsi="http://www.w3.org/2001/XMLSchema-instance"
    xmlns:crs="http://example.com/higheredtestprep/course/ns">

...

</crs:course>
```

Unlike element names, there is no default namespace for attribute names. Default namespaces apply to elements, but not to attributes. An attribute name without a prefix is assumed to belong to the same namespace as the element that contains it. This means you could write the code listed above without the `crs:` prefix before the `courseID` attribute name and have the same result. In the code that follows, the `courseID` attribute is automatically assumed to belong to the course namespace, even though it lacks the `crs` prefix:

```
<crs:course courseID="PSAT-080-5"
     xmlns:xsi="http://www.w3.org/2001/XMLSchema-instance"
     xmlns:crs="http://example.com/higheredtestprep/course/ns">
...
</crs:course>
```

Because an attribute is automatically associated with the namespace of its element, you rarely need to qualify an attribute name. The only exception occurs when an attribute from one namespace needs to be used in an element from another namespace. For example, XHTML uses the `class` attribute to associate elements belonging to a common group or class. You could attach the `class` attribute from the XHTML namespace to elements from other namespaces. Because the `class` attribute is often used in CSS to apply common formats to groups of elements, using the `class` attribute in other XML elements would apply this feature of CSS to those elements as well.

For Gabby's document, there is no need to assign attributes to namespaces, so you will not specify namespaces for the attributes in the psatstudents.xml file.

Now that you've specified namespaces for the root elements of the two vocabularies you're using, you'll use an XML validator to validate your compound document.

To validate the compound document:

▶ 1. Use an XML validator to validate the **psatstudents.xml** document. The validator returns a number of errors.

▶ 2. Examine the text of the error messages for the reported errors. The first error message says that the target namespace of the schema document is 'null.'

   Trouble? If you're using Exchanger XML Editor and your first error message doesn't say that the target namespace of the schema document is 'null', compare your code to Figures 4-13 and 4-14, fix any errors you find, and then revalidate until the target namespace error is the first error.

Gabby's compound document is invalid because even though the namespaces in the compound document are associated with URIs, the schemas themselves are not. For the instance document to be valid, you must add this information to each schema file associated with it.

Associating a Schema with a Namespace

So far, you've specified the URI http://example.com/higheredtestprep/course/ns as the URI for the course vocabulary and the URI

http://example.com/higheredtestprep/students/ns

as the URI for the students vocabulary in the psatstudents.xml compound document. Next, you need to place the schemas themselves in the namespaces.

Targeting a Namespace

To associate the rules of a schema with a namespace, you declare the namespace of the instance document in the schema element and then make that namespace the target of the schema using the `targetNamespace` attribute. The code to set the schema namespace is

```
<xs:schema xmlns:xs="http://www.w3.org/2001/XMLSchema"
           xmlns:prefix="uri"
           targetNamespace="uri">
...
</xs:schema>
```

where *prefix* is the prefix of the namespace and *uri* is the URI of the namespace. The *prefix* value is optional. You can omit it to make the namespace of the instance document the default namespace. For example, to associate Gabby's studentsvb.xsd schema file with the namespace of the students vocabulary, you would modify the schema element as follows:

```
<xsi:schema xmlns:xsi="http://www.w3.org/2001/XMLSchema"
            xmlns="http://example.com/higheredtestprep/students/ns"
            targetNamespace="http://example.com/higheredtestprep/students/ns">
...
</xsi:schema>
```

Any customized data types, named types, elements, element groups, or attributes created in the schema are considered part of the target namespace. This allows you to make validation rules part of an XML vocabulary. For example, the `pretest` element is part of the students vocabulary, as is the rule that the `pretest` element must have a minimum value of 0 and a maximum value of 80.

REFERENCE

Targeting a Namespace in a Schema and Applying the Namespace to an Instance Document

- To target a schema to a namespace, add the attributes

```
xmlns:prefix="uri"
targetNamespace="uri"
```

to the `schema` element, where *prefix* is the optional prefix of the namespace and *uri* is the URI of the namespace.

- To apply a schema to a document with a namespace, add the attributes

```
xmlns:xsi="http://www.w3.org/2001/XMLSchema-instance"
xmlns:prefix="uri"
xsi:schemaLocation="uri schema"
```

to the instance document's root element, where *prefix* is the namespace prefix, *uri* is the URI of the namespace, and *schema* is the schema file. All global elements and attributes declared in the schema must be qualified in the instance document.

If you use the vocabulary's namespace as the default namespace for the schema, you do not have to qualify any references to those customized objects. On the other hand, if you apply a prefix to the namespace, references to those objects must be qualified by that prefix. Figure 4-15 shows both possibilities—one in which references to objects from the XML Schema vocabulary are qualified, and the other in which XML Schema is the default namespace and references to customized objects are qualified.

Figure 4-15   **A schema with and without qualified XML Schema object names**

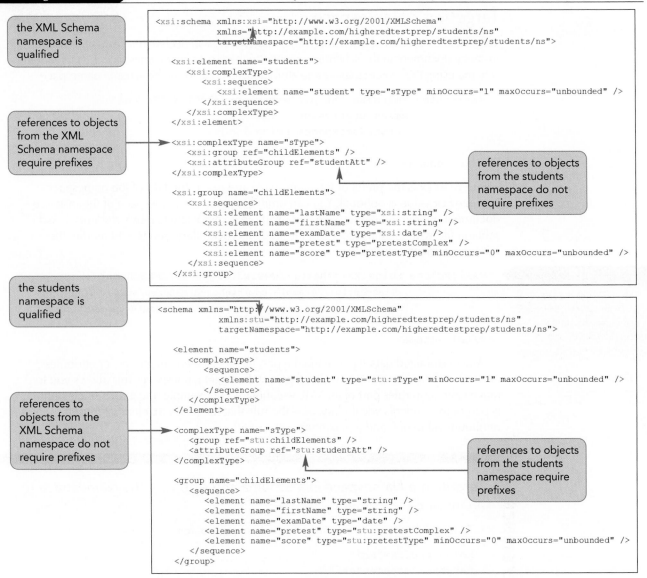

the XML Schema namespace is qualified

references to objects from the XML Schema namespace require prefixes

references to objects from the students namespace do not require prefixes

the students namespace is qualified

references to objects from the XML Schema namespace do not require prefixes

references to objects from the students namespace require prefixes

You will modify Gabby's studentsvb.xsd schema file, using `http://example.com/higheredtestprep/students/ns` as the default and target namespace of the schema. You'll also modify the course.xsd schema file using `http://example.com/higheredtestprep/course/ns`.

To associate each schema with a namespace:

1. Return to the **studentsvb.xsd** document in your XML editor.

2. In the file, add the following attributes to the root `schema` element:

```
xmlns="http://example.com/higheredtestprep/students/ns"
targetNamespace="http://example.com/higheredtestprep/students/ns"
```

Figure 4-16 shows the attributes inserted in the code.

Figure 4-16	Associating the students schema with a namespace

```
<xsi:schema xmlns:xsi="http://www.w3.org/2001/XMLSchema"
          xmlns="http://example.com/higheredtestprep/students/ns"
          targetNamespace="http://example.com/higheredtestprep/students/ns">

  <xsi:element name="students">
```

3. Save your changes to the **studentsvb.xsd** file.

4. In the **course.xsd** file, add the following attributes to the root `schema` element:

```
xmlns="http://example.com/higheredtestprep/course/ns"
targetNamespace="http://example.com/higheredtestprep/course/ns"
```

Figure 4-17 shows the attributes inserted in the code.

Figure 4-17	Associating the course schema with a namespace

```
<xs:schema xmlns:xs="http://www.w3.org/2001/XMLSchema"
         xmlns="http://example.com/higheredtestprep/course/ns"
         targetNamespace="http://example.com/higheredtestprep/course/ns">

  <xs:element name="course">
```

5. Save your changes to the **course.xsd** file, return to **psatstudents.xml** in your XML validator, and then validate the document. The document still fails validation, this time with a message about `stu:students` not being expected as a child element.

Trouble? If you receive any validation errors other than the error described in Step 5, compare your code against the preceding figures, fix any errors you find, and then revalidate until you receive only the error described in Step 5.

Gabby is pleased that you've been able to combine both the course and the students namespaces in a single instance document. Your final step will be to combine the schema information for both namespaces in the course.xsd schema document. XML Schema includes two methods for achieving this—including and importing schemas.

Including and Importing Schemas

You include a schema file when you want to combine schema files from the same namespace. This might be the case if one schema file contains a collection of customized data types that you want shared among many different files, and another schema file contains a collection of elements and attributes that define the structure of a particular document. To include a schema, you add the element

```
<xsi:include schemaLocation="schema" />
```

as a child of the root `schema` element, where *schema* is the name of the schema file to be included. The effect is to combine the two schema files into a single schema that can then be applied to a specific instance document. In an environment in which large and complex XML vocabularies are developed, different teams might work on different parts of the schema, using the `include` element to combine the different parts into a finished product. Rather than having one large and complex schema file, you can break the schema into smaller, more manageable files that can be shared and combined.

The other way to combine schemas is through importing, which is used when the schemas come from different namespaces. The syntax of the `import` element is

```
<xsi:import namespace="uri" schemaLocation="schema" />
```

where *uri* is the URI of the namespace for the imported schema and *schema* is again the name of the schema file. For example, to import the contents of the students schema into Gabby's course schema, you would add the following `import` element to the course.xsd schema file:

```
<xsi:import
    namespace="http://example.com/higheredtestprep/students/ns"
    schemaLocation="studentsvb.xsd" />
```

A schema can contain any number of `include` and `import` elements. Each must be globally declared as a direct child of the root `schema` element.

REFERENCE

Including and Importing Schemas

- To combine schemas from the same namespace, add the element

```
<xsi:include schemaLocation="schema" />
```

as a child of the schema element, where *schema* is the name of the schema file.
- To combine schemas from different namespaces, use

```
<xsi:import namespace="uri" schemaLocation="schema" />
```

where *uri* is the URI of the imported schema's namespace and *schema* is the name of the schema file.

You will use the `import` element to import the studentsvb.xsd schema file into the course.xsd file.

To import the *studentsvb.xsd* schema file:

1. Return to the **course.xsd** file in your XML editor.

2. Directly below the opening tag of the schema element, insert the following import element:

```
<xs:import
    namespace="http://example.com/higheredtestprep/students/ns"
    schemaLocation="studentsvb.xsd" />
```

Figure 4-18 shows the import element inserted in the code.

Figure 4-18   **Importing a schema file**

```
<xs:schema xmlns:xs="http://www.w3.org/2001/XMLSchema"
           xmlns="http://example.com/higheredtestprep/course/ns"
           targetNamespace="http://example.com/higheredtestprep/course/ns">

  <xs:import namespace="http://example.com/higheredtestprep/students/ns"
             schemaLocation="studentsvb.xsd" />
  <xs:element name="course">
```

This element assigns the namespace

http://example.com/higheredtestprep/students/ns

to the contents of the studentsvb.xsd schema document.

3. Save your work, validate the file, and then if necessary troubleshoot any validation errors until the file validates.

Referencing Objects from Other Schemas

After a schema is imported into another schema file, any objects it contains with global scope can be referenced in that file. To reference an object from an imported schema, you must declare the namespace of the imported schema in the schema element. You can then reference the object using the ref attribute or the type attribute for customized simple and complex types.

Gabby wants the students element to be placed directly after the instructor element in this schema, to match the location where you placed the students element and its content in the instance document. You will add the reference to the students element to the schema now.

To reference the students element in the *course.xsd* file:

TIP

When referencing elements in an imported schema file, the prefix does not have to match the prefix used in the imported schema file.

1. In the **course.xsd** file, add the following namespace declaration to the root schema element:

```
xmlns:stu="http://example.com/higheredtestprep/students/ns"
```

2. Insert the following element reference directly below the closing `</xs:element>` tag for the instructor element declaration:

```
<xs:element ref="stu:students" />
```

This code tells validators that in the sequence of elements within the course element, the students element from the students namespace should follow the instructor element from the course namespace. The element reference is qualified with a namespace prefix to indicate to validators that this reference points to a global object found in the students namespace. Figure 4-19 shows the revised schema code.

Figure 4-19	The course and students schemas combined in a single file

```xml
<xs:schema xmlns:xs="http://www.w3.org/2001/XMLSchema"
           xmlns="http://example.com/higheredtestprep/course/ns"
           targetNamespace="http://example.com/higheredtestprep/course/ns"
           xmlns:stu="http://example.com/higheredtestprep/students/ns">

  <xs:import namespace="http://example.com/higheredtestprep/students/ns"
             schemaLocation="studentsvb.xsd" />
  <xs:element name="course">
    <xs:complexType>
      <xs:sequence>
        <xs:element name="name">
          <xs:complexType>
            <xs:sequence>
              <xs:element name="title" type="xs:string" />
              <xs:element name="session" type="xs:string" />
            </xs:sequence>
          </xs:complexType>
        </xs:element>
        <xs:element name="description" type="xs:string" />
        <xs:element name="instructor">
          <xs:complexType>
            <xs:sequence>
              <xs:element name="firstName" type="xs:string" />
              <xs:element name="lastName" type="xs:string" />
            </xs:sequence>
          </xs:complexType>
        </xs:element>
        <xs:element ref="stu:students" />
      </xs:sequence>
      <xs:attribute name="courseID" type="xs:ID" />
    </xs:complexType>
  </xs:element>

</xs:schema>
```

3. Save the changes to the **course.xsd** document.

4. Return to **psatstudents.xml** in your XML editor.

5. Validate the XML content against the schema. The document passes validation, with the validator drawing rules for content and structure from the two different schema files.

   Trouble? If your psatstudents.xml document doesn't validate, compare your course.xsd file to Figure 4-19, and then edit your code as necessary until the psatstudents.xml document validates.

This example provides a glimpse of the power and flexibility of schemas in working with multiple vocabularies and namespaces. In more advanced applications, large schema structures can be created to validate equally complex XML environments involving dozens of documents and vocabularies. The XML Schema language is also flexible enough to provide control over which elements and attributes are validated, and how they are validated.

Gabby is pleased with the work you have done on creating a schema for the compound document describing the features of the PSAT Mathematics Course and the list of students enrolled in that course. She'll use the document as a model for creating compound documents for other courses.

PROSKILLS

Problem Solving: To Namespace or Not to Namespace?

XML documents can have any format unless specifically tied to a vocabulary. The question of whether or not to namespace often arises. Because namespaces must be added to both the XML document and any associated CSS, adding a namespace prefix requires quite a bit of document customization. Some programmers feel that using namespaces in XML and CSS documents "clutters" the code, and they argue that it would be better to modify any custom vocabularies as much as possible to avoid name collision problems. This would allow the XML and CSS documents to remain more flexible. To avoid namespace collisions, the name of one item (typically the one used less often) would need to be changed to some other name. Although this seems like a simple solution, it could be difficult to implement because there is no master list of all element and attribute names for XML vocabularies. Therefore, you may not always be able to predetermine where every possible name collision will occur. Another approach would be to put unique characters before the names so that the names differ and further name collisions are unlikely to happen. Regardless of which approach you take to avoid namespace collisions, it should be applied consistently throughout the system.

Combining Standard Vocabularies

So far you've worked only with the custom XML vocabularies that Gabby has created for Higher Ed Test Prep. The standard vocabularies that are shared throughout the world, such as XHTML, RSS, and MathML, can also be combined within a single compound document. Many of these standard vocabularies have unique URIs, some of which are listed in Figure 4-20.

| Figure 4-20 | Namespace URIs for standard vocabularies |

Vocabulary	Namespace URI
CML	http://www.xml-cml.org/schema
MathML	http://www.w3.org/1998/Math/MathML
iTunes Podcast	http://www.itunes.com/dtds/podcast-1.0.dtd
SMIL	http://www.w3.org/2001/SMIL20/Language
SVG	http://www.w3.org/2000/svg
VoiceML	http://www.w3.org/2001/vxml
XForms	http://www.w3.org/2002/xforms
XHTML	http://www.w3.org/1999/xhtml

TIP

Internet Explorer versions before IE9 support the combination of MathML with other languages only if an add-in is installed.

As XML has developed as a standard language for sharing markup data, web browsers have extended and improved their ability to support documents that combine multiple vocabularies. For example, current versions of Internet Explorer, Firefox, Chrome, Safari, and Opera support documents that combine both the XHTML and MathML languages.

INSIGHT

Compound Documents and Podcasting

Podcasting is an area where compound documents are used. Information about the location and content of podcasts is written in the XML vocabulary language RSS. As you learned in an earlier tutorial, RSS is used for syndicating text, video, or audio content. However, if you want to list your podcast on Apple's iTunes Music Store to make it more accessible to the general population, you must add elements that are specific to the needs of iTunes but that are not part of RSS. Therefore, the final podcast document contains elements from both RSS and the iTunes vocabulary.

To declare the iTunes namespace, you add the following attribute to the root `rss` element of the podcast document:

```
<rss version="2.0"
xmlns:itunes="http://www.itunes.com/dtds/podcast-1.0.dtd">
```

After you have declared the iTunes namespace, you can populate the rest of the document with iTunes-specific elements. The following text shows a portion of a compound document describing a podcast channel using elements from both RSS and iTunes:

```
<channel>
    <title>Jazz Pod Sessions</title>
    <link>http://example.com</link>
    <description>Enjoy jazz music from JPS</description>
    <itunes:author>David Hmong</itunes:author>
    <itunes:category text="Music">
       <itunes:category text="Jazz" />
    </itunes:category>
...
</channel>
```

The iTunes-specific elements listed here—author and category—will be displayed in Apple's iTunes Music Store, providing additional information to potential subscribers of the feed. To augment the descriptions of individual episodes, you add iTunes-specific elements to each `<item>` tag in the RSS document. The following shows part of the code for one episode of a podcast:

```
<item>
    <title>Jazz at Carnegie Hall</title>
    <itunes:subtitle>Famous Concerts</itunes:subtitle>
    <itunes:summary>Jazz from Carnegie Hall</itunes:summary>
    <itunes:author>Various</itunes:author>
    <itunes:duration>59:23</itunes:duration>
...
</item>
```

This particular episode highlights famous jazz concerts at Carnegie Hall. The code uses iTunes-specific elements to provide a subtitle for the show, a summary, the show's author, and the duration of the show in minutes and seconds.

The iTunes elements listed here represent only a fraction of the elements you can add to podcast code. You can learn more about podcasting and how to write compound documents involving both RSS and iTunes by visiting Apple's website.

REVIEW

Session 4.2 Quick Check

1. What is a name collision?
2. How do namespaces prevent the problem of name collisions?
3. If an attribute name is unqualified, what namespace is it presumed to belong to?
4. How does importing a schema file differ from including a schema file, with respect to the namespace of the schema?
5. How do you reference an object with global scope from an imported schema?

Session 4.3 Visual Overview:

To link multiple style sheets to a compound document, you add a separate processing instruction for each style sheet.

```
<?xml-stylesheet type="text/css" href="students.css" ?>
<?xml-stylesheet type="text/css" href="course.css" ?>

<crs:course courseID="PSAT-080-5"
        xmlns:xsi="http://www.w3.org/2001/XMLSchema-instance"
        xmlns:crs="http://example.com/higheredtestprep/course/ns"
        xsi:schemaLocation="http://example.com/higheredtestprep/course/ns course.xsd">

    <name>
        <title>PSAT Mathematics Course</title>
        <session>5</session>
    </name>
    <description>
        This is a focused course for students who
        have previously taken the PSAT exam as a sophomore
        but did not receive a desired score on the mathematics
        portion or students who will be taking the PSAT and
        wish to strengthen their skills in the mathematics
        area. Outcomes of the course will be measured using
        the original PSAT mathematics score or the course
        pre-test compared to the and the score of the PSAT
        mathematics score along with a course post-test.
    </description>
    <instructor>
        <crs:firstName>Rachel</crs:firstName>
        <crs:lastName>Polygoni</crs:lastName>
    </instructor>
    <stu:students xmlns:stu="http://example.com/higheredtestprep/students/ns"
                xsi:schemaLocation="http://example.com/higheredtestprep/students/ns studentsvb.xsd">
        <student stuID="I8900-041" courseID="PSAT-080-5">
            <stu:lastName>Garcia</stu:lastName>
            <stu:firstName>Georgianna</stu:firstName>
            <examDate>2017-10-17</examDate>
            <pretest level="M">55</pretest>
            <score>51</score>
        </student>

        ...

    </stu:students>
</crs:course>
```

Elements in an instance document must be qualified to be styled by linked style sheet rules.

The lastName and firstName elements in the course vocabulary are qualified with the `crs:` prefix and formatted by the style sheet for the course vocabulary.

The lastName and firstName elements in the students vocabulary are qualified with the `stu:` prefix and formatted by the style sheet for the students vocabulary.

Styling a Compound Document

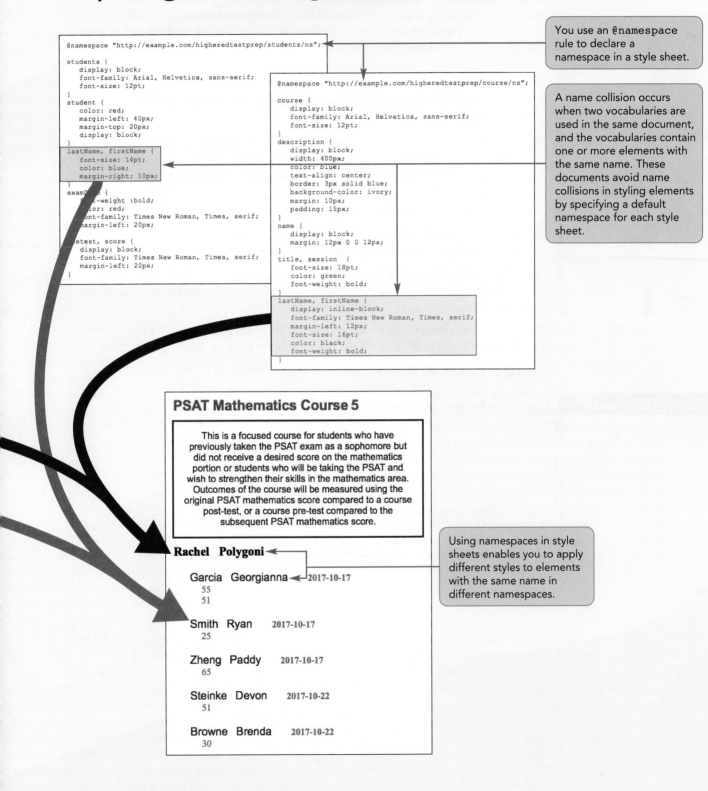

You use an @namespace rule to declare a namespace in a style sheet.

```
@namespace "http://example.com/higheredtestprep/students/ns";

students {
    display: block;
    font-family: Arial, Helvetica, sans-serif;
    font-size: 12pt;
}
student {
    color: red;
    margin-left: 40px;
    margin-top: 20px;
    display: block;
}
lastName, firstName {
    font-size: 14pt;
    color: blue;
    margin-right: 10px;
}
examDate {
    font-weight :bold;
    color: red;
    font-family: Times New Roman, Times, serif;
    margin-left: 20px;
}
pretest, score {
    display: block;
    font-family: Times New Roman, Times, serif;
    margin-left: 20px;
}
```

```
@namespace "http://example.com/higheredtestprep/course/ns";

course {
    display: block;
    font-family: Arial, Helvetica, sans-serif;
    font-size: 12pt;
}
description {
    display: block;
    width: 400px;
    color: blue;
    text-align: center;
    border: 3px solid blue;
    background-color: ivory;
    margin: 10px;
    padding: 15px;
}
name {
    display: block;
    margin: 12px 0 0 12px;
}
title, session  {
    font-size: 18pt;
    color: green;
    font-weight: bold;
}
lastName, firstName {
    display: inline-block;
    font-family: Times New Roman, Times, serif;
    margin-left: 12px;
    font-size: 16pt;
    color: black;
    font-weight: bold;
}
```

A name collision occurs when two vocabularies are used in the same document, and the vocabularies contain one or more elements with the same name. These documents avoid name collisions in styling elements by specifying a default namespace for each style sheet.

PSAT Mathematics Course 5

This is a focused course for students who have previously taken the PSAT exam as a sophomore but did not receive a desired score on the mathematics portion or students who will be taking the PSAT and wish to strengthen their skills in the mathematics area. Outcomes of the course will be measured using the original PSAT mathematics score compared to a course post-test, or a course pre-test compared to the subsequent PSAT mathematics score.

Rachel Polygoni

Garcia Georgianna   2017-10-17
55
51

Smith Ryan   2017-10-17
25

Zheng Paddy   2017-10-17
65

Steinke Devon   2017-10-22
51

Browne Brenda   2017-10-22
30

Using namespaces in style sheets enables you to apply different styles to elements with the same name in different namespaces.

Adding a Namespace to a Style Sheet

In the previous session, you added namespaces to Gabby's new psatstudents.xml compound document. To display the contents of this compound document, Gabby wants you to use styles from style sheets that she already uses for the students and course vocabularies. You'll link these files now to the psatstudents.xml compound document.

To link the *students.css* and *course.css* style sheets to the psatstudents.xml file:

▶ 1. Use your XML editor to open **studentstxt.css** and **coursetxt.css** from the xml04 ▸ tutorial folder, enter **your name** and **today's date** in the comment section, and then save the files as **students.css** and **course.css**, respectively, in the same folder.

▶ 2. Examine the contents of the students.css and course.css files.

▶ 3. If you took a break after the previous session, make sure the **psatstudents.xml** document from the xml04 ▸ tutorial folder is open in your XML editor.

▶ 4. In the **psatstudents.xml** file, immediately below the comment section, enter the following two processing instructions to link the students.css and course.css style sheets to the psatstudents.xml document:

```
<?xml-stylesheet type="text/css" href="students.css" ?>
<?xml-stylesheet type="text/css" href="course.css" ?>
```

Figure 4-21 shows the processing instructions inserted in the code.

Figure 4-21	Linking the instance document to the style sheets

```
    Filename:          psatstudents.xml
    Supporting Files: course.css, course.xsd, students.css, studentvb.xsd
-->
<?xml-stylesheet type="text/css" href="students.css" ?>
<?xml-stylesheet type="text/css" href="course.css" ?>

<crs:course courseID="PSAT-080-5"
```

▶ 5. Save your changes to the **psatstudents.xml** file, and then open the **psatstudents.xml** file in your browser. See Figure 4-22.

Figure 4-22	Compound document with default style sheets applied

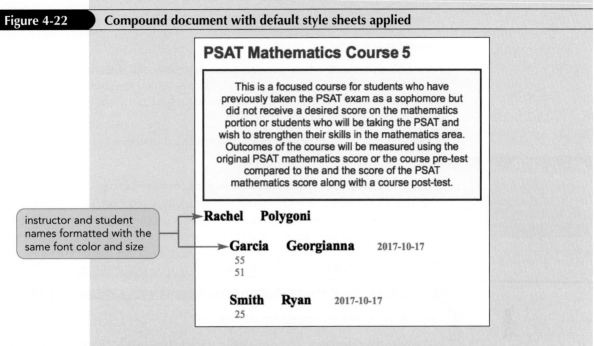

instructor and student names formatted with the same font color and size

Trouble? If the instructor name and the student names are displayed in blue instead of black in your browser, you entered the link to the course.css style sheet before the link to the students.css style sheet. To make your code match the figure, edit the code you just added to the instance document so the line referencing students.css is first, followed by the line referencing course.css, as in Figure 4-21.

The first and last names of the instructor and the students are displayed in the same color, size, and font. Instead, Gabby wants the instructor's name to be visually distinct from the students' names, as shown in the rendered document in Visual Overview 4.3.

The document's appearance is different than expected because the rules in the style sheet documents don't take into account the namespaces of the different elements in the instance document. Your next task is to add namespace support to the style sheets.

Recall that to apply a CSS style to an XML element, you use the style declaration

```
selector {attribute1:value1; attribute2:value2; ...}
```

where `selector` references an element or elements in the XML document. So, to set the width of the `student` element, you could enter the following style declaration:

```
student {width: 150px}
```

If an element has a qualified name such as `stu:student`, you do *not* include the prefix in the selector name, as follows:

Invalid code

```
stu:student {width: 150px}
```

This doesn't work with style sheets because CSS reserves the colon character for pseudo-elements and pseudo-classes. Instead, you must declare a namespace in the style sheet and then reference that namespace in the selector using a different syntax.

Declaring a Namespace in a Style Sheet

To declare a namespace in a style sheet, you add the rule

```
@namespace prefix "uri";
```

to the CSS style sheet, where *prefix* is the namespace prefix and *uri* is the URI of the namespace. Both the prefix and the URI must match the prefix and URI used in the XML document. So, to declare the students namespace in Gabby's students.css style sheet, you would add the following rule:

```
@namespace stu "http://example.com/higheredtestprep/students/ns";
```

TIP

If a namespace prefix is declared more than once, only the last instance is used in the style sheet.

Note that the prefix (stu) and the URI

```
http://example.com/higheredtestprep/students/ns
```

match the prefix and URI you entered in the previous session.

As with XML documents, the namespace prefix is optional. If the namespace prefix is omitted, the URI in the @namespace rule is considered to be the default namespace for the selectors in the style sheet. Any @namespace rules in the style sheet must come after all @import and @charset rules, and before any style declarations.

INSIGHT

Applying a Namespace to a Selector

After you have declared a namespace in a style sheet, you can associate selectors with that namespace by adding the namespace prefix to each selector name separated with the | symbol, as follows:

```
prefix|selector {attribute1: value1; attribute2: value2; ...}
```

For example, the style declaration

```
stu|lastname {width: 150px}
```

applies a width value of 150px to all lastname elements that belong to the stu namespace. You can also use the wildcard symbol (*) to apply a style to any element within a namespace or to elements across different namespaces. For example, the style declaration

```
stu|* {font-size: 12pt}
```

applies the specified font-size value to any element within the stu namespace. Similarly, the declaration

```
*|student {width: 150px}
```

sets a width of 150 pixels for any element named student from any namespace. If you omit the namespace prefix from a selector, its style is also applied to all namespaces. For example, the declaration

```
student {width: 150px}
```

applies to all elements named student in any namespace.

In the psatstudents.xml instance document, the namespace collisions are occurring between the students and course vocabularies. As a result, styles intended for the firstName and lastName elements from one vocabulary are being applied to those elements in the other vocabulary as well. You'll add code to each style sheet now to associate it with a namespace.

REFERENCE

Declaring and Applying a Namespace in a CSS Style Sheet

- To declare a namespace in a CSS style sheet, add the rule

  `@namespace prefix "uri";`

  before any style declarations, where *prefix* is the namespace prefix and *uri* is the namespace URI. If no prefix is specified, the namespace URI is the default namespace for selectors in the style sheet.

- To apply a namespace to a selector, use the form

  `prefix|selector {attribute1: value1; attribute2: value2; ...}`

  where *prefix* is the namespace prefix and *selector* is a selector for an element or group of elements in the document.

You will add `@namespace` rules to the style sheets in the students.css and course.css files now.

To declare and apply namespaces in the *students.css* and *course.css* style sheets:

▶ **1.** In the **students.css** style sheet, directly after the comment section, insert the following namespace declaration:

   `@namespace "http://example.com/higheredtestprep/students/ns";`

   Figure 4-23 shows the namespace declaration inserted in the code.

Figure 4-23   **Default namespace declared in students.css style sheet**

```
*/
@namespace "http://example.com/higheredtestprep/students/ns";

students {
    display: block;
    font-family: Arial, Helvetica, sans-serif;
    font-size: 12pt;
}
```

This code specifies http://example.com/higheredtestprep/students/ns as the default namespace for all selectors in the students.css document.

▶ **2.** Save your changes to the file.

▶ **3.** In the **course.css** style sheet in your XML editor, directly after the comment section, insert the following namespace declaration:

   `@namespace "http://example.com/higheredtestprep/course/ns";`

   This code specifies http://example.com/higheredtestprep/course/ns as the default namespace for all selectors in the course.css document. Figure 4-24 shows the namespace declaration inserted in the code.

| Figure 4-24 | Default namespace declared in course.css style sheet |

```
*/
@namespace "http://example.com/higheredtestprep/course/ns";

course {
    display: block;
    font-family: Arial, Helvetica, sans-serif;
    font-size: 12pt;
}
```

4. Save your changes to the **course.css** style sheet, and then reload **psatstudents.xml** in your browser. As shown in Figure 4-25, none of the text from either namespace is formatted.

| Figure 4-25 | Unformatted document in browser after declaring style sheet namespaces |

PSAT Mathematics Course 5 This is a focused course for students who have previously taken the PSAT exam as a sophomore but did not receive a desired score on the mathematics portion or students who will be taking the PSAT and wish to strengthen their skills in the mathematics area. Outcomes of the course will be measured using the original PSAT mathematics score or the course pre-test compared to the and the score of the PSAT mathematics score along with a course post-test. Rachel Polygoni Garcia Georgianna 2017-10-17 55 51 Smith Ryan 2017-10-17 25 Zheng Paddy 2017-10-17 65 Steinke Devon 2017-10-22 51 Browne Brenda 2017-10-22 30

You need to make a couple more changes to your code to enable both schemas and style sheets to work together in your instance document.

As you saw earlier in the tutorial, parsers can associate child elements with namespaces and validate those elements against schemas, based only on a prefix designated for the parent element. However, when browsers apply CSS styles to a default namespace, such as those you declared for the students.css and course.css style sheets, the browsers expect the name of each element being styled to be qualified. Because all of the elements that you want to style in your instance document are currently inheriting their namespace designations from their parent elements, rather than being qualified themselves, the browser didn't associate any of the styles in the style sheets with elements in the instance document. You'll make two changes in your code to make the elements styleable.

Qualifying Elements and Attributes by Default

You can force all elements and attributes to be qualified, regardless of their scope, by adding the `elementFormDefault` and `attributeFormDefault` attributes

```
<xs:schema
    elementFormDefault="qualify"
    attributeFormDefault="qualify">
...
</xs:schema>
```

to the root `schema` element in the schema file, where *qualify* is either `qualified` or `unqualified`, specifying whether all the elements and attributes of the instance document must be qualified. The default value of both of these attributes is `unqualified` except for globally defined elements and attributes, which must always be qualified. To require all elements to be qualified but not all attributes (other than globally declared attributes), you enter the following code into the schema element:

```
<xs:schema
    elementFormDefault="qualified"
    attributeFormDefault="unqualified">


...
</xs:schema>
```

This is a common setup when you want to explicitly qualify each element name with a namespace prefix.

You can also set the qualification for individual elements or attributes by applying the `form` attribute

```
<xs:element name="name" form="qualify" />
<xs:attribute name="name" form="qualify" />
```

to the definitions in the schema, where *qualify* is again either `qualified` or `unqualified`. For example, the element declaration

```
<xs:element name="student" form="qualified" />
```

requires the `student` element to be qualified in the instance document, whether it has been declared globally or locally in the schema.

Browsers are looking for qualified element names in your instance document, but your schema is configured to expect unqualified names. To make your instance document work with both schemas and style sheets, you'll first add code to the course.xsd schema document to specify that all elements should be qualified. Then in your instance document, you'll make all elements qualified by adding prefixes to all elements.

To specify that elements should be qualified and then qualify all elements:

1. In the **course.xsd** schema file, within the opening <schema> tag, insert the following attributes, and then save your changes:

   ```
   elementFormDefault="qualified"
   attributeFormDefault="unqualified"
   ```

   Figure 4-26 shows the attributes inserted in the code.

Figure 4-26   Attributes added to course.xsd schema file

```
<xs:schema xmlns:xs="http://www.w3.org/2001/XMLSchema"
           xmlns="http://example.com/higheredtestprep/course/ns"
           targetNamespace="http://example.com/higheredtestprep/course/ns"
           xmlns:stu="http://example.com/higheredtestprep/students/ns"
           elementFormDefault="qualified" attributeFormDefault="unqualified">

   <xs:import namespace="http://example.com/higheredtestprep/students/ns"
           schemaLocation="studentsvb.xsd" />
```

This code specifies that the schema expects all elements in an instance document to be qualified, and that it does not expect attributes in an instance document to be qualified.

2. In the **studentsvb.xsd** schema file, within the opening <schema> tag, insert the following attributes, and then save your changes:

   ```
   elementFormDefault="qualified"
   attributeFormDefault="unqualified"
   ```

   Figure 4-27 shows the attributes inserted in the code.

Figure 4-27   Attributes added to studentsvb.xsd schema file

```
<xsi:schema xmlns:xsi="http://www.w3.org/2001/XMLSchema"
            xmlns="http://example.com/higheredtestprep/students/ns"
            targetNamespace="http://example.com/higheredtestprep/students/ns"
            elementFormDefault="qualified" attributeFormDefault="unqualified">

   <xsi:element name="students">
```

3. In the **psatstudents.xml** instance document, add the `stu:` prefix to the opening and closing tags of all elements nested within the `students` element, add the `crs:` prefix to the opening and closing tags of all elements within the root `course` element that are not already qualified with the `stu:` prefix, and then save your changes. See Figure 4-28.

Figure 4-28	Namespace prefixes added to elements in compound document

```
<crs:course courseID="PSAT-080-5"
        xmlns:xsi="http://www.w3.org/2001/XMLSchema-instance"
        xmlns:crs="http://example.com/higheredtestprep/course/ns"
        xsi:schemaLocation="http://example.com/higheredtestprep/course/ns course.xsd">

  <crs:name>
     <crs:title>PSAT Mathematics Course</crs:title>
     <crs:session>5</crs:session>
  </crs:name>
  <crs:description>
     This is a focused course for students who
     have previously taken the PSAT exam as a sophomore
     but did not receive a desired score on the mathematics
     portion or students who will be taking the PSAT and
     wish to strengthen their skills in the mathematics
     area. Outcomes of the course will be measured using
     the original PSAT mathematics score or the course
     pre-test compared to the and the score of the PSAT
     mathematics score along with a course post-test.
  </crs:description>
  <crs:instructor>
     <crs:firstName>Rachel</crs:firstName>
     <crs:lastName>Polygoni</crs:lastName>
  </crs:instructor>

  <stu:students xmlns:stu="http://example.com/higheredtestprep/students/ns"
        xsi:schemaLocation="http://example.com/higheredtestprep/students/ns studentsvb.xsd">
  <stu:student stuID="I8900-041" courseID="PSAT-080-5">
     <stu:lastName>Garcia</stu:lastName>
     <stu:firstName>Georgianna</stu:firstName>
     <stu:examDate>2017-10-17</stu:examDate>
     <stu:pretest level="M">55</stu:pretest>
     <stu:score>51</stu:score>
  </stu:student>

  <stu:student stuID="I7711-121" courseID="PSAT-080-5">
     <stu:lastName>Smith</stu:lastName>
     <stu:firstName>Ryan</stu:firstName>
     <stu:examDate>2017-10-17</stu:examDate>
     <stu:pretest level="L">25</stu:pretest>
  </stu:student>

  <stu:student stuID="I7012-891" courseID="PSAT-080-5">
     <stu:lastName>Zheng</stu:lastName>
     <stu:firstName>Paddy</stu:firstName>
     <stu:examDate>2017-10-17</stu:examDate>
     <stu:pretest level="H">65</stu:pretest>
  </stu:student>

  <stu:student stuID="I8053-891" courseID="PSAT-080-5">
     <stu:lastName>Steinke</stu:lastName>
     <stu:firstName>Devon</stu:firstName>
     <stu:examDate>2017-10-22</stu:examDate>
     <stu:pretest level="M">51</stu:pretest>
  </stu:student>

  <stu:student stuID="I8154-741" courseID="PSAT-080-5">
     <stu:lastName>Browne</stu:lastName>
     <stu:firstName>Brenda</stu:firstName>
     <stu:examDate>2017-10-22</stu:examDate>
     <stu:pretest level="L">30</stu:pretest>
  </stu:student>

  </stu:students>
</crs:course>
```

crs: prefix added to opening and closing tags for all elements in the course namespace

stu: prefix added to opening and closing tags for all elements in the students namespace

4. Reload **psatstudents.xml** in your browser. Now that all the elements are qualified, the `lastName` and `firstName` elements for the instructor and the students are formatted using the rules for the course and students namespaces, respectively, as shown in Visual Overview 4.3.

INSIGHT

Defining Namespaces with the Escape Character

Not all browsers support the use of the @namespace rule. When the specifications for XML 1.0 were first posted, no support existed for namespaces. Several competing proposals were circulated for adding namespace support to XML and CSS. One proposal, which was not adopted but was implemented in the Internet Explorer browser before version 9, was to insert the backslash escape character (\ ) before the colon character in the namespace prefix. So, for older versions of Internet Explorer to apply a style to an element from a particular namespace, you use the declaration

```
prefix\:selector {attribute1:value1; attribute2:value2; ...}
```

where *prefix* is the namespace prefix used in the XML document. For example, the declaration for the title element in a products namespace that uses the prd prefix is as follows:

```
prd\:title {width: 150px}
```

You can apply the same style to several elements in the namespace by using the * symbol. For example, the following declaration sets the width of all elements in the products namespace to 150 pixels:

```
prd\:* {width: 150px}
```

Other browsers such as Firefox, Opera, and Safari do not support this method with XML documents. If you want to support the widest range of browsers, you must duplicate the styles in the style sheet using both methods.

Gabby is pleased that you were able to apply namespaces to the style sheets and the namespaces. The web page contains all the data that Gabby wants and is displayed in the way she intended. She'll base future documents for Higher Ed Test Prep on the model document you created.

REVIEW

Session 4.3 Quick Check

1. What code would you add to an XML instance document to link it to the branding.css style sheet?
2. What rule would you add to a CSS style sheet to declare a namespace with the URI *http://ns.doc.student* and the namespace prefix `student`?
3. What rule would you add to a CSS style sheet to make the namespace in Question 2 the default namespace for all selectors in the style sheet?
4. In a style sheet that includes the namespace rule in Question 2, how would you modify the selector for the `lastname` element to indicate that it belongs to the namespace with the URI *http://ns.doc.student*?
5. What code would you add to a schema file to force all elements and all attributes to be qualified by default?

PRACTICE

Review Assignments

Data Files needed for the Review Assignments: coursetxt.css, coursetxt.xsd, psattxt.xml, sessionstxt.css, sessionstxt.xml, sessionstxt.xsd

Gabby would like your help with creating another compound document and styling it with CSS. She would like to create a document that combines the description of a single course, using the course vocabulary, with a list of session descriptions for that course, using the sessions vocabulary. She then wants to apply the course.css and sessions.css styles to the content to produce formatted content in a web browser. Figure 4-29 shows a preview of the completed document.

Figure 4-29   **Final PSAT Writing Skills Course compound document**

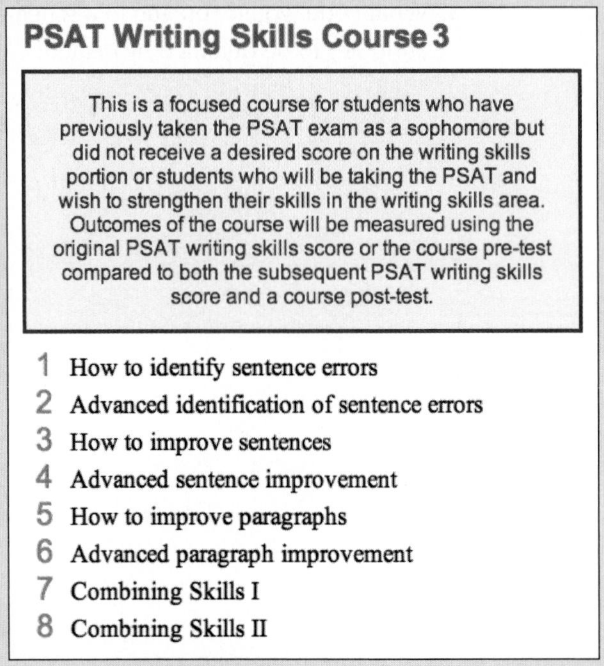

PSAT Writing Skills Course 3

This is a focused course for students who have previously taken the PSAT exam as a sophomore but did not receive a desired score on the writing skills portion or students who will be taking the PSAT and wish to strengthen their skills in the writing skills area. Outcomes of the course will be measured using the original PSAT writing skills score or the course pre-test compared to both the subsequent PSAT writing skills score and a course post-test.

1 How to identify sentence errors
2 Advanced identification of sentence errors
3 How to improve sentences
4 Advanced sentence improvement
5 How to improve paragraphs
6 Advanced paragraph improvement
7 Combining Skills I
8 Combining Skills II

Gabby has already created separate XML documents for the course and sessions content schemas to validate each vocabulary, and style sheets for the different elements in both vocabularies. She needs you to combine the content into a single document, import the sessions schema into the course schema, and edit the style sheets so that they support namespaces.

Complete the following:

1. In your XML editor, open the **psattxt.xml** and **sessionstxt.xml** documents and the **coursetxt.xsd** and **sessionstxt.xsd** schema files located in the xml04 ▶ review folder, enter *your name* and *today's date* in the comment section of each file, and then save the files as **psat.xml**, **sessions.xml**, **course.xsd**, and **sessions.xsd**, respectively, in the same folder. Validate the psat.xml and sessions.xml files to confirm that they're valid.

2. In the sessions.xml file, copy the content from the opening `<sessions>` tag through the closing `</sessions>` tag, and then in psat.xml, paste the copied content directly before the closing `</course>` tag. Save the file as psatsessions.xml. Close the sessions.xml file.

3. In psatsessions.xml, in the opening `<course>` tag, keep the attribute and value that declare the XML Schema namespace, and then edit the attributes to declare the namespace http://example.com/higheredtestprep/course/ns for the course vocabulary, declare the namespace http://example.com/higheredtestprep/sessions/ns for the sessions vocabulary, and specify the location of the course.xsd schema file. Specify the prefix `crs` for the course namespace and the prefix `ses` for the sessions namespace. In the opening `<sessions>` tag, remove all attributes.

4. Qualify the `course` element and the `sessions` element using the prefixes declared in the previous step, and then save your work.

5. In the course.xsd file, specify the namespace

   http://example.com/higheredtestprep/course/ns

   for all unqualified names in the schema, and then specify the same namespace as the target namespace. Repeat for the sessions.xsd file, using the namespace http://example.com/higheredtestprep/sessions/ns.

6. In the course.xsd file, import the sessions.xsd file, specifying the http://example.com/higheredtestprep/sessions/ns namespace, declare the prefix `ses` for the sessions namespace, and then add a reference to the `sessions` element from the sessions namespace immediately after the declaration of the `description` element.

7. Save your work in all open files, and then validate psatsessions.xml.

8. In your XML editor, open the **coursetxt.css** and **sessionstxt.css** style sheets from the xml04 ▸ review folder, enter ***your name*** and ***today's date*** in the comment section of each file, and then save the files as **course.css** and **sessions.css**, respectively, in the same folder.

9. In the course.css style sheet, declare

   http://example.com/higheredtestprep/course/ns

   as the default namespace. In the sessions.css style sheet, declare

   http://example.com/higheredtestprep/sessions/ns

   as the default namespace. Save your changes to both files.

10. In the course.xsd and sessions.xsd files, specify that elements are qualified by default, and that attributes are unqualified by default. Save your changes to both files.

11. In the psatsessions.xml file, add instructions to link to the course.css and sessions.css style sheets, and then qualify all elements. Save your work and validate the file.

12. Open psatsessions.xml in your browser and verify that it matches Figure 4-29.

Case Problem 1

Data Files needed for this Case Problem: sitemapPS.xml, sitemapVS.xml, sitemapWFS.xml, sitestxt.xml, sitestxt.xsd

Weekend Fun Snacks   Cleo Coal created and maintains a website called Weekend Fun Snacks, which lists her picks of the best and easiest recipes for kids to cook. The site's popularity convinced her there was room for more specialty recipe sites, so she created two additional websites—Primal Snacks, which features snacks appropriate for a paleo or primal diet, and Veg Snacks, which includes quick bites suitable for vegetarians.

Cleo also created a Sitemaps file for each site, which is a document written in XML that provides basic information about each page in a website, as well as how all the pages are related. Cleo has submitted her Sitemaps files to Google and other search services to help them better index her sites. However, she also thinks that the Sitemaps content she's created would be useful in a compound document with a custom vocabulary, which would allow her to view information about all the pages on all of her sites in a single page. Cleo asks for your help with creating this compound document.

Figure 4-30 shows a tree diagram highlighting some of the elements from both vocabularies that you'll place in the document.

Figure 4-30   **Tree diagrams of Sitemaps and sites vocabularies**

Sitemaps vocabulary

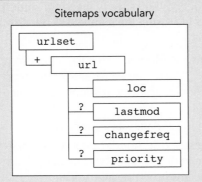

sites vocabulary

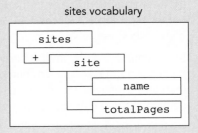

Cleo has provided you with a truncated version of the Sitemaps file for each of her three websites as well as another XML file containing the administrative information on her sites. Your job will be to create a compound document combining the features of the two vocabularies.

Complete the following:

1. In your XML editor, open the **sitestxt.xml** and **sitestxt.xsd** files from the xml04 ▸ case1 folder, enter *your name* and *today's date* in the comment section of each file, and then save the files as **sites.xml** and **sites.xsd**, respectively, in the same folder.

2. In the sites.xml file, add a namespace declaration to the root `sites` element, associating the `xs` prefix with the URI for the XML Schema namespace. Specify the default namespace http://example.com/weekendfunsnacks/sites for the file. Specify sites.xsd as the location of the schema for the default namespace.

3. In your XML editor, open the **sitemapPS.xml**, **sitemapVS.xml**, and **sitemapWFS.xml** files from the xml04 ▸ case1 folder. These files contain the Sitemaps for Cleo's three websites. In the sitemapWFS.xml file, copy the contents from the opening `<urlset>` tag through the closing `</urlset>` tag to the Clipboard, and then paste them into the sites.xml file just before the closing `</site>` tag for the Weekend Fun Snacks site. Repeat to copy and paste the content from the sitemapPS.xml file into the `site` element for the Paleo Snacks site, and the content from the sitemapVS.xml file into the `site` element for the Veg Snacks site. Save your changes to the sites.xml file.

4. In each of the opening `<urlset>` tags you pasted in the previous step, remove the XML Schema namespace declaration and the schema location, leaving the default namespace declaration for each element. Save your work.

5. In the sites.xsd file, in the root element, specify the target namespace as http://example.com/weekendfunsnacks/sites, and then associate the prefix `cc` with the target namespace. Associate the prefix `sm` with the namespace http://www.sitemaps.org/schemas/sitemap/0.9. Specify that elements are qualified by default, and that attributes are unqualified by default.

6. Add code to import the schema for the
   http://www.sitemaps.org/schemas/sitemap/0.9
   namespace from the location
   http://www.sitemaps.org/schemas/sitemap/0.9/sitemap.xsd.

7. Immediately following the declaration of the `totalPages` element, add a reference to the `urlset` element from the
   http://www.sitemaps.org/schemas/sitemap/0.9 namespace.
   Save your work.

8. Validate the sites.xml file, and then, if necessary, fix any validation errors.

CREATE

Case Problem 2

Data Files needed for this Case Problem: menutxt.css, menutxt.xml, recipetxt.css, recipetxt.xml

Chester's Restaurant   Chester's Restaurant is located in Hartland, Minnesota. Jasmine Pup, the owner and operator, has all the menu information stored in XML files. She also has the recipes for all the menu items stored in XML. She'd like to combine the menu and recipe information for each item into a document formatted with CSS, which would give her an easy-to-read overview of the description and ingredients of each menu item.

Jasmine has asked you to combine the menu and recipe information about one menu item for her approval. Figure 4-31 shows tree diagrams of the subsets of the menu and recipe vocabularies that you'll be using.

Figure 4-31   **Tree diagrams of menu and recipe subsets**

menu vocabulary

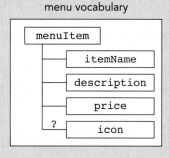

recipe vocabulary

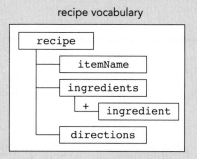

Figure 4-32 shows a preview of the page that you will create.

Figure 4-32   **Preview of menu and recipe document in browser**

Oatmeal Breakfast
Our oatmeal is served warm with fresh fruit, pecans, raisins, and 100% maple syrup. Available all day.
6.95 ♠ ♥

1/3 c steel cut oats
1-1/4 c water
1/4 t salt

Bring water to a boil. Add salt and oats, stir, and lower heat to lowest setting. Cover and let stand 2 hours.

Complete the following:

1. In your XML editor, open **menutxt.xml** and **recipetxt.xml** from the xml04 ▸ case2 folder, enter *your name* and *today's date* in the comment section of each file, and then save the documents as **menu.xml** and **recipe.xml**, respectively, in the same folder.

2. Review the contents of menu.xml, and then create a schema file for the menu vocabulary using the Russian Doll design. Save the schema file to the xml04 ▸ case2 folder as **menu.xsd**. Specify the target namespace for the schema and save your changes. In menu.xml, specify the location of the schema file and save your changes. Validate menu.xml against the schema and then, if necessary, fix any validation errors.

3. Review the contents of recipe.xml, and then create a schema file for the recipe vocabulary using the Russian Doll design. Save the schema file to the xml04 ▸ case2 folder as **recipe.xsd**. Specify the target namespace for the schema and save your changes. In recipe.xml, specify the location of the schema file and save your changes. Validate recipe.xml against the schema and then, if necessary, fix any validation errors.

4. In the recipe.xml file, copy the `recipe` element and its contents to the Clipboard, and then in the menu.xml file, paste the recipe contents directly before the closing `</menuItem>` tag. Save a copy of the file as **menurecipe.xml**, and then change the filename listed in the comment section to match.

5. In menurecipe.xml, select and assign a prefix to the XML Schema namespace. Select and assign a prefix to the menu namespace specified in the root element of the menu.xml file.

6. Select and assign a prefix to the recipe namespace specified in the root element of the menurecipe.xml file. Specify the location of the schema file for the menu namespace.

7. Qualify all elements in the menurecipe.xml file using the prefixes you defined.

8. In menu.xsd, specify that elements are qualified by default and attributes are unqualified by default. Specify the namespace of the menu vocabulary as the target namespace. Assign a prefix to the namespace for the recipe vocabulary. Import the recipe.xsd file, and then add a reference to the `recipe` element from the recipe namespace immediately after the definition of the `icon` element. Save your work.

9. In your XML editor, open **menutxt.css** and **recipetxt.css** from the xml04 ▸ case2 folder, enter *your name* and *today's date* in the comment section of each file, and then save the documents as **menu.css** and **recipe.css**, respectively, in the same folder.

10. In menu.css, specify the namespace for the menu vocabulary as the default namespace, and then save your changes.

11. In recipe.css, specify the namespace for the recipe vocabulary as the default namespace, and then save your changes.

12. In menurecipe.xml, directly below the comment section, insert a processing instruction that links the document to the **menu.css** style sheet. Insert another processing instruction that links the document to the **recipe.css** style sheet. Save your changes.

13. Validate the menurecipe.xml file and then, if necessary, fix any validation errors.

14. Open menurecipe.xml in your browser and verify that its appearance matches Figure 4-32.

CHALLENGE

Case Problem 3

Data Files needed for this Case Problem: atclectxt.xml, ituneselem.txt

Austin Technical College   Pia Zhou is a community relations officer for the School of Information Technology at Austin Technical College (ATC) in Austin, Utah. Pia is part of an interdepartmental task force exploring ways to make more ATC courses available online. Her current task is to explore making lectures from a single class available through iTunes U, which is an Apple application that lets instructors distribute course content to students. Pia has asked for your help with creating an initial demonstration document.

iTunes U content is formatted in XML using the RSS vocabulary, supplemented with elements from the custom iTunes and iTunes U vocabularies.

Figure 4-33 shows tree diagrams highlighting some of the elements from the vocabularies that you'll place in the document.

Figure 4-33   **Tree diagrams of RSS and iTunes vocabularies**

RSS 2.0 vocabulary

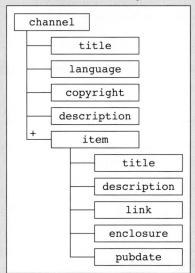

iTunes and iTunes U vocabularies

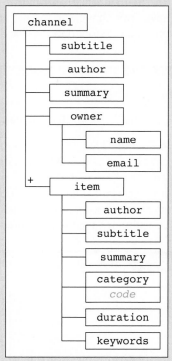

You've already received an RSS file containing the RSS elements and a text file containing iTunes U-related information on the course and lectures. Your job will be to create a compound document combining the features of the two vocabularies. Note that by convention, RSS documents do not declare the RSS namespace.

Complete the following:

1. In your XML editor, open the **atclectxt.xml** file from the xml04 ▸ case3 folder, enter *your name* and *today's date* in the comment section, and then save the file as **atclecture.xml** in the same folder.

2. Add a namespace declaration to the root `rss` element declaring the iTunes namespace http://www.itunes.com/dtds/podcast-1.0.dtd. Use `itunes` as the namespace prefix. Add a second namespace declaration to the root `rss` element declaring the iTunes U namespace http://www.itunesu.com/feed. Use `itunesu` as the namespace prefix.

⊕ **EXPLORE** 3. In your XML editor, open the **ituneselem.txt** file from the xml04 ▸ case3 folder. This file contains the content for the different iTunes and iTunes U elements. Using this file as a reference, complete the rest of the content in the RSS document.

4. Return to the atclecture.xml file in your XML editor. Add the `subtitle`, `author`, and `summary` iTunes elements as child elements of the `channel` element. Place all three elements in the iTunes namespace, and use the text indicated in the ituneselem.txt file as the content of the three elements.

5. Below the `description` element, insert the iTunes `owner` element. The `owner` element indicates the owner of the podcast for the iTunes Store. Within the `owner` element, insert two elements named `name` and `email` containing Zakia Choudhry's name and email address, respectively. Make sure these elements belong to the iTunes namespace.

6. Add iTunes elements that describe each lecture in the series. Each lecture is marked with the `item` element. Zakia's document includes four lectures. Add the `author`, `subtitle`, `summary`, `duration`, and `keywords` elements for each of the four lectures.

7. Specify the category of each lecture using the iTunes U `category` element. The name of the category is contained in an attribute of the `category` element named `code`. The `code` attribute for each lecture should have a value of 101102, which corresponds to computer science.

8. Save your changes to the file, and then load atclecture.xml in your web browser. Verify that no errors are reported in the document.

Case Problem 4

Data Files needed for this Case Problem: carstxt.css, carstxt.xml, teamstxt.css, teamstxt.xml

CREATE

South Racing   Danika Francis tracks team cars for South Racing's racing teams. As part of her job, she has created several XML vocabularies dealing with team series and the cars available to race in them. She has created an XML document containing information on two teams, and another document on cars. She wants to combine this information to create a compound document that includes team information and lists each team's cars. She has already developed a style sheet for each vocabulary. Figure 4-34 shows the tree structures of the teams and cars vocabularies.

Figure 4-34   **Tree diagrams of combined teams and cars vocabularies**

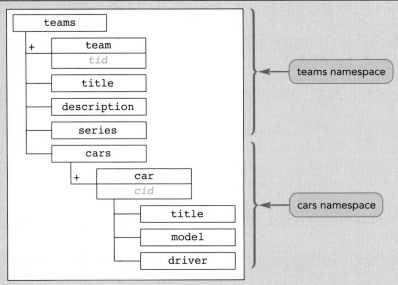

Danika has asked you to create schema documents to validate both vocabularies, and a compound document that incorporates the information and style sheet formatting from both vocabularies. There is some overlap in the element names from the two vocabularies, so you'll have to use namespaces to distinguish the elements from the two vocabularies. Figure 4-35 shows a preview of the page you'll create.

Figure 4-35   Completed South Racing document in browser

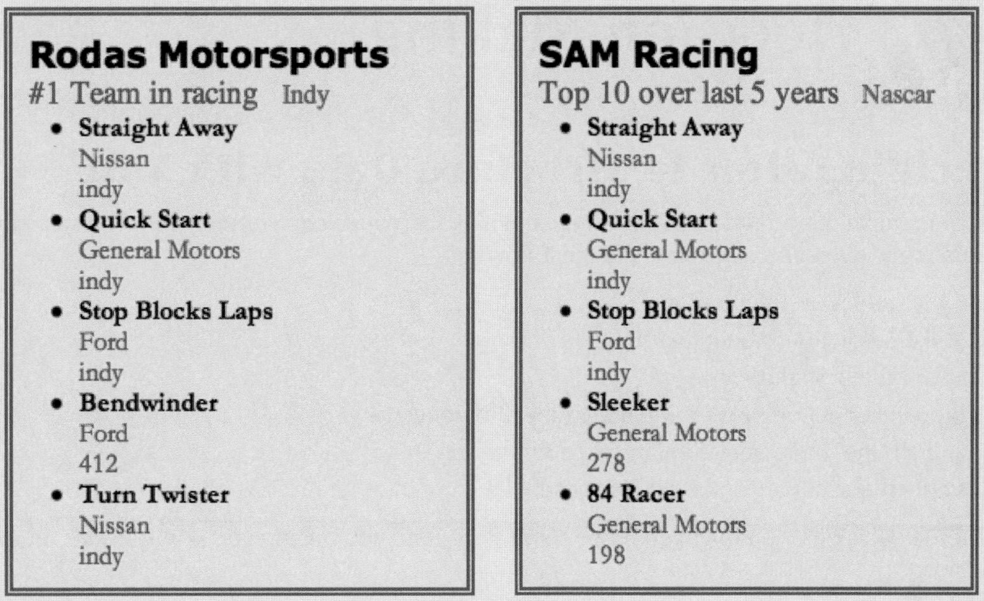

Rodas Motorsports
#1 Team in racing   Indy
- **Straight Away**
  Nissan
  indy
- **Quick Start**
  General Motors
  indy
- **Stop Blocks Laps**
  Ford
  indy
- **Bendwinder**
  Ford
  412
- **Turn Twister**
  Nissan
  indy

SAM Racing
Top 10 over last 5 years   Nascar
- **Straight Away**
  Nissan
  indy
- **Quick Start**
  General Motors
  indy
- **Stop Blocks Laps**
  Ford
  indy
- **Sleeker**
  General Motors
  278
- **84 Racer**
  General Motors
  198

Complete the following:

1. In your XML editor, open the **carstxt.css**, **carstxt.xml**, **teamstxt.css**, and **teamstxt.xml** files from the xml04 ▶ case4 folder, enter *your name* and *today's date* in the comment section of each file, and then save the files as **cars.css**, **cars.xml**, **teams.css**, and **teams.xml**, respectively, in the same folder.

2. Create a schema file for each of the two XML files using whichever schema design you choose, and selecting appropriate filenames and namespaces. Validate each XML file against its schema file, and then correct any errors, if necessary, until both instance documents validate.

3. Add a `cars` element after the `series` element for both of the teams. Copy and paste the relevant `cars` elements, along with their children, for each team, as shown in Figure 4-34. Save the compound document as **teamscars.xml**.

4. Associate the schema information with the compound document.

5. Specify the default namespace for each style sheet, and then link the compound document to both style sheets.

6. Validate the compound document and then correct any errors, if necessary, until it validates. Open the document in your browser and verify that it matches Figure 4-35.

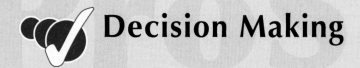 **Decision Making**

Deciding How to Structure Data with XML

Decision making is a process of choosing between alternative courses of action. The steps involved in evaluating a given alternative include the following:

1. Obtain relevant information.
2. Make predictions about the future.
3. Select the best alternative.
4. Prepare an action plan to implement the alternative.
5. Launch the implementation and monitor the result.
6. Verify the accuracy of the decision and take corrective action, if needed.

For some decisions, you might combine some steps, and you might even skip steps for the simplest decisions.

Obtaining Information, Making Predictions, and Selecting the Best Alternative

In order to effectively evaluate a potential course of action, data and information must be gathered. The relevant information may include quantitative financial factors that can be expressed in monetary or numerical terms, and qualitative factors that cannot be measured in numerical terms. For example, a company thinking about switching to a new system for maintaining electronic data will gather quantitative information related to the costs of the current system, such as staff time, salaried positions, software licensing, and hardware requirements. Additional information may include qualitative information related to factors such as employee morale.

After collecting relevant information, a decision model can be used to help make predictions about how the costs, behaviors, and states of nature beyond the control of the decision maker may influence outcomes. Excel spreadsheets are well suited to the quantitative portion of this task; qualitative variables may be assigned numerical weights so they, too, can be part of the decision model used for predicting potential outcomes.

Using quantitative approaches to making a decision can lead to greater confidence in the choice, but you should not ignore the value of qualitative information. After modeling the decision alternatives and calculating outcomes, selection of the best alternative may require asking additional questions, such as:

- What qualitative factors must be considered in addition to the quantitative analysis, and do they carry enough weight to discount one or more options?
- Does this alternative make sense for the long term?
- Can this alternative be realistically implemented? Think about resources and time frame, for example.
- Will the alternative be acceptable even if the outcome is not perfect, or if some unconsidered factors emerge after implementation?

Preparing an Implementation Action Plan

Once the decision has been made, the steps necessary to implement the decision must be determined. The decision maker should have a pretty good idea of what the final outcome should be in order to consider all relevant steps. For example, in the case of moving to a new data storage system, the final outcome is new software and hardware in use company-wide.

One key consideration is the time table for implementation. When will it start? How long will each task take? What tasks must be completed before others start? Can tasks be performed concurrently?

A project manager also must be chosen to help develop and manage the implementation action plan. This person will be held accountable for all tasks, resources, and scheduling to assure the decision is implemented as originally designed.

Key milestones for the implementation must be determined so that successful completion can be tracked. Determining who will be accountable for these milestones can help keep track of completion. The project manager may have overall responsibility for keeping the implementation on budget and on time, but others will play a supporting role in getting work done.

What resources are required for successful implementation? Money? Personnel? Facilities? Are these available in-house, or does external expertise need to be sourced?

Often, the most challenging part of implementing some decisions is dealing with the human and behavioral aspects. Part of the action plan must consider regular communication with all affected parties, including weekly project status updates, scheduled training sessions, and mechanisms for handling inquiries, feedback, or opposition.

Taking Action and Monitoring Results

Once the decision is made, approvals are received, and the action plan is developed, the actual implementation of the plan can begin. As progress is made, completion of the predetermined tasks can be documented and assessed against the schedule. The project manager can then compare actual completion activity against planned activity to be sure the implementation stays on track.

Occasionally, the best-laid plans do veer off-course. In this case, the project manager must be able to determine why, when, and where the tasks fell behind schedule to help set them back on course.

Verifying the Accuracy of the Decision

Once the action plan has been implemented, it is essential to verify that the decision was the correct course of action. The decision maker can assess the effect of the implemented decision by collecting feedback about the changes in operations. For example, in the case of the new electronic data storage system, were the anticipated cost savings achieved? Was the retraining of affected staff managed appropriately?

PROSKILLS

Design and Implement a Custom XML Vocabulary

XML is a powerful tool for developing structured documents whose content can be tested against a collection of rules defined in a DTD or schema. In this exercise, you'll use XML to create a vocabulary, and then you'll create and validate an XML document using your vocabulary by applying the XML skills you've learned in these tutorials.

Note: Please be sure *not* to include any personal information of a sensitive nature in the documents you create to be submitted to your instructor for this exercise. Later on, you can update the data in your database with such information for your own personal use.

1. Design your own XML vocabulary for a field of study that interests you. Your vocabulary should include the following features:
   a. Elements containing textual content
   b. Elements containing child elements
   c. Attributes containing textual content
   d. XML-supported entities
2. Write a summary documenting your vocabulary for other users.

3. Create an instance document based on your XML vocabulary.

4. Write a DTD to validate your instance document based on your vocabulary. Confirm that your instance document passes validation.

5. Write a schema to validate your instance document. Your schema should include the following features:

   a. One or more custom data types

   b. A named complex type

   c. Schema contents laid out in a Venetian Blind design

6. Apply your schema to your instance document and verify that your instance document passes validation.

7. Create a second XML vocabulary in the same field of study as your first. Document your vocabulary for other users.

8. Create a namespace for each of your vocabularies.

9. Create a compound document combining elements and attributes from both of your vocabularies.

10. Create a second schema file to validate the contents of your second XML vocabulary.

11. Apply your combined schemas to your compound document and confirm that the compound document passes validation.

12. Document your code and describe what you've learned from creating your own system of XML documents.

TUTORIAL 5

Transforming XML with XSLT and XPath

Writing XML Data to an Output File

OBJECTIVES

Session 5.1
- Learn the history and theory of XSLT
- Understand XPath and examine a node tree
- Create and attach an XSLT style sheet
- Create a root template
- Generate a result document from an XSLT style sheet

Session 5.2
- Create and apply templates to different nodes
- Extract and display the value of an element
- Extract and display the value of an attribute
- Explore XSLT's built-in templates

Session 5.3
- Set the value of an attribute in a result document
- Create conditional output using the `if` and `choose` elements
- Create an XPath expression using predicates
- Use XSLT to generate elements and attributes

Case | *Chesterton Financial*

Chesterton Financial is a brokerage firm in Burlington, Vermont. As part of its investment services business, the company advises clients on their investment portfolios. Rafael Garcia, a Chesterton Financial analyst, has created a sample XML document containing financial data on 15 different stocks. An XML document is useful for data storage but that data can sometimes be difficult to read and interpret. Rafael would like the content of his document displayed in an easier-to-read format.

One way of achieving Rafael's goal is to transform his XML data into a new file format. Rafael would like to see his stock market data placed within an HTML file that can be easily displayed in a web browser. He's asked your help in creating this transformation.

STARTING DATA FILES

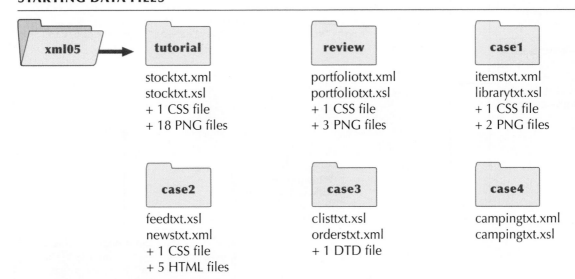

xml05 → **tutorial**
stocktxt.xml
stocktxt.xsl
+ 1 CSS file
+ 18 PNG files

review
portfoliotxt.xml
portfoliotxt.xsl
+ 1 CSS file
+ 3 PNG files

case1
itemstxt.xml
librarytxt.xsl
+ 1 CSS file
+ 2 PNG files

case2
feedtxt.xsl
newstxt.xml
+ 1 CSS file
+ 5 HTML files

case3
clisttxt.xsl
orderstxt.xml
+ 1 DTD file

case4
campingtxt.xml
campingtxt.xsl

Session 5.1 Visual Overview:

The **source document** contains the data that will be transformed using a style sheet.

```xml
<?xml version="1.0" encoding="UTF-8" ?>

<?xml-stylesheet type="text/xsl" href="stock.xsl" ?>
<portfolio>

   <author>Rafael Garcia</author>
   <date>4/17/2017</date>
   <time>13:17</time>

   <stock>
      <sName symbol="BA">Boeing Company</sName>
      <description>The Boeing Company engages in the design, development,
      manufacture, sale, and support of commercial jetliners, military
      aircraft, satellites, missile defense, human space flight, and
      launch systems and services worldwide. It also offers aviation
      services support, aircraft modifications, spares, training, maintenance
      documents, and technical advice to commercial and government customers.
      Its financing portfolio consists of equipment under operating leases,
      finance leases, notes and other receivables, assets held for sale or
      re-lease, and investments. The Boeing Company was founded in 1916
      and is based in Chicago, Illinois.
      </description>
      <category>Industrials</category>
```

The root element of an XSLT style sheet is stylesheet.

XSLT style sheets must be placed in the *http://www.w3.org/1999/XSL/Transform* namespace.

The **output element** is used to define the format of the result document.

This shows the output format for an HTML5 document.

The **root template** defines styles for the source document's root node.

Literal result elements are any elements that are not part of the XSLT vocabulary but instead are sent directly to the result document as raw text.

```xml
<xsl:stylesheet version="1.0"
    xmlns:xsl="http://www.w3.org/1999/XSL/Transform">

   <xsl:output method="html"
      doctype-system="about:legacy-compat"
      encoding="UTF-8"
      indent="yes" />

   <xsl:template match="/">
      <html>
         <head>
            <title>Portfolio Stocks</title>
            <link href="stock.css" rel="stylesheet" type="text/css" />
         </head>

         <body>

            <header>
               <h1>Chesterton Financial</h1>
               <h2>Portfolio Stocks</h2>
            </header>
         </body>

      </html>
   </xsl:template>

</xsl:stylesheet>
```

This shows the code written to the result document.

An **XSLT style sheet** is an XML document used to transform the contents of the source document into a new format, which appears in the result document.

Creating an XSLT Style Sheet

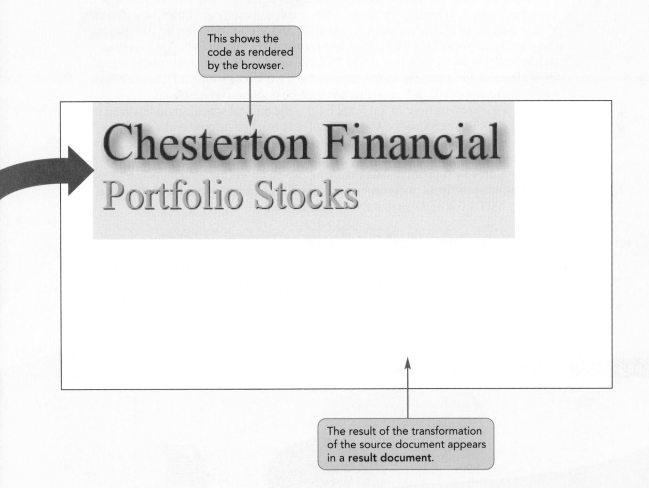

This shows the code as rendered by the browser.

Chesterton Financial
Portfolio Stocks

The result of the transformation of the source document appears in a **result document**.

Introducing XSL and XSLT

A challenge of working with data stored in XML is presenting that data in an easily readable format. One way of achieving this is by using **Extensible Stylesheet Language** or **XSL**. XSL is used to transform the contents of a source XML document containing data into a result document written in a new format. XSL is itself an XML vocabulary, so you can apply much of what you've learned in writing XML code toward writing your first XSL style sheet. XSL is organized into two languages:

- **XSL-FO** (**Extensible Stylesheet Language – Formatting Objects**) is used for the layout of paginated documents.
- **XSLT** (**Extensible Stylesheet Language Transformations**) is used to transform the contents of an XML document into another document format.

XSL-FO describes the precise layout of text on a page, indicating the placement of individual pages, text blocks, horizontal rules, headers, footers, and other page elements. XSLT is used for text-based output such as HTML and XHTML (for creating web pages), Portable Document Format (PDF), Rich Text Format (RTF), and so forth. XSLT can also take an XML file and rewrite it as a new XML document with a different structure and set of elements and attributes. In this tutorial you'll work only with XSLT, transforming a source document into HTML code that can then be displayed on a website.

There are several versions of XSLT. XSLT 1.0 is the original specification finalized by the W3C in 1999. The follow-up version, XSLT 2.0, reached recommendation status in 2007. Support for XSLT 2.0 was slow to develop; thus, it is not unusual at this time to find legacy applications based solely on XSLT 1.0 standards. XSLT 3.0 extends the language further by supporting data streaming, which allows the output document to be processed as the input document is read, resulting in greater speed and efficiency. Currently XSLT 3.0 is in the draft stage of development.

XSLT Style Sheets and Processors

Because XSLT is itself an XML vocabulary, you can create an XSLT style sheet using a basic text editor. XSLT style sheets have the filename extension .xsl to distinguish them from other XML documents. Once your style sheet is written, an XSLT processor is used to transform the contents of the source document into a new format (see Figure 5-1), which appears as the result document.

Figure 5-1   **Transforming a source document**

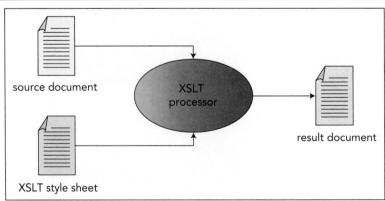

The transformation can be performed on a server or a client. In a **server-side transformation**, a server receives a request from a client to generate the result document. The server applies the style sheet to the source document and returns the result document to the client, often as a new file. In a server-side transformation, the client does not need an XSLT processor because all of the work is done on the server. This makes the process more accessible to a wide variety of users who may not have access to an XSLT processor. A disadvantage to server-side transformations is the heavy load they can place on a server as it attempts to handle transformation requests from multiple clients.

In a **client-side transformation**, a client requests retrieval of both a source document and a style sheet from the server. The client then performs the transformation and generates its own result document. There are several client-side XSLT processors available, including the following:

- Altova Raptor/XML Server is a processor sold with XMLSpy and supports XSLT 1.0, 2.0, and 3.0.
- libxslt is a free library of functions written in C supporting XSLT 1.0 and used within WebKit to run transformations within the Safari and Google Chrome browsers.
- MSXML is a set of application services supporting XSLT 1.0 that was developed by Microsoft and is included with Internet Explorer.
- Saxon is an open source standalone processor supporting XSLT 2.0 that can be used with Java and JavaScript applications.
- Xalan Apache is an open-source component that supports XSLT 1.0 and was developed by the Apache Software Foundation for both the Java and C++ programming languages.

TIP

For security reasons, Google Chrome displays transformations only for files stored on a server but not for files saved locally.

Most current browsers have built-in XSLT processors supporting XSLT 1.0. Thus, to view the results of a transformation, you only need to open the source XML document within your browser. If you want the transformed document stored as a separate file or if you want to use XSLT 2.0, you will need an XML editor. There are several free and commercial editors that support XSLT 1.0 and 2.0; the most prominent at the time of this writing is the free home edition of the Saxon processor.

Attaching an XSLT Style Sheet

An XSLT style sheet is attached to an XML document by adding the following processing instruction near the top of the XML document prior to the root element:

```
<?xml-stylesheet type="text/xsl" href="url" ?>
```

where *url* is the URL pointing to the location of the XSLT style sheet file.

Now that you have learned the basics about XSLT, you'll begin helping Rafael to develop an XSLT style sheet for displaying his stock market data. Rafael has a source XML document containing data from 15 different stocks in a sample portfolio. He wants to display this information in a web page, generating the HTML code with his XSLT style sheet. You'll start developing the XSLT style sheet by adding a processing instruction to Rafael's source document, linking that file to a proposed style sheet file.

To add the processing instruction:

1. Use your text editor to open **stocktxt.xml** from the xml05 ▶ tutorial folder. Enter **your name** and the **date** in the comment section at the top of the file, and save the file as **stock.xml**.

2. Insert the following processing instruction directly above the opening `<portfolio>` tag at the top of the file:

```
<?xml-stylesheet type="text/xsl" href="stock.xsl" ?>
```

Figure 5-2 shows the newly added processing instruction.

Figure 5-2 Attaching a style sheet

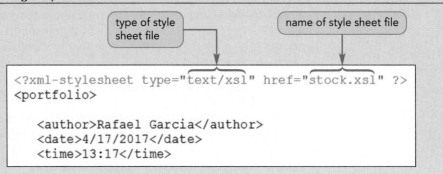

```
<?xml-stylesheet type="text/xsl" href="stock.xsl" ?>
<portfolio>

    <author>Rafael Garcia</author>
    <date>4/17/2017</date>
    <time>13:17</time>
```

Next, you and Rafael discuss how he wants to have the data in the stock.xml file transformed into an HTML document. First you need to study the current content and layout of the source file. Figure 5-3 shows the document's structure.

Figure 5-3 Structure of the stock.xml file

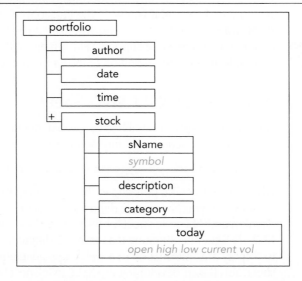

The content and purpose of each element and attribute is described in Figure 5-4.

Figure 5-4 Contents of the stock.xml file

Element	Description
portfolio	The root element
author	The author of the document
date	The date of the document contents
time	The time the document was last updated, in 24 hour format
stock	Information for an individual stock
sName	The name of the stock, containing an attribute named symbol that stores the stock ticker symbol
description	A description of the stock
category	The category for the stock: Industrials, Transportation, or Utilities
today	The opening, high, low, current, and volume values of the stock, stored in the following attributes: open, high, low, current, and vol

Take a few minutes now to review the contents of the file, comparing the structure and content to Figures 5-3 and 5-4.

To review the stock.xml file:

▶ **1.** Scroll down through the stock.xml file using your editor, paying attention to the use of elements and attributes throughout the document.

▶ **2.** After you have finished reviewing the document, close the file, saving your changes.

Figure 5-5 previews how Rafael wants the data in the stock.xml to be transformed into a web page. The date and time values are placed at the top-right corner of the page so that readers can quickly determine how current the data is. The stock's name, description, and ticker symbol are drawn from the sName and description elements, and the symbol attribute. Attributes from the today element are used to populate the table of current stock values. An inline image displaying a chart of the last three months of stock activity has been added to the web page. Finally, note that Rafael wants the stocks sorted into different stock categories (Industrials, Transportation, or Utilities) so stocks that share common characteristics appear together.

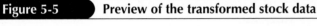

Figure 5-5   **Preview of the transformed stock data**

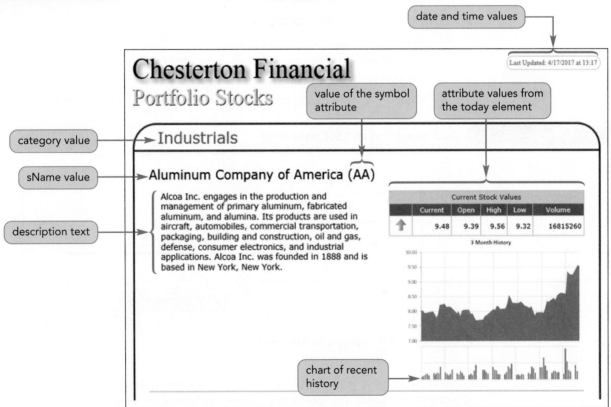

Now that you've seen how Rafael wants the output document to appear, you can begin writing the XSLT style sheet file to generate the HTML code.

Starting an XSLT Style Sheet

Because XSLT style sheets are XML documents, XSLT documents start with an xml declaration and a root element named stylesheet. The `stylesheet` element needs to be placed in the *http://www.w3.org/1999/XSL/Transform* namespace. Thus, every XSLT stylesheet has the following basic structure:

```
<?xml version="1.0" ?>
<xsl:stylesheet version="value"
     xmlns:xsl="http://www.w3.org/1999/XSL/Transform">
  style sheet contents
</xsl:stylesheet>
```

where *value* is the XSLT version and *style sheet contents* are the elements and attributes specific to the style sheet.

For Rafael's project you'll use a version number of "1.0" to indicate to the XSLT processor that this file should be compliant with XSLT 1.0 standards. You create the stock.xsl style sheet file now.

To create the XSLT style sheet:

▶ **1.** Use your text editor to open **stocktxt.xsl** from the xml05 ▶ tutorial folder. Enter **your name** and the **date** in the comment section at the top of the file, and save the file as **stock.xsl**.

▶ **2.** Below the comment section insert the following tags:

```
<xsl:stylesheet version="1.0"
     xmlns:xsl="http://www.w3.org/1999/XSL/Transform">
</xsl:stylesheet>
```

Figure 5-6 highlights the root `stylesheet` element used in the document.

Figure 5-6 | **Root element of an XSLT style sheet**

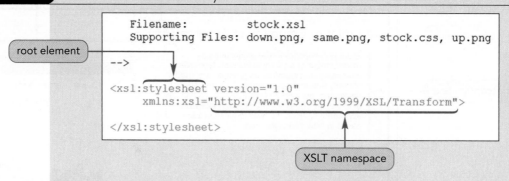

▶ **3.** Save your changes to the stock.xsl file.

With the initial structure of the XSLT file in place and linked to the XML source document, stock.xml, you can begin working with the style sheet design. To do this, you first need to learn how to access the source document content from within the style sheet.

Introducing XPath

While XML data is stored in text files, the contents are read into memory and stored in a hierarchal tree structure. The **XPath** language, which was introduced by W3C, is used to access and navigate the contents of that data tree. Like XSLT, XPath has gone through several versions, usually paired with enhancements of XSLT. The initial version, XPath 1.0, was released in 1999 and enjoys universal support with XML processors and web browsers. XPath 2.0 reached Recommendation status in 2007 and is the most current version of the language. Processors that support XSLT 2.0 will also support most, if not all, features of XPath 2.0. None of the major web browsers provides built-in support for XPath 2.0 at the time of this writing. XPath 3.0, like XSLT 3.0, is only in the candidate stage of language development and is not widely supported by XML processors or web browsers.

Working with Nodes

XPath operates by expressing the contents of the source document in terms of nodes. A **node** is any item within the tree structure of the document. A collection of nodes is called a **node set**. Any of the following objects from an XML document are considered nodes of that document:

- An element
- The text contained within an element
- An element attribute
- A comment statement
- A processing instruction
- A defined namespace
- The entire source document itself

Nodes are referred to based on the type of objects they contain. Thus, an **element node** refers to an element from the source document, an **attribute node** refers to an element's attribute, and so forth.

However, not everything within the source document is a node. The following are *not* considered nodes:

- The XML declaration
- A DOCTYPE declaration
- A CDATA section
- An entity reference

The various nodes from the source document are organized into a **node tree**, with the **root node** or **document node** at the top of the tree. The root node contains all other nodes. It is also the node that represents the source document; this should not be confused with the root element, which is the element at the top of the hierarchy of elements. Figure 5-7 shows the node tree for a sample XML document. Note that although the XML declaration in the first line of the document is not treated as a node, the other lines of code in the document have corresponding entries in the node tree.

Figure 5-7 A sample node tree

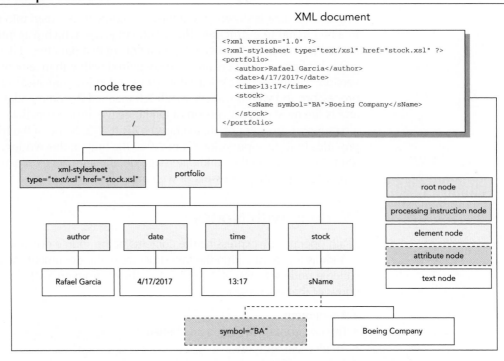

The relationship among the nodes in a node tree is based on a familial structure. A node that contains other nodes is called a **parent node**, and the nodes contained in a parent node are called **child nodes**. Nodes that share a common parent are called **sibling nodes**. Note that a node can have only one parent. As you progress further down the tree, any node found at a level below another node is referred to as a **descendant** of that node. The node at the top of the branch is referred to as the **ancestor** of all nodes that lie beneath it. In the sample document shown in Figure 5-7, the portfolio node is the parent of the child nodes author, date, time, and stock. Further down the node tree is the sName node, which is a descendant of both the portfolio and stock nodes. The root node has only two child nodes—the portfolio node and the processing instruction that links the XML document to the stock.xsl style sheet.

Absolute and Relative Location Paths

One of the functions of XPath is to translate this hierarchical structure into an expression called a **location path** that references a specific node or node set from the source document. You can think of a location path as the directions that lead you through the node tree.

The location path can be written in either absolute or relative terms. An **absolute path** is a path that always starts from the root node and descends down through the node tree to a particular node or node set. The root node is identified by an initial forward slash (/), and then each level down the tree is marked by additional forward slashes. An absolute path that extends down the node tree from the root node has the following general form:

```
/child1/child2/child3/...
```

where `child1`, `child2`, `child3`, and so forth are the descendants of the root node. For example, the absolute path to the sName node from Figure 5-7 is

```
/portfolio/stock/sName
```

starting from the root node through the portfolio element and then the stock element within that and finally the sName element within the stock element. This particular location path returns a node set that references all of the sName element nodes in the source document. Note that element nodes are identified by the element name.

A large document can have a long and complicated hierarchy. In order to avoid listing all of the levels of the node tree, you can use a double forward slash (//) with the syntax

> //descendant

where descendant is the name of the descendant node. For example, the path

> //sName

returns a node set containing all of the sName element nodes in the document, no matter where they're located.

Absolute paths can be long and cumbersome for large and complicated node trees. Therefore, most locations are written using **relative paths** in which the location path starts from a particular node (not necessarily the root node) called the **context node**. Rather than working through a path that navigates through the entire node tree, the XSLT processor needs only to work with a fragment of the tree. Figure 5-8 describes some of the common relative path expressions in XPath.

Figure 5-8   XPath expressions for relative paths

Relative Path	Description
.	Refers to the context node itself
..	Refers to the parent of the context node
child	Refers to the child of the context node named child
child1/child2	Refers to the child2 node, a child of the child1 node beneath the context node
../sibling	Refers to a sibling of the context node named sibling
.//descendant	Refers to a descendant of the context node named descendant
../..	Refers to the parent of the parent of the context node

For example, if the portfolio element shown in Figure 5-7 is the context node, then the relative path that starts from the portfolio element and goes to the sName element has the path expression

> stock/sName

Figure 5-9 provides other examples of the relative paths in the node tree from Figure 5-7 using the stock element as the context node. Take some time to study these expressions because relative paths are an important part of XPath.

Figure 5-9   Resolving an XPath expression relative to a context node

Context Node	Relative Path	Description
stock	.	Refers to the stock element
	..	Refers to the portfolio element, the parent of the stock element
	sName	Refers to the sName element, a child of the stock element
	../date	Refers to the date element, a sibling of the stock element
	.//sName	Refers to all descendent elements of the stock element named sName
	../..	Refers to the parent of the parent of the stock element (in this case the root node)

Identifying Nodes with Location Paths

For Absolute Paths

• To create an absolute reference to a node, use the location path expression

   `/child1/child2/child3/...`

   where `child1`, `child2`, `child3`, and so on are descendants of the root node.

For Relative Paths

• To reference a node without regard to its location in the node tree, use the expression

   `//descendant`

   where `descendant` is the name of the descendant node.
• To reference the context node, use

   `.`

• To reference the parent of the context node, use

   `..`

• To reference a child of the context node, use

   `child`

   where `child` is the name of the child node.
• To reference a sibling of the context node, use

   `../sibling`

   where `sibling` is the name of the sibling node.

XPath supports the wildcard character (*) to reference nodes of any type or name. For example, the XPath expression

   `/portfolio/*`

is an absolute reference that references all of the child nodes of the portfolio element. To select all of the nodes in the node tree, you can use the path

   `//*`

In this expression, the (*) symbol matches any node, and the (//) symbol sets the scope of the path to include all of the descendants of the root node.

Text, Comment, and Process Instruction Nodes

As you've seen, element nodes are referenced using the element's name. To reference a **text node**, which is the text contained within an element, you use the XPath expression:

   `text()`

For example, the following location path returns a node set that contains all of the text nodes within the sName element node:

   `//sName/text()`

Note that, because there are no nodes for character or entity references, if the element text contains an entity or character reference, then that reference is resolved by the XSLT processor before the text node is created.

Comments and processing instruction nodes can be referenced using the XPath expressions

```
comment()
```

and

```
processing-instruction()
```

Thus, the following location path returns a node set of all of the comments in the source document:

```
//comment()
```

There is usually little need for referencing comments or processing instructions in the source document until you get to more advanced XSLT applications.

You've barely scratched the surface of all that can be done with XPath. As you continue to work on XSLT style sheets in this and future tutorials, you'll return to XPath periodically to explore the various facets of this language. However, what you've learned is enough to start adding content to Rafael's style sheet that he will use to generate his stock market report.

Introducing XSLT Templates

The basic building block of an XSLT style sheet is the template. A **template** is a collection of styles that are applied to a specific node set within the source document. The general syntax of an XSLT template is

```
<xsl:template match="node set">
    styles
</xsl:template>
```

where *node set* is an XPath expression that references a node set from the source document and *styles* are the XSLT styles applied to those nodes. An XSLT style sheet will usually have several templates with each template matching a particular node set. Templates simplify the process of creating a style sheet because the programmer only needs to write a style for a single set of nodes rather than the entire node tree. The final style sheet is therefore the sum total of individual templates.

The Root Template

The fundamental template in the XSLT style sheet is the root template, which defines styles for the source document's root node. Because the root node refers to the source document itself (and *not* the root element), the root template sets the initial styles for the entire result document. The syntax for the root template is

```
<xsl:template match="/">
    styles
</xsl:template>
```

Note that the value of the `match` attribute is set to `"/"`, which is the XPath expression for the root node. The root template can be located anywhere between the opening and closing `<xsl:stylesheet>` tags of the XSLT document. However, it is customary to put the root template at the top of the document, directly after the opening `<xsl:stylesheet>` tag.

Creating a Template

- To create an XSLT template that matches a specified node set from the source document, insert

```
<xsl:template match="node set">
    styles
</xsl:template>
```

where *node set* is an XPath expression that references the node set and *styles* are the XSLT styles defined for those node(s).
- To create a template for the root node, enter

```
<xsl:template match="/">
    styles
</xsl:template>
```

You add a root template to the stock.xsl file now.

To create the root template:

1. Return to the **stock.xsl** file in your text editor.

2. Within the stylesheet element, insert the following content:

```
<xsl:template match="/">
</xsl:template>
```

Figure 5-10 shows the initial code for the root template.

Figure 5-10 **Inserting the template element**

```
<xsl:stylesheet version="1.0"
    xmlns:xsl="http://www.w3.org/1999/XSL/Transform">

    <xsl:template match="/">

    </xsl:template>

</xsl:stylesheet>
```

> XPath expression matching the root element of the source document

Next you'll insert XSLT elements into the root template that will generate the contents of the result document.

Literal Result Elements

Content is written to the result document through the use of XSLT elements and literal result elements. An **XSLT element** is any element that is part of the XSLT vocabulary. An XSLT element will usually contain instructions to the processor regarding how to interpret and render the contents from the source document. XSLT elements must be placed within the XSLT namespace, usually with the namespace prefix xsl.

A literal result element is any element that is not part of the XSLT vocabulary but is sent directly into the result document as raw text. For example, any HTML tags in a style sheet are considered a literal result because they are ignored by XSLT processors and written into the result document.

Rafael wants to create a web page based on the contents of the stock.xml file. He provides you with the following initial HTML code for his document:

```
<html>
   <head>
      <title>Portfolio Stocks</title>
      <link href="stock.css" rel="stylesheet" type="text/css" />
   </head>

   <body>
      <header>
         <h1>Chesterton Financial</h1>
         <h2>Portfolio Stocks</h2>
      </header>
   </body>

</html>
```

TIP

Even though HTML tags are treated as text, they still must follow XML syntax for well-formedness to be accepted by the XSLT processor.

All of the HTML elements in this code sample are literal result elements because they do not involve any of the elements associated with XSLT. The XSLT processor will write the HTML code directly into the result document without modification, creating an HTML document in the process.

To insert the HTML tags:

1. Within the root template, insert the following content immediately following the `<xsl:template>` tag:

```
<html>
   <head>
      <title>Portfolio Stocks</title>
      <link href="stock.css" rel="stylesheet" type="text/css" />
   </head>

   <body>
      <header>
         <h1>Chesterton Financial</h1>
         <h2>Portfolio Stocks</h2>
      </header>
   </body>
</html>
```

Figure 5-11 highlights the initial code from the root template.

Figure 5-11	Literal result elements placed within the root template

```
<xsl:template match="/">
   <html>
      <head>
         <title>Portfolio Stocks</title>
         <link href="stock.css" rel="stylesheet" type="text/css" />
      </head>

      <body>
         <header>
            <h1>Chesterton Financial</h1>
            <h2>Portfolio Stocks</h2>
         </header>
      </body>
   </html>
</xsl:template>
```

HTML code to be written directly to the result document

2. Save your changes to the file.

Note that Rafael has already created an external CSS style sheet named stock.css to format the appearance of his web page. If you want to review CSS usage, you can examine the contents of stock.css to see how the headings are formatted.

You've entered the initial code that you want written to the result document, but how does the processor know to create an HTML file based on this code rather than an XML file or a basic text file? You can control the type of file created by specifying the output method.

Defining the Output Format

By default, an XSLT processor will create a result document as an XML file. There are two exceptions to this default behavior:

- If the root element in the result document is the `html` element, then the result document will be created as an HTML file.
- If the root element in the result document is the `html` element and it is placed in the XHTML namespace, *http://www.w3.org/1999/xhtml*, then the result document will be created as an XHTML file.

To explicitly define the format of the result document, you can add the following `output` element to the style sheet:

```
<xsl:output attributes />
```

where *attributes* is the list of attributes that control how the processor writes the result document. The `output` element should be placed directly after the opening `<xsl:stylesheet>` tag before any templates. Figure 5-12 describes the different attributes associated with this element.

Figure 5-12   **Attributes of the output element**

Attribute	Description
`method="xml|html|text"`	Defines the output format as xml (the default), html, or text
`version="number"`	Specifies the version of the output
`encoding="text"`	Specifies the character encoding
`omit-xml-declaration="yes|no"`	Specifies whether to omit an XML declaration in the first line of the result document
`standalone="yes|no"`	Specifies whether a standalone attribute should be included in the output and sets its value
`doctype-public="text"`	Sets the URI for the public identifier in the `<!DOCTYPE>` declaration
`doctype-system="text"`	Sets the system identifier in the `<!DOCTYPE>` declaration
`cdata-section-elements="list"`	Specifies a list of element names whose content should be output in CDATA sections
`indent="yes|no"`	Specifies whether the output should be indented to better display its structure
`media-type="mime-type"`	Sets the MIME type of the output

For example, to create a file based on the strict XHTML DTD, you would include the following output element as part of your style sheet:

```
<xsl:output method="xml"
   indent="yes"
   encoding="UTF-8"
   doctype-system="http://www.w3.org/TR/xhtml1/DTD/xhtml1-strict.dtd"
   doctype-public="-//W3C//DTD XHTML 1.0 Strict//EN" />
```

When the XSLT processor generates the result document it automatically adds the following XML declaration and a DOCTYPE to the beginning of the file, creating a XHTML file that can be validated against the strict XHTML DTD:

```
<?xml version="1.0" encoding="UTF-8" ?>
<!DOCTYPE html PUBLIC "-//W3C//DTD XHTML 1.0 Strict//EN"
   "http://www.w3.org/TR/xhtml1/DTD/xhtml1-strict.dtd">
```

If you need to only to create an HTML file but do not need to have it validated, you can employ the following output element:

```
<xsl:output method="html"
   indent="yes"
   encoding="UTF-8"
   version="4.0" />
```

and the processor will generate code that is compliant with HTML 4.0, but the file will include neither an XML declaration nor a DOCTYPE.

For some applications, the result document will require only XML elements and attributes but not an XML declaration. Because it lacks an XML declaration, the result document is not a true XML document but rather an **XML fragment** containing part of a full XML document. XML fragments are created by including the following omit-xml-declaration attribute in the output statement:

```
<xsl:output method="xml"
   version="1.0"
   omit-xml-declaration="yes" />
```

Finally, to create documents that contain only text values, use the following output element with the method attribute set to "text":

```
<xsl:output method="text" />
```

This format could be used for creating Rich Text Format (RTF), which is a format supported by most word processors. To create an RTF file, you insert code for the RTF file into the style sheet. XSLT processors then pass the code through as text, without checking the document for well-formedness or validity or added XML tags.

Rafael's document will be written in the language of HTML5. He wants the file to conform to valid HTML5 standards, which include the presence of a DOCTYPE statement but do not include an XML processing instruction. To create an HTML5 file, you would use the following output element with the value of the doctype-system attribute set to "about:legacy-compat"

```
<xsl:output method="html"
   doctype-system="about:legacy-compat"
   encoding="UTF-8"
   indent="yes" />
```

You add this element now to Rafael's style sheet.

To specify the output format of the result document:

▶ **1.** Insert the following code immediately after the opening `<xsl:stylesheet>` element located at the top of the stock.xsl file:

```
<xsl:output method="html"
    doctype-system="about:legacy-compat"
    encoding="UTF-8"
    indent="yes" />
```

Figure 5-13 highlights the `output` element to create a result document in HTML5 format.

Figure 5-13 ▶ **Setting the output format to HTML5**

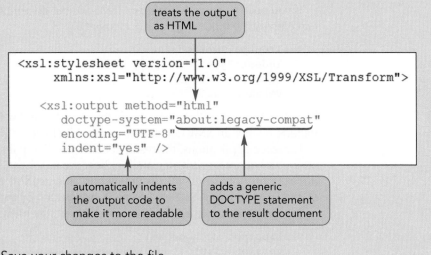

treats the output as HTML

```
<xsl:stylesheet version="1.0"
    xmlns:xsl="http://www.w3.org/1999/XSL/Transform">

  <xsl:output method="html"
    doctype-system="about:legacy-compat"
    encoding="UTF-8"
    indent="yes" />
```

automatically indents the output code to make it more readable

adds a generic DOCTYPE statement to the result document

▶ **2.** Save your changes to the file.

Now that you've specified an output method, you can view the initial result document generated by the XSLT style sheet.

Transforming a Document

The simplest way to view a web page generated by an XSLT 1.0 style sheet is to open the source document in your web browser. Because most browsers have a built-in XSLT processor, the browser will automatically apply the XSLT style sheet to the source file and display the HTML file as rendered by the browser. If you want to view the underlying HTML code that was generated by the XSLT style sheet, you must use the developer tools available on your browser.

To review your progress in developing a style sheet for Rafael's stock report, you'll use your browser to open the stock.xml file and view its content as transformed by the stock.xsl style sheet. You can then use the developer's tools provided by your browser to view the actual HTML code generated by the style sheet.

To view the result document:

▶ **1.** Use your browser to open **stock.xml** from the xml05 ▶ tutorial folder. Your browser should display a main heading with the text "Chesterton Financial" and a subheading with the text "Portfolio Stocks".

Trouble? If no page content appears you might have made a mistake in the XSLT file. Check your code against the code shown in Figure 5-11. If you are using Google Chrome, you will have to upload your files to a web server to view the result document.

2. Use the developer tools in your browser to view the HTML code generated by the style sheet. In Internet Explorer you open the developer tools by pressing the **F12** key. In Firefox and Google Chrome, you can view the HTML code by pressing **Ctrl+Shift+I**. For other web browsers, check the browser's online help for information on displaying the developer tools.

Figure 5-14 shows the appearance of the web page and the underling HTML code written by the style sheet as viewed under Internet Explorer.

Figure 5-14   **Viewing the result document within Internet Explorer**

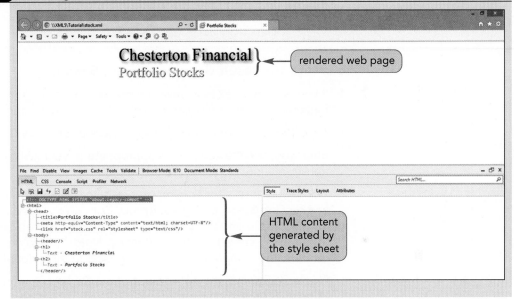

Running Transformations Using Saxon

Another way to view the result document is to generate the document as a separate file using an XSLT processor. While it is not necessary to generate this file, the advantage of creating a separate file is that you can easily review the code generated by the style sheet and locate any errors in the output. You can also share the result document with other users who might not have access to an XSLT processor. A disadvantage is that every time you make a change to the style sheet you have to recreate the result file.

In the steps that follow, you perform the transformation using the Saxon XSLT processor in Java command line mode. The free home edition of the Saxon XSLT processor can be downloaded from *saxon.sourceforge.net*. To use Saxon you must also have Java or the .NET framework installed on your computer. You can download these programming environments freely from *www.java.com* or *www.microsoft.com/net/downloads*. The most current installation instructions for these programs are provided on the websites.

Once you have installed and configured both Java and Saxon on your computer, you can apply a transformation in Saxon Java command line mode by running the following command within a command prompt window:

```
java net.sf.saxon.Transform –s:source –xsl:style –o:output
```

where *source* is the XML source file, *style* is the XSLT style sheet file, and *output* is the result file. You can omit the **-s:** and **-xsl:** prefixes provided that the source and style sheet file are listed prior to the output file and other Saxon command line parameters. For example, the following command applies the style sheet transformation from the stock.xsl file to the stock.xml file, storing the result document in the portfolio.html file:

```
java net.sf.saxon.Transform stock.xml stock.xsl -o:portfolio.html
```

If you are using Saxon on the .NET platform, the equivalent command line is

```
Transform -s:source -xsl:style -o:output
```

where, once again, you can omit the -s: and -xsl: prefixes provided the source and style sheet file are listed prior to the output file and other Saxon command line parameters. Thus, the same transformation under Saxon on the .NET platform is entered as

```
Transform stock.xml stock.xsl -o:portfolio.html
```

You use an XSLT processor now to create the result document in the portfolio.html file. If you have access to an editor other than Saxon using Java or the .NET platform, review the steps that follow and apply the corresponding commands available from your own editor to the task of generating a result document.

To create the result document using Saxon:

▶ 1. If you are using Saxon in Java command line mode, go to the xml05 ▶ tutorial folder and run the following command from within a command window:

```
java net.sf.saxon.Transform stock.xml stock.xsl -o:portfolio.html
```

otherwise, use the commands appropriate to your XSLT processor to run the transformation and generate the result document.

Talk to your instructor or computer resource person for help in installing and running Saxon or any XSLT processor on your system. If you do not have access to an XSLT processor other than your web browser, you can review these steps for future reference. *Note: You do not need a standalone processor to complete the remaining tasks in this tutorial.*

Figure 5-15 shows the appearance of the Saxon command as it appears on a Windows command line.

| Figure 5-15 | **Running a transformation using Saxon in Java command line mode** |

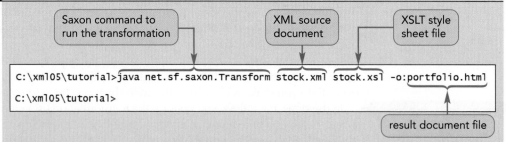

Trouble? If Saxon returns the warning that you are running an XSLT 1 style sheet in an XSLT 2 processor, you can safely ignore the warning. Most of XSLT 2.0 is backward compatible with XSLT 1.0.

 2. Open the **portfolio.html** file from the xml05 ▸ tutorial folder in a text editor and verify that the code matches that shown in Figure 5-16.

Figure 5-16	Result document code

```
<!DOCTYPE html
  SYSTEM "about:legacy-compat">
<html>
   <head>
      <meta http-equiv="Content-Type" content="text/html; charset=UTF-8">

      <title>Portfolio Stocks</title>
      <link href="stock.css" rel="stylesheet" type="text/css">
   </head>
   <body>
      <header>
         <h1>Chesterton Financial</h1>
         <h2>Portfolio Stocks</h2>
      </header>
   </body>
</html>
```

 3. Close your text editor.

When you viewed the contents of the portfolio.html file, you may have noticed that the XSLT processor added the following extra line to the document:

```
<meta http-equiv="Content-Type" content="text/html; charset=UTF-8">
```

The meta element makes it clear to any application opening this file what type of content the file contains and how the characters are encoded.

Problem Solving: Debugging your Style Sheet

When you start creating your own style sheets you will invariably encounter a transformation that results in an error in which no code is sent to the result document or the code that is sent is missing key features and values. To debug your style sheets you should look for these common sources of error:

- **Attach the Style Sheet**. If your transformation is not being applied to the source document, confirm that you have attached the style sheet using the `<?xml-stylesheet>` processing instruction.
- **Validate**. XSLT files have to adhere to well-formed and valid XML. Test both the source document and the XSLT file for errors in structure or content before running your transformation.
- **Typos**. The names of elements and attributes in your XPath expressions must exactly match the names of elements and attributes in the source document, including upper- and lowercase letters.
- **Context matters**. Many errors occur because of mistakes in an XPath expression. Make sure your XPath expression makes sense based on the location of the context node.
- **Namespace Issues**. Make sure that all of your elements belong to the correct namespace and that the namespace has the correct prefix and URI.

If you still can't find the source of error, remember that most XML editors include debugging tools to locate errors in code or style sheet structure. Invest in an editor with a good debugger to quickly find the source of your mistakes.

At this point, you have not placed any content from the source document into the result document. All of the content of the result document has been literal result elements. In the next session, you'll learn how to retrieve data values from the source file and display them in the result document.

REVIEW

Session 5.1 Quick Check

1. What are XSLT, XPath, and XSL-FO?
2. Provide the processing instruction to link an XML document to an XSLT style sheet named styles.xsl.
3. Using the node tree diagram in Figure 5-7, provide the absolute path to the author element node.
4. Using the node tree diagram in Figure 5-7, if the context node is the author element node, provide the relative path to the sName element node.
5. Provide an XPath expression to return a node set of all author elements, regardless of their location in the source document.
6. What is a literal result element?
7. Provide the XSLT element to specify that the result document should be a transitional XHTML file with a system DTD sent to "http://www.w3.org/TR/xhtml1/DTD/xhtml1-transitional.dtd" and the public DTD set to "-//W3C//DTD XHTML 1.0 Transitional//EN". Include an attribute to have the XSLT processor indent the output to make it easier to read.

Session 5.2 Visual Overview:

```
<body>

    <header>

        <section>
           Last Updated:
           <xsl:value-of select="portfolio/date" />
           at
           <xsl:value-of select="portfolio/time" />
        </section>

        <h1>Chesterton Financial</h1>
        <h2>Portfolio Stocks</h2>

    </header>

    <section>
       <xsl:apply-templates select="portfolio/stock" />
    </section>

</body>
```

The **xsl:value-of** element writes the value of the selected nodes.

The **xsl:apply-templates** element applies a template for the selected nodes.

This is the value of the sName element and the @symbol attribute.

This is the value of the description element.

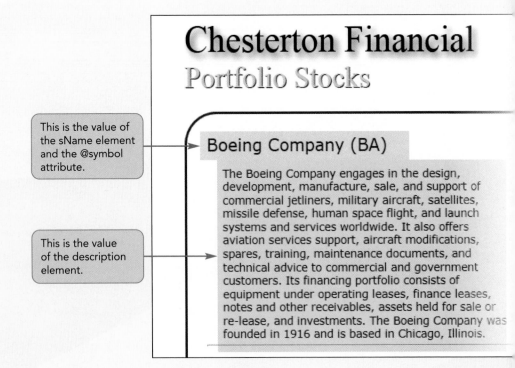

Chesterton Financial
Portfolio Stocks

Boeing Company (BA)

The Boeing Company engages in the design, development, manufacture, sale, and support of commercial jetliners, military aircraft, satellites, missile defense, human space flight, and launch systems and services worldwide. It also offers aviation services support, aircraft modifications, spares, training, maintenance documents, and technical advice to commercial and government customers. Its financing portfolio consists of equipment under operating leases, finance leases, notes and other receivables, assets held for sale or re-lease, and investments. The Boeing Company was founded in 1916 and is based in Chicago, Illinois.

Applying Templates to Document Nodes

The **match** attribute of the xsl:template element is used to design the output format for the specified node set.

Attribute nodes are referenced using the path expression @*att* where *att* is the name of the attribute.

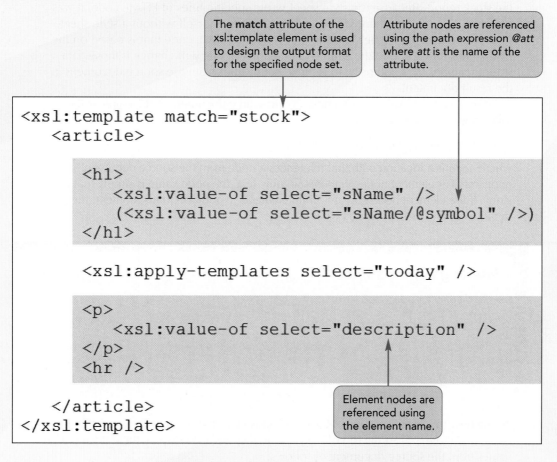

```
<xsl:template match="stock">
   <article>

      <h1>
         <xsl:value-of select="sName" />
         (<xsl:value-of select="sName/@symbol" />)
      </h1>

      <xsl:apply-templates select="today" />

      <p>
         <xsl:value-of select="description" />
      </p>
      <hr />

   </article>
</xsl:template>
```

Element nodes are referenced using the element name.

Last Updated: 4/17/2017 at 13:17

This is the value of the date and time elements.

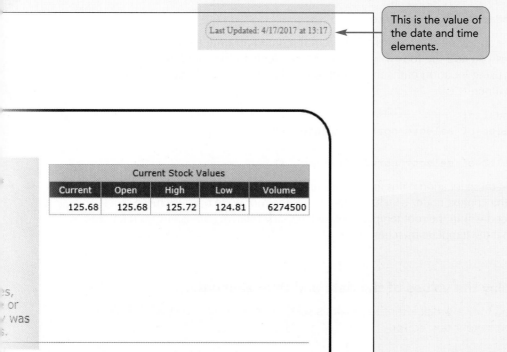

Current Stock Values				
Current	Open	High	Low	Volume
125.68	125.68	125.72	124.81	6274500

Extracting Element Values

In the last session you worked with Rafael to create the initial XSLT style sheet for the stock report. Because the style sheet wrote specific lines of HTML code, it was not any more efficient than writing the HTML code yourself without a style sheet. However, Rafael wants the style sheet to generate HTML code that is based on the data values found within the source document and that will change if those data values change. Thus you need to retrieve data values from the source document in the result document.

To display a data value from a node in the source document, XSLT employs the following value-of element:

```
<xsl:value-of select="node" />
```

where *node* is a location path that references a node from the source document's node tree. For element nodes that contain only text, the node value is simply that text string. If the element node contains child elements in addition to text content, the text in those child nodes appears as well.

To see how this works, return to Rafael's proposed sketch of his web page, shown earlier in Figure 5-5. At the top of the page, Rafael wants to display the date and time values from the source document as follows:

```
Last Updated: date at time
```

where *date* and *time* are values taken from the date and time elements. To display these values you add the following value-of elements to the root template of the style sheet using location paths that point to the date and time elements in the source document:

```
Last Updated:
<xsl:value-of select="portfolio/date" />
at
<xsl:value-of select="portfolio/time" />
```

Note that these location paths are relative and not absolute paths. They are expressed relative to the context node, which, in this case, is the root node because these styles will be placed within the root template. By default, any relative path is always relative to the node that the template matches.

To display the values of the date and time elements:

▶ **1.** If you took a break after the previous session, make sure the **stock.xsl** file is open in your text editor.

2. Insert the following code within the header element inside of the root template:

```
<section>
   Last Updated:
   <xsl:value-of select="portfolio/date" />
   at
   <xsl:value-of select="portfolio/time" />
</section>
```

Figure 5-17 shows the location of the style code within the root template.

Figure 5-17   **Displaying the value of the date and time elements**

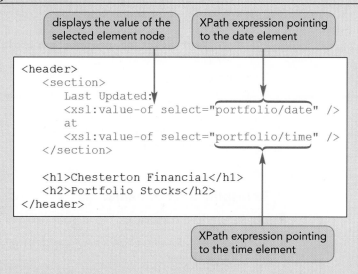

displays the value of the selected element node

XPath expression pointing to the date element

```
<header>
    <section>
       Last Updated:
       <xsl:value-of select="portfolio/date" />
       at
       <xsl:value-of select="portfolio/time" />
    </section>

    <h1>Chesterton Financial</h1>
    <h2>Portfolio Stocks</h2>
</header>
```

XPath expression pointing to the time element

3. Save your changes to the file.

4. Using either your browser (if it contains a built-in XSLT processor) or an XSLT processor, generate the revised result document.

Note: If you use the editor, follow the techniques described in the last session to update the contents of the portfolio.html file. You will need to update the portfolio.html file each time if you want to keep the file current.

Figure 5-18 shows the appearance of the revised web page with the date and time values retrieved from the stock.xml file.

Figure 5-18   **Revised result document**

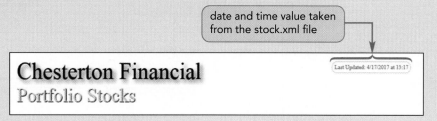

date and time value taken from the stock.xml file

Chesterton Financial
Portfolio Stocks

Last Updated: 4/17/2017 at 13:17

The stock.xml file contains the names of 15 stocks. Next, you'll display the name of each stock as an h1 heading in the document and placed within its own article by writing the following HTML5 code to the result document:

```
<section>
   <article>
       <h1>stock name</h1>
   </article>
</section>
```

where *stock name* is the name of the stock, as retrieved from the sName element. To generate this code you'll add the following code to the root template:

```
<section>
   <article>
       <h1>
           <xsl:value-of select="portfolio/stock/sName" />
       </h1>
   </article>
</section>
```

If you're unclear about the location path used in this expression, refer to the source document or to the tree diagram shown earlier in Figure 5-3. You'll add this code now to the stock.xsl style sheet.

To display a stock name:

1. Return to the **stock.xsl** file in your text editor.

2. Insert the following code above the closing **</body>** tag within the root template:

```
<section>
   <article>
       <h1>
           <xsl:value-of select="portfolio/stock/sName" />
       </h1>
   </article>
</section>
```

Figure 5-19 shows the code used to display the names of the stock in the portfolio.

Figure 5-19	Code to display the stock name

HTML5 article element

location path referencing the sName element

```
<section>
   <article>
       <h1>
           <xsl:value-of select="portfolio/stock/sName" />
       </h1>
   </article>
</section>

</body>
```

3. Save your changes to the stock.xsl file, and regenerate the result document (either within your web browser or by using an XML editor.) Figure 5-20 shows the revised result document.

Figure 5-20   **Name of the first stock in the portfolio**

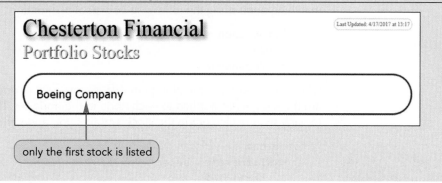

The first stock name listed in the stock.xml file appears in the document, but where are the other 14 stocks? In XSLT 1.0, when the location path returns more than one possible node, the value-of element will display only the value of the first node in that node set (in XSLT 2.0 the values of all of the matching nodes are displayed.)

Thus, to list the names of the stocks in the portfolio, you'll revise the style sheet to go through each stock element in the node tree.

INSIGHT

Using XSLT with HTML Markup Tags

XSLT can be used to transform data from documents written in any XML vocabulary, including RSS news feeds. Some RSS news feeds will store news items within HTML tags placed inside CDATA sections. Thus, one challenge for transforming data from a news feed is to retain the HTML tag structure in the result document. For example, the following code from an RSS feed uses a CDATA section to store the heading for a news story within an h1 element used for marking main web page headings.

```
<description><![CDATA[
    <h1>News Story</h1>
]]></description>
```

When the XSLT processor encounters this HTML code, it will replace all of the HTML tags with escape characters, writing the following text to the result document:

```
&lt;h1&gt;News Story&lt;/h1&gt;
```

and losing the h1 heading tag in the process.

To overcome this problem, you can disable the replacement of HTML tags with escape characters using the disable-output-escaping attribute. The following code shows how to write the HTML code in the description element directly without escaping:

```
<xsl:value-of select="description" disable-output-
escaping="yes" />
```

Now the processor will send the HTML code directly to the result document as it is stored in the CDATA section, including all of the HTML markup tags. This technique is particularly useful when you need to place large sections of HTML code in the result document without losing the HTML tags in the process.

Using the `for-each` Element

If there are multiple nodes that match the location path, you can create a style for each matching node using the following `for-each` instruction:

```
<xsl:for-each select="node set">
    styles
</xsl:for-each>
```

where *node set* is a location path that returns a set of one or more nodes and *styles* are the XSLT styles applied to each node in the node set. Thus, to apply the same style to each sName element in the stock.xml file, you apply the following code:

```
<section>
    <xsl:for-each select="portfolio/stock">
        <article>
            <h1>
                <xsl:value-of select="sName" />
            </h1>
        </article>
    </xsl:for-each>
</section>
```

As the XSLT processor goes through the source document's node tree, it stops at each occurrence of a portfolio/stock node and writes the HTML code enclosing the value of the sName element. Note that the statement `<xsl:value-of select="sName" />` uses a relative path reference to point to the sName element because, in this situation, the context node is the portfolio/stock element node.

REFERENCE

Applying a Style for each Node in a Node Set

- To apply a style to each occurrence of a node, use

```
<xsl:for-each select="node set">
    styles
</xsl:for-each>
```

where *node set* is an XPath expression that matches several nodes from the source document's node tree and *styles* are styles that are applied to each node matching that XPath expression.

Next, you use the `for-each` instruction to display all of the stock names from the source document.

To display multiple stock names:

1. Return to the **stock.xsl** file in your text editor.

2. Replace the five lines of code within the section element containing the `<xsl:for-each select="portfolio/stock">` tag with the following:

```
<xsl:for-each select="portfolio/stock">
    <article>
        <h1>
            <xsl:value-of select="sName" />
        </h1>
    </article>
</xsl:for-each>
```

Figure 5-21 shows the application of the `for-each` instruction to display the value of each sName element.

| Figure 5-21 | **Name of the first stock in the portfolio** |

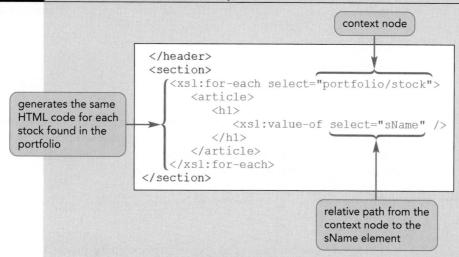

3. Save your changes to the file and then regenerate the result document using either your web browser or an XML editor. Verify that all 15 stock names are now displayed in the document. The stock names are listed in the order they appear in the source document.

The `for-each` instruction is one way to apply styles to each node from a node set. A more versatile approach is to create a template.

Working with Templates

You've already created a template for the source document's root node. However templates can be defined for any node set specified by an XPath expression. For example, a template that displays the value of the sName element could be entered as

```
<xsl:template match="stock">
   <article>
      <h1>
         <xsl:value-of select="sName" />
      </h1>
   </article>
</xsl:template>
```

This template matches every occurrence of the stock element in the source document, creating a style that displays the value of the sName elment as an h1 heading within an article element. The node specified in the `match` attribute sets the context for any location paths defined within the template. In this example, all location paths within the stock template are interpreted relative to the position of the stock element. Thus, the XPath expression `select="sName"` is interpreted by the XSLT processor as referencing "the sName element that is a child of the stock element."

Simply creating a template does not force the XSLT processor to use it with the result document. You must also indicate where you want that template applied.

Applying a Template

To apply a template, use the following `apply-templates` instruction:

```
<xsl:apply-templates select="node set" />
```

where *node set* is a location path that references a node set in the source document. The XSLT processor then searches the XSLT style sheet for a template matching that node set. For example, the following code applies the template written for the stock element:

```
<xsl:template match="portfolio">
   <xsl:apply-templates select="stock" />
</xsl:template>
```

Because the context node for this template is the portfolio element, the `apply-templates` instruction matches the stock element nested within the portfolio element and the XSLT processor will apply any styles written for that particular node. However, the following template would have the same effect:

```
<xsl:template match="/">
   <xsl:apply-templates select="portfolio/stock" />
</xsl:template>
```

Here, the root from the source document is the context node and the stock template is applied for every occurrence of the portfolio/stock node set within the root node. In both cases, the XSLT processor searches the XSLT style sheet for a template that matches the stock node, no matter how the location path is specified by the `select` attribute in the `apply-templates` instruction. The template is then applied each time a matching node is found in the source document. This is why templates can be used in place of the `for-each` instruction.

REFERENCE

Applying a Template

- To apply a template, use the XSLT instruction

  ```
  <xsl:apply-templates select="node set" />
  ```

  where *node set* is an XPath expression matching a node set from the source document.

You'll replace the `for-each` instruction with a template for the stock element and then apply that template in the style sheet.

To create and apply a template:

▶ **1.** Return to the **stock.xsl** file in your text editor.

▶ **2.** Delete the for-each construction from within the section element (all of the lines shown in red in Figure 5-21), and replace it with the following line:

```
<xsl:apply-templates select="portfolio/stock" />
```

3. Insert the following code immediately above the closing
`</xsl:stylesheet>` tag:

```
<xsl:template match="stock">
   <article>
      <h1>
         <xsl:value-of select="sName" />
      </h1>
   </article>
</xsl:template>
```

Figure 5-22 shows the revised file employing the use of templates in place of
for-each instructions.

Figure 5-22 **Applying the stock template**

template applies to the
nodes at this location in
the source document

applying the
stock template

```
         <section>
            <xsl:apply-templates select="portfolio/stock" />
         </section>

      </body>

   </html>
</xsl:template>

<xsl:template match="stock">
   <article>
      <h1>
         <xsl:value-of select="sName" />
      </h1>
   </article>
</xsl:template>

</xsl:stylesheet>
```

stock template

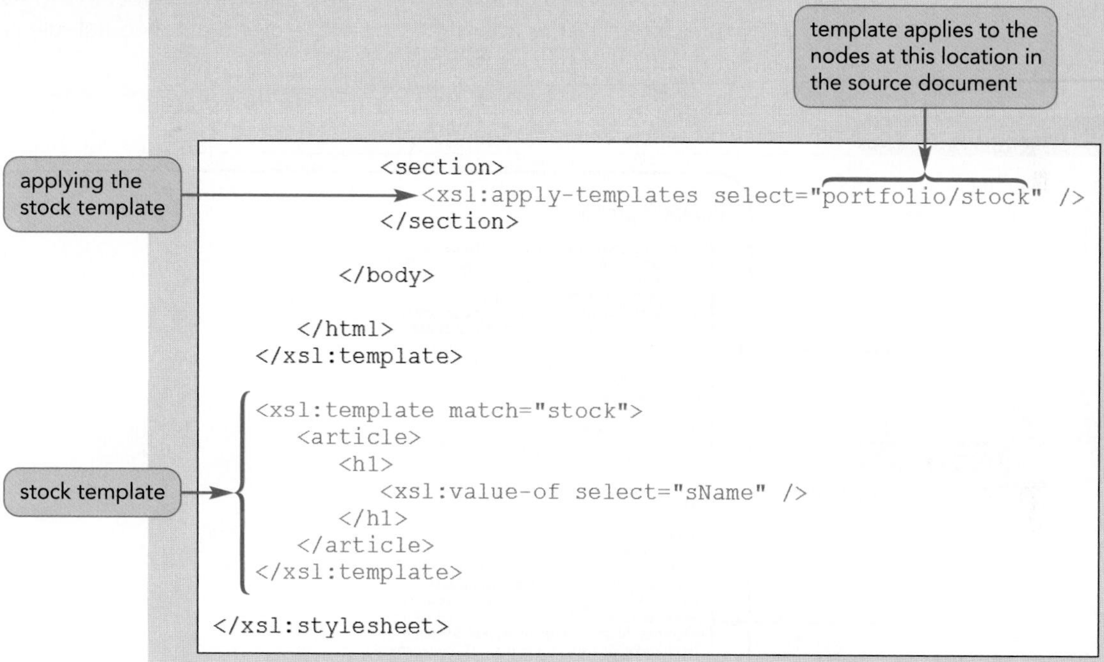

4. Save your changes to the file, and regenerate the result document,
verifying that the result document once again shows the names of all
15 stocks in the portfolio.

Rafael wants you to add a paragraph to each article describing the stock and its
history. This information is stored within the description element. So, next, you add the
value of this element to the stock template displayed within a paragraph. You also add a
horizontal rule after the paragraph using the `<hr />` tag.

To display a paragraph of descriptive text:

1. Return to the **stock.xsl** file in your text editor.

2. Directly above the closing `</article>` tag, insert the following:

```
<p>
   <xsl:value-of select="description" />
</p>
<hr />
```

Figure 5-23 shows the placement of the paragraph tag and horizontal rule.

Figure 5-23 **Revised stock template**

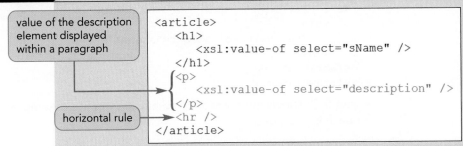

value of the description element displayed within a paragraph

horizontal rule

```
<article>
    <h1>
        <xsl:value-of select="sName" />
    </h1>
    <p>
        <xsl:value-of select="description" />
    </p>
    <hr />
</article>
```

▶ **3.** Save your changes to the file and regenerate the result document. As shown in Figure 5-24, a paragraph of descriptive text and a horizontal rule is included with the output for each company.

Figure 5-24 **List of stocks with descriptive paragraphs**

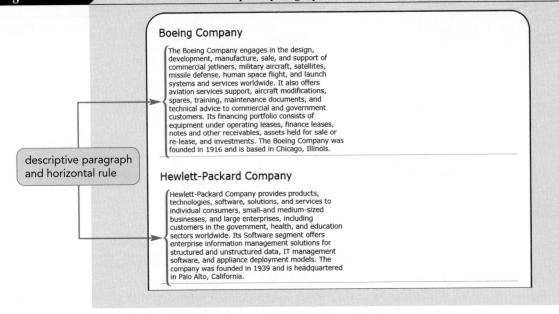

descriptive paragraph and horizontal rule

Boeing Company

The Boeing Company engages in the design, development, manufacture, sale, and support of commercial jetliners, military aircraft, satellites, missile defense, human space flight, and launch systems and services worldwide. It also offers aviation services support, aircraft modifications, spares, training, maintenance documents, and technical advice to commercial and government customers. Its financing portfolio consists of equipment under operating leases, finance leases, notes and other receivables, assets held for sale or re-lease, and investments. The Boeing Company was founded in 1916 and is based in Chicago, Illinois.

Hewlett-Packard Company

Hewlett-Packard Company provides products, technologies, software, solutions, and services to individual consumers, small-and medium-sized businesses, and large enterprises, including customers in the government, health, and education sectors worldwide. Its Software segment offers enterprise information management solutions for structured and unstructured data, IT management software, and appliance deployment models. The company was founded in 1939 and is headquartered in Palo Alto, California.

Stocks are identified both by their stock name and their ticker symbol. For example, the stock symbol for the Boeing Company is "BA". Rafael wants to include the ticker symbol in his report. To add that information, you'll have to work with attribute nodes.

INSIGHT

Applying Templates without a `Select` *Attribute*

The `select` attribute is not required with the `<xsl:apply-templates>` tag. When the `select` attribute is omitted the `apply-templates` instruction automatically processes all of the children of the context node, including any text nodes. For example, if the stock element document contains the child elements

```
<stock>
    <sName>Boeing Company</sName>
    <category>Transportation</category>
</stock>
```

you can apply templates to each child element with

```
<xsl:template match="stock">
    <xsl:apply-templates select="sName" />
    <xsl:apply-templates select="category" />
</xsl:template>
```

Or, more efficiently you can omit the `select` attribute and use

```
<xsl:template match="stock">
    <xsl:apply-templates />
</xsl:template>
```

Both the sName and category templates will be automatically applied by the processor, but the code will be more efficient and run more quickly by omitting the select `attribute` and using the `<xsl:apply-templates />` tag.

Displaying Attribute Values

The location paths you've seen so far have been concerned only with element nodes, but attributes can also be included in a location path using the XPath expression:

`node@attribute`

where *node* is an element node and *attribute* is the name of an attribute for that node. For example, the sName element has a single attribute named symbol. The absolute reference to this attribute is

`/portfolio/stock/sName/@symbol`

Attribute nodes can also be used in relative paths. Thus, if the stock element is the context node, then the relative path to the symbol attribute now becomes

`sName/@symbol`

Rafael wants the name of each stock to include the ticker symbol as follows:

stock name (*ticker symbol*)

where *stock name* is drawn from the sName element and *ticker symbol* is drawn from the symbol attribute of the sName element. The code to display these values is therefore

```
<xsl:value-of select="sName" />
(<xsl:value-of select="sName/@symbol" />)
```

You modify the sName template now, adding the value of the symbol attribute.

To display the `symbol` attribute value:

1. Return to the **stock.xsl** file in your text editor.

2. Insert the following code immediately above the closing `</h1>` tag in the stock template:

   `(<xsl:value-of select="sName/@symbol" />)`

   Figure 5-25 highlights the code to display the value of the symbol attribute.

Figure 5-25	List of stocks with descriptive paragraphs

```
<article>
    <h1>
        <xsl:value-of select="sName" />
        (<xsl:value-of select="sName/@symbol" />)
    </h1>
```

XPath expression referencing the symbol attribute within the sName element

3. Save your changes to the style sheet, and regenerate the result document. Verify that the ticker symbol for each stock appears in parentheses after the stock name.

Next, Rafael wants to display the current values of each stock. This information is stored as attributes of the today element. For example, the opening, high, low, current, and volume values of the Boeing Company stock are entered in the stock.xml file as:

```
<today open="125.68" high="125.72" low="124.81" current="125.68"
vol="6274500" />
```

Rafael wants this data displayed in a table. The HTML code for creating the table header is

```
<table>
    <thead>
        <tr>
            <th colspan="5">Current Stock Values</th>
        </tr>
        <tr>
            <th>Current</th>
            <th>Open</th>
            <th>High</th>
            <th>Low</th>
            <th>Volume</th>
        </tr>
    </thead>
</table>
```

Next, you insert this code into a new template matching the today element.

To start creating the today template:

1. Return to the **stock.xsl** file in your text editor.

2. Go to the end of the file and directly before the closing `</xsl:stylesheet>` tag, insert the following template matching the today element:

```
<xsl:template match="today">
   <table>
      <thead>
         <tr>
            <th colspan="5">Current Stock Values</th>
         </tr>
         <tr>
            <th>Current</th>
            <th>Open</th>
            <th>High</th>
            <th>Low</th>
            <th>Volume</th>
         </tr>
      </thead>
   </table>
</xsl:template>
```

Figure 5-26 shows the complete code for the header row of the today table.

Figure 5-26   **Initial today template**

```
<xsl:template match="today">
   <table>
      <thead>
         <tr>
            <th colspan="5">Current Stock Values</th>
         </tr>
         <tr>
            <th>Current</th>
            <th>Open</th>
            <th>High</th>
            <th>Low</th>
            <th>Volume</th>
         </tr>
      </thead>
   </table>
</xsl:template>

</xsl:stylesheet>
```

The table body will consist of a single row with each cell in the row displaying a different stock attribute. The HTML code for the table body is

```
<tbody>
   <tr>
      <td>current</td>
      <td>open</td>
      <td>high</td>
      <td>low</td>
      <td>volume</td>
   </tr>
</tbody>
```

where *current*, *open*, *high*, *low*, and *volume* are the corresponding attributes from the today element. Notice that the five table cells have essentially the same code aside from the value being displayed. It would be more efficient to write this code by applying the same template to the different attribute values. You can do this by combining different node sets into a single location path.

Combining Node Sets

Multiple nodes sets can be combined into a single location path using the union (|) operator. For example, the expression

```
/portfolio/date | /portfolio/time
```

defines a location path that matches both the date and time elements nested within the portfolio element. Similarly, the expression

```
@open|@high|@low|@current|@vol
```

matches the open, high, low, current, and vol attributes. Thus, the following template matches all five attributes of the today element:

```
<xsl:template match="@open|@high|@low|@current|@vol">
   <td><xsl:value-of select="." /></td>
</xsl:template>
```

Note that the template displays the attribute value by using the XSLT element tag `<xsl:value-of select="." />` to return the value of the context node, which, in this case, is the value of the open, high, low, current, or vol attribute.

To display the attribute values as table cells, you would then apply the template as follows:

```
<tbody>
   <tr>
      <xsl:apply-templates select="@current" />
      <xsl:apply-templates select="@open" />
      <xsl:apply-templates select="@high" />
      <xsl:apply-templates select="@low" />
      <xsl:apply-templates select="@vol" />
   </tr>
</tbody>
```

Next, you add this code to the today template to write the body of the today table and then apply it.

To complete the today template:

▶ 1. In the stock.xls file, directly above the closing `</table>` tag in the today template, insert the following code:

```
<tbody>
   <tr>
      <xsl:apply-templates select="@current" />
      <xsl:apply-templates select="@open" />
      <xsl:apply-templates select="@high" />
      <xsl:apply-templates select="@low" />
      <xsl:apply-templates select="@vol" />
   </tr>
</tbody>
```

2. Directly above the closing `</xsl:stylesheet>` tag, insert the following code to create the template for the attribute values:

```
<xsl:template match="@open|@high|@low|@current|@vol">
   <td><xsl:value-of select="." /></td>
</xsl:template>
```

Figure 5-27 shows the revised code.

Figure 5-27   **Template for displaying attribute values**

```
         </thead>
         <tbody>
            <tr>
               <xsl:apply-templates select="@current" />
               <xsl:apply-templates select="@open" />
               <xsl:apply-templates select="@high" />
               <xsl:apply-templates select="@low" />
               <xsl:apply-templates select="@vol" />
            </tr>
         </tbody>
      </table>
   </xsl:template>

   <xsl:template match="@open|@high|@low|@current|@vol">
      <td><xsl:value-of select="." /></td>
   </xsl:template>

</xsl:stylesheet>
```

applies the template to display the table cells

matches the current, open, high, low, and vol attributes

template to display the attribute value within table cells

3. Next you'll apply the today template to display the table of current stock values for each stock listed in the result document.

4. Scroll up to the stock template and, directly after the closing `</h1>` tag and before the `<p>` tag, insert

```
<xsl:apply-templates select="today" />
```

Figure 5-28 highlights the apply-templates instruction in the today template.

Figure 5-28   **Applying the today template**

```
<xsl:template match="stock">
   <article>
      <h1>
         <xsl:value-of select="sName" />
         (<xsl:value-of select="sName/@symbol" />)
      </h1>
      <xsl:apply-templates select="today" />
      <p>
         <xsl:value-of select="description" />
      </p>
      <hr />
   </article>
</xsl:template>
```

displays the table of current stock values

5. Save your changes to the file and then regenerate the result document. The table of current stock values appears alongside the description of the stock, as shown in Figure 5-29.

Figure 5-29	Table of current stock values

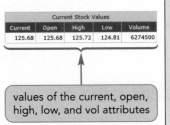

Boeing Company (BA)

The Boeing Company engages in the design, development, manufacture, sale, and support of commercial jetliners, military aircraft, satellites, missile defense, human space flight, and launch systems and services worldwide. It also offers aviation services support, aircraft modifications, spares, training, maintenance documents, and technical advice to commercial and government customers. Its financing portfolio consists of equipment under operating leases, finance leases, notes and other receivables, assets held for sale or re-lease, and investments. The Boeing Company was founded in 1916 and is based in Chicago, Illinois.

Current Stock Values				
Current	Open	High	Low	Volume
125.68	125.68	125.72	124.81	6274500

values of the current, open, high, low, and vol attributes

INSIGHT

Built-In Templates

XSLT supports several **built-in templates** that specify how the values of different nodes are displayed, by default. For example, the following built-in template defines how the values of all text nodes and all attribute nodes from the source document are displayed:

```
<xsl:template match="text()|@*">
   <xsl:value-of select="." />
</xsl:template>
```

For this built-in template to be invoked, the element and attribute nodes from the source document have to be assigned a template written by the programmer. Once such a template is assigned, the XSLT processor automatically applies this built-in template, rendering the text of the element or attribute within the result document.

Comments and processing instruction nodes have the following built-in template:

```
<xsl:template match="comment()|processing-instruction()" />
```

Because the purpose of this template is to keep comments and processing instructions from appearing in the result document, no values are ever sent to the result document. Note that this `template` element appears in a one-sided tag because it contains no content.

The most fundamental built-in template is the following:

```
<xsl:template match="*|/">
   <xsl:apply-templates />
<xsl:template>
```

which applies to all element nodes and the root node. No `select` attribute is given for the `apply-templates` instruction, which causes the XSLT processor to locate all of the element nodes from the source document. The result is that the processor navigates the entire node tree, searching for templates to apply, including those written by the style sheet's author.

At this point, you've added all of the stock data that Rafael wants to show in the result document. In the next session, you'll insert attribute values and learn how to modify the appearance of the document by sorting the nodes of the node tree and creating conditional nodes.

REVIEW

Session 5.2 Quick Check

1. Provide the command to display the value of the book element nested within the catalog element.
2. Provide the command to display the value of the context node.
3. Provide the command to display the value of the parent of the context node.
4. Provide the code to apply a template for the location path "catalog/books".
5. Provide the code to apply a template for either the "catalog/books" or "catalog/authors" node sets.
6. Provide the code to display the value of the ISBN attribute of the book element.
7. What is a built-in template?

Session 5.3 Visual Overview:

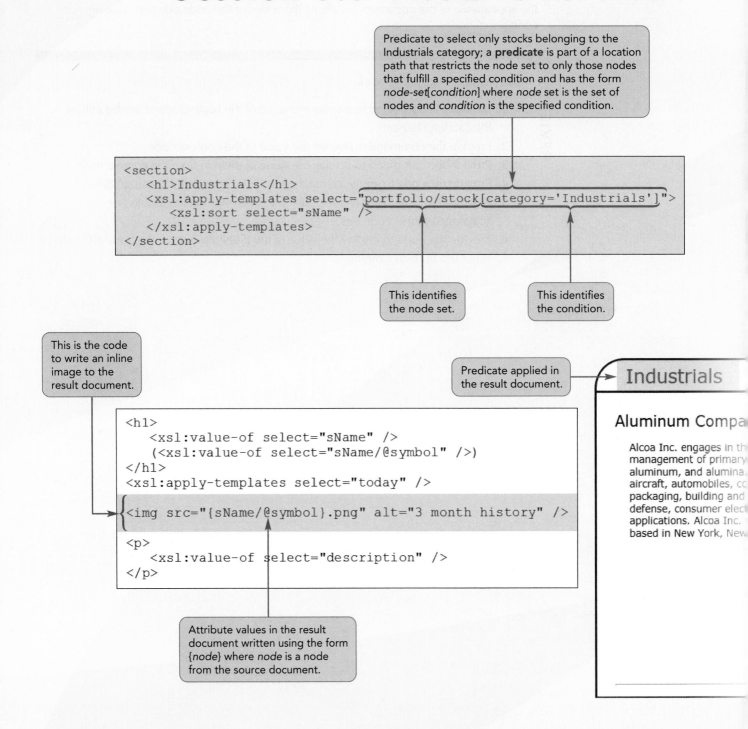

Predicate to select only stocks belonging to the Industrials category; a **predicate** is part of a location path that restricts the node set to only those nodes that fulfill a specified condition and has the form *node-set*[*condition*] where *node* set is the set of nodes and *condition* is the specified condition.

```
<section>
   <h1>Industrials</h1>
   <xsl:apply-templates select="portfolio/stock[category='Industrials']">
      <xsl:sort select="sName" />
   </xsl:apply-templates>
</section>
```

This identifies the node set.

This identifies the condition.

This is the code to write an inline image to the result document.

Predicate applied in the result document.

Industrials

```
<h1>
   <xsl:value-of select="sName" />
   (<xsl:value-of select="sName/@symbol" />)
</h1>
<xsl:apply-templates select="today" />
<img src="{sName/@symbol}.png" alt="3 month history" />
<p>
   <xsl:value-of select="description" />
</p>
```

Aluminum Compa

Alcoa Inc. engages in th
management of primary
aluminum, and alumina.
aircraft, automobiles, cc
packaging, building and
defense, consumer elect
applications. Alcoa Inc.
based in New York, New

Attribute values in the result document written using the form {*node*} where *node* is a node from the source document.

Applying a Conditional Expression

The **xsl:choose** element chooses among different possible styles to apply to the result document.

The **test** attribute tests whether the XPath expression returns a value of true or false; if it is true the enclosed style is applied.

Conditional processing is a programming technique that applies different styles based on the values from the source document using either xsl:if or xsl:choose elements.

The **xsl:when** element provides a condition to choose from.

The **xsl:otherwise** element is applied when no conditions are satisfied.

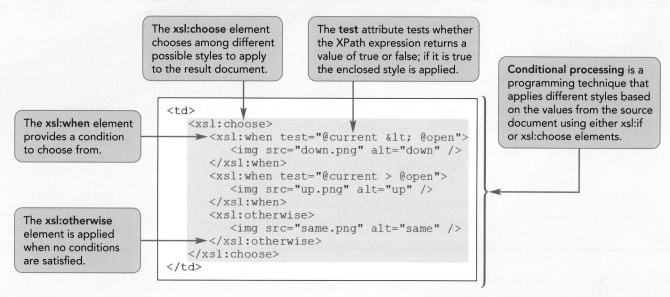

```
<td>
   <xsl:choose>
     <xsl:when test="@current &lt; @open">
        <img src="down.png" alt="down" />
     </xsl:when>
     <xsl:when test="@current > @open">
        <img src="up.png" alt="up" />
     </xsl:when>
     <xsl:otherwise>
        <img src="same.png" alt="same" />
     </xsl:otherwise>
   </xsl:choose>
</td>
```

The icon to be displayed is chosen using the xsl:choose element.

Inline image with its source determined by the value of the symbol attribute.

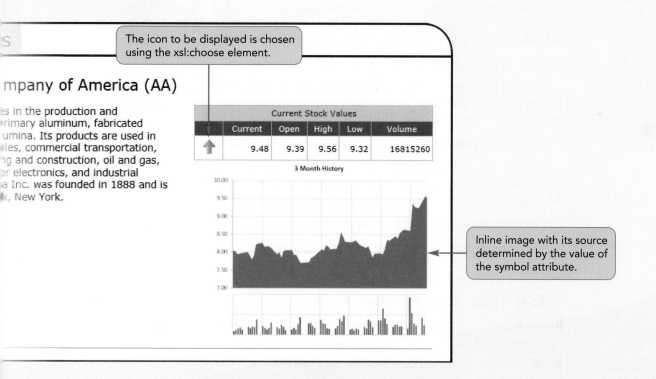

...mpany of America (AA)

...s in the production and ...rimary aluminum, fabricated ...umina. Its products are used in ...iles, commercial transportation, ...ng and construction, oil and gas, ...r electronics, and industrial ...a Inc. was founded in 1888 and is ...k, New York.

Current Stock Values				
Current	Open	High	Low	Volume
9.48	9.39	9.56	9.32	16815260

3 Month History

Inserting a Value into an Attribute

In the last session, you learned how to write values into the elements of the result document. You can also use XSLT to write values in the attributes of those elements by enclosing an XPath expression within a set of curly braces using the general form:

```
<element attribute="{expression}">
```

where *element* is the name of the element written to the result document, *attribute* is the element's attribute, and *expression* is an XPath expression that sets the attribute's value. For example, the following code writes a hypertext link using the value of the link node as the URL of the link:

```
<a href="{link}">
    Stock Report
</a>
```

If the value of the link node contains the text "http://www.example.com/stockreports", the XSLT processor will generate the following HTML code:

```
<a href="http://www.example.com/stockreports">
    Stock Report
</a>
```

Rafael wants his web page to include graphic images charting stock values from the past three months. He has provided you with 15 image files—one for each stock in the portfolio. The image files are named *ticker*.png where *ticker* is the stock's ticker symbol, such as BA.png for the Boeing Company chart. Rafael wants the style sheet to write the following inline image tag for each stock in the portfolio:

```
<img src="ticker.png" alt="3 month history" />
```

Because the ticker symbol is an attribute of the sName element, you can write this image tag by enclosing the sName/@symbol path within curly braces for the src attribute in the following style sheet statement:

```
<img src="{sName/@symbol}.png" alt="3 month history" />
```

Thus, for the Boeing Company stock, which has the ticker symbol BA, the style sheet will write the following HTML inline image tag with the src attribute value equal to BA.png:

```
<img src="BA.png" alt="3 month history" />
```

You revise the style sheet now to write this code for each stock in the portfolio.

To write an attribute value:

1. Return to the **stock.xsl** file in your text editor and scroll down to the stock template.

2. Directly above the opening <p> tag, insert the following:

```
<img src="{sName/@symbol}.png" alt="3 month history" />
```

Figure 5-30 highlights the newly added code in the style sheet.

When writing a value to an XML attribute, you must enclose the XPath expression within curly braces.

Figure 5-30 | **Writing an attribute value**

```
<xsl:template match="stock">
    <article>
        <h1>
            <xsl:value-of select="sName" />
            (<xsl:value-of select="sName/@symbol" />)
        </h1>
        <xsl:apply-templates select="today" />
        <img src="{sName/@symbol}.png" alt="3 month history" />
        <p>
            <xsl:value-of select="description" />
        </p>
        <hr />
    </article>
</xsl:template>
```

displays an inline image of the stock's recent performance

inserts the value of the symbol attribute

▶ **3.** Save your changes to the file and then regenerate the result document. Figure 5-31 shows the appearance of the stock alongside the 3-month history chart.

Figure 5-31 | **Stock information with the 3 year history chart**

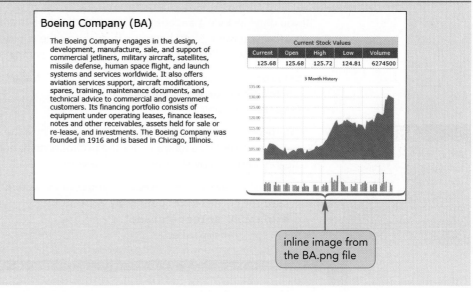

inline image from the BA.png file

Sorting Node Sets

Nodes are displayed in the result document in the same order in which they appear in the source document's node tree. To sort the nodes in a different order, you can apply the following sort instruction in the style sheet:

```
<xsl:sort select="node set" data-type="text|number|qname"
          order="ascending|descending"
          case-order="upper-first|lower-first"
          lang="language" />
```

where *node set* is an XPath expression that returns a set of nodes, the data-type attribute specifies the type of data to be sorted (text, number, or qname for qualified XML names), the order attribute defines whether to sort in ascending or descending order, the case-order attribute specifies whether uppercase or lowercase characters are to be sorted first, and the `lang` attribute defines the language used to determine sort order. For example, the following `sort` instruction sorts the sName element in descending order with lowercase characters sorted prior to uppercase letters:

```
<xsl:sort select="sName" order="descending"
    case-order="lower-first" />
```

All of the attributes are optional. If no attribute values are specified then the nodes are sorted in ascending order with uppercase characters sorted first and the language determined by the operating system.

The `sort` instruction is always used within an `<xsl:for-each>` or `<xsl:apply-templates>` tag. The following code adds the `sort` instruction to a `for-each` instruction so that the values from the portfolio/stock node set are sorted in descending order of the sName element:

```
<xsl:for-each select="portfolio/stock">
    <xsl:sort select="sName" order="descending" />
    <xsl:value-of select="sName" />
</xsl:for-each>
```

When sorting is applied to a template, the `<xsl:apply-templates>` tag is entered as a two-sided tag as demonstrated in the following code:

```
<xsl:apply-templates select="portfolio/stock">
    <xsl:sort select="sName" order="descending" />
</xsl:apply-templates>
```

If you don't include a `select` attribute with the `sort` instruction, the XSLT processor will assume that you want to sort based on the value of the context node. Thus, the following code sorts the portfolio/stock/sName node set in descending order of the sName element:

```
<xsl:for-each select="portfolio/stock/sName">
    <xsl:sort order="descending" />
</xsl:for-each>
```

TIP

Always set the data type to number when sorting numeric values; otherwise, the numeric values will be sorted in alphabetical order with a value such as 123 listed before 24.

If you need to sort by more than one factor, you nest the `sort` instructions. The following code applies a template for the portfolio/stock node set, sorting the results first by category and then by sName within category:

```
<xsl:apply-templates select="portfolio/stock">
    <xsl:sort select="category" />
    <xsl:sort select="sName" />
</xsl:apply-templates>
```

REFERENCE

Sorting a Node Set

• To sort a node set, apply

```
<xsl:sort select="node set" data-type="text|number|qname"
        order="ascending|descending"
        case-order="upper-first|lower-first"
        lang="language" />
```

where *node set* is an XPath expression, the `data-type` attribute specifies the type of data to be sorted, the `order` attribute defines whether to sort in ascending or descending order, the `case-order` attribute specifies whether uppercase or lowercase characters are to be sorted first, and the *lang* attribute defines the language used to determine sort order.

The `sort` instruction can only be used within the `<xsl:for-each>` tag or the `<xsl:apply-templates>` tag.

Rafael has also noticed that the report lists the stocks in the same order in which they appear in the stock.xml file. He wants to see stocks reported alphabetically by stock name. You make this change now by applying the sort instruction to the `<xsl:apply-templates>` tag.

To sort the stocks by order of name:

1. Return to the **stock.xsl** file in your text editor.

2. Go to the root template near the top of the style sheet and replace the `apply-templates` instruction with the following code:

```
<xsl:apply-templates select="portfolio/stock">
   <xsl:sort select="sName" />
</xsl:apply-templates>
```

   Figure 5-32 highlights the modified code to sort the applied templates by the sName element.

Figure 5-32   **Applying a template in sorted order**

```
         <h1>Chesterton Financial</h1>
         <h2>Portfolio Stocks</h2>

      </header>
      <section>
        <xsl:apply-templates select="portfolio/stock">
            <xsl:sort select="sName" />
        </xsl:apply-templates>
      </section>
    </body>
  </html>

</xsl:template>
```

applies the template for the portfolio/stock node set sorted by the value of the sName element

3. Save your changes to the style sheet and then regenerate the result document in your web browser or XML editor.

4. Verify that the stocks are now listed in ascending order of name with the Aluminum Company of America listed first, followed by the American Electric Power Company, and so forth.

   Trouble? Make sure that you change the `<xsl:apply-templates>` tag from an empty tag to a two-sided tag by removing the (/) character at the end of the opening tag.

Rafael wants to know whether a particular stock is increasing or decreasing in value from its opening price. While this information can be gleaned from examining the Current Stock Values table, he would like the style sheet to provide this information graphically. This can be accomplished using conditional processing.

Conditional Processing

Conditional processing is a programming technique that applies different styles based on the values from the source document. For example, the style sheet would write one result if a node from the source document has one particular value and a different result if that node has a different value. One way of accomplishing this is with the following `if` instruction:

```
<xsl:if test="expression">
    styles
</xsl:if>
```

where *expression* is an XPath expression that is either true or false and *styles* are XSLT styles that are applied if the expression is true. To create an expression that returns a true or false value, you need to work with comparison operators.

Using Comparison Operators and Functions

XPath supports several different **comparison operators** to compare one value to another. The most commonly used comparison operator is the equals symbol (=), which is used to test whether the two values are equal. For example, the following `if` statement tests whether the symbol attribute of the sName element is equal to "BA":

```
if test="sName/@symbol='BA'"
```

Note that when you nest a text string within the test attribute you need to use single quotes for the text string and double quotes for the test attribute or double quotes for the test string and single quotes for the test attribute.

Figure 5-33 describes other comparison operators supported by the test attribute used to compare text strings and numeric values.

| Figure 5-33 | Comparison operators in XSLT |

Operator	Description	Example
=	Tests whether two values are equal to each other	@symbol = "BA"
!=	Tests whether two values are unequal	@symbol != "BA"
&lt;	Tests whether one value is less than another	day < 5
<=	Tests whether one value is less than or equal to another	day <= 5
>	Tests whether one value is greater than another	day > 1
>=	Tests whether one value is greater than or equal to another	day >= 1
and	Combines two expressions, returning a value of true only if both expressions are true	@symbol = "BA" and day > 1
or	Combines two expressions, returning a value of true if either expression is true	@symbol = "BA" or @symbol = "UCL"
not	Negates the value of the expression, changing true to false or false to true	not(day >= 1)

TIP

Be careful when comparing node sets and single values. When multiple values are involved, the expression is true if any of the values in the node set satisfy the test condition.

Because XSLT treats the left angle bracket character (<) as the opening character for an element tag, you must use the text string `&lt;` when you want to make less-than comparisons. XSLT doesn't have a problem with the right angle bracket character (>), however. As a result, one way to avoid using the `&lt;` expression is to reverse the order of a comparison. For example, instead of writing a comparison as

```
day &lt; 5
```

to test whether the value of the day element is less than 5, you write it as

```
5 > day
```

which gives the equivalent result, testing whether 5 is greater than the value of the day element. Comparison tests can be combined using the and and or operators. For example, the expression

```
day > 2 and day &lt; 5
```

tests whether the value of the day element lies between 2 and 5. Similarly, the expression

```
@symbol = "BA" or @symbol = "AEP"
```

tests whether the value of the symbol attribute is equal to "BA" or "AEP". You can reverse the true/false value of an expression using the not() function. The expression

```
not(@symbol = "BA")
```

returns a value of false if the value of the symbol attribute is equal to "BA" and true if the symbol attribute is not equal to "BA".

REFERENCE

Testing a Condition with the if Element

- To test for a single condition, use the following if instruction:

```
<xsl:if test="expression">
    styles
</xsl:if>
```

where *expression* is an XPath expression that is either true or false and *styles* are XSLT commands that are run if the expression is true.

You can also test for the presence or absence of an attribute or element by entering the attribute or element name without any comparison operator. The following code tests for the presence of the symbol attribute. If the context node has that attribute, then the attribute's value is displayed; otherwise, nothing is done.

```
<xsl:if test="@symbol">
    <xsl:value-of select="@symbol" />
</xsl:if>
```

Verifying the presence or absence of an element or attribute is often used to avoid errors that would cause a transformation to fail. For example, if the style sheet had attempted to return the value of a missing symbol attribute, the processor would have halted the transformation and returned an error message. Using a comparison test avoids this problem.

Testing for Multiple Conditions

Unlike other programming languages, XSLT doesn't support an else-if construction. This means that the if instruction tests for only one condition and allows for only one outcome. If you want to test for multiple conditions and display different outcomes, you need to apply the following choose structure:

```
<xsl:choose>
    <xsl:when test="expression1">
        styles
    </xsl:when>
    <xsl:when test="expression2">
        styles
    </xsl:when>
    ...
```

```
      <xsl:otherwise>
         styles
      </xsl:otherwise>
   </xsl:choose>
```

where *expression1*, *expression2*, and so forth are expressions that are either true or false. The XSLT processor proceeds through the list of expressions one at a time and, when it encounters an expression that is true, it processes the corresponding style and stops. If it reaches the last expression without finding one that is true, the style contained in the `otherwise` instruction is processed.

REFERENCE

Testing Multiple Conditions with the choose Element

- To test multiple conditions, use the following **choose** element:

```
<xsl:choose>
   <xsl:when test="expression1">
      styles
   </xsl:when>
   <xsl:when test="expression2">
      styles
   </xsl:when>
   ...
   <xsl:otherwise>
      styles
   </xsl:otherwise>
</xsl:choose>
```

where *expression1*, *expression2*, and so forth are expressions that are either true or false.

Rafael wants to use the choose structure to test whether the stock's value is rising from its opening value. In other words, he wants to test whether the value of the current attribute of the today element is less than, greater than, or equal to the value of the open attribute. Depending on the result of the test, he wants the table of current stock values to display either a down-arrow image, an up-arrow image, or an even level image. He has three graphic files named down.png, up.png, and same.png for this purpose. Thus, to display different image files based on the change in the stock price, you'll employ the following choose structure:

```
<xsl:choose>
   <xsl:when test="@current &lt; @open">
      <img src="down.png" alt="down" />
   </xsl:when>
   <xsl:when test="@current > @open">
      <img src="up.png" alt="up" />
   </xsl:when>
   <xsl:otherwise>
      <img src="same.png" alt="same" />
   </xsl:otherwise>
</xsl:choose>
```

You add this choose structure to the style sheet, creating a table cell that displays different icons based on the comparison of the stock's current value to its opening value.

To apply the **choose** element:

1. Return to the **stock.xsl** file in your editor and go to the today template.

2. Within the `<th>` tag for the Current Stock Values, change the value of the colspan attribute to **6** because you'll be adding a sixth cell to the table row.

3. Insert a new table heading cell in the second row of the table by adding the tag `<th></th>`, which creates a blank table cell to the left of the Current column heading.

4. Scroll down to the table body and insert the following code for a new table cell displaying one of three possible icon images:

```
<td>
   <xsl:choose>
      <xsl:when test="@current &lt; @open">
         <img src="down.png" alt="down" />
      </xsl:when>
      <xsl:when test="@current > @open">
         <img src="up.png" alt="up" />
      </xsl:when>
      <xsl:otherwise>
         <img src="same.png" alt="same" />
      </xsl:otherwise>
   </xsl:choose>
</td>
```

Figure 5-34 shows the revised code in the style sheet.

| Figure 5-34 | Applying the choose structure to display different inline images |

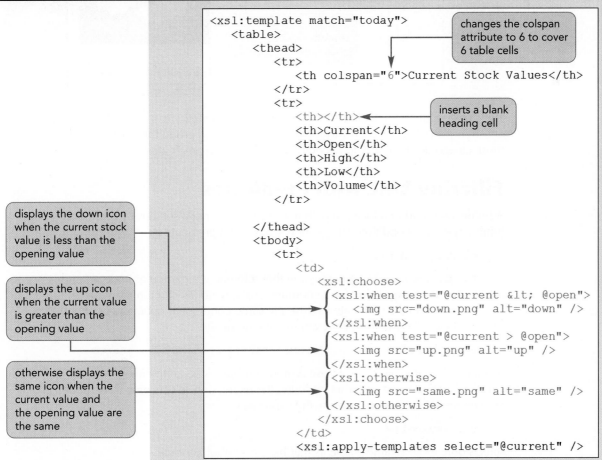

displays the down icon when the current stock value is less than the opening value

displays the up icon when the current value is greater than the opening value

otherwise displays the same icon when the current value and the opening value are the same

```
<xsl:template match="today">
   <table>
      <thead>
         <tr>
            <th colspan="6">Current Stock Values</th>
         </tr>
         <tr>
            <th></th>
            <th>Current</th>
            <th>Open</th>
            <th>High</th>
            <th>Low</th>
            <th>Volume</th>
         </tr>

      </thead>
      <tbody>
         <tr>
            <td>
               <xsl:choose>
                  <xsl:when test="@current &lt; @open">
                     <img src="down.png" alt="down" />
                  </xsl:when>
                  <xsl:when test="@current > @open">
                     <img src="up.png" alt="up" />
                  </xsl:when>
                  <xsl:otherwise>
                     <img src="same.png" alt="same" />
                  </xsl:otherwise>
               </xsl:choose>
            </td>
            <xsl:apply-templates select="@current" />
```

changes the colspan attribute to 6 to cover 6 table cells

inserts a blank heading cell

5. Save your changes to the file and then regenerate the result document. Figure 5-35 shows the newly added icon for the first two stocks listed in the web page.

Figure 5-35   **Icons representing the change in stock price**

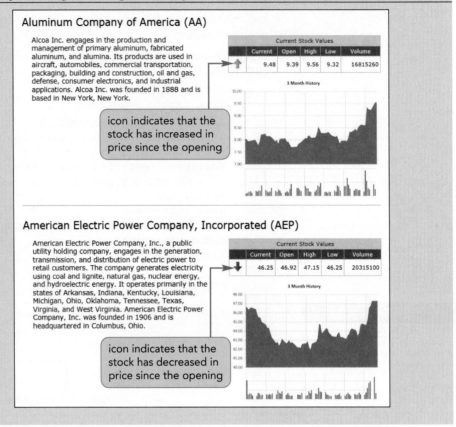

The stocks in the stock.xml file are placed into three categories—Industrials, Utilities, and Transportation. Rafael wants the result document to group the stocks based on those categories. One way to accomplish this is to use predicates.

Filtering XML with Predicates

A predicate is part of a location path that restricts the node set to only those nodes that fulfill a specified condition. The general syntax for a predicate is

```
node-set[condition]
```

where *node-set* is an XPath expression that references a particular node set and *condition* is an expression for a condition that any nodes in the node set must fulfill. The expression in the predicate can use the same conditional operators used with the `if` and `choose` instructions. For example, the predicate

```
sName[@symbol = "BA" or @symbol="AEP"]
```

matches all sName elements whose symbol attribute is equal to either "BA" or "AEP". If you don't include a value for an attribute, the expression selects only those nodes that contain the attribute. For example, the expression

```
sName[@symbol]
```

selects only those sName elements that have a symbol attribute.

Predicates and Node Position

A predicate can also indicate the position of a node in the node tree. The general syntax is

```
node-set[position]
```

where *position* is an integer indicating the position of the node. For example, the expression

```
stock[3]
```

selects the third stock element from the source document. The union operator (|) can also be used to select multiple positions. Thus, the expression

```
stock[3|5]
```

selects the third and fifth stock elements.

Predicates and Functions

A predicate can also contain an XPath function. The two functions that you'll explore in this tutorial are the `last()` and `position()` functions. The `last()` function returns the last node in the node tree. Thus, the expression

```
stock[last()]
```

returns the last stock element from the source document's node tree. The `position()` function returns the position value of the node. For example, the following expression selects the second stock element:

```
stock[position()=2]
```

and is equivalent to the expression `stock[2]`. The `position()` function is useful when combined with comparison operators to select ranges of nodes. The following expression combines the `position()` function with comparison operators to select the second through fifth stock nodes:

```
stock[position()>=2 and position()&lt;=5]
```

Finally, predicates can be used within longer location paths. For example, the following code returns the value of the sName element but only for the second stock listed in the source document:

```
<xsl:value-of select="stock[position()=2]/sName" />
```

REFERENCE

Using Node Predicates

- To select a subset of nodes from the node tree, combine the node set with a predicate using the syntax

  ```
  node-set[condition]
  ```

  where *node-set* is an XPath expression that references a particular node set and *condition* is an expression for a condition that nodes in the node set must fulfill.
- To process only the first node from a branch of the node tree, use the expression

  ```
  node-set[1]
  ```

- To process only the nth node from a branch of the node tree, use the expression

  ```
  node-set[n]
  ```

- To process only the last node from a branch of the node tree, use the expression

  ```
  node-set[last()]
  ```

- To process a node from a specific location in the node's tree branch, use the expression

  ```
  node-set[position()=value]
  ```

  where *value* is an integer indicating the node's location in the branch.

Rafael wants to display the name of each stock category using an h1 heading. Under each heading, Rafael wants to display the stocks that belong to that category (Industrials, Utilities, Transportation) sorted in alphabetical order by stock name. The code to display the industrial stocks uses the following predicate with the `apply-templates` element:

```
<h1>Industrials</h1>
<xsl:apply-templates
    select="portfolio/stock[category='Industrials']">
    <xsl:sort select="sName" />
</xsl:apply-templates>
```

The code to display stocks that belong to the Utilities and Transportation categories is similar. You add this code to the root template of the stock.xsl style sheet.

To apply a predicate to the selection of stock nodes:

1. Return to the **stock.xsl** file in your text editor and go to the root template, replacing the contents within the second section element (the one immediately following the `</header>` tag) with the following:

   ```
   <h1>Industrials</h1>
   <xsl:apply-templates
       select="portfolio/stock[category='Industrials']">
       <xsl:sort select="sName" />
   </xsl:apply-templates>
   ```

2. Copy the section element you just created including the opening and closing section tags and paste the code as a new section under the section that contains the code for the Industrials head, replacing Industrials with **Utilities** in both the h1 heading and the predicate category.

3. Paste a third section under the section you just created for the Utilities with **Transportation** for the h1 heading and the predicate category.

Figure 5-36 highlights the new and revised code in the style sheet.

Figure 5-36   **Limiting node sets using a predicate**

applies the template only
to stocks belonging to
the Industrials category

```
    </header>
    <section>
        <h1>Industrials</h1>
        <xsl:apply-templates
            select="portfolio/stock[category='Industrials']">
            <xsl:sort select="sName" />
        </xsl:apply-templates>
    </section>

    <section>
        <h1>Utilities</h1>
        <xsl:apply-templates
            select="portfolio/stock[category='Utilities']">
            <xsl:sort select="sName" />
        </xsl:apply-templates>
    </section>

    <section>
        <h1>Transportation</h1>
        <xsl:apply-templates
            select="portfolio/stock[category='Transportation']">
            <xsl:sort select="sName" />
        </xsl:apply-templates>
    </section>

    </body>
</html>
```

applies the template only
to stocks belonging to
the Utilities category

applies the template only
to stocks belonging to the
Transportation category

4. Save your changes.

5. Use your web browser or XML editor to regenerate the result document. Verify that the stocks are now grouped into categories and that, within each category, stocks are listed alphabetically (see Figure 5-37, which shows the first stock in the Industrials category).

Figure 5-37 | **Final appearance of the Web page**

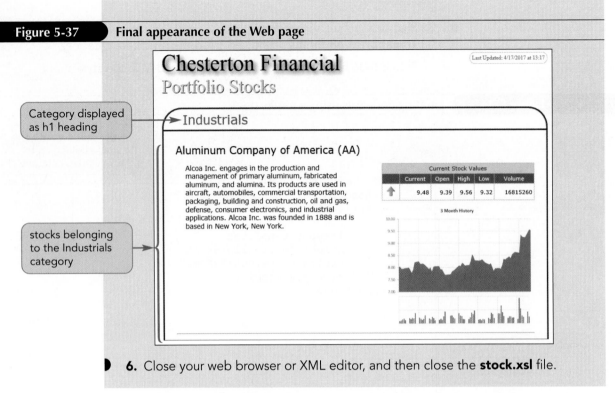

6. Close your web browser or XML editor, and then close the **stock.xsl** file.

In addition to categorizing nodes, you can use predicates for many other applications. In future tutorials you'll examine ways to write predicates to create more advanced and dynamic node structures.

Aa

Written Communication: Writing Effective XSLT Style Sheets

XSLT style sheets need to be written clearly both to make the code easier for your colleagues to read and interpret and to minimize the chance of coding mistakes. Here are some tips to keep in mind as you develop your own style sheets.

- Build up your style sheet incrementally by adding only a few templates at a time. Verify that the style sheet works at each stage before introducing additional complexity.
- Add comments to your style sheet document to aid yourself and others in interpreting and revising the style sheet at a later time.
- Use templates in preference to the `<xsl:for-each />` tag whenever possible. Templates are faster to process, easier to debug, and can be reused in different contexts throughout the style sheet.
- Use relative path expressions within templates and for-each loops. Any XPath expression should be interpreted relative to the context node and not rely on nodes defined outside of the template or for-each loop.
- Reduce errors and speed up processing by using the `indent="no"` attribute with the `<xsl:output />` tag. This will remove extra white space and reduce the size of the result document. Note that the default value for HTML files is `indent="yes"`, while for XML documents the default is `indent="no"`.
- Use an XML editor and avoid coding by hand. This will cut down on typos and syntax errors.
- Use the `<xsl:comment />` tag to add comments to the result document, making it easier for others to interpret the code in that file.
- The web contains a wealth of free XSLT libraries. Before trying to solve a coding problem, check these libraries to see if a solution is already available.

A well-written style sheet will also be processed quicker, which is an important consideration when transforming large files containing thousands of records.

Constructing Elements and Attributes with XSLT

In writing the code for the stock report, you entered the HTML tags for the elements and attributes that were part of the final result document. In the process of creating the HTML file, the XSLT processor used these HTML tags to create a **result tree**, which is composed of the element, attribute, text, and other nodes.

For some projects, you might need to have a result tree whose nodes are defined explicitly based on contents of the source document. This happens most often when changing the structure of one XML document into another. For example, the source document might contain the following elements and attributes:

```
<stock>
   <sName symbol="BA">Boeing Company</sName>
   <values>
      <day>124.81</day>
      <day>125.22</day>
   </values>
</stock>
```

which you want to restructure as

```
<stock>
   <stockName>Boeing Company</stockName>
   <stockSymbol>BA</stockSymbol>
   <stockValues day1="124.81" day2="125.22" />
</stock>
```

To create this document you can have XSLT construct the element and attribute nodes, rather than entering them as literal result elements.

Constructing an Element Node

To construct an element node in the result tree, XSLT uses the following <xsl:element> tag:

```
<xsl:element name="text" namespace="uri">
   styles
</xsl:element>
```

where the name attribute assigns a name to the element and the namespace attribute provides a namespace. For example, to convert the sName element and symbol attribute into elements named stockName and stockSymbol you could apply the following code:

```
<xsl:element name="stockName">
   <xsl:value-of select="sName" />
</xsl:element>
<xsl:element name="stockSymbol">
   <xsl:value-of select="sName/@symbol" />
</xsl:element>
```

Under this transformation, the source document code

```
<sName symbol="BA">Boeing Company</sName>
```

is transformed into

```
<stockName>Boeing Company</stockName>
<stockSymbol>BA</stockSymbol>
```

TIP

If you need to create a one-sided element, you use a one-sided <xsl:element /> tag.

New elements can be combined with predicates, conditional statements, and the for-each instruction to create a subset of the original source document in a new structure. For example, to create an XML document containing a list of the stock symbols for transportation stocks, you could apply the following template:

```
<xsl:template match="portfolio">
   <xsl:element name="Transportation">
      <xsl:for-each select="stock[category='Transportation']">
         <xsl:element name="stockSymbol">
            <xsl:value-of select="sName/@symbol" />
         </xsl:element>
      </xsl:for-each>
   </xsl:element>
</xsl:template>
```

After transforming the stock.xml document, an XSLT processor generates the following Transportation element containing symbols of all of the transportation stocks:

```
<Transportation>
   <stockSymbol>CNI</stockSymbol>
   <stockSymbol>DAL</stockSymbol>
   <stockSymbol>R</stockSymbol>
   <stockSymbol>LUV</stockSymbol>
   <stockSymbol>UNP</stockSymbol>
</Transportation>
```

Constructing Attributes and Attribute Sets

Attributes are constructed in XSLT using the following `<xsl:attribute />` tag:

```
<xsl:attribute name="text" namespace="uri">
   styles
</xsl:attribute>
```

where the `name` attribute specifies the name of the attribute and the `namespace` attribute indicates the namespace. Attributes are nested within `<xsl:element>` tags so that the attribute is added to the newly created element. For example, to convert this collection of nodes

```
<values>
   <day>124.81</day>
   <day>125.22</day>
</values>
```

into a single element node with the following attributes:

```
<stockValues day1="124.81" day2="125.22" />
```

you can apply the following transformation:

```
<xsl:element name="stockValues">
   <xsl:attribute name="day1">
      <xsl:value-of select="day[1]" />
   </xsl:attribute>
   <xsl:attribute name="day2">
      <xsl:value-of select="day[2]" />
   </xsl:attribute>
</xsl:element>
```

Rather than nesting the entire collection of attributes, those attributes can be grouped within an **attribute set**, which allows you to add several attributes to the same element without having a long nested statement. To create an attribute set you apply the following `attribute-set` element:

```
<xsl:attribute-set name="text" use-attribute-sets="name-list">
   <xsl:attribute name="text">styles</xsl:attribute>
   <xsl:attribute name="text">styles</xsl:attribute>
   ...
</xsl:attribute-set>
```

where the `name` attribute contains the name of the set and then the names of the individual attributes created within that set. You can also refer to other attribute sets by specifying their names in the *name-list* parameter, allowing you to build a collection of attribute sets by combining one with another. For example, the following code creates an attribute set named dayAttributes, which consists of values for the day element:

```
<xsl:attribute-set name="dayAttributes">
   <xsl:attribute name="day1">
      <xsl:value-of select="day[1]" />
   <xsl:attribute>
   <xsl:attribute name="day2">
      <xsl:value-of select="day[2]" />
   <xsl:attribute>
</xsl:attribute>
```

The attribute set is then applied to an element by applying the `attribute-set` attribute. The following code demonstrates how to apply the dayAttributes attribute-set to the stockValues element:

```
<xsl:element name="stockValues" attribute-set="dayAttributes" />
```

REFERENCE

Creating Elements and Attributes with XSLT

- To create an element, use the XSLT element

```
<xsl:element name="text" namespace="uri"
    use-attribute-sets="namelist">
  styles
</xsl:element>
```

where the `name` attribute assigns a name to the element, the `namespace` attribute provides a namespace, and `use-attribute-sets` provides a list of attribute sets.
- To create a one-sided or empty element, use

```
<xsl:element attributes />
```

- To create an attribute, use

```
<xsl:attribute name="text" namespace="uri">
  styles
</xsl:attribute>
```

where the `name` attribute specifies the name of the attribute and the `namespace` attribute indicates the namespace.
- To create a set of attributes, use

```
<xsl:attribute-set name="text" use-attribute-sets="name-list">
  <xsl:attribute name="text">styles</xsl:attribute>
  <xsl:attribute name="text">styles</xsl:attribute>
  ...
</xsl:attribute-set>
```

where the `name` attribute is the name of the set and `use-attribute-sets` can refer to the contents of another attribute set.

Constructing Comments and Processing Instructions

XSLT also includes elements to write comments and processing instructions to the result tree. To construct a comment node, use the element

```
<xsl:comment>
  comment text
</xsl:comment>
```

where *comment text* is the text that should be placed within a comment tag. For example, the code

```
<xsl:comment>
  Sample Stock Portfolio
</xsl:comment>
```

creates the following comment in the result document:

```
<!-- Sample Stock Portfolio -->
```

To create a processing instruction node, use the element

```
<xsl:processing-instruction name="text">
   attributes
</xsl:processing-instruction>
```

where the `name` attribute provides the name of the processing instruction and `attributes` are attributes contained within the processing instruction. For example, if you want to add a processing instruction to attach the styles.css style sheet to the result document, you use the code

```
<xsl:processing-instruction name="xml-stylesheet">
   href="styles.css" type="text/css"
</xsl:processing-instruction>
```

which generates the following tag in the result document:

```
<?xml-stylesheet href="styles.css" type="text.css"?>
```

The `processing-instruction` element contains the attributes of the processing instruction to be placed in the result document.

REFERENCE

Creating Comments and Processing Instructions

- To add a comment to the result document, use

```
<xsl:comment>
   comment text
</xsl:comment>
```

where `comment text` is the text to be placed in the comment.
- To add a processing instruction to the result document, use

```
<xsl:processing-instruction name="text">
   attributes
</xsl:processing-instruction>
```

where the `name` attribute provides the name of the processing instruction and `attributes` are attributes and attribute values contained in the processing instruction.

You don't have to use XSLT to create elements, attributes, comments, or processing instructions in Rafael's stock report, but you keep these features of XSLT in mind for future projects. For now, you've completed your work on the stock report. Rafael will examine the document and discuss the results with his colleagues. If he needs to make changes, he'll contact you.

Session 5.3 Quick Check

REVIEW

1. An XML document contains the root element named books, which has a single child element named book. Each book element has two child elements named title and author. Using the XSLT's for-each instruction, sort the book elements in alphabetical order based on the title.

2. By default, does the `<xsl:sort>` element sort items numerically or alphabetically?

3. The book element has a single attribute named category. The value of category can be either fiction or nonfiction. Write an if construction that displays the book title only if it is a nonfiction book.

4. Use a choose construction that displays book titles in an h3 heading if they are fiction and an h2 heading if otherwise.

5. Correct the following expression so that it doesn't result in an error:

   ```
   test="sales < 20000"
   ```

6. What code do you use to select the first book from the XML document described in Question 1? What do you use to select the last book?

7. What code do you use to create an element named inventory that contains the value 15000?

8. What code do you use to create an empty element named inventory that contains a single attribute named amount with the value 15000?

Review Assignments

PRACTICE

Data Files needed for the Review Assignments: portfoliotxt.xml, portfoliotxt.xsl, +1 CSS file, +3 PNG files

Rafael Garcia has worked with the stock report you generated and has made a few modifications to the source document. Rafael has added a few more elements providing information on each stock's high and low value over the previous year, the stock's P/E ratio, earnings per share (EPS), dividend, and yield. He's also included the URL to the company's website.

Rafael wants to try a new design, in which these new stock values appear in a table alongside a description of the stock. He also wants to show the current stock value and whether it's rising, falling, or remaining level, which is to be prominently displayed below the company name. Figure 5-38 shows a preview of the revised content and layout of the report.

Figure 5-38   **Revised stock report design**

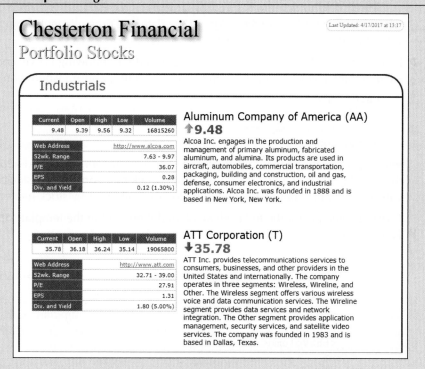

Rafael has already created the CSS style sheet for this web page, but he needs you to create the XSLT style sheet, which will generate the HTML code used in the report.

Because creating a style sheet can be complicated, it is strongly recommended that you save your changes and generate the result document as you complete each step below to check on your progress and detect any problems early. Complete the following:

1. Using your text editor, open the **portfoliotxt.xml** and **portfoliotxt.xsl** files from the xml05 ▶ review folder. Enter *your name* and the *date* in the comment section of each file, and save them as **portfolio.xml** and **portfolio.xsl**, respectively.

2. Go to the **portfolio.xml** file in your text editor. Take some time to review the content of the file and its structure. Add a processing instruction after the comment section that attaches the portfolio.xsl style sheet to this XML document. Close the file, saving your changes.

3. Go to the **portfolio.xsl** file in your text editor. Below the comment section, set up this document as an XSLT style sheet by adding a stylesheet root element and declaring the XSLT namespace using the namespace prefix xsl.

4. Add an `output` element to indicate to the XSLT processor that the transformed file should be in HTML5 format.

Design an XSLT style sheet to write the HTML code for John's report. Complete the following:

1. Using your text editor, open the **campingtxt.xml** and **campingtxt.xsl** files from the xml05 ▸ case4 folder. Enter *your name* and the *date* in the comment section of each file, and save them as **camping.xml** and **camping.xsl**, respectively.

2. Go to the **camping.xml** file in your text editor. Take some time to study the content and structure of the document. Note that every customer can have multiple orders on file and within each order are multiple items. Attach the camping.xsl style sheet to this XML document. Close the file, saving your changes.

3. Go to the **camping.xsl** file in your text editor and begin designing your XSLT style sheet. John wants the report to include the following features:
   - The name of the store as a main heading.
   - A customer ID table providing each customer's name, address, and ID, with customers listed alphabetically by customer name.
   - Order tables following each customer ID table with the order information for that customer; the order tables are listed in descending order by the order ID.
   - Each order table should include the date of the order and the order ID.
   - Each order table should list the items purchased with the items purchased in the largest quantities listed first. If two products have the same quantity of items ordered, the products should be arranged alphabetically by the item ID.

4. The web page code can be written to HTML5, XHTML, or HTML4 standards. Include the appropriate `output` element specifying how to render the result code.

5. The layout of the page is up to you. You may attach an external style sheet of your own design to make your report easier to read and interpret.

6. Generate your result document using either an XML editor or your web browser. Verify that the page layout and content fulfill all of John's criteria.

OBJECTIVES

Session 6.1
- Create and apply XSLT variables
- Copy nodes into the result document
- Retrieve data from XML documents
- Access external style sheets

Session 6.2
- Create a lookup table
- Use XPath 1.0 numeric functions and operators
- Apply a number format
- Extract and combine text strings

Session 6.3
- Create global and local parameters
- Explore the principals of functional programming
- Create a recursive template

Functional Programming with XSLT and XPath 1.0

Designing a Product Review Page

Case | *Harpe Gaming Store*

Sean Greer manages web development for the *Harpe Gaming Store*, an online store specializing in digital and board games. He's currently working on a redesign of the web pages that describe the different games sold by the company. Sean would like the page to include customer reviews. Each customer can write a short review of a game and rate that game from one star (poor) up to five stars (great).

Information about the games, the customers, and the customer reviews are stored in a database. Those data are then exported into different formats, including XML documents. Sean has stored this information in three XML files that he wants to use as source documents for an XSLT style sheet that will provide a summary of each game. He's asked you to complete the style sheet by adding functions and templates that will provide a numerical overview of customer opinion on two sample games he's selected.

STARTING DATA FILES

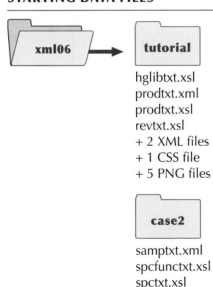

tutorial

hglibtxt.xsl
prodtxt.xml
prodtxt.xsl
revtxt.xsl
+ 2 XML files
+ 1 CSS file
+ 5 PNG files

review

gamestxt.xml
gamestxt.xsl
+ 2 XML files
+ 1 XSL file
+ 1 CSS file
+ 3 PNG files

case1

congresstxt.xml
electiontxt.xsl
+ 1 XML file
+ 1 CSS file
+ 1 PNG file

case2

samptxt.xml
spcfunctxt.xsl
spctxt.xsl
+ 1 CSS file
+ 5 PNG files

case3

hdfunctxt.xsl
hdorderstxt.xml
hdorderstxt.xsl
+ 2 XML files
+ 1 CSS file
+ 1 PNG file

case4

brwstorestxt.xml
brwstorestxt.xsl
+ 2 XML files
+ 1 CSS file
+ 4 PNG files

Session 6.1 Visual Overview:

The **xsl:include** element includes the contents of an external style sheet file in the current style sheet.

```
<xsl:stylesheet version="1.0"
    xmlns:xsl="http://www.w3.org/1999/XSL/Transform"
    xmlns:r="http://example.com/reviews">

  <xsl:include href="reviews.xsl" />

  <xsl:variable name="productID" select="'vg10551'" />

  <xsl:variable name="reviewList"
    select="document('reviews.xml')/r:reviews/r:review[@pid=$productID]" />
```

The **xsl:variable** element creates a **variable** as a user-defined name that stores a value or an object.

The **document()** function is an XSLT 1.0 function used to access the contents of an external XML file.

```
<section id="productSummary">
  <xsl:apply-templates select="products/product[@pid=$productID]" />
</section>

<section id="reviews">
  <h1>Customer Reviews</h1>

  <xsl:apply-templates select="$reviewList"/>
</section>
```

Variables are accessed using the reference $*name* where *name* is the variable name.

Variables and External Documents

```
    <tr>
        <th>Review Date:</th>
        <td>
            <xsl:apply-templates select="r:reviewDate" />
        </td>
    </tr>
</table>

<xsl:copy-of select="r:description" />
```

> The **xsl:copy-of** element is used to copy a node set into the output document.

Dance Off VII

By: Anasta Games

Product ID:	vg10551
List Price:	29.95
Media:	Video Game
Release Date:	2017-09-28

> This shows the value of the *productID* variable.

Challenge Yourself with Dance

Dance Off VII is the highly-anticipated sequel in the *Dance Off* line of dance games, brings even more fun and challenges to your gaming console. Take advantage of your motion-control platform and 50 of the hottest dance tracks to challenge the world - or your best friends - to *Dance Off*.

You wanted the top stars and hit songs and we got 'em for this new release. But don't think we dropped your old favorites and standards. Every track from *Dance Off III* is available and fully compatible with the new release. An added bonus: downloadable tracks from the top songs on the charts, so you can dance off to current hits.

Dance Off VII is the ultimate party game. The challenges are endless. Let the boys challenge the girls or the kids challenge the parents. Go international and stage your own Dance Off Olympics against friends from around the world. Dancers can track their standings on global leader boards and follow stats from dancers around the world.

Customer Reviews

My Favorite Workout Video and Workout Game

Review Date: 2017-11-18

I've owned all of the Dance Off releases from the beginning. It's my favorite workout video every morning. I have lost 12 pounds with very little modification of my diet.

Dance Off just gets better with every release. The song tracks are great. There is a wonderful selection of new and old tracks from around the world; some obscure and others more popular, including several that are in heavy rotation on the radio right now. Most tracks have several choreographic alternatives that can be unlocked by earning in-game dance points.

> Styles and content retrieved from an external document.

Using XSLT Variables

Like most programming languages, XSLT supports the creation and use of variables. A variable is a user-defined name that stores a value or an object. In XSLT, a variable can store any of the following:

- A numeric value
- A text string
- A node set from an XML document
- A Boolean value (either true or false)
- A section of code

Once a variable has been created, it can be used in place of the value or object it represents, resulting in code that is more compact and easier to maintain and revise.

Creating a Variable

XSLT variables are created using the following `variable` element

```
<xsl:variable name="name" select="expression" />
```

where *name* is the variable's name and *expression* is a numeric value, text string, Boolean value (`true` or `false`), or node set. For example, the following statement creates the *price* variable storing the numeric value 29.95:

```
<xsl:variable name="price" select="29.95" />
```

A text string is stored within a variable using either the empty element or the two-sided element format. If you choose to use an empty element, you must enclose the text string within its own set of quotation marks. The following code shows the two ways of storing the text string "The Harpe Gaming Store" within the *company* variable.

As an empty element:

```
<xsl:variable name="company" select="'The Harpe Gaming Store'" />
```

As a two-sided element:

```
<xsl:variable name="company">
The Harpe Gaming Store
</xsl:variable>
```

If you omit the quotation marks around the text string in the empty element form, XSLT processors treat the variable value as a reference to a node from the source document. If no such node exists, the processor will not report an error; instead, the processor will store a blank value in the variable.

To store a node set within a variable, you enter the location path for the node set. For example, the following *productList* variable references the node set defined by the products/product location path.

```
<xsl:variable name="productList" select="products/product" />
```

A node set can also be stored directly within a variable by placing the element tags within a two-sided `<xsl:variable>` tag. Thus, the following *mainHeading* variable stores HTML code for an h1 heading containing the element text "Harpe Gaming Store".

```
<xsl:variable name="mainHeading">
   <h1>Harpe Gaming Store</h1>
</xsl:variable>
```

Well-formed code that is stored in this fashion is known as a **result tree fragment** and is often used in projects in which the same code samples need to be repeatedly written to the result document.

XSLT variables act more like constants because the value of an XSLT variable can only be defined once and it cannot be further updated. As you'll see later, this has a profound effect on writing code that takes advantage of variable values. While variables in XSLT 1.0 are limited to the number, text string, Boolean, and node-set data types, XSLT 2.0 variables can be based on the data types defined in the XML Schema language or in user-defined schemas. You'll explore this topic in more detail in Tutorial 8.

Understanding Variable Scope

The locations in the style sheet where a variable can be referenced are known as the variable's **scope**. The scope is determined by where the variable is defined. In general, a variable can only be referenced within the element in which it is defined. Variables are said to have either global or local scope.

A variable with **global scope**, also known as a **global variable**, can be referenced from anywhere within a style sheet. To create a global variable, the `<xsl:variable>` tag must be at the top level of the style sheet, as a direct child of the `stylesheet` element. Because global variables are referenced anywhere in a style sheet, each global variable must have a unique variable name to avoid conflicts with variable names defined with the same name elsewhere in the style sheet. The advantage of a global variable is that it can be referenced within any template in the style sheet.

A variable that is created within an element such as a template is known as a **local variable**, has **local scope**, and can be referenced only within that element or template. Unlike global variables, local variables can share the same variable name if they are declared in different elements or templates. You can also assign the same name to a global variable and a local variable. In this case, an XSLT processor uses the local variable within the element in which it is defined and the global variable anyplace else it is referenced. Even though the same variable name can be used in the situation just described, it is best practice to give each variable a unique name, regardless of whether it is a global or a local variable, in order to avoid confusion.

You'll use variables extensively in the Harpe Gaming Store products page. You'll examine that page now.

Applying a Variable

Sean has created a sample XML document named products.xml containing information on two digital games sold by the Harpe Gaming Store. Figure 6-1 shows the structure of the products.xml document.

Figure 6-1   **Structure of the products XML document**

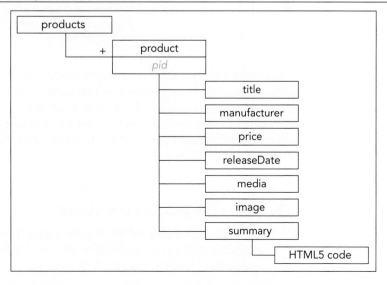

The two digital games described in this document are the *Dance Off* dancing game and the basketball simulation game *Net Force*. Sean has already begun creating an XSLT style sheet for the data from the products document. You open both the source document and style sheet document now and view the current state of the web page.

To open the source document and style sheet:

▶ **1.** Use your editor to open the **prodtxt.xml** and **prodtxt.xsl** files from the xml06 ▶ tutorial folder. Enter **your name** and the **date** in the comment section of each file and save them as **products.xml** and **products.xsl**, respectively.

▶ **2.** Go the **products.xml** file in your editor. Take some time to study the contents and structure of the document.

▶ **3.** Directly below the comment section, insert the following line to attach the products.xsl style sheet to the products.xml file:

```
<?xml-stylesheet type="text/xsl" href="products.xsl" ?>
```

▶ **4.** Close the file, saving your changes.

▶ **5.** Open the **products.xml** file in your web browser or use an XSLT processor to generate a result document based on the products.xsl style sheet. Figure 6-2 shows the initial appearance of the page.

Figure 6-2   **Initial appearance of the products page**

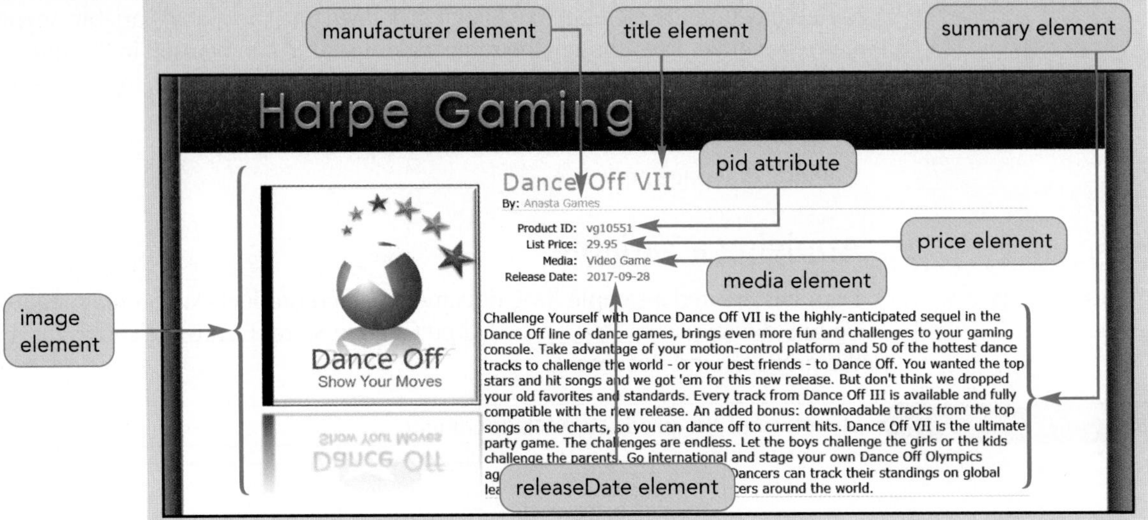

Currently, the style sheet only shows product information for the *Dance Off* digital game. Ultimately, this style sheet will be used to generate reports based on hundreds of games sold by the company. Each game is identified by its `pid` (product ID) attribute. Sean wants to store the `pid` value within a global variable named *productID*. You will create this variable now and set its initial value to the text string 'vg10551' – the product ID of the *Dance Off* game.

To create the *productID* variable:

▶ **1.** Go to the **products.xsl** file in your editor. Take some time to study the contents of the style sheet to understand how the styles from the style sheet are used in forming the result document.

> **Variables that contain text strings should enclose those text strings within a separate set of quotation marks.**

2. Go to the top of the document and, directly after the opening `<xsl:stylesheet>` tag, insert the following code to create the *productID* variable:

```
<xsl:variable name="productID" select="'vg10551'" />
```

Figure 6-3 shows the code to create the *productID* variable.

Figure 6-3 **Creating the productID variable**

3. Save your changes to the file.

Now that you've created the *productID* variable and set its value, you'll learn how to reference it elsewhere in the style sheet.

Referencing a Variable

Once a variable is created, it can be referenced using the expression

```
$name
```

where *name* is the variable's name. For example, the following code displays the value of the *price* variable:

```
The price of the item is
<xsl:value-of select="$price" />.
```

If the value of the *price* variable is 29.95, the text string "The price of the item is 29.95" is written to the result document.

If the variable references a node set, you can use the variable in place of the node-set reference. The following code demonstrates how a variable can be used to store a node set and then accessed to apply a template to that node set:

```
<xsl:variable name="customerList" select="customers/customer" />
<xsl:apply-templates select="$customerList" />
```

One of the advantages of using variables to store node sets is that you can replace long and complicated location paths with compact variable names, making your code easier to manage.

REFERENCE

Declaring and Referencing Variables in XSLT 1.0

• To declare a variable, use the XSLT element

```
<xsl:variable name="name" select="expression" />
```

where *name* is the variable's name and *expression* is a value or an object stored by the variable.

• To reference a variable, use the expression

```
$name
```

Now, you return to the products.xsl style sheet to replace the two locations where the value of the pid attribute is set to 'vg10551' with references to the value of the *productID* variable.

To reference the *productID* variable:

▶ **1.** Within the **products.xsl** file, scroll down to the root template and replace predicate [@pid='vg10551'] with **[@pid=$productID]** in both the title element and with the apply-templates element (see Figure 6-4).

| Figure 6-4 | Referencing the productID variable |

```
<html>
  <head>
    <title><xsl:value-of select="products/product[@pid=$productID]/title" /></title>
    <link href="harpe.css" rel="stylesheet" type="text/css" />
  </head>

  <body>
    <div id="wrap">
    <header>
      <h1>Harpe Gaming</h1>
    </header>
    <section id="productSummary">
      <xsl:apply-templates select="products/product[@pid=$productID]" />
    </section>
```

> returns the product whose pid attribute matches the value of the productID variable

▶ **2.** Save your changes to the file.

▶ **3.** Recreate the result document using either your web browser or an XML editor. Verify that the page remains unchanged, still showing product information for the *Dance Off* game since that is the game with the product ID vg10551.

Next, you change the style sheet so that it displays information for the *Net Force* digital game by changing the value of the *productID* variable to vg10552.

▶ **4.** Return to the **products.xsl** file in your editor. At the top of the file, change the value of the *productID* variable from 'vg10551' to **'vg10552'**. Save your changes to the file.

▶ **5.** Rerun the transformation of the source document using either your browser or an XSLT processor. As shown in Figure 6-5, the result document shows product information on the *Net Force* digital game.

| Figure 6-5 | The products page for the *Net Force* video game |

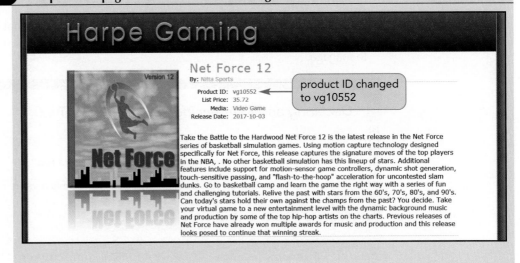

6. For now, you'll continue to work with the contents of the *Dance Off* game. Return to the **products.xsl** file in your editor. Change the value of the *productID* variable back to **'vg10551'** and save your changes.

7. Rerun the transformation to once again display information on the *Dance Off* game.

Notice, that in switching the report between different games, you only had to make one change to the value of the *productID* variable rather than multiple changes throughout the style sheet, demonstrating one of the advantages of global variables.

After studying the web page, Sean notices that the summary information is not formatted correctly. In the products.xml file, he had entered this information as HTML code with different topical sections separated into headings and paragraphs. However, Sean notices that the web page shows the text with no formatting. What happened to the HTML code? Why isn't the formatting showing?

Copying Nodes

The following `value-of` instruction writes the value of the summary element:

```
<xsl:value-of select="summary" />
```

but that value will only include the text of the summary element and its child elements, not the element tags themselves. For example, if the summary element contains the following HTML code:

```
<summary>
   <h3>Challenge Yourself with Dance</h3>
</summary>
```

the XSLT processor will only write the text "Challenge Yourself with Dance" and it will not include <h3> tags. If you are writing this content to a web page, that important piece of markup information will be lost. This is why the result document for Sean's products file included the text of the summary element but none of the markup.

One approach to including the markup tags as part of the element's value is to place the HTML code within a CDATA section as follows:

```
<summary><![CDATA[
   <h3>Challenge Yourself with Dance</h3>
]]></summary>
```

The XSLT processor will then write the entire enclosure including the markup tags into the result document. You will see this approach used in some legacy applications, but it is considered a misuse of the CDATA section, which was designed to represent non-markup data and thus should not be used to enclose markup tags. In fact, many XSLT processors, including the processor built into the Firefox browser, will enforce this principle by not writing markup tags even if they are enclosed within a CDATA section.

Another approach is to copy the HTML code directly into the result document as a result tree fragment, thus preserving both the text and the element markup. This is done through either the XSLT `copy` instruction or the `copy-of` element.

The copy Element

The copy element copies a node from the source document using the following syntax:

```
<xsl:copy use-attribute-sets="list">
   content template
</xsl:copy>
```

where *list* is a white-space-separated list of attributes (see Tutorial 5 for a discussion of attribute sets) that will be copied along with the node, and *content template* applies the template for the node set in the source document to be copied. For example, the following code copies the contents of the summary element:

```
<xsl:copy>
   <xsl:apply-templates select="summary" />
</xsl:copy>
```

The copy element creates a **shallow copy** limited to only the active node and does not include the children, descendants, or attributes of that node. Thus, in this example, the XSLT processor will copy the summary element into the result document but not any descendants or attributes of the summary element.

INSIGHT

Using the Identity Template

In many style sheets, you will want to copy entire branches of the source document's node tree into the result document. One way of accomplishing this is with the **identity template**, which matches any kind of node (including attribute nodes) in the source document and copies them to the result document. The identity template has the form

```
<xsl:template match="@* | node()">
   <xsl:copy>
      <xsl:apply-templates select="@* | node()" />
   </xsl:copy>
</xsl:template>
```

The identity template navigates the entire node tree and every time it encounters a node, it copies that node to the result tree. The only exceptions are namespace nodes and the document node.

To omit a branch of the source tree, write a separate template for that particular branch that does nothing. For example, the following code

```
<xsl:template match="@* | node()">
   <xsl:copy>
      <xsl:apply-templates select="@* | node()" />
   </xsl:copy>
</xsl:template>

<xsl:template match="appendix" />
```

copies every attribute and node from the source document unless it encounters the appendix element. For that node (and thus its descendants), the appendix template overrides the identity template and nothing is done, including no copying. The result is a document that includes all elements and attributes of the source document except the appendix element and its descendants and attributes.

The identity template is one of the basic tools used in XSLT style sheets and allows for several variations, including the ability to rename or combine elements and attributes from the source document.

The `copy-of` Element

The `copy-of` element differs from the `copy` element by creating a **deep copy** of a node set, including all descendant nodes and attributes. The syntax of the `copy-of` element is

```
<xsl:copy-of select="expression" />
```

where *expression* is an XPath expression for a node set or a value to be copied to the result document. If the expression is a number or Boolean value, the `copy-of` element converts the expression to a text string and the text is output to the result document. For example, to create a copy of the summary element including any children, descendants, or attributes, you would enter the instruction

```
<xsl:copy-of select="summary" />
```

If you only want to copy the descendent elements and attributes of the summary element but not the summary element itself, use the wildcard character (*) and enter the `copy-of` element as

```
<xsl:copy-of select="summary/*" />
```

REFERENCE

Creating a Copy of a Node Set

- To create a shallow copy of the active node (one that does not include the node's children, descendants, and attributes), use the XSLT `copy` element

```
<xsl:copy use-attribute-sets="list">
   content template
</xsl:copy>
```

where *list* is a white-space-separated list of attributes that will be copied along with the node, and *content template* references of the node set in the source document to be copied.
- To create a deep copy of a node set (including all children, descendants, and attributes), use the `copy-of` element

```
<xsl:copy-of select="expression" />
```

where *expression* is an XPath expression for a node set of a value that should be copied to the result document.

You will use the `copy-of` element to copy the contents of the summary element, including any HTML tags found within that element, to the source document.

To copy a node set to the result document:

▶ 1. Return to the **products.xsl** file in your editor.

▶ 2. Scroll down to the end of the product template and replace the tag
`<xsl:value-of select="summary" />` with
`<xsl:copy-of select="summary/*" />` as shown in Figure 6-6.

Figure 6-6	Creating a deep copy of a node set

```
        <tr>
           <th>Release Date: </th>
           <td>
              <xsl:value-of select="releaseDate" />
           </td>
        </tr>
     </table>

     <xsl:copy-of select="summary/*" />
  </xsl:template>

</xsl:stylesheet>
```

> copies all of the elements and attributes nested within the summary element and inserts that copy into the result document

> **3.** Save your changes to the style sheet and then apply the transformation to recreate the result document using either your web browser or an XML editor. Figure 6-7 shows the revised appearance of the summary text, now marked with the HTML tags from the summary element of the products.xml file.

Figure 6-7	Result document showing formatted summary text

contents of the summary element

```
<summary>
  <h3>Challenge Yourself with Dance</h3>

  <p><i>Dance Off VII</i> is the highly-anticipated sequel in the
  <i>Dance Off</i> line of dance games, brings even more fun and
  challenges to your gaming console. Take advantage of your motion-control
  platform and 50 of the hottest dance tracks to challenge
  the world - or your best friends - to <i>Dance Off</i>.</p>
  <p>You wanted the top stars and hit songs and we got 'em for this new release.
  But don't think we dropped your old favorites and standards. Every
  track from <i>Dance Off III</i> is available and fully compatible with
  the new release. An added bonus: downloadable tracks from the top
  songs on the charts, so you can dance off to current hits.</p>

  <p><i>Dance Off VII</i> is the ultimate party game. The challenges are
  endless. Let the boys challenge the girls or the kids challenge the
  parents. Go international and stage your own Dance Off Olympics against
  friends from around the world. Dancers can track their standings on
  global leader boards and follow stats from dancers around the world.</p>
</summary>
```

summary element as rendered in the result document

Challenge Yourself with Dance

Dance Off VII is the highly-anticipated sequel in the *Dance Off* line of dance games, brings even more fun and challenges to your gaming console. Take advantage of your motion-control platform and 50 of the hottest dance tracks to challenge the world - or your best friends - to *Dance Off*.

You wanted the top stars and hit songs and we got 'em for this new release. But don't think we dropped your old favorites and standards. Every track from *Dance Off III* is available and fully compatible with the new release. An added bonus: downloadable tracks from the top songs on the charts, so you can dance off to current hits.

Dance Off VII is the ultimate party game. The challenges are endless. Let the boys challenge the girls or the kids challenge the parents. Go international and stage your own Dance Off Olympics against friends from around the world. Dancers can track their standings on global leader boards and follow stats from dancers around the world.

INSIGHT

Copying Nodes in XSLT 2.0

XSLT 2.0 made several enhancements to the `copy` and `copy-of` elements, including the ability to add namespaces and apply schema validation to copied node sets. Under XSLT 2.0, the following attributes have been added to the `copy` and `copy-of` elements:

```
copy-namespace="yes|no"
validation="strict|lax|preserve|strip"
type="type"
```

The `copy-namespace` attribute indicates whether the namespace of a selected node should be copied to the result tree. The `validation` attribute indicates whether and how the copied nodes should receive strict or lax validation against a schema, or whether existing type annotations should be preserved or removed (stripped). The `type` attribute identifies the data type, either built-in or from a schema, that the copied nodes should be validated against.

The `copy` element under XSLT 2.0 also supports the following inherit-namespace attribute:

```
inherit-namespace="yes|no"
```

indicating whether the children of the copied nodes should inherit the namespace of the parent.

Sam also wants his report to include the reviews of customers who purchased the game. Those reviews are not part of the products.xml file and thus to bring in that information, you'll have to include data from a second source document in your style sheet.

Retrieving Data from Multiple Files

XML data is often spread among several XML files in order to keep each XML document to a manageable size and complexity. For example, in a sales database, one XML document might describe the different products sold by the company, another file might store data on product sales, a third document might contain information on the employees who processed those sales, and a fourth document might store data on the customers who purchased those products. Each document is therefore focused on a specific area of information and there is no need to duplicate the same data across several different documents.

There are three ways of accessing data from multiple source documents within an XSLT style sheet:

- the XSLT 1.0 `document()` function
- the XPath 2.0 `doc()` function
- the XSLT 2.0 `unparsed-text()` function

The XSLT 1.0 `document()` and XPath 2.0 `doc()` functions perform similar tasks and are used to retrieve node sets from XML source documents. The `unparsed-text()` function is used to access non-XML content stored within a text file, such as a CSV or comma-separated values text file. You'll examine each method in more detail.

The `document()` and `doc()` Functions

The syntax of the `document()` function is

```
document(uri [,base-node])
```

TIP

You must enter the URI for a path on the local machine prefaced with file:///, and any spaces or special characters must be replaced with escape codes.

where *uri* provides the location of an external XML document and *base-node* is an optional attribute representing a node whose base URI is used to resolve any relative URIs. For example, the following expression

```
document("customers.xml")
```

retrieves the customer.xml file, assuming that the customer.xml file shares the same folder with the active style sheet. To retrieve the same document from the web, include the web address as in the following example:

```
document("http://www.example.com/customers.xml")
```

The syntax of XPath 2.0's `doc()` function is similar to the `document()` function:

```
doc(uri)
```

TIP

Use the `document()` function when you are writing an XSLT 1.0-compliant style sheet. Use the `doc()` function for XSLT 2.0 style sheets or when you are using XPath for non-XSLT applications such as database queries.

where once again *uri* provides the location and filename of the external document. Thus, you can also retrieve the customers.xml file using

```
doc("customers.xml")
```

Both the `document()` and `doc()` functions return the root node of the specified document. From this root node, you can append an XPath expression just as you would with location paths in the source document. For example, the expression

```
document("customers.xml")/customers/customer/name
```

accesses the location path customers/customer/name within the customers.xml file. You can also use the `document()` and `doc()` functions to access the root node and location paths within the active style sheet by entering a blank text string for the document's URI. For example, the expression

```
document('')/xsl:stylesheet/xsl:template
```

references the node set of template elements within the style sheet. This technique of referencing the style sheet is useful when the active style sheet contains important data such as a table of values to be used in the result document.

Applying the `document()` Function

Sean wants to retrieve customer reviews from the reviews.xml file. Figure 6-8 shows the structure of this document.

Figure 6-8   **Structure of the reviews document**

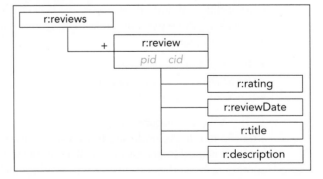

The reviews document contains reviews for the products sold by the store. Each review is identified by its `pid` attribute, which provides the ID of the product being reviewed, and the `cid` attribute, which provides the ID of the customer writing the review. The rating element stores the customer rating from one star (poor) to five stars (great). The `reviewDate` element provides the date that the review was submitted, the `title` element gives the title of the review, and the description element stores the review text. Note that the elements of this document are placed within the http://example.com/reviews namespace with the prefix "r".

To make the customer reviews accessible to Sean's style sheet, you'll add the following global variable to the products.xsl document:

```
<xsl:variable name="reviewList"
 select="document('reviews.xml')/r:reviews/r:review
[@pid=$productID]" />
```

The *reviewList* variable stores a node set of all of the customer reviews for the current product (as identified by the *productID* variable). Thus, when the value of the *productID* variable changes to display a new product, the reviewList node set will automatically display the relevant reviews.

You add the *reviewList* variable to the products.xsl style sheet.

To retrieve a document with the document() function:

1. Return to the **products.xsl** file and scroll to the top of the document.

2. Because you are accessing nodes from the reviews namespace, declare the namespace by adding the following attribute within the opening tag of the `<xsl:stylesheet>` tag directly after the declaration of the xsl namespace:

   ```
   xmlns:r="http://example.com/reviews"
   ```

3. Below the statement that declares the *productID* variable, insert the following variable element that references the reviews/review path from the reviews.xml file:

   ```
   <xsl:variable name="reviewList"
   select="document('reviews.xml')/r:reviews/r:review
   [@pid=$productID]" />
   ```

   Figure 6-9 shows the revised code of the style sheet.

Figure 6-9	Accessing the reviews.xml document

```
<xsl:stylesheet version="1.0"
    xmlns:xsl="http://www.w3.org/1999/XSL/Transform"
    xmlns:r="http://example.com/reviews">                name of the
                                                          reviewList variable
  <xsl:variable name="productID" select="'vg10551'" />
  <xsl:variable name="reviewList"
    select="document('reviews.xml')/r:reviews/r:review[@pid=$productID]" />
```

namespace for the reviews document

stores the node set of reviews from the reviews.xml file for the specified product

4. Save your changes to the file.

Retrieving Data from a non-XML File

Files accessed with the `document()` and `doc()` functions must be well-formed XML documents. XSLT 2.0 also supports the following `unparsed-text()` function to retrieve non-XML data:

```
unparsed-text(uri [,encoding])
```

where `uri` is the URI of the text file and `encoding` is an optional attribute that defines the character encoding used in the file. For example, the following expression retrieves the contents of the sales.txt file, formatted using the ISO-8859-1 encoding.

```
unparsed-text("sales.txt", "ISO-8859-1")
```

The data retrieved using the `unparsed-text()` function is read as a long text string. From that text string, you can use text functions from XPath and XSLT to retrieve specific data values.

The `unparsed-text()` function can also be used to read HTML files, including those files that are not well-formed and would cause an error if copied directly into XML. The following expression reads the contents of the reports.html file and then outputs the HTML code as raw text to the result document.

```
<xsl:value-of select="unparsed-text('reports.html')"
  disable-output-escaping="yes" />
```

Remember, however, that many editors, including the Firefox browser, do not support the `disable-output-escaping` attribute and will instead display the text of the file, including the HTML markup tags. So, before using this attribute, you have to first determine whether your browser supports this attribute. You'll learn more about the `unparsed-text()` function in Tutorial 8.

PROSKILLS

Problem Solving: Checking for the Existence of an External Document

A well-designed style sheet catches errors before they occur. If your XSLT application attempts to retrieve a document that is either not there or is not well-formed XML, the processor will halt the transformation. To catch this error before it causes the transformation to fail, you can use the following functions to test for the existence of XML and non-XML documents:

```
doc-available(uri)
unparsed-text-available(uri, encoding)
```

Both functions will return a value of true if the document exists and, in the case of the `doc-available()` function, is well-formed. A value of false indicates that the document is not readable. For example, the following code tests to see whether the customers.xml file is readable before attempting to read it:

```
if (doc-available("customers.xml")) then

doc("customers.xml") else ()
```

If this test returns a value of false, the processor skips trying to import the customers.xml file but continues with the rest of the transformation. Note that both the `doc-available()` and `unparsed-text-available()` functions require an XSLT 2.0 style sheet processor.

Now that you've used the `document()` function to access the reviews.xml file from within the products.xsl style sheet file, you can display the customer reviews on the web page. Sean has already started work on a style sheet named reviews.xsl to display those reviews. Next, you'll learn how to add that style sheet to the products.xsl file.

Accessing an External Style Sheet

As an XML application grows larger, the XSLT style sheet becomes longer and more unwieldy. Many applications break up the style sheet into separate files that can be managed more easily. This also allows the project to use only those style elements that are relevant to the current project and to mix different style sheets to create new applications.

XSLT supports two ways of accessing an external style sheet file: the `include` element and the `import` element.

Including a Style Sheet

To include an external style sheet file in the active style sheet, add the following `include` element as a child of the `stylesheet` element:

```
<xsl:include href="uri" />
```

where `uri` provides the location and name of the style sheet file. For example, to include the style sheet file library.xsl within the active style sheet file you apply the instruction

```
<xsl:include href="library.xsl" />
```

Including a style sheet has the same effect as inserting the style sheet code at the location where the `include` element is placed. This can cause a problem if components in the included style sheet conflict with components in the active style sheet. When the processor has to resolve conflicts between two style components, it picks the one that is defined *last* in the style sheet. Thus, if you place the `include` element at the end of your style sheet it will have precedence over the active style sheet; on the other hand, when the `include` element is placed at the top of the style sheet, any components in the active style sheet will have precedence.

Importing a Style Sheet

TIP

If you're concerned about name conflicts and want the active style sheet to always have precedence over the external sheet, always use the `import` element.

Another way to access an external style sheet file is with the following `import` element:

```
<xsl:import href="uri" />
```

Unlike the `include` element, which can be placed anywhere within the style sheet as long as it is a child of the `stylesheet` element, the `import` element must be placed as the first child of the `stylesheet` element. Because it is defined first, the active style sheet will have precedence if any conflicts arise.

REFERENCE

Including and Importing Style Sheets

- To include a style sheet, place the following element as a child of the `stylesheet` element:

```
<xsl:include href="uri" />
```

where `uri` defines the name and location of the external style sheet file to be included in the active sheet.
- To import a style sheet, place the following element as the first child of the `stylesheet` element:

```
<xsl:import href="uri" />
```

You'll use the `include` element to include the reviews.xml style sheet in the products.xsl style sheet.

To include the reviews.xsl style sheet:

1. Use your editor to open the **revtxt.xsl** file from the xml06 ▸ tutorial folder. Enter **your name** and the **date** in the comment section and save the file as **reviews.xsl**.

2. Take some time to study the content and structure of the style sheet and then close the file.

3. Return to the **products.xsl** file in your editor.

4. Directly below the opening tag for the `<xsl:stylesheet>` element, insert the following `include` element:

   ```
   <xsl:include href="reviews.xsl" />
   ```

   Next, you'll revise the root template to show the list of reviews. A template for the review element has already been created in the reviews.xsl file, so you'll only need to apply that template.

5. Scroll down to the end of the root template and, directly above the closing `</div>` tag, insert

   ```
   <section id="reviews">
      <h1>Customer Reviews</h1>
      <xsl:apply-templates select="$reviewList"/>
   </section>
   ```

   Figure 6-10 highlights the revised code in the products.xsl file.

Figure 6-10	Including the reviews.xsl style sheet

includes the reviews.xsl style sheet file in the current style sheet

```
<xsl:stylesheet version="1.0"
      xmlns:xsl="http://www.w3.org/1999/XSL/Transform"
      xmlns:r="http://example.com/reviews">
<xsl:include href="reviews.xsl" />
```

```
      <section id="reviews">
         <h1>Customer Reviews</h1>
         <xsl:apply-templates select="$reviewList"/>
      </section>

      </div>
   </body>
</html>
</xsl:template>
```

applies the review template from the reviews.xsl file to the list of reviews stored in the reviewList variable

6. Save your changes to the file and recreate the result document using either your web browser or your XML editor. Figure 6-11 shows the revised products page with the list of customer reviews appended to the product description.

Figure 6-11	Customer reviews displayed in the products page

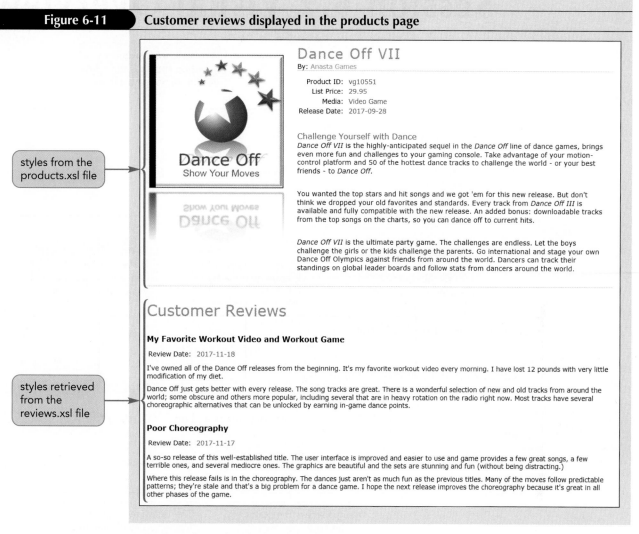

styles from the products.xsl file

styles retrieved from the reviews.xsl file

Sean is pleased with the web page so far. In the next session, you add information about the reviewers and you calculate the average rating given to selected digital games.

Session 6.1 Quick Check

REVIEW

1. Create a variable named *OrderDate* containing the text '10/14/2017'.
2. Provide the code to display the value of the *OrderDate* variable.
3. What is variable scope? What is the difference between local scope and global scope and how do you declare a variable having each type of scope?
4. Provide the code to create a deep copy of the `customers` element.
5. Provide the function to import the sales.xml file under the XSLT 1.0 processor. What function would you use under XPath 2.0?
6. Provide a function to import the sales.txt document with UTF-8 encoding.
7. Provide the function to check whether the XML document sales.xml exists and is well-formed.
8. Provide the code to import the sales.xsl style sheet in the active style sheet. Where should this element be placed?

Session 6.2 Visual Overview:

The `format-number()` **function** specifies the text format of numeric values.

```
<tr>
   <th>List Price: </th>
   <td>
      <xsl:value-of select="format-number(price,'$#,#0.00')" />
   </td>
</tr>
```

The `sum()` function calculates the sum of the numeric values in a node set.

The div keyword is used to divide one numeric value by another.

The `count()` function is used to count the number of numeric values in a node set.

```
<h1>Customer Reviews</h1>

<p>
  <xsl:variable name="avgRating"
   select="sum($reviewList/r:rating) div count($reviewList/r:rating)" />

  <xsl:value-of select="format-number($avgRating, '0.00')" />
  out of 5 stars

  (<xsl:value-of select="count($reviewList)" /> reviews)
</p>
```

This shows the count of the customer review.

The rating average formatted to display the value to 2 decimal points.

The `current()` function returns the current node being processed.

```
<th>By:</th>
<td>
   <xsl:variable name="customerID" select="current()/@cid" />
   <xsl:value-of select="$customerList[@cid=$customerID]/c:nickname" />
   (<xsl:value-of select="$customerList[@cid=$customerID]/c:city" />,
   <xsl:value-of select="$customerList[@cid=$customerID]/c:state" />)
</td>
```

Values from an external document can be looked up by comparing key values in that document with the value of the current node.

Calculations and Formatting

Dance Off VII

By: Anasta Games

Product ID: vg10551
List Price: $29.95
Media: Video Game
Release Date: September 28, 2017

Price value displayed as currency.

Challenge Yourself with Dance

Dance Off VII is the highly-anticipated sequel in the *Dance Off* line of dance games, brings even more fun and challenges to your gaming console. Take advantage of your motion-control platform and 50 of the hottest dance tracks to challenge the world - or your best friends - to *Dance Off*.

You wanted the top stars and hit songs and we got 'em for this new release. But don't think we dropped your old favorites and standards. Every track from *Dance Off III* is available and fully compatible with the new release. An added bonus: downloadable tracks from the top songs on the charts, so you can dance off to current hits.

Dance Off VII is the ultimate party game. The challenges are endless. Let the boys challenge the girls or the kids challenge the parents. Go international and stage your own Dance Off Olympics against friends from around the world. Dancers can track their standings on global leader boards and follow stats from dancers around the world.

This shows the count of reviews.

Customer Reviews

4.21 out of 5 stars (19 reviews)

My Favorite Workout Video and Workout Game

By: WillHa85 (Galway, New York)
Review Date: November 18, 2017

Customer information looked up in an external XML document.

I've owned all of the Dance Off releases from the beginning. It's my favorite workout video every morning. I have lost 12 pounds with very little modification of my diet.

Dance Off just gets better with every release. The song tracks are great. There is a wonderful selection of new and old tracks from around the world; some obscure and others more popular, including several that are in heavy rotation on the radio right now. Most tracks have several choreographic alternatives that can be unlocked by earning in-game dance points.

Average customer rating calculated by dividing the sum of the ratings by the count.

Creating a Lookup Table in XSLT

A **lookup table** is a collection of data values that can be searched in order to return data that matches a supplied key value. For example, a lookup table could contain a list of zip codes matched with a state name. A program would then submit a zip code and the lookup table would return the state in which that zip code originated.

Lookup tables are a key feature of many XSLT applications in which the table is stored as part of a node tree in an external document and the style sheet retrieves data values by searching through the node tree looking for matching values.

One way to create a lookup table is to use the `current()` function, which returns the active node being processed in the style sheet. For example, the following two expressions are equivalent in that they can be used to display the value of the active node.

```
<xsl:value-of select="." />
<xsl:value-of select="current()" />
```

Now, you'll examine how the `current()` function can be used to look up values from a data source. In this example, every store has a ZIP element providing the zip code of the store location. But the store data doesn't include the state name. However, another element, the `states` element, lists zip codes along with their state name. By going through the list of stores, we can match the zip code of the current store with a zip code in the states node set. The template looks as follows:

```
<xsl:template match="store">
   <xsl:variable name="storeZip" select="current()/ZIP" />
   <xsl:value-of select="states/state[ZIP=$storeZip]/name" />
</xsl:template>
```

The template uses the `current()` function to retrieve the zip code of the store currently being processed by the template, saving that value in the *storeZip* local variable. The next line of the template uses a predicate to look up the name of the state whose zip code matches the value of *storeZip*, retrieving this information from the states/state node set.

Sean wants you to use this approach to retrieve data on the customers who wrote reviews for the Harpe Gaming Store. Every review stored in the reviews.xml file contains two attributes: the `pid` attribute, which identifies the product being reviewed, and the `cid` attribute, which provides the ID of the customer submitting the review. Customer data is stored in a separate XML document named customers.xml. The structure of this document is shown in Figure 6-12.

Figure 6-12	Structure of the customers document

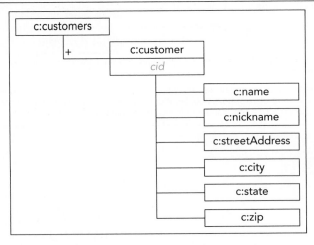

The customers.xml file records each customer's name; a nickname used for reviews (to ensure anonymity); the customer's street address, city, state of residence, and the zip code. Note that the document also uses the `cid` attribute to uniquely identify each customer. You add access to the customers.xml document to the reviews.xsl style sheet, storing the reference under the global variable named *customerList*.

To access the customers.xml file:

1. Return to the **reviews.xsl** document in your editor.

Because the customer data is placed in the http://www.example.com/customers namespace, you must first declare this namespace and prefix in the style sheet.

2. Add the following attribute to the opening `<xsl:stylesheet>` tag directly after the attribute that declares the namespace for product reviews:

```
xmlns:c="http://example.com/customers"
```

3. Directly below the stylesheet element, insert the following global variable to save the list of customers from the customers.xml in the *customerList* variable:

```
<xsl:variable name="customerList"
  select="document('customers.xml')/c:customers/c:customer" />
```

Figure 6-13 shows the revised code.

Figure 6-13   **Retrieving the customers.xml file**

```
<xsl:stylesheet version="1.0"
    xmlns:xsl="http://www.w3.org/1999/XSL/Transform"
    xmlns:r="http://example.com/reviews"
    xmlns:c="http://example.com/customers">

    <xsl:variable name="customerList"
      select="document('customers.xml')/c:customers/c:customer" />
```

name of the customerList variable

namespace for the customers document

stores the node set listing Harpe Gaming Store customers

Next, you'll display the customer nickname, city, and state alongside each review. You'll match the value of the `cid` attribute assigned to the customer with the customer ID specified in the review.

To retrieve customer data for each review:

1. Scroll down to the review template within the reviews.xsl file.

2. Directly after the opening `<table id="reviewTable">` tag, insert the following:

```
<tr>
   <th>By:</th>
   <td>
      <xsl:variable name="customerID" select="current()/@cid" />
```

```
    <xsl:value-of
      select="$customerList[@cid=$customerID]/c:nickname" />
    (<xsl:value-of
      select="$customerList[@cid=$customerID]/c:city" />,
    <xsl:value-of
      select="$customerList[@cid=$customerID]/c:state" />)
  </td>
</tr>
```

Figure 6-14 shows the table cells with the data pulled from the customers.xml file.

Figure 6-14	Looking up the customer nickname and location

customerID stores the value of the cid attribute for current review

```
<table id="reviewTable">
  <tr>
    <th>By:</th>
    <td>
      <xsl:variable name="customerID" select="current()/@cid" />
      <xsl:value-of select="$customerList[@cid=$customerID]/c:nickname" />
      (<xsl:value-of select="$customerList[@cid=$customerID]/c:city" />,
      <xsl:value-of select="$customerList[@cid=$customerID]/c:state" />)
    </td>
  </tr>
```

displays the value of the nickname, city, and state elements for the customer whose cid attribute matches customerID

3. Save your changes to the style sheet and then regenerate the result document for the products.xml file using either your web browser or an XML editor. Figure 6-15 shows the review list with the customer data added from the customers.xml file.

Figure 6-15	Customer reviews with reviewer nicknames and addresses

Customer Reviews

nickname element

My Favorite Workout Video and Workout Game

By: WillHa85 (Galway, New York)
Review Date: 2017-11-18

city and state elements

I've owned all of the Dance Off releases from the beginning. It's my favorite workout video every morning. I have lost 12 pounds with very little modification of my diet.

Dance Off just gets better with every release. The song tracks are great. There is a wonderful selection of new and old tracks from around the world; some obscure and others more popular, including several that are in heavy rotation on the radio right now. Most tracks have several choreographic alternatives that can be unlocked by earning in-game dance points.

Poor Choreography

By: GoldFry26 (Sea Island, Georgia)
Review Date: 2017-11-17

A so-so release of this well-established title. The user interface is improved and easier to use and game provides a few great songs, a few terrible ones, and several mediocre ones. The graphics are beautiful and the sets are stunning and fun (without being distracting.)

Where this release fails is in the choreography. The dances just aren't as much fun as the previous titles. Many of the moves follow predictable patterns; they're stale and that's a big problem for a dance game. I hope the next release improves the choreography because it's great in all other phases of the game.

Sean also wants the page to summarize the customer reviews. He would like to display the total number of reviews and average rating. To display this information, you'll work with XSLT and XPath's numeric functions.

TIP

If XPath is unable to calculate a value because of an error in the style sheet, it will return the text string "NaN" (Not a Number).

Working with Numeric Functions

XPath 1.0 supports several functions to perform numeric calculations on node sets. Using these functions you can count the number of items in the node set, determine the sum of numeric values, and round values to the next-lowest or next-highest integer. Figure 6-16 summarizes the numeric functions supported by XPath 1.0.

Figure 6-16   **XPath 1.0 numeric functions**

Function	Description
`ceiling(number)`	Rounds *number* up to the next integer
`count(values)`	Counts the number of items in *values*
`floor(number)`	Rounds *number* down to the next integer
`last(values)`	Returns the last item from *values*
`number(text)`	Returns the numeric value indicated by *text*
`position()`	Returns the position of context node
`round(number)`	Rounds *number* to the nearest integer
`sum(values)`	Returns the sum of the items in *values*

You'll use the `count()` function to display the total number of reviews submitted by customers on the selected product.

To apply the `count()` function:

▶ 1. Return to the **products.xsl** file in your editor.

▶ 2. Directly after the `<h1>Customer Reviews</h1>` tag in the root template, insert the following code to display the count of reviews stored in the *reviewList* variable:

```
<p>
   (<xsl:value-of select="count($reviewList)" /> reviews)
</p>
```

Figure 6-17 shows the application of the `count()` function.

Figure 6-17   **Applying the count() function**

applies the count() function to count the number of nodes stored in the reviewList variable

```
<section id="reviews">
   <h1>Customer Reviews</h1>

   <p>
     (<xsl:value-of select="count($reviewList)" /> reviews)
   </p>

   <xsl:apply-templates select="$reviewList"/>
</section>
```

▶ 3. Save your changes to the style sheet and then regenerate the result document using either your web browser or an XML editor.

> **4.** Verify that the text "(19 reviews)" appears below the Customer Reviews heading, indicating that there were 19 reviews submitted for the *Dance Off* digital game.

While there are only 19 reviews in this sample document, a complete report might include hundreds of reviews for some products. Sean wants to limit the number of reviews displayed in the product overview page to the first 5 reviews listed in the reviews.xml file.

The `position()` function was introduced along with predicates in Tutorial 5 as a way of returning the position of individual nodes within a node set. You can also use the `position()` function to return the position of the context node from the result document using the following expression:

```
<xsl:value-of select="position()" />
```

The `position()` function can also be used in an `if` element to test whether a node occupies a particular position in the result document. For example, the following `if` element tests whether the context node is in the third position in the result document:

```
<xsl:if test="position()=3" />
```

You'll use the `position()` function now to limit the reviews to the first five reviews listed in the products page.

To apply the `position()` function:

> **1.** Return to the **products.xsl** file in your editor.

> **2.** Go to the root template and change the apply-templates instruction that displays the reviews in the *reviewList* variable by adding the predicate

> ```
> [position() &lt;= 5]
> ```

> Figure 6-18 highlights the addition of the predicate to the *reviewList* variable.

Figure 6-18	Applying the position() function

```
<section id="reviews">
   <h1>Customer Reviews</h1>                    displays only the first five
                                                reviews in the products page

   <p>
      (<xsl:value-of select="count($reviewList)" /> reviews)
   </p>

   <xsl:apply-templates select="$reviewList[position() &lt;= 5]"/>
</section>
```

> **3.** Save your changes to the style sheet, and then regenerate the result document and verify that only the first five reviews from the reviews.xml file are listed on the page.

Notice that while only the 5 most recent reviews are displayed on the page, the count of total number of reviews is still 19. This is because the `count()` function is applied to the entire node set of customer reviews, while the apply-templates instruction that displays the text of the reviews is only applied to the first 5 reviews listed in the reviews.xml file.

INSIGHT

Using the number Element

The `position()` function returns the position of the node as it is displayed within the result document, not necessarily the position of the node in the source document. For example, if the style sheet displays the nodes in sorted order, the `position()` function will reflect the sorted positions. If you want to retrieve the position values of the nodes as they appeared in the source document, you can use the following `number` element:

```
<xsl:number select="expression" />
```

where *expression* is an XPath expression that indicates which nodes in the source document are being numbered. The `select` attribute is optional; however, if omitted the `number` element generates numbering for the context node. For example, the following code displays the node number alongside the review title:

```
<xsl:for each select="reviews/review">
   <xsl:number />.
   <xsl:value-of select="title" />
</xsl:for>
```

producing the following text:

```
1. My Favorite Workout Video and Workout Game
2. Poor Choreography
3. A Great Gift
…
```

Because the `number` element counts nodes based on the source document, even if you sort the nodes in the result document, the value returned by the `number` element will still reflect the original order from the source file. For example, if you sort the review titles alphabetically and display the number value alongside the title text, the resulting numbering will still reflect the document order:

```
3. A Great Gift
1. My Favorite Workout Video and Workout Game
2. Poor Choreography
…
```

In general, you should use the `position()` function for numbering the nodes in the result document and use the `number` element for reporting on the node's position in the source file.

In addition to calculating the total number of reviews, Sean wants you to calculate the average customer rating of the game. XPath 1.0 does not provide a function to calculate an average, but you can calculate this value using a mathematical expression.

Applying Mathematical Operators

The XPath 1.0 list of numeric functions is very limited (a more extensive list is provided in XPath 2.0). To perform calculations not covered by an XPath 1.0 function, you have to write a mathematical expression. XPath 1.0 provides six mathematical operators, as described in Figure 6-19.

Figure 6-19 | **XPath 1.0 mathematical operators**

Operator	Description	Example	Result
+	Adds two numbers together	3 + 5	8
–	Subtracts one number from another	5 – 3	2
*	Multiplies two numbers together	5 * 3	15
div	Divides one number by another	15 div 3	5
mod	Provides the remainder after performing a division of one number by another	15 mod 4	3
–	Negates a single number	–2	-2

Averages are calculated by the dividing the sum of a set of values by its count. Thus, you can calculate the average rating in the following expression, which divides the sum of the customer ratings by the count:

```
sum($reviewList/r:rating) div count($reviewList/r:rating)
```

You'll add the expression to the style sheet to calculate the average customer rating of the game.

To calculate the average rating:

1. Return to the **products.xsl** file in your editor and go to the root template.

2. Directly above the line that displays the total number of customer reviews, insert the following code to create the *avgRating* variable and display its value:

```
<xsl:variable name="avgRating"
  select="sum($reviewList/r:rating) div
          count($reviewList/r:rating)" />

<xsl:value-of select="$avgRating" />
out of 5 stars
```

Figure 6-20 shows the code to calculate the average customer rating.

> Mathematical division can only be done with the div keyword and not the / symbol because that symbol is reserved by XPath for use in location paths.

Figure 6-20 | **Calculating the average rating**

calculates the sum of the ratings for the selected product

calculates the count of the ratings for the selected product

displays the value of the avgRating variable

division operator

```
<section id="reviews">
  <h1>Customer Reviews</h1>

  <p>
    <xsl:variable name="avgRating"
      select="sum($reviewList/r:rating) div count($reviewList/r:rating)" />

    <xsl:value-of select="$avgRating" />
    out of 5 stars

    (<xsl:value-of select="count($reviewList)" /> reviews)
  </p>

  <xsl:apply-templates select="$reviewList[position() &lt;= 5]"/>
</section>
```

3. Save your changes to the style sheet and then regenerate the result document using either your web browser or an XML editor. Figure 6-21 shows the average rating of the *Dance Off* digital game based on 19 reviews.

Figure 6-21   **Average customer rating**

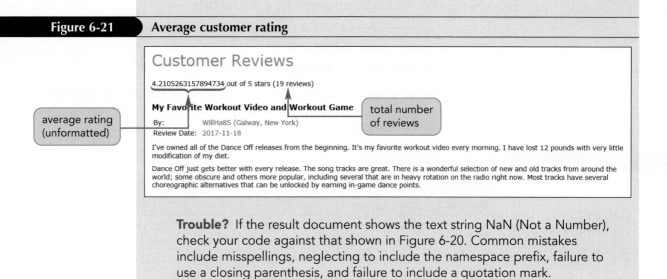

Trouble? If the result document shows the text string NaN (Not a Number), check your code against that shown in Figure 6-20. Common mistakes include misspellings, neglecting to include the namespace prefix, failure to use a closing parenthesis, and failure to include a quotation mark.

Numerical Calculations in XPath 2.0

XPath 2.0 adds several new mathematical functions to expand that language's ability to perform numeric calculations. Figure 6-22 describes some of the numeric functions added in XPath 2.0. In addition to these functions, XPath 2.0 still supports all of the XPath 1.0 functions.

Figure 6-22   **XPath 2.0 numeric functions**

Function	Description
`abs(number)`	Returns the absolute value of `number`
`avg(values)`	Calculates the average of `values`
`max(values)`	Returns the maximum of `values`
`min(values)`	Returns the minimum of `values`
`round-half-to-even(number, precision)`	Rounds `number` to the number of digits specified by `precision`; if `precision` is negative, `number` is rounded to the number of zeroes left of the decimal point and, if there are two possible values that are equally close, the function chooses the even value

For example, if you were designing an XSLT 2.0 style sheet for Sean, you could calculate the average customer rating using the following `avg()` function:

```
avg(reviewList$r:rating)
```

You'll learn more about XPath 2.0 numeric functions and how to apply them in Tutorial 8 and Tutorial 9.

Formatting Numeric Values

XSLT and XPath 1.0 support only one data type for numbers, **double precision floating point**, in which the data values are stored using 8 bytes of computer storage in order to achieve greater precision with calculations. This can sometimes lead to "too much" precision, as is displayed in Figure 6-21, in which the customer rating is displayed to the 16th decimal place. You rarely need an average calculated to that level of precision!

Using the `format-number()` Function

To display numeric values to a more manageable level of precision you can use the following `format-number()` function:

```
format-number(value, format)
```

where *value* is the numeric value and *format* is a pattern that indicates how the number should appear. Figure 6-23 describes the symbols that can be used in creating the number format pattern.

Figure 6-23	Number format symbols

Symbol	Description
#	Placeholder that displays an optional number of digits in the formatted number and is usually used as the far left symbol in the number format
0	Placeholder that displays required digits in the formatted number
.	Separates the integer digits from the fractional digits
,	Separates groups of digits in the number
;	Separates the pattern for positive numbers from the pattern for negative numbers
−	Shows the location of the minus symbol for negative numbers
%	Displays the value as a percentage (parts per hundred)
‰	Displays the value as per-mill (parts per thousand)

For example, the pattern

```
format-number(56823.847, '#,##0.00')
```

displays the number as 56,823.85. Note that the processor rounds the value if the number contains digits other than those provided by the number format. For values that can be either positive or negative, you can specify different patterns using a semicolon symbol (;) to separate the two patterns. The expression

```
format-number(-238.2, '#,##0.0;(#,##0.0)')
```

displays the value –238.2 as (238.2). Any characters not listed in Figure 6-23 appear as part of the number format. To display the number 152.25 as currency, for example, you could use the number format

```
format-number(152.25, '$#,##0.00')
```

which the processor displays as $152.25.

International Number Formats

The numbering scheme used by the `format-number()` function follows the American system, in which decimal places are represented by a period (.), and the thousands separator is represented by a comma (,). If you plan to create an international document, you may need to support the numbering schemes of other countries. Some European countries, for example, use a comma as the decimal point and a period to separate groups of three digits. To define a different numbering scheme or to make modifications in how numbers are represented in your document, you apply the following element to the style sheet:

```
<xsl:decimal-format attributes />
```

where *attributes* is a list of attributes that define the numbering scheme that XSLT processors should employ when rendering numeric values. Because the `decimal-format` element defines behavior for the entire style sheet, it must be entered as a direct child of the `stylesheet` element and cannot be placed within a template. Figure 6-24 describes the different attributes of the `decimal-format` element.

| Figure 6-24 | Attributes of the decimal-format element |

Attribute	Description
name	Name of the decimal format; if you omit a name, the numbering scheme becomes the default format for the document
decimal-separator	Character used to separate the integer and fractional parts of the number; the default is "."
grouping-separator	Character used to separate groups of digits; the default is ","
infinity	Text string used to represent infinite values; the default is "infinity"
minus-sign	Character used to represent negative values; the default is "-"
NaN	Text used to represent entries that are not numbers; the default is "NaN"
percent	Character used to represent numbers as percentages; the default is "%"
per-mille	Character used to represent numbers in parts per 1000; the default is "‰"
zero-digit	Character used to indicate a required digit in the number format pattern; the default is "0"
digit	Character used to indicate an optional digit in the number format pattern; the default is "#"
pattern-separator	Character used to separate positive number patterns from negative number patterns in the number format; the default is ";"

To create a numbering scheme for some European countries, you can insert the following element at the beginning of the XSLT style sheet:

```
<xsl:decimal-format name="Europe"
    decimal-separator="," grouping-separator="." />
```

To use this numbering scheme in your number formats, you include the name of the scheme as part of the `format-number()` function. Thus, to employ the Europe number scheme, you enter the number format as

```
format-number(56823.847, '#.##0,00', 'Europe')
```

and the processor displays the value as 56.823,85.

REFERENCE

Formatting Numeric Values

- To format a number, use the XPath function

  ```
  format-number(value, format)
  ```

  where *value* is the numeric value and *format* is a pattern that indicates how the number should be displayed.
- To set the default number formats for the style sheet, use the XSLT element

  ```
  <xsl:decimal-format attributes />
  ```

  where *attributes* is a list of attributes that define the numbering scheme that XSLT processors should employ when rendering numeric values.

Sean suggests that you format the averaging rating value, showing the value to two decimal places. He also wants the price of the digital game to be displayed as currency.

To apply a number format:

▶ **1.** Return to the **products.xsl** file in your editor.

▶ **2.** Go to the root template and change the statement to display the value of the *avgRating* variable to

```
<xsl:value-of select="format-number($avgRating, '0.00')" />
```

▶ **3.** Scroll down to the product template and change the line to display the price element to

```
<xsl:value-of select="format-number(price,'$#,#0.00')" />
```

Figure 6-25 highlights the newly added code in the style sheet.

Figure 6-25 ▶ **Formatting the average rating and sales price**

displays the average rating
to two decimal places

```
<p>
  <xsl:variable name="avgRating"
  select="sum($reviewList/r:rating) div count($reviewList/r:rating)" />

  <xsl:value-of select="format-number($avgRating, '0.00')" />
  out of 5 stars

  (<xsl:value-of select="count($reviewList)" /> reviews)
</p>
```

displays the sales price with
a dollar symbol and a
thousands separator and ...

```
<tr>
   <th>List Price: </th>
   <td>
      <xsl:value-of select="format-number(price,'$#,#0.00')" />
   </td>
</tr>
```

... as currency to
two decimal places

▶ **4.** Save your changes to the file and then regenerate the result document using either your web browser or an XML editor. The price of the *Dance Off* digital game should now be displayed as $29.95 and the average customer rating as 4.21.

Trouble? If your style sheet doesn't work, make sure that you have enclosed the number formats within a set of single quotation marks because the entire value of the select attribute is enclosed in double quotation marks.

Sean also wants you to format the date values for the release date of the digital game and the date of each customer's review. Because XPath 1.0 and XSLT 1.0 don't support date formats, you'll use XPath's text string functions.

Working with Text Strings

XPath supports several functions for manipulating text strings. Figure 6-26 describes the different text string functions supported in XPath 1.0.

Figure 6-26   **XPath 1.0 text string functions**

Function	Description
concat(*string1*, *string2*, *string3*, …)	Combines *string1*, *string2*, *string3*, … into a single text string
contains(*string1*, *string2*)	Returns true if *string1* contains *string2*, and false if otherwise
normalize-space(*string*)	Returns *string* with leading and trailing white space characters stripped
starts-with(*string1*, *string2*)	Returns value true if *string1* begins with the characters defined in *string2*, and false if otherwise
string(*item*)	Converts *item* to a text string; if *item* is not specified, returns the string value of the context node
string-length(*string*)	Returns the number of characters in *string*
substring(*string*, *start*, *length*)	Returns a substring from *string*, starting with the character in the *start* position and continuing for *length* characters; if no *length* is specified, the substring goes to the end of the original text *string*
substring-after(*string1*, *string2*)	Returns a substring of *string1* consisting of everything occurring after the characters defined in *string2*
substring-before(*string1*, *string2*)	Returns a substring of *string1* consisting of everything occurring before the characters defined in *string2*
translate(*string1*, *string2*, *string3*)	Returns *string1* with occurrences of characters listed in *string2* replaced by characters in *string3*

Many of the XPath functions work with sections of text strings called **substrings**. For example, the following expression uses the substring() function to extract a substring from the text string "Harpe Gaming Store," starting with the seventh character in the text string and extending through the next six characters:

```
substring("Harpe Gaming Store", 7, 6)
```

resulting in the substring "Gaming". In some applications, you may need to test whether a text string contains a specified substring. The following expression uses the contains() function to test whether the text of the title element contains the substring "Store":

```
contains(title, "Store")
```

The contains() function returns the Boolean value true if the title text contains "Store" and false if otherwise.

Extracting and Combining Text Strings

Another approach to extracting a substring is to search for a specified character that marks the beginning or end of the string. Consider, for example, the following text string containing a date in the *yyyy-mm-dd* format.

```
2017-10-05
```

If you want to extract the year, month, and day value, you have to locate the positions of the "-" character. To extract the year value (2017), you use the following substring-before() function:

```
substring-before("2017-10-05", "-")
```

and XPath will extract a substring consisting of all of the characters *before* the first occurrence of the "-" character. The resulting string will contain the text "2017". To find the month value, you have to extract the substring between the two "-" characters. To do this, you first create a substring of all the characters *after* the first occurrence of the "-" character using the function:

```
substring-after("2017-10-05", "-")
```

and XPath returns the substring "10-05". Now, apply the substring-before() function to this substring to return the month value consisting of the characters before the "-" symbol. You can do this in one expression by nesting the two functions as follows:

```
substring-before(substring-after("2017-10-05", "-"), "-")
```

XPath returns the substring "10". Finally, to return the day value, you need to extract the substring after the second occurrence of the "-" character. You can do this by nesting two substring-after() functions:

```
substring-after(substring-after("2017-10-05", "-"), "-")
```

and XPath returns the substring "05".

Another important task is to combine or **concatenate** two or more text strings into a single text string. This can be achieved using the following concat() function:

```
concat("October ", "10, ", "2017")
```

After running this function, XPath will return the text string "October 10, 2017". Similarly, the following expression concatenates the text of the city element, a comma, and the text of the state element into a single string:

```
concat(city, ", ", state)
```

If the city element contains the text "Galway" and the state element contains the text "New York", the resulting text string is "Galway, New York".

Formatting a Date String

Sean wants to convert all of the dates displayed in the products page from the current *yyyy-mm-dd* format into the *Month Day, Year* format. For example, he wants the 2017-10-05 date to be displayed as "October 10, 2017". Because XPath 1.0 doesn't support a function to change a date format, he'll use an external style sheet to modify the date text using XSLT 1.0 text functions. The style sheet has already been created for you, stored in the hglibrary.xsl file. The contents of the style sheet are shown in Figure 6-27. Before importing this style sheet into the products.xsl style sheet, you'll examine the code.

Figure 6-27	Style sheet to format dates

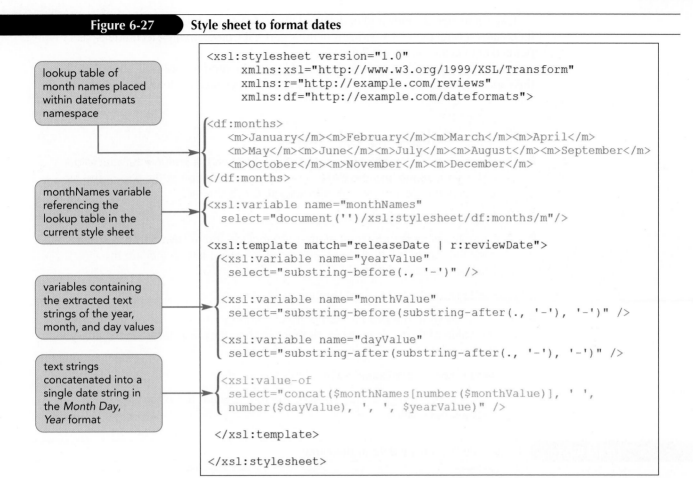

lookup table of month names placed within dateformats namespace

monthNames variable referencing the lookup table in the current style sheet

variables containing the extracted text strings of the year, month, and day values

text strings concatenated into a single date string in the *Month Day, Year* format

```
<xsl:stylesheet version="1.0"
    xmlns:xsl="http://www.w3.org/1999/XSL/Transform"
    xmlns:r="http://example.com/reviews"
    xmlns:df="http://example.com/dateformats">

<df:months>
    <m>January</m><m>February</m><m>March</m><m>April</m>
    <m>May</m><m>June</m><m>July</m><m>August</m><m>September</m>
    <m>October</m><m>November</m><m>December</m>
</df:months>

<xsl:variable name="monthNames"
  select="document('')/xsl:stylesheet/df:months/m"/>

<xsl:template match="releaseDate | r:reviewDate">
  <xsl:variable name="yearValue"
    select="substring-before(., '-')" />

  <xsl:variable name="monthValue"
    select="substring-before(substring-after(., '-'), '-')" />

  <xsl:variable name="dayValue"
    select="substring-after(substring-after(., '-'), '-')" />

  <xsl:value-of
    select="concat($monthNames[number($monthValue)], ' ',
    number($dayValue), ', ', $yearValue)" />

  </xsl:template>

</xsl:stylesheet>
```

The first page of the style sheet creates a lookup table consisting of the names of the two months. Notice that to avoid name collisions with other elements in other XML documents, the lookup table has been placed in the http://example.com/dateformats namespace with the df prefix. The node set containing those 12 names is stored as part of the *monthNames* variable. The variable uses the **document()** function with a blank filename to reference the contents of the active style sheet.

Date text for both the release date of the game and the date of the customer review is stored in the *yyyy-mm-dd* format. The template extracts the year, month, and day values from the date text and stores them in three local variables named *yearValue*, *monthValue*, and *dayValue*.

The last part of this template concatenates the text strings stored in the *yearValue*, *monthValue*, and *dayValue* variables into a single string. The month names are retrieved by looking up the values from the *monthNames* variable using the predicate expression

```
$monthNames[index]
```

where *index* is a value from 1 to 12 that indicates the position of the node. For example, the expression

```
$monthNames[8]
```

returns the eighth node containing the text string "August". Note that, because the *monthValue* variable stores a text string, it must first be converted to a numeric value using the XPath **number()** function. The *dayValue* variable is also converted to a number to remove any leading zeroes. For example, if the *dayValue* variable contains the text string "09", that text string is converted to the numeric value 9. After the three variables are concatenated, the template returns a text string with a date in the *Month Day, Year* format.

Take some time to study and understand the code used in this template because it contains several useful text string functions and XSLT programming techniques, as pointed out via the callouts in Figure 6-27.

You'll import the hglibrary.xsl style sheet file into the products.xsl style sheet. You'll then apply the template to both the releaseDate and reviewDate elements.

To apply the hglibrary style sheet:

▶ 1. Use your editor to open the **hglibtxt.xsl** file from the xml06 ▶ tutorial folder. Enter **your name** and the **date** in the comment section at the top of the file and save the document as **hglibrary.xsl**. Close the file.

▶ 2. Return to the **products.xsl** file in your editor.

▶ 3. Directly above the `include` element to include the reviews.xsl style sheet near the top of the document, insert the following line to include the hglibrary.xsl style sheet:

```
<xsl:include href="hglibrary.xsl" />
```

▶ 4. Scroll down to the product template and change the expression to display the value of the `releaseDate` element to the following statement to apply the template for the `releaseDate` element:

```
<xsl:apply-templates select="releaseDate" />
```

Figure 6-28 highlights the revised code to apply the template to the `releaseDate` value.

Figure 6-28	Displaying the release date of the game

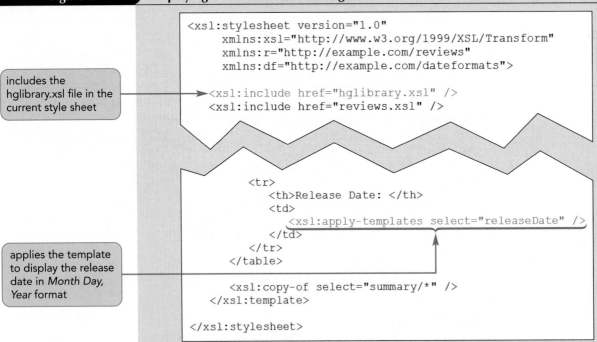

includes the hglibrary.xsl file in the current style sheet

applies the template to display the release date in *Month Day, Year* format

```
<xsl:stylesheet version="1.0"
    xmlns:xsl="http://www.w3.org/1999/XSL/Transform"
    xmlns:r="http://example.com/reviews"
    xmlns:df="http://example.com/dateformats">

<xsl:include href="hglibrary.xsl" />
<xsl:include href="reviews.xsl" />

        <tr>
            <th>Release Date: </th>
            <td>
                <xsl:apply-templates select="releaseDate" />
            </td>
        </tr>
    </table>

    <xsl:copy-of select="summary/*" />
</xsl:template>

</xsl:stylesheet>
```

▶ 5. Save your changes to the file and then go to the **reviews.xsl** file in your editor.

▶ 6. Within the review template, change the expression that displays the value of the `reviewDate` element to

```
<xsl:apply-templates select="r:reviewDate" />
```

Figure 6-29 highlights the revised code to apply the template to the `reviewDate` value.

Figure 6-29   **Displaying the date of the customer review**

```
<tr>
    <th>Review Date:</th>
    <td>
        <xsl:apply-templates select="r:reviewDate" />
    </td>
</tr>
</table>

<xsl:copy-of select="r:description/*" />
```

applies the template to display the review date in *Month Day, Year* format

7. Save your changes to the reviews style sheet and then regenerate the result document using your web browser or an XML editor. Figure 6-30 shows the revised date format displayed in the result document.

Figure 6-30   **Formatted text and values in the product page**

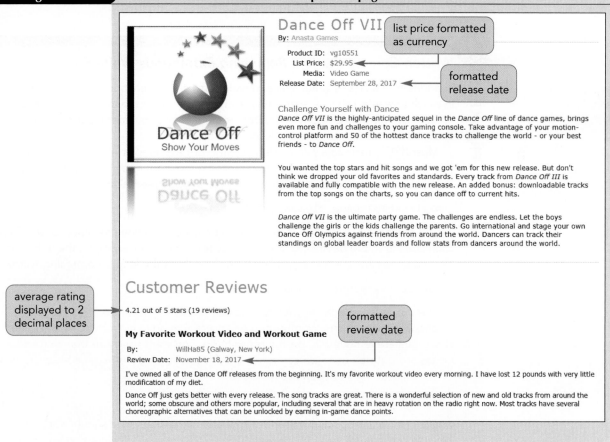

XPath 2.0 includes several new functions for manipulating text strings and working with dates and durations. You can also use third-party style sheets and functions to gain more control over the formatting of values, text, and dates.

Working with White Space

Another issue that can come up with text strings is the use of white space. For example, consider the following code that displays the text of the `city` and `state` elements:

```
<xsl:value-of select="city" /> <xsl:value-of select="state" />
```

Even though a blank space separates the two tags, when the result document is produced the space is omitted, resulting in a text string like "GalwayNew York". The reason for this is that some XSLT processors will strip **white space nodes**, which are nodes that contain only white space characters such as blanks, line returns, or tabs.

One way to insert a white space node without it being stripped is to use the character entity ` ` to explicitly place a blank space between the two elements as follows:

```
<xsl:value-of select="city" /> <xsl:value-of select="state" />
```

Note that if you want multiple blank spaces, you need to include multiple ` ` entity references. Another way is to insert a text node element enclosing a blank text string between the two elements:

```
<xsl:value-of select="city" /><xsl:text> </xsl:text><xsl:value-of
select="state" />
```

Because the blank space is nested within a text node, it is treated as a white space node.

> **TIP**
>
> Do not use the ` ` entity even if you are generating HTML code because that entity will not be recognized by the XSLT processor.

PROSKILLS

Written Communication: Removing Extraneous White Space

In addition to a lack of white space, developers can also encounter excess white space in which unwanted spaces, extra lines, and tabs are written to the result document. This process can result in a poorly formatted or unreadable document. Extraneous white space nodes will also unnecessarily increase file size.

Most XSLT processors will, by default, strip out extraneous white space nodes, but you can explicitly indicate to the processor to remove them by adding the following `strip-space` element as a direct child of the `stylesheet` element:

```
<xsl:strip-space elements="*" />
```

The **normalize-space()** function can also be used to remove extraneous white space characters from the beginning or end of any text string. For example, the following expression returns the text string "goodbye", without the leading or trailing spaces:

```
normalize-space("   goodbye   ")
```

The `normalize-space()` function is commonly used with text values, such as passwords, in which it is important to ensure that any inadvertent white space characters are removed. If, on the other hand, you want to insure that white space nodes are not deleted, you can apply the following **preserve-space** element as a direct child of the `stylesheet` element:

```
<xsl:preserve-space elements="list" />
```

where *list* is a list of elements in which the white space nodes should not be deleted. Thus, to preserve all white space text nodes, you add the following `preserve-space` element to the style sheet:

```
<xsl:preserve-space elements="*" />
```

Stripping out all white space nodes does not impact any white space characters found in the text of an element or attribute and it can result in a cleaner, more compact document.

You've completed your work formatting the values and text from the products page. In the next session, Sean wants to add a few more graphical elements to this page including ratings displayed by a list of stars and a bar chart showing the distribution of the customer ratings. He also wants to make it possible to switch the output from one digital game to another without having to rewrite the style sheet code. If you want to take a break, you can close any files or applications now.

Session 6.2 Quick Check

1. Provide two ways of displaying the value of the active node.
2. Provide an expression to divide the sum of the *demVotes* variable by the sum of the *allVotes* variable and then to multiply that quotient by 100.
3. Provide an expression to display the value of the *votePerc* variable accurate to two decimal places to the right of the decimal point.
4. Provide an expression to determine whether the *fileName* variable contains the substring ".xls".
5. Provide an expression to extract a five-character substring from the *fileURL* variable starting with the eighth character.
6. Provide an expression to combine the *lastName* and *firstName* variables in a single text string, separated by the ", " substring.
7. Provide an expression to remove leading and trailing spaces from the *password* variable.

Session 6.3 Visual Overview:

A **named template** is a template that is not matched to a node set but instead acts like a function to display a calculated value or perform an operation.

Parameters are similar to variables except that their values can be passed to them from outside their scope; a **template parameter** is defined and referenced within a template.

A **recursive template** is a template that continually calls itself until a specified stopping condition or base case is reached.

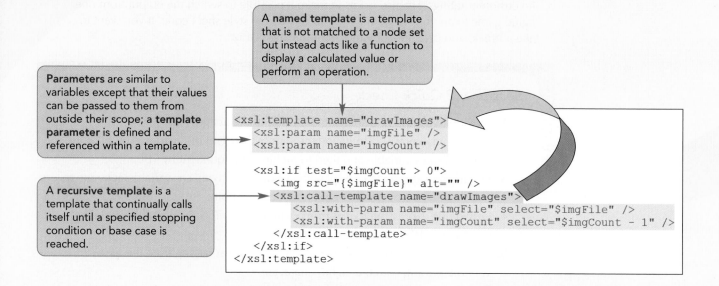

```
<xsl:template name="drawImages">
  <xsl:param name="imgFile" />
  <xsl:param name="imgCount" />

  <xsl:if test="$imgCount > 0">
    <img src="{$imgFile}" alt="" />
    <xsl:call-template name="drawImages">
      <xsl:with-param name="imgFile" select="$imgFile" />
      <xsl:with-param name="imgCount" select="$imgCount - 1" />
    </xsl:call-template>
  </xsl:if>
</xsl:template>
```

The **xsl:call-template** element is used to call and execute the commands contained within a named template.

The **xsl:with-param** element sets the value of the template parameters defined within a named template.

The **xsl:text** element can be used to insert a text node into the result document.

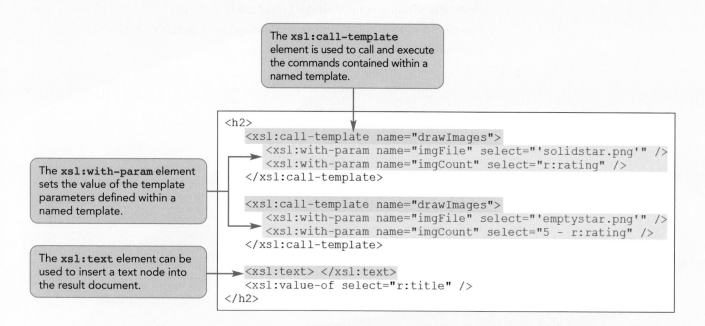

```
<h2>
  <xsl:call-template name="drawImages">
    <xsl:with-param name="imgFile" select="'solidstar.png'" />
    <xsl:with-param name="imgCount" select="r:rating" />
  </xsl:call-template>

  <xsl:call-template name="drawImages">
    <xsl:with-param name="imgFile" select="'emptystar.png'" />
    <xsl:with-param name="imgCount" select="5 - r:rating" />
  </xsl:call-template>

  <xsl:text> </xsl:text>
  <xsl:value-of select="r:title" />
</h2>
```

Parameters and Recursive Templates

Solid stars show the average customer ranking.

Repeated images can be generated by using a recursive template that continually inserts an inline image until a stopping condition or base state is reached.

Customer Reviews

★★★★☆
4.21 out of 5 stars (19 reviews)

5 star (11)
4 star (3)
3 star (4)
2 star (0)
1 star (1)

★★★★★ **My Favorite Workout Video and Workout Game**

By: WillHa85 (Galway, New York)
Review Date: November 18, 2017

I've owned all of the Dance Off releases from the beginning. It's my favorite workout video every morning. I have lost 12 pounds with very little modification of my diet.

Dance Off just gets better with every release. The song tracks are great. There is a wonderful selection of new and old tracks from around the world; some obscure and others more popular, including several that are in heavy rotation on the radio right now. Most tracks have several choreographic alternatives that can be unlocked by earning in-game dance points.

★★★☆☆ **Poor Choreography**

By: GoldFry26 (Sea Island, Georgia)
Review Date: November 17, 2017

A so-so release of this well-established title. The user interface is improved and easier to use and game provides a few great songs, a few terrible ones, and several mediocre ones. The graphics are beautiful and the sets are stunning and fun (without being distracting.)

Where this release fails is in the choreography. The dances just aren't as much fun as the previous titles. Many of the moves follow predictable patterns; they're stale and that's a big problem for a dance game. I hope the next release improves the choreography because it's great in all other phases of the game.

For this review, the recursive template stopped after filling in three stars to match the reviewer's rating.

Introducing Parameters

A major limitation of the XSLT variable is that its value can only be defined once and only from within the style sheet. Every time Sean wants to create a product report for a different digital game, he has to edit the products.xsl file and regenerate the result document for a different product ID. It would be much more efficient to specify the product ID when the report is generated without having to edit the style sheet file.

Sean can accomplish this through the use of parameters, which are similar to variables except that their values can be passed to them from outside their scope. A **global parameter** is a parameter with global scope and can be accessed anywhere within the style sheet, while a **local parameter** or template parameter is a parameter limited in scope to the template in which it's defined.

Parameters are defined using the following `param` element:

```
<xsl:param name="name" select="value" />
```

where *name* is the parameter name and *value* is the parameter's default value. The `select` attribute is optional and is used only when no value has been passed to the parameter by the processor or outside source.

The following code is used to create a parameter named *productID* with a default value of 'vg10551':

```
<xsl:param name="productID" select="'vg10551'" />
```

This parameter code has a similar syntax to the code used to create the *productID* variable, except that in this case the `select` attribute provides a default value that can be replaced. As with variables, parameter values containing text strings must be enclosed within a second set of quotation marks.

Parameters are referenced using the same syntax that is applied to variables. Thus, the value of the *productID* parameter would be displayed with the instruction

```
<xsl:value-of select="$productID" />
```

TIP

Parameters created in XSLT 2.0 also support the as attribute to define the data type of the parameter value.

REFERENCE

Creating and Using Parameters

- To declare a parameter, use the XSLT element

  ```
  <xsl:param name="name" select="value" />
  ```

  where *name* is the parameter name and *value* is the parameter's default value used when no value is passed to the parameter from outside its scope.
- To reference a parameter, use the expression

  ```
  $name
  ```

  where *name* is the name of the parameter.

You'll change the *productID* variable in the products.xsl style sheet to a parameter with the same name, leaving the default value of the parameter as 'vg10551'.

To create a global parameter:

▶ 1. If you took a break after the last session, return to the **products.xsl** file in your editor.

▶ 2. Replace the line `<xsl:variable name="productID" select="'vg10551'" />` that declares the *productID* variable with the following line to create the *productID* parameter:

```
<xsl:param name="productID" select="'vg10551'" />
```

Figure 6-31 shows the code to create the *productID* parameter.

| Figure 6-31 | Creating the productID parameter |

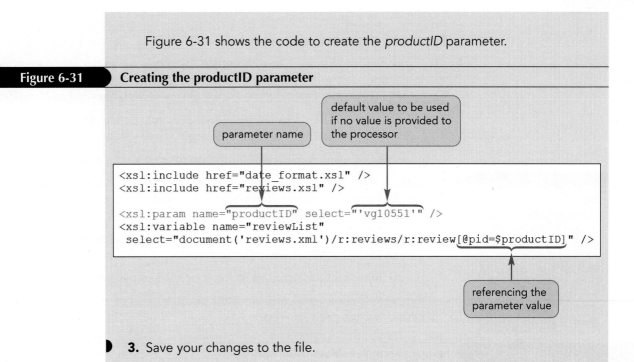

3. Save your changes to the file.

Now that you've defined a global parameter, you will set its value and generate a result document.

Setting a Global Parameter Value

Because parameters have their values passed to them from outside their scope, global parameters have their values set by the processor itself. The exact steps in setting a global parameter value depend on the processor being used to run the transformation. A server-side framework such as Apache Cocoon allows developers to pass a parameter's value as part of the web page's URL.

If you are using the Saxon XSLT processor with Java, you can set the parameter value using the command

```
java net.sf.saxon.Transform source style param=value -o:output
```

where *source* is the source document, *style* is the XSLT style sheet, *param* is the XSLT parameter, *value* is the parameter value, and *output* is the result document. The equivalent command using Saxon with the .NET platform is

```
transform source style param=value -o:output
```

The XSLT processors built into web browsers do not allow users to set parameter values directly at this time. However, you can set parameter values by running a JavaScript program from within the browser. That topic, however, is beyond the scope of this tutorial.

You'll use an XSLT processor now to generate a result document by setting the value of the *productID* parameter. The steps that follow assume the Saxon XSLT processor is in Java command line mode.

To create the result document:

1. If you are using Saxon in Java command line mode, go to the xml06 ▸ tutorial folder and run the following command from within a command window to create the product report for the *Dance Off* game with the product ID vg10551:

   ```
   java net.sf.saxon.Transform products.xml products.xsl
   productID="vg10551" -o:vg10551.html
   ```

   otherwise, run the command appropriate to your XSLT processor.

TIP

Make sure that the parameter name matches the name of the parameter. If you mistype the name, an XSLT processor does not pass the value but it also does not return an error message indicating that a mistake was made.

2. Next, using Saxon in Java command line mode (if that is your XSLT processor), run the following command to create the product report for *Net Force 12* with the product ID vg10552:

   ```
   java net.sf.saxon.Transform products.xml products.xsl
   productID="vg10552" -o:vg10552.html
   ```

   or run the appropriate command for your XSLT processor.

   Figure 6-32 shows the commands for Saxon in Java command line mode to create the two product reports.

Figure 6-32	Setting parameter values using Saxon

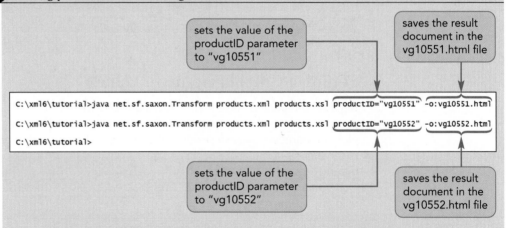

Trouble? Talk to your instructor or computer resource person for help in installing and running an XSLT processor on your system. If you do not have access to an XSLT processor other than your web browser, you can use the default parameter value set within the style sheet to complete the remaining tasks in the rest of this tutorial, viewing the results in your browser.

3. Open the **vg10552.html** file in your web browser. As shown in Figure 6-33, your browser should display product information and reviews for the *Net Force* digital game.

Figure 6-33 | **Product report for the Net Force video game**

Take the Battle to the Hardwood

Net Force 12 is the latest release in the Net Force series of basketball simulation games. Using motion capture technology designed specifically for *Net Force*, this release captures the signature moves of the top players in the NBA, . No other basketball simulation has this lineup of stars. Additional features include support for motion-sensor game controllers, dynamic shot generation, touch-sensitive passing, and "flash-to-the-hoop" acceleration for uncontested slam dunks.

Go to basketball camp and learn the game the right way with a series of fun and challenging tutorials. Relive the past with stars from the 60's, 70's, 80's, and 90's. Can today's stars hold their own against the champs from the past? You decide.

Take your virtual game to a new entertainment level with the dynamic background music and production by some of the top hip-hop artists on the charts. Previous releases of *Net Force* have already won multiple awards for music and production and this release looks posed to continue that winning streak.

Customer Reviews

2.71 out of 5 stars (14 reviews)

Another Great Edition in a Great Series

By: LottsoGame81 (Copper Harbor, Michigan)
Review Date: November 18, 2017

I'm a big fan of this product. As great as Version 11 was, I think this version is more realistic and responsive. It's not perfect. I found the controller system still a bit too complicated. Muscle memory helps a bit, but it could still use some improvement.

But that's a minor complaint. Compared to other games on the market, this is a great game at a great price.

The music I can take or leave. I know that some players really get into the sound track. To me it's a lot of noise and very repetitive. I recommend picking this game up, even if you own Version 11. It's a substantial upgrade and well worth the price.

4. Open the **vg10551.html** file in your web browser and verify that the file displays information for the *Dance Off* digital game.

Next, you'll examine how to create and apply a template parameter.

Exploring Template Parameters

As with local variables, the scope of a template parameter is limited to the template in which it is created. The parameter value, however, can be passed to the template parameter from outside of the template. The general syntax to pass a value to a template parameter is

```
<xsl:apply-templates select="expression">
   <xsl:with-param name="name" select="value" />
</xsl:apply-templates>
```

where *name* is the name of a parameter declared within the template and *value* is the value passed to the parameter. If you don't include the select attribute, the template uses the parameter's default value. For example, in the following sample code, the customer template is called with a value of C101, which is passed to the *custID* parameter within the customer template:

```
<xsl:apply-templates select="customer">
   <xsl:with-param name="custID" select="C101" />
</xsl:apply-templates>

...

<xsl:template match="customer">
   <xsl:param name="custID" />
   styles
</xsl:template>
```

Note that a template parameter must be declared prior to any other XSLT or literal result elements within the template in which it is used.

REFERENCE

Passing a Value to a Template Parameter

- To set the value of a template parameter, use the `with-param` element as in the following code:

```
<xsl:apply-templates select="expression">
   <xsl:with-param name="name" select="value" />
</xsl:apply-templates>
```

where *name* is the parameter's name and *value* is the value that is passed to the parameter. Note that the `with-param` element must be the first child of the `apply-templates` element.

One use of template parameters is in the creation and application of named templates.

Using Named Templates

So far, all of the templates you've created have been matched to specific nodes using the match attribute. A named template is a template that is not matched to a node set but instead acts like a function to display a calculated value or perform an operation. Named templates are created using the structure

```
<xsl:template name="name">
   parameters
   XSLT elements
</xsl:template>
```

where *name* is the name of the template. Within the named template, you first insert local parameters used in the template and then include any XSLT elements to generate a result. For example, the following drawImages template is used to generate an inline image tag using the image filename specified in the *imgFile* parameter:

```
<xsl:template name="drawImages">
   <xsl:param name="imgFile" />
   <img src="{$imgFile}" alt="" />
</xsl:template>
```

Because a named template is not matched to a node set, it has to be called rather than applied using the following `call-template` element:

```
<xsl:call-template name="name">
   <xsl:with-param name="param1" select="value1" />
   <xsl:with-param name="param2" select="value2" />
   ...
</xsl:call-template>
```

where *name* is the name of the template; *param1*, *param2*, and so forth are parameters used within the template; and *value1, value2*, and so forth are the values passed to each template parameter. The following code calls the drawImages template described above using the text string value 'star.png' for the *imgFile* parameter:

```
<xs:call-template name="drawImages">
   <xsl:with-param name="imgFile" select="'star.png'" />
</xsl:call-template>
```

The only element that the `call-template` element can contain is the `with-param` element. If you don't specify a parameter value, the template parameter assumes its default value when the template is called.

REFERENCE

Creating and Calling Named Templates

- To create a named template, apply the following:

```
<xsl:template name="name">
   parameters
   XSLT elements
</xsl:template>
```

where *name* is the name of the template.
- To call a named template, apply the following:

```
<xsl:call-template name="name">
   <xsl:with-param name="param1" select="value1" />
   <xsl:with-param name="param2" select="value2" />
   ...
</xsl:call-template>
```

where *name* is the name of the template; *param1*, *param2*, and so forth are parameters used within the template; and *value1*, *value2*, and so forth are the values passed to the template parameters.

Sean wants to display each customer rating with a row of stars matching the number of stars given by each customer to each digital game. To create this row of stars, you'll use named templates and template parameters that employ the techniques of functional programming.

Introducing Functional Programming

XSLT is an example of **functional programming**, which relies on the evaluation of functions and expressions, rather than on the sequential execution of commands. You might find functional programming to be quite different from other computer languages you have worked with in the past. Perhaps the best way to explain functional programming is to first show what it is not.

The following is an example of a generic code structure (it doesn't correspond to any particular programming language) used to create a function that calculates the sum of items within a list:

```
function calcSum(list)
   totalValue = 0

   for each item in list
      totalValue = item + totalValue;
   next item;

   return totalValue;
end function
```

This structure uses a program loop in which the processor goes through every item in the list and adds that item's value to the *totalValue* variable. After the last item has been added, the function returns the value of the *totalValue* variable, representing the total sum. This type of structure is not compatible with XSLT 1.0 because the XSLT language does not allow variables to be redefined after they've been created. Remember that an XSLT variable or a parameter can only be defined once. The value of the *totalValue* variable in this structure is defined twice: once before the program loop and then a second time within the loop.

Functional programming languages such as XSLT are instead designed around the following principles:

- The main program consists entirely of functions with well-defined inputs.
- The results of the program are defined in terms of outputs from functions.
- When a variable is defined, its definition cannot be changed.
- Because the program consists only of function calls, the order of the execution is irrelevant.

The important overall principle to keep in mind with functional programs is to think of tasks in terms of functions rather than loops and assignment statements.

PROSKILLS

Problem Solving: Choosing Functional Programming

Proponents of functional programming argue that adherence to these principles results in code that is easier to maintain and less susceptible to error. It is their belief that statements that impose a specific order of execution on the code can lead to complications. They also believe that a variable whose value is constantly changing makes it necessary to understand the whole code structure to interpret even the simplest equations. For example, the interpretation of a simple equation such as $x = x + 1$ depends on several factors, including the initial value of x and how often the statement is run. In complex applications, it is often necessary to use sophisticated debugging tools to track the value of a variable as it changes throughout the execution of the code.

However, in functional programming, each time a function is called it does the same thing, regardless of how many times it has already been called or the condition of other variables in the style sheet. With functional programming, it is important to think about the desired end result, rather than the sequential steps needed to achieve that effect.

You've already been applying the principles of functional programming when creating and applying templates. Each template can be thought of as a function, with the input being the specified node set and the output being the result text generated by XSLT. In fact, an entire style sheet can be considered a single function with the input being the source document and the output being the result document.

The benefits of functional programming are by no means accepted universally, and many programmers believe that some tasks can only be done using assignment statements, updatable variables, and sequential commands.

Understanding Recursion

Because programs loops are invalid under functional programming, commands are repeated through recursion. **Recursion** is the process by which a function calls itself. We can recast the function shown earlier to calculate the *totalValue* variable as the following recursive function:

```
totalValue = 0

function calcSum(totalValue, list)

   if (list has at least one item)
      newList = list without the first item
      calcSum(totalValue + first_item, newList)
   else
      return totalValue


end function
```

The `calcSum` function has two parameters: the *totalValue* parameter containing a running total and a *list* parameter containing a list of items to sum. If there are no items in the list, the function simply returns the value of *totalValue*; otherwise, it reruns the function with two important changes: the value of the first item in the list is added to *totalValue*, and a new list is used without the first item.

In this structure, the `calcSum()` function keeps calling itself, reducing the number of items in the list until no items are left. When that happens, the value of all of the items in the list have been added to *totalValue*, and that final value is returned to the user.

Every recursive function needs to have the following three features:

- A **base case** that represents a stopping condition. In the `calcSum()` function the base case is reached when there are no items left in the list.
- A **change of state** that occurs when the base case has not been reached. The `calcSum()` function changes state by increasing the *totalValue* parameter by the value of the first item and then removing that item.
- The function must call itself employing the change of state. To operate recursively, the `calcSum()` function must be rerun each time with a new list and an updated *totalValue*.

It's important to include a base case so that there is an end to all the recursion. If you fail to provide a base case, you run the risk of endless recursion as the function calls itself indefinitely. The `calcSum()` function just described could be created using the following calcSum template with template parameters named *totalValue* and *list*:

```
<xsl:template name="calcSum">
   <xsl:param name="totalValue" select="0" />
   <xsl:param name="list" />

   <xsl:choose>

      <xsl:when test="count($list) > 0">
         <xsl:call-template select="calcSum">
            <xsl:with-param name="totalValue"
                select="$totalValue + $list[1]" />
            <xsl:with-param name="list"
                select="$list[position() > 1]" />
         </xsl:call-template>
      </xsl:when>
```

```
      <xsl:otherwise>
         <xsl:value-of select="$totalValue" />
      </xsl:otherwise>

   </xsl:choose>
</xsl:template>
```

Like the generic code described earlier, the calcSum template calls itself as long as the count of items in the *list* parameter is greater than 0. Each time it calls itself, it sets the value of the *totalValue* parameter to the current *totalValue* plus the value of the first item and reduces the size of the list by excluding the first item. Eventually, there will be no items left in the list and the template will cease calling itself; at that point it displays the value of the *totalValue* parameter.

Creating a Recursive Template

You'll create a recursive template for Sean's project that displays multiple star images with the number of stars determined by a parameter named *imgCount*. Sean envisions using this template for a variety of projects, so you'll place the template in the hglibrary.xsl file.

To create the drawImages template:

1. Use your editor to open the **hglibrary.xsl** file from the xml06 ▸ tutorial folder.

2. Directly above the closing `</xsl:stylesheet>` tag, insert the following drawImages template:

```
<xsl:template name="drawImages">
  <xsl:param name="imgFile" />
  <xsl:param name="imgCount" />

  <xsl:if test="$imgCount > 0">
    <img src="{$imgFile}" alt="" />
    <xsl:call-template name="drawImages">
      <xsl:with-param name="imgFile" select="$imgFile" />
      <xsl:with-param name="imgCount" select="$imgCount - 1" />
    </xsl:call-template>
  </xsl:if>

</xsl:template>
```

Figure 6-34 shows the complete code and description of the drawImages template.

> When recursively calling a template, be sure you include all template parameter values using the with-param element.

Figure 6-34   **drawImages template**

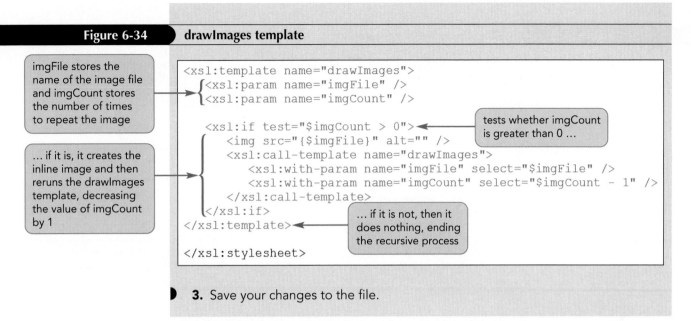

imgFile stores the name of the image file and imgCount stores the number of times to repeat the image

... if it is, it creates the inline image and then reruns the drawImages template, decreasing the value of imgCount by 1

tests whether imgCount is greater than 0 ...

... if it is not, then it does nothing, ending the recursive process

```
<xsl:template name="drawImages">
  <xsl:param name="imgFile" />
  <xsl:param name="imgCount" />

  <xsl:if test="$imgCount > 0">
    <img src="{$imgFile}" alt="" />
    <xsl:call-template name="drawImages">
      <xsl:with-param name="imgFile" select="$imgFile" />
      <xsl:with-param name="imgCount" select="$imgCount - 1" />
    </xsl:call-template>
  </xsl:if>
</xsl:template>

</xsl:stylesheet>
```

3. Save your changes to the file.

The drawImages template has two parameters: the *imgFile* parameter provides the name of the image file to be displayed and the *imgCount* parameter indicates the number of duplicates of the image. As long as *imgCount* is greater than 0, the template continues to call itself, drawing an image and decreasing the *imgCount* value by 1 each time. Note that even though the *imgFile* parameter is not changing, it still needs to be included when drawImages is called so that the *imgFile* value is passed to the template.

You've already created a link to the hglibrary.xsl file, so this template is ready to be used in the products page and the list of reviews. You'll run it now using the solidstar.png file for the *imgFile* parameter and the value of rating element for the *imgCount* parameter.

To run the drawImages template:

1. Go to the **reviews.xsl** file in your editor.

2. Scroll down to the review template and insert the following code directly below the opening <h2> tag to call the drawImages template using 'solidstar.png' for the *imgFile* parameter and r:rating for the value of the *imgCount* parameter.

```
<xsl:call-template name="drawImages">
  <xsl:with-param name="imgFile" select="'solidstar.png'" />
  <xsl:with-param name="imgCount" select="r:rating" />
</xsl:call-template>
```

Figure 6-35 highlights the code to call the drawImages template.

Figure 6-35 Calling the drawImages template

> draws repeated images of the solidstar.png file

```
<xsl:template match="r:review">
   <h2>
      <xsl:call-template name="drawImages">
         <xsl:with-param name="imgFile" select="'solidstar.png'" />
         <xsl:with-param name="imgCount" select="r:rating" />
      </xsl:call-template>
      <xsl:value-of select="r:title" />
   </h2>
```

> repeats the image the number of times equal to the customer's rating of the game

3. Save your changes to the file and then regenerate the result document for the vg10551 product ID (the *Dance Off* game). Figure 6-36 shows a list of the first few customer reviews with the customer rating displayed graphically with the solidstar.png image.

Figure 6-36 Stars representing each customer's rating

Customer Reviews

4.21 out of 5 stars (19 reviews)

★★★★★My Favorite Workout Video and Workout Game

By: WillHa85 (Galway, New York)
Review Date: November 18, 2017

I've owned all of the Dance Off releases from the beginning. It's my favorite workout video every morning. I have lost 12 pounds with very little modification of my diet.

Dance Off just gets better with every release. The song tracks are great. There is a wonderful selection of new and old tracks from around the world; some obscure and others more popular, including several that are in heavy rotation on the radio right now. Most tracks have several choreographic alternatives that can be unlocked by earning in-game dance points.

★★★Poor Choreography

By: GoldFry26 (Sea Island, Georgia)
Review Date: November 17, 2017

A so-so release of this well-established title. The user interface is improved and easier to use and game provides a few great songs, a few terrible ones, and several mediocre ones. The graphics are beautiful and the sets are stunning and fun (without being distracting.)

Where this release fails is in the choreography. The dances just aren't as much fun as the previous titles. Many of the moves follow predictable patterns; they're stale and that's a big problem for a dance game. I hope the next release improves the choreography because it's great in all other phases of the game.

★★★★★A Great Gift

By: Mittens41 (Atlanta, Georgia)
Review Date: November 17, 2017

I bought this for my 13 year old daughter and her friends. They had exhausted the songs from the earlier releases and looking for a new challenge. This release includes the most current songs with GREAT new moves. My daughter also likes the new format and is getting hours of fun (and exercise!) out of the game.

Sean wants the titles of the customer reviews to be lined up on the page. Because every rating is on a five-star scale, he can line up the titles by including empty stars when the rating is less than five stars. For example, a three-star rating should be displayed with three solid stars and two empty stars. Also, he wants you to include a blank space between the row of stars and the review title. The empty star image is stored in the emptystar.png file. You'll use the drawImages template to generate the correct number of empty stars, and you'll use the `<xsl:text>` element to create a blank space between the stars and the review title. You edit the reviews.xsl file now.

To modify the row of stars:

1. Return to the **reviews.xsl** file in your editor.

2. Directly below the code you just entered to create the solid row of stars, insert the following code to create a similar row of empty stars followed by a blank space enclosed within the `text` element:

```
<xsl:call-template name="drawImages">
   <xsl:with-param name="imgFile" select="'emptystar.png'" />
   <xsl:with-param name="imgCount" select="5 - r:rating" />
</xsl:call-template>
<xsl:text> </xsl:text>
```

Note that the number of empty stars is equal to five (the maximum possible rating) minus the customer rating.

Figure 6-37 shows the revised code in the style sheet to create the row of blank stars followed by a blank space.

Figure 6-37 | **Drawing empty stars**

calls the drawImages template with the emptystar.png image file

```
<xsl:template match="r:review">
   <h2>
      <xsl:call-template name="drawImages">
         <xsl:with-param name="imgFile" select="'solidstar.png'" />
         <xsl:with-param name="imgCount" select="r:rating" />
      </xsl:call-template>
      <xsl:call-template name="drawImages">
         <xsl:with-param name="imgFile" select="'emptystar.png'" />
         <xsl:with-param name="imgCount" select="5 - r:rating" />
      </xsl:call-template>
      <xsl:text> </xsl:text>
      <xsl:value-of select="r:title" />
   </h2>
```

adds a blank space between the star images and the review title

the number of empty stars is five minus the customer rating

3. Save your changes to the file and then regenerate the result document for the *Dance Off* digital game. Figure 6-38 shows the revised appearance of the row of stars.

Figure 6-38 **A row of five filled or empty stars is displayed for every customer review**

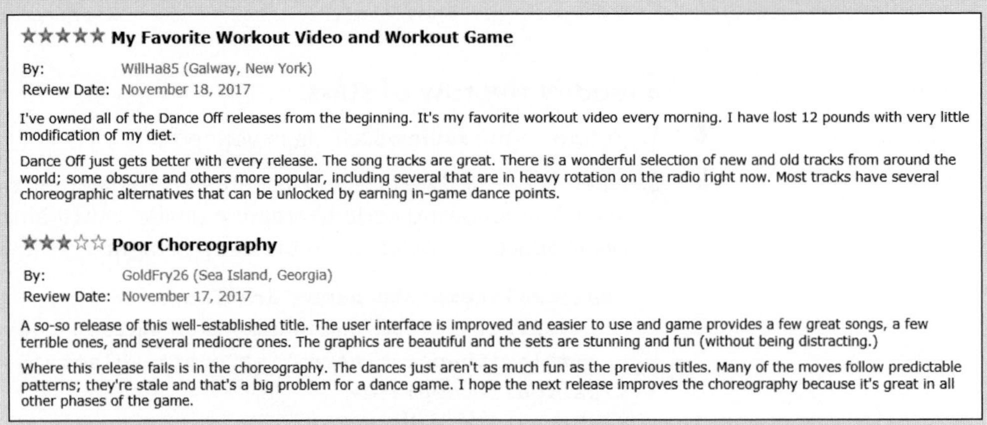

★★★★★ **My Favorite Workout Video and Workout Game**

By: WillHa85 (Galway, New York)
Review Date: November 18, 2017

I've owned all of the Dance Off releases from the beginning. It's my favorite workout video every morning. I have lost 12 pounds with very little modification of my diet.

Dance Off just gets better with every release. The song tracks are great. There is a wonderful selection of new and old tracks from around the world; some obscure and others more popular, including several that are in heavy rotation on the radio right now. Most tracks have several choreographic alternatives that can be unlocked by earning in-game dance points.

★★★☆☆ **Poor Choreography**

By: GoldFry26 (Sea Island, Georgia)
Review Date: November 17, 2017

A so-so release of this well-established title. The user interface is improved and easier to use and game provides a few great songs, a few terrible ones, and several mediocre ones. The graphics are beautiful and the sets are stunning and fun (without being distracting.)

Where this release fails is in the choreography. The dances just aren't as much fun as the previous titles. Many of the moves follow predictable patterns; they're stale and that's a big problem for a dance game. I hope the next release improves the choreography because it's great in all other phases of the game.

Sean also wants the average rating to appear with the row of stars graphic. You add this graphic now next to the average rating score.

To display the average rating:

1. Return to the **products.xsl** file in your editor.

2. Scroll down to the end of the root template and, directly after the declaration of the *avgRating* variable, insert the following code to create rows of stars based on the average customer rating:

```
<xsl:call-template name="drawImages">
   <xsl:with-param name="imgFile" select="'solidstar.png'" />
   <xsl:with-param name="imgCount" select="round($avgRating)" />
</xsl:call-template>
<xsl:call-template name="drawImages">
   <xsl:with-param name="imgFile" select="'emptystar.png'" />
   <xsl:with-param name="imgCount"
    select="5 - round($avgRating)" />
</xsl:call-template>
<br />
```

Note that the code uses the round() function to round the average rating to the nearest integer value (because we don't have a way to display a fraction of a star). Figure 6-39 shows the revised code.

Figure 6-39	Displaying a row of stars for the average rating

rounds the average rating to the nearest integer

inserts a line break between the stars and the average rating value

```
<p>
  <xsl:variable name="avgRating"
   select="sum($reviewList/r:rating) div count($reviewList/r:rating)" />

  <xsl:call-template name="drawImages">
     <xsl:with-param name="imgFile" select="'solidstar.png'" />
     <xsl:with-param name="imgCount" select="round($avgRating)" />
  </xsl:call-template>
  <xsl:call-template name="drawImages">
     <xsl:with-param name="imgFile" select="'emptystar.png'" />
     <xsl:with-param name="imgCount" select="5 - round($avgRating)" />
  </xsl:call-template>
  <br />

  <xsl:value-of select="format-number($avgRating, '0.00')" />
  out of 5 stars
```

3. Save your changes to the file and then regenerate the result document for the *Dance Off* game. Verify that five stars (four solid stars and one blank star) are displayed in the line above the average customer rating.

INSIGHT

Returning Variables Values with Named Templates

Named templates can be used to store variable values by having the last action of the template use the value-of element to set the variable value. For example, the following recursive template is used to calculate the factorial of a number (a factorial is equal to the product of an integer with all positive integers below it, for example, factorial(4) = 4 × 3 × 2 × 1 = 24):

```
<xsl:template name = "factorial">
   <xsl:param name = "n" />
   <xsl:param name = "fact" select = "1" />
   <xsl:if test = "$n > 1">
      <xsl:call-template name = "factorial">
         <xsl:with-param name = "n" select = "$n - 1" />
         <xsl:with-param name = "fact" select = "$n * $fact" />
      </xsl:call-template>
      <xsl:if test ="$n = 1">
         <xsl:value-of select="$fact" />
      </xsl:if>
   </xsl:if>
```

The recursive template continues to call itself, decreasing the value of $n by one with each call, until $n equals 1. At that point, it returns the value of the *$fact* parameter. To use this template to set the value of a variable, you call the template within the variable definition. For example, the following calculates the value of factorial(4):

```
<xsl:variable name = "nfact">
   <xsl:call-template name="factorial">
      <xsl:with-param name="n" select="4" />
   </xsl:call-template>
</xsl:variable>
```

After this code is run, the *nfact* variable will have a value of 24.

Averages, while useful for summarizing large sets of numeric data, can be misleading. Sean is aware that a mostly popular game might still show a low average score if a few customers give the game a single star. Thus, he wants the web page to show the distribution of the customer ratings so that users can see at a glance how many customers gave the game five stars, four stars, and so forth. Such distributions are often shown as bar charts in which the length of each bar is related to the number of votes within each category.

Sean's last task for you is to create a bar chart of all of the customer ratings. You'll place the chart within a web table with each row of the table displaying a separate bar. You start now by inserting the web table.

To create the web table for the bar chart:

1. Return to the **products.xsl** file in your editor and go to the end of the root template.

2. Directly above the closing `</p>` tag insert the following code to call the makeBarChart template (which you'll create shortly). There are no parameters for this template.

   ```
   <xsl:call-template name="makeBarChart">
   </xsl:call-template>
   ```

3. Scroll down to the bottom of the file and, directly above the closing `</xsl:stylesheet>` tag, insert the following template:

   ```
   <xsl:template name="makeBarChart">
       <table id="barChart">
       </table>
   </xsl:template>
   ```

Figure 6-40 highlights the newly added code and shows its location in the file.

Figure 6-40 **Creating and calling the makeBarChart template**

calls the makeBarChart template directly above the list of customer reviews

```
    <xsl:call-template name="makeBarChart">
    </xsl:call-template>
  </p>

  <xsl:apply-templates select="$reviewList[position() &lt;= 5]"/>
</section>
```

```
    <xsl:template name="makeBarChart">
        <table id="barChart">
        </table>
    </xsl:template>

</xsl:stylesheet>
```

inserts the makeBarChart template containing a web table

Next, you'll create a recursive template named drawBars that writes a table row for each of the five possible stars that customers can give the selected product.

To insert the drawBars template:

▶ **1.** Within the table element of the makeBarChart template in the products.xsl file, insert the following code to call the drawBars template using an initial value for the *stars* parameter of 5:

```
<xsl:call-template name="drawBars">
   <xsl:with-param name="stars" select="5" />
</xsl:call-template>
```

The *stars* parameter will be used to count down the possible customer ratings, starting with five stars and going down to one star.

▶ **2.** Insert the following initial code for the drawBars template directly after the makeBarChart template:

```
<xsl:template name="drawBars">
   <xsl:param name="stars" />
   <xsl:if test="$stars > 0">
      <tr>
         <th>
         </th>
         <td>
         </td>
      </tr>

      <xsl:call-template name="drawBars">
         <xsl:with-param name="stars" select="$stars - 1" />
      </xsl:call-template>
   </xsl:if>
</xsl:template>
```

Note that the drawBars template is called recursively until the value of the *stars* parameter drops to zero, at which point the template stops. Each time the template is run, a table row containing a single table header cell and table data cell is written to the result document. See Figure 6-41.

| Figure 6-41 | Adding rows to the barChart table |

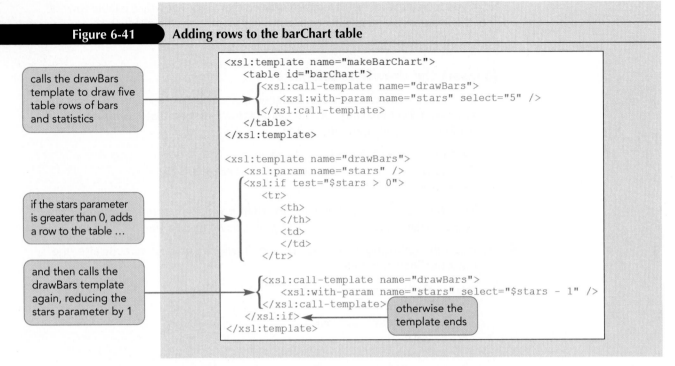

calls the drawBars template to draw five table rows of bars and statistics

if the stars parameter is greater than 0, adds a row to the table …

and then calls the drawBars template again, reducing the stars parameter by 1

otherwise the template ends

```
<xsl:template name="makeBarChart">
   <table id="barChart">
      <xsl:call-template name="drawBars">
         <xsl:with-param name="stars" select="5" />
      </xsl:call-template>
   </table>
</xsl:template>

<xsl:template name="drawBars">
   <xsl:param name="stars" />
   <xsl:if test="$stars > 0">
      <tr>
         <th>
         </th>
         <td>
         </td>
      </tr>

      <xsl:call-template name="drawBars">
         <xsl:with-param name="stars" select="$stars - 1" />
      </xsl:call-template>
   </xsl:if>
</xsl:template>
```

Sean wants the table header in each row to display the following text:

n star (*count*)

where *n* is a rating (from five down to one star) and *count* is the number of customers who gave the game that rating. You calculate the number of customers using the following count function and predicate that references both the *reviewList* variable containing a list of all of the reviews for the selected game and the *stars* parameter, which has a value of five stars down to one.

```
count($reviewList[r:rating=$stars])
```

You'll store this calculated value in the *dataCount* variable. You add this code to the drawBars template.

To display the counts for each possible rating:

▶ 1. In the drawBars template of the products.xsl file, add the following code to create the *dataCount* variable directly below the if element that tests whether the *stars* parameter is greater than 0:

```
<xsl:variable name="dataCount"
 select="count($reviewList[r:rating=$stars])" />
```

▶ 2. Within the <th> tag, insert the following code to display the current value of the *stars* parameter and the number of customers who gave the game that star rating:

```
<xsl:value-of select="$stars" /> star
(<xsl:value-of select="$dataCount" />)
```

Figure 6-42 shows newly added code in the drawBars template.

Figure 6-42   **Adding rows to the barChart table**

the dataCount variable stores the number of reviews matching the stars rating

```
<xsl:template name="drawBars">
  <xsl:param name="stars" />
  <xsl:if test="$stars > 0">
    <xsl:variable name="dataCount" select="count($reviewList[r:rating=$stars])" />
    <tr>
      <th>
        <xsl:value-of select="$stars" /> star
        (<xsl:value-of select="$dataCount" />)
      </th>
      <td>
      </td>
    </tr>
```

displays the value of the stars parameter and the value of the dataCount variable

3. Save your changes to the file and then regenerate the result document for the *Dance Off* digital game. Figure 6-43 shows the distribution of the 19 customer ratings from Sean's sample document.

Figure 6-43   **Distribution of the customer ratings for the Dance Off video game**

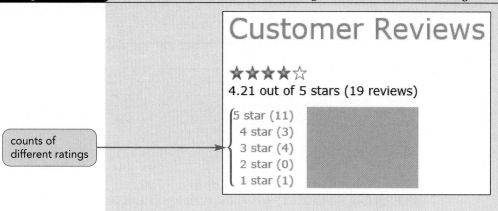

counts of different ratings

To complete the bar chart, you'll add an inline image to the five table data cells. The width of the image will be equal to the percentage of customers who gave the digital game each rating. For example, if 54% of the customers gave the game a 5-star rating, the width of the bar will be 54 pixels.

To complete the bar chart:

1. Return to the **products.xsl** file in your editor.

2. Within the drawBars template, create the following *percent* variable calculating the percentage of customers that gave the digital game the current stars by dividing the *dataCount* variable by the total number of customer reviews and multiplying that value by 100. Place the following code to create the inline image between the `<td></td>` tags:

```
<xsl:variable name="percent"
  select="100*($dataCount div count($reviewList))" />
```

3. Create an inline image of a width equal to the *percent* variable by adding the following code to the template, directly below the code you just added in Step 2:

```
<img src="solidbar.png" alt="" height="18px"
 width="{concat($percent, 'px')}" />
```

Note that the code uses the `concat()` function to append the text string "px" to the value of the *percent* variable so that the width is expressed in pixels. Figure 6-44 highlights the newly added code in the template.

Figure 6-44 **Displaying bars as inline images**

```
<xsl:template name="drawBars">
  <xsl:param name="stars" />          calculates the percentage by dividing
  <xsl:if test="$stars > 0">           the dataCount variable by the total
                                        number of customer reviews
  <xsl:variable name="dataCount" select="count($reviewList[r:rating=$stars])" />
     <tr>
        <th>
           <xsl:value-of select="$stars" /> star
           (<xsl:value-of select="$dataCount" />)
        </th>
        <td>
           <xsl:variable name="percent"
            select="100*($dataCount div count($reviewList))" />

           <img src="solidbar.png" alt="" height="18px"
            width="{concat($percent, 'px')}" />
        </td>
     </tr>
```

sets the width of the inline image
to the value of the percent
variable, expressed in pixels

---

4. Save your changes to the file.

5. Use an XSLT processor to generate the result for the *Dance Off* digital game with the product ID "**vg10551**" saving the result document in the **vg10551.html** file.

6. Create a result document for the *Net Force* digital game with the product ID "**vg10552**" saving the result in the **vg10552.html** file. Figure 6-45 shows the distribution of customer scores for both games.

Figure 6-45   Customer scores for the two video games

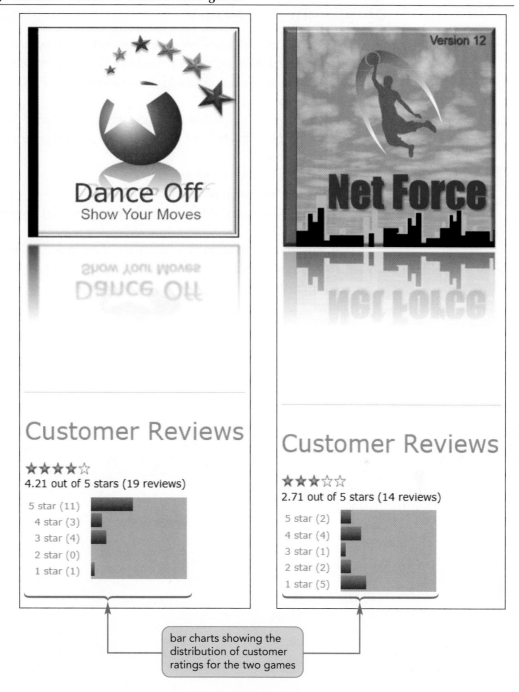

bar charts showing the distribution of customer ratings for the two games

You've completed your work on the products page for two of the games sold by the Harpe Gaming Store. Sean will continue to work with your files and develop other pages for products offered by the company. You can close any open files and applications now.

REVIEW

Session 6.3 Quick Check

1. What is the difference between a parameter and a variable?
2. In general, how are values passed to a global parameter?
3. Provide the code to create a parameter named *dateValue*, setting its default value to "11/18/2017".
4. You want to call the Date template, setting the value of the *dateValue* parameter within the template to the value 12/4/2017. What code would you use in your style sheet?
5. What is a named template?
6. What is functional programming?
7. What is recursion? What are the three fundamental features of any recursive function?
8. Provide code to create a recursive template named countdown that shows values of a parameter named *levelValue* counting backward from 100 in steps of 10, stopping when *levelValue* reaches zero.

PRACTICE

Review Assignments

Data Files needed for the Review Assignments: gamestxt.xml, gamestxt.xsl, +2 XML files, +1 XSL file, +3 PNG files, +1 CSS file

Sean has a new project for you to work on. In addition to digital games, the Harpe Gaming Store also sells board games. Sean is working on a page describing a few sample board games. He has created an XML document named games.xml that contains the description of two games, as well as scores the store has given the games on a 1 to 10 scale in seven categories. Sean also has an XML document named game_reviews.xml containing reviews written up in other gaming websites and an XML document named reviewers.xml that describes those websites.

Sean wants all of this information collected and displayed using a customized style sheet. He would like the style sheet to calculate the average score given to the selected board game and wants all numeric values and dates to be nicely formatted. Figure 6-46 shows a preview of the completed project.

Figure 6-46   Board game reviews

Complete the following:

1. Using your editor, open the **gamestxt.xml** and **gamestxt.xsl** file from xml06 ▸ review folder. Enter *your name* and the *date* in the comment section of each file and save them as **games.xml** and **games.xsl**, respectively.

2. Go the **games.xml** file in your editor. Take some time to review the contents of the file and then link the games.xsl style sheet file to the file. Close the games.xml file, saving your changes.

3. View the contents of the **game_reviews.xml** and **reviewers.xml** file in your editor, taking note of the structure and content of each document. Close the files. You do not have to save any changes to these documents.

4. Sean also has created a library of functions you'll use in this project. Open the **hgfunctions.xsl** file in your editor and study the contents. The document has two templates. One template matching the `releaseDate` element is used to convert date values from the *mm/dd/yyyy* format to the *Month Day, Year* format. The second template, named imageRow, is used to create a row of inline images. The imageRow template has two parameters: the *imgFile* parameter specifies the name of the image file, and the *imgCount* parameter specifies the number of images to be displayed. After studying the files, close the document. You don't have to save any changes.

5. Go to the **games.xsl** file in your editor. Directly after the opening `<xsl:stylesheet>` tag, use the `include` element to include the contents of the hgfunctions.xsl style sheet.

6. Directly after the `include` element, create the following global parameters and variables:

   a. The **gameID** parameter with a default value of 'bg210'. This parameter will be used to select different board games to display in the web page.

   b. The **currentGame** variable containing the /games/game[@gid=$gameID] node set. This variable will be used to select the game to display in the report.

   c. The **externalReviews** variable containing the /reviews/review[@gid=$gameID] node set from the game_reviews.xml file. (*Hint*: Use the `document()` function.) This variable will be used to access customer reviews for the current game.

   d. The **externalReviewers** variable containing the /reviewers node set from the reviewers.xml file. This variable will be used to access the list of reviewers for the report.

7. Go to the root template and make the following style changes so that the report displays information for the current game selected by the user:

   a. Go to the `<title>` tag within the head section of the HTML file and change the node set for the `value-of` element to $currentGame/title in order to display the title of the current game.

   b. Go to the gameSummary section and change the `select` attribute of the `apply-templates` element so that it applies the template for the *currentGame* variable.

8. Go to the game template and make the following style changes:

   a. Locate the table cell in the List Price row that displays the value of the price element and format the price value so that it appears in the $#,##0.00 format.

   b. Change the table cell in the Release Date row that displays the value of the `releaseDate` element so that it applies the template for the `releaseDate` element found in the hgfunctions.xsl file.

9. Next, within the game template, you need to display the summary information on the game taken from the summary element in the games.xml file. Below the summaryTable web table `</table>` tag in the game template, use the `copy-of` element to copy the node-set summary/* into the result document.

10. Sean wants the report to display the score for each game. Directly after the `copy-of` element you just created within the game template, create a variable named **avgScore** that returns the average scores contained in the scores/score node set. (*Hint*: Divide the sum of the values in the scores/score node set by the count of values in that node set.)

11. Finally, within the game template, insert the following web table structure for a web table that displays the scores from each gaming category and a final row that displays the average score from all gaming categories:

```
<table id="scoreTable">
   score template
   <tr>
      <th>OVERALL
         (avgScore / 10)
      </th>
      <td>
         row of token images
      </td>
   </tr>
</table>
```

where *score template* applies the template for the scores/score node set to display scores from each gaming category and *avgScore* is the value of the *avgScore* variable displayed with the 0.00 number format. Create the *row of token images* by calling the imageRow template from the hgfunctions.xsl file using the 'token.png' file for the *imgFile* parameter and the value of the *avgScore* variable rounded to the nearest integer for the *imgCount* parameter.

12. Directly below the game template, create a template for the `score` element. The template will display a table row for each category of gaming score by writing the following HTML code:

```
<tr>
   <th>
      category (current score/10)
   </th>
   <td>
      row of token images
   </td>
</tr>
```

where *category* is the value of category attribute, *current score* is the value returned by the `current()` function, and *row of token images* is created by calling the imageRow template using 'token.png' for the *imgFile* parameter and the value returned by the `current()` function for the *imgCount* parameter.

13. Scroll up to the game template and, directly below the `<img>` tag, insert a command to apply the template to the *externalReviews* variable you created in Step 6.

14. Go back to the bottom of the style sheet to the review template used to display external reviews of the current game. This template has two local variables: the *reviewerTitle* variable contains the title of the review, and the *reviewerURL* variable contains the URL of the reviewer's website. Add the following HTML code to the template:

```
<section class="review">
   summary nodes
   <p>
      reviewerTitle
      <br />
      (<a href="reviewerURL">reviewerURL</a>)
   </p>
</section>
```

where *summary nodes* is a copy of the summary/* node set using the `copy-of` element, *reviewerTitle* is the value of the *reviewerTitle* variable, and *reviewerURL* is the value of the *reviewerURL* variable.

15. Save your changes to the style sheet.

16. Generate a result document using **bg210** and **bg211** for the values of the *gameID* parameter, storing the results in files named **bg210.html** and **bg211.html**, respectively.

Case Problem 1

APPLY

Data Files needed for this Case Problem: congresstxt.xml, electiontxt.xsl, +1 XML file, + 1 CSS file, + 1 PNG file

Voter Web   Pam Carls is a manager for the website Voter Web, which compiles statistics from local and national elections. Pam has the results from recent congressional elections from eight districts in Minnesota stored in an XML document named congress.xml. The candidates.xml document stores information about the candidates. The structures of both documents is shown in Figure 6-47.

Figure 6-47 **Structure of the congress.xml and candidates.xml documents**

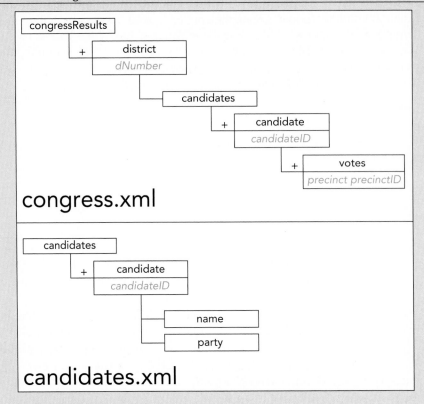

Pam wants to summarize the results from each district's election with tables that show the total votes cast for each candidate, the percentage of the total vote, and a bar chart that graphically displays the percentage. Figure 6-48 shows a preview of the final web page.

Figure 6-48 **Voter web election results**

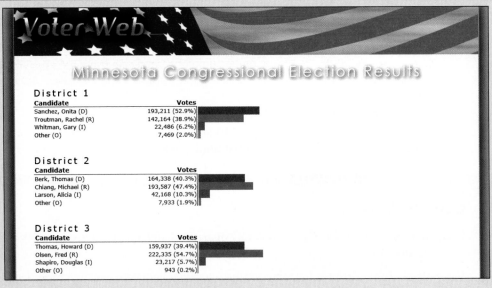

Pam has already started work on the style sheet and created a template named drawCells to create the bar chart, but she needs you to complete the style sheet. Complete the following:

1. Using your editor, open the **congresstxt.xml** and **electiontxt.xsl** files from the xml06 ▸ case1 folder. Enter *your name* and the *date* in the comment section of each file, and save them as **congress.xml** and **election.xsl,** respectively.

2. Go to the **congress.xml** file in your editor. Review the content of the file and its structure and then link the election.xsl style sheet to the file. Close the file, saving your changes.

3. Go to the **election.xsl** file in your editor. Directly after the output element, create the global variable **candidateInfo** to store information about each candidate by referencing the /candidates/candidate node set from the candidates.xml file.

4. Scroll down to the candidate template at the bottom of the file. The candidate template will display a table row containing the names of each candidate and votes he or she received, as well as a bar whose length is equal to the vote percentage of the candidate. At the top of the template, create the following local variables:

    a. **candidateVotes** equal to the number of votes placed for the current candidate with the value "sum(votes)"

    b. **totalVotes** equal to the number of votes placed within the current district with the value "sum(..//votes)"

    c. **candidatePercent** containing the percent of votes assigned to the candidate, calculated by dividing *candidateVotes* by *totalVotes*

    d. **candidateName** containing the name of the candidate, determined by looking up the value of the `name` element in the candidateInfo node set using the value "$candidateInfo[@candidateID=current()/@candidateID]/name"

    e. **candidateParty** containing the party affiliation of the candidate, obtained by looking up the `party` element for the matching candidate in the candidateInfo node set using the value "$candidateInfo[@candidateID=current()/@candidateID]/party"

5. Write the following HTML code within the `<tr>` element in the candidate template:

```
<th>
   candidateName (candidateParty)
</th>
```

where `candidateName` is the value of the *candidateName* variable and `candidateParty` is the value of the *candidateParty* variable.

6. Add the following code to the table row:

```
<th>
   candidateVotes (candidatePercent)
</th>
```

where `candidateVotes` is the value of the *candidateVotes* variable displayed with the '###,##0' number format and `candidatePercent` is the value of the *candidatePercent* variable displayed with the '#0.0%' number format.

7. Create the bar that displays the percentage of votes given to the candidate by adding the following table data cell to the table row:

```
<td>
   drawCells
</td>
```

where `drawCells` calls the drawCells template using two parameter values: **cellCount** equal to the value of the *candidatePercent* variable multiplied by 100 and rounded to the nearest integer, and **party** equal to the value of the *candidateParty* variable.

8. Close the election.xsl file, saving your changes.

9. View the results of the transformation by opening the **congress.xml** file in your web browser. Verify that the layout and content of your web page resembles that shown in Figure 6-48.

Case Problem 2

APPLY

Data Files needed for this Case Problem: samptxt.xml, spcfunctxt.xsl, spctxt.xsl, +1 CSS file, +5 PNG files

Karleton Manufacturing   Carmen Garza is a quality control manager at Karleton Manufacturing, a manufacturing plant located in Trotwood, Ohio. One project that Carmen oversees is the manufacture of tin cans for a major food company. According to specifications for the project, the width of the tin can walls should be close to 65 millimeters; however, as the manufacturing process continues throughout the day, the tools become worn and the pressure behind the tools automatically increases to compensate. This can result in varying can widths. Thus, every day Carmen takes a few sample batches, testing whether the width of the tin can wall stays close to an optimal 65 millimeter value. This information is stored in an XML document. Carmen wants to display this information in an HTML format that she can quickly display on her browser. She wants the page to display the maximum, minimum, average, and standard error of each sample batch. She also wants to display sample values in a quality control chart. A preview of the page that Carmen needs to create is shown in Figure 6-49.

| Figure 6-49 | Quality control analysis |

Carmen has also started work on the XSLT style sheet to create this project, and she has compiled some XSLT templates to calculate minimum, maximum, and standard error values. Your job will be to finish the project for her. Complete the following:

1. Using your editor, open the **samptxt.xml**, **spctxt.xsl**, and **spcfunctxt.xsl** from the xml06 ▸ case2 folder. Enter *your name* and the *date* in the comment section of each file, and save them as **samples.xml**, **spc.xsl**, and **spcfunctions.xsl**, respectively.

2. Go to the **samples.xml** file in your editor. Study the content and structure of the document and then link the spc.xsl style sheet to the file. Close the file, saving your changes.

3. Go to the **spcfunctions.xsl** file in your editor. The document contains templates to calculate the minimum, maximum, and standard error of a list of values. It also includes a template to calculate the square root of a given value. Directly after the opening `<xsl:stylesheet>` tag, insert a template named **average** to calculate the average value from a node set specified in a parameter named **list**. Close the file, saving your changes.

4. Go to the **spc.xsl** file in your editor. Create a global parameter named **sampleID** that will contain the ID of the quality control sample that Carmen wants to display. Set the default value of the parameter to the text string 'A100'.

5. After the *sampleID* variable, use the `include` element to include the spcfunctions.xsl file in the style sheet.

6. Go to the root template and, after the h1 heading, use the `apply-templates` element to apply the template for the node set "samples/sample[@sampleID=$sampleID]" in order to display sample data for the current quality control sample.

7. Go to the sample template, which displays summary statistics for the current quality sample, and add the following code to the template:

```
<h2>Sample: sampleID</h2>
<table id="batchTable">
    <thead>
        <tr>
            <th>Batch</th>
            <th>Sample Size</th>
            <th>Minimum</th>
            <th>Maximum</th>
            <th>Average</th>
            <th>Standard Error</th>
            <th><img src="grid.png" alt="" /></th>
        </tr>
    </thead>
    <tbody>
        batch template
    </tbody>
</table>
```

where *sampleID* is the value of the `sampleID` attribute and *batch template* applies the template for the `batch` element.

8. Go to the batch template and insert the following local variables to calculate the summary statistics for the tin can widths:

   a. **minWidth** storing the minimum value of the width node set by calling the minimum template

   b. **maxWidth** storing the maximum value of the width node set by calling the maximum template

   c. **avgWidth** storing the average width value by calling the average template

   d. **stdErrWidth** storing the standard error of the width values by calling the stdErr template

   e. **lowerCI** storing the expression *average* − 1.96×*standard_error* where *average* is the value of the *avgWidth* variable and *standard_error* is the value of the *stdErrWidth* variable

   f. **upperCI** storing the expression *average* + 1.96×*standard_error* where once again *average* is the value of the *avgWidth* variable and *standard_error* is the value of the *stdErrWidth* variable

9. After the variable declarations within the batch template, write the following HTML code to the result document:

```
<tr>
    <td>batch ID</td>
    <td>count</td>
    <td>minimum</td>
    <td>maximum</td>
    <td>average</td>
    <td>standard error</td>
</tr>
```

where *batch ID* is the value of the `batchID` attribute, `count` is the number of recorded widths in the batch calculated using the `count()` function, *minimum* is value of the *minWidth* variable using the number format '#0.00', *maximum* is the value of the *maxWidth* variable using the number format '#0.00', *average* is the value of the *avgWidth* variable using the number format '#0.00', and *standard error* is the value of the *stdErrWidth* variable using the number format '#0.000'.

10. Directly after the table cell for the standard error value, insert the following table cell that creates the graphic representation of the range of tin can widths:

```
<td>
    <img src="background.png" height="22px"
    width="25×(lowerCI - 58)" alt="lowerCI" />

    <img src="lowerbar.png" height="22px"
    width="25×(average - lowerCI)" alt="average" />

    <img src="upperbar.png" height="22px"
    width="25×(upperCI - average)" alt="upperCI" />

    <img src="background.png" height="22px"
    width="25×(72 - upperCI)" alt="" />

</td>
```

where *lowerCI* is the value of the *lowerCI* variable, *average* is the value of the *avgWidth* variable, and *upperCI* is the value of the *upperCI* variable. Use the concat() function to append each width value in the different <img> tags with the text string "px."

11. Save your changes to the style sheet.

12. Generate a result document using **A100** and **B100** for the values of the *sampleID* parameter, storing the results in files named **a100.html** and **b100.html**, respectively.

CHALLENGE

Case Problem 3

Data Files needed for this Case Problem: hdfunctxt.xsl, hdorderstxt.xml, hdorderstxt.xsl, + 2 XML files, +1 CSS file, + 1 PNG file

Homes of Dreams   Larry Helt is a sales manager at Homes of Dreams, a company that manufactures and sells custom dollhouses. Orders are stored in a database, and from that database Larry can extract sample information and place it into XML documents. He has created three sample XML documents: hdorders.xml, which contains a list of recent orders; hdcustomers.xml, which provides information about Homes of Dreams customers; and finally hdproducts.xml, which describes the products sold by the company.

Larry wants your help in creating an XSLT style sheet to view information about customer orders in his web browser. The web page should list all of the orders placed by a selected customer, calculating the total cost charged to each order. A preview of the web page is shown in Figure 6-50.

Figure 6-50   **Customer order report**

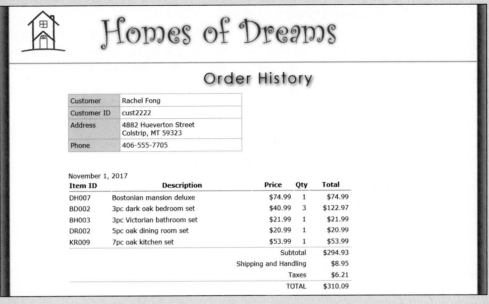

Complete the following:

1. Using your editor, open **hdfunctxt.xsl**, **hdorderstxt.xml**, and **hdorderstxt.xsl** from the xml06 ▸ case3 folder. Enter *your name* and the *date* in the comment section of each file, and save them as **hdfunctions.xsl**, **hdorders.xml**, and **hdorders.xsl**, respectively.

2. Go to the **hdorders.xml** file in your editor and review the contents and structure of the file. Link the hdorders.xsl style sheet to the file. Close the file, saving your changes.

3. Using your editor, open **hdproducts.xml** and **hdcustomers.xml** from the xml06 ▸ case3 folder. Review the contents of the hdproducts.xml file containing the list of products sold by the company and the hdcustomers.xml file containing information about the company's customers. Close the two files without saving any changes.

4. Go to the **hdfunctions.xsl** file in your editor. The style sheet already has one template named formatDate used to convert date text stored in the text string *mm/dd/yyyy* to the format `Month Day, Year` where `Month` is the name of the month, `Day` is the day of the month, and `Year` is the year value. Take some time to study the code for the template.

✥ **EXPLORE**   5. Directly after the formatDate template, create a template named **sumProduct**. The purpose of this recursive template is to multiply two number lists by returning the sum of the products of each matching item in the two lists. The template has two parameters named **list1** and **list2** containing the node sets of the two number lists. Do not specify a default value for the parameters. Create a third parameter named **sumProductTotal** with a default value of **0**. Use the `choose` element to apply the following recursive code to the template:

   a. Test whether the count of items in the list1 and list2 nodes is greater than 0 to determine whether the two lists are empty.

   b. If neither list is empty, then recursively call the sumProduct template. Let the *sumProductTotal* parameter value be equal to the product of the first item in the two lists plus the current value of the *sumProductTotal* parameter. Let the *list1* parameter value contain the node set of the *list1* parameter other than the first item. Similarly, let the *list2* parameter value contain the list2 node set other than the first item. Thus, every time the sumProduct template is called, the size of the list1 and list2 node sets is reduced by 1.

   c. If the two lists are empty, then use the `value-of` element to display the value of the *sumProductTotal* parameter.

6. Close the **hdfunctions.xsl** file, saving your changes.

7. Go to the **hdorders.xsl** file in your editor. Directly after the `<xsl:output>` tag, create a global parameter named **customerID** with the default value 'cust2222'. The purpose of this parameter will be to set the ID of the customer to be displayed in the order report.

8. Create a global variable named ***reportCustomer***, which will be used to look up information on each customer. The variable should reference the node set "/cust:customers/cust:customer[@custID=$customerID]" from the hdcustomers.xml file.

9. Use the `include` element to include the hdfunctions.xsl style sheet in the active style sheet.

✦ **EXPLORE** 10. Go to the root template and, directly below the h1 heading, insert the following HTML code to create a web table providing contact information for the current customer:

```
<table id="customerTable">
   <tr>
      <th>Customer</th>
      <td>First Last</td>
   </tr>
   <tr>
      <th>Customer ID</th>
      <td>ID</td>
   <tr>
      <th>Address</th>
      <td>Street <br />
         City, State  ZIP
      </td>
   </tr>
   <tr>
      <th>Phone</th>
      <td>Phone</td>
   </tr>
</table>
```

where `First`, `Last`, `Street`, `City`, `State`, `ZIP`, and `Phone` are values of the `First_Name`, `Last_Name`, `Street`, `City`, `State`, and `ZIP` elements looked up from the reportCustomer node set, and `ID` is the value of the *customerID* parameter. Use a text element to insert a blank space between the customer's first and last name and between the state name and the ZIP code.

11. Below the web table, apply the template for the node set "orders/order[@custID=$customerID]" in order to display the orders made by the current customer.

✦ **EXPLORE** 12. Go to the order template. Within this template, you'll write the code that displays the orders made by the customer. At the top of the template is the subTotal variable that will contain the total cost of each item ordered multiplied by the quantity ordered. To calculate this value within the `<xsl:variable></xsl:variable>` tags, use the `call-template` element to call the sumProduct template using the node set "item/@qty" for the value of the *list1* parameter and the node set "item/@price" for the value of the *list2* parameter.

13. Directly after the *subTotal* variable, add the following HTML code to the order template:

```
<table class="orderTable">
   <caption>formatted date</caption>
   <thead>
      <tr>
         <th>Item ID</th>
         <th>Description</th>
         <th>Price</th>
         <th>Qty</th>
         <th>Total</th>
      </tr>
   </thead>
</table>
```

where `formatted date` is the order date formatted by calling the formatDate template using the value of the `orderDate` attribute for the *date* parameter.

14. Directly below the closing `</thead>` tag, insert the following code to create a footer for the web table to display the summary values for the customer order:

```
<tfoot>
    <tr>
        <th colspan="4">Subtotal</th>
        <th>subtotal</th>
    </tr>
    <tr>
        <th colspan="4">Shipping and Handling</th>
        <th>shipping</th>
    </tr>
    <tr>
        <th colspan="4">Taxes</th>
        <th>tax</th>
    </tr>
    <tr>
        <th colspan="4">TOTAL</th>
        <th>total cost</th>
    </tr>
</tfoot>
```

where *subtotal* is the value of the *subTotal* variable, *shipping* is the value of the `shipping` attribute, *tax* is the value of the `tax` attribute, and *total cost* is the sum of the *subtotal*, *shipping*, and *tax* values. Display each value using the number format $###,##0.00.

15. Below the closing `</tfoot>` tag, insert the following HTML code for the table body:

```
<tbody>
    items
</tbody>
```

where *items* applies the template for the `item` element.

16. Go to the item template. The purpose of this template is to display the list of items ordered by the customer. First, create a local variable named ***reportItem*** that stores the node set "/prod:items/prod:item[@itemID=current()/@itemID]" from the hdproducts.xml file. The purpose of this variable is to look up descriptive information about the items sold by the company.

17. Directly after the *reportItem* variable, insert the following HTML code within the item template:

```
<tr>
    <td>item ID</td>
    <td>description</td>
    <td>price</td>
    <td>qty</td>
    <td>total price</td>
</tr>
```

where *item ID* is the value of the `itemID` attribute, *description* is the item's description taken from the `description` element in the *reportItem* variable, *price* is the value of the `price` attribute, *qty* is the value of the `qty` attribute, and *total price* is the product of *price* and *qty*. Display the price and total price values using the number format $###,##0.00.

18. Save your changes to the style sheet.

19. Generate result documents using **cust2222**, **cust1140**, **cust2917**, and **cust2855** for the values of the *customerID* parameter, storing the results in files named **cust2222.html**, **cust1140.html**, **cust2917.html**, and **cust2855.html**, respectively.

CREATE

Case Problem 4

Data Files needed for this Case Problem: brwstorestxt.xml, brwstorestxt.xsl, + 2 XML files, + 1 CSS file, +4 PNG files

Big Red Wraps   Michael Dean handles sales reports and market analyses for *Big Red Wraps*, a Midwest restaurant chain that specializes in made-to-order sandwich wraps, seasonal soups, and fresh salads. Sales data and market research for the 20 *Big Red Wraps* stores has been stored in several XML documents. The brwstores.xml file contains contact information about each of the 20 franchise stores. The brwreviews.xml file contains a rating of each store in 5 different categories, scored on a 1 to 10 scale. The brwsales.xml file contains monthly gross sales figures for each store.

Michael wants you to create an XSLT style sheet that converts these data into an easily readable HTML file. One possible design for the report is shown in Figure 6-51.

Figure 6-51   **Store report**

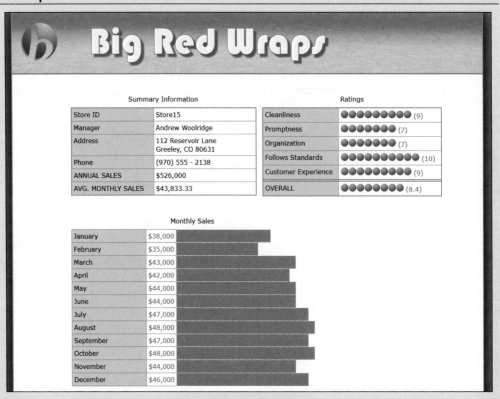

Complete the following:

1. Using your editor, open the **brwstorestxt.xml** and **brwstorestxt.xsl** files from the xml06 ▸ case4 folder. Enter *your name* and the *date* in the comment section of each file, and save them as **brwstores.xml** and **brwstores.xsl**, respectively.

2. Go to the **brwstores.xml**, **brwreviews.xml**, and **brwsales.xsl** files in your editor. Take some time to study the content and structure of the three documents.

3. Within the **brwstores.xml** file, insert a link to the brwstores.xsl style sheet file.

4. Go to the **brwstores.xsl** file in your editor and begin designing your XSLT style sheet. The style sheet design is up to you, but it should display a selected store's contact information, ratings in five categories, and monthly sales, and it should employ the following features:

   a. A global parameter in which the user can specify the ID of the store to be displayed in the report

   b. Variables that access the contents of the brwreviews.xml and brwsales.xml files

   c. One or more external style sheet files included within the brwstores.xsl file

   d. Data retrieved from a lookup table

   e. Number formatting that displays currency values as currency and calculated values in an easy-to-read format

   f. Summary statistics that display the selected store's total annual and average monthly gross sales

   g. Summary statistics that display the average overall rating of the selected store

   h. Recursive template that is called until a stopping condition is met

5. The web page code can be written to HTML5, XHTML, or HTML4 standards. Include the appropriate output element specifying how to render the result code.

6. You are free to include whatever CSS style sheet or external graphics you wish to complete the look of the final page. A sample CSS style sheet, brwstyles.css, is provided for you, but you may substitute that one with one of your own.

7. Test your code by generating result documents for the following stores: Store 1, Store 4, Store 8, Store 12, Store 16, and Store 20. Save the result documents under the names **store1.html**, **store4.html**, **store8.html**, **store12.html**, **store16.html**, and **store20.html**.

TUTORIAL 7

Building an XSLT Application

Working with IDs, Keys, and Groups

OBJECTIVES

Session 7.1
- Work with step patterns
- Write a step pattern to create an element group
- Create and apply the mode attribute

Session 7.2
- Work with ID attributes
- Create reference keys
- Generate an ID automatically
- Understand how to apply Muenchian Grouping
- Explore extension functions and elements

Case | *Bowline Realty*

Bowline Realty is a real estate agency located in Longmont, Colorado that handles property in Longmont and other communities along the Front Range. Web designer Lisa Riccio is working on one of the company's web pages that displays new home listings for eastern Colorado. She is working on an XSLT style sheet that will collect information from XML documents describing newly listed properties, as well as the agents and real estate companies that manage them.

To make it easier for homebuyers to locate specific properties, Lisa wants the web page to display the listings organized by city. However, the contents of the source document are not organized by city, and Lisa does not have the ability to modify the source document; therefore, any changes to the web page have to be done by modifying the style sheet. She has come to you for help in creating a style sheet that groups real estate listings by city.

STARTING DATA FILES

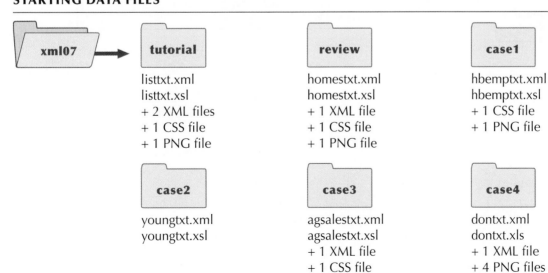

xml07 → tutorial
listtxt.xml
listtxt.xsl
+ 2 XML files
+ 1 CSS file
+ 1 PNG file

review
homestxt.xml
homestxt.xsl
+ 1 XML file
+ 1 CSS file
+ 1 PNG file

case1
hbemptxt.xml
hbemptxt.xsl
+ 1 CSS file
+ 1 PNG file

case2
youngtxt.xml
youngtxt.xsl

case3
agsalestxt.xml
agsalestxt.xsl
+ 1 XML file
+ 1 CSS file
+ 1 PNG file

case4
dontxt.xml
dontxt.xls
+ 1 XML file
+ 4 PNG files

Session 7.1 Visual Overview:

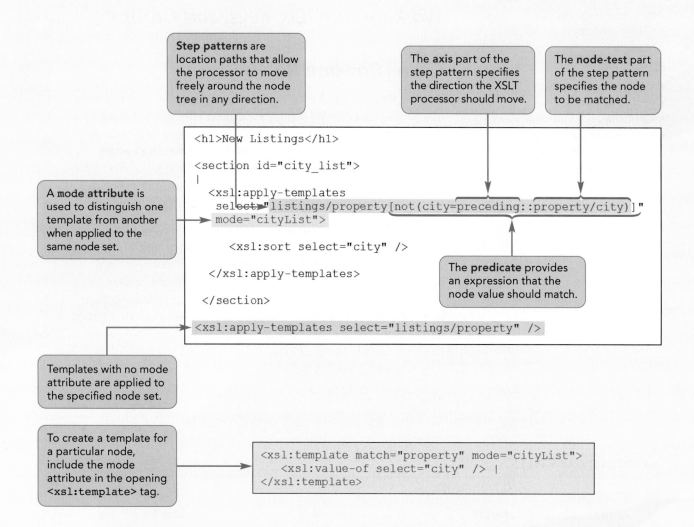

Step patterns are location paths that allow the processor to move freely around the node tree in any direction.

The **axis** part of the step pattern specifies the direction the XSLT processor should move.

The **node-test** part of the step pattern specifies the node to be matched.

A mode **attribute** is used to distinguish one template from another when applied to the same node set.

```
<h1>New Listings</h1>

<section id="city_list">
  |
  <xsl:apply-templates
   select="listings/property[not(city=preceding::property/city)]"
   mode="cityList">

    <xsl:sort select="city" />

  </xsl:apply-templates>

</section>

<xsl:apply-templates select="listings/property" />
```

The **predicate** provides an expression that the node value should match.

Templates with no mode attribute are applied to the specified node set.

To create a template for a particular node, include the mode attribute in the opening <xsl:template> tag.

```
<xsl:template match="property" mode="cityList">
   <xsl:value-of select="city" /> |
</xsl:template>
```

Step Patterns and the mode Attribute

This shows the application of the cityList template for the property node.

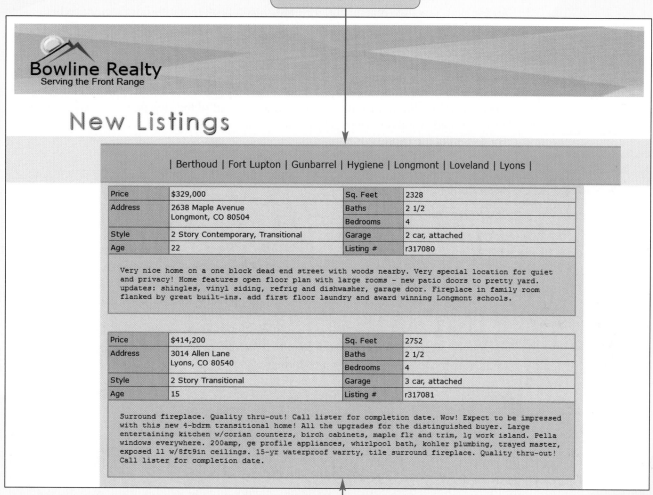

This is the default template for the property node.

Working with Step Patterns

As you learned in Tutorial 5, a location path is an XPath expression that defines a path through the node tree to a particular node or set of nodes. Up until now, you've been using location paths that only allow processors to travel up and down the node tree from a starting point, called the context node, going either up to the context node's ancestors or down to the context node's descendants. However, XPath supports more complicated expressions called step patterns that allow processors to move in almost any direction from the context node through the node tree. A step pattern is composed of three parts: an axis, a node test, and a predicate. The axis specifies the direction in which the processor should move through the node tree, the node test specifies a node for the step pattern to match, and the predicate defines properties of the node to be matched. The general syntax of a step pattern is

```
axis::node-test[predicate]
```

where *axis* is the direction that the XSLT processor should move from the context node, *node-test* is the node to be matched, and *predicate* is the expression that the node value should match. Only the node-test part of the step pattern is required. You've already used node tests and predicates in your previous XPath expressions. For example, the expression

```
property[city="Longmont"]
```

has a node test of

```
property
```

and a predicate of

```
city="Longmont"
```

When an XSLT processor encounters this expression, it selects all of the children of the context node that are property elements and, within those property elements, it only selects nodes from the city of Longmont. Note that by default the processor starts from the context node and moves down the node tree. To move in a direction, for example to siblings or ancestor elements rather than to the children of the context node, you must work with the axis part of the step pattern.

REFERENCE

Working with Step Patterns

• To create a step pattern, use the XPath expression

```
axis::node-test[predicate]
```

where *axis* defines how to move through the node tree, *node-test* specifies the node for the step pattern to match, and *predicate* defines properties of the node to be matched.

Working with Axes

XPath supports 13 values for the axis part of the step pattern. Figure 7-1 describes the axis values that can be used in any XPath step pattern.

| Figure 7-1 | Axis values in an Xpath step pattern |

Axis	Selects
ancestor	All nodes that are ancestors of the context node, starting with the context node's parents and moving up the node tree
ancestor-or-self	All nodes that are ancestors of the context node, starting with the context node and moving up the node tree
attribute	All of the attribute nodes of the context node
child	All children of the context node
descendant	All nodes that are descendants of the context node, starting with the node's immediate children and moving down the node tree
descendant-or-self	All nodes that are descendants of the context node, starting with the context node and moving down the node tree
following	All nodes that appear after the context node in the source document, excluding the context node's own descendants
following-sibling	All siblings of the context node that appear after the context node in the source document
namespace	All namespace nodes of the context node
parent	The parent of the context node
preceding	All nodes that appear before the context node in the source document, excluding the context node's own ancestors
preceding-sibling	All siblings of the context node that appear before the context node in the source document
self	The context node

The default value for the axis portion of the step pattern is `child`, which instructs processors to select the context node children that match the node-test and the predicate. Thus, from the perspective of a processor, the following two expressions are equivalent:

```
property[city="Longmont"]
child::property[city="Longmont"]
```

In both cases, the processor selects element nodes named `property` that are children of the context node and that match the specified predicate.

To go in a different direction from the context node you change the axis value. Figure 7-2 charts the effect of the different axis values on both the nodes selected and the order in which they're selected. The context node is indicated in blue, and the objects in the node set that are selected by the XPath expression are numbered, with lower node numbers selected first in the node set. Note that, when the axis value includes self, the context node is included in the node set and numbered as the first selected item.

| Figure 7-2 | Node numbers from different step patterns |

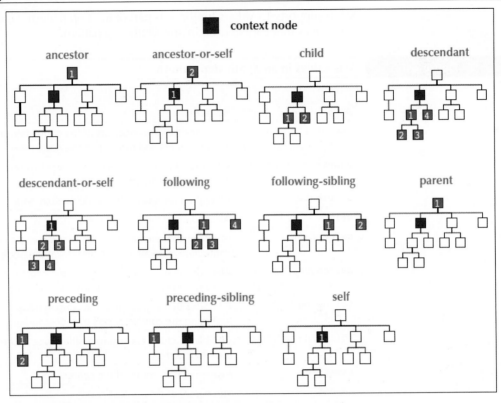

For example, the following location path moves up the node tree from the context node, selecting all of the elements (parent, grandparent, and so on) that are property elements from the city of Longmont:

```
ancestor::property[city="Longmont"]
```

To move left or right from the context node, you use a sibling axis. The following location path moves to the right of the context node, selecting all of the property elements for the city of Longmont:

```
following-sibling::property[city="Longmont"]
```

Finally, you can move both right and down from the context node, using the following axis within the location path:

```
following::property[city="Longmont"]
```

To move to the left of the context node, you would use the `preceding-sibling` axis and to move to the left and down, you would use the `preceding` axis.

As the processor follows the location path, it creates a node set of all of the nodes that match the conditions of the path. The order in which objects are placed into the node set is determined by the direction the processor takes as it navigates the node tree. The processor moves up and down the node tree before moving left or right.

You can use node numbers in the predicate to select specific items from the node set generated by the location path. For example, the following location path selects the second property element that follows the context node as a sibling:

```
following-sibling::property[2]
```

For some step patterns, processors recognize an abbreviated form. Figure 7-3 displays additional examples of step patterns using their complete syntax, including the axis, node test, and predicate, as well as the familiar abbreviated form for each complete syntax.

Figure 7-3   **Abbreviated location paths**

Step pattern	Abbreviated as
`self::node()`	`.`
`parent::node()`	`..`
`child::property/child::city`	`property/city`
`child::listings/descendant::city`	`listings//city`
`property/attribute::firm`	`property/@firm`
`parent::node()/property/attribute::firm`	`../property/@firm`

Step patterns provide the programmer with great flexibility in selecting node sets from the source document. One use of step patterns is to construct lists of unique values from node items.

Combining Node Sets

INSIGHT

In some applications, you will want to combine two or more node sets. There are three possible combinations of two node sets, which are labeled using the variables $n1 and $n2 in the examples that follow:

- Union—includes a node if it appears in either $n1 or $n2
- Intersection—includes a node only if it appears in both $n1 and $n2
- Difference—includes a node only if it appears in $n1 but not in $n2

To create a union of two node sets, use the | operator in the XPath expression as follows:

```
$n1 | $n2
```

XPath 1.0 does not provide a built-in method of creating the intersection or difference of two node sets. However, Michael Kay discovered the following expression, which is known as the Kaysian Method, using the count() method to return the intersection of two node sets:

```
$n1[count(. | $n2) = count($n2)]
```

The expression for returning the difference of the $n1 and $n2 node sets is similar:

```
$n1[count(. | $n2) != count($n2)]
```

XPath 2.0 provides operators for the intersection and difference of node sets, which are named intersect and except, so these expressions can be written more simply in XPath 2.0 as

```
$n1 intersect $n2
$n1 except $n2
```

There are also third-party function libraries that provide tools for combining node sets in a variety of ways.

Creating Unique Lists with Step Patterns

Lisa has already created a sample XML document and begun working on a style sheet for her real estate report. You open her documents now.

To open Lisa's documents:

▶ 1. Use your editor to open the **listtxt.xml** file from the xlm07 ▶ tutorial folder. Enter **your name** and the **date** in the comment section at the top of the file, and save the file as **listings.xml**.

▶ 2. Review the contents of the file, noting the document structure. Below the comment section, insert a processing instruction to attach the **listings.xsl** style sheet to this document.

▶ 3. Close the file, saving your changes.

▶ 4. Open the **listtxt.xsl** file in your editor. Enter **your name** and the **date** in the comment section, and save the file as **listings.xsl**.

▶ 5. Use your web browser or an XLST processor to generate the result document for the listings.xml file based on the listings.xsl style sheet. Figure 7-4 shows the appearance of Lisa's property report.

Figure 7-4 **Initial appearance of the new listings.xml page**

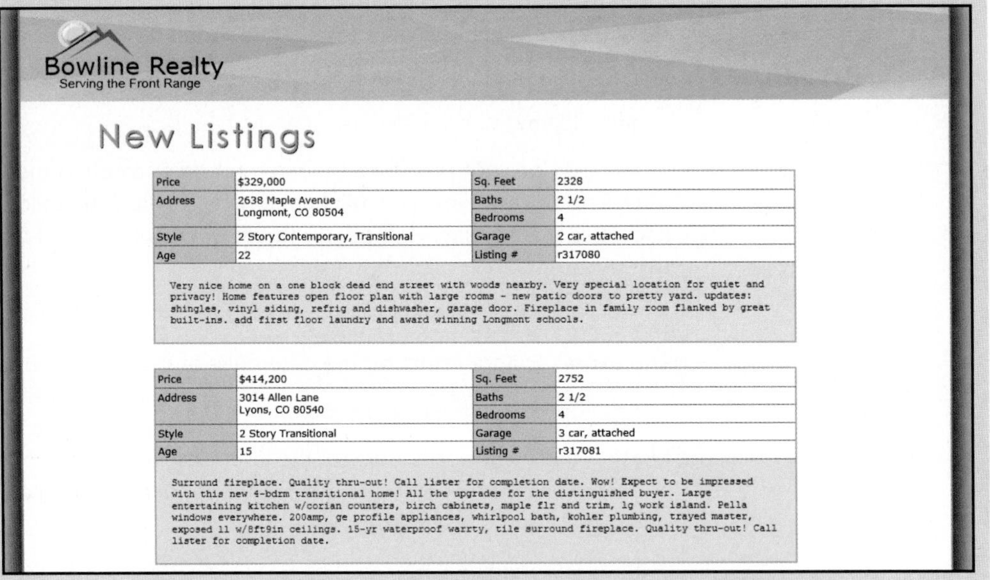

For each property, Lisa has recorded the property's price, address, style, age, size (in square feet), number of bathrooms, number of bedrooms, garage size and type, listing #, and a description. Figure 7-5 shows the structure of the document.

Figure 7-5 **Structure of the listings.xml document**

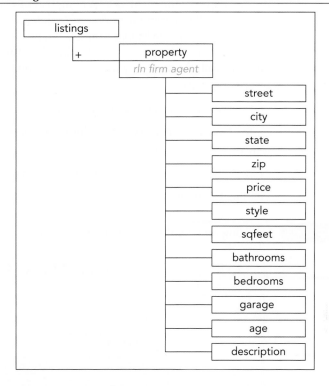

Currently, Lisa's report displays information about each property, but there is no feature that summarizes this information. Specifically, Lisa would like her report to list the cities in which the properties reside, including the number of properties listed within each city. The following location path could be used to create a node set of all of the city elements:

```
listings/property[city]
```

The problem with this approach is that it selects every property element that contains a city element (see Figure 7-6). Although this would certainly allow you to create a list of all of the city names, many city names would be duplicated.

Figure 7-6 **Selecting all city elements from the source document**

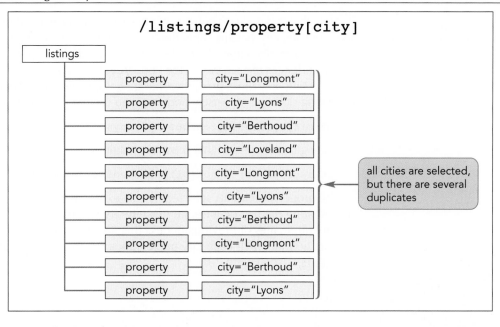

Lisa wants to identify only one property from each city in order to create a list of the city names. One method to accomplish this is to locate all of the duplicate entries and remove them from the node set. To determine which nodes are duplicates, you first create a step pattern that instructs the processor to select only those properties that have a preceding sibling containing the same city name. To check for a preceding property with the same city name, you use the following expression, which utilizes the `preceding` axis:

```
city=preceding::property/city
```

To create a node set based on this expression, you add it to the predicate of the following location path

```
listings/property[city=preceding::property/city]
```

yielding the node set shown in Figure 7-7.

Figure 7-7   Selecting only duplicate city nodes

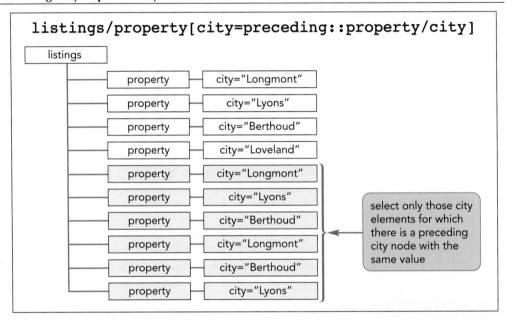

Note that this node set consists of the second occurrence, third occurrence, and so on of each city, because only these nodes have a preceding property element with the same city name. The nodes that don't fulfill this expression represent the first occurrences of each city in the node tree. Thus, you want to reverse this node set, selecting only those properties that do *not* contain a city name duplicated in a preceding sibling. To reverse a node set, you use the following XPath `not()` function:

```
not(city=preceding::property/city)
```

Adding this expression to a predicate results in the following location path:

```
listings/property[not(city=preceding::property/city)]
```

The property elements selected by this expression include only those properties representing the first occurrence of each city name—in other words, the nodes that are not duplicates of previous nodes. This also means that the node set contains a collection in which each city name appears only once and all city names are represented (see Figure 7-8).

| Figure 7-8 | Selecting the initial occurrence of each city property |

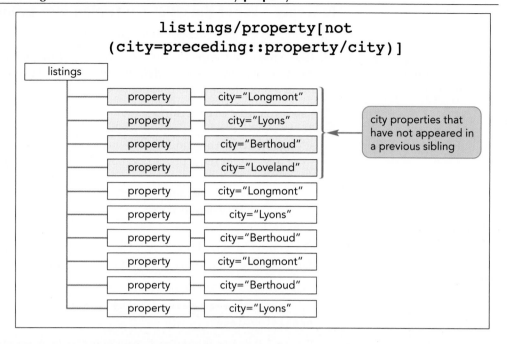

Creating a List Using Step Patterns

- To create a list of unique values using step patterns, use the following syntax to select the first occurrence of each unique node value:

  `not(node=preceding::node set)`

  where *node* is a specific node in the source document and *node set* is the complete set of values for that node in the source document.

- Once you generate the list of unique values, you can use the `apply-templates` element or the `for` element to write code to the result document for each unique value.

You can associate a template that only applies to the first property listed for each city to this location path. The code is

```
<xsl:apply-templates
 select="listings/property[not(city=preceding::property/city)]">
   <xsl:sort select="city" />
</xsl:apply-templates>
```

Note that the `sort` element is used to sort those properties by order of their city names. The following template then creates a list of each city name separated by the | character:

```
<xsl:template match="property">
   <xsl:value-of select="city" /> |
</xsl:template>
```

You'll create this template now and apply it to Lisa's document.

To create a list of the cities containing new properties:

1. Return to the **listings.xsl** file in your editor.

Remember, in a predicate, the expressions are resolved relative to the context node.

2. Go to the root template and, between the New Listings h1 heading and the `<xsl:apply-templates>` element, insert the following code to generate a node set containing the unique list of cities:

```
<section id="city_list">
   |
   <xsl:apply-templates
   select="listings/property[not(city=preceding::property/city)]">

      <xsl:sort select="city" />
   </xsl:apply-templates>
</section>
```

3. Go to the bottom of the file and insert the following template directly before the closing `</xsl:stylesheet>` tag to display the list of each city name:

```
<xsl:template match="property">
   <xsl:value-of select="city" /> |
</xsl:template>
```

Figure 7-9 shows the revised code in the style sheet file.

Figure 7-9   Creating the city list template

```
<body>
   <div id="wrap">
      <header>
         <img src="brlogo.png" alt="Bowline Realty" />
      </header>

      <h1>New Listings</h1>

      <section id="city_list">
         |
         <xsl:apply-templates
         select="listings/property[not(city=preceding::property/city)]">

            <xsl:sort select="city" />
         </xsl:apply-templates>
      </section>

      <xsl:apply-templates select="listings/property" />

   </div>
</body>
```

applies the template to the first property listed for each city in the source document

```
   <xsl:template match="property">
      <xsl:value-of select="city" /> |
   </xsl:template>

</xsl:stylesheet>
```

displays the name of the city

4. Save your changes to the file, and regenerate the result document using your web browser, the Exchanger XML Editor, or another XSLT processor. Figure 7-10 shows the revised appearance of the properties document.

| Figure 7-10 | The city list |

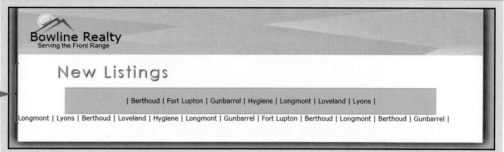

the same template is applied to every occurrence of the property element

Trouble? The list of city names may appear wrapped to a second line in some browsers.

The list of city names appears as expected, but what happened to the property descriptions? The problem is that the style sheet has two templates that apply to the property element. The first property template contains a table describing each property, and the second template, the one that you just created, displays the list of city names associated with those properties. When an XSLT processor encounters two templates with the same name, it uses the last one defined in the style sheet, which, in this case, is the template that displays the list of cities. You need to distinguish one template from the other.

Using the mode Attribute

When two templates can be applied to the same node set, you distinguish them by adding the following mode attribute within the <xsl:template> tag:

```
<xsl:template match="node set" mode="mode">
    styles
</xsl:template>
```

where *node set* is the node set in the source document, *mode* identifies the template, and *styles* is the XSLT code applied to that node set under the specified mode. For example, to indicate that a property template is used to display the list of cities within those properties, you can add the mode attribute to the template element, setting its value to cityList:

```
<xsl:template match="property" mode="cityList">
```

REFERENCE

Identifying Templates with the mode Attribute

- To mark the template's mode, use the following mode attribute:

```
<xsl:template match="node set" mode="mode">
   styles
</xsl:template>
```

where *node set* is the node set in the source document, *mode* is the name of the mode, and *styles* is the XSLT code applied to that node set under the specified mode.

- To apply a template of a specified mode, use the mode attribute in the apply-templates element:

```
<xsl:apply-templates select="node set" mode="mode" />
```

The mode attribute distinguishes this template from the other property template in Lisa's style sheet. To apply a template based on the value of the mode attribute, you include the mode's value in the apply-templates element as follows:

```
<xsl:apply-templates select="node set" mode="mode">
```

When an XSLT processor encounters this element, it applies only those templates that match both the node set and the mode name. For example, you can apply the cityList template using the following code:

```
<xsl:apply-templates
 select="listings/property[not(city=preceding::property/city)]"
 mode="cityList">
```

When an XSLT processor encounters this element, it applies the template for the property node set under the cityList mode. If no mode attribute is specified as in the following code:

```
<xsl:apply-templates select="listings/property" />
```

the processor applies the default template for the property element, which for Lisa's document displays the description of the property being sold.

To apply the mode attribute:

1. Return to the **listings.xsl** file in your editor.

2. Go to the root template, and add the following attribute to the apply-templates element that applies the template for the city list:

   `mode="cityList"`

3. Go to the template that creates the city list at the bottom of the style sheet, and add the following attribute to the template element:

   `mode="cityList"`

   Figure 7-11 shows the revised code for the style sheet.

Figure 7-11   **Setting the template mode**

```
<section id="city_list">
 |
  <xsl:apply-templates
   select="listings/property[not(city=preceding::property/city)]"
    mode="cityList">

    <xsl:sort select="city" />
  </xsl:apply-templates>
 </section>

<xsl:apply-templates select="listings/property" />



    <xsl:template match="property" mode="cityList">
       <xsl:value-of select="city" /> |
    </xsl:template>

</xsl:stylesheet>
```

> mode of the template to be applied to the node set

> template mode

4. Save your changes to the style sheet file, and regenerate the result document using your web browser or XSLT processor.

Figure 7-12 shows the revised result document with the cityList template displaying the list of city names and the default template displaying the property descriptions.

Figure 7-12   **The city list and the property description**

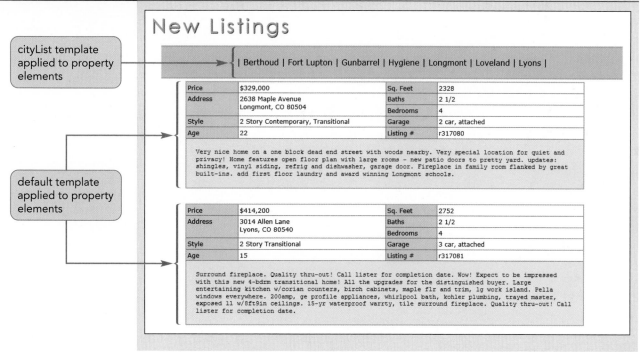

cityList template applied to property elements

default template applied to property elements

New Listings

| Berthoud | Fort Lupton | Gunbarrel | Hygiene | Longmont | Loveland | Lyons |

Price	$329,000	Sq. Feet	2328
Address	2638 Maple Avenue Longmont, CO 80504	Baths	2 1/2
		Bedrooms	4
Style	2 Story Contemporary, Transitional	Garage	2 car, attached
Age	22	Listing #	r317080

Very nice home on a one block dead end street with woods nearby. Very special location for quiet and privacy! Home features open floor plan with large rooms - new patio doors to pretty yard. updates: shingles, vinyl siding, refrig and dishwasher, garage door. Fireplace in family room flanked by great built-ins. add first floor laundry and award winning Longmont schools.

Price	$414,200	Sq. Feet	2752
Address	3014 Allen Lane Lyons, CO 80540	Baths	2 1/2
		Bedrooms	4
Style	2 Story Transitional	Garage	3 car, attached
Age	15	Listing #	r317081

Surround fireplace. Quality thru-out! Call lister for completion date. Wow! Expect to be impressed with this new 4-bdrm transitional home! All the upgrades for the distinguished buyer. Large entertaining kitchen w/corian counters, birch cabinets, maple flr and trim, lg work island. Pella windows everywhere. 200amp, ge profile appliances, whirlpool bath, kohler plumbing, trayed master, exposed ll w/8ft9in ceilings. 15-yr waterproof warrty, tile surround fireplace. Quality thru-out! Call lister for completion date.

Problem Solving: Understanding Template Priority

Because only one template can be processed with any node, the processor must choose between competing templates for the same node. Using the `mode` attribute is one way of explicitly assigning a template to a specific node; another way is by assigning a template priority.

The XSLT processor assigns a priority number to each template it encounters; templates assigned to the same node set that have a higher priority number are given precedence over templates that have lower-priority numbers. The default priority numbering uses the following rules:

- Templates with paths that match nodes based on their context in the source document, such as the location path `property/city`, have a priority number of +0.5. These templates have the greatest priority.
- Templates with paths that match nodes specifically by name, such as the location path `city`, have a priority number of 0.
- Built-in templates and templates with location paths that match a class of nodes, such as with the wildcard `*` character, have a priority number of –0.5. These templates have the lowest priority.

If two templates have the same priority number, the last one defined in the style sheet is the one applied by the processor. You can also use the `priority` attribute to define your own priority numbers. Thus, the following template:

```
<xsl:template match="property/city" priority="2">
    ...
</xsl:template>
```

has a priority of 2 and will be given precedence over any template with a lower priority. To avoid confusion when using multiple templates that could be assigned to the same node, you should always use either the `mode` attribute or the `priority` attribute.

You show the result document to Lisa, and she is pleased with your progress. Your next task is to group the individual property descriptions by city and to create links between the names in the city list and the property listings for each city. You'll work on this task in the next session.

REVIEW

Session 7.1 Quick Check

1. Describe the three parts of a step pattern.
2. What location path do you use to select the context node only? Provide the extended, not the abbreviated, expression.
3. Express the following location path as a step pattern in long form: /property/city.
4. Provide the abbreviated form of the following step pattern: child::property/attribute::rln.
5. When do you use the `mode` attribute as part of a template?
6. Provide the code to create a template for the property node that belongs to the propertyList mode.
7. Provide the code to apply the propertyList template from the previous question to the /listings/property node set.
8. Provide the priority value assigned to the location path: listings/property/city.

Session 7.2 Visual Overview:

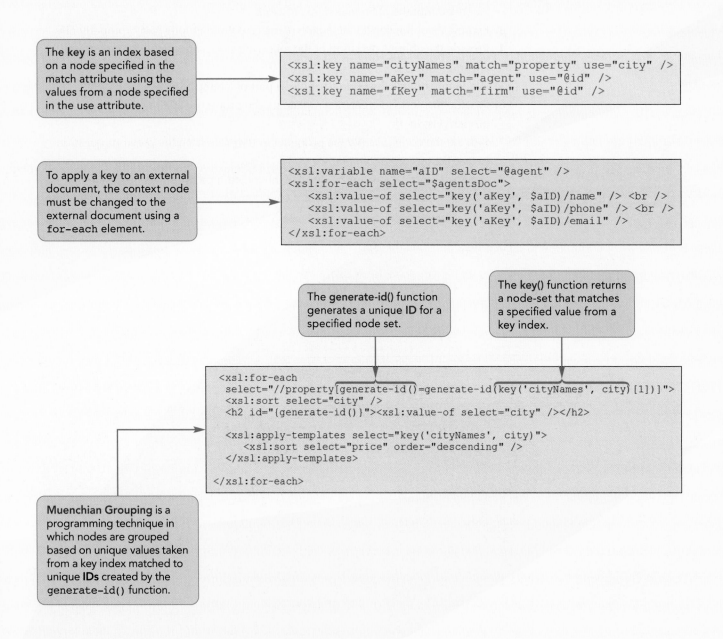

The **key** is an index based on a node specified in the match attribute using the values from a node specified in the use attribute.

```
<xsl:key name="cityNames" match="property" use="city" />
<xsl:key name="aKey" match="agent" use="@id" />
<xsl:key name="fKey" match="firm" use="@id" />
```

To apply a key to an external document, the context node must be changed to the external document using a for-each element.

```
<xsl:variable name="aID" select="@agent" />
<xsl:for-each select="$agentsDoc">
   <xsl:value-of select="key('aKey', $aID)/name" /> <br />
   <xsl:value-of select="key('aKey', $aID)/phone" /> <br />
   <xsl:value-of select="key('aKey', $aID)/email" />
</xsl:for-each>
```

The **generate-id()** function generates a unique **ID** for a specified node set.

The **key()** function returns a node-set that matches a specified value from a key index.

```
<xsl:for-each
  select="//property[generate-id()=generate-id(key('cityNames', city)[1])]">
 <xsl:sort select="city" />
 <h2 id="{generate-id()}"><xsl:value-of select="city" /></h2>

 <xsl:apply-templates select="key('cityNames', city)">
    <xsl:sort select="price" order="descending" />
 </xsl:apply-templates>

</xsl:for-each>
```

Muenchian Grouping is a programming technique in which nodes are grouped based on unique values taken from a key index matched to unique **IDs** created by the generate-id() function.

Muenchian Grouping and Keys

New Listings

| Berthoud (2) | Fort Lupton (1) | Gunbarrel (2) | Hygiene (1) | Longmont (3) | Loveland (1) | Lyons (1) |

Berthoud

Price	$461,500		Sq. Feet	3360
Address	9 Alston Court Berthoud, CO 80513		Baths	3
			Bedrooms	4

Great curb appeal in this 9 yr old transitional w/2 story entry, tile flr. Formal lr and dr w/12' ceilings. Beautiful oak cabinetry w/center island, wet bar and dinette.

Real Estate Agency	Agent
The Rawlings Company 678 Grimble Street Lyons, CO 80540	Allan Lee (303) 555-8900 adlee@example.com/rawlingscompany

Price	$405,200		Sq. Feet	2900
Address	505 Brandit Road Berthoud, CO 80513		Baths	2
			Bedrooms	4

A picture perfect home in a fantastic location. 4 bedrooms, formal dining and living room, a family room with wood burning fireplace and a lower level rec room.

Real Estate Agency	Agent
The Rawlings Company 678 Grimble Street Lyons, CO 80540	Lawrence Rao (414) 555-8580 lkrao@example.com/rawlingscompany

Fort Lupton

Price	$429,900		Sq. Feet	2770
Address	57 East Raulston Lane Fort Lupton, CO 80621		Baths	2 1/2
			Bedrooms	4

Wonderful 2 story colonial in super area. Homestead builder quality with custom cabinetry, oak trim, 6 panel doors, crown molding, elegant 2 story foyer.

Real Estate Agency	Agent
Toffer Realty 311 Allen Court Berthoud, CO 80513	Karen Fawkes (303) 555-3414 karen_fawkes@example.com/tofferrealty

Properties are grouped by city using Muenchian grouping.

Values retrieved from an external file using a key index.

Working with IDs

In the last session, you saw how to use step patterns to navigate through the contents of the source document to create a list of unique city names. While this process worked well for a small sample document consisting of 12 properties, it can become slow and cumbersome when applied to documents that might contain thousands of nodes. There are several techniques that you can use to search through the contents of your source document more efficiently. One of these involves the use of IDs.

As you learned in Tutorial 3, XML allows you to validate the contents of an XML document by creating a DTD (document type definition). One item you can declare in a DTD is the ID attribute, which provides a way to uniquely identify a particular item in the source document. Recall that the syntax for declaring the ID attribute is either

```
<!ATTLIST element attribute ID #REQUIRED>
```

or

```
<!ATTLIST element attribute ID #IMPLIED>
```

depending on whether the use of an ID is required (#REQUIRED) or optional (#IMPLIED). For example, every property listed in Lisa's document has an rln attribute, which stores that property's real estate listing number. If Lisa wants to declare the rln attribute as an ID and require every property element to have an rln attribute, she can create a DTD containing the following declaration:

```
<!ATTLIST property rln ID #REQUIRED>
```

A benefit of declaring an ID is that any XML processor that parses the document must verify that all ID values are unique, even if they are associated with different elements in the source document. Thus, if Lisa's document has two or more properties with the same rln, an XML processor will reject the document as invalid, providing a useful check for Lisa as she compiles real estate listings.

The process of ensuring unique ID values has an additional benefit: the XML processor creates an index that matches each element to a specific ID. You can search the contents of this index using the following XPath function:

```
id(value)
```

where value is the value of the ID. The id() function returns the element node whose attribute matches the ID value. For example, if the rln attribute is declared as an ID in a DTD for the listings.xml document, the expression

```
id("r317087")
```

returns the property whose listing number is r317087. This expression is identical to the following location path, which explicitly returns the property element whose listing number is r317087:

```
//property[@rln="r317087"]
```

While both expressions return the same node set, the expression using the id() function is more efficient because it takes advantage of an index that has already been set up by the processor. On the other hand, when the processor encounters the explicit reference used in the location path, it has to search every property element in the node tree for the element with the specified listing number. If a document contains thousands of properties, this would be a time-consuming process and, if that location path is repeated elsewhere in the style sheet, the processor repeats the search all over again because it does not permanently store the search results for use in other expressions.

An important point to remember about IDs is that all IDs belong to the same index, even if they are associated with different attributes. Thus, a source document containing the following two attribute declarations places both the firmID and agentID attributes within a single index:

```
<!ATTLIST firm firmID ID #REQUIRED>
<!ATTLIST agent agentID ID #REQUIRED>
```

The implication of this is that the following code is invalid because the ID value a2140 is not unique, even though it is the value for different attributes:

```
<firm firmID="a2140">
   <agent agentID="a2140" />
</firm>
```

Declaring and Finding an ID

- To declare an ID attribute in the source document's DTD, use either of the following expressions:

  ```
  <!ATTLIST element attribute ID #REQUIRED>
  ```

  or

  ```
  <!ATTLIST element attribute ID #IMPLIED>
  ```

  depending on whether use of the attribute is required (#REQUIRED) or optional (#IMPLIED).
- To reference the element node containing an ID attribute with the specified value, use the XPath function

  ```
  id(value)
  ```

  where *value* is the value of the ID attribute.

While the id() function is a more efficient tool than step patterns for searching through the contents of a source document, there are several limitations you need to consider:

- IDs can be associated only with attributes. An index cannot be created based on the values of an element or values of the children of an element. For example, Lisa cannot use the real estate listing number as an element in her source document if she also wants to use it as an ID.
- You must create a unique ID for each of the ID attributes, even if they are associated with different elements. This can be a time-consuming and difficult process for large documents.
- ID attributes must be valid XML names and, therefore, they cannot contain spaces or begin with numbers. Because of this requirement, traditional IDs, such as Social Security numbers or ISBNs, cannot be declared as ID attributes.

Another way of working with IDs is to generate them within your XSLT style sheet.

Generating an ID Value

The id() function returns a node set based on IDs defined in the document's DTD; but, with some style sheets, you will want to do the opposite—generate an ID that identifies a specific node or node set within the source document. To create such an ID, XPath provides the following generate-id() function:

```
generate-id(node set)
```

where *node set* is the node set for which you want to create an ID. If you omit a node set, the function is applied to the current context node. The `generate-id()` function returns an arbitrary text string starting with an alphanumeric character and followed by several more alphanumeric characters. The exact ID is generated by the XSLT processor and, depending on the processor, a different arbitrary alphanumeric string might be created for a given node set in each session in which the style sheet is accessed.

However, different node sets always have different IDs. Thus, if two node sets share the same generated ID, they must be the same node set. Therefore, one use of the `generate-id()` function is to determine whether two variables refer to the same node set. For example, if you designate one node set as `$n1` and the other as `$n2`, the following expression:

```
generate-id($n1) = generate-id($n2)
```

returns a value of `true` if the node set referenced by `$n1` is the same as the node set referenced by `$n2`.

REFERENCE

Generating an ID Value

- To generate an ID value for a node set, use the XPath expression:

  ```
  generate-id(node set)
  ```

  where *node set* is the node set for which you want to create an ID. If you omit a node set, the function is applied to the current context node.
- To compare whether two variables point to the same node set, use the expression:

  ```
  generate-id($n1) = generate-id($n2)
  ```

  where `$n1` is a variable that references the first node set and `$n2` references the second node set.

Indexes are one way of returning a node set based on a set of values. Another, and more flexible, way of achieving the same result is with a key.

Working with Keys

A key is an index that creates a node set based on the values of an attribute or child element. Keys can be thought of as generalized IDs, without their limitations. Unlike IDs, keys have the following characteristics:

- Keys are declared in the style sheet, not in the DTD of the source document.
- Keys have names as well as values, allowing the style sheet author to create multiple distinct keys rather than rely on a single index.
- Keys can be associated with node sets that contain attribute and element values.
- Keys are not limited to valid XML names and thus can be based on commonly used IDs, such as Social Security numbers.

As you'll see later in this tutorial, keys can also be used to group node sets in a way that is often more efficient than step patterns.

Creating a Key

To create a key, add the following `key` element at the top level of the style sheet as a child of the `stylesheet` element:

```
<xsl:key name="name" match="node set" use="expression" />
```

where *name* is the name of the key, *node set* is the set of nodes in the source document to which the key is applied, and *expression* is an XPath expression that indicates the values to be used in the key's index table. When an XSLT processor encounters a `key` element, it creates an index based on the unique values found within the key. Thus, keys create the same type of indexes that are created when IDs are declared in a DTD associated with the source document, except that with keys the index is generated by the style sheet.

For example, to create a key named listNumber based on each property's listing number, you add the following `key` element to the style sheet:

```
<xsl:key name="listNumber" match="//property" use="@rln" />
```

The listNumber key indexes all of the property elements in the source document based on the value of their rln attributes. Note that the expression in the `use` attribute is based on the context node provided by the `match` attribute and thus, in this example, the rln attribute is assumed to be an attribute of the property element.

Because keys are not limited to attributes, you can also create a key based on the value of a child element. If you wanted to create a cityNames key based on the city associated with each property, you would create the following `key` element:

```
<xsl:key name="cityNames" match="//property" use="city" />
```

In this code, the cityNames key indexes all of the property elements based on the value of the city element. The code for this key assumes that city is a child of the property element, which is true in the case of the listings.xml file.

You'll add the cityNames key to the listings.xsl file.

To create a key:

1. If you took a break after the previous session, make sure the **listings.xsl** file is open in your editor.

2. Insert the following code directly below the opening `<xsl:stylesheet>` tag:

   ```
   <xsl:key name="cityNames" match="property" use="city" />
   ```

   Figure 7-13 shows the code to create the cityNames key based on the unique names of the cities associated with all of the listed properties.

Figure 7-13   **Adding the cityNames key**

3. Save your changes to the file.

Now that you've defined a key and thereby created an index of all of the city names in the listings.xml file, you'll learn how to reference node sets based on the key.

Applying the `key()` Function

To reference a node set based on a key value you apply the following `key()` function:

```
key(name, value)
```

where *name* is the name of the key and *value* is the key's value. The `key()` function works the same as the `id()` function for IDs. For example, to use the listNumber key to return the property with the real estate listing r317087, you use the `key()` function

```
key("listNumber", "r317087")
```

which is equivalent to the location path

```
//property[@rln="r317087"]
```

As with the `id()` function, a processor using the `key()` function can search the index faster than it can search through the entire node tree. Unlike IDs, a key can point to more than one node because the key values are not required to be unique in the source document. Thus, the cityNames key defined previously can be used to return all property elements from a specified city. The expression

```
key("cityNames", "Longmont")
```

is equivalent to the location path

```
//property[city="Longmont"]
```

The `key()` function can also be used with a predicate to select a specific node from a node set. The following expression selects the first property element from the city of Longmont:

```
key("cityNames", "Longmont")[1]
```

Finally, the `key()` function can be nested within other XPath functions. The following expression uses a nested `key()` function to return the count of all property elements from the city of Longmont:

```
count(key("cityNames", "Longmont"))
```

The key value itself does not have to be entered explicitly; it can also be inserted as a reference to a node in the source document. The following template for the property element displays the name of the city in which the property resides, followed by the total count of properties listed within that city:

```
<xsl:template match="property">
   <xsl:value-of select="city" />:
   <xsl:value-of select="count(key('cityNames', city))" />
</xsl:template>
```

For example, if three properties are listed for the city of Longmont, this template will write the text "Longmont: 3" to the result document.

REFERENCE

Creating and Using Keys

- To create a key, use the key element:

  ```
  <xsl:key name="name" match="node set" use="expression" />
  ```

  where *name* is the name of the key, *node set* is the set of nodes in the source document to which the key is applied, and *expression* is an XPath expression that indicates the values to be used as part of the key index.
- To reference a node set based on a key value, use the key() function:

  ```
  key(name, value)
  ```

  where *name* is the name of the key and *value* is the key's value.

Lisa wants the city list at the top of the property report to include a count of the number of properties within each city. You decide to add this information with a key() function using the cityNames key you've already created.

To apply the key() function:

1. Go to the property template belonging to the cityList mode at the bottom of the style sheet in the listings.xsl file.

2. Directly before the | character, insert the following code, leaving a space before the | character:

   ```
   (<xsl:value-of select="count(key('cityNames', city))" />)
   ```

   Figure 7-14 shows application of the key() function to the template.

Figure 7-14   **Using the key() function**

```
<xsl:template match="property" mode="cityList">
   <xsl:value-of select="city" />
   (<xsl:value-of select="count(key('cityNames', city))" />) |
</xsl:template>

</xsl:stylesheet>
```

counts the number of cities matching the city specified in the cityNames key

3. Save your changes to the file, and regenerate the result document using your web browser or an XSLT processor. Figure 7-15 shows the revised city list with the count of properties displayed alongside the city name.

Figure 7-15 **Number of properties found within each city**

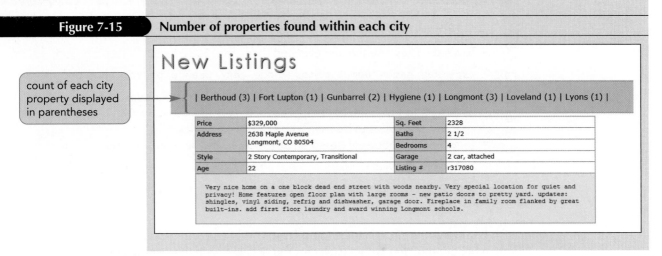

count of each city
property displayed
in parentheses

From the city list, Lisa can see at a glance that she has only one new listing from the cities of Fort Lupton, Hygiene, Loveland, and Lyons, but three new properties listed in the cities of Berthoud and Longmont. The city of Gunbarrel has two new listings.

Using Keys with External Documents

The `key()` function can also be used with data from external documents. Lisa has stored data on the agents and real estate firms that list the properties contained in her report. The information has been saved in the agents.xml and firms.xml files, and the structure of the two documents is shown in Figure 7-16.

Figure 7-16 **Structure of the agents.xml and firms.xml documents**

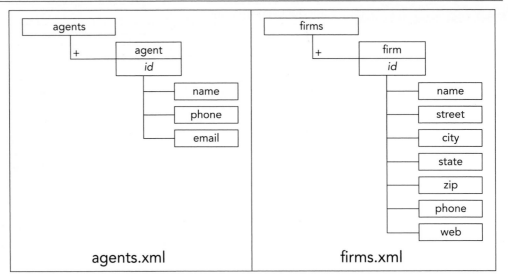

Lisa wants her report to include the name and contact information for the listing agents and firms associated with each new property. To access this data, you'll use the `document()` function introduced in the last tutorial to create global variables that reference the root nodes of the agents.xml and firms.xml documents.

To access the agents.xml and firms.xml files:

1. Return to the **listings.xsl** file in your editor.

2. Directly below the opening `<xsl:stylesheet>` tag, insert the following code to create the *agentsDoc* and *firmsDoc* variables, pulling the node sets from the agents.xml and firms.xml files:

```
<xsl:variable name="agentsDoc" select="document('agents.xml')" />
<xsl:variable name="firmsDoc" select="document('firms.xml')" />
```

3. Next, define keys based on the values of the `id` attribute for the agent and firm elements by entering the following code directly below the line that defines the cityNames key:

```
<xsl:key name="aKey" match="agent" use="@id" />
<xsl:key name="fKey" match="firm" use="@id" />
```

Figure 7-17 highlights the revised code in the file.

Figure 7-17   **Creating keys for external documents**

retrieves the document nodes from the agents.xml and firms.xml files

creates keys based on the id attributes of the agent and firm elements

```
<xsl:stylesheet version="1.0"
    xmlns:xsl="http://www.w3.org/1999/XSL/Transform">
  <xsl:variable name="agentsDoc" select="document('agents.xml')" />
  <xsl:variable name="firmsDoc" select="document('firms.xml')" />

  <xsl:key name="cityNames" match="property" use="city" />
  <xsl:key name="aKey" match="agent" use="@id" />
  <xsl:key name="fKey" match="firm" use="@id" />
```

Note that the `match` attributes of the aKey and fKey keys don't indicate in which document the agent and firm elements reside. This is because, in XPath 1.0, you cannot use the `document()` function or variables in a key element's `match` attribute.

Because you can't specify the document as part of the definition of the key, the processor will evaluate the `key()` function relative to the context node. Thus, if you want to use keys with an external document, you have to first change the context node so that it points to a location path within that document. In the case of the aKey and fKey keys, you have to change the context node to the root element of the agents.xml and firms.xml files, respectively. One way of doing this is by placing the `key()` function within a `for-each` element that selects the external document. For example, the following code uses the fKey key to display the name of firm f102 from the firms.xml file:

```
<xsl:for-each select="$firmsDoc">
   <xsl:value-of select="key('fKey', 'f102')/name" />
</xsl:for-each>
```

The `for-each` element in this example changes the context node to the root node of the firms.xml file. There's only one root node, so the processor executes this `for-each` element once, but that's okay because you're only retrieving information from that single document.

The challenge is to match up each property with its corresponding agency. As shown in Figure 7-5, the ID of the firm handling the property is stored in the firm attribute of the property element in the listings.xml document, but once you switch the context node to the root node of the firms.xml document, you no longer have access to that information. To get around this problem, you can store the value of the firm attribute in a variable before the for-each element is invoked. The revised code is

```
<xsl:variable name="fID" select="@firm" />
<xsl:for-each select="$firmsDoc">
   <xsl:value-of select="key('fKey', $fID)/name" />
</xsl:for-each>
```

so that the *fID* variable stores the ID of the firm and the key() function retrieves the name of the firm from the firms.xml file.

You'll use the for-each element with the key() function to retrieve the contact information from the firms.xml document and display that data in new table cells added to each property table.

To display data from the real estate firm:

1. Return to the **listings.xsl** file in your editor and scroll down to the property template.

2. Scroll down to the property template and, directly above the closing </table> tag, insert the following HTML code to create additional table rows and cells.

```
<tr>
   <th colspan="2">Real Estate Agency</th>
</tr>
<tr>
   <td colspan="2">
   </td>
</tr>
```

To access a key in an external file, you have to use the for-each element to change the context node.

3. Next, enter the following code within the second table cell to display the name and contact information of the firm:

```
<xsl:variable name="fID" select="@firm" />
<xsl:for-each select="$firmsDoc">
  <xsl:value-of select="key('fKey', $fID)/name" /> <br />
  <xsl:value-of select="key('fKey', $fID)/street" /> <br />
  <xsl:value-of select="key('fKey', $fID)/city" />,
  <xsl:value-of select="key('fKey', $fID)/state" />  
  <xsl:value-of select="key('fKey', $fID)/zip" /><br />
  <xsl:value-of select="key('fKey', $fID)/phone" /><br />
  <xsl:value-of select="key('fKey', $fID)/web" />
</xsl:for-each>
```

Figure 7-18 highlights the revised code in the file.

Figure 7-18   Retrieving the contact information for the firm

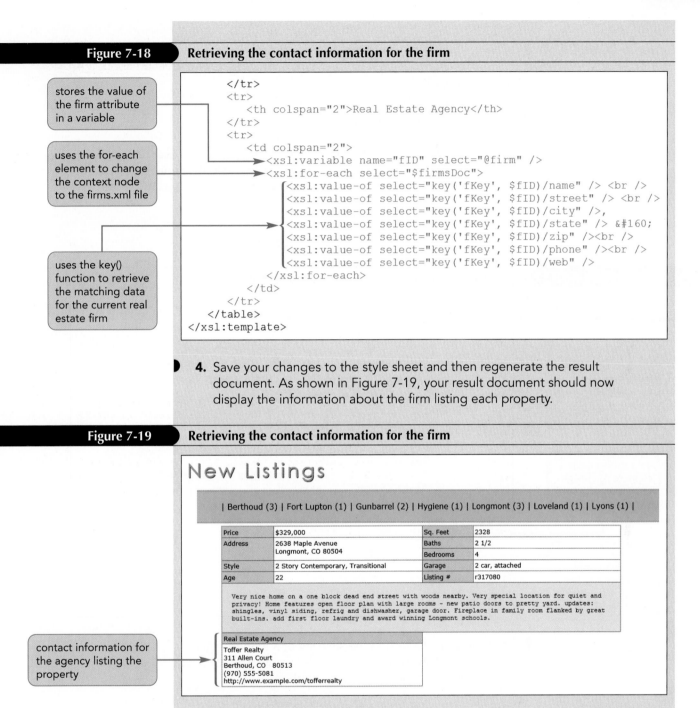

stores the value of the firm attribute in a variable

uses the for-each element to change the context node to the firms.xml file

uses the key() function to retrieve the matching data for the current real estate firm

```
    </tr>
    <tr>
      <th colspan="2">Real Estate Agency</th>
    </tr>
    <tr>
      <td colspan="2">
        <xsl:variable name="fID" select="@firm" />
        <xsl:for-each select="$firmsDoc">
          <xsl:value-of select="key('fKey', $fID)/name" /> <br />
          <xsl:value-of select="key('fKey', $fID)/street" /> <br />
          <xsl:value-of select="key('fKey', $fID)/city" />,
          <xsl:value-of select="key('fKey', $fID)/state" />  
          <xsl:value-of select="key('fKey', $fID)/zip" /><br />
          <xsl:value-of select="key('fKey', $fID)/phone" /><br />
          <xsl:value-of select="key('fKey', $fID)/web" />
        </xsl:for-each>
      </td>
    </tr>
  </table>
</xsl:template>
```

4. Save your changes to the style sheet and then regenerate the result document. As shown in Figure 7-19, your result document should now display the information about the firm listing each property.

Figure 7-19   Retrieving the contact information for the firm

New Listings

| Berthoud (3) | Fort Lupton (1) | Gunbarrel (2) | Hygiene (1) | Longmont (3) | Loveland (1) | Lyons (1) |

Price	$329,000	Sq. Feet	2328
Address	2638 Maple Avenue Longmont, CO 80504	Baths	2 1/2
		Bedrooms	4
Style	2 Story Contemporary, Transitional	Garage	2 car, attached
Age	22	Listing #	r317080

Very nice home on a one block dead end street with woods nearby. Very special location for quiet and privacy! Home features open floor plan with large rooms - new patio doors to pretty yard. updates: shingles, vinyl siding, refrig and dishwasher, garage door. Fireplace in family room flanked by great built-ins. add first floor laundry and award winning Longmont schools.

Real Estate Agency
Toffer Realty
311 Allen Court
Berthoud, CO   80513
(970) 555-5081
http://www.example.com/tofferrealty

contact information for the agency listing the property

You'll employ the same technique to display information about the agent handling the property.

To display data about the agent:

1. Return to the **listings.xsl** file in your editor and scroll down to the property template.

2. Directly below the line `<th colspan="2">Real Estate Agency</th>`, insert the following HTML code to create a table heading for the listing agent:

   `<th colspan="2">Agent</th>`

3. Scroll down to the bottom of the template and, directly before the last closing `</tr>` tag, insert the following table cell to display information about the listing agent:

```
<td colspan="2">
  <xsl:variable name="aID" select="@agent" />
  <xsl:for-each select="$agentsDoc">
    <xsl:value-of select="key('aKey', $aID)/name" /> <br />
    <xsl:value-of select="key('aKey', $aID)/phone" /> <br />
    <xsl:value-of select="key('aKey', $aID)/email" />
  </xsl:for-each>
</td>
```

Figure 7-20 highlights the revised code in the file.

Figure 7-20 | **Retrieving the contact information for the agent**

stores the value of the agent attribute in a variable

uses the for-each element to change the context node to the agents.xml file

uses the key() function to retrieve the matching data for the real estate agent

```
<tr>
   <th colspan="2">Real Estate Agency</th>
   <th colspan="2">Agent</th>
</tr>
<tr>
   <td colspan="2">
      <xsl:variable name="fID" select="@firm" />
      <xsl:for-each select="$firmsDoc">
         <xsl:value-of select="key('fKey', $fID)/name" /> <br />
         <xsl:value-of select="key('fKey', $fID)/street" /> <br />
         <xsl:value-of select="key('fKey', $fID)/city" />,
         <xsl:value-of select="key('fKey', $fID)/state" />  
         <xsl:value-of select="key('fKey', $fID)/zip" /><br />
         <xsl:value-of select="key('fKey', $fID)/phone" /><br />
         <xsl:value-of select="key('fKey', $fID)/web" />
      </xsl:for-each>
   </td>
   <td colspan="2">
      <xsl:variable name="aID" select="@agent" />
      <xsl:for-each select="$agentsDoc">
         <xsl:value-of select="key('aKey', $aID)/name" /> <br />
         <xsl:value-of select="key('aKey', $aID)/phone" /> <br />
         <xsl:value-of select="key('aKey', $aID)/email" />
      </xsl:for-each>
   </td>
</tr>
```

4. Save your changes to the style sheet and then regenerate the result document. As shown in Figure 7-21, contact information for the listing agent is included in the property description.

Figure 7-21	Retrieving the contact information for the agent

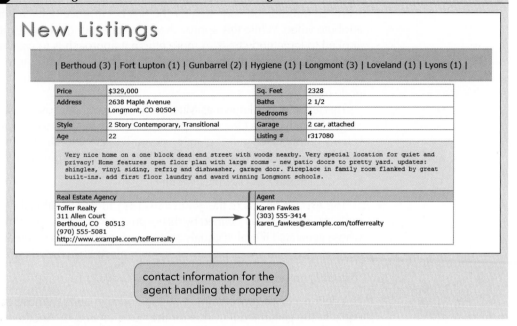

contact information for the
agent handling the property

Lisa is pleased with the information that the report now provides about the property, the listing agency, and the agent handling the property. Next, you'll explore how to group the information in this real estate report by city.

Using Keys in XPath 2.0

XPath 2.0 modified the syntax of the `key()` function to allow keys to be associated with specific nodes and documents. The revised syntax of the `key()` function is

```
key(name, value, node)
```

where *name* is the key name, *value* is the value to be searched, and *node* is an optional parameter that specifies the node tree to be searched. For example, the following expression searches the cityNames key for properties from the city of Lyons, but it limits the search to only the first 50 property elements:

```
key('cityNames', 'Lyons', //property[position() <= 50])
```

The revised `key()` function also makes it much easier to search external documents without having to use a `for-each` element to change the context node. Thus, the following expression:

```
key('fKey', 'f102', document('firms.xml'))
```

returns a node set using the fKey key with a search value of 'f102', searching the contents of the firms.xml file starting from the root node. Note that XPath 2.0 is not supported by all XSLT processors, so you need to confirm your processor's support for XPath 2.0 before using the `key()` function in this way.

Organizing Nodes with Muenchian Grouping

In the last session, you created groups of node sets by using a step pattern that searched through the node tree for the first occurrence of each unique element or attribute value. While this approach works for small documents, it is slow when applied to large node trees. A more efficient approach is to use the `generate-id()` and `key()` functions to create indexes of element and attribute values that the processor can search in much less time than is required when searching the entire node tree.

This technique is known as Muenchian grouping because it was first formulated by Steve Muench of the Oracle Corporation. The expression used in Muenchian grouping is fairly complicated at first glance, so you'll begin with the basics and build up to the final expression. You'll start with the following XPath expression:

```
node1[generate-id()=IDvalue]
```

This expression places the `generate-id()` function within the predicate for the *node1* node set. The node set defined by this expression consists only of those nodes in *node1* whose generated ID value equals *IDvalue*. Though you can't predict what ID value will be generated by an XSLT processor, if you replace *IDvalue* in the expression with

```
node1[generate-id()=generate-id(node2)]
```

you define a node set containing all the nodes in *node1* whose generated ID value is equal to the generated ID value for the node set *node2*. Another way to think about this is the node set defined by this expression consists of the intersection of *node1* and *node2*, containing only the nodes in *node1* that are also present in *node2*. For example, the expression

```
property[generate-id()=generate-id(//property[city="Berthoud"])]
```

returns a node set of all the property elements whose generated ID equals the generated ID of the Berthoud properties. This is in essence the node set of all property elements from the city of Berthoud (see Figure 7-22).

Figure 7-22   **Selecting nodes with the generate-id() function**

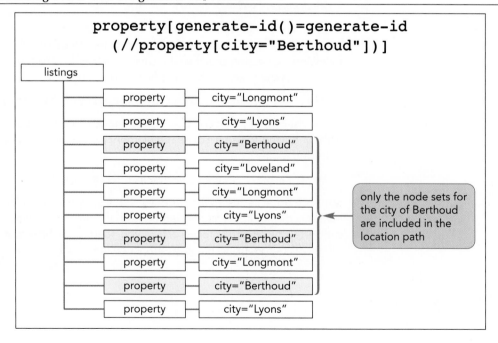

However, for a large source document, it is more efficient to define *node2* using keys instead of a predicate expression. You've already created the cityNames key for the list of cities, so the node set for *node2* can be defined using the XPath function `key("cityNames", "Berthoud")`, resulting in the following expression:

```
property[generate-id()=generate-id(key("cityNames","Berthoud"))]
```

Figure 7-23 shows the result of the path expression that selects all of the Berthoud properties from the node set.

Figure 7-23   **Selecting nodes with the generate-id() and key() functions**

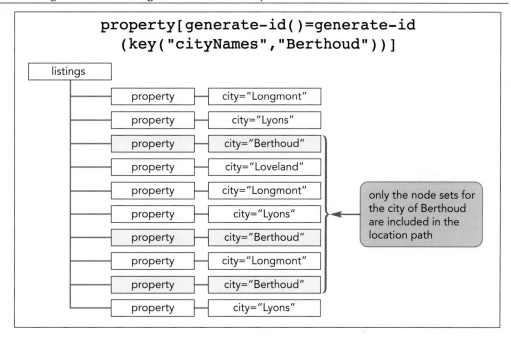

At this point, your node set still selects all the Berthoud properties, but you can limit *node2* to only the first property from Berthoud by adding a predicate containing the node number. Thus, you change

```
key("cityNames", "Berthoud")
```

to

```
key("cityNames", "Berthoud")[1]
```

and the new expression becomes

```
property[generate-id()=generate-id(key("cityNames","Berthoud")[1])]
```

creating a node set that contains only the first Berthoud property (see Figure 7-24).

Figure 7-24   Selecting the first Berthoud property

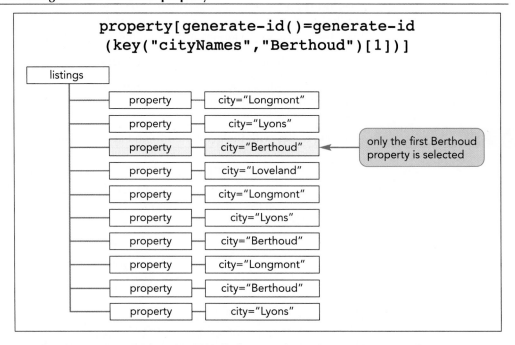

So far, this may seem like a lot of work for a node set that can be created using a step pattern. However, the final step in Muenchian grouping is to apply this expression to all of the cities in the source document—not just Berthoud. To accomplish this, you replace Berthoud with the city element itself:

```
property[generate-id()=generate-id(key("cityNames",city)[1])]
```

This complete expression is the Muenchian grouping that returns a node set consisting of the unique values of the city element for each property element in the node tree (see Figure 7-25). This is the same result you obtained in the last session using step patterns (see Figure 7-8). The advantage, though, is that for larger node trees this expression is much more efficient than the step pattern.

Figure 7-25   Using Muenchian Grouping to select the first property listed for each city

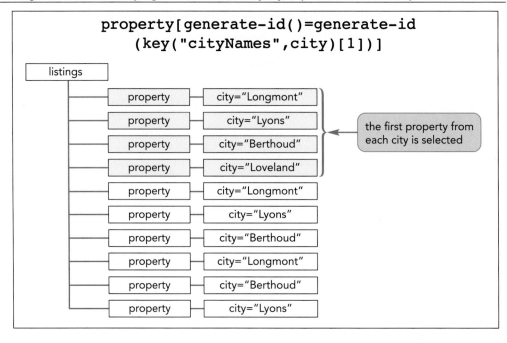

Employing Muenchian Grouping

- First, create a key for the element or attribute that you want to group using the `key` element

  ```
  <xsl:key name="name" match="node set" use="expression" />
  ```

  where *name* is the name of the key, *node set* is the node set that you want to group, and *expression* is an XPath expression that references the element or attribute on which to group.
- Next, add the following expression to the select attribute of a `for-each` or an `apply-templates` element:

  ```
  node set[generate-id()=generate-id(key(name,expression)[1])]
  ```

  where *node set*, *name*, and *expression* are the same values and node sets used in creating the key. This expression returns the first occurrence of each node in the node set for the index defined in the key.
- Finally, within the `for-each or apply-templates` element, you can reference the group value using

  ```
  expression
  ```

  where *expression* is the element or attribute used to group the node set.

Now that you have seen how to use Muenchian grouping to group the different property elements by city, you'll apply that grouping to the result document so that the property listing is organized by city. You'll display the properties from each city using a `for-each` element sorted alphabetically by city with the city name displayed using an `<h2>` heading tag. The complete code for the `for-each` element is

```
<xsl:for-each
 select="//property[generate-id()=generate-id(key('cityNames',
city)[1])]">
    <xsl:sort select="city" />
    <h2><xsl:value-of select="city" /></h2>
</xsl:for-each>
```

You'll add this code to the listings.xsl style sheet.

To apply Muenchian grouping:

1. Return to the **listings.xsl** file in your editor.
2. Go to the root template and, directly above the closing `</div>` tag, delete the statement:

   ```
   <xsl:apply-templates select="listings/property" />
   ```

3. Replace the deleted line with the following for-each loop:

   ```
   <xsl:for-each
    select="//property[generate-id()=generate-id(key('cityNames',
   city)[1])]">
       <xsl:sort select="city" />
       <h2><xsl:value-of select="city" /></h2>
   </xsl:for-each>
   ```

   Figure 7-26 shows the code to apply Muenchian grouping to the list of properties.

Figure 7-26 | **Applying the h2 heading to each city name**

generates output for
each unique city name

```
        <xsl:sort select="city" />
    </xsl:apply-templates>
    </section>

    <xsl:for-each
    select="//property[generate-id()=generate-id(key('cityNames', city)[1])]">
    <xsl:sort select="city" />
    <h2><xsl:value-of select="city" /></h2>
    </xsl:for-each>
    </div>
</body>
```

displays the name of each
city as an h2 heading

▶ **4.** Save your changes to the file, and regenerate the result document in your web browser or XSLT processor. Figure 7-27 shows the current state of the property report with the different city name headings.

Figure 7-27 | **City name headings**

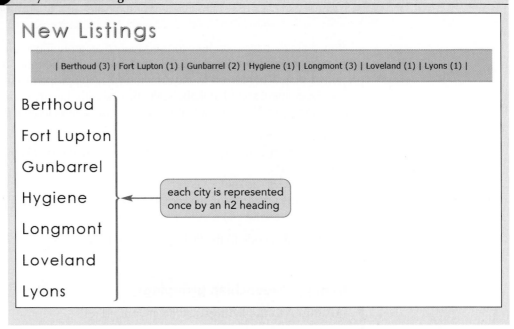

New Listings

| Berthoud (3) | Fort Lupton (1) | Gunbarrel (2) | Hygiene (1) | Longmont (3) | Loveland (1) | Lyons (1) |

Berthoud

Fort Lupton

Gunbarrel

Hygiene

Longmont

Loveland

Lyons

each city is represented
once by an h2 heading

Next, you display the property descriptions from each city, sorted in descending order by price. Because the property descriptions have already been created in the property template, you only need to apply that template within the `for-each` element. The code to apply the property template is

```
<xsl:apply-templates select="key('cityNames', city)">
    <xsl:sort select="price" order="descending" />
</xsl:apply-templates>
```

Note that this code uses the cityNames key to include only those properties from a selected city. Add this code to the `for-each` element you created in the last set of steps.

To display the property descriptions within each city:

1. Return to the **listings.xsl** in your editor.

2. Within the for-each element in the root template, insert the following code below the h2 heading:

```
<xsl:apply-templates select="key('cityNames', city)">
   <xsl:sort select="price" order="descending" />
</xsl:apply-templates>
```

Figure 7-28 highlights the code to apply the template for each property within each city.

Figure 7-28	Applying the property template within each city group

```
         <xsl:for-each
          select="//property[generate-id()=generate-id(key('cityNames', city)[1])]">
          <xsl:sort select="city" />
          <h2><xsl:value-of select="city" /></h2>

         {<xsl:apply-templates select="key('cityNames', city)">
             <xsl:sort select="price" order="descending" />
          {</xsl:apply-templates>

          </xsl:for-each>
        </div>
   </body>
```

applies a template to display information on each property within the currently selected city

3. Save your changes to the style sheet, and regenerate the result document. Figure 7-29 shows the property reports nested within each city and sorted in descending order of price. Verify that your property report is organized in the same way.

Figure 7-29   **Property report grouped by city**

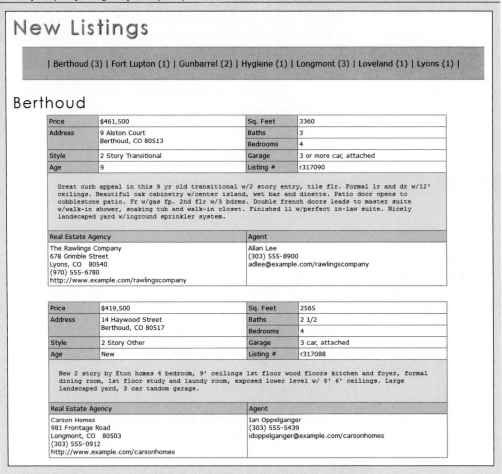

Muenchian grouping can appear daunting at first, so take some time to examine the code you've just entered to understand how the different city groups and property descriptions within each city are generated.

Grouping in XSLT 2.0

Grouping nodes, a difficult and cumbersome task in XSLT 1.0, is made much easier in XSLT 2.0 with the introduction of the following `for-each-group` element:

```
<xsl:for-each-group select="expression" group-by="expression">
</xsl:for-each-group>
```

where the `select` attribute specifies the sequence or node set that will be grouped and the `group-by` attribute specifies the value by which to group the selected items. For example, the following code groups the values of the `property` element by the value of the city element:

```
<xsl:for-each-group select="listings/property" group-by="city">
<xsl:for-each-group>
```

The `for-each-group` element acts like the `for-each` element except that you specify styles and commands to each `for-each-group` element. When using the `for-each-group` element, the current group being examined is referenced using the XPath 2.0 `current-group()` function, while the value associated with that group is returned using the XPath 2.0 `current-group-key()` function. The following code displays the value of each city name as an h2 heading and then applies a template to the property elements within each city group, replacing what was done previously using Muenchian grouping under an XSLT 1.0 processor:

```
<xsl:for-each-group select="listings/property" group-by="city">
   <h2><xsl:value-of select="current-group-key()" /></h2>
   <xsl:apply-templates select="current-group()" />
</xsl:for-each-group>
```

As with the `for-each` element, you can include the `sort` element within the `for-each-group` element to sort your groups in ascending or descending order. You'll learn more about grouping nodes under XSLT 2.0 in Tutorial 8.

Lisa likes the work you've done in grouping the property descriptions by city. To complete the report, she wants you to create links between the names in the city list at the top of the report and the section of the report that lists all of the new properties for sale within that city.

Creating Links with Generated IDs

You can use the `generate-id()` function to create links for specific locations within a web page. In HTML, these links are created using the `<a>` tag along with an ID attribute in the target of the link. The basic syntax is

```
<a href="#id">linked text</a>
...
<elem id="id">target of link</elem>
```

where *id* identifies the location of the target within the web page, *linked text* is the text of the link, *elem* is the HTML element that acts as the link's target, and *target of link* is the content of the link's target. If the source document contains ID attributes, you can use the values of those attributes as link targets. However, if there are no appropriate link targets, you can generate your own IDs using the `generate-id()` function as in the following sample code:

```
<a href="#{generate-id(node)}">linked text</a>
...
<elem id="{generate-id(node)}">target of link</elem>
```

where *node* is a node in the source document that uniquely identifies the target of the link. The only requirement is that the node used in the link be the same as the node used in the link's target. For example, an XSLT processor might generate the following HTML code to create links between a city name and the h2 heading of that city:

```
<a href="#AE1804Z">Cutler</a>
...
<h2 id="AE1804Z">Cutler</h2>
```

Note that the ID values are random text strings generated by the XSLT processor and might not have the same value the next time the page is generated. For this reason, generated IDs are useful for hypertext links within a single page but not when the link has to reference an external page or website.

REFERENCE

Creating Links and Targets

- To generate ID values for internal targets and links, use the `generate-id()` function as follows:

```
<a href="#{generate-id(node)}">linked text</a>
...
<elem id="{generate-id(node)}">target of link</elem>
```

where *node* is a node in the source document, *linked text* is the text of the link, *elem* is an HTML element that acts as the link's target, and *target of link* is the content of the link's target.

You'll use the `generate-id()` function to generate an internal link between the city names listed at the top of the page and the h2 headings that mark each city group in Lisa's report.

To create the links:

1. Return to **listings.xsl** in your editor.

2. Go to the property template belonging to the cityList mode at the bottom of the file and, directly before the tag `<xsl:value-of select="city" />`, insert the following tag to change the city text to a hypertext link using a generated ID value for the link target:

   ```
   <a href="#{generate-id()}">
   ```

3. Add a closing `</a>` directly after the `value-of` element.

   Figure 7-30 shows the revised code in the style sheet.

Figure 7-30	Generating an id for a hypertext link

```
<xsl:template match="property" mode="cityList">
   <a href="#{generate-id()}">
   <xsl:value-of select="city" />
   </a>
   (<xsl:value-of select="count(key('cityNames', city))" /> |
</xsl:template>
```

4. Go up to the root template and, within the opening `<h2>` tag that displays the city name, insert the following attribute to mark these h2 headings as targets of the hypertext links:

```
id="{generate-id()}"
```

Figure 7-31 highlights the newly added attribute in the h2 heading.

Figure 7-31 | **Generating an id for the target of a hypertext link**

```
<xsl:for-each
 select="//property[generate-id()=generate-id(key('cityNames', city)[1])]">
<xsl:sort select="city" />
<h2 id="{generate-id()}"><xsl:value-of select="city" /></h2>
```

5. Save your changes to **listings.xsl**, and regenerate the result document. As shown in Figure 7-32, each name in the city list should now be underlined, indicating that it acts as a link within the report.

Figure 7-32 | **Hypertext links in the city list**

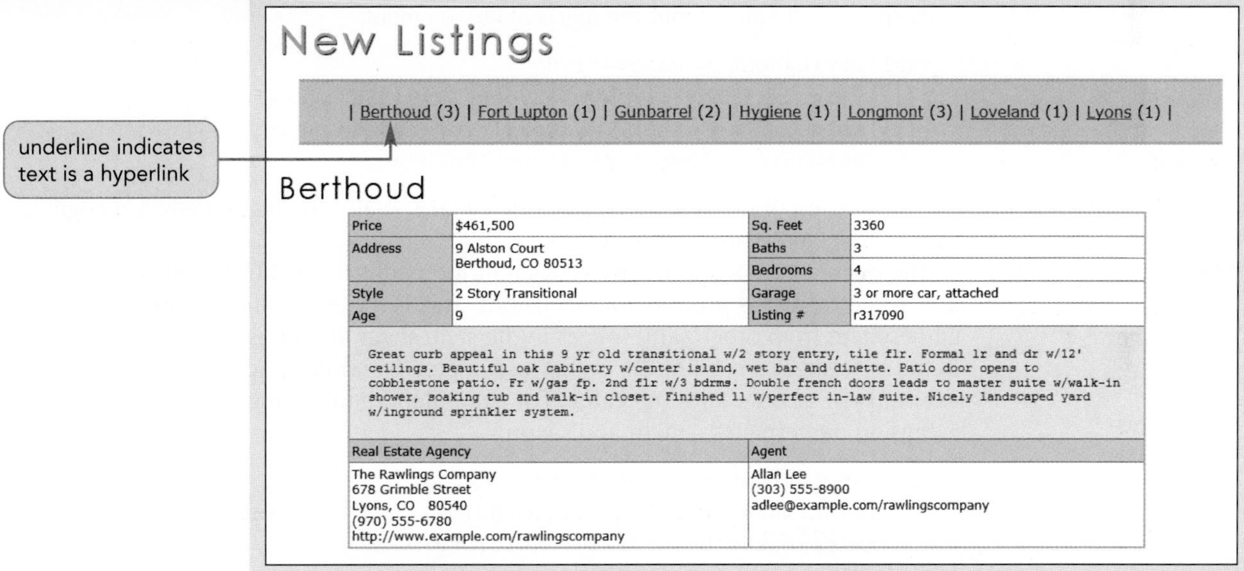

underline indicates text is a hyperlink

6. Click each of the links in the city list, and verify that the web browser jumps to the section of the report describing the new listings within that city.

You are finished with Lisa's project and you can close any open files or applications now.

Introducing Extension Functions

TIP

Before using any XSLT extension, check the documentation for your XSLT processor to ensure that the extension is supported.

There are many ways of going beyond the elements, attributes, and functions provided with the XSLT 1.0 language. One option is to create your style sheets using XSLT 2.0, which includes more robust tools for doing calculations, managing text strings, and generating output. You have already been introduced to some XSLT 2.0 features and you will explore the language in more detail in the next tutorial. Another option to enhance your style sheets is with extensions to the XSLT and XPath languages. Many XSLT processors support the following extensions:

- **Extension functions** that extend the list of functions available to XPath and XSLT expressions
- **Extension elements** that extend the list of elements that can be used in an XSLT style sheet
- **Extension attributes** that extend the list of attributes associated with XSLT elements
- **Extension attribute values** that extend the data types associated with XSLT attributes

A community of XSLT developers created a standard collection of extension elements and extension functions called **EXSLT**. Many XSLT processors support the EXSLT standard, allowing for greater flexibility in designing XSLT style sheets. You'll explore a few features of EXSLT now.

Defining the Extension Namespace

The first step in using extensions is to define an extension's namespace within the `stylesheet` element. Different extensions use different namespaces, so you must refer to the extension's documentation to determine how the extension should be applied. For example, the math functions provided by EXSLT are associated with the namespace www.exslt.org/math. To define this extension in the style sheet, you insert the following namespace declarations into the `stylesheet` element:

```
<xsl:stylesheet version="1.0"
    xmlns:xsl="http://www.w3.org/1999/XSL/Transform"
    xmlns:math="http://www.exslt.org/math"
    extension-element-prefixes="math">
```

Any function or element in the style sheet that contains the math prefix is recognized by the processor as an EXSLT extension.

The `extension-element-prefixes` attribute tells the XSLT processor which prefixes to regard as prefixes for extensions. This is a way to differentiate extension namespaces from other namespaces in the style sheet. If you use several extensions in the style sheet, list all of the prefixes separated by white space in the `extension-element-prefixes` attribute value. For example, the following code references two extension namespaces—math and saxon:

```
<xsl:stylesheet version="1.0"
    xmlns:xsl="http://www.w3.org/1999/XSL/Transform"
    xmlns:math="http://www.exslt.org/math"
    xmlns:saxon="http://icl.com/saxon"
    extension-element-prefixes="math saxon">
```

Using an Extension Function

Once a prefix for an extension has been defined, you can use the extension function or extension element in your style sheet, assuming that your processor supports the extension. Figure 7-33 describes some of the mathematical functions supported by EXSLT.

Figure 7-33   **Math extension functions in EXSLT**

EXSLT Function	Description
math.abs(*number*)	absolute value of *number*
math.cos(*number*)	cosine of *number*
math.highest(*node-set*)	nodes with the highest value in *node-set*
math.lowest(*node-set*)	nodes with the lowest value in *node-set*
math.max(*node-set*)	maximum value from *node-set*
math.min(*node-set*)	minimum value from *node-set*
math.power(*base, number*)	value of *base* raised to the *number* power
math.random()	random number between 0 and 1
math.sin(*number*)	sine of *number*
math.sqrt(*number*)	square root of *number*
math.tan(*number*)	tangent of *number*

For example, there is no function in XSLT 1.0 to calculate minimum values; however, under the EXSLT math extension, you can apply the following `math.min()` function to perform that calculation:

```
<xsl:value-of select="math.min(stores/expenses)" />
```

In this example, the processor will return the minimum value from the expenses element in the stores/expenses node set. To do the same calculation in XSLT 1.0 and XPath 1.0, you would have to use a recursive template.

Writing an Extension Function

In addition to using existing extension functions, you can create your own. In MSXML, the processor used by Internet Explorer, you can write an extension in any scripting language supported by the HTML script element. These include both JavaScript and VBScript.

Extension functions for the MSXML processor are created by adding the following `script` element at the top of the style sheet:

```
<msxsl:script language="language" implements-prefix="prefix">
    script commands
</msxsl:script>
```

where *language* is the language of the script, *prefix* is the namespace prefix you want to assign to the extension functions you create, and the phrase *script commands* refers to the commands needed to create the extension function. Note that the `<script>` tag is placed in the MSXSL namespace using the msxsl namespace prefix. The prefix should be associated with the namespace urn:schemas-microsoft-com:xslt in the `stylesheet` element of the XSLT file.

For example, XPath does not provide a function to generate random numbers, but JavaScript does with its `Math.random()` function. Thus, if you wanted to create an extension function to generate random numbers with the MSXML processor, you could take advantage of that function using the following code:

TIP

You can also use the `min()` function in XSLT 2.0 and XPath 2.0 to calculate the minimum value from a node set and the `max()` function to calculate maximum values.

```
<xsl:stylesheet version="1.0"
    xmlns:xsl="http://www.w3.org/1999/XSL/Transform"
    xmlns:jsext="http://javascript-extensions"
    xmlns:msxsl="urn:schemas-microsoft-com:xslt"
    extension-element-prefixes="jsext msxsl">

<msxsl:script implements-prefix="jsext" language="javascript">
    function random() {
        return Math.random();
    }
</msxsl:script>
```

To run the extension function, you call the function within the value-of element as follows:

```
<xsl:value-of select="jsext:random()" />
```

The result document would display a random number between 0 and 1. This specific technique works only with the MSXML processor. If you are using another processor, refer to the processor's documentation to learn how to create the extension functions that it recognizes.

Applying Extension Elements and Attributes

In addition to extension functions, you can also use extension elements and attributes in your style sheets. Similar to extension functions, extension elements and attributes must be associated with namespaces. You must also identify which namespaces are extension namespaces using the extension-element-prefixes attribute in the stylesheet element. Using the extension-element-prefixes attribute is critical because it tells XSLT processors how to differentiate extension elements and attributes from literal result elements.

Changing a Variable's Value

XSLT's inability to change a variable's value can be frustrating. You can get around this limitation by using an extension supported by the Saxon XSLT processor that allows variable values to be changed on the fly. To reference the saxon extension namespace, you insert the following attributes into the stylesheet element:

```
<xsl:stylesheet version="1.0"
    xmlns:xsl="http://www.w3.org/1999/XSL/Transform"
    xmlns:saxon="http://ic1.com/saxon"
    extension-element-prefixes="saxon">
```

To create a variable that can be assigned a value after it is declared, you enter the following extension attribute to XSLT's variable element:

```
<xsl:variable name="name" saxon:assignable="yes" />
```

where *name* is the name of the variable and the assignable attribute tells processors that this variable can be assigned a different value later in the style sheet. To assign a new value to the variable, use the following assign extension:

```
<saxon:assign name="name" select="expression" />
```

where *expression* is a new value assigned to the variable. For example, the following code creates a variable named *CVar* that stores a customer's ID, which in this case is C1:

```
<xsl:variable name="CVar" saxon:assignable="yes" select="C1" />
```

Later in the style sheet, the following code changes the value of the *CVar* variable from C1 to B2 using the statement:

```
<saxon:assign name="CVar" select="B2" />
```

Creating a Loop

If you find it difficult to work with recursive templates, you can instead create loops in Saxon using the following `while` extension:

```
<saxon:while test="condition">
    commands
</saxon:while>
```

where `condition` is an expression that must be true for the loop to continue and run the `commands` contained within the `while` element. By combining the Saxon `assign` and `while` extensions, you can create the following loop to update the value of the *i* variable:

```
<xsl:variable name="i" select="1" saxon:assignable="yes" />
<saxon:while test="$i &lt;= 3">
    The value of i is <xsl:value-of select="$i" />
    <saxon:assign name="i" select="$i+1" />
</saxon:while>
```

The result document would display the text:

```
The value of i is 1
The value of i is 2
The value of i is 3
```

Testing Function Availability

▶ Because keeping track of all of the extensions supported by a given XSLT processor is an arduous task, you can have your processor test whether it supports a particular extension function, using the following `function-available()` function:

```
function-available("prefix:function")
```

TIP

You can often find named templates on the web to duplicate the capabilities of EXSLT extension functions. Many such templates are not free and must be purchased before they can be used.

where `prefix` is the namespace prefix of the extension function and `function` is the function name. The `function-available()` function returns the Boolean value `true` if it supports the function and `false` if it does not. For example, the following code uses `function-available()` to test whether the `math.min()` function is supported by the XSLT processor. If it isn't, the processor writes a text string indicating that the extension function is required:

```
<xsl:choose>
    <xsl:when test="function-available('math.min')">
        <xsl:value-of select="math.min(values/item)" />
    </xsl:when>
    <xsl:otherwise>
        <xsl:value-of select="Extension function required." />
    </xsl:otherwise>
</xsl:choose>
```

Testing Element Availability

As with extension functions, you can test whether a processor supports a particular extension element or attribute, using the following `element-available()` function:

```
element-available("extension")
```

where *extension* is the name of the extension element or attribute. For example, the following code tests whether a processor supports Saxon's `while` extension before attempting to run a program loop:

```
<xsl:if test="element-available("saxon.while")">
   <xsl:variable name="i" select="1" saxon:assignable="yes" />|
   <saxon:while test="$i &lt;= 3">
      The value of i is <xsl:value-of select="$i"/>
      <saxon:assign name="i" select="$i+1"/>
   </saxon:while>
</xsl:if>
```

If the processor does not support the `while` extension, it skips the program loop and does not attempt to run the code enclosed within the `if` element.

You can support processors that don't recognize an extension element or attribute by using the `fallback` element. When a processor encounters an extension element it doesn't recognize, it searches inside of that element for the `fallback` element. If it finds it, it processes the code contained within that element, rather than reporting an error. The following code uses the `fallback` element to provide an alternate set of instructions for processors that do not support Saxon's `while` extension:

```
<xsl:variable name="i" select="1" saxon:assignable="yes" />
<saxon:while test="$i &lt;= 3">
   The value of i is <xsl:value-of select="$i"/>
   <saxon:assign name="i" select="$i+1"/>
   <xsl:fallback>
      <xsl:value-of select="This style sheet requires Saxon." />
   </xsl:fallback>
</saxon:while>
```

Under Saxon, the while loop is run; otherwise, other processors run the fallback code and display the text "This style sheet requires Saxon."

PROSKILLS

Problem Solving: Debugging with the *message* Element

The first task in debugging a style sheet is determining the location of the error. One useful tool for this task is the following XSLT 1.0 `message` element, which can be used to send messages about errors in the style sheet code:

```
<xsl:message select="expression" terminate="yes|no">
    message
</xsl:message>
```

where `select` is an optional XSLT 2.0 attribute used to produce the content of the message and *message* is the text of the message that will be sent to the XSLT processor. The `terminate` attribute specifies whether the processor should halt the style sheet; the default is no. For example, the following command tests whether the value of the `count(property/city)` expression returns the text string "NaN"; if it does, the message "Invalid City Count" is sent to the XSLT processor and the processor stops processing the style sheet at this point:

```
<xsl:if test="string(count(property/city))='NaN'">
    <xsl:message terminate="yes">
        <xsl:text>Invalid City Count</xsl:text>
    <xsl:message>
</xsl:if>
```

There is nothing in the XSLT standard that specifies how the message will be handled by the processor. Some processors will display a dialog box with the error message, other processors will write the message to the result document. You have to test your code against your specific process to see how it handles this element.

Lisa is pleased with your work on the real estate property report. She has a few other reports that she will want your help in creating that will involve working with XSLT's and XPath's step patterns and grouping functions. You'll examine these reports in the review assignment.

REVIEW

Session 7.2 Quick Check

1. What XPath expression would you use to select nodes whose agentID attribute equals "f102"? Assume that the agentID attribute has been defined in the document's DTD.

2. What is a key? How does a key differ from an ID?

3. The agent element has a single child element named `agentName` that stores the name of the real estate agent. What code would you use to create a key named agentKey applied to the agent element with key values based on agentName?

4. What code would you use to create a node set using agentKey for agents named "Howard"?

5. What XPath expression would you enter to generate an ID based on the agentName element? Assume that agent is the context node.

6. Using Muenchian grouping, what expression would you use to create a node set for the agent element grouped by the agentName element?

7. Provide the general code structure to access a key used in the stores.xml document.

8. You wish to use extensions supported by the Xalan processor. The namespace for Xalan is xml.apache.org/xslt. What attributes would you add to the `stylesheet` element to reference these extensions? Use the namespace prefix lxslt.

Review Assignments

Data Files needed for the Review Assignments: homestxt.xml, homestxt.xsl, +1 XML file, +1 CSS file, +1 PNG file

Lisa asks you to design another style sheet for her. Many of her clients are not looking for a house in a particular geographic area as much as they are looking for one of a particular style. She wants you to create a new style sheet based on her property data that groups the property report by housing style. She has already created the style sheet for the property report, but she needs your help in grouping the properties.

The property report should also contain information on the real estate agencies and agents handling the properties. Since working on her last project, Lisa has placed all of this information within a single file. Figure 7-34 shows the structure of the new agencies file. You have to extract information from this second source document to complete the report.

Figure 7-34   **Structure of the agencies.xml document**

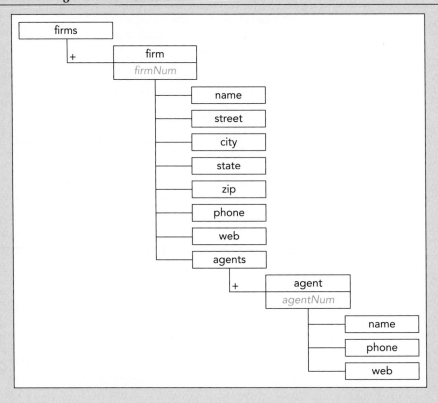

Figure 7-35 shows a preview of the report you'll help Lisa create.

Figure 7-35   **Report grouped by house style**

Complete the following:

1. Using your editor, open **homestxt.xml** and **homestxt.xsl** from the xml07 ▸ review folder. Enter *your name* and the *date* in the comment section of each file, and save them as **homes.xml** and **homes.xsl**, respectively.

2. Go to the **homes.xml** file in your editor. Add a processing instruction after the comment section that attaches the homes.xsl style sheet to the document. Close the file, saving your changes.

3. Go to the **homes.xsl** file in your editor, and review the content of the style sheet and the different templates it contains. At the top of the file, directly below the opening `<xsl:stylesheet>` tag, do the following:

    a. Create a variable named **agencies** that selects the agencies.xml file.

    b. Create a key named **agentID** that matches the agent element, using values of the agentNum attribute to generate the key index.

c. Create a key named **firmID** that matches the firm element, using values of the firmNum attribute to generate the key index.

d. Create a key named **houseStyles** that matches the property element, using values of the style element to generate the key index.

4. At the bottom of the style sheet, insert a template with a mode value of **styleList** that matches the property element. The purpose of this template is to create a list of the different housing styles associated with the properties in the style.xml document. Have the template write the following code:

```
<a href="#id">style</a> (count) |
```

where *id* is an ID value generated automatically by the XSLT processor using the `generate-id()` function, *style* is the value of the style element, and *count* is the number of properties that contain that style. (*Hint*: Use the `key()` function and the houseStyles key to retrieve the node set of properties belonging to a particular style, and use the `count()` function to calculate the number of properties in that node set.)

5. Go to the root template. Within the style_list section after the | character, apply a template of the styleList mode to the step pattern: "listings/property[not(style=preceding::property/style)]" in order to display a list of unique housing styles. Sort the application of the template by order of the style element.

6. Directly below the closing `</section>` tag in the root template, insert a `for-each` element using the Muenchian grouping with the location path "//property[generate-id()=generate-id(key('houseStyles', style)[1])]" for the `select` attribute in order to select each housing style. Within the `for-each` element, add

a. Sort the output by values of the style element.

b. For each unique housing style, write the following code to the result document:

```
<h2 id="id">style</h2>
```

where *id* is an ID value generated automatically by the XSLT processor using the `generate-id()` function and *style* is the value of the style element.

c. Apply a template for each property belonging to the selected housing style. (*Hint*: Use the `key()` function with the houseStyles key and the value of the style element.) Sort the applied template by the sqfeet element in descending order.

7. Go to the property template. The purpose of this template is to write the HTML code for a web table describing each property. Most of the contents of the table have already been created for you. Your task is to insert the firm and agent data into the table in the appropriate cells. Within the table cell following the comment "Place information about the firm here", add the following styles to display information about the listing firm in the result document:

a. Declare a variable named **fID**, containing the value of the firm attribute.

b. Insert a `for-each` element, selecting the value of the *agencies* variable to change the context node to the agencies.xml file.

c. Within the `for-each` element, write the following firm contact information:

```
name <br /> street <br /> city, state   zip <br />
phone <br /> web
```

where *name*, *street*, *city*, *state*, *zip*, *phone*, and *web* are the values of the name, street, city, state, zip, phone, and web elements for the selected firm in the agencies.xml file. (*Hint*: Use the `key()` function with the firmID key and the value of the *fID* variable to select the appropriate firm element from the agencies.xml file.)

8. Scroll down the web table and, within the table cell directly after the comment "Place information about the agent here", add the following styles:

a. Declare a variable named **aID**, selecting the value of the agent attribute.

b. Insert a `for-each` element, selecting the value of the *agencies* variable in order to change the context node to the agencies.xml file.

c. Within the `for-each` element, write the following code to the result document:

```
name <br />
phone <br />
email
```

where `name`, `phone`, and `email` are the values of the name, phone, and email elements for the selected agent in the agencies.xml file.

9. Save your changes to the homes.xsl file.

10. Use your web browser or your XSLT processor to generate the result document. Verify that the property report displays each property grouped by housing style, that the list of housing styles includes a count of the number of each property within each style, that links within the style list jump the browser to the appropriate style section in the report, and that the agent and firm data are correctly retrieved from the agencies.xml file.

Case Problem 1

APPLY

Data Files needed for this Case Problem: hbemptxt.xml, hbemptxt.xsl, +1 CSS file, +1 PNG file

Harris and Barnes   Pamela Curry is the director of personnel for Harris and Barnes, a medical software firm located in Chandler, Arizona. Pamela has information about Harris and Barnes employees saved to an XML document. She wants to create a web page that displays the employee data, grouped by department (Management, Marketing, Production, and so on) and sorted within each department in descending order by salary. A preview of the page is shown in Figure 7-36.

Figure 7-36   **Employment report grouped by department**

Harris and Barnes
Medical Software and Diagnostics

Employee Report

Management

Name	Position	Salary	Phone	Gender	Marital Status	Work Status
Heffner, Marian	Chief Operating Officer	$262,000	x10962	female	married	Full Time
Spaulding, Marjorie	Mgr Site Services	$186,000	x31758	female	single	Full Time
Molina, Albert	Mgr Proj Del	$175,000	x18621	male	single	Full Time
Pierce, Jeffrey	Mgr Fin Rpts Budgets	$111,000	x27519	male	married	Contract
Dixon, Matthew	Accountant	$91,000	x32019	male	single	Full Time
Medina, Shirley	Exec Asst	$84,500	x15138	female	single	Contract
Vecchio, Art	Line Worker	$83,000	x12125	male	married	Part Time
Curry, Pamela	Exec Asst	$83,000	x31732	female	single	Full Time
Bush, Virginia	Mech Mt A HD Repair	$82,000	x06843	female	married	Full Time
Murphy, Mark	Elec Maint A	$80,000	x31594	male	single	Contract
Mcdowell, Janice	Term Mtce A	$79,500	x13827	female	married	Full Time
Binion, Johnnie	Mtce Plng Clk	$76,500	x29795	male	married	Contract
Lindeman, Julius	Gen Maint B	$69,500	x06108	male	married	Full Time
Rice, Gary	Mobile Eq Opr	$67,500	x03557	male	single	Full Time
Kimbrough, Alexander	Dsl Sys Rep	$56,500	x17370	male	single	Full Time
Hicks, Helen	Asset Spec Lines Stns	$54,500	x22873	female	married	Part Time
Haggerty, Vernon	Elec Maint A	$52,500	x05826	male	married	Full Time
Higgins, Peter	Fire Sec Off	$49,500	x12112	male	single	Part Time

Marketing

Name	Position	Salary	Phone	Gender	Marital Status	Work Status
Davis, Robert	Mgr Ther Gen	$196,000	x18451	male	married	Full Time
Pina, Alfred	Pur Admin Sv	$129,500	x17880	male	married	Full Time
Calvillo, Blanca	Stn Opr	$95,000	x01941	female	married	Full Time
Paul, Henry	Mech Mt A Welder	$94,000	x27285	male	married	Contract
Merrick, Hector	Technologist	$93,500	x20137	male	single	Full Time
Arrington, Rita	Line Wrker A	$92,000	x19508	female	married	Full Time
Knapp, Jane	Sec Off	$89,000	x13382	female	single	Full Time
		$79,500		female	married	

Pamela has asked you to complete the XSLT style sheet and write the code to group and summarize the employment data. Complete the following:

1. Using your editor, open the **hbemptxt.xml** and **hbemptxt.xsl** files from the xml07 ▸ case1 folder. Enter *your name* and the *date* in the comment section of each file, and save them as **hbemployees.xml** and **hbemployees.xsl**, respectively.

2. Go to the **hbemployees.xml** file in your editor and link the hbemployees.xsl style sheet to the document. Close the file, saving your changes.

3. Go to the **hbemployees.xsl** file in your editor. Directly after the opening `stylesheet` element, create the **departments** key, matching the employee element and using the department element for the key index. The purpose of this key will be to group the employees by department.

4. Directly after the h1 Employee Report heading, insert a `for-each` element that that uses Muenchian grouping to select each unique department by using the location path:
   "//employee[generate-id()=generate-id(key('departments', department)[1])]"
   then sort the results by department.

5. Each time through the for-each loop, write the following HTML code to the result document:

```
<table class="employeeList">
    <caption>department</caption>
    <thead>
        <tr>
            <th>Name</th>
            <th>Position</th>
            <th>Salary</th>
            <th>Phone</th>
            <th>Gender</th>
            <th>Marital Status</th>
            <th>Work Status</th>
        </tr>
    </thead>
    <tbody>
    </tbody>
</table>
```

where *department* is the value of the department element.

6. Within the `tbody` element of the HTML code you just wrote, apply a template using the departments key with the current value of the department element in order to display information on each employee within the currently displayed department. Sort the applied template by descending order of the salary element.

7. Directly after the root template, insert a new template matching the employee element. The purpose of this template will be to write a table row containing information on a selected employee. Have the template write the following HTML code to the result document:

```
<tr>
    <td>name</td>
    <td>position</td>
    <td>salary</td>
    <td>phone</td>
    <td>gender</td>
    <td>marital status</td>
    <td>working status</td>
</tr>
```

where *name*, *position*, *salary*, *phone*, *gender*, *marital status*, and *working status* are the values of the name, position, salary, phone, gender, martialStatus, and workingStatus elements. Format *salary* so that it is displayed as currency.

8. Save your changes, then generate the result document using either your web browser or your XSLT processor. Verify that the layout and content of your web page resembles that shown in Figure 7-36.

Case Problem 2

APPLY

Data Files needed for this Case Problem: youngtxt.xml, youngtxt.xsl

Youngston Office Supply   Andrei Koshkin is a manager at Youngston Office Supply, located in Youngston, Ohio. The company keeps records of the daily orders in a database. Andrei has received this information in an XML document named youngston.xml with the structure shown in Figure 7-37.

Figure 7-37   **Structure of the youngston.xml document**

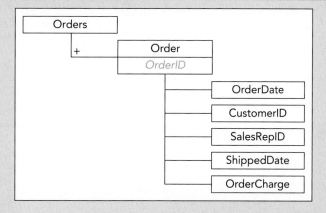

However, Andrei wants the data to be organized by customer so he can track each customer's order history. Figure 7-38 shows how he wants the data organized in a result document named yoscustomers.xml.

Figure 7-38   **Revised structure of the yoscustomers.xml document**

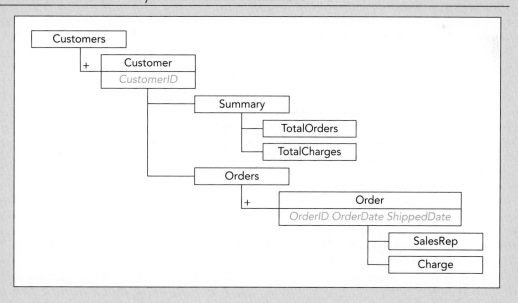

Andrei wants you to write an XSLT style sheet to automatically transform his source data and create the yoscustomers.xml file. Complete the following:

1. Using your editor, open the **youngtxt.xml** and **youngtxt.xsl** files from the xml07 ► case2 folder. Enter *your name* and the *date* in the comment section of each file, and save them as **youngston.xml** and **youngston.xsl**, respectively.

2. Go to the **youngston.xml** file in your editor. Link the youngston.xsl style sheet to the document. Close the file, saving your changes.

3. Go to the **youngston.xsl** file in your editor. Add an output element to specify that the style sheet output should be an xml version 1.0 file, encoded in UTF-8 with the text indented for readability.

4. Create a key named **CustomerList** that matches the Order element using value of CustomerID as the index.

5. Within the root template, write the following code, creating Customers as the root element of the result document:

```
<Customers>
</Customers>
```

6. Within the Customers element you just created, insert a `for-each` element that uses Muenchian grouping to loop through the unique values of the CustomerID element within the CustomerList key. Sort the for-each loop by the values of the CustomerID element.

7. Each time through the for-each loop, write the following code to the result document to provide information on each customer:

```
<Customer CustomerID="ID">
    <Summary>
        <TotalOrders>count</TotalOrders>
        <TotalCharges>charges</TotalCharges>
    </Summary>
</Customer>
```

where *ID* is the value of the CustomerID element, *count* is the count of orders within the CustomerList key for the current CustomerID, and *charges* is the sum of the OrderCharge element within the CustomerList key for the current CustomerID. Format *charges* as currency.

8. Below the root template, create a new template to match the Order element. The purpose of this template will be to write the tags describing all of the orders made by a customer. Write the following XML code into the template:

```
<Order OrderID="ID" OrderDate="date" ShippedDate="ship">
    <SalesRep>RepID</SalesRep>
    <Charge>OrderCharge</Charge>
</Order>
```

where *ID* is the value of the OrderID attribute from Figure 7-37, *date* is the value of the OrderDate element, *ship* is the value of the ShippedDate element, *RepID* is the value of the SalesRepID element, and *OrderCharge* is the value of the OrderCharge element. Write the value of *OrderCharge* in a currency format.

9. Scroll back up to the root template and, directly after the closing `</Summary>` tag, insert the following code to display the orders made by the current customer:

```
<Orders>
    Order
</Orders>
```

where *Order* applies the Order template for the node set returned by the CustomerList key for the current CustomerID.

10. Save your changes.

11. Using an XSLT processor, generate a result document by applying the youngston.xsl style sheet to the youngston.xml source file. Save the result document as **yoscustomers.xml**.

Case Problem 3

Data Files needed for this Case Problem: agsalestxt.xml, agsalestxt.xsl, +1 XML file, +1 CSS file, +1 PNG file

CHALLENGE

Asian Gardens   The Asian Gardens is a chain of Chinese restaurants located in the Pacific Northwest. Richard Hayes, a sales manager for the company, is working with a database of daily sales figures from 10 restaurants in Oregon and Washington. The data has been transferred to an XML document and Richard wants you to transform the contents of this document in a web table displaying annual revenue broken down by month and restaurant location. A preview of the completed table is shown in Figure 7-39.

Figure 7-39   **Total revenue grouped by month and restaurant**

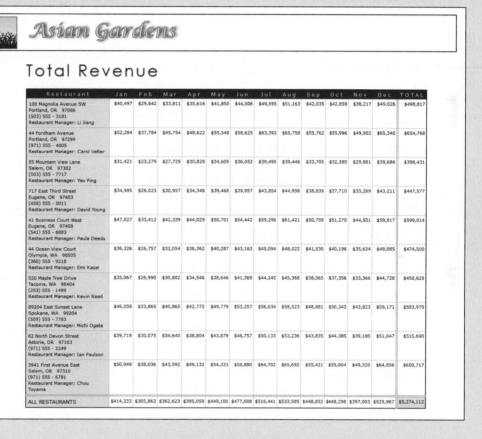

Complete the following:

1. Using your editor, open the **agsalestxt.xml** and **agsalestxt.xsl** files from the xml07 ▸ case3 folder. Enter ***your name*** and the ***date*** in the comment section of each file, and save them as **agsales.xml** and **agsales.xsl**, respectively.

2. Go to the **agsales.xml** file in your editor. This file contains information about each of the 10 restaurants in the chain. Study the content and structure of the document. Note that each sales element includes the date and month in which the sales were generated. The revenue collected from each restaurant is saved in the revenue attribute, and the restaurant ID is identified in the ID attribute. Link the agsales.xsl style sheet to the document and then close the file, saving your changes.

3. Go to the **agsales.xsl** file in your editor. Create a global variable named **restaurantsDoc** that uses the `document()` function to reference the /restaurants/restaurant node set from the ag.xml file.

4. Create the following keys:

   a. The **restaurantSales** key matching the sales element using the ID attribute. The purpose of this key will be to group the sales data by restaurant.

   b. The **monthSales** key matching the sales element using the month attribute. The purpose of this key will be to group the sales data by month.

5. Go to the bottom of the style sheet and create a template named **showSales** and with a single parameter named **salesNode**, which will be used to reference a node set of sales data. Have the template display the sum of sales revenue for the selected node set by writing the sum of the location path "$salesNode/@revenue" in currency format.

6. Next you'll start creating the web table to show sales revenue by month and restaurant. You'll first create the column headings. Return to the root template and write the following HTML tags within the `<thead></thead>` tag:

```
<tr>
   <th>Restaurant</th>
   <th>TOTAL</th>
</tr>
```

7. Next, you'll create column headings for each month of the year shown in Figure 7-39. Between the two table heading cells you just created, insert a `for-each` element that uses Muenchian grouping to loop through all of the unique values of the monthSales key. Each time through the loop, write the following HTML code:

```
<th>month</th>
```

   where *month* is the value of the month attribute.

8. Next, you'll calculate and display the monthly revenue for each restaurant. Within the `<tfoot></tfoot>` tag, insert the following HTML code:

```
<tr>
   <th>ALL RESTAURANTS</th>
   <td>total revenue</td>
</tr>
```

   where *total revenue* is the sum of all sales from all of the restaurants. Calculate *total revenue* using the showSales template with all of the sales elements in the source document as the *salesNode* parameter.

9. Next, you'll calculate and display the total sales for each month. Directly after the `<th>ALL RESTAURANTS</th>` tag, insert a `for-each` element that uses Muenchian grouping to loop through the unique values of the monthSales key. For each month, write the following HTML code:

```
<td>monthly revenue</td>
```

   where *monthly revenue* is the revenue for the current month calculated by calling the showSales template with the *salesNode* parameter referencing all of the sales elements for the current month. Use the monthSales key with the month attribute to create the appropriate node set.

10. The table body displays the monthly revenue for each restaurant on a separate table row. To create the table rows within the `<tbody></tbody>` tag, insert a `for-each` element that uses Muenchian grouping with the restaurantSales key to loop through the unique restaurant IDs. Each time through the loop, write the following HTML code to create the table rows:

```
<tr>
   <th>
       address <br />
       city, state zip <br />
       phone <br />
       Restaurant Manager: manager
   </th>
</tr>
```

where *address*, *city*, *state*, *zip*, *phone*, and *manager* are the values of the address, city, state, zip, phone and manager elements looked up from the values in the ag.xml file using the current ID attribute as the lookup value.

⊕ **EXPLORE** 11. Next, within each table row, you'll display the monthly sales of the current restaurant in separate table cells. To calculate the monthly sales for each restaurant you need to generate a node set representing the intersection of every combination of restaurant and month. You'll do this with a nested `for-each` element.

    a. After the closing `</th>` tag, create a local variable named **restaurantNode** using the restaurantSales key to reference the node set containing all of the restaurants matching the value of the current restaurant ID.

    b. Insert a nested `for-each` element that uses Muenchian grouping to loop through the unique values of the monthSales key.

    c. Within the nested `for-each` element create a local variable named **monthNode** using the monthSales key to reference the node set containing all of the sales elements matching the current value of the month attribute.

    d. Use the Kaysian method described in the Combining Node Sets Insight box to create the intersection of the *restaurantNode* and *monthNode* variables. Save the resulting node set in a local variable named **monthRestaurant**.

    e. Write the following HTML code to the result document:

```
<td>revenue</td>
```

    where *revenue* is the value returned by the showSales template using the value of the *monthRestaurant* variable as the value of the *salesNode* parameter.

12. After the nested for-each loop, display the total sales for the current restaurant by writing the following code to the result document:

```
<td>restaurant revenue</td>
```

where *restaurant revenue* is the value returned by the showSales template using the value of the *restaurantNode* variable for the *salesNode* parameter.

13. Save your changes to the style sheet and generate the result document using either your browser or an XML editor. Verify that the total revenue for each restaurant, each month, and each combination of month and restaurant matches the values shown in Figure 7-39.

Case Problem 4

CREATE

Data Files needed for this Case Problem: dontxt.xml, dontxt.xsl, +1 XML file, +4 PNG files

Appalachian House   Kendrick Thorne is the fundraising coordinator for Appalachian House, a charitable organization located in central Kentucky. One of his responsibilities is to report on the progress Appalachian House is making in soliciting donations. Kendrick has two XML documents. The donations.xml file lists all of the donations received over the past 5 months, while the donors.xml file contains contact information for the donors over that time period.

Kendrick wants you to create an XSLT style sheet that will generate an HTML file that will report on the total donations grouped by donation level. The report should calculate the total amount from all donors, calculate the number of donors at each donation level, and provide contact information for each donor. A possible solution is shown in Figure 7-40.

Figure 7-40   Donations grouped by donation level

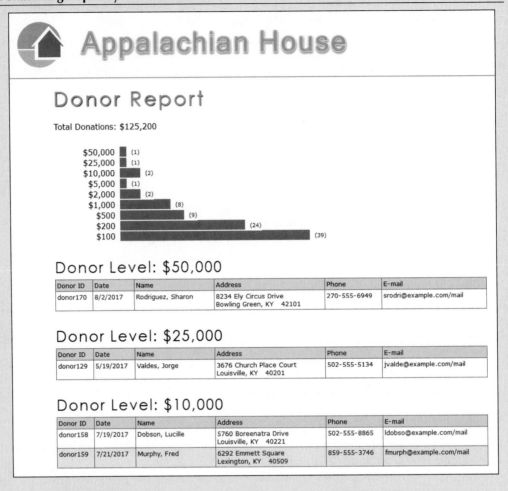

Complete the following:

1. Using your editor, open **dontxt.xml** and **dontxt.xsl** from the xml07 ▶ case4 folder. Enter *your name* and the *date* in the comment section of each file, and save them as **donations.xml** and **donations.xsl**, respectively.

2. Attach the donations.xsl style sheet to the donations.xml file.

3. Add styles to the donations.xsl style sheet to generate the contribution report. The style and layout of the report is left up to you, but it must include the following features:

   a. The total amount of the donations

   b. The number of donors within each contribution level

   c. The contact information for each donor within each contribution level

   d. An example of the use of step patterns

   e. An example of a key used with the source document and an external document

   f. An example of the use of Muenchian Grouping

4. You are free to augment your completed project with any graphics or CSS styles of your choosing.

5. Test your style sheet using your web browser or an XSLT processor, and verify that all required elements are displayed and that the contributor list is properly grouped.

TUTORIAL **8**

OBJECTIVES

Session 8.1
- Create an XSLT 2.0 style sheet
- Use multiple source documents with a style sheet
- Work with XPath 2.0 date functions and values
- Apply XSLT 2.0 sequences in your style sheet

Session 8.2
- Create custom functions in XSLT 2.0
- Work with XPath 2.0 conditional expressions
- Use XSLT 2.0 grouping elements
- Use the `doc()` function

Session 8.3
- Work with XPath 2.0 string functions
- Explore regular expressions in XSLT 2.0
- Import data from non-XML files

Building Applications with XSLT 2.0

Exploring XSLT 2.0 and XPath 2.0

Case | *Illuminated Fixtures*

Illuminated Fixtures is an online seller of lamps, lights, light bulbs, and other electronic home furnishings. William Garson manages the shipping department. Part of his job is to track orders and review customer information. Often his job also requires him to work with XML documents. He wants your help in creating a report that analyzes recent shipments based on date, items ordered, and the customer submitting the order. Some of the calculations he needs to add to this report are not easily done in XSLT 1.0, so he's asked for your help in creating an XSLT 2.0 style sheet to transform his data.

STARTING DATA FILES

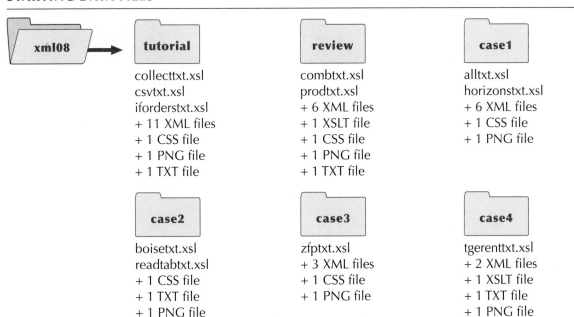

xml08 → **tutorial**
collecttxt.xsl
csvtxt.xsl
iforderstxt.xsl
+ 11 XML files
+ 1 CSS file
+ 1 PNG file
+ 1 TXT file

review
combtxt.xsl
prodtxt.xsl
+ 6 XML files
+ 1 XSLT file
+ 1 CSS file
+ 1 PNG file
+ 1 TXT file

case1
alltxt.xsl
horizonstxt.xsl
+ 6 XML files
+ 1 CSS file
+ 1 PNG file

case2
boisetxt.xsl
readtabtxt.xsl
+ 1 CSS file
+ 1 TXT file
+ 1 PNG file

case3
zfptxt.xsl
+ 3 XML files
+ 1 CSS file
+ 1 PNG file

case4
tgerenttxt.xsl
+ 2 XML files
+ 1 XSLT file
+ 1 TXT file
+ 1 PNG file

Session 8.1 Visual Overview:

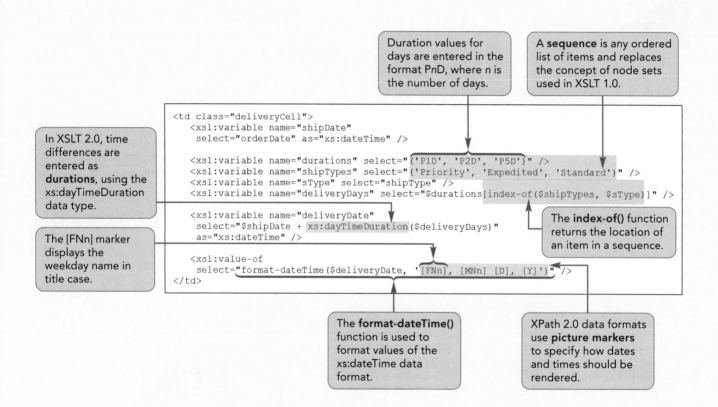

Duration values for days are entered in the format P*n*D, where *n* is the number of days.

A **sequence** is any ordered list of items and replaces the concept of node sets used in XSLT 1.0.

In XSLT 2.0, time differences are entered as **durations**, using the xs:dayTimeDuration data type.

The [FNn] marker displays the weekday name in title case.

```
<td class="deliveryCell">
   <xsl:variable name="shipDate"
    select="orderDate" as="xs:dateTime" />

   <xsl:variable name="durations" select="('P1D', 'P2D', 'P5D')" />
   <xsl:variable name="shipTypes" select="('Priority', 'Expedited', 'Standard')" />
   <xsl:variable name="sType" select="shipType" />
   <xsl:variable name="deliveryDays" select="$durations[index-of($shipTypes, $sType)]" />

   <xsl:variable name="deliveryDate"
    select="$shipDate + xs:dayTimeDuration($deliveryDays)"
    as="xs:dateTime" />

   <xsl:value-of
    select="format-dateTime($deliveryDate, '[FNn], [MNn] [D], [Y]')" />
</td>
```

The **index-of()** function returns the location of an item in a sequence.

The **format-dateTime()** function is used to format values of the xs:dateTime data format.

XPath 2.0 data formats use **picture markers** to specify how dates and times should be rendered.

Data Types and Sequences

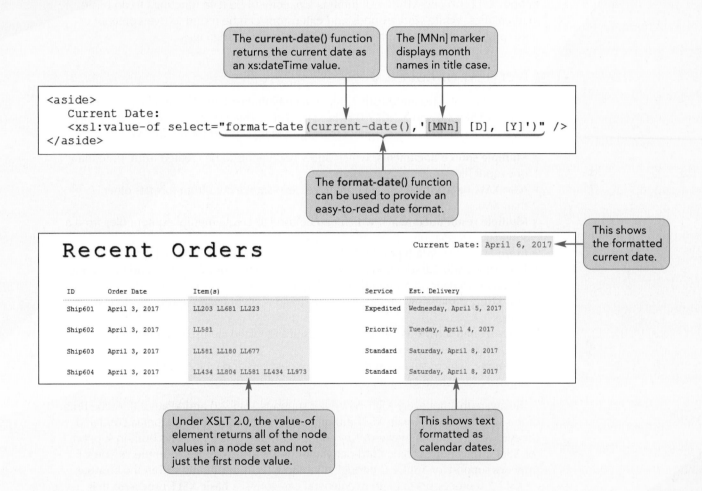

The **current-date()** function returns the current date as an xs:dateTime value.

The [MNn] marker displays month names in title case.

```
<aside>
   Current Date:
   <xsl:value-of select="format-date(current-date(),'[MNn] [D], [Y]')" />
</aside>
```

The **format-date()** function can be used to provide an easy-to-read date format.

This shows the formatted current date.

Recent Orders   Current Date: April 6, 2017

ID	Order Date	Item(s)	Service	Est. Delivery
Ship601	April 3, 2017	LL203 LL681 LL223	Expedited	Wednesday, April 5, 2017
Ship602	April 3, 2017	LL581	Priority	Tuesday, April 4, 2017
Ship603	April 3, 2017	LL581 LL180 LL677	Standard	Saturday, April 8, 2017
Ship604	April 3, 2017	LL434 LL804 LL581 LL434 LL973	Standard	Saturday, April 8, 2017

Under XSLT 2.0, the value-of element returns all of the node values in a node set and not just the first node value.

This shows text formatted as calendar dates.

Introducing XSLT 2.0

XSLT 1.0 combined with XPath 1.0 is a powerful tool for document manipulation, allowing the programmer to transform a source document into a wide variety of output formats. Yet, these languages are not without their problems. One huge challenge to the programming community is the complexity of the XSLT 1.0 language, especially for those who are used to working with non-functional programming languages, such as C or Java. Another challenge is that XPath 1.0 is limited to essentially three data types—text, numbers, and Boolean values—with no native support for common data types such as integers, date values, and time durations. In both XSLT 1.0 and XPath 1.0, there is a paucity of built-in functions to do basic mathematics. While workarounds and extensions can be found to overcome all of these problems, they do limit the appeal of those two languages.

Overview of XSLT 2.0

To deal with XSLT 1.0 and XPath 1.0 language limitations, the XSL working group approved XSLT 2.0 and XPath 2.0 in January, 2007. The 2.0 version of these languages are very different from their predecessors, providing support for the following:

- **Multiple source documents**, which allow documents to be created from more than one input file
- **Non-XML data**, which can be used to retrieve source data from formats other than XML
- **Multiple result documents**, which can be used to create multiple output files from a single transformation
- **More extensive data types**, including data types defined in XML Schema
- **Powerful XPath 2.0 functions**, which can be used to work with date and time values as well as to perform arithmetic calculations
- **Text string processing**, including the ability to apply regular expressions to text strings
- **User-defined functions**, which can be used to replace the use of named templates and recursive templates
- **Grouping**, which can be used to organize data sets and which can be used to replace Muenchian grouping

Be aware that not every XSLT processor supports XSLT 2.0 and XPath 2.0. At the time of this writing, the two main XSLT 2.0 processors are Saxon (*www.saxonica.com*) and the Altova XSLT Engine (*www.xmlspy.com*). No web browser provides built-in support for XSLT 2.0, although some third-party add-ins are available. For example, Saxon-CE provides support for XSLT 2.0 through a JavaScript add-in running within the browser.

XSLT 2.0 processors fall into two general categories: a **basic XSLT processor** that supports the core functionality of XSLT 2.0 and a **schema-aware XSLT processor** that supports data types defined in user-created schemas, in addition to the core functionality of XSLT 2.0. The current free home edition of Saxon (Saxon-HE) provides all of the features of XSLT 2.0 and XPath 2.0, except schema-aware processing.

Creating an XSLT 2.0 Style Sheet

The first step in converting an existing XSLT 1.0 style sheet into an XSLT 2.0 is to set the version number in the `stylesheet` element to 2.0. This signals an XSLT 2.0-aware processor to treat the style sheet code as conforming to the 2.0 standard.

William wants to create an XSLT 2.0 style sheet to display a sample list of orders that have been shipped by Illuminated Fixtures over the last few days. You'll start converting his style sheet to the 2.0 standard by inserting the `stylesheet` element with the `version` attribute set to 2.0.

To begin an XSLT style sheet:

▶ **1.** Use your text editor to open the **collecttxt.xsl** file from the xml08 ▸ tutorial folder. Enter *your name* and the *date* in the comment section at the top of the file, and save the file as **collection.xsl**.

▶ **2.** Directly below the comment section, insert the following opening and closing stylesheet tags:

```
<xsl:stylesheet version="2.0"
    xmlns:xsl="http://www.w3.org/1999/XSL/Transform">
</xsl:stylesheet>
```

Figure 8-1 shows the `stylesheet` element for XSLT 2.0.

Figure 8-1	Opening stylesheet element for XSLT 2.0

sets the version to 2.0

```
<xsl:stylesheet version="2.0"
    xmlns:xsl="http://www.w3.org/1999/XSL/Transform">
</xsl:stylesheet>
```

▶ **3.** Save your changes to the file.

William's style sheet will have one basic task: to pull in shipping data from multiple XML files and combine those data into a single XML document.

Transforming Data from Multiple Sources

TIP

The implementation of the `collection()` function might differ between XSLT 2.0 processors, so you have to check your processor's documentation before applying the function.

XPath 2.0 allows the programmer to retrieve data from multiple document sources using the following `collection()` function:

```
collection(uri)
```

where `uri` provides the name and location of the documents to be transformed by the style sheet. The URI will usually include a select query string to select files based on a specified criteria. For example, the following `collection()` function:

```
collection('file:///c:/data/?select=*.xml')
```

returns a node set from a collection of files that have the .xml file extension from the c: ▸ data folder on the local machine.

A relative URI can also be used to select files from a folder location relative to the location of the style sheet file. Thus, the following `collection()` function:

```
collection('.?select=*.xml')
```

uses the "." character to reference the folder of the current style sheet and returns a collection of all files in the current folder that have the .xml file extension.

Using a Catalog File

Another way to specify a collection is to use a **catalog file** that contains a collection of the files that you want to retrieve into the style sheet. For example, the following `collection()` function retrieves the files listed in the catalog.xml file, which is located in the c: ▸ report folder:

```
collection('file:///c:/report/catalog.xml')
```

Thus, if the catalog.xml file contains the following collection and doc elements, the processor will load the report1.xml through report4.xml files:

```
<collection>
    <doc href="data/report1.xml" />
    <doc href="data/report2.xml" />
    <doc href="data/report3.xml" />
    <doc href="data/report4.xml" />
</collection>
```

REFERENCE

Importing Data from Multiple Documents

- To retrieve data from multiple document sources, use the XPath 2.0 `collection()` function

  `collection(uri)`

  where *uri* provides the name and location of the documents to be transformed by the style sheet.

Applying the `collection()` Function

TIP

A common practice is to place XPath 2.0 functions within the *http://www.w3.org/2005/xpath-functions* namespace using the `fn` namespace prefix.

To apply a style to each file in a collection, you can use the `collection()` function within the following `for-each` element:

```
<xsl:for-each select="collection(uri)">
    styles
</xsl:for-each>
```

where *styles* are styles used to transform the contents of each file in the collection to a result document.

William wants to retrieve information from each shipping label that accompanies every shipment from Illuminated Fixtures. The shipping labels include a shipping ID, the date and time that the shipment was made, the shipping dispatcher and the location from which the order was shipped, information about the customer receiving the shipment, and finally a list of items shipped to the customer. Shipping labels are stored as XML documents, and William has retrieved a sample of ten shipping labels from the last several days. The files are named shipdoc601.xml through shipdoc610.xml. Figure 8-2 shows the contents and structure of the shipdoc601.xml file, representing one particular shipment sent out on April 3, 2017, at 9:45 a.m.

Figure 8-2   **Contents of the shipdoc601.xml document**

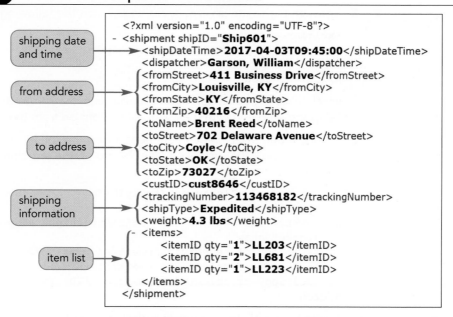

The other documents follow the same structure. William wants to combine data from these ten files into a single result file that will contain information on ten shipments made in the last several days. The structure of this result file is shown in Figure 8-3.

Figure 8-3   **Structure of the shipping orders document**

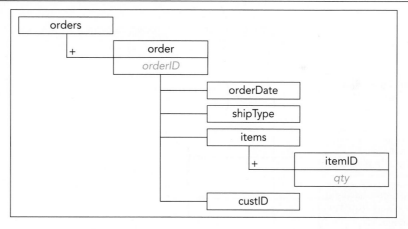

Because there is no single source file for this transformation and thus no root node, you'll place the commands to retrieve and process these ten shipping files within a named template in the collection.xsl style sheet.

To apply the `collection()` function:

1. Within the `stylesheet` element in the collection.xsl file, insert the following named template to create the orders element:

```
<xsl:template name="list">
   <orders>
   </orders>
</xsl:template>
```

2. Between the `<orders></orders>` tags, insert the following code:

```
<xsl:for-each
 select="collection('.?select=shipdoc*.xml')">

</xsl:for-each>
```

which loads the collection of XML documents that start with the text string "shipdoc" and end with the ".xml" file extension from the current folder.

3. Finally, within the `for-each` element, insert the following code that writes the contents of the orders element based on the structure shown earlier in Figure 8-3:

```
<order orderID="{shipment/@shipID}">
   <orderDate>
      <xsl:value-of select="shipment/shipDateTime" />
   </orderDate>
   <xsl:copy-of select="shipment/shipType" />
   <xsl:copy-of select="shipment/items" />
   <xsl:copy-of select="shipment/custID" />
</order>
```

Figure 8-4 highlights the newly added code to retrieve the data files and create the elements in the result document.

Figure 8-4	Applying the collection() function

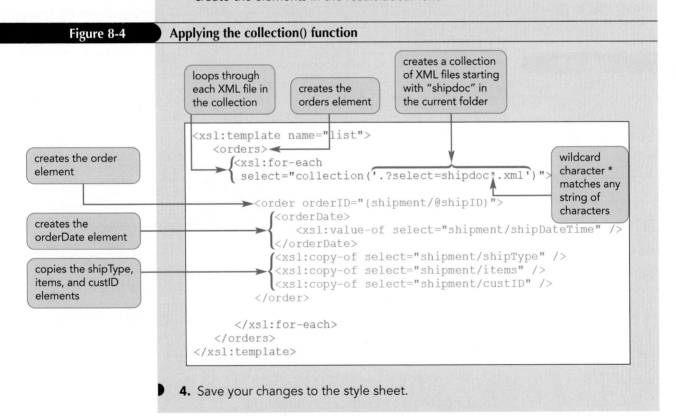

4. Save your changes to the style sheet.

You'll run this style sheet using an XSLT 2.0 processor. In the steps that follow, you'll perform the transformation using Saxon in Java command line mode. If you are using a different XSLT 2.0 processor, check your processor's documentation and modify your steps accordingly.

To apply a transformation that involves a named template using Saxon in Java command line mode, enter the following command within a command prompt window:

```
java net.sf.saxon.Transform –it:template style –o:output
```

where *template* is the initial or named template in the style sheet to be executed, *style* is the XSLT style sheet file, and *output* is the name of the result document. Note that in this case there is no source document specified because the source documents are loaded as part of the `collection()` function defined within *template*. If you are using Saxon on the .NET platform, the equivalent command line is

```
Transform -it:template style -o:output
```

You'll run the transformation now with the XSLT 2.0 processor of your choice.

TIP

You can open a command prompt window in Windows 8 by opening File Explorer, going to the xml08 ▶ tutorial folder, and clicking the Open command prompt from the File tab.

To run the transformation:

1. Open a command prompt window and go to the xml08 ▶ tutorial folder.

2. If you're using Saxon in Java command line mode, enter the following command on a single line:

   ```
   java net.sf.saxon.Transform -it:list collection.xsl
   -o:iforders.xml
   ```

   Figure 8-5 shows the Saxon command entered on a single line.

Figure 8-5   **Running the transformation to create the iforders.xml file**

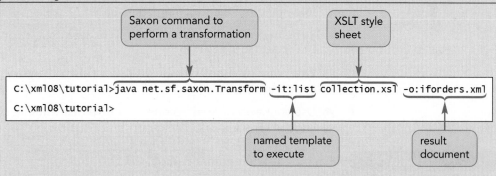

3. Press **Enter** to generate the result document **iforders.xml**.

4. Open the **iforders.xml** file in your text editor or within a browser. As shown in Figure 8-6, the document should contain the order data from the ten shipping documents.

Figure 8-6   **Contents and structure of the iforders.xml file**

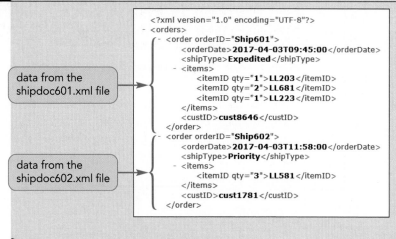

5. Close the iforders.xml file.

The iforders.xml file provides William with the single document he needs to summarize customer orders from the past several days. William has already created an XSLT 2.0 style sheet to display the contents of this result document as a web page. If you are using Saxon in Java command line mode, you can run the command

```
java net.sf.saxon.Transform source style -o:output
```

where *source* is the XML source file, *style* is the XSLT style sheet, and *output* is the result file. If you are using Saxon on the .NET platform, the equivalent command line is

```
Transform source style -o:output
```

You'll generate the HTML file now with the XSLT 2.0 processor of your choice.

To generate the HTML file:

1. Use your text editor to open the **iforderstxt.xsl** file from the xml08 ▸ tutorial folder. Enter **your name** and the **date** in the comment section of the file and then save document as **iforders.xsl**.

2. Take some time to review the contents of the style sheet to become familiar with its code and structure.

3. If you are using Saxon in Java command line mode, go to the xml08 ▸ tutorial folder and run the following command:

   ```
   java net.sf.saxon.Transform iforders.xml iforders.xsl
   -o:orderlist.html
   ```

   Otherwise, use the commands appropriate to your XSLT 2.0 processor to run the transformation.

4. Use your web browser to open the **orderlist.html** file. Figure 8-7 shows the current appearance of the report.

| Figure 8-7 | Illuminated Fixtures order report |

ID	Order Date	Item(s)	Ordered By	Service
Ship601	2017-04-03T09:45:00	LL203 LL681 LL223	cust8646	Expedited
Ship602	2017-04-03T11:58:00	LL581	cust1781	Priority
Ship603	2017-04-03T15:14:00	LL581 LL180 LL677	cust4031	Standard
Ship604	2017-04-03T17:26:00	LL434 LL804 LL581 LL434 LL973	cust4373	Standard
Ship605	2017-04-04T10:43:00	LL511	cust4031	Expedited
Ship606	2017-04-04T12:18:00	LL489 LL804 LL157 LL612	cust8646	Expedited
Ship607	2017-04-04T15:55:00	LL223 LL511 LL282	cust1781	Standard
Ship608	2017-04-04T17:21:00	LL587 LL282 LL265	cust4653	Expedited
Ship609	2017-04-05T08:22:00	LL170	cust1781	Standard
Ship610	2017-04-05T11:14:00	LL886 LL579 LL844	cust4031	Priority

xsl:value-of instruction returns all node values in XSLT 2.0

One important thing to note in this report is the list of items in the third column of the web table. Note that each item in the third column is associated with an item ID. The XSLT instruction in the iforders.xsl file to display the value of the itemID element is

```
<td class="itemCell">
   <xsl:value-of select="items/itemID" />
</td>
```

If this were an XSLT 1.0 style sheet, only the first itemID value would be displayed; however, under XSLT 2.0, the *value-of* element displays all items that match the expression in the `select` attribute. This is because XSTL 2.0 works on sequences rather than node sets. You'll explore the topic of sequences later in this session.

Exploring Atomic Values and Data Types

There are several important differences between the data model used with XPath 1.0 and the one used with XPath 2.0. XPath 1.0 functions were built around the concept of manipulating a wide variety of node types, including element nodes, text nodes, comment nodes, and processing instruction nodes. XPath 2.0 is fundamentally based on **atomic values**, which are values that cannot be broken into smaller parts. For example, an integer value or a text string is an atomic value but a node set is not because it can be broken down into a collection of individual nodes.

Each atomic value has a **data type** that describes the kind of data it contains. In XPath 1.0, data types were limited to text strings, numbers, Boolean values, and result tree fragments. XPath 2.0 has an extensive library of data types including all of the simple and derived data types defined within XML Schema. For example, date and time values can be stored using the XML Schema `xs:dateTime` data type, an integer value can be stored using the `xs:integer` data type, and a positive integer can be stored using the derived XML Schema data type `xs:positiveInteger`.

The data type of an atomic value is specified using the `as` attribute. Thus, the following expression creates the *month* variable storing the value 12 as an `xs:positiveInteger` data type:

```
<variable name="month" select="12" as="xs:positiveInteger" />
```

Note that the data type includes the prefix `xs` to indicate that this data type is derived from the XML Schema namespace (*http://www.w3.org/2001/XMLSchema*). A data type can also be applied to a node set. In the following expression:

```
<variable name="qty" select="orders/total" as="xs:positiveInteger" />
```

the *qty* variable stores the value of the orders/total node as a positive integer. When this data is handled by the XSLT processor, the orders/total value will be converted into an atomic value with the data type `xs:positiveInteger`.

The advantage of specifying the data type is that the processor will catch errors when improper data values are used in an expression, such as when a negative value is passed to an expression in which a positive integer is required or a numeric value is passed to a function that is expecting a text string.

Constructor Functions

You can create atomic values based on XML Schema data types using the following **constructor function**:

```
xs:dataType(value)
```

where *dataType* is an XML Schema data type and *value* is the value assigned to that data type. For example, the following expression uses a constructor function to store the date April 6, 2017, using the *xs:date* data type:

```
<xsl:variable name="thisDate" select="xs:date('2017-04-06')" />
```

The XSLT processor will return an error if the value entered into the constructor function doesn't match the data type. Thus, the statement

```
<xs:variable name="thisDate" select="xs:date('the 6th of April')" />
```

will result in a runtime error because this text string is not supported by the `xs:date()` constructor function.

Now that you've been introduced to the concepts of atomic values and data types, you'll use them to work with the dates and times in the Illuminated Fixtures style sheet. William wants to add the current date to the report, and he wants to display the Order Date values shown in the report in an easier-to-read format. To do this, you'll work with functions and attributes of date and time data types from XML Schema.

Displaying Dates and Times

XPath 1.0 has no built-in functions to work with dates and times. The only way to manipulate a date or time value is to treat the value as a text string and use XPath 1.0's string functions to extract the text of the date and time values. This can result in complicated code, which can be difficult to interpret and apply. On the other hand, XPath 2.0 supports a large library of date and time functions based on date and time data types. A few of these functions are described in Figure 8-8.

Figure 8-8 XPath 2.0 date and time functions

Function	Description
current-date() current-dateTime() current-time()	Returns the current date, date time, or time as an xs:date, xs:dateTime, or xs:time data type
dateTime(*date, time*)	Returns an xs:dateTime data value based on an xs:date and xs:time value
day-from-date(*date*) day-from-dateTime(*dateTime*)	Returns the day component from an xs:date or xs:dateTime value
month-from-date(*date*) month-from-dateTime(*dateTime*)	Returns the month component from an xs:date or xs:dateTime value
year-from-date(*date*) year-from-dateTime(*dateTime*)	Returns the year component from an xs:date or xs:dateTime value
seconds-from-time(*time*) seconds-from-dateTime(*dateTime*)	Returns the seconds component from an xs:time or xs:dateTime value
hours-from-time(*time*) hours-from-time(*dateTime*)	Returns the hours component from an xs:time or xs:dateTime value
timezone-from-time(*time*) timezone-from-dateTime(*dateTime*)	Returns the time zone component from an xs:time or xs:dateTime value

Note that the input and output from many of the XPath 2.0 functions are based on data types from XML Schema. For example, the `current-date()` function returns a value using the XML Schema `xs:date` type, and the `day-from-dateTime()` assumes that the input values correspond to values from the `xs:dateTime` data type. Thus, to use these functions, you must first declare the namespace for XML Schema in the style sheet.

REFERENCE

Displaying the Current Date and Time

- To display the current date and time, use the following XPath 2.0 function:

  `current-date()`

  which returns a value in the xs:dateTime format.

You will apply the `current-date()` function now to William's style sheet in order to display the current date in the upper-right corner of the report.

To apply the `current-date()` function:

1. Return to the **iforders.xsl** file in your text editor.

2. Declare the XML Schema namespace in the `stylesheet` element at the top of the file:

   `xmlns:xs="http://www.w3.org/2001/XMLSchema"`

3. You don't need to write the XML Schema namespace to the result file, so you add the following attribute to the `stylesheet` element to exclude the XML Schema namespace from the result document:

   `exclude-result-prefixes="xs"`

4. Scroll down to the root template and, directly below the closing `</header>` tag, insert the following code to display the current date within an aside element:

   ```
   <aside>
      Current Date:
      <xsl:value-of select="current-date()" />
   </aside>
   ```

   Figure 8-9 highlights the newly added code to the file.

Figure 8-9	Displaying the current date

excludes the XML Schema namespace from the result file

namespace for XML Schema data types

```
<xsl:stylesheet version="2.0"
    xmlns:xsl="http://www.w3.org/1999/XSL/Transform"
    xmlns:xs="http://www.w3.org/2001/XMLSchema"
    exclude-result-prefixes="xs">

    <xsl:output method="html"
        doctype-system="about:legacy-compat"
        encoding="UTF-8"
        indent="yes" />


    <xsl:template match="/">
        <html>
            <head>
                <title>Recent Orders</title>
                <link href="ifstyles.css" rel="stylesheet" type="text/css" />
            </head>

            <body>
                <div id="wrap">
                    <header>
                        <img src="iflogo.png" alt="Illuminated Fixtures" />
                    </header>

                    <aside>
                        Current Date:
                        <xsl:value-of select="current-date()" />
                    </aside>
```

displays the current date

TIP

If you are working in command line mode, you can keep the Command window open and press the up arrow on your keyboard to recall the previous command rather than retyping it.

5. Save your changes to the style sheet and then regenerate the result document orderlist.html using the following command if you are running Saxon in Java command line mode:

   ```
   java net.sf.saxon.Transform iforders.xml iforders.xsl
   -o:orderlist.html
   ```

   If you are not running Saxon in Java command line mode, use the command specific to your XSLT 2.0 processor.

6. Reload the **orderlist.html** file in your web browser and verify that the current date and time is shown in the upper-right corner of the web page. See Figure 8-10.

Figure 8-10	Displaying the current date and time

The current date provides a context for the report, but William would like to see this information displayed in a more readable format.

Formatting Date Values

The current date is displayed using the default XPath date format

   yyyy-mm-dd-tz

where *yyyy* is the year number, *mm* is the two-digit month value, *dd* is the two-digit day of the month, and *tz* is the time zone offset from Greenwich Mean Time. For example, the current date shown in Figure 8-10 corresponds to April 6, 2017, 5 hours prior to Greenwich Mean Time.

The order dates in the second column of the Recent Orders table display both the date and the time of the shipment with the format used with the `xs:dateTime` data type

   yyyy-mm-ddThh:mm:ss

where *hh* is the 2-digit hour value in 24-hour time, *mm* is the 2-digit minutes value, and *ss* is the 2-digit seconds value. The `T` symbol is used to separate the date from the time. Thus, the first shipment listed in the table left the warehouse on April 3, 2017, at 9:45 a.m.

XPath 2.0 provides the following three functions to format date and time values to make them more readable:

```
format-date(date, picture)
format-dateTime(dateTime, picture)
format-time(time, picture)
```

where *date* is a date value entered as an `xs:date` data type, *dateTime* is an `xs:dateTime` value, *time* is an `xs:time` value, and *picture* is a text string identifying the components to be output and their text format. The general format of the *picture* argument is

   [*marker1*] [*marker2*] [*marker3*] …

where *marker1*, *marker2*, *marker3*, and so on indicate the date and time components to be added to the output string and the format in which they are to be displayed. Any text outside of the square brackets is treated as literal text and is written directly to the date format. For example, the following picture argument:

   [M]/[D]/[Y]

would display a date such as April 6, 2017, as 4/6/2017. Figure 8-11 describes some of the different markers that can be used with date and time formats.

Figure 8-11 Date and time formats

Letter	Component	Default Format
Y	Year	4 digit value
M	Month	Integer: 1 – 12
D	Day of Month	Integer: 1 – 31
d	Day of Year	Integer: 1 – 366
F	Day of Week	Name of day
W	Week of Year	Integer: 1 – 52
w	Week of Month	Integer: 1 – 5
H	Hour (24 hour)	Integer: 00 – 23
h	Hour (12 hour)	Integer: 1 – 12
P	A.M. or P.M.	Text string
m	Minutes in hour	Integer: 00 – 59
s	Seconds in minute	Integer: 00 – 59
f	Fractional seconds	Numeric, one decimal place
Z	Timezone	Numeric, such as +6:00
z	Timezone	GMT+n
C	Calendar	Name of calendar
E	Era	Text string describing era such as A.D.

Each component can be augmented by one or more modifiers that indicate how the component should be displayed. For example, the marker [MN] displays the month name in uppercase letters (APRIL) while the marker [MNn] displays the month name in title case (April). Figure 8-12 describes the modifiers supported by XPath 2.0.

Figure 8-12 Date and time modifiers

Modifier	Format	Picture	Sample output
1	Decimal number	[M1]-[D1]	4-6
I	Uppercase Roman numeral	[MI]-[DI]	IV-VI
i	Lowercase Roman numeral	[Mi]-[Di]	iv-vi
W	Uppercase number in words	[MW]-[DW]	FOUR-SIX
w	Lowercase number in words	[Mw]-[Dw]	four-six
Ww	Title-case number in words	[MWw]-[DWw]	Four-Six
N	Uppercase name	[MN] [D1]	APRIL 6
n	Lowercase name	[Mn] [D1]	april 6
Nn	Title-case name	[MNn] [D1]	April 6
o	Ordinal numbering	[MNn] [D1o]	April 6th
,width	Display *width* characters	[MN,3] [D,2]	APR 06
,min-max	Display *min* up to *max* characters	[MN,3-4] [D,1-2]	APR 6
			JULY 14

REFERENCE

Formatting Date and Time Values

- To format a date and time value, apply one of the following XPath 2.0 functions:

```
format-date(date, picture)
format-dateTime(dateTime, picture)
format-time(time, picture)
```

where *date* is a date value entered as an *xs:date* data type, *dateTime* is an xs:dateTime value, *time* is an xs:time value, and *picture* is a text string identifying the components to be output and their text format.
- To specify the picture format, use the general form

```
[marker1] [marker2] [marker3] …
```

where *marker1*, *marker2*, *marker3*, and so on indicate the date and time components to be added to the picture format.

William suggests you apply a date format to the current date and order dates to display the full month name followed by the day of the month and the year.

To apply a date format:

1. Return to the **iforders.xsl** file in your text editor.

2. Return to the `value-of` element within the aside element (scrolling down as needed) and change the value of the `select` attribute to

```
format-date(current-date(),'[MNn] [D], [Y]')
```

Figure 8-13 highlights the code to format the current date value.

Figure 8-13	Formatting the current date

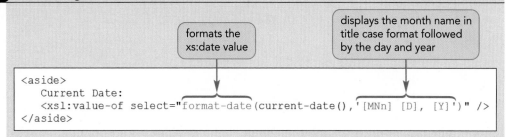

formats the
xs:date value

displays the month name in
title case format followed
by the day and year

```
<aside>
   Current Date:
   <xsl:value-of select="format-date(current-date(),'[MNn] [D], [Y]')" />
</aside>
```

Make sure you use the
`format-dateTime()`
function only with
values of the data type
`xs:dateTime`.

3. The order dates are stored as `xs:dateTime` data types. Scroll down to the order template and change the value displayed in the dateCell to

```
format-dateTime(orderDate, '[MNn] [D], [Y]')
```

Figure 8-14 highlights the code to format the date of each order.

Figure 8-14 Formatting the order date

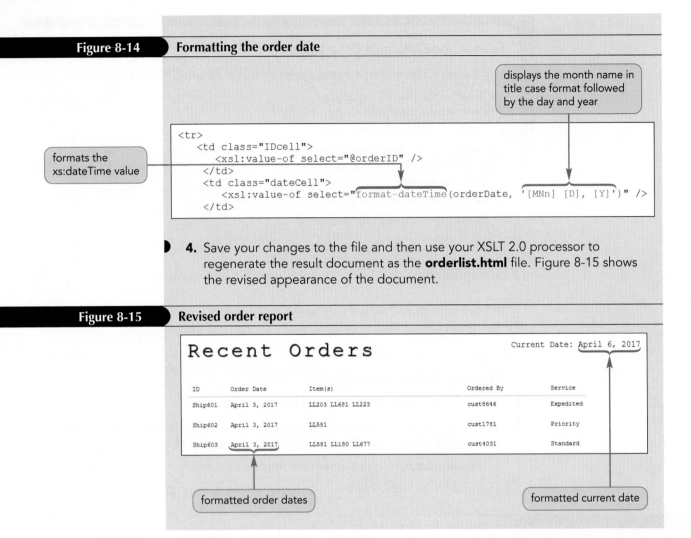

displays the month name in title case format followed by the day and year

formats the xs:dateTime value

```
<tr>
   <td class="IDcell">
      <xsl:value-of select="@orderID" />
   </td>
   <td class="dateCell">
      <xsl:value-of select="format-dateTime(orderDate, '[MNn] [D], [Y]')" />
   </td>
```

4. Save your changes to the file and then use your XSLT 2.0 processor to regenerate the result document as the **orderlist.html** file. Figure 8-15 shows the revised appearance of the document.

Figure 8-15 Revised order report

Current Date: April 6, 2017

Recent Orders

ID	Order Date	Item(s)	Ordered By	Service
Ship601	April 3, 2017	LL203 LL681 LL223	cust8646	Expedited
Ship602	April 3, 2017	LL581	cust1781	Priority
Ship603	April 3, 2017	LL581 LL180 LL677	cust4031	Standard

formatted order dates

formatted current date

Written Communication: Using XPath 2.0 to Display International Dates

The `format-date()`, `format-dateTime()`, and `format-time()` functions can be used with international dates and times. Each of the functions supports the following optional arguments:

```
language = "string"
calendar = "string"
country = "string"
```

where the `language` argument specifies the language to be used, the `calendar` argument provides a code for the calendar type, and the `country` argument identifies the country in which the dated event took place. While these three arguments are optional, they must be either all supplied or all omitted; however, you can use an empty set of parentheses to signify a missing value, leaving the processor to supply the default value.

For example, the following `format-date()` function is used to display a date format using the Hebrew calendar:

```
format-date('2002-12-31', '[D] [Mn] [Y]', 'he', 'AM', ())
```

returning the date string "26 טבת 5763" representing the date 2002-12-31 in the Hebrew language ('he') and the Jewish Calendar ('AM'). There is no country value specified.

The actual implementation and support for international date formats depends on the XSLT 2.0 processor. Be aware that not every processor supports this feature, so you have to check your processor's documentation for the specific code to apply international date formats.

Calculating Date and Time Durations

XPath 2.0 supports the XML Schema `xs:duration` data type for storing changes in dates and times. The general format of duration value is

```
PyYmMdDThHmMsS
```

where yY specifies the change in years, mM specifies the change in month, dD specifies the change in days, hH specifies the change in hours, mM specifies the change in minutes, and finally, sS specifies the change in seconds. For example, the following duration string specifies a duration of 5 years, 3 months, 10 days, 4 hours, 5 minutes, and 15 seconds:

```
P5Y3M10DT4H5M15S
```

You are not required to include all of the duration values in the text string. Thus, the text string

```
P3Y
```

sets the duration value to 3 years, while the text string

```
P3YT2H24M
```

sets the duration value to 3 years, 2 hours, and 24 minutes. You can extract specific components from the duration value using the XPath 2.0 functions described in Figure 8-16.

Figure 8-16	XPath 2.0 duration functions

Function	Description
years-from-duration(*duration*) months-from-duration(*duration*) days-from-duration(*duration*)	Returns the years, months, or days component from an xs:duration value
hours-from-duration(*duration*) minutes-from-duration(*duration*) seconds-from-duration(*duration*)	Returns the hours, minutes, or seconds component from an xs:duration value
duration(*string*)	Constructs an xs:duration data type based on the value specified in *string*
yearMonthDuration(*string*)	Constructs an xs:duration data type limited to the year and month components
dayTimeDuration(*string*)	Constructs an xs:duration data type limited to the days, hours, minutes, and seconds components

For example, the XPath expression

```
months-from-duration('P3Y4MT2H13M18S')
```

returns the value 4 because that is the number of months in a total duration of 3 years, 4 months, 2 hours, 13 minutes, and 18 seconds, while the expression

```
hours-from-duration('P3Y4MT2H13M18S')
```

returns the value 2 because there are 2 hours specified in the duration.

One of the uses of the durations is to increase a date or time value by a specified amount. XPath separates duration calculations into two constructor functions: one that deals only with days and times (hours, minutes, and seconds) and the other that focuses on years and months. This is done to avoid confusion between months and days, such as a duration that is entered as 4 months and 65 days with the day component itself extending beyond 2 months.

To add 5 days to the current date, you would apply the following `xs:dayTimeDuration()` constructor function:

```
current-date() + xs:dayTimeDuration('P5D')
```

To add 2 years and 4 months to the current date, you would apply the following `xs:yearMonthDuration()` constructor function:

```
current-date() + xs:yearMonthDuration('P2Y4M')
```

William wants his report to display the estimated arrival date of each item shipped. For now, you'll simply assume that the arrival date is five days after the order was placed; however, you will revise this later to allow for different and faster shipping times. You will add a new column to the Orders table that displays the estimated arrival date of the customer orders.

To estimate the delivery dates:

1. Return to the **iforders.xsl** file in your text editor.

2. Go to the root template and directly after the `<th>Service</th>` tag, insert the following table heading cell for the new column showing the estimated delivery dates:

```
<th>Est. Delivery</th>
```

3. Scroll down to the order template and, directly above the closing `</tr>` tag, insert the following table cell that will contain the estimated delivery dates in each table row:

```
<td class="deliveryCell">
</td>
```

4. Within the deliveryCell table cell, declare the following *shipDate* variable containing the atomic value of the orderDate node as an `xs:dateTime` data type:

```
<xsl:variable name="shipDate"
 select="orderDate" as="xs:dateTime" />
```

5. Declare the *deliveryDate* variable with a value equal to shipDate plus a duration of 5 days using the following XSLT instruction:

```
<xsl:variable name="deliveryDate"
 select="$shipDate + xs:dayTimeDuration('P5D')"
 as="xs:dateTime" />
```

6. Finally, display the value of the *deliveryDate* variable formatted to display the day of the week, month name, day, and year value using the following XSLT instruction:

```
<xsl:value-of select="format-dateTime($deliveryDate, '[FNn],
 [MNn] [D], [Y]')" />
```

Figure 8-17 highlights the revised code in the file to calculate and format the estimated delivery date.

Figure 8-17	Calculating a 5-day delivery date

7. Save your changes to the file and then use your XSLT 2.0 processor to regenerate the result file, storing the document in the orderlist.html file.

Figure 8-18 shows the estimated delivery dates for the orders in the order report.

Figure 8-18 Estimated arrival dates assuming 5-day delivery

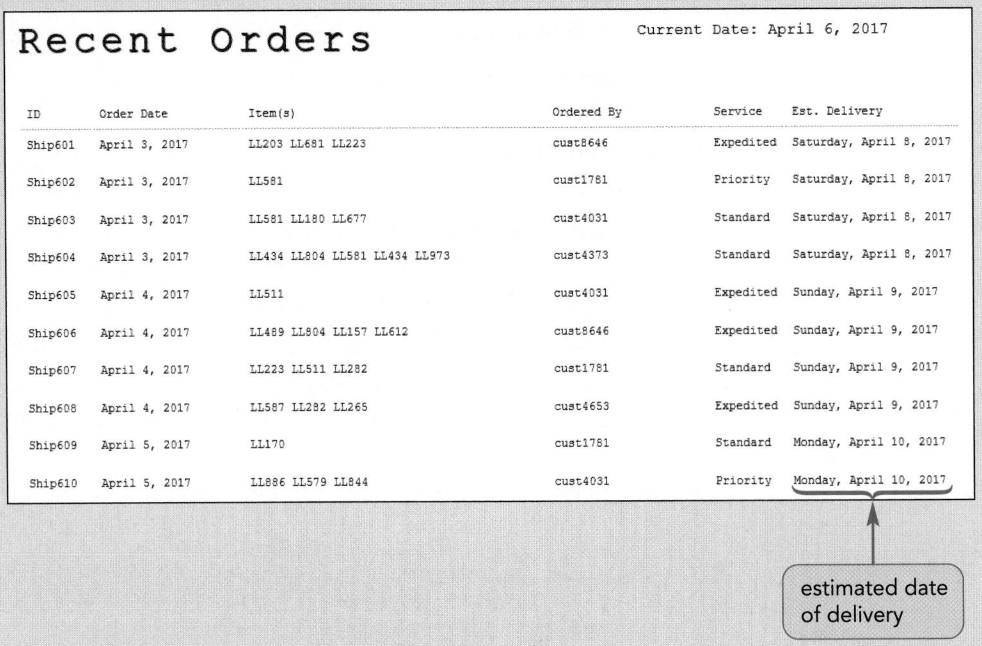

Recent Orders

Current Date: April 6, 2017

ID	Order Date	Item(s)	Ordered By	Service	Est. Delivery
Ship601	April 3, 2017	LL203 LL681 LL223	cust8646	Expedited	Saturday, April 8, 2017
Ship602	April 3, 2017	LL581	cust1781	Priority	Saturday, April 8, 2017
Ship603	April 3, 2017	LL581 LL180 LL677	cust4031	Standard	Saturday, April 8, 2017
Ship604	April 3, 2017	LL434 LL804 LL581 LL434 LL973	cust4373	Standard	Saturday, April 8, 2017
Ship605	April 4, 2017	LL511	cust4031	Expedited	Sunday, April 9, 2017
Ship606	April 4, 2017	LL489 LL804 LL157 LL612	cust8646	Expedited	Sunday, April 9, 2017
Ship607	April 4, 2017	LL223 LL511 LL282	cust1781	Standard	Sunday, April 9, 2017
Ship608	April 4, 2017	LL587 LL282 LL265	cust4653	Expedited	Sunday, April 9, 2017
Ship609	April 5, 2017	LL170	cust1781	Standard	Monday, April 10, 2017
Ship610	April 5, 2017	LL886 LL579 LL844	cust4031	Priority	Monday, April 10, 2017

This report assumes that all deliveries are completed in exactly five days; however, in practice Illuminated Fixtures provides three delivery options: Priority with overnight delivery, Expedited with two-day delivery, and Standard with a delivery time of up to five days. To modify this order report to use these delivery schedules, you'll first have to learn about sequences in XPath 2.0.

Introducing Sequences

> **TIP**
> Empty sequences are entered as ().

XPath 2.0 replaces the XPath 1.0 concept of the node set with sequences, where a sequence is any ordered list of items. Sequences can be entered directly as a comma-separated list of values enclosed within a set of parentheses. The values do not need to have the same data type; for example, the following sequence contains a list of four items: a text string, an integer value, a Boolean value, and a date:

```
('Fixtures', 3, true(), xs:date('2017-04-06'))
```

> **TIP**
> The expression `(100 to 1)` creates a sequence of integers starting at 100 and ending at 1.

Sequences of integers can be created more compactly using the notation

```
(start to finish)
```

where ***`start`*** is the initial integer value and ***`finish`*** is the ending integer. Thus, the expression

```
(1 to 100)
```

creates a sequence of integers starting with 1 and ending at 100.

Sequences are treated as flat lists and thus you cannot nest one sequence within another. The result will always be treated as a single list. The following sequence of integers

```
(1, 2, (6, 4), 5, (3, 8))
```

is equivalent to

```
(1, 2, 6, 4, 5, 3, 8)
```

Even though it has multiple values, a sequence also has a data type. To indicate the sequence's data type, add an occurrence indicator to the data type using the symbol * for zero to many, + for one to many, and ? for zero-to-one values. For example, the following data type is used for a sequence that contains one or more `xs:dateTime` values:

```
xs:dateTime+
```

while the data type

```
xs:date*
```

is used for any sequence that contains zero or more dates. If no occurrence indicator is provided, the sequence is assumed to have only one item.

Sequences and Node Sets

In the XPath 2.0 data model, everything is a sequence, including node sets. While XPath 2.0 still supports the node set operations from XPath 1.0, there are a few important differences in how node sets are handled. In the XPath 1.0 data model, nodes are processed in document order, while in the XPath 2.0 data model, nodes can be arranged in any order within a sequence. For example, the following XPath 2.0 expression creates a variable named employees containing a sequence of all of the fullTime elements in the document, followed by all of the partTime elements.

```
<xsl:variable name="employees" select="(//fullTime, //partTime)" />
```

An XPath 2.0 sequence also does not need to be confined to nodes from the same document. In the following statements, the variable *employees* is associated with a sequence of elements containing fulltime and then part-time employee data, which is drawn from two separate documents referenced in the *emp1* and *emp2* variables.

```
<xsl:variable name="emp1" select="document('full.xml')//emp" />
<xsl:variable name="emp2" select="document('part.xml')//emp" />
<xsl:variable name="employees" select="($emp1, $emp2)" />
```

Another important difference from XPath 1.0 is that an XPath 2.0 sequence can contain duplicate nodes. Thus, the following XPath 2.0 sequence consists of all of the fullTime elements followed by all of the partTime elements and then concluding with the fullTime elements.

```
(//fullTime, //partTime, //fullTime)
```

This type of arrangement is not possible in XPath 1.0 because that data model does not allow node sets to contain the same node more than once.

Depending on the data type, XPath can treat node sets either as a sequence of atomic values or a sequence of nodes. Figure 8-19 describes the data types associated with XML nodes.

| Figure 8-19 | Data types associated with XML nodes |

Data Type	Description
element()	An element node
element(*elem*)	An element named *elem*
attribute()	An attribute node
attribute(*att*)	An attribute named *att*
text()	A text node
node()	Any type of XML node
item()	Either a node or an atomic value

For example, the following variable *empData* contains a sequence of zero to many element nodes referenced by the XPath expression //employees.

```
<xs:variable name="empData" select="//employees" as="element()*" />
```

On the other hand, the same variable *empData* can create a sequence of zero to many string data types from the nodes in the //employees location path:

```
<xs:variable name="empData" select="//employees" as="xs:string*" />
```

By treating the values from the //employees location path as a sequence of text strings, XPath 2.0 can apply string functions to those values.

XPath 2.0 makes it easy to combine several different sequences into a single sequence. You've already seen that the comma symbol (,) acts as a concatenation operator by combining two sequences while maintaining the sequence order. The union | operator returns the union of two sequences, removing any duplicates. Thus, the XPath 2.0 expression that applies the union operator to two sequences

```
($node1, $node2, $node3) | ($node3, $node4, $node5)
```

results in the single sequence

```
($node1, $node2, $node3, $node4, $node5)
```

The intersect operator returns the intersection of two sequences, once again removing duplicates. When applied to the following sequence:

```
($node1, $node2, $node3) intersect ($node3, $node4, $node5)
```

XPath 2.0 returns items common to both sequences, which in this case is the single item sequence

```
($node3)
```

Finally, the `except` operator returns every item from the first sequence that is not present in the second sequence. Thus, the expression

```
($node1, $node2, $node3) except ($node3, $node4, $node5)
```

returns the sequence

```
($node1, $node2)
```

Each of these node set operations is much more difficult to achieve under the XPath 1.0 data model.

Looping Through a Sequence

Just as you could use the `for-each` element to loop through the contents of a node set under XSTL 1.0, you can apply the `for-each` element under XSLT 2.0 to loop through the items within a sequence. For example, if a sequence has the following state abbreviations

```
<xsl:variable name="state"
  select="('AZ', 'CA', 'OR', 'WA')" />
```

then you can reference each item value in the following loop:

```
<xsl:for-each select="$state">
   <xsl:value-of select="." />
   <br />
</xsl:for-each>
```

The loop returns the following lines of code:

```
AZ<br />CA<br />OR<br />WA<br />
```

Note that the symbol "`.`", which in XPath 1.0 represents the context node, represents the current item in the sequence that is being processed in XPath 2.0.

Sequence Operations

Everything you've learned about predicates from XPath1.0 can be applied to sequences in XPath 2.0. Applying a predicate to a sequence returns a new sequence containing only those items that satisfy the conditions of the predicate. The following expression demonstrates the use of a predicate to return the second item from a sequence of text strings:

```
('P1D', 'P2D', 'P5D')[2]
```

resulting in a sequence containing the single item 'P2D'. A predicate can also apply a conditional expression to each item in the sequence. In the following expression, each item in the sequence is tested to see whether its value is greater than 3:

```
(3, 8, 4, 2, 1)[. > 3]
```

After applying the predicate, XPath 2.0 returns the sequence

```
(8, 4)
```

Notice that the conditional expression is applied in item order starting from the first sequence item (8) and ending at the last (4) that meets the condition and, notice once again, that the "`.`" symbol is used to indicate the current item in the sequence.

The opposite problem is to determine the position of a specified value within a sequence. This can be accomplished using the following `index-of()` operator:

```
index-of(sequence, value)
```

where `index-of` returns the position integer based on sequence and `value`, `sequence` is a sequence of items, and `value` is the value to search for within the sequence. For example, the following expression finds the position of the text string value 'P2D' within the sequence ('P1D', 'P2D', 'P5D'):

```
index-of(('P1D', 'P2D', 'P5D'),'P2D')
```

returning the integer value, 2, indicating the position of 'P2D', which is the second item in the sequence. If the sequence returns multiple instances of the specified value, the `index-of()` operator returns a sequence that contains every index value, which is the position value of each instance. If the sequence doesn't contain the specified value, the `index-of()` operator returns an empty sequence.

REFERENCE

Applying Sequence Operations

- To return the index value, which is the position of an item in a sequence, use the XPath 2.0 function

  ```
  index-of(sequence, value)
  ```

  where *sequence* is a sequence of items and *value* is the value to search for within the sequence.
- To return a sequence item by its position, use the predicate

  ```
  sequence[position]
  ```

  where *position* is the index value of the item in the sequence.

At this point, you've learned enough about sequences to apply them to the Illuminated Fixture's order report. Recall that William wants to revise the order report so that the estimated delivery date has a duration of 1 day for Priority deliveries, 2 days for Expedited deliveries, and 5 days for Standard deliveries. Assigning the right duration to each delivery type can be done using a set of conditional expressions, but it can be done more compactly with sequences. First, you'll define two variables named *durations* and *deliveryTypes*. The *durations* variable will contain a sequence of durations (1 day, 2 days, and 5 days), while the *deliveryTypes* variable will contain a sequence of the delivery types. The code is

```
<xsl:variable name="durations"
 select="('P1D', 'P2D', 'P5D')" />
<xsl:variable name="deliveryTypes"
 select="('Priority', 'Expedited', 'Standard')" />
```

Then, you'll retrieve the value of the shipType element from the source document and store it in the *sType* variable to determine how each order is to be delivered. Finally, you'll determine the index value of the *sType* variable within the *deliveryTypes* sequence and apply that index value in a predicate to the *durations* sequence:

```
<xsl:variable name="sType" select="shipType" />
<xsl:variable name="deliveryDays"
 select="$durations[index-of($deliveryTypes, $sType)]" />
```

The end result is that the *deliveryDays* variable will return the number of days until the order is to be delivered to the customer.

You will now enter this code into the iforders.xsl file to calculate the estimated delivery dates for each item in the order report.

To estimate the delivery dates:

1. Return to the **iforders.xsl** file in your text editor.

2. Scroll down to the deliveryCell within the order template and, directly after the *shipDate* variable, insert the following code to define the *durations*, *deliveryTypes*, *sType*, and *deliveryDays* variables:

```
<xsl:variable name="durations" select="('P1D', 'P2D', 'P5D')" />
<xsl:variable name="deliveryTypes"
 select="('Priority', 'Expedited', 'Standard')" />
<xsl:variable name="sType" select="shipType" />
<xsl:variable name="deliveryDays"
 select="$durations[index-of($deliveryTypes, $sType)]" />
```

3. Within the statement to create the *deliveryDate* variable, change the duration value from the text string 'P5D' to **$deliveryDays** to use the value of the *deliveryDays* variable in estimating the date of delivery.

Figure 8-20 highlights the revised code in the style sheet to create these four variables.

Figure 8-20   **Creating and applying sequences**

sequence of duration values

sequences of durations and delivery types

calculates the estimated date of delivery based on shipping type

uses the index-of() operator to match a duration with a shipping type

```
<td class="deliveryCell">
  <xsl:variable name="shipDate"
   select="orderDate" as="xs:dateTime" />

  <xsl:variable name="durations" select="('P1D', 'P2D', 'P5D')" />
  <xsl:variable name="deliveryTypes" select="('Priority', 'Expedited', 'Standard')" />
  <xsl:variable name="sType" select="shipType" />
  <xsl:variable name="deliveryDays" select="$durations[index-of($deliveryTypes, $sType)]" />

  <xsl:variable name="deliveryDate"
   select="$shipDate + xs:dayTimeDuration($deliveryDays)"
   as="xs:dateTime" />

  <xsl:value-of select="format-dateTime($deliveryDate, '[FNn], [MNn] [D], [Y]')" />
</td>
```

4. Use your XSLT 2.0 processor to regenerate the result document, saving the document as **orderlist.html**.

> **5.** Reopen **orderlist.html** in your web browser. Figure 8-21 shows the current list of orders and their estimated delivery dates.

Figure 8-21	Estimated dates of delivery

Recent Orders   Current Date: April 6, 2017

ID	Order Date	Item(s)	Ordered By	Service	Est. Delivery
Ship601	April 3, 2017	LL203 LL681 LL223	cust8646	Expedited	Wednesday, April 5, 2017
Ship602	April 3, 2017	LL581	cust1781	Priority	Tuesday, April 4, 2017
Ship603	April 3, 2017	LL581 LL180 LL677	cust4031	Standard	Saturday, April 8, 2017
Ship604	April 3, 2017	LL434 LL804 LL581 LL434 LL973	cust4373	Standard	Saturday, April 8, 2017
Ship605	April 4, 2017	LL511	cust4031	Expedited	Thursday, April 6, 2017
Ship606	April 4, 2017	LL489 LL804 LL157 LL612	cust8646	Expedited	Thursday, April 6, 2017
Ship607	April 4, 2017	LL223 LL511 LL282	cust1781	Standard	Sunday, April 9, 2017
Ship608	April 4, 2017	LL587 LL282 LL265	cust4653	Expedited	Thursday, April 6, 2017
Ship609	April 5, 2017	LL170	cust1781	Standard	Monday, April 10, 2017
Ship610	April 5, 2017	LL886 LL579 LL844	cust4031	Priority	Thursday, April 6, 2017

order and shipping date

delivery type (1 day for Priority, 2 days for Expedited, 5 days for Standard)

estimated date of delivery

You show the revised order report to William, who notes that your report shows some estimated delivery dates occurring on Saturday and Sunday. He tells you that the shipping company does not deliver on those days and wants you to revise your code to take this into account. You'll work on that revision in the next session.

Session 8.1 Quick Check

REVIEW

1. Provide code to retrieve every file from the current style sheet folder that starts with the text string "data" and ends with the .xml file extension.
2. How does the implementation of the XSLT `value-of` element differ between XSLT 1.0 and XSLT 2.0 when applied to element nodes?
3. Provide code to store the value of the location path //orderQty as a non-negative integer data type from XML Schema in a variable named *Orders*.
4. Provide code to display the current date in the format *Weekday, Month Day, Year*.
5. Assuming the *orderDate* variable contains an `xs:dateTime` value, provide code to create the *expireDate* variable containing an `xs:dateTime` value 1 year and 6 months after *orderDate*.
6. Provide an expression to create a sequence of the first 50 integers, starting with 50 and going down to 1.
7. Provide an expression to retrieve the third item from the sequence: ('Detroit', 'Chicago', 'Dallas', 'Boston').
8. Provide the sequence returned by the expression
   ```
   index-of(('A', 'B', 'C', 'A', 'A', 'B'),'A')
   ```

Session 8.2 Visual Overview:

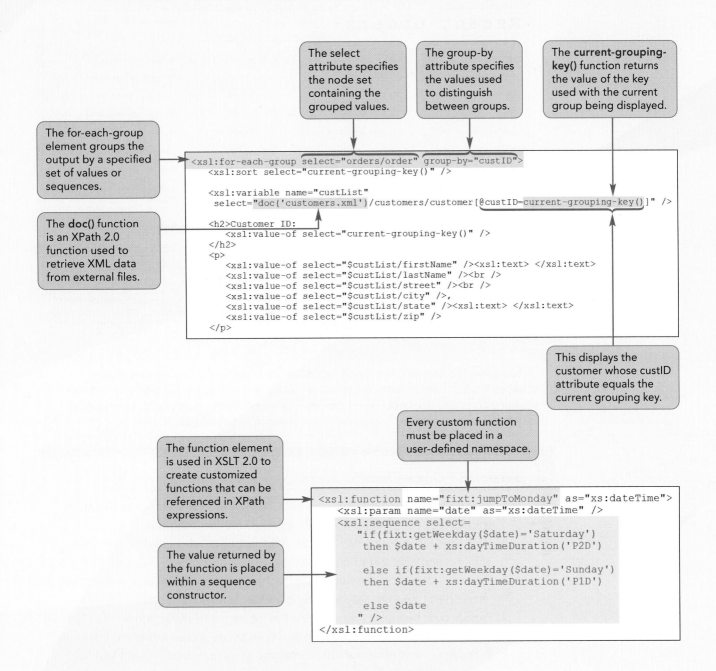

The select attribute specifies the node set containing the grouped values.

The group-by attribute specifies the values used to distinguish between groups.

The **current-grouping-key()** function returns the value of the key used with the current group being displayed.

The for-each-group element groups the output by a specified set of values or sequences.

The **doc()** function is an XPath 2.0 function used to retrieve XML data from external files.

```
<xsl:for-each-group select="orders/order" group-by="custID">
    <xsl:sort select="current-grouping-key()" />

    <xsl:variable name="custList"
     select="doc('customers.xml')/customers/customer[@custID=current-grouping-key()]" />

    <h2>Customer ID:
        <xsl:value-of select="current-grouping-key()" />
    </h2>
    <p>
        <xsl:value-of select="$custList/firstName" /><xsl:text> </xsl:text>
        <xsl:value-of select="$custList/lastName" /><br />
        <xsl:value-of select="$custList/street" /><br />
        <xsl:value-of select="$custList/city" />,
        <xsl:value-of select="$custList/state" /><xsl:text> </xsl:text>
        <xsl:value-of select="$custList/zip" />
    </p>
```

This displays the customer whose custID attribute equals the current grouping key.

Every custom function must be placed in a user-defined namespace.

The function element is used in XSLT 2.0 to create customized functions that can be referenced in XPath expressions.

The value returned by the function is placed within a sequence constructor.

```
<xsl:function name="fixt:jumpToMonday" as="xs:dateTime">
    <xsl:param name="date" as="xs:dateTime" />
    <xsl:sequence select=
        "if(fixt:getWeekday($date)='Saturday')
        then $date + xs:dayTimeDuration('P2D')

        else if(fixt:getWeekday($date)='Sunday')
        then $date + xs:dayTimeDuration('P1D')

        else $date
        " />
</xsl:function>
```

Functions and Grouping

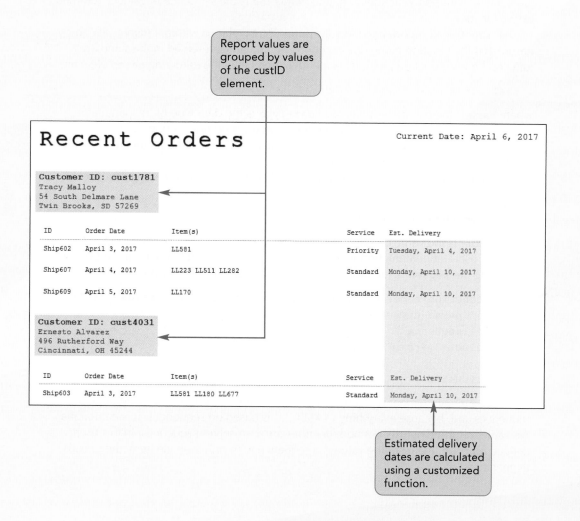

Report values are grouped by values of the custID element.

Recent Orders

Current Date: April 6, 2017

Customer ID: cust1781
Tracy Malloy
54 South Delmare Lane
Twin Brooks, SD 57269

ID	Order Date	Item(s)	Service	Est. Delivery
Ship602	April 3, 2017	LL581	Priority	Tuesday, April 4, 2017
Ship607	April 4, 2017	LL223 LL511 LL282	Standard	Monday, April 10, 2017
Ship609	April 5, 2017	LL170	Standard	Monday, April 10, 2017

Customer ID: cust4031
Ernesto Alvarez
496 Rutherford Way
Cincinnati, OH 45244

ID	Order Date	Item(s)	Service	Est. Delivery
Ship603	April 3, 2017	LL581 LL180 LL677	Standard	Monday, April 10, 2017

Estimated delivery dates are calculated using a customized function.

Creating Functions with XSLT 2.0

XSLT 1.0 used named templates as a way of performing calculations and manipulating node sets. XPath 2.0 still supports named templates, but much of their utility has been supplemented with the following user-defined function:

```
<xsl:function name="prefix:name" as="dataType">
   parameters
   sequence
</xsl:function>
```

where *prefix:name* is the name of the function and the prefix identifies its namespace, *dataType* is the type of data value(s) returned by the function, *parameters* are the parameters required by the function, and *sequence* is the sequence of value(s) returned by the function.

The names of all user-defined functions need to be placed within a namespace to ensure that the function name doesn't conflict with names reserved in the standard function library. Function parameters are identified using the following `param` element:

```
<xsl:param name="name" as="dataType" />
```

where *name* is the parameter name and *dataType* is the data type of the parameter value. Unlike named templates, user-defined functions do not support optional parameters; thus, any parameter listed within the function must be included when the function is called or else an error will result.

The value(s) returned by the function are enclosed within the following sequence constructor:

```
<xsl:sequence select="value" />
```

where *value* is the value or values returned by the function. For example, the following user-defined function is used to convert a Fahrenheit temperature to Celsius, employing the `sequence` element to return the calculated Celsius value.

```
<xsl:function name="myfunc:farhenheitToCelsius" as="xs:decimal">
   <xsl:param name="tempF" as="xs:decimal" />
   <xsl:sequence
    select="($tempF - 32) div 1.8"
   />
</xsl:function>
```

The `sequence` element is a general XSTL 2.0 element used to define and populate sequences and, because everything in XSLT 2.0 is based on sequences, it is natural that the values returned by user-defined functions are themselves sequences. In this user-defined function, the resulting value is a sequence with only a single item (the Celsius temperature value).

Creating a User-Defined Function

- To create a user-defined function, enter the following structure:

```
<xsl:function name="prefix:name" as="dataType">
   parameters
   sequence
</xsl:function>
```

where *prefix:name* is the name of the function and the prefix identifies its namespace, *dataType* is the type of data value(s) returned by the function, *parameters* are the parameters required by the function, and *sequence* is the sequence of value(s) returned by the function.

- To define the function parameter, use the element

```
<xsl:param name="name" as="dataType" />
```

where *name* is the parameter name and *dataType* is the data type of the parameter value.

- To define the sequence value returned by the function, use the constructor

```
<xsl:sequence select="value" />
```

where *value* is the value or values returned by the function.

Writing an XSLT 2.0 Function

William wants a function that returns the day of the week for a specified date and time. There is no built-in XPath 2.0 function that returns this value, but you can create one by returning the formatted date text as a text string from the function.

To create a function in XSLT 2.0

1. If you took a break after the previous session, make sure the **iforders.xsl** document is open in your text editor.

2. Near the top of the file, insert the following namespace declaration immediately before the `exclude-result-prefixes` attribute within the `stylesheet` element:

   xmlns:fixt="http://example.com/illumfixtures"

3. Add the **fixt** namespace prefix to the `exclude-result-prefixes` attribute. See Figure 8-22.

Figure 8-22 **Defining the namespace for user functions**

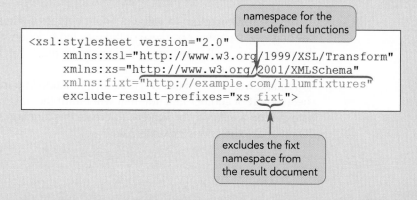

namespace for the user-defined functions

```
<xsl:stylesheet version="2.0"
    xmlns:xsl="http://www.w3.org/1999/XSL/Transform"
    xmlns:xs="http://www.w3.org/2001/XMLSchema"
    xmlns:fixt="http://example.com/illumfixtures"
    exclude-result-prefixes="xs fixt">
```

excludes the fixt namespace from the result document

Be sure to enclose the select attribute of the sequence constructor within a set of quotation marks.

4. Scroll down to the bottom of the style sheet file and, directly after the order template, insert the following function:

```
<xsl:function name="fixt:getWeekday" as="xs:string">
   <xsl:param name="dateValue" as="xs:dateTime" />
   <xsl:sequence select="
     format-dateTime($dateValue, '[FNn]')
     " />
</xsl:function>
```

See Figure 8-23.

Figure 8-23 ▶ **Creating the getWeekday() function**

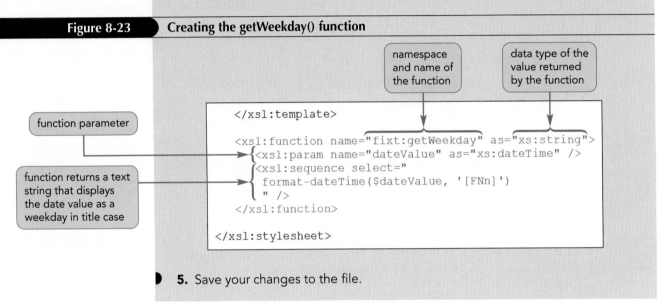

5. Save your changes to the file.

Running an XSLT 2.0 Function

User-defined functions are treated like built-in functions and thus can be run from within an XPath 2.0 expression. The general syntax is

```
prefix:name(value1, value2, …)
```

where *prefix:name* is the namespace prefix and name of the user-defined function and *value1, value2,* and so on are values assigned to the function's parameters. Because there are no optional parameters allowed in user-defined functions, the number of parameter values must match the number of `param` elements within the function. For example, the following XPath expression calls the farhenheitToCelsius() function defined earlier with the value 58 for the *tempF* parameter:

```
myfunc:farhenheitToCelsius(58)
```

This expression returns a value of 14.44 degrees Celsius. Notice that this expression has only one parameter because of the way the function was defined earlier. Note that the namespace prefix, myfunc in this example, must match the namespace prefix used when defining the function.

William wants to call the getWeekday() function you inserted in the iforders.xsl style sheet as part of another function that will return the next business day if the specified date falls on a Saturday or Sunday. To create this function, you'll explore how to write conditional expressions in XPath 2.0.

Creating Conditional Expressions in XPath 2.0

Under XSLT 1.0, conditional expressions are created using the `if` and `choose` elements. One problem with this approach is that it sometimes results in long and complicated code. XSLT 2.0 provides a more compact approach in which conditional tests can be entered within a single XPath expression using the following `if` operator:

```
if (test) then result1 else result2
```

where *test* is a conditional test that evaluates the condition as either `true` or `false`, *result1* is the returned value if true, and *result2* is the returned value if false.

For example, the value of the following *discount* variable is determined using an `if` operator that tests whether the value of the *qty* variable is greater than 10. If so, it sets the value of the variable to 0.10; otherwise, the value is set to 0.

```
<xsl:variable name="discount"
 select="if ($qty > 10) then 0.1 else 0" />
```

Note that both the `then` and `else` keywords need to be present to avoid a syntax error. If there is no else condition, enter an empty sequence as follows:

```
if (test) then result else ()
```

XPath 2.0 also allows for multiple conditional tests by stringing together several if operators:

```
if (test1) then result1
else if (test2) then result2
else if (test3) then result3
else result4
```

XPath conditional expressions are often used to test whether a node value exists before attempting to perform a calculation. The following expression returns the sum of customer orders but only if the location path $customer/orders exists; otherwise, it returns the value 'NaN' indicating that no such sum exists.

```
if ($customer/orders) then
sum($customer/orders) else number('NaN')
```

By using this conditional expression, the programmer avoids the possibility of an error that would cause the style sheet to crash due to a missing customer order.

You'll use a conditional expression now in a function named jumpToMonday() that tests whether a specified date stored in the *date* variable falls on the weekend. If *date* is Saturday the function returns the date of the following Monday (2 days later), else if *date* is a Sunday the function returns the date of the following Monday (1 day later). If *date* does not fall on a weekend, then the function simply returns the value of *date*. The conditional expression used in the function is

```
if(fixt:getWeekday($date) = 'Saturday')
then $date + xs:dayTimeDuration('P2D')
else
if(fixt:getWeekday($date) = 'Sunday')
then $date + xs:dayTimeDuration('P1D')
else $date
```

Note that this function calls the getWeekday() function you created earlier to determine the day of the week. You'll create the jumpToMonday() function now.

To write a conditional expression in XPath 2.0:

1. Add the following function directly after the getWeekday( ) function in the iforders.xsl style sheet file:

```
<xsl:function name="fixt:jumpToMonday" as="xs:dateTime">
  <xsl:param name="date" as="xs:dateTime" />
  <xsl:sequence select=
   "if(fixt:getWeekday($date)='Saturday')
    then $date + xs:dayTimeDuration('P2D')

    else if(fixt:getWeekday($date)='Sunday')
    then $date + xs:dayTimeDuration('P1D')

    else $date
   " />
</xsl:function>
```

Figure 8-24 shows the complete code of the jumpToMonday() function.

Figure 8-24 **Creating the jumpToMonday() function**

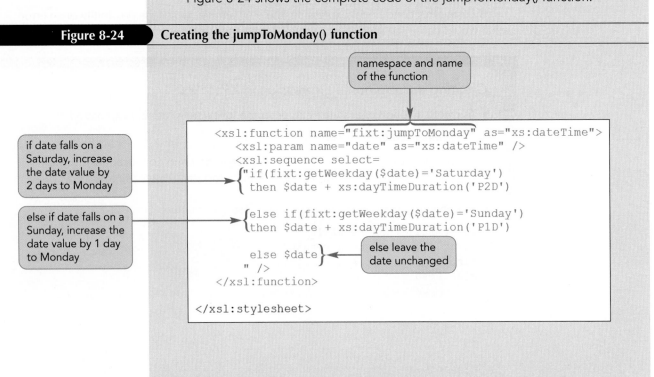

2. Scroll up to the order template and revise the expression to display the value of the *deliveryDate* variable by calling the jumpToMonday() function using *deliveryDate* for the parameter value, as shown in Figure 8-25. You might want to revise the line breaks within the expression to make your code easier to read.

Figure 8-25	Calling the jumpToMonday() function

applies the jumpToMonday() function to deliveryDate

```
<xsl:variable name="deliveryDate"
  select="$shipDate + xs:dayTimeDuration($deliveryDays)"
  as="xs:dateTime" />

<xsl:value-of select="format-dateTime(fixt:jumpToMonday($deliveryDate),
                      '[FNn], [MNn] [D], [Y]')" />
</td>
```

3. Save your changes to the style sheet and then regenerate the result document into the **orderlist.html** file using your XSLT 2.0 processor. Figure 8-26 shows the revised estimated delivery dates for the recent orders made to Illuminated Fixtures.

Figure 8-26	Delivery dates with weekends excluded

estimated delivery dates moved to the following Monday

Note that three of the orders were shifted from weekend deliveries to Monday.

Summary Calculations with XPath 2.0

Summary functions in XPath 1.0 were limited to the `sum()` and `count()` functions to return the sum and count from a set of numeric values. XPath 2.0 expanded on this by including the `avg()`, `max()`, and `min()` functions to calculate averages, maximums, and minimums. Beyond these new functions, the XPath 2.0 data model supports summarizing items across a sequence of calculated values. For example, to calculate the total cost of an order that is equal to the price of each item multiplied by its quantity, you can apply the following XPath 2.0 expression:

```
<xsl:variable name="totalOrderCost"
   select="sum(item/(@price * @quantity))" />
```

where price and quantity are both attributes of the item element. XPath 2.0 automatically generates a temporary sequence of each product of price and quantity and then applies the `sum()` function to that sequence of calculated values. To do the same calculation in XPath 1.0 would require a recursive template in which price and quantity is multiplied for each item and then a running total is updated through the recursion process. XSLT 2.0 provides a much simpler and more direct approach.

Having calculated the estimated delivery for each order, William would like the report grouped by customer. To modify the report, you'll use the grouping functions introduced in XSLT 2.0.

Grouping Data in XSLT 2.0

Grouping data, a laborious task in XSLT 1.0, is made much easier in XSLT 2.0 with the following `for-each-group` element:

```
<xsl:for-each-group select="items" grouping-method>
   styles
</xsl:for-each-group>
```

where *items* is the sequence of items to be grouped, also known as the **population**, and *grouping-method* defines the method by which items in the sequence are assigned to their group. The `for-each-group` element implicitly creates a grouping key and assigns each item in the population to a group based on that key. The processor then loops through the grouping key values, applying styles to the items within each group.

Grouping Methods

XSLT 2.0 supports two general grouping methods: grouping by value and grouping in sequence. With **grouping by value**, all items from the population that share the same grouping key value are grouped together. One way to define the grouping key is by the following `group-by` attribute:

```
group-by="expression"
```

where *expression* is an XPath expression containing the grouping key. For example, the following code groups items in an employees node set based on distinct values of the status attribute.

```
<xsl:for-each-group select="//employees" group-by="@status">
...
</xsl:for-each-group>
```

The *group-by* attribute allocates items to group regardless of their position in the population. In some applications, you may want to group items only if they share a common value and are adjacent to each other in the population order. To group items using this method, apply the following *group-adjacent* attribute:

```
group-adjacent="expression"
```

Consider a sorted population of dated events extending across several weeks in which you want to group each event by day of the week but you want to retain the date order so that not all Monday events are grouped together. By applying the following *for-each-group* element you can group each event by the weekday attribute but not place all Monday events in a single group unless they are listed adjacently in the population:

```
<xsl:for-each-group select="//event" group-adjacent="@weekday">
...
</xsl:for-each-group>
```

The **grouping in sequence** option does not rely on item values but rather their position in the sequence. Values are evaluated in population order, and the beginning or ending of each group is marked by a specified pattern. The attribute to mark the beginning of each group is

```
group-starting-with="pattern"
```

where a new group is started for each item in the population that matches *pattern*. For example, if the population contains a collection of time-ordered events marked by the day of the week, you can create weekly groups starting with Monday of each week using the following code:

```
<xsl:for-each-group select="//event"
  group-starting-with="@weekday='Monday'">
...
</xsl:for-each-group>
```

Thus, every group will contain the events starting from Monday through the end of the week with a new group starting when the next Monday event is encountered in the sequence. To mark the ending of each group use the group-ending-with attribute

```
group-ending-with="pattern"
```

where a new group is started with the first item that follows an item matching *pattern*. To group weekly based on events ending with Sunday, you would use the following code:

```
<xsl:for-each-group select="//event"
  group-ending-with="@weekday='Sunday'">
...
</xsl:for-each-group>
```

In this case, each time the processor encounters a Sunday event, the next item in the population (presumably Monday) is marked as the beginning of a new group.

Because William wants to organize the Recent Orders report by customer, you'll use the for-each-group element now to organize the report based on customer ID using the group-by attribute.

To group the order list by customer ID:

1. Return to the **iforders.xsl** file in your text editor.

2. Go to the root template and, directly below the `<h1>Recent Orders</h1>` tag, insert the following statement to group the orders/order sequence based on the value of the custID element.

```
<xsl:for-each-group select="orders/order" group-by="custID">
```

3. Scroll down and, directly below the closing `</table>` tag, insert

`</xsl:for-each-group>`

to close off the opening tag.

Figure 8-27 shows the code to group the order report by customer ID.

Figure 8-27	Creating groups with the for-each-group element

```
<h1>Recent Orders</h1>
<xsl:for-each-group select="orders/order" group-by="custID">

<table id="shipmentList">
    <thead>
        <tr>
            <th>ID</th>
            <th>Order Date</th>
            <th>Item(s)</th>
            <th>Ordered By</th>
            <th>Service</th>
            <th>Est. Delivery</th>
        </tr>
    </thead>
    <tbody>
        <xsl:apply-templates select="orders/order" />
    </tbody>
</table>

</xsl:for-each-group>
</div>
```

groups the contents of the orders/order node set

groups by distinct values of the custID element

Next, you'll explore how to apply styles to the items within a group.

Applying Styles to a Group

When the processor encounters the `for-each-group` element, it creates sequences drawn from the items in the population that belong to each group. As the processor creates each group, the current group being created is referenced using the following XPath 2.0 function:

`current-group()`

To apply a template to the items within the current group, you use the `current-group()` function as part of the `select` attribute in the following `apply-templates` element:

`<xsl:apply-templates select="current-group()" />`

This approach assumes that a template has been created that will match the node set referenced by the current group.

When groups are based on a value using either the `group-by` or `group-adjacent` attribute, the key value associated with the current group is returned using the XPath 2.0 function

`current-grouping-key()`

For example, if you group a sequence of nodes based on the customer ID value, the `current-grouping-key()` function will return the ID for whatever customer is currently being processed by the style sheet. Thus, the statement

`<h2><xsl:value-of select="current-grouping-key()" /></h2>`

displays the customer ID from each customer as an h2 heading.

You can sort the grouped values by using the `current-group-key()` function as the value for the `select` attribute in the following `sort` element:

```
<xsl:sort select="current-grouping-key()" />
```

In the case of customer IDs, this statement will display the customers by order of the ID value.

REFERENCE

Grouping Data in XSLT 2.0

- To create group data, enter the structure

```
<xsl:for-each-group select="items" grouping-method>
    styles
</xsl:for-each-group>
```

where *items* is the population of items to be grouped and *grouping-method* defines the method by which items in the sequence are assigned to their group. XSLT 2.0 supports the grouping methods group-by, group-adjacent, group-starting-with, and group-ending-with.

- To reference the current group, use the XPath 2.0 function

```
current-group()
```

which returns the sequence of values for the current group being processed in the *for-each-group* instruction.

- To display the value of the key associated with the current group, use the XPath 2.0 function

```
current-grouping-key()
```

William wants the customer ID for each group of orders to be displayed in an h2 heading. He also wants the order template to be applied to each group of customers. You'll use the `current-group()` and `current-grouping-key()` functions now to display the grouped values in the Recent Orders report, sorted by the grouping key.

To display the grouped items:

1. Scroll up to the root template in the iforders.xsl file and, directly above the opening `<table id="shipmentList">` tag in the root template, insert the following code to sort the groups in ascending order by the grouping key and to display the value by the grouping key as an h2 heading:

```
<xsl:sort select="current-grouping-key()" />
<h2>Customer ID:
    <xsl:value-of select="current-grouping-key()" />
</h2>
```

2. Scroll down to the `apply-templates` element within the `<tbody></tbody>` tag and change the value of the `select` attribute from orders/order to **current-group()** in order to apply the template to the node set defined by the current group being processed.

3. Because you are displaying the customer ID within an h2 heading, there is no need to display the customer ID information in the table. Delete `<th>Ordered By</th>` from the table heading.

Figure 8-28 highlights the code used to display the grouping information.

Figure 8-28 Displaying the values of the current group

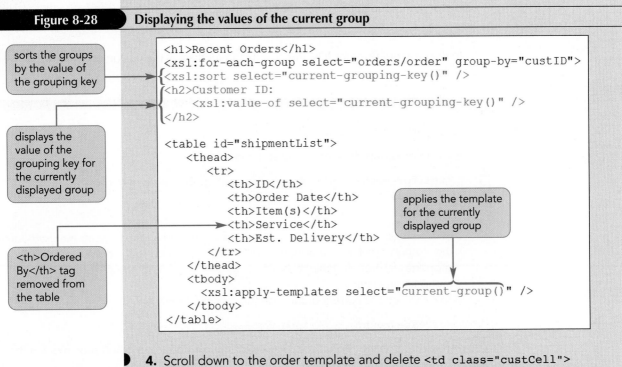

sorts the groups by the value of the grouping key

displays the value of the grouping key for the currently displayed group

applies the template for the currently displayed group

`<th>Ordered By</th>` tag removed from the table

```
<h1>Recent Orders</h1>
<xsl:for-each-group select="orders/order" group-by="custID">
<xsl:sort select="current-grouping-key()" />
<h2>Customer ID:
    <xsl:value-of select="current-grouping-key()" />
</h2>

<table id="shipmentList">
    <thead>
        <tr>
            <th>ID</th>
            <th>Order Date</th>
            <th>Item(s)</th>
            <th>Service</th>
            <th>Est. Delivery</th>
        </tr>
    </thead>
    <tbody>
        <xsl:apply-templates select="current-group()" />
    </tbody>
</table>
```

4. Scroll down to the order template and delete `<td class="custCell">` `<xsl:value-of select="custID" /></td>` from the table row.

5. Save your changes to the file and then regenerate the result document, writing the result to the orderlist.html file.

Figure 8-29 shows the Recent Orders report grouped by customer ID for the first two customers in the report.

Figure 8-29 Recent orders grouped by customer ID

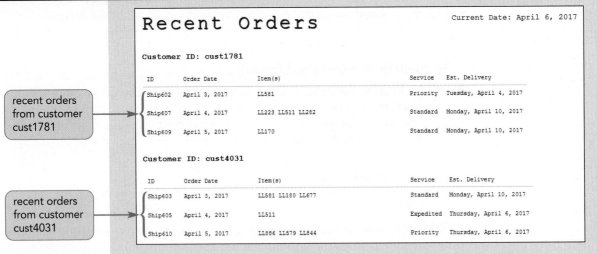

recent orders from customer cust1781

recent orders from customer cust4031

Applying Multilevel Grouping

You can nest one `for-each-group` element within another one to create multiple grouping levels. The general structure for a two-level group is

```
<xsl:for-each-group select="items" grouping-method>
   styles
   <xsl:for-each-group select="current-group()" grouping-method>
      styles
   </xsl:for-each-group>
</xsl:for-each-group>
```

The items will be grouped first by the outer loop and then by the inner loop. Note that the `select` attribute for the inner group employs the `current-group()` function. There is no requirement that the same grouping method be used on each level. For example, you can use the `group-by` attribute in the outer group and apply `group-ending-with` in the inner level.

Another way to create a multi-level group is to use a single grouping key that concatenates two elements into a single text string separated by a symbol, such as a comma. The general structure is

```
<xsl:for-each-group select="items"
  group-by="concat(category1, ',', category2)">
     styles
</xsl:for-each-group>
```

where *category1* and *category2* are the grouping elements. The processor will first group the population by *category2* nested within *category1*. The grouping key value will contain the concatenated text string combining both categories.

William would like to include the contact information for each customer in the report. To add this information, you'll use the table lookup features of XPath 2.0.

Creating Lookup Tables with the doc() Function

XPath 2.0 introduced the following doc() function to retrieve data from external XML files:

```
doc(uri)
```

where *uri* provides the location and filename of the external document. The doc() function is a simplified version of the document() function introduced in XSLT 1.0. There are a few important differences between the doc() and document() functions:

- The document() function can work with a node set or sequence, while the doc() function takes a single string as its argument.
- The document() function can return a set of nodes from multiple documents, while the doc() function returns a document node from a single XML document.
- The document() function supports relative URLs, while the base URI of the doc() function is always the base URI of the style sheet.
- The document() function supports URLs that include fragment identifiers (such as http://www.example.com/#data), while the doc() function must work through the document node.

Thus, the document() function is more flexible than the doc() function. However, the doc() function works very well in most cases except for those just described and, as you'll learn in the next tutorial, can be used with the XQuery language to retrieve data from external documents.

You'll explore the doc() function to display information about Illuminated Fixtures customers by looking up data from the customers.xml file. The lookup value will be based on the value of the custID element, accessed through the current-grouping-key() function.

To look up customer data:

▶ **1.** Return to the **iforders.xsl** file in your text editor and go to the root template.

▶ **2.** Directly below the `<xsl:sort>` tag and under the `<h1>` Recent Orders `</h1>` tag, insert the following *custList* variable to access the customers/customer node set from the customers.xml file using the current grouping key value:

```
<xsl:variable name="custList"
 select="doc('customers.xml')/customers/customer
[@custID=current-grouping-key()]" />
```

▶ **3.** Below the closing `</h2>` tag, insert the following paragraph displaying customer contact information based on the current group:

```
<p>
    <xsl:value-of select="$custList/firstName" />
    <xsl:text> </xsl:text>
    <xsl:value-of select="$custList/lastName" /><br />
    <xsl:value-of select="$custList/street" /><br />
    <xsl:value-of select="$custList/city" />,
    <xsl:value-of select="$custList/state" />
    <xsl:text> </xsl:text>
    <xsl:value-of select="$custList/zip" />
</p>
```

Figure 8-30 highlights the code to retrieve customer information from the customers.xml file.

Figure 8-30	Looking up customer contact data

accessing the customers.xml file using the doc() function with the current-grouping-key() function providing the lookup value

displaying customer data

```
<h1>Recent Orders</h1>
<xsl:for-each-group select="orders/order" group-by="custID">
<xsl:sort select="current-grouping-key()" />

<xsl:variable name="custList"
 select="doc('customers.xml')/customers/customer[@custID=current-grouping-key()]" />

<h2>Customer ID:
    <xsl:value-of select="current-grouping-key()" />
</h2>
<p>
    <xsl:value-of select="$custList/firstName" /><xsl:text> </xsl:text>
    <xsl:value-of select="$custList/lastName" /><br />
    <xsl:value-of select="$custList/street" /><br />
    <xsl:value-of select="$custList/city" />,
    <xsl:value-of select="$custList/state" /><xsl:text> </xsl:text>
    <xsl:value-of select="$custList/zip" />
</p>
```

▶ **4.** Save your changes to the file and then regenerate the result document as orderlist.html. Figure 8-31 shows the contact data for the first customer in the report.

Figure 8-31 **Customer information in the Recent Orders report**

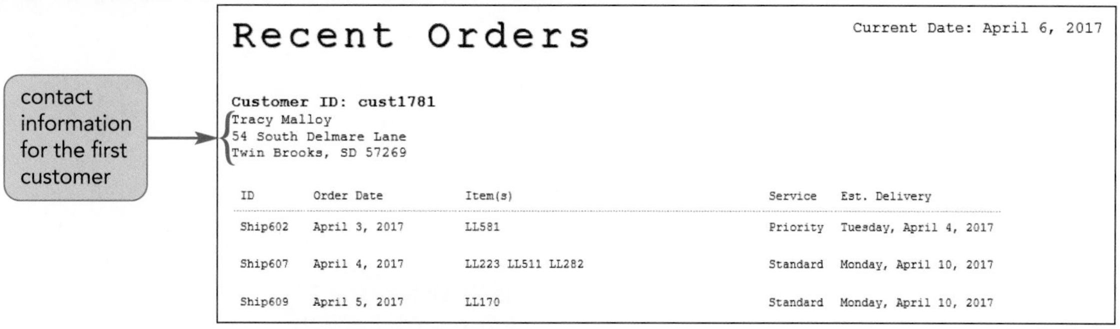

William appreciates the addition of the customer data to the Recent Orders report. In the next session, you'll explore how to work with text strings in XPath 2.0 and how to import data from non-XML documents.

Session 8.2 Quick Check

REVIEW

1. Provide code to create a custom function named taxesDue() that returns a decimal value. The function has the myAccount namespace prefix and includes a single parameter named *netIncome*, which stores the decimal data type. Have the function return the value of netIncome multiplied by 0.17.

2. Provide code to call the taxesDue() function from the previous question using 82147.41 as the *netIncome* value. Store the result in a variable named *myTaxes*.

3. Create a variable named *taxResult* that displays the text string "Tax Due" if the *myTaxes* variable is positive and the value "Refund" otherwise.

4. Describe the two general ways of grouping data in XSLT 2.0.

5. Provide code to group by value the contents of the /orders/order node set using the value of the orderDate attribute.

6. Provide code to display the value of the current grouping key within an h3 heading.

7. Provide code to apply a template to the sequence referenced by the current group.

8. Provide an XPath 2.0 expression to retrieve the contents of the /orders/order node set from the transactions.xml document.

Session 8.3 Visual Overview:

In a **CSV file**, data values are separated by commas on a single line.

The first line contains the element names.

```
itemID,item description,item size, item price
LL511,EcoLight 702107 - 7.5 Watt S11 Light Bulb,12-Pack,11.45
LL467,Dearborn 417071 Compact Fluorescent 13-Watt,8-Pack,15.28
LL729,J5 40 Watt Globe G25 Light Bulb,6-Pack,6.91
LL359,LMC Lighting 75368 Spiral Compact Fluorescent Bulb,6-Pack,30.25
LL282,Wittmore 10489 60-Watt Household Bulb,24-Pack,26.26
LL856,Dearborn 423798 Indoor Flood LED Light Bulb,12-Pack,20.97
LL515,100 Watt LMC Soft White Incandescent Light Bulb,48-Pack,47.99
LL102,EcoLight 14-Watt Fluorescent Light Bulbs,4-Pack,10.65
LL587,EcoLight 14-Watt LED Flood Light Bulb,12-Pack,41.23
```

This shows data values in a structured XML document.

```xml
<?xml version="1.0" encoding="UTF-8"?>
- <items>
  - <item>
      <itemID>LL511</itemID>
      <item_description>EcoLight 702107 - 7.5 Watt S11 Light Bulb</item_description>
      <item_size>12-Pack</item_size>
      <item_price>11.45</item_price>
    </item>
  - <item>
      <itemID>LL467</itemID>
      <item_description>Dearborn 417071 Compact Fluorescent 13-Watt</item_description>
      <item_size>8-Pack</item_size>
      <item_price>15.28</item_price>
    </item>
  - <item>
      <itemID>LL729</itemID>
      <item_description>J5 40 Watt Globe G25 Light Bulb</item_description>
      <item_size>6-Pack</item_size>
      <item_price>6.91</item_price>
    </item>
```

Importing CSV Files

The *rows* variable contains a sequence of text strings containing each line from the CSV file.

The **tokenize()** function is an XPath 2.0 function that splits a text string into a sequence of substrings at every occurrence of a regular expression pattern.

This shows a regular expression matching 0 or more carriage returns followed by the newline character.

This shows a regular expression matching a comma followed by zero or more white space characters.

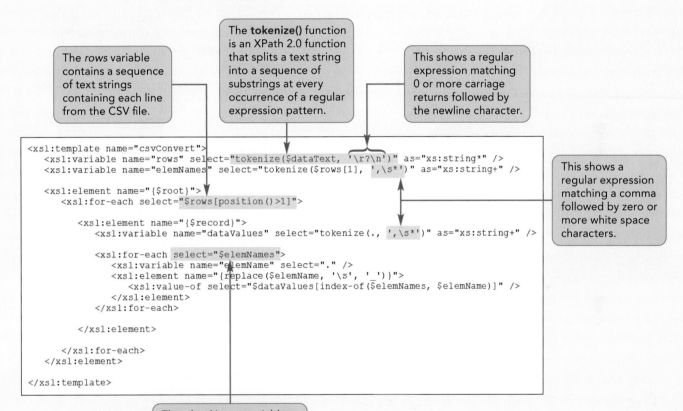

```
<xsl:template name="csvConvert">
    <xsl:variable name="rows" select="tokenize($dataText, '\r?\n')" as="xs:string*" />
    <xsl:variable name="elemNames" select="tokenize($rows[1], ',\s*')" as="xs:string+" />

    <xsl:element name="{$root}">
        <xsl:for-each select="$rows[position()>1]">

            <xsl:element name="{$record}">
                <xsl:variable name="dataValues" select="tokenize(., ',\s*')" as="xs:string+" />

                <xsl:for-each select="$elemNames">
                    <xsl:variable name="elemName" select="." />
                    <xsl:element name="{replace($elemName, '\s', '_')}">
                        <xsl:value-of select="$dataValues[index-of($elemNames, $elemName)]" />
                    </xsl:element>
                </xsl:for-each>

            </xsl:element>

        </xsl:for-each>
    </xsl:element>

</xsl:template>
```

The *elemNames* variable contains a sequence of text strings containing each element name specified in the first row of the CSV file.

Working with Text Strings in XSLT 2.0

Text strings are perhaps the most commonly used data type in XML. As you saw in Tutorial 6, XPath 1.0 provides several functions to manipulate text strings. XPath 2.0 expands on that functionality with several new functions described in Figure 8-32.

Figure 8-32	String functions in XPath 2.0

Function	Description
`codepoints-to-string(code)`	Converts every integer listed in *code* to the corresponding Unicode character, concatenating the results into a single string
`compare(string1, string2, collation)`	Compares *string1* to *string2* returning 0 if they are the same, -1 if *string1* is less than *string2*, and 1 if *string1* is greater than *string2*
`ends-with(string1, string2)`	Returns true if *string1* ends with *string2* and false if otherwise
`lower-case(string)`	Returns *string* in lowercase characters
`matches(string, regex)`	Returns true if *string* matches the regular expression *regex* and false if otherwise
`normalize-unicode(string, norm_form)`	Applies a Unicode normalization algorithm to *string*, returning the normalized string where *norm_form* specifies the normalization algorithm
`replace(string1, regex, string2, flags)`	Replaces all substrings within *string1* that match the regular expression, *regex*, with *string2*; the *flags* parameter specifies how the matching is to be performed
`string-join(string1, string2, …, separator)`	Joins *string1*, *string2*, … into a single string where *separator* is the separation character
`string-to-codepoints(string)`	Returns a sequence of integers representing the Unicode codepoints for each character in *string*
`tokenize(string, regex, flags)`	Splits *string* into a sequence of substrings using the separation defined in the regular expression *regex*; the *flags* parameter defines how the matching is performed
`upper-case(string)`	Returns *string* in uppercase characters

These functions greatly simplify many string manipulation tasks that were too cumbersome to do in XPath 1.0. For example, to convert a text string from lowercase to uppercase letters, you would have to apply the following XPath 1.0 `translate()` function:

```
translate(string, 'abcdefghijklmnopqrstuvwxyz',
'ABCDEFGHIJKLMNOPQRSTUVWXYZ')
```

where *string* is the text string to be converted. Using the `translate()` function this way, every occurrence of a lowercase letter is replaced by its corresponding uppercase letter specified in the third argument of the function. Yet, this task is more easily written using the following XPath 2.0 `upper-case()` function:

```
upper-case(string)
```

In the same way, converting text strings to lowercase letters is more easily accomplished using the XPath 2.0 `lower-case()` function.

Regular Expressions with XPath 2.0

TIP

You can learn more about regular expressions in Appendix F.

The most important addition in XPath 2.0 is the ability to work with regular expressions. Recall from Tutorial 3 that a regular expression is a text string that specifies a character pattern. For example, the regular expression

```
^\(\d{3}\) \d{3}-\d{4}$
```

represents a phone number pattern of (###) ###-#### including the area code in parentheses. You can test whether a text string matches the pattern specified in a regular expression using the following XPath 2.0 `matches()` function:

```
matches(string, regex)
```

where *string* is the text string to be examined and *regex* is the regular expression pattern. Thus, the following function returns `true` if the `phone` element contains a text string that matches the pattern and `false` if otherwise:

```
match(phone, '^\(\d{3}\) \d{3}-\d{4}$')
```

The `replace()` function can be used to replace any substrings within a text string that match a regular expression pattern. The syntax of the `replace()` function is

```
replace(string1, regex, string2, flags)
```

where *string1* is a text string containing substrings to be replaced, *regex* is the regular expression that will match the substrings in *string1*, *string2* is the replacement for the substrings, and *flags* are optional parameters that control how the regular expression pattern is applied. For example, the following `replace()` function replaces all occurrences of "i" with "*" in the text string "Illuminated Fixtures":

```
replace('Illuminated Fixtures', 'i', '*')
```

returning the text string "Illum*nated F*xtures". Note that the capital 'I' is not replaced because the replacement is case-sensitive and distinguishes between "i" and "I". To ignore character case you can use the i flag as described in Figure 8-33.

| Figure 8-33 | Regular expression flags |

Flag	Description
i	Matches should be carried out without respect to upper- or lowercase
s	Matches should be applied so that the "." character will match any character in the text string
m	Matches should be carried out in multiline mode so that the ^ character marks the beginning of a line and the $ character marks the ending of a line
x	White space characters within the regular expression should be ignored

TIP

For long and complicated expressions, use the m flag so that you can place the regular expression pattern on more than one line without adding unwanted white space characters.

Thus, the following `replace()` function:

```
replace('Illuminated Fixtures', 'i', '*', i)
```

returns the text string "*llum*nated F*xtures" with every occurrence of the i character replaced with an asterisk regardless of case. The `replace()` function can also be applied to variables or element nodes. The following `replace()` function replaces every occurrence of the text string "april" with "April" within the month element:

```
replace(month, 'april', 'April', i)
```

The final XPath 2.0 text function that supports regular expressions is the following `tokenize()` function:

```
tokenize(string, regex, flags)
```

which splits *string* into a sequence of separate substrings at any occurrence of characters that match the regular expression *regex*. For example, the following function splits the contents of the products element into a sequence of strings at every occurrence of a white space character such as a blank space, tab, or newline character:

```
tokenize(products, '\s+')
```

TIP

Regular expression symbols have opposite meanings when expressed in uppercase letters: \S is the opposite of \s and thus matches non-white space characters such as any number, letter, or symbol.

Note that this function uses the `\s+` character to represent one or more consecutive occurrences of any white space character.

Once you have extracted a sequence of substrings using the `tokenize()` function, you can use XSLT's `for-each` element to apply styles to each substring in the sequence. For example, the following code first creates a sequence of substrings from the contents of the products element by breaking the products element text at every occurrence of one or more white space characters; then the text of each substring is modified using the commands specified in *styles*.

```
<xsl:for-each select="tokenize(products, '\s+')">
    styles
</xsl:for-each>
```

Note that if the text contained within the products element begins or ends with a white space character, the first (or last) substring will be an empty text string. You can prevent this problem by applying the XPath 1.0 `normalize-space()` function to strip out leading and trailing white space characters before tokenizing the text string. The revised code would be

```
<xsl:for-each select="tokenize(normalize-space(products), '\s+')">
    styles
</xsl:for-each>
```

Using the `normalize-space()` function is a useful technique to avoid the appearance of empty text strings in the style sheet output.

REFERENCE

Regular Expressions with XPath 2.0

- To determine where a text string matches a regular expression pattern, use the function

  ```
  matches(string, regex)
  ```

  where *string* is the text string to be examined and *regex* is the regular expression pattern.

- To replace a substring within a text string, use

  ```
  replace(string1, regex, string2, flags)
  ```

  where *string1* is the text string, *regex* is the regular expression, *string2* is the replacement string, and *flags* are optional parameters that control how the regular expression pattern is applied.

- To split a text string into a sequence of substrings at every occurrence of a regular expression pattern, use

  ```
  tokenize(string, regex, flags)
  ```

  where *string* is the text string, *regex* is the regular expression that matches the locations where the text string should be split, and *flags* control how the regular expression is applied.

Analyzing Text Strings in XSLT 2.0

One of the limitations of XPath 2.0 when working with text strings and regular expressions is that XPath 2.0 functions do not allow the programmer to create structured content in which resulting text strings are placed with element or attribute nodes. To create structured content, you can use the following XSLT 2.0 `analyze-string` element:

```
<xsl:analyze-string select="expression" regex="regex" flags="flags">
   <xsl:matching-substring>
      styles
   </xsl:matching-substring>
   <xsl:non-matching-substring>
      styles
   </xsl:non-matching-substring>
   <xsl:fall-back>
      styles
   </xsl:fall-back>
</xsl:analyze-string>
```

where *expression* is a sequence or node set to be analyzed, *regex* is a regular expression, and *flags* are regular expression flags. The XSLT 2.0 processor analyzes the content specified in the *select* attribute. Each time the processor finds a substring that matches the regular expression pattern, it applies the styles defined within the `matching-substring` element and, for each substring that does not match the pattern, the processor applies the styles defined within the `non-matching-substring` element. The `fall-back` element is used if you need to support XSLT 1.0 processors by providing styles for those processors to apply; otherwise, it can be omitted.

For example, consider the contact element containing address information stored on several lines:

```
<contact>
   Ian White
   14 South Lane
   Boulder, CO 80302
</contact>
```

If you were writing the text to a web page, you might want to retain the line returns; however, HTML doesn't recognize line returns and instead uses the `<br />` tag to start text on a new line. You can use the following `analyze-string` element to replace every occurrence of the new line character with a `<br />` tag:

```
<xsl:analyze-string select="contact" regex="\n">
   <xsl:matching-substring>
      <br />
   </xsl:matching-substring>
   <xsl:non-matching-substring>
      <xsl:value-of select="normalize-space(.)" />
   </xsl:non-matching>
</xsl:analyze-string>
```

The `analyze-string` element moves through the contact text, locating newline characters as indicated the `\n` regular expression. When a newline character is encountered, the `<br />` element is written to the result document. Any substring that is not a newline character is normalized to remove leading and trailing white space and then written to the result document. The final result is a single text string in which all newline characters have been replaced with the `<br />` tag.

```
Ian White<br />14 South Lane<br />Bouder, CO 80302<br />
```

In analyzing a text string, the `analyze-string` element creates a sequence of substrings that match the regular expression in the `regex` parameter. You can reference each substring in that sequence through the `regex-group()` function. The first substring is referenced by `regex-group(1)`, the second by `regex-group(2)`, and so forth. Thus, you can apply a different style to each substring in the sequence. For example, the following code displays the content of the first substring in uppercase letters, while the subsequent substrings are displayed without the case being changed:

```
<xsl:matching-substring>
   <xsl:choose>
      <xsl:when test="regex-group(1)">
         <xsl:value-of select="upper-case(regex-group(1))" />
      </xsl:when>
      <xsl:otherwise>
         <xsl:value-of select="." />
      </xsl:otherwise>
   </xsl:choose>
</xsl:matching-substring>
```

Note that it's not necessary to have both the `matching-substring` and `non-matching-substring` elements. You can have one or the other but, if both appear, they should appear in the order of the `matching-substring` element first followed by the `non-matching-substring`.

Writing to Multiple Output Files

In addition to supporting multiple input files, XSLT 2.0 also supports writing to multiple result documents. To specify multiple destinations for the transformation result use the following `result-document` element:

```
<xsl:result-document href="uri">
   styles
</xsl:result-document>
```

where *uri* is the URI of the output file(s) and *styles* are styles applied to the result document. The `href` attribute can contain variable values to write the output to different files. For example, the following template creates a different result document for each customer based on the customer's ID:

```
<xsl:template match="customer">
   <xsl:result-document href="{@custID}.xml" method="xml">
      styles
   </xsl:result-document>
</xsl:template>
```

Thus, a customer with the id cust4418 will have a result document written to the cust4418.xml file. The `result-document` element supports the same attributes that can be applied with the `output` element, which means you can specify the output method, encoding, media type, and whether or not to apply indenting, among other attributes, to the result document.

Importing non-XML Data

The new string functions and elements available within XSLT 2.0 make it easier to convert data from non-XML files into XML format. A very common non-XML format used for transferring data from one application to another is the **CSV** or **comma-separated values** format, in which each data record is written on a separate line and data values within each record are separated by commas.

William wants to display the names of the products ordered by the customers in his order report. However, that information is not available to him as an XML file; instead, it's available as a CSV file named itemlist.txt containing each item's ID code, description, and price. Figure 8-34 shows a preview of the first few lines of the itemlist.txt file.

Figure 8-34	itemlist.txt file containing product information in CSV format

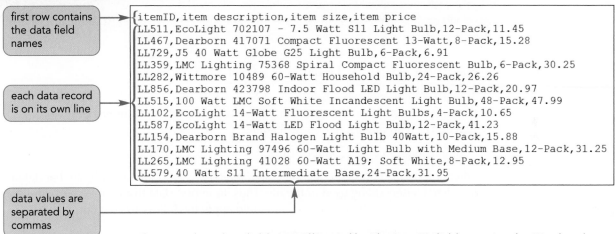

first row contains the data field names

each data record is on its own line

```
itemID,item description,item size,item price
LL511,EcoLight 702107 - 7.5 Watt S11 Light Bulb,12-Pack,11.45
LL467,Dearborn 417071 Compact Fluorescent 13-Watt,8-Pack,15.28
LL729,J5 40 Watt Globe G25 Light Bulb,6-Pack,6.91
LL359,LMC Lighting 75368 Spiral Compact Fluorescent Bulb,6-Pack,30.25
LL282,Wittmore 10489 60-Watt Household Bulb,24-Pack,26.26
LL856,Dearborn 423798 Indoor Flood LED Light Bulb,12-Pack,20.97
LL515,100 Watt LMC Soft White Incandescent Light Bulb,48-Pack,47.99
LL102,EcoLight 14-Watt Fluorescent Light Bulbs,4-Pack,10.65
LL587,EcoLight 14-Watt LED Flood Light Bulb,12-Pack,41.23
LL154,Dearborn Brand Halogen Light Bulb 40Watt,10-Pack,15.88
LL170,LMC Lighting 97496 60-Watt Light Bulb with Medium Base,12-Pack,31.25
LL265,LMC Lighting 41028 60-Watt A19; Soft White,8-Pack,12.95
LL579,40 Watt S11 Intermediate Base,24-Pack,31.95
```

data values are separated by commas

There are four data fields in William's file. The itemID field contains the ID of each product sold by Illuminated Fixtures, the item description providing a short description of each product, the item size storing the number of bulbs in each pack, and the item price field indicating the sales price. William wants you to create a style sheet to read the contents of this file and convert the data into an XML document having the structure shown in Figure 8-35.

Figure 8-35	Structure of the proposed XML document

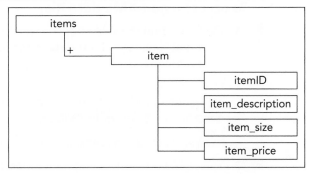

Converting a CSV File to XML Format

- Read the content of the CSV file into a single text string using the `unparsed-text()` function.
- Use the `tokenize()` function with the `\r?\n` regular expression to split the individual lines of the text string into a sequence of substrings.
- Use the `tokenize()` function with the `,\s*` regular expression to split an item from the sequence of substrings into another sequence of substrings at each occurrence of a comma character followed by zero or more white space characters.
- Use the sequence of values from the first line of the CSV file as the element names, replacing any white space characters in the element names with the underscore (_) character.
- Match the data values from the subsequent lines of the CSV file with their corresponding element names and write those element and element values to the result document.

Reading from an Unparsed Text File

The first step in importing data from a CSV file is to read the content of the file into the style sheet as a text string. XPath 2.0 provides the following `unparsed-text()` function to read unparsed (non-XML) data:

```
unparsed-text(uri, encoding)
```

where *uri* is the URI of the text file and *encoding* is an optional attribute that defines the character encoding used in the file. Thus, to import data from the itemlist.txt file and store it as a single text string you would apply the following function:

```
unparsed-text('itemlist.txt')
```

Once the text string has been created, it can be split into separate substrings and the content of each substring can be written to an XML document as elements and element values.

You'll use the `unparsed-text()` function now as part of a new style sheet to import the itemlist.txt file containing information on the products sold by Illuminated Fixtures.

To access a non-XML data file:

1. Open the **csvtxt.xsl** file from the xml08 ▸ tutorial folder in your text editor. Enter **your name** and the **date** in the comment section of the file and save it as **csvconvert.xsl**.

2. Directly below the opening `stylesheet` element, insert the following `output` element to specify that the result document will be in XML format with UTF-8 encoding and the contents indented for readability.

   ```
   <xsl:output method="xml" encoding="UTF-8" indent="yes" />
   ```

3. The style sheet will have the following three global parameters: the *csvFile* parameter will store the name of the CSV file to be imported, the *root* parameter will be used to specify the name of the `root` element in the result document, and the *record* parameter will be used to specify the element name enclosing the data from each line in the CSV file. Enter the following code after the `output` element:

   ```
   <xsl:param name="csvFile" as="xs:string" />
   <xsl:param name="root" as="xs:string" />
   <xsl:param name="record" as="xs:string" />
   ```

> **4.** Finally, after the *record* parameter, create the following *dataText* variable that contains the imported content of the CSV file as a single text string:

```
<xsl:variable name="dataText"
 select="unparsed-text($csvFile)" as="xs:string" />
```

Figure 8-36 shows the initial code in the style sheet to import the contents of a CSV file into a single text string.

Figure 8-36	**Reading unparsed data**

using global parameters to specify the name of the CSV file, the name of the root element, and the element name used for each line of the CSV file

```
<xsl:stylesheet version="2.0"
    xmlns:xsl="http://www.w3.org/1999/XSL/Transform"
    xmlns:xs="http://www.w3.org/2001/XMLSchema"
    exclude-result-prefixes="xs">

  <xsl:output method="xml" encoding="UTF-8" indent="yes" />

  <xsl:param name="csvFile" as="xs:string" />
  <xsl:param name="root" as="xs:string" />
  <xsl:param name="record" as="xs:string" />

  <xsl:variable name="dataText" select="unparsed-text($csvFile)" as="xs:string" />
```

outputs the contents to a result document in XML format

dateText variable contains the contents of the csvFile as a single text string

> **5.** Save your changes to the file.

Because the *dataText* variable is a single text string containing all of the text found in the original data file, you need to split that text string into several substrings with each substring containing the text from a single line in the data file. To split a text string between each line of text, use the `tokenize()` function described earlier with the regular expression \r?\n, which matches zero or more carriage return characters followed by one newline character. The result will be a sequence of substrings with each text string containing the text of a single line. The following code uses the `tokenize()` function to store that sequence of substrings in a variable named *rows*:

```
<xsl:variable name="rows"
 select=tokenize($dataText, '\r?\n') as="xs:string*" />
```

Because the *rows* variable contains a sequence of substrings, rows[1] will store the text of the first line of the data file, rows[2] will store the text of the second line, and so forth. As indicated in Figure 8-34, the first line of the itemlist.txt file, and thus rows[1], contains the text of the element names. To extract those element names, you'll split the contents of the first line at every occurrence of a comma, using another `tokenize()` function, and store the sequence of substrings in a variable named *elemNames*.

```
<xsl:variable name="elemNames"
 select="tokenize($rows[1], ',\s*')" as="xs:string+" />
```

In this code, the regular expression ,\s* matches any occurrences of a comma followed by zero or more white space characters. The result of applying the `tokenize()` function is a sequence of substrings in which every substring contains the text of one element name.

You'll add code now to the csvconvert.xsl file to create the *rows* and *elemNames* variables. You'll place these variables within a new template named csvConvert.

To create the csvConvert template:

1. Within the csvconvert.xsl file, insert the following csvConvert template and variables directly below the declaration of the *dataText* variable:

```
<xsl:template name="csvConvert">
  <xsl:variable name="rows"
   select="tokenize($dataText, '\r?\n')"
   as="xs:string*" />

  <xsl:variable name="elemNames"
   select="tokenize($rows[1], ',\s*')"
   as="xs:string+" />

</xsl:template>
```

> When using the `tokenize()` function to create a sequence of text strings, specify xs:string* or xs:string+ as the data type.

Figure 8-37 highlights code for the creation of the *rows* and *elemNames* local variables.

Figure 8-37	Creating sequences of substrings

the *rows* variable stores a sequence of substrings containing the text of each line in the CSV file

```
<xsl:variable name="dataText" select="unparsed-text($csvFile)" as="xs:string" />

<xsl:template name="csvConvert">
  <xsl:variable name="rows" select="tokenize($dataText, '\r?\n')" as="xs:string*" />
  <xsl:variable name="elemNames" select="tokenize($rows[1], ',\s*')" as="xs:string+" />

</xsl:template>
```

the *elemNames* variable stores a sequence of substrings containing each element name from the first line of the CSV file

2. Save your changes to the file.

You are now ready to begin writing the contents of the XML document that will contain the contents of the itemlist.txt file. First, you'll create a root element for the XML document using the name specified in the *root* parameter. Within the root element, you'll create one record for each row in the CSV file after the initial row, which contains the list of element names.

To create the csvConvert template:

▶ **1.** Within the csvConvert template and after the *elemNames* variable, insert the following code to create the root element using the *root* parameter as the element name:

```
<xsl:element name="{$root}">
</xsl:element>
```

▶ **2.** Within the root element, insert the following `for-each` structure to create one record element for each row in the CSV file after the initial row:

```
<xsl:for-each select="$rows[position()>1]">
   <xsl:element name="{$record}">
   </xsl:element>
</xsl:for-each>
```

Figure 8-38 highlights the code to create the root and record elements.

Figure 8-38   **Writing the root element and record elements**

creates the root element in the result document

creates a record element for every item in the rows sequence after the first item

```
<xsl:template name="csvConvert">
  <xsl:variable name="rows" select="tokenize($dataText, '\r?\n')" as="xs:string*" />
  <xsl:variable name="elemNames" select="tokenize($rows[1], ',\s*')" as="xs:string+" />

  <xsl:element name="{$root}">
     <xsl:for-each select="$rows[position()>1]">

        <xsl:element name="{$record}">

        </xsl:element>

     </xsl:for-each>
  </xsl:element>

</xsl:template>
```

▶ **3.** Save the file.

The final step in this process is to write the data values. Because the source is a CSV file with the data value separated by commas, you'll write the values by splitting the text string of each row at every occurrence of a comma. The element names of the data values will be taken from the sequence of text strings stored in the *elemNames* variable. You'll use the `index-of()` function to match each data value with its corresponding element name.

To write the data values:

▶ **1.** Within the `<xsl:element name="{$record}"></xsl:element>` tag, insert the following code to create the *dataValues* variable containing the sequence of data values from the current record, split at every occurrence of a comma followed by zero or more white space characters:

```
<xsl:variable name="dataValues"
 select="tokenize(., ',\s*')"
 as="xs:string+" />
```

Next, you'll go through each element name in the *elemNames* sequence, and for each element name you'll write the corresponding data value. Note that some element names from the CSV file contain spaces, which is an illegal character for an XML name. You'll use the `replace()` function to replace each white space character in the element name with an underscore (_).

▶ **2.** Enter the following code directly after the code that creates the *dataValues* variable:

```
<xsl:for-each select="$elemNames">
   <xsl:variable name="elemName" select="." />
   <xsl:element name="{replace($elemName, '\s', '_')}">
      <xsl:value-of
         select="$dataValues[index-of($elemNames, $elemName)]" />
   </xsl:element>
</xsl:for-each>
```

Figure 8-39 highlights the code to write the data values to the result document.

| Figure 8-39 | Writing individual data values |

creates a sequence of individual data values by splitting the *dataValues* variable at each comma character

replaces any white space characters in the element name with an underscore

matches each element name with the corresponding data value and writes the element value to the result document

```
<xsl:element name="{$record}">
   <xsl:variable name="dataValues" select="tokenize(., ',\s*')" as="xs:string+" />

   <xsl:for-each select="$elemNames">
      <xsl:variable name="elemName" select="." />
      <xsl:element name="{replace($elemName, '\s', '_')}">
         <xsl:value-of select="$dataValues[index-of($elemNames, $elemName)]" />
      </xsl:element>
   </xsl:for-each>

</xsl:element>
```

▶ **3.** Save your changes to the file.

You can now run the style sheet to convert the itemlist.txt file to an XML document. You'll set the value of the *root* parameter to "items" and the value of the *record* to "item". Use itemlist.txt as the source file for the transformation by setting the value of the *csvFile* parameter to "itemlist.txt". The result of the transformation should be sent to the itemlist.xml file.

To run the style sheet transformation:

▶ **1.** Open a command prompt window and go to the xml08 ▶ tutorial folder.

▶ **2.** If you're using Saxon in Java command line mode, enter the following command on a single line:

```
java net.sf.saxon.Transform –it:csvConvert csvconvert.xsl
 root=items record=item csvFile=itemlist.txt
 –o:itemlist.xml
```

Trouble? If you are using Saxon on the .NET platform, enter the single-line command

```
Transform –it:csvConvert csvconvert.xsl
 root=items record=item csvFile=itemlist.txt
 –o:itemlist.xml
```

Otherwise, enter the command appropriate to your XSLT 2.0 processor.

> **3.** Press **Enter** to generate the result document **itemlist.xml**.

> **4.** Open the **itemlist.xml** file in your text editor or within a browser. Figure 8-40 shows the content and structure of the document.

| Figure 8-40 | XML document containing product information |

```
<?xml version="1.0" encoding="UTF-8"?>
<items>
  <item>
    <itemID>LL511</itemID>
    <item_description>EcoLight 702107 - 7.5 Watt S11 Light Bulb</item_description>
    <item_size>12-Pack</item_size>
    <item_price>11.45</item_price>
  </item>
  <item>
    <itemID>LL467</itemID>
    <item_description>Dearborn 417071 Compact Fluorescent 13-Watt</item_description>
    <item_size>8-Pack</item_size>
    <item_price>15.28</item_price>
  </item>
  <item>
    <itemID>LL729</itemID>
    <item_description>J5 40 Watt Globe G25 Light Bulb</item_description>
    <item_size>6-Pack</item_size>
    <item_price>6.91</item_price>
  </item>
```

root element

record elements

> **5.** Close the itemlist.xml file.

One of the advantages of creating the csvConvert.xsl file is that it can be reused again to convert other CSV documents. You only need to set the values of the *row*, *record*, and *csvFile* parameters when running the transformation and make sure that the first line of the text file contains the element names you want applied to the XML document.

Now that the itemlist.xml file has been created, you can use that file to look up the information on each item ordered by Illuminated Fixtures customers and display them in the final version of William's order report.

To display product information in the orders report:

> **1.** Return to the **iforders.xsl** file in your text editor.

> **2.** Go to the order template and, within the `<td class="itemCell"></td>` tag, replace the `<xsl:value-of select="items/itemID" />` tag with the following `apply-templates` element:

```
<xsl:apply-templates select="items/itemID" />
```

> **3.** Directly below the order template, insert the following template to look up and display product information from the itemlist.xml file:

```
<xsl:template match="itemID">
  <xsl:variable name="itemList"
   select="doc('itemlist.xml')/items/item[itemID=current()]" />
  <xsl:value-of select="current()" />:
  <xsl:value-of select="$itemList/item_description" />
  [<xsl:value-of select="$itemList/item_size" />]
  <br /><br />
</xsl:template>
```

Figure 8-41 highlights the code to look up data from the itemlist.xml file.

Figure 8-41   Looking up product information

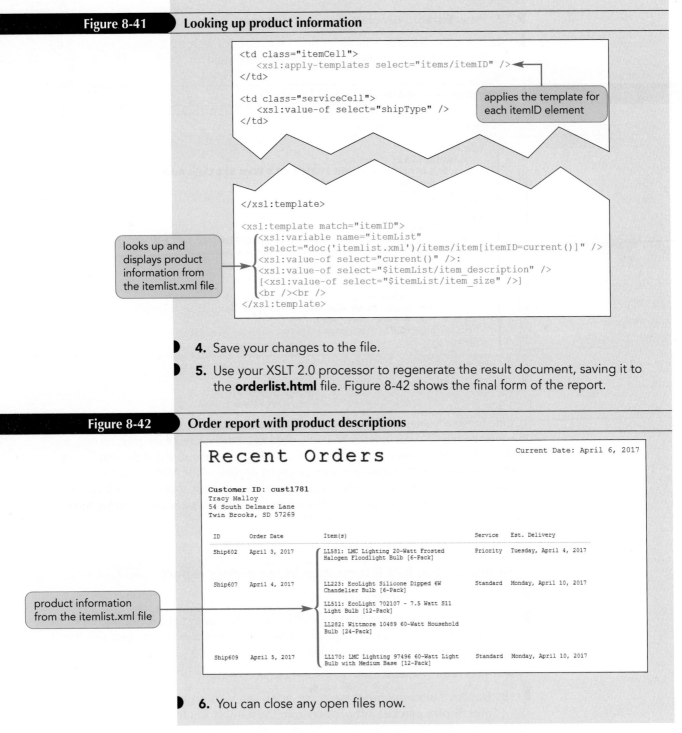

```
<td class="itemCell">
   <xsl:apply-templates select="items/itemID" />
</td>

<td class="serviceCell">
   <xsl:value-of select="shipType" />
</td>
```

applies the template for each itemID element

```
</xsl:template>

<xsl:template match="itemID">
   <xsl:variable name="itemList"
     select="doc('itemlist.xml')/items/item[itemID=current()]" />
   <xsl:value-of select="current()" />:
   <xsl:value-of select="$itemList/item_description" />
   [<xsl:value-of select="$itemList/item_size" />]
   <br /><br />
</xsl:template>
```

looks up and displays product information from the itemlist.xml file

4. Save your changes to the file.

5. Use your XSLT 2.0 processor to regenerate the result document, saving it to the **orderlist.html** file. Figure 8-42 shows the final form of the report.

Figure 8-42   Order report with product descriptions

Recent Orders

Current Date: April 6, 2017

Customer ID: cust1781
Tracy Malloy
54 South Delmare Lane
Twin Brooks, SD 57269

ID	Order Date	Item(s)	Service	Est. Delivery
Ship602	April 3, 2017	LL581: LMC Lighting 20-Watt Frosted Halogen Floodlight Bulb [6-Pack]	Priority	Tuesday, April 4, 2017
Ship607	April 4, 2017	LL223: EcoLight Silicone Dipped 6W Chandelier Bulb [6-Pack]	Standard	Monday, April 10, 2017
		LL511: EcoLight 702107 - 7.5 Watt S11 Light Bulb [12-Pack]		
		LL282: Wittmore 10489 60-Watt Household Bulb [24-Pack]		
Ship609	April 5, 2017	LL170: LMC Lighting 97496 60-Watt Light Bulb with Medium Base [12-Pack]	Standard	Monday, April 10, 2017

product information from the itemlist.xml file

6. You can close any open files now.

With the final version of the report, William can now view exactly what each customer ordered, as well as the estimated date of each order's delivery.

PROSKILLS

Problem Solving: Migrating from XSLT 1.0 to XSLT 2.0

XSTL 2.0 has many advantages over XSLT 1.0, so it is natural to want to upgrade existing style sheets to work under the 2.0 standard. The first step in making the transition is simple: change the version number to 2.0 and see what happens when you run the style sheet. Here are some possible sources of error you may encounter.

- **Data Type Mismatches**. XSTL 1.0 is much less strict in enforcing data types. For example, the XPath 1.0 expression `substring-before(54812, 8)` will return the text string "54" implicitly recasting the values 54812 and 8 as text strings. XSLT 2.0, however, will return an error message. To avoid this, you need to recast numeric values as text strings, replacing that XPath 1.0 expression with this XPath 2.0 expression:

  `substring-before(string(54812), string(8))`.

- **Passing Node Sets as Values**. When XSLT 1.0 encounters a node set as an argument, it takes the value of the first node and ignores the rest. In this same situation, XSLT 2.0 will attempt to apply the expression to all nodes in the set. This will result in an error if the expression expects only a single value. For example, the `generate-id()` function will return an error when applied to several nodes. To avoid this problem, explicitly add the predicate [1] to any node set to ensure that only the first node is evaluated.

- **Undefined Template Parameters**. In XSLT 1.0, you do not have to provide a value for every template parameter. Any undefined parameters are ignored by the processor. In XSLT 2.0, the number of parameter values specified within the `call-template` element needs to match the number of parameters in the template.

- **Calculations with Numeric Values**. In XSLT 1.0, all numbers have the simple number data type. But in XSLT 2.0, there are several numeric data types including `xs:integer`, `xs:decimal`, `xs:float`, and `xs:double`. Even simple calculations involving division will return different answers if the integer data type is used in place of the `xs:decimal` or `xs:float` data types, for example.

One way to ease the migration from version 1.0 to version 2.0 is to add the `version="1.0"` attribute to different templates in the style sheet to indicate that those templates should be processed under the 1.0 standard. You can then gradually revise parts of the style sheet to the 2.0 standard, isolating and fixing errors as you go.

You've completed your work on William's report of recent orders made to Illuminated Fixtures. William will apply your work on these sample orders to a larger set of customer orders, and he'll explore other ways to use XSLT 2.0 and XPath 2.0 to monitor customer orders and shipping activity.

PROSKILLS

Problem Solving: Learning about your XSLT Processor

Because there are many XSLT 1.0 legacy applications, ideally an XSLT processor should support both XSLT 1.0 and 2.0. This can present a challenge because the data model in Version 1.0 differs in many important respects from the 2.0 data model. You can learn information about your processor and what it supports by running the following `system-property()` function within your style sheet:

```
system-property(property)
```

where *property* specifies the aspect of the processor upon which to report. Possible values for property include `xsl:version` for the XSLT version supported by the processor, `xsl:vendor` to identify the processor being used, and `xsl:vendor-url` to retrieve the URL of your XSLT processor. One application of the `system-property()` function is to create separate styles for 1.0 and 2.0 processors. The following code demonstrates a choose structure that applies one set of styles if the processor supports XSLT 2.0 and another if it only supports XSLT 1.0:

```
<xsl:choose>
    <xsl:when test="number(system-property('xsl:version')) = 1.0">
       XSLT 1.0 styles
    </xsl:when>
    <xsl:otherwise>
      Non 1.0 styles
    </xsl:otherwise>
</xsl:choose>
```

Your processor might support other properties as well. Check your processor's documentation for more information on its capabilities and features. Note that if you attempt to get information on a property that is not supported by your processor the `system-property()` function will return an empty text string.

REVIEW

Session 8.3 Quick Check

1. Provide an XPath expression to return the text of the *customerID* variable in lowercase letters.
2. Tabs are indicated by the `\t` regular expression character. Provide the code to replace every occurrence of a comma in the text string store in variable *sampleDoc* with a tab, saving the revised text string in the *revisedDoc* variable.
3. Provide code to split the *revisedDoc* variable at every occurrence of the tab character. Store the sequence of substrings in a variable named *docValues*.
4. Show how to use the `analyze-string` element to analyze the structure of the custAddress element, replacing every occurrence of a newline character with the *<p>* tag.
5. Provide code to write a result document to the file *pid*.xml, where *pid* is the value of the pid attribute found within the products/product node set.
6. Show how to use the `unparsed-text()` function to retrieve the contents of the products.txt file as a single non-XML text string. Store the text string in the *dataFile* variable.
7. Provide the code to split the *dataFile* variable at each occurrence of the regular expression `\r?\n`. Store the sequence of substrings in the *dataLines* variable.

Review Assignments

Data Files needed for the Review Assignments: combtxt.xsl, prodtxt.xsl, + 6 XML files, +1 XSLT file +1 CSS file, +1 PNG file, +1 TXT file

PRACTICE

William has approached you with a new project. He wants to create an XSLT 2.0 application that will report on the products that have been recently shipped by Illuminated Fixtures. The report should organize the products by product ID and display the order ID and customer ID, the quantity of each product ordered, the date it was ordered, the location it was sent to, and the estimated date of delivery. Figure 8-43 shows a preview of the completed report for some data supplied to William.

Figure 8-43   Illuminated Fixtures product report

To complete this application, you'll first combine product information from several XML documents into a single file. You'll then use the date and time functions from XPath 2.0 to display the current date and to calculate the estimated delivery date for each order. William has also received a CSV file containing customer IDs and addresses, which you'll have to convert to XML in order to display the city and state to where each order will be delivered.

Complete the following:

1. Using your text editor, open **combtxt.xsl** and **prodtxt.xsl** from the xml08 ▸ review folder. Enter **your name** and the **date** in the comment section of each file, and save them as **combine.xsl** and **productlist.xsl**, respectively.

2. Go to the **combine.xsl** file in your text editor. This style sheet will be used to combine several XML documents into a single file. Create a template named **pList**. Within the template, insert an element named **products** that will be the root element of the XML document you'll create. Within the products element, use the `collection()` function to retrieve content from every XML document that matches the filename pattern prod_*.xml. For each file, use the `copy-of` element to copy the contents of the product element into the result document.

3. Save your changes to the file.

4. Use an XSLT 2.0 processor to run a transformation that applies the pList template from the combine.xsl style sheet, writing the output to the **productlist.xml** file.

5. View the contents of the **productlist.xml** file and verify that it contains products as the root element and, within the products element, five product elements with information on each product, including a list of orders and order IDs made on that product.

6. William has provided you with the readcsv.xsl style sheet, which you will use to convert a text file in the CSV format into XML format. The style sheet has three global parameters: the *csvSource* parameter specifies the filename of the CSV file, the *main* parameter sets the name of the main or root element, and the *entry* parameter specifies the name of each record. Use your XSLT 2.0 processor to convert the contacts.txt file into the custlist.xml document by running the transformation with the *csvSource* equal to contacts.txt, *main* equal to customers, and *entry* equal to contact. Use the template csvTransform as the initial template, and have your processor send the output to the **custlist.xml** file.

7. Take some time to study the contents and structure of the **productorders.xml** file containing a list of orders made by Illuminated Fixtures customers. You'll display this information in the report you'll generate for William.

8. The format of the product report will be generated using the productlist.xsl style sheet. Open **productlist.xsl** in your text editor. Within the `stylesheet` element declare the namespace "http://example.com/illumfixtures" using the namespace prefix "illf". Exclude this namespace from result documents generated with this style sheet.

9. Go to the root template and, directly below the CURRENT DATE: line in the aside element, use the `current-date()` function to display the current date formatted as *Month Day, Year*, where *Month* is the name of the month in title case, *Day* is the day number displayed with ordinal numbering, and *Year* is the four-digit year value.

10. Directly below the `<h1>Recently Shipped Products</h1>` tag, use the `for-each-group` element to group the contents of the products/product node set based on key values of the pID attribute. Sort the group by the current grouping key using the `current-grouping-key()` function.

11. Within the `for-each-group` element you created in the last step, write the following HTML code:

```
<h2>Product: id</h2>
<p>
   summary<br />
   Manufacturer: manufacturer<br />
   Size: size
</p>
```

where *id* is the value of the current grouping key, *summary* is the value of the summary element within the current group, *manufacturer* is the value of the manufacturer element within the current group, and *size* is the value of the size element within the current group.

12. Next, within the `for-each-group` element, you'll display a table that lists the orders made for each listed product. Write the following HTML code for each group:

```
<table id="orderTable">
    <thead>
        <tr>
            <th>Order ID</th>
            <th>Customer ID</th>
            <th>Quantity</th>
            <th>Order Date</th>
            <th>Delivered To</th>
            <th>Shipping</th>
            <th>Est. Delivery</th>
        </tr>
    </thead>
    <tbody>
        order template
    </tbody>
</table>
```

where *order template* is the application of the template for the orders/order node set within the current group.

13. Go to the order template, and within the template define the **IDValue** variable, setting it equal to the value of the orderID attribute.

14. Information about each order is stored in the productorders.xml file. Create a variable named **orderInfo** using the `doc()` function to access the node set "/orders/order[@orderID=$IDValue" from the productorders.xml file.

15. Create the **customer** variable storing the value of the `by` element from within the *orderInfo* node set.

16. Information about the customers is stored in the custlist.xml file you created in Step 6. Define the **custInfo** variable using the `doc()` function to reference the node set "/customers/contact[custID=$customer]" from the custlist.xml file.

17. Next, within the order template, write the following HTML code to the result document to display information about the orders and the customers:

```
<tr>
    <td>orderID</td>
    <td>customer</td>
    <td>qty</td>
    <td>date</td>
    <td>city, state</td>
    <td>ship</td>
    <td></td>
</tr>
```

where *orderID* is the value of the orderID attribute; *customer* is the value of the *customer* variable; *qty* is the value of the qty element from within the *orderInfo* node set; *date* is the value of date element from within the *orderInfo* node set displayed in the date format mm/dd/yyyy; *city, state* are the values of the city and state elements from within the *custInfo* node set; and *ship* is the value of the ship element from within the *orderInfo* node set.

18. Within the last `<td></td>` tag in the table row from the previous step, create a variable named **deliveryDate** equal to the value returned by the illf:estDelivery() function using the value of the date element within the *orderInfo* node set as the first parameter value and the value of the ship element within the *orderInfo* node set as the second parameter value. Display the value of the *deliveryDate* variable in the table cell in the *wDay, Month day, Year* format where *wDay* is the day of the week, *Month* is name of the month, *day* is the day of the month, and *Year* is the year.

19. Save your changes to the productlist.xsl file.

20. Use your XSLT 2.0 processor to transform the productlist.xml file using the productlist.xsl style sheet, storing the result in the **productlist.html** file.

Case Problem 1

APPLY

Data Files needed for this Case Problem: alltxt.xsl, horizonstxt.xsl, +6 XML files, +1 CSS file, +1 PNG file

Horizons TechNet   Lucy di Prima is the employment officer at Horizons TechNet, a technology firm located in Provo, Utah. Periodically, she has to compile reports on employee compensation by gender, where compensation is defined as the sum of each employee's salary, bonuses, and any sales commissions.

Lucy has received sample employee data from several departments in the form of XML documents. She wants to compile these XML documents into a single XML document and then she wants to display the total compensation for each employee and calculate the average compensation across all employees by gender. Figure 8-44 shows a preview of her report.

| Figure 8-44 | Horizons TechNet employment report |

Lucy has asked you to use XSLT 2.0 and XPath 2.0 to write this report. Complete the following:

1. Using your text editor, open the **alltxt.xsl** and **horizonstxt.xsl** files from the xml08 ► case1 folder. Enter *your name* and the *date* in the comment section of each file, and save them as **alldepartments.xsl** and **horizons.xsl**, respectively.

2. Go to the **alldepartments.xsl** file in your text editor. The purpose of this template is to create a single XML document listing all of the employees from each department. First, create a template named **getEmployees**.

3. Within the getEmployees template, create a variable named **depts** containing a sequence of the following text strings representing the department codes for Lucy's sample data: 'a00', 'c01', 'd11', 'd21', 'e11', and 'e21'.

4. After the line to create the *depts* variable, create the **departments** element.

5. Within the departments element, insert a for-each loop that loops through each entry in the *depts* sequence.

6. For each entry in the *depts* sequence do the following:

   a. Create a variable named **currentDept** equal to the current item in the *depts* sequence.

   b. Create an element named **department** with an attribute named **deptID** whose value is equal to the value of the *currentDept* variable.

   c. Use the `doc()` function to reference the "dept*current*.xml" file, where *current* is the value of the *currentDept* variable. (*Hint*: Use the `concat()` function to combine the text strings for "dept", the *currentDept* variable, and the text string ".xml".)

   d. Use the `copy-of` element to copy the contents of the employees element and its descendants to the department element.

7. Save your changes to the file and then use your XSLT 2.0 processor to generate the result document **horizons.xml** by applying the getEmployees template within the alldepartments.xsl style sheet.

8. Next, you'll display the employee data in an HTML file. Go to the **horizons.xsl** file in your text editor.

9. Directly below the `<h1>Employment Report</h1>` tag, insert a `for-each-group` element that selects all of the employee elements in the source document and groups them by the gender element.

10. Within the `for-each-group` loop, write the following code to the result document:

```
<table id="summary">
   <tr>
      <th>Gender</th>
      <td>key</td>
   </tr>
   <tr>
      <th>Employees</th>
      <td>count</td>
   </tr>
   <tr>
      <th>Average Compensation</th>
      <td>average</td>
   </tr>
</table>
```

where *key* is the value of the current grouping key, *count* is the number of items in the current group, and *average* uses the XPath 2.0 `avg()` function to calculate the average value of the sum of the salary + bonus + commission elements within the current group. Format the average compensation as a currency value.

11. Next, write the following HTML table to the result document:

```
<table id="emptable">
   <tr>
      <th>ID</th>
      <th>Department</th>
      <th>Title</th>
      <th>Education Level</th>
      <th>Total Compensation</th>
   </tr>
   current group template
</table>
```

where `current group template` is application of the template for the current group, displaying information on each employee in a separate table row sorted in descending order of the sum of salary + bonus + commission. (*Hint*: Be sure to specify the data type for the `sort` element as `xs:number`.)

12. Create the template for the employee element. The purpose of this template is to display information on each employee. Within the template, write the following table row:

```
<tr>
    <td>empID</td>
    <td>department</td>
    <td>title</td>
    <td>edLevel</td>
    <td>compensation</td>
</tr>
```

where *empID* is the value of the empID attribute, *department* is the value of the department element, *title* is the value of the title element, *edLevel* is the value of the edLevel element, and *compensation* is the sum of the salary, bonus, and commission elements.

13. Save your changes to the file.

14. Use your XSLT 2.0 processor with the horizons.xml source document and the horizons.xsl style sheet to generate an output file named **horizons.html**.

15. Open the **horizons.html** file in your web browser and verify that its contents and layout resemble that shown in Figure 8-44.

Case Problem 2

Data Files needed for this Case Problem: boise.txt, readtabtxt.xsl. +1 CSS file, +1 XSLT file, +1 PNG file

Idaho Climate Research Council   Paul Rao works for the Idaho Climate Research Council, a research institute located in Boise, Idaho, that is investigating issues surrounding climate and weather. Paul has the job of developing a report summarizing temperature, precipitation, wind, and other weather factors taken from a weather research station outside of Boise.

His first job is to summarize daily temperature readings from 1995 to 2013. As an initial step, he wants to create a table showing average, maximum, and minimum temperature values as summary statistics for each month. He also wants his table to calculate the range of temperatures (equal to the maximum value minus the minimum value). Figure 8-45 shows a preview of the completed report.

Figure 8-45   Boise, Idaho temperature summary

Boise, Idaho
Annual Temperature Summary

Month	Average	Minimum	Maximum	Range
January	32.12	6.0	54.0	48.0
February	36.52	7.3	53.1	45.8
March	44.19	26.7	62.8	36.1
April	50.07	35.4	75.7	40.3
May	58.97	40.4	80.2	39.8
June	67.57	44.0	88.6	44.6
July	78.20	56.8	94.2	37.4
August	75.97	54.2	89.2	35.0
September	66.23	46.2	85.1	38.9
October	52.42	23.4	79.1	55.7
November	40.83	15.2	63.1	47.9
December	32.10	3.1	55.8	52.7

The data source that Paul has been given is in tab-delimited format, which means one column is separated from another by the tab character. He wants your help in converting this file to an XML document. He then wants you to use the features of XSTL 2.0 and XPath 2.0 to calculate the summary statistics for his temperature data.

Complete the following:

1. Using your text editor, open the **boisetxt.xsl** and **readtabtxt.xsl** files from the xml08 ▸ case2 folder. Enter *your name* and the *date* in the comment section of each file, and save them as **boise.xsl** and **readtab.xsl**, respectively.

2. Go to the **readtab.xsl** file in your text editor. The purpose of this style sheet is to convert the contents of the boise.txt file to XML format. Below the `output` element, declare the **tempDataset** variable, importing the text from the boise.txt file using the `unparsed-text()` function.

3. Create the **tabConvert** template that will be used to convert the text of the boise.txt file to XML format.

4. Within the tabConvert template create the **records** variable containing a sequence of substrings drawn from the *tempDataset* variable, split at each occurrence of the regular expression \r?\n. Set the data type of the sequence to `xs:string*`.

5. Within the tabConvert template create an element named **annual**.

6. Within the annual element, insert a `for-each` loop for each item in the *records* sequence. Within the loop, create an element named **daily**.

7. Within the daily element, create a variable named **dailyValues** containing a sequence of text string values split from the current item in the *records* variable at every occurrence of a tab character followed by zero or more white space characters. (*Hint*: Use the \t symbol to represent a tab character.)

8. Within the daily element, create the **temperature** element containing the value of the first item in the *dailyValues* sequence. Create the **date** element containing the value of the second item in the *dailyValues* sequence.

9. Save your changes to the style sheet and then use your XSLT 2.0 processor to generate the result document **boise.xml** by applying the tabConvert template within the readtab.xsl style sheet.

10. Go the **boise.xsl** style sheet in your text editor. This style sheet will be used to generate the report that summarizes the temperature data. Within the `stylesheet` element, declare the namespace for XML Schema using the prefix "xs". Also declare the namespace for a customized function that you'll create using the URI *http://example.com/idaho* and the prefix icrc. Add an attribute to the `stylesheet` element to exclude these two namespaces from the result document.

11. Scroll to the bottom of the file and insert a custom function named **icrc:rangeValue** that returns a value with the data type `xs:double`. The function has a single parameter named **dataValues** with no specified data type. Have the function return the maximum of the *dataValues* parameter minus the minimum value of the *dataValues* parameter by using the XPath 2.0 `max()` and `min()` functions.

12. Return to the root template. Within the tbody element, declare a variable named **monthNames** containing the sequence of month names starting with January and concluding with December.

13. Insert a for-each-group loop that selects all of the daily elements from the source document grouping them by the year value retrieved from the date element. (*Hint*: Apply the `year-from-date()` function to the date element to get 12 distinct month numbers from all of the dates in the source document.)

14. Within the for-each-group loop, declare a variable named **tempValues** referencing the temperature element from within the current group. Then, on the next line, declare a variable named **monthNumber** equal to the integer value of the current grouping key. (*Hint*: Use the `xs:integer()` constructor function.)

15. Write the following HTML code for every group within the for-each-group loop:

```
<tr>
    <td>Month Name</td>
    <td>average</td>
    <td>minimum</td>
    <td>maximum</td>
    <td>range</td>
</tr>
```

where `Month Name` is the name of the month taken from the *monthNames* sequence using the value of the *monthNumber* variable as the index number, `average` is the average value of the *tempValues* variable, `minimum` is the minimum value of the *tempValues* variable, `maximum` is maximum value of *tempValues*, and `range` is the range of values in *tempValues* calculated using the icrc:rangeValue() function. Format the summary statistics so that they are easy to read.

16. Save your changes to the style sheet and then use your XSLT 2.0 processor along with the boise.xml source file and the boise.xsl style sheet to generate the **boise.html** result document containing the summary statistics grouped by month.

Case Problem 3

CHALLENGE

Data Files needed for this Case Problem: zfptxt.xsl, +3 XML files, +1 CSS file, +1 PNG file

The Zocalo Fire Pit   Luis Nieves is an accounts manager at The Zocalo Fire Pit, an online distributor of gourmet meats and other dishes and beverages. He's asked for your help in developing an XML application that will take an XML document containing a list of recent orders and use it to generate several HTML files so that each document details the recent order history of a selected customer. A preview of one of the web pages is shown in Figure 8-46.

Figure 8-46	Recent customer orders from the Zocalo Fire Pit

The Zocalo Fire Pit
Gourmet Meats and Dishes

Customer   Lorena Parsons
Customer ID   c92115
Address   202 Nixon Way
              Bergen, NY 14416

Recent Orders

August 14, 2017

Product ID	Product	Box Size	Quantity	Price	Total
filet740-7f	Bacon-Wrapped Filet Mignon (6 oz.)	6	1	89.99	89.99
wine452-2w	Cabernet Sauvignon	1	1	39.99	39.99
				Subtotal	129.98
				Shipping	0.00
				Tax	6.50
				TOTAL	$136.48

August 18, 2017

Product ID	Product	Box Size	Quantity	Price	Total
sauce557-6s	Lemon Dill Tartar Sauce (6 oz.)	1	1	5.99	5.99
seafo553-4s	Salmon Fillets (6 oz.)	4	3	29.99	89.97
wine304-6w	Sauvignon Blanc	1	1	21.99	21.99
				Subtotal	117.95
				Shipping	5.00
				Tax	6.15
				TOTAL	$129.10

To create this collection of result documents, you'll use the XSLT 2.0 `result-document` element. You'll also explore how to work with multi-level grouping, first you'll group the list of orders by customer ID and then, within each customer report, you'll group the orders by order date.

Complete the following:

1. Using your text editor, open the **zfptxt.xsl** file from the xml08 ► case3 folder. Enter **your name** and the **date** in the comment section in the file and save it as **zfp.xsl**.

2. Take some time to review the data content in the **zfpcustomers.xml**, **zfporders.xml**, and **zfpproducts.xml** files. You'll use the zfporders.xml file to generate the result documents. The other two files will be used as lookup tables for the customer and product information displayed in the reports.

3. Return to the **zfp.xsl** file in your text editor and go to the root template. Surround the opening `<html>` tag and the closing `</html>` tag with a `for-each-group` element, selecting all of the order elements from the source document and grouping them by the value of the custID element.

✪ **EXPLORE** 4. Within the for-each-group loop, surround the opening `<html>` tag and closing `</html>` tag with a `result-document` element to generate a result document named **key.html** where **key** is the value of the current grouping key. Specify "html" as the method for the result document, and have the processor indent the code in the result file to make it more readable.

5. Directly above the `<table id="customerTable">` tag, insert a variable named **custInfo** containing a reference to the customers/customer node set in the zfpcustomers.xml file for which the value of the custID attribute is equal to the value of the current grouping key.

6. Write the following HTML code within the customerTable:

```
<tr>
    <th>Customer</th>
    <td>firstName lastName</td>
</tr>
<tr>
    <th>Customer ID</th>
    <td>custID</td>
</tr>
<tr>
    <th>Address</th>
    <td>address</td>
</tr>
```

where *firstName* and *lastName* is the customer name looked up from the *custInfo* node set, *custID* is the value of the current grouping key, and *address* is the customer's street address, city and state of residence, and postal code as retrieved from the *custInfo* node set.

✪ **EXPLORE** 7. Directly below the `<h1>Recent Orders</h1>` tag, insert a nested `for-each-group` that groups the current group by the value of the orderID attribute. Within the `for-each-group`, apply a template with the `select` attribute equal to the nested current group.

8. Go to the order template. This template will be used to display individual customer orders. Within the `<h3></h3>` tags, display the value of the orderDate element formatted as *Month Day, Year*.

9. Go to the `<tbody></tbody>` tag, which will be used to display each individual product purchased in the current order. Within these tags, apply a template to the products/product node set.

10. Go to the product template. This template will be used to display a table row describing a specific product sold by the company. Within the template, define a variable named **currentProd** equal to the value of the pID attribute.

11. Next, within the template write the following HTML code to the result document(s):

```
<tr>
    <td>product ID</td>
    <td>description</td>
    <td>box size</td>
    <td>qty</td>
    <td>price</td>
    <td>total</td>
</tr>
```

where *product ID* is the value of the *currentProd* variable, *description* is the product description retrieved from the zfpproducts.xml file using *currentProd* as the lookup value, *box size* is the value of the boxSize element looked up from the zfpproducts.xml file, *qty* and *price* are the values of the qty and price attributes, and *total* is the value of qty multiplied by price.

12. Go to the `<tfoot></tfoot>` tags in the order template. Within these tags, you'll provide summary calculations for each order. The company provides free shipping for any orders of more than $120 in price; otherwise, it charges a flat fee of $5. Also the store charges a 5% tax on the cost of the products and shipping cost. The total cost of the order is equal to the cost of the products plus the shipping cost plus the taxes due.

✦ **EXPLORE** 13. Directly after the opening `<tfoot>` tag, create the following variables:

   a. **subtotal** equal to the sum of the node set "products/product/(@qty*@price)"

   b. **shipping** equal to 0 if *subtotal* is greater than 120 and 5 otherwise

   c. **tax** equal to 5% of the sum of the *subtotal* and *shipping* values

   d. **total** equal to the sum of the *subtotal*, *shipping*, and *tax* values

14. Directly after the declaration of the *total* variable, write the following HTML code:

```
<tr>
    <td colspan="5">Subtotal</td>
    <td>subtotal</td>
</tr>
<tr>
    <td colspan="5">Shipping</td>
    <td>shipping</td>
</tr>
<tr>
    <td colspan="5">Tax</td>
    <td>tax</td>
</tr>
<tr>
    <td colspan="5">TOTAL</td>
    <td>total</td>
</tr>
```

where *subtotal*, *shipping*, *tax*, and *total* are the values of the *subtotal*, *shipping*, *tax*, and *total* variables. Format the subtotal, shipping, and tax values to display two decimal places. Format the total value as currency.

15. Save your changes to the file.

16. Using an XSLT 2.0 processor run the zfp.xsl style sheet using zfporders.xml as the source document. Do not specify a result document because that is provided for by the `result-document` element in the style sheet.

17. Verify that the processor generates five HTML files named **c10224.html**, **c28153.html**, **c49060.html**, **c61673.html**, and **c92115.html**. Open the files and confirm that they show the recent order history for each of the five customers in Luis's sample data set.

Case Problem 4

CREATE

Data Files needed for this Case Problem: tgerenttxt.xsl, +2 XML files, +1 XSLT file, +1 TXT file, +1 PNG file

The Good Earth   Melissa Gauthier is an equipment manager at The Good Earth, a landscaping and rental company near Shreveport, Louisiana. Melissa is preparing a document listing several pieces of equipment the company is currently renting out. She wants to generate a report detailing the equipment that has been rented, who is renting it, the estimated date of return of the equipment, and the estimated cost of the rental. To make this report, she'll have to work with data stored in several different formats including XML documents and a CSV file. She has asked for your assistance in creating an XSLT 2.0 style sheet to generate the result document. A possible solution is shown in Figure 8-47.

Figure 8-47   **Rental schedule at The Good Earth**

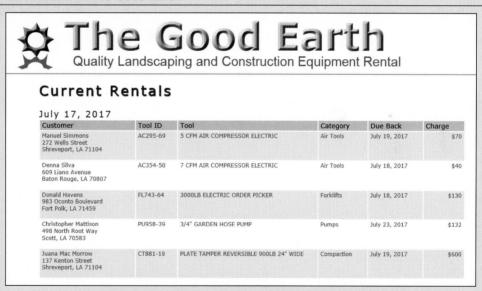

Complete the following:

1. Using your text editor, open the **tgerenttxt.xsl** file from the xml08 ► case4 folder. Enter *your name* and the *date* in the comment section of the file, and save it as **tgerentals.xsl**.

2. Use the **importcsv.xsl** style sheet to transform the CSV file **tgerentals.txt** into the XML file **tgerentals.xml**.

3. Edit the **tgerentals.xsl** to create a style sheet that generates a result document displaying information about rentals from The Good Earth over the last several days. The style and layout of the result document is left up to you, but your style sheet must include the following features:

   a. Grouping your report by the date using the XSLT 2.0 grouping elements.

   b. Use of the `current-grouping-key()` to display the value of the current key.

   c. Data value lookups using the XPath 2.0 `doc()` function.

   d. Date formats using the XPath 2.0 picture formats.

   e. Application of an XML Schema data type to a variable and a function.

   f. A custom function that calculates the date at which each piece of equipment is due to be returned to the company.

   g. Calculation of the total rental charge equal to the number of weeks in which the equipment is rented at the weekly rate plus the number of days at the daily rate.

4. Augment your completed project with any graphics or CSS styles of your choosing.

5. Use an XSLT 2.0 processor to generate an HTML file named **tgerentals.html** containing the completed report on rented equipment.

6. Test your style sheet on your web browser or an XSLT processor, and verify that all required elements are displayed, that the report correctly calculates the total rental fee, and that the date the equipment should be returned is displayed.

TUTORIAL **9**

Exploring Data with XQuery

Querying Sales Totals from a Database

OBJECTIVES

Session 9.1
- Create an XQuery document
- Create an XQuery variable
- Design a query with a path expression
- Design a FLWOR query

Session 9.2
- Work with nested FLWOR queries
- Create a grouped Query
- Create and run a user-defined function
- Create and import a library module

Case | *Green Jersey Cycling*

Jessica Otter is an accounts manager at Green Jersey Cycling, a small but growing cycling and recreational company with several stores at different locations in the Midwest, West, and Pacific regions. Recently, Jessica received a sample database containing information on customer orders for a selection of Green Jersey Cycling products written in XML format. Jessica wants to use these XML files to summarize total revenue from these sales for different GJC stores and products. She's asked for your help in working with XQuery to retrieve this information.

STARTING DATA FILES

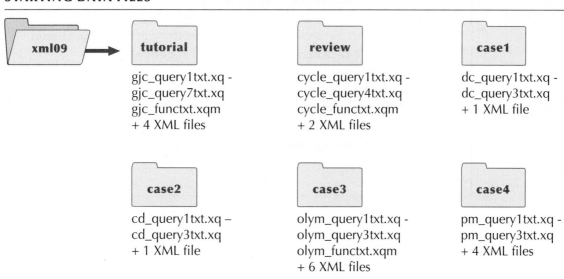

xml09 →

tutorial
gjc_query1txt.xq -
gjc_query7txt.xq
gjc_functxt.xqm
+ 4 XML files

review
cycle_query1txt.xq -
cycle_query4txt.xq
cycle_functxt.xqm
+ 2 XML files

case1
dc_query1txt.xq -
dc_query3txt.xq
+ 1 XML file

case2
cd_query1txt.xq –
cd_query3txt.xq
+ 1 XML file

case3
olym_query1txt.xq -
olym_query3txt.xq
olym_functxt.xqm
+ 6 XML files

case4
pm_query1txt.xq -
pm_query3txt.xq
+ 4 XML files

Session 9.1 Visual Overview:

The **external** keyword allows the variable value to be set by the processor when the query is run.

This shows the value of the *$stores* global variable.

The *declare* variable statement defines a global variable.

Element values are enclosed within a set of curly braces.

This shows the query result when the *$s* variable equals "AZ".

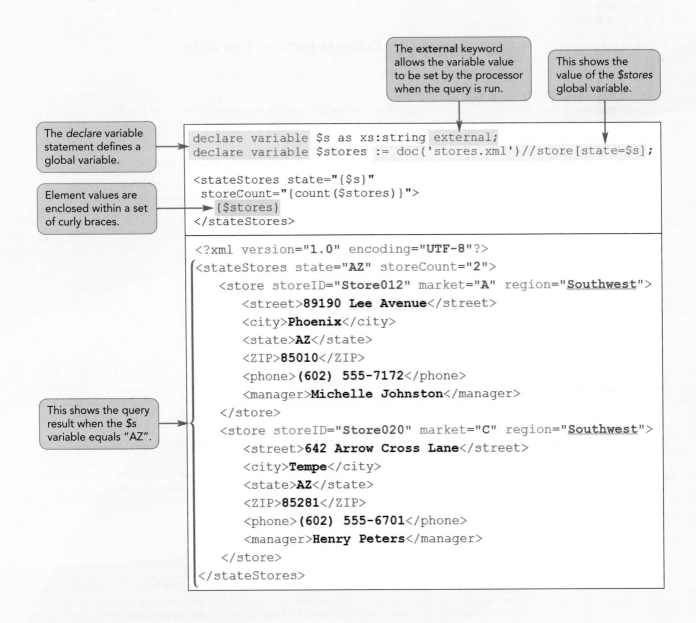

```
declare variable $s as xs:string external;
declare variable $stores := doc('stores.xml')//store[state=$s];

<stateStores state="{$s}"
 storeCount="{count($stores)}">
   {$stores}
</stateStores>
```

```xml
<?xml version="1.0" encoding="UTF-8"?>
<stateStores state="AZ" storeCount="2">
   <store storeID="Store012" market="A" region="Southwest">
      <street>89190 Lee Avenue</street>
      <city>Phoenix</city>
      <state>AZ</state>
      <ZIP>85010</ZIP>
      <phone>(602) 555-7172</phone>
      <manager>Michelle Johnston</manager>
   </store>
   <store storeID="Store020" market="C" region="Southwest">
      <street>642 Arrow Cross Lane</street>
      <city>Tempe</city>
      <state>AZ</state>
      <ZIP>85281</ZIP>
      <phone>(602) 555-6701</phone>
      <manager>Henry Peters</manager>
   </store>
</stateStores>
```

Queries and Results

A **FLWOR** query is an XQuery structure built around for, let, where, order by, and return clauses.

The **for clause** iterates through a sequence of nodes or atomic values.

The **let clause** is the local variable used in the query.

The **where clause** filters the result of the query.

The **order by clause** sorts the query result.

The **return clause** specifies the format and structure of the query result.

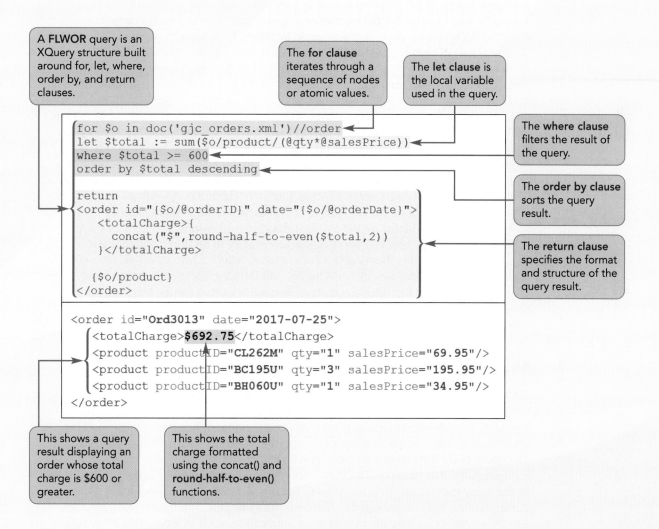

```
for $o in doc('gjc_orders.xml')//order
let $total := sum($o/product/(@qty*@salesPrice))
where $total >= 600
order by $total descending

return
<order id="{$o/@orderID}" date="{$o/@orderDate}">
   <totalCharge>{
      concat("$",round-half-to-even($total,2))
   }</totalCharge>

   {$o/product}
</order>
```

```
<order id="Ord3013" date="2017-07-25">
   <totalCharge>$692.75</totalCharge>
   <product productID="CL262M" qty="1" salesPrice="69.95"/>
   <product productID="BC195U" qty="3" salesPrice="195.95"/>
   <product productID="BH060U" qty="1" salesPrice="34.95"/>
</order>
```

This shows a query result displaying an order whose total charge is $600 or greater.

This shows the total charge formatted using the concat() and **round-half-to-even()** functions.

Introducing XQuery

XML can be used to store an enormous amount of structured information but, when encountering a large database, it's usually necessary to retrieve only those data that match some specified search criteria or to summarize a large amount of data as a collection of summary statistics. **XQuery** is a database query language developed by the W3C to meet these needs. With XQuery, the user can do the following:

- Select data based on search criteria.
- Join data from multiple tables and documents.
- Sort and group data.
- Summarize data with aggregate functions.

Because there is considerable overlap between XSLT and XQuery, you can use XQuery in place of XSLT to transform a source document, just as you can use XSLT to perform a query on the contents of one or more XML source files. Whether you use XSLT or XQuery is a matter of personal preference, but those users who come from database backgrounds often find it easier to transition to XQuery in place of XSLT. A general rule of thumb is that XSLT is used when working with the complete XML document, while XQuery is used with fragments of an XML document. Also, for larger documents and more complicated search criteria, it's generally easier and more efficient to use XQuery.

Currently, there are two W3C recommended standards for XQuery: the specifications for XQuery 1.0 were released in January 2007, while the specifications for XQuery 3.0 were released in April 2014 (there is no XQuery 2.0). The XQuery 1.0 and 3.0 data models are identical to the data model used in XPath 2.0; in addition, XQuery supports many of the same functions and operators used in XPath 2.0. This is by design because XPath 2.0 is essentially a subset of XQuery. Thus, a background in XPath 2.0 leaves you well on the way to understanding how to write queries in the XQuery language.

XQuery is written in text format as a collection of expressions. Unlike XSLT, XQuery is not an XML vocabulary. This allows an XQuery query to be stored within a text document, embedded within program code, placed within a hypertext link, or used within a relational database, such as Oracle, IMB DB2, or the Microsoft SQL Server. In the examples used in this tutorial, you'll write queries as stand-alone text files, but you should be aware that the techniques you learn have much wider application as database commands within other programming environments.

Writing an XQuery Document

An XQuery file consists of two parts. The **prolog** is an optional section that is placed at the beginning of the query and is used to set up fundamental properties of the query including identifying declarations, such as variables, that define the XQuery working environment; establishing namespaces; importing schemas; and defining functions. The **query body** consists of a single expression (though that expression may contain multiple parts) that retrieves data from a source document based on criteria provided in the query expression. Thus, an XQuery document is usually smaller in size than a corresponding XSLT document that performs the same task. The results from the query can be written to an XML file or sent to an application, such as a database program, for further processing.

Declarations in the Query Prolog

The prolog contains a series of declarations with each declaration terminated with a semi-colon. The first statement in the prolog defines the version of XQuery and the text encoding using the following declaration:

```
xquery version "version" encoding="enctype";
```

where *version* is either 1.0 for XQuery 1.0 or 3.0 for XQuery 3.0 and *enctype* is an optional attribute value that specifies the text encoding such as utf-8. The next part of the prolog contains declarations that define the XQuery working environment. Figure 9-1 describes the different prolog declarations.

Figure 9-1   **XQuery prolog declarations**

Declaration	Description
declare boundary-space strip | preserve;	Specifies whether white space is stripped when elements are constructed in the query or preserved
declare ordering ordered | unordered;	Specifies whether the query processor ignores ordering of nodes (unordered) or applies ordering (ordered)
declare default order greatest | least;	Specifies whether empty elements should appear last (greatest) in any node ordering or first (least)
declare copy-namespace preserve | no-preserve, inherit | no-inherit;	Controls whether namespace declarations are preserved from the source document and/or inherited from the parent node
declare construction strip | preserve;	Specifies whether constructed elements have untyped data types (strip) or are constructed as xs:anyType data types (preserve)
declare default collation *type*	Defines the collation used in constructing the query where *type* is the name of the collation
declare base-uri *uri*;	Provides the *uri* used in resolving relative references
declare namespace *prefix=uri*;	Defines a namespace and namespace prefix for the query
declare default element namespace *uri*	Declares the default namespace for elements and types
declare default function namespace *uri*	Declares the default namespace for functions used in the query

For example, the following declaration defines a namespace using the URI http://www.example.com/greenjersey and the namespace prefix gjc:

```
declare namespace gjc="http://www.example.com/greenjersey";
```

Note that namespaces need to be declared in the prolog prior to their use in any XQuery statement; however, XQuery supports the following built-in namespaces and namespace prefixes, which do not have to be declared within the prolog.

```
xml = http://www.w3.org/XML/1998/namespace
xs = http://www.w3.org/2001/XMLSchema
xsi = http://www.w3.org/2001/XMLSchema-instance
fn = http://www.w3.org/2005/xpath-functions
local = http://www.w3.org/2005/xquery-local-functions
```

The `local` namespace is used for creating user-defined functions, while the `fn` namespace is preserved for functions from XPath 1.0 and 2.0. For most XQuery processors, you will not have to include the `fn` prefix when using XPath functions because that namespace is assumed for any XPath function.

Writing the XQuery Prolog

- To define the XQuery version and text encoding, insert the following statement at the top of the XQuery file:

```
xquery version "version" encoding="enctype";
```

where *version* is either 1.0 for XQuery 1.0 or 3.0 for XQuery 3.0 and *enctype* is an optional attribute that specifies the text encoding.
- To define a namespace for the query, include the following statement in the prolog:

```
declare namespace prefix=uri;
```

where *prefix* is the namespace prefix and *uri* is the URI of the namespace.

Commenting Text in XQuery

As with any program, you'll want to document your query for others with several lines of comments. You can add comments to any part of the XQuery file using the following statement:

```
(: comment :)
```

TIP

XQuery comments can be nested within one another to provide more information to the user.

where *comment* is the text of the comment. The comment text can span multiple lines and be placed anywhere within the query file that allows for insignificant white space, such as the empty lines between XQuery expressions.

XML comments can also be constructed as they would be in an XML document with the following tag:

```
<!-- comment -->
```

A constructed XML comment will be written to the result document alongside the results of the query. Note that an XQuery comment is not written to the result document so, if you want to include your comments alongside the query results, you will want to use an XML comment tag.

INSIGHT

Enhanced Commenting with xqdoc

You can automatically generate comments for your query through the use of **xqdoc** comments, which are a standard method for creating structured documentation. The general format for an xqdoc comment is

```
(:~
: comments
:)
```

where *comments* contains the text of user comments. Comments that belong to specific categories are marked by the @ symbol. The xqdoc standard supports comment categories such as the document's author, its file version, and where to go for additional information. These marked comments become elements in the result document. For example, the xqdoc comment

```
(:~
: A sales report for GJC
: @author Jessica Otter
: @version 1.0
: @see http://example.com/gjc
:)
```

will generate the following XML fragment when scanned by a processor that supports xqdoc:

```
<xqdoc:xqdoc xmlns:xqdoc="http://www.xqdoc.org/1.0">
...
  <xqdoc:comment>
    <xqdoc:description>A sales report for GJC</xqdoc:description>
    <xqdoc:author>Jessica Otter</xqdoc:author>
    <xqdoc:version>1.0</xqdoc:version>
    <xqdoc:see>http://example.com/gjc</xqdoc:see>
  </xqdoc:comment>
</xqdoc:xqdoc>
```

Note that general comments that are not marked with the @ symbol are placed in the description. Once in the xqdoc form, comments can be easily transformed into other output formats such as HTML5 or PDF. You can learn more about xqdoc at *http://www.xqdoc.org*.

Jessica has already created a query file containing some of the information about the report you'll generate. You'll open her document and edit the XQuery comments in the file to include your name and the date.

To open the XQuery file:

1. Use your editor to open the **gjc_query1txt.xq** file from the xml09 ▸ tutorial folder. Enter *your name* and the *date* in the comment section at the top of the file. See Figure 9-2.

Figure 9-2	XQuery comments

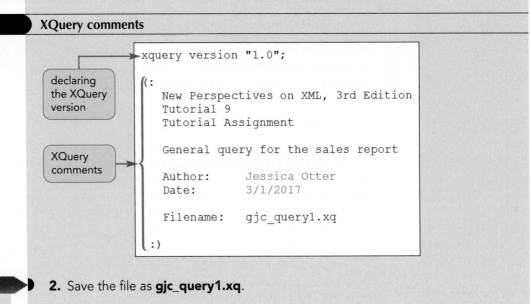

```
xquery version "1.0";

(:
    New Perspectives on XML, 3rd Edition
    Tutorial 9
    Tutorial Assignment

    General query for the sales report

    Author:     Jessica Otter
    Date:       3/1/2017

    Filename:   gjc_query1.xq
:)
```

declaring the XQuery version

XQuery comments

2. Save the file as **gjc_query1.xq**.

Next, you'll add an expression to the query file to retrieve XML data for the sales report. Jessica has created the following four XML source documents for your investigation:

- **gjc_customers.xml** containing contact information on 1791 Green Jersey Cycling customers
- **gjc_orders.xml** listing 2468 items purchased by those customers over the past 2 months
- **gjc_products.xml** describing 129 different products sold by the company
- **gjc_stores.xml** providing information on 20 Green Jersey Cycling stores located in the Midwest, West, and Pacific regions

Figure 9-3 summarizes the contents of each file.

Figure 9-3	Sample XML documents from Green Jersey Cycling

Table	Elements and Attributes

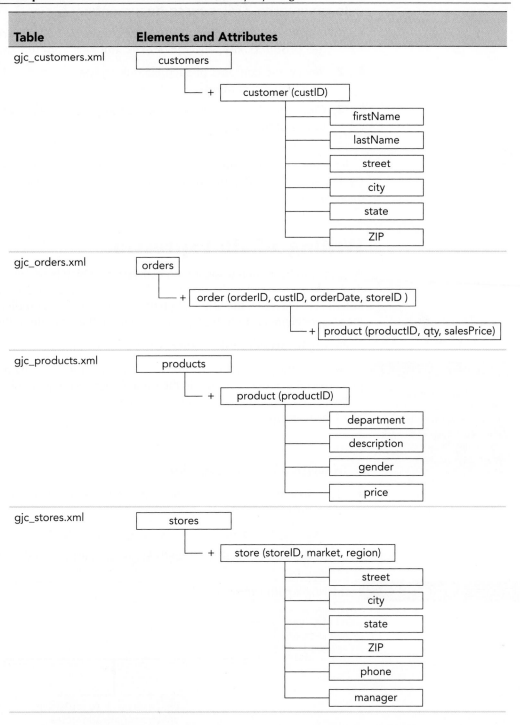

Each file contains one or more elements that can be used to join it with one of the other documents. For example, each customer is marked with a unique custID attribute, each store with the storeID attribute, and finally each product sold by the company with the productID attribute. By combining these files, you'll be able to determine what products each customer bought, where they bought them, and how much they spent at the store. Take some time now to review the contents and structure of these XML documents.

To review the XML source documents:

1. Use your editor to open the **gjc_customers.xml**, **gjc_orders.xml**, **gjc_products.xml**, and **gjc_stores.xml** files from the xml09 ▸ tutorial folder.

2. Review the contents of each file, taking special note of the document structure and contents.

3. Close the files without saving any changes you may have inadvertently made to any of the documents.

Jessica wants you to start by developing a basic query that lists the Green Jersey Cycling stores located in different states. To create such a query, you'll work with XPath expressions within XQuery.

Writing a Path Expression

A query can be written using a **path expression**, which is simply an XPath expression that retrieves element and attribute nodes from a source document based on specified criteria. For example, the following path expression uses a predicate to select only those store elements from the gjc_stores.xml file that operate in the state of Colorado.

```
doc('gjc_stores.xml')//store[state='CO']
```

Note that the path to the gjc_stores.xml file is not required by most XQuery processors if that file is located in the same folder as the query file.

Jessica asks you to use this path expression in order to generate a query that displays all of the Colorado stores.

TIP

The XSLT document() function is not supported in XQuery, which means you must use the XPath doc() function to reference a document source.

To write a path expression:

1. Below the comment section of the gjc_query1.xq file, enter the following expression:

```
doc('gjc_stores.xml')//store[state='CO']
```

Figure 9-4 highlights the path expression added to the XQuery document.

Figure 9-4   **Entering a path expression**

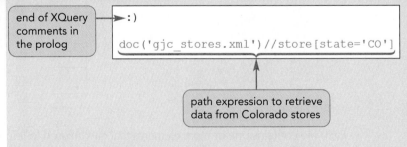

end of XQuery comments in the prolog → `:)`

`doc('gjc_stores.xml')//store[state='CO']`

path expression to retrieve data from Colorado stores

2. Save your changes to the file.

To see the results of a query, you need to run the query.

Running a Query

To run a query, you need a **query processor** that parses, analyzes, and evaluates the query. Because XPath 2.0 is a subset of XQuery, a processor that supports XSLT 2.0 and XPath 2.0 will usually also support XQuery. At the time of this writing, popular query processors include BaseX, Saxon XSLT, XMLSpy, and Zorba; all support XQuery 1.0, and a few provide support for XQuery 3.0. The Java programming language supports XQuery through the XQuery API for Java (or XQJ), allowing programmers to query XML source documents from within their Java applications.

In the examples that follow, you'll use the free version of the Saxon command-line processor to run your queries, but you can substitute your own XQuery processor if you have one. To run a query using Saxon in command line mode, enter the following command within a command prompt window:

```
java net.sf.saxon.Query -s:source -q:query -o:output
```

TIP

If you don't specify an output file, Saxon will display the query result in the command window.

where *source* is the XML source document, query is the XQuery query file, and *output* contains the query result. If you are using Saxon on the .NET platform, the equivalent command line is

```
Query -s:source -q:query -o:output
```

If you reference the source document in the query file using the `doc()` function, you can use the following more simplified Saxon command, which assumes the first file listed in the command is the query file:

```
java net.sf.saxon.Query query -o:output
```

Finally, instead of using a query file, you can enter the text of the query as part of the command using the statement

```
java net.sf.saxon.Query -qs:query -o:output
```

where *query* is the text of the XQuery expression. For example, the following statement inserts the query expression directly into the command and sends the result of the query to the output.xml file:

```
java net.sf.saxon.Query -qs:doc('gjc_stores.xml')
//store[state='CO'] -o:output.xml
```

Formatting the Query Output

Unlike XSLT, XQuery does not have the tools to create formatted output, and there is no standard way to indent or format the results. This is by design because the query results might be written to a separate output file or they might be transferred directly as a single text string to a database application or website for further processing. Many XQuery processors have their own mechanisms to format the query result. For example, if you're using Saxon from the command line, you can include the parameter `!indent=yes` to create indented and easily readable result text.

Another option to format the query results is to add the following declaration to the XQuery prolog, which preserves all of the white space characters from the XQuery file and writes them to the result document:

```
declare boundary-space preserve;
```

Using this declaration you can preserve the formats and indenting from the query file in the result document. However, this approach does not always result in nicely formatted text because the white space characters you use in writing the query document may not be what you want to see in the result file.

You'll run the query now using the XQuery processor of your choice to display a list of the GJC stores in Colorado. If you are using the Saxon XQuery processor, you'll use the `!indent=yes` option to create nicely formatted and indented output.

To run the query:

▶ **1.** Open a command prompt window within the xml09 ▸ tutorial folder.

▶ **2.** If you're using Saxon in Java command line mode, enter the following command on a single line to run the query and place the results in the gjc_results1.xml file:

```
java net.sf.saxon.Query !indent=yes gjc_query1.xq –o:gjc_
results1.xml
```

Figure 9-5 shows the text of the query command using the Saxon XQuery processor in Java command mode.

| Figure 9-5 | **Running a query from the Saxon command line** |

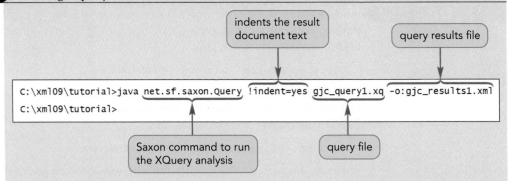

▶ **3.** Press **Enter** to run the command.

Trouble?   If the processor indicates that it can't find the gjc_stores.xml file, the cause might be that your XQuery processor does not automatically assume that the query file is in the same folder as the gjc_stores.xml file. You can fix this problem by adding the `declare base-uri uri;` declaration to the query file directly after the version statement where *uri* is the URI of your data folder.

▶ **4.** Open the **gjc_results1.xml** file in your editor. As shown in Figure 9-6, the document should contain an XML fragment listing the Green Jersey Cycling stores located in Colorado.

Figure 9-6	**XML fragment containing the result of the query**

```
<?xml version="1.0" encoding="UTF-8"?>
<store storeID="Store005" market="B" region="Mountain">
        <street>1440 Segall Avenue</street>
        <city>Boulder</city>
        <state>CO</state>
        <ZIP>80301</ZIP>
        <phone>(303) 555-4381</phone>
        <manager>Tiffany Hurst</manager>
    </store>
<store storeID="Store006" market="A" region="Mountain">
        <street>5181 Pike Drive</street>
        <city>Colorado Springs</city>
        <state>CO</state>
        <ZIP>80904</ZIP>
        <phone>(720) 555-6122</phone>
        <manager>Sofia Gonzales</manager>
    </store>
<store storeID="Store008" market="A" region="Mountain">
        <street>1552 Pointe Street</street>
        <city>Denver</city>
        <state>CO</state>
        <ZIP>80229</ZIP>
        <phone>(303) 555-8371</phone>
        <manager>Peter Higgins</manager>
    </store>
```

data on Colorado stores

5. Close the gjc_results1.xml file.

XQuery returns a document containing an XML fragment, but it lacks a root element. To create a valid XML document, you will have to add a root element to the query code in much the same way you would add elements to the result documents from an XSLT transformation.

Adding Elements and Attributes to a Query Result

You can add an element to a query through a **direct element constructor**, which uses XML-like syntax to insert the element markup tags directly into the query expression. The general syntax to insert an element and its value into the query is

```
<elem>{expression}</elem>
```

where `elem` is the element name and `expression` is a query expression that returns a sequence of atomic values or nodes. For example, the following query will add the root element stateStores to the query results, creating a valid XML document:

```
<stateStores state="CO">
    {
    doc('gjc_stores.xml')//store[state='CO']
    }
</stateStores>
```

Notice that the state="CO" attribute of the stateStores element is passed directly to the query result. Essentially any text in the query that is not part of an expression is treated as **literal text** and displayed as part of the query result without modification.

To place the value of an expression within an attribute, you once again enclose the expression within a set of curly braces as follows:

```
<elem att="{expression}">...</elem>
```

where *att* is the name of the attribute and *expression* is an XPath expression that returns a single value or a sequence of atomic values. For example, the following query adds the storeCount attribute, using the XPath *count( )* function to display a count of the number of Colorado stores:

```
<stateStores state="CO"
  storeCount="{
    count(doc('gjc_stores.xml')//store[state='CO'])
    }">
    {
    doc('gjc_stores.xml')//store[state='CO']
    }
</stateStores>
```

REFERENCE

Adding Elements and Attributes to a Query Result

- To write an element into the query result, insert the following statement into the query:

  ```
  <elem>{expression}</elem>
  ```

  where *elem* is the element name and *expression* is a query expression that returns a sequence of atomic values or nodes.

- To write an element attribute to the query result, apply the following statement:

  ```
  <elem att="{expression}">…</elem>
  ```

  where *att* is the name of the attribute and *expression* is an XPath expression that returns a single value or a sequence of atomic values.

You modify your query now by adding the stateStores element to your query result, as well as the state and storeCount attributes.

To add elements and attributes to a query:

1. Return to the **gjc_query1.xq** file in your editor.

2. Directly above the XPath expression that displays the Colorado store data, insert the following opening tag:

   ```
   <stateStores state="CO"
     storeCount="{
       count(doc('gjc_stores.xml')//store[state='CO'])
       }">
       {
   ```

3. Indent the XPath expression that displays the Colorado store data to offset that code from the enclosing curly braces.

4. After the XPath expression that displays the Colorado store data, insert the following closing brace and closing tag to complete the revisions to the query element.

   ```
       }
   </stateStores>
   ```

   Figure 9-7 highlights the newly added code in the query.

> XPath expressions need to be enclosed within curly braces so that the results of the expression are displayed.

| Figure 9-7 | Adding an element and attribute to a query |

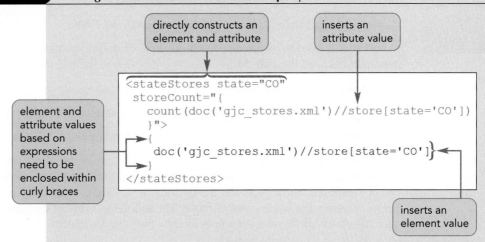

5. Save your changes to the file and then rerun the **gjc_query1.xq** query using your XQuery processor, saving the result document to the **gjc_results1.xml** file. If you are using the Saxon processor, include the !indent=yes option to indent the elements in the result document.

6. View the contents of the query result in your web browser or editor. As shown in Figure 9-8, the query result should now appear as a valid XML document with the stateStores root element and a count of the number of stores returned by the query.

| Figure 9-8 | Query result showing count of Colorado stores |

```
<?xml version="1.0" encoding="UTF-8"?>
<stateStores state="CO" storeCount="3">
    <store storeID="Store005" market="B" region="Mountain">
        <street>1440 Segall Avenue</street>
        <city>Boulder</city>
        <state>CO</state>
        <ZIP>80301</ZIP>
        <phone>(303) 555-4381</phone>
        <manager>Tiffany Hurst</manager>
    </store>
```

Trouble? Figure 9-8 shows the appearance of the gjc_results1.xml file as rendered by the Notepad++ text editor. If you are using a different program to view the XML document, your screen might differ in how it presents the data. In some editors, the text will appear on a single line; other editors will show the XML data in a structured outline.

Jessica wants you to simplify your XQuery code. Rather than repeating the path expression that selects the Colorado stores from the gjc_stores.xml document, she wants you to save that expression within a variable.

Declaring XQuery Variables

Variables can be created within the XQuery prolog using the following declaration:

```
declare variable $name as=type := expression;
```

TIP

If you don't specify a data type, XQuery applies the xs:anyType data type, allowing the variable to contain any type of data.

where *name* is the variable name, *type* is the data type, and *expression* sets the variable value. For example, the following statement declares the *price* variable using the xs:decimal data type, setting its value to 29.95:

```
declare variable $price as=xs:decimal :=29.95;
```

Text strings need to be enclosed within single or double quotes; thus, the following statement declares the *state* variable, setting its value to the text string 'AZ' for Arizona:

```
declare variable $state as=xs:string :='AZ';
```

A variable can also contain a path expression as the following statement demonstrates:

```
declare variable $storeList :=doc('gjc_stores.xml')//store;
```

Because XQuery is a declarative programming language like XSLT, variable values can be assigned only once. Variables defined within the prolog have global scope and can be referenced throughout the query document. Variables are referenced using $*name*, where *name* is the variable name. The following *storeList* variable retrieves store information for whatever state is specified by the *state* variable:

```
declare variable $storeList
  :=doc('gjc_stores.xml')//store[state=$state];
```

You'll add the *state* and *storeList* variables to your query now with the *state* variable containing the text string 'AZ' and the *storeList* variable containing the list of stores from Arizona.

To declare and reference an XQuery variable:

TIP

A common error in defining the variable value is to use the = symbol instead of :=.

1. Return to the **gjc_query1.xq** document in your editor.

2. Directly below the comment section, insert the following commands to declare the *state* and *storeList* variables:

   ```
   declare variable $state as xs:string :='AZ';
   declare variable $storeList
   := doc('gjc_stores.xml')//store[state=$state];
   ```

3. In the stateStores element, replace the text state="CO" with state="{$state}".

4. Replace the location paths to the list of stores with the **$storeList** variable in both the count() function and the value of the stateStores element. Figure 9-9 highlights the new and revised text in the query.

Figure 9-9 Declaring XQuery variables in the query prolog

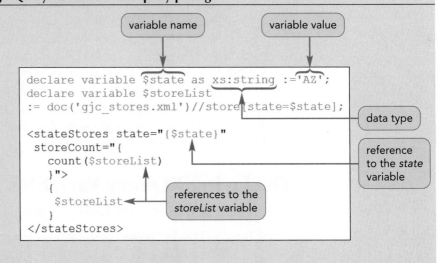

▶ **5.** Save your changes to the query.

▶ **6.** Use your XQuery processor to rerun the query, saving the result in the gjc_results1.xml file. View the result in your XML editor and confirm that the query returns the two Arizona Green Jersey Cycling stores as displayed in Figure 9-10.

Figure 9-10 ▶ **Query result for Arizona stores**

```xml
<?xml version="1.0" encoding="UTF-8"?>
<stateStores state="AZ" storeCount="2">
   <store storeID="Store012" market="A" region="Southwest">
      <street>89190 Lee Avenue</street>
      <city>Phoenix</city>
      <state>AZ</state>
      <ZIP>85010</ZIP>
      <phone>(602) 555-7172</phone>
      <manager>Michelle Johnston</manager>
   </store>
   <store storeID="Store020" market="C" region="Southwest">
      <street>642 Arrow Cross Lane</street>
      <city>Tempe</city>
      <state>AZ</state>
      <ZIP>85281</ZIP>
      <phone>(602) 555-6701</phone>
      <manager>Henry Peters</manager>
   </store>
</stateStores>
```

Trouble? If your query processor returns an error, it could be due to a mistake in your code. Common mistakes include not ending your declaration statements with a semicolon, not enclosing a text string within quotes, and not including closing curly braces in your path expressions.

You can change the query result by altering the value of the *state* variable in the gjc_query1.xq file and then rerunning the query. However, rather than constantly editing the query file, you can also set the value of the *state* variable from your XQuery processor at the time you run the query by using external variables.

Using External Variables

External variables are variables whose values are determined when the query is run by the processor. To declare an external variable, add the keyword `external` to the variable declaration, which tells the processor that the variable value can be set from a source external to the query file.

Jessica wants you to complete your work on the store list query by making the *state* variable an external variable so that she can define which state she wants to view whenever she runs the query, freeing her from having to edit the query file itself.

To declare an external variable:

▶ **1.** Return to the **gjc_query1.xq** document in your editor.

▶ **2.** Go to the declaration for the *state* variable, remove its initial value, and insert the keyword **external**. Figure 9-11 highlights the new code in the variable declaration.

| Figure 9-11 | Binding a variable to external input |

sets the variable value from the XQuery processor

```
declare variable $state as xs:string external;
declare variable $storeList
:= doc('gjc_stores.xml')//store[state=$state];
```

3. Save your change to the query.

REFERENCE

Declaring a Query Variable

- To declare a query variable insert the following statement into the prolog:

  `declare variable $name as=type := expression;`

  where *name* is the variable name, *type* is the data type, and *expression* sets the variable value.
- To reference a variable, use the following expression:

  `$name`

  where *name* is the name of the variable.
- To create a parameter whose value is assigned by the XQuery processor when the query is run, add the keyword **external** to the declaration of the variable in the query prolog.

To set the value of an external variable using Saxon, add *parameter=value* to the command line running the query where *parameter* is the name of the external variable (without the $ symbol) and *value* is the variable value.

You run Jessica's query now to display the list of Oregon stores using the state abbreviation OR.

To display the list of Oregon stores:

1. If you are using Saxon in Java command line mode, open a command prompt window within the xml09 ► tutorial folder and enter the following command on a single line:

```
java net.sf.saxon.Query gjc_query1.xq !indent=yes
state=OR -o:gjc_results1.xml
```

2. Press **Enter** to run the command.

Trouble? If you are using a different XQuery processor, refer to your processor's documentation about setting query parameter values. Send the output of your query to the **gjc_results1.xml** file.

3. Open the **gjc_results1.xml** file in your editor. Confirm that the query result returns three Oregon stores located in Beaverton, Bend, and Portland (see Figure 9-12). Note that the specific appearance of the file will depend on your editor.

| Figure 9-12 | Query result for Oregon stores |

```xml
<?xml version="1.0" encoding="UTF-8"?>
<stateStores state="OR" storeCount="3">
    <store storeID="Store002" market="C" region="Pacific">
        <street>21 Mountain Drive</street>
        <city>Beaverton</city>
        <state>OR</state>
        <ZIP>97005</ZIP>
        <phone>(971) 555-2101</phone>
        <manager>Roy Sexton</manager>
    </store>
    <store storeID="Store004" market="B" region="Pacific">
        <street>71 North Umberland Way</street>
        <city>Bend</city>
        <state>OR</state>
        <ZIP>97702</ZIP>
        <phone>(458) 555-7689</phone>
        <manager>Janice Callahan</manager>
    </store>
    <store storeID="Store014" market="A" region="Pacific">
        <street>7662 Faulk Street</street>
        <city>Portland</city>
        <state>OR</state>
        <ZIP>97202</ZIP>
        <phone>(503) 555-3371</phone>
        <manager>Beverly Estes</manager>
    </store>
</stateStores>
```

4. Close the gjc_results1.xml file.

Using this query file, Jessica can view information on Green Jersey Cycling stores by state location. She can also use this query inside database programs, such as SQL Server, to extract information about the stores and present it within the database program using the database's reporting tools.

INSIGHT

Computing Elements and Attributes

Elements can be constructed with both the element name and content determined dynamically from variables and XPath expressions. The general syntax of an element constructor is

```
element {name} {expression}
```

where *name* is the name of the element computed through an expression and *expression* is the value stored within the element.

Attributes can be computed using the constructor

```
attribute {name} {expression}
```

where *name* is the name of the attribute and *expression* is the attribute value. The attribute constructor must be nested within an element constructor. For example, the following code creates an element named Colorado and an attribute named state based on values stored in the *elemName* and *attName* variables.

```
declare $elemName as xs:string :='Colorado';
declare $attName as xs:string :='state';
element {$elemName}
    {
    attribute {$attName} {'CO'}
    store data
    }
```

The resulting query has the XML content

```
<Colorado state='CO'>
    store data
</Colorado>
```

Element constructors can be nested within other element constructors to create a hierarchy of element nodes. The element and attribute names can also be drawn dynamically from the source document using XPath expressions.

Introducing FLWOR

Path expressions can be used in many queries, but they are limited and difficult to apply when the query involves multiple source documents or when they are used with long and complicated criteria. In addition, you cannot sort the results of a query created using a path expression. To overcome the limitations of path expressions, XQuery supports queries written in a FLWOR structure.

The Syntax of FLWOR

FLWOR (pronounced "flower") is an XQuery structure containing the following parts:

- **for** clause, which iterates through a sequence of values, calculating an expression for each item in the sequence
- **let** clause, which declares a variable and gives it an initial value
- **where** clause, which specifies a condition by which the items in the iterated sequence are filtered
- **order by** clause, which sorts the items in the sequence based on a supplied expression
- **return** clause, which returns values from each item in the sequence

The general structure of a FLWOR query is

```
for expression
let expression
where expression
order by expression
return expression
```

where *expression* returns a sequence of values or performs a calculation on a sequence. Every FLWOR structure needs to have at least one `for` or `let` clause and exactly one `return` clause. The `where` and `order by` clauses are optional.

Previously, to retrieve the list of Colorado stores, you employed the following path expression:

```
doc('gjc_stores.xml')//store[state='CO']
```

However, you could have constructed the same query with the following FLWOR structure:

```
for $stores in doc('gjc_stores.xml')//store
where $stores/state='CO'
return $stores
```

This FLWOR structure starts with the `for` clause iterating through every store element in the gjc_stores.xml file. At each step in the iteration, the *stores* variable is bound to the current store element with the `where` clause limiting the iteration to only those store elements whose state value equals 'CO'. Finally, at each step in the iteration, the `return` clause returns the current value of the *stores* variable. The result of the query is a sequence of store elements containing data on the Green Jersey Cycling stores in Colorado.

A FLWOR query is treated as a single XQuery statement. Thus, you can construct a valid XML result document by placing the FLWOR query within the result document's root element. The following code demonstrates how to generate a valid XML result document with stateStores as the root element:

```
<stateStores state="CO">{
    for $stores in doc('gjc_stores.xml')//store
    where $stores/state='CO'
    return $stores
}</stateStores>
```

Note that the FLWOR structure needs to be enclosed within a set of curly braces so that the XQuery processor evaluates the expression before writing the query result into the stateStores element.

Because many queries can be written using either path expressions or FLWOR, which approach you use is often a matter of personal preference and experience. A path expression is usually more compact and easier to apply for simple queries, but the FLWOR structure will allow greater flexibility in writing more complicated queries. Programmers coming from database backgrounds and who are new to XQuery will find a FLWOR query very similar to the following SELECT statement from the SQL query language:

```
SELECT stores.store FROM stores WHERE stores.state='CO'
```

Next, you'll examine each part of the FLWOR structure in more detail, starting with the `for` clause.

Working with the `for` Clause

The `for` clause iterates through a sequence of nodes or atomic values, following the syntax

```
for $variable as type in expression
```

where $variable is the variable that is bound to each item in the sequence defined by expression. The type attribute is optional and specifies the data type of the variable. For example, the following FLWOR query iterates through a sequence of integers from 1 to 3 and returns the square of each integer:

```
<list>{
    for $i in (1 to 3)
    return <square>{$i*$i}</square>
}</list>
```

writing the following result:

```
<list>
    <square>1</square>
    <square>4</square>
    <square>9</square>
</list>
```

You can also use multiple for clauses to create nested sequences. The following code iterates through the numeric sequence (1, 2) and, within that iteration, returns each item from the (a,b) sequence:

```
<list>{
    for $i in (1, 2)
    for $j in ('a', 'b')
    return <item>{concat($i, ',', $j)}</item>
}</list>
```

writing the following result:

```
<list>
    <item>1,a</item>
    <item>1,b</item>
    <item>2,a</item>
    <item>2,b</item>
</list>
```

Nested for clauses can be written more compactly with the sequences entered in a comma-separated list. The previous query can also be written as

```
<list>{
    for $i in (1, 2), $j in ('a', 'b')
    return <item>{concat($i, ',', $j)}</item>
}</list>
```

You'll explore nested for clauses in more detail in the next session when examining queries involving multiple source documents.

Defining Variables with the let Clause

The let clause defines a local variable using the following statement:

```
let $variable as type := expression
```

where variable is the variable name, type is the optional variable data type, and expression is the variable value. Variables defined in the for clause update their value at each step in the iteration, but a variable defined in the let clause has a single unchanged value. The let clause is primarily used to simplify the query code by storing long expressions within an easy-to-use variable name. For example, the following let clause is used to store the list of store elements within the *stores* variable and the state name within the *state* variable:

```
let $stores := doc('gjc_stores.xml')//store
for $store in $stores
let $state := 'CO'
where $store/state=$state
return $store
```

Note that a query can support any number of `for` and `let` clauses, and they can be placed in any order. As with the `for` clause, you can combine several `let` clauses into a single comma-separated statement, as the following query demonstrates in defining both the *stores* and *state* variables within a single statement:

```
let $stores := doc('gjc_stores.xml')//store,
    $state :='CO'
for $store in $stores
where $store/state=$state
return $store
```

Filtering with the `where` Clause

The `where` clause filters the result of the query and can replace the long and complicated predicates found in path expressions. Thus, the statement

```
with $price > 150
```

filters the query to include only those records for which the *price* variable is greater than 150. Only one `where` clause is allowed per query, and it must be placed after all of the `for` and `let` clauses. If you need to include several filter conditions, you can combine them using the `and` and `or` keywords. For example, Jessica could use the following `where` clause to retrieve a list of women's shorts or women's jerseys sold by Green Jersey Cycling:

```
let $products := doc('gjc_products.xml')//product
for $prod in $products
where $prod/gender='Women'
  and
  (contains($prod/description, 'Shorts')
  or
  contains($prod/description, 'Jersey')
  )
return $prod
```

The same query written as a path expression using a predicate would be expressed as

```
doc('gjc_products.xml')//product[gender='Women' and
(contains(description, 'Shorts') or contains(description, 'Jersey'))]
```

One important difference between conditions stored within a predicate and conditions stored within a `where` clause is that predicates are interpreted relative to a context node and a condition in a `where` clause requires a complete path to define its context. Thus, the predicate just shown contains the expression `gender='Women'` using the product element as the context node, while the `where` clause requires the complete path `$prod/gender='Women'` to apply the same query condition.

Sorting with the `order by` Clause

A FLWOR query returns results based on the order of the sequence specified in the `for` clause. If the sequence is a location path, the results will appear in document order unless a different order is specified by the following `order by` clause:

```
order by expression modifier
```

where *expression* defines the value(s) by which the query result is to be ordered and *modifier* controls how that ordering is applied. For example, the following query returns a list of women's products sold by Green Jersey Cycling, sorted by product ID:

```
let $products := doc('gjc_products.xml')//product
for $prod in $products
where $prod/gender='Women'
order by $prod/@productID
return $prod
```

The default is to sort items in ascending order. To sort the query by product ID in descending order, add the following `descending` modifier:

```
order by $prod/@productID descending
```

TIP

To explicitly specify ascending order, add the keyword `ascending` to the `order by` clause.

Another way to change the sorting order is to apply the `reverse()` function. For example, the following expression

```
order by reverse($prod/@productID)
```

sorts the query in reverse document order.

To sort by more than one factor, you can include multiple expressions in a comma-separated list. Thus, the following statement sorts the product list first by department and then within each department by product ID:

```
order by $prod/department, $prod/@productID
```

Some sorting expressions will contain empty or missing values. XQuery gives you two choices to handle missing values. To sort the sequence so that empty items are listed first, include the modifier `empty greatest` in the `order by` clause, and to list the empty items last use the modifier `empty least`. You can set the default ordering for all `order by` clauses in the query by adding the `declare default order` declaration to the query prolog and setting its value to `empty greatest` or `empty least`.

Displaying Results with the `return` Clause

The last statement in the FLWOR structure is always the `return` clause, which is evaluated once per iteration through the `for` clause. The `return` clause can pass either a single value or a sequence of values, and it can contain any valid XPath expression. For example, the following query employs a `return` clause that displays a sequence of elements at each iteration in the for loop:

```
let $products := doc('gjc_products.xml')//product
for $prod in $products
where $prod/gender='Women'
return $prod[contains(description,'Jersey') or
             contains(description,'Shorts')]
```

The query iterates through all of the Green Jersey Cycling products sold to women, returning only those products containing the text string "Jersey" or "Shorts". The result is a list of women's jerseys and shorts sold by the company. Note that the `return` clause uses a predicate within a path expression. Remember that XPath is a subset of XQuery; thus, any valid XPath expression can be used within any XQuery statement.

Writing a FLWOR Query

Now that you've examined some of the fundamentals of working with FLWOR queries, Jessica wants you to create a query for the customer orders from the last two months of sample data. She's interested in tracking information about large orders and wants you to query the gjc_orders.xml document, returning a list of orders of $500 or greater. Referring to Figure 9-3, note that each order contains a list of products ordered by the customer, including the quantity purchased of each product and the sales price. To calculate the total cost of the order you have to sum the quantity of each product purchased multiplied by the sales price. The XPath 2.0 expression to return this total is

```
sum(product/(@qty*@salesPrice))
```

The first two lines in the FLWOR query will contain a for clause that uses the *o* variable to iterate through all of the order elements in the gjc_orders.xml and a let clause to store the total cost of each order in the *total* variable:

```
for $o in doc('gjc_orders.xml')//order
let $total := sum($o/product/(@qty*@salesPrice))
```

To limit the query to only those orders with totals of $500 or greater, add the following with clause:

```
with $total >= 500
```

To list the largest orders first, use the following expression to sort the query by the *total* variable in descending order:

```
order by $total descending
```

Finally, the query returns each order that matches Jessica's query. She wants to display the order ID, order date, total revenue from all of the orders, and the list of the products ordered by the customer. The return clause used to include all of this information appears as

```
return
  <order
   orderID="{$o/@orderID}"
   orderDate="{$o/@orderDate}">

    <revenue>
    {
      $total
    }
    </revenue>

    {$o/product}
  </order>
```

Next, you'll add this query to a new XQuery document named gjc_query2.xq and then run it.

To write a FLWOR query:

1. Use your editor to open the **gjc_query2txt.xq** file from the xml09 ▸ tutorial folder. Enter **your name** and the **date** in the comment section at the top of the file. Save the file as **gjc_query2.xq** to the same folder.

2. Below the comment section, insert the following FLWOR query:

```
<results>{

    for $o in doc('gjc_orders.xml')//order
    let $total := sum($o/product/(@qty*@salesPrice))
    where $total >= 500
    order by $total descending

    return
      <order
        orderID="{$o/@orderID}"
        orderDate="{$o/@orderDate}">
```

```
        <revenue>{
           $total
        }</revenue>

       {$o/product}
     </order>

}</results>
```

Figure 9-13 shows the complete code of the FLWOR query.

Figure 9-13 | **FLWOR query to display large customer orders**

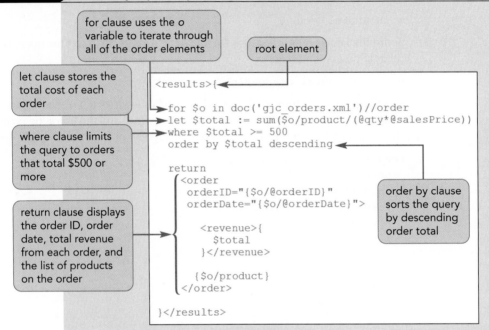

3. Save your changes to the query file.

4. Using your XQuery processor, run the query from the **gjc_query2.xq** file, saving the results to the **gjc_results2.xml** file.

5. Use your browser or editor to view the contents of the gjc_results2.xml file. Figure 9-14 shows the list of customer orders that totaled $500 or more as rendered in the gjc_results2.xml file.

Figure 9-14   **Query result showing large orders**

total revenue
generated
from the order

3 customer
orders totaled
$500 or more
in revenue

```xml
<?xml version="1.0" encoding="UTF-8"?>
<results>
   <order orderID="Ord3013" orderDate="2017-07-25">
       <revenue>692.75</revenue>
       <product productID="CL262M" qty="1" salesPrice="69.95"/>
       <product productID="BC195U" qty="3" salesPrice="195.95"/>
       <product productID="BH060U" qty="1" salesPrice="34.95"/>
   </order>
   <order orderID="Ord4553" orderDate="2017-07-28">
       <revenue>587.8499999999999</revenue>
       <product productID="BC195U" qty="3" salesPrice="195.95"/>
   </order>
   <order orderID="Ord4061" orderDate="2017-06-12">
       <revenue>576.8499999999999</revenue>
       <product productID="CL406M" qty="2" salesPrice="75.50"/>
       <product productID="CC020U" qty="3" salesPrice="141.95"/>
   </order>
</results>
```

Trouble? If you receive an error message, check your code. Common mistakes include not enclosing XPath expressions within a set of curly braces, forgetting closing tags, and forgetting closing quotation marks.

Based on the results of the query, Jessica learns that 3 orders over the past 2 months totaled at least $500 in sales. The largest order was for $692.75. She also notices that the second order is for $587.8499999999999. Jessica is concerned that the value shown in the revenue element is difficult to read for some records and she would like to have it displayed as currency. In XSLT, you can do this using the `format-number()` function, but that function is not supported in XQuery 1.0. However, the `format-number()` function is supported in XQuery 3.0 and in XQuery 1.0 through the use of extension functions.

As an alternative, you'll round the revenue element to the nearest cent using the `round-half-to-even()` function, which is similar to the `round()` function except that when the number to be rounded is halfway between two values it rounds to whatever value is even. This type of rounding is often used in financial applications in which a list of rounded numbers needs to be accurately summed. The syntax of the function is

```
round-half-to-even(number, precision)
```

where *number* is the number to be rounded and *precision* is the decimal value to round to. For example, the expression

```
round-half-to-even(812.486, 2)
```

returns the value to 812.49, rounded to the 2nd decimal point. In addition to this function, you can use the `concat()` function to insert a "$" symbol before the calculated total charge for each order. You'll revise your query now to use these two functions and rerun the query.

To format the revenue value:

▶ **1.** Return to the **gjc_query2.xq** file in your editor.

▶ **2.** Scroll down to the revenue element and change the expression within the element from `$total` to

```
concat("$",round-half-to-even($total,2))
```

Figure 9-15 highlights the code to format the value of the *total* variable.

Figure 9-15	Formatting the revenue value

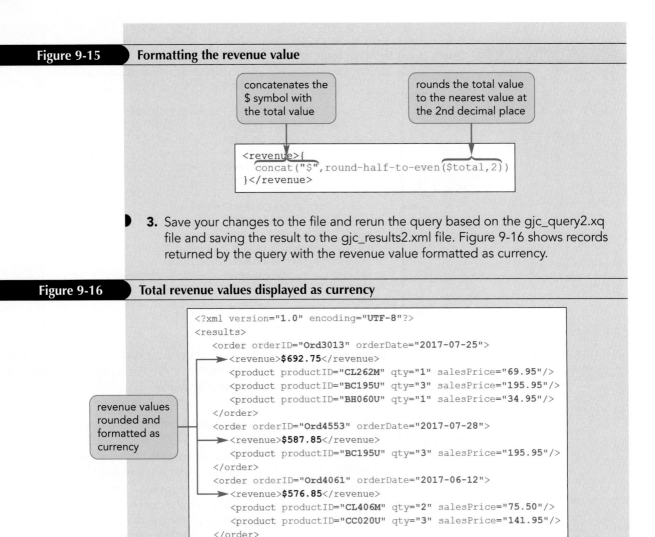

3. Save your changes to the file and rerun the query based on the gjc_query2.xq file and saving the result to the gjc_results2.xml file. Figure 9-16 shows records returned by the query with the revenue value formatted as currency.

Figure 9-16	Total revenue values displayed as currency

```xml
<?xml version="1.0" encoding="UTF-8"?>
<results>
   <order orderID="Ord3013" orderDate="2017-07-25">
      <revenue>$692.75</revenue>
      <product productID="CL262M" qty="1" salesPrice="69.95"/>
      <product productID="BC195U" qty="3" salesPrice="195.95"/>
      <product productID="BH060U" qty="1" salesPrice="34.95"/>
   </order>
   <order orderID="Ord4553" orderDate="2017-07-28">
      <revenue>$587.85</revenue>
      <product productID="BC195U" qty="3" salesPrice="195.95"/>
   </order>
   <order orderID="Ord4061" orderDate="2017-06-12">
      <revenue>$576.85</revenue>
      <product productID="CL406M" qty="2" salesPrice="75.50"/>
      <product productID="CC020U" qty="3" salesPrice="141.95"/>
   </order>
</results>
```

revenue values rounded and formatted as currency

Note that there are limits to number formatting with the `round-half-to-even()` function. For example, if the number that is rounded ends with 0, such as 45.20, XQuery will display the numeric value 45.2. XQuery was designed to return numeric values and text strings; it was not designed for creating formatted reports. For more sophisticated numeric formats, such as including thousands separators and adding ending zeroes to decimal values, you have to work with text string functions available in XPath. The code to perform this string manipulation is beyond the scope of this tutorial.

Jessica asks you to write a query that returns the total charge on all customer orders from her sample database. In order to do this, you will need to learn about calculating summary statistics.

Calculating Summary Statistics

You can use the XPath 2.0 numeric functions to include summary statistics as part of the query results. To calculate a summary statistic like a total, enclose the query expression within the `sum()` function as follows:

```
sum(expression)
```

where *expression* is an expression that returns a sequence of numeric values. Because a FLWOR query is simply an expression, you can use it within an XPath function as long as the result of the query is a sequence of values with a data type matching the syntax of the function.

You'll use the XPath `sum()` function now to calculate the sum of the revenue from all customer orders, formatting the result with the `concat()` and `round-half-to-even()` functions you used in the previous query.

To calculate the total revenue:

▶ **1.** Use your editor to open the **gjc_query3txt.xq** file from the xml09 ▶ tutorial folder. Enter **your name** and the **date** in the comment section at the top of the file. Save the file as **gjc_query3.xq** to the same folder.

▶ **2.** Below the comment section, insert the following FLWOR query:

```
<revenue>{
concat("$",
  round-half-to-even(
    sum(
      for $o in doc('gjc_orders.xml')//order
      let $total := sum($o/product/(@qty*@salesPrice))
      return $total
      )
    ,2)
  )
}</revenue>
```

Figure 9-17 shows the code to calculate the total revenue from all stores.

Figure 9-17 Calculating the total revenue from all orders

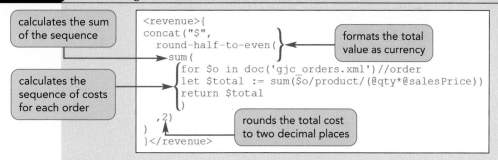

calculates the sum of the sequence

calculates the sequence of costs for each order

formats the total value as currency

rounds the total cost to two decimal places

```
<revenue>{
concat("$",
  round-half-to-even(
    sum(
      for $o in doc('gjc_orders.xml')//order
      let $total := sum($o/product/(@qty*@salesPrice))
      return $total
      )
    ,2)
  )
}</revenue>
```

▶ **3.** Save your changes to the query file and then, using your XQuery processor, run the query from the gjc_query3.xq file, saving the results to the **gjc_results3.xml** file.

▶ **4.** Use your editor to view the contents of the query. As shown in Figure 9-18, the total revenue from all of the customer orders was $109,318.55.

Figure 9-18 Total revenue from the customer orders

total revenue from all orders was $109,318.55

```
<?xml version="1.0" encoding="UTF-8"?>
<revenue>$109318.55</revenue>
```

Problem Solving: Common XQuery Mistakes

PROSKILLS

When you write your own XQuery documents, watch out for the following common XQuery mistakes in your code:

- **Missing or Mismatched Quotation Marks**. All string values and file references need to be enclosed within matching quotation marks.
- **Neglecting Curly Braces**. Remember that XPath expressions that return a value or an XML fragment need to be enclosed in curly braces; otherwise, your processor will return the query code and not the query value.
- **Using = instead of :=**. Unlike other programming languages, variables are not assigned using the = symbol; instead, they are all assigned using :=.
- **Misusing the Semicolon**. All declarations in the query prolog need to terminate with a semicolon, but query expressions should never terminate with a semicolon.
- **Neglecting the $ Symbol**. Variable names must always start with the $ symbol even when they are being initially declared.
- **Mismatched Data Types**. Errors will occur when functions and expressions are applied to incorrect data types. Explicitly assign data types to your variables to catch these errors.

One way to catch many errors is to use a schema-aware processor that will support user-defined schemas when writing and running your queries.

Jessica now knows the total revenue from all customer orders in her sample sales database. She would like to know how the different stores and products contributed to this total. In the next session, you'll expand your work with XQuery by writing queries that join data from multiple documents so that Jessica can compare sales across stores and products. For now, you can take a break before starting the next session.

REVIEW

Session 9.1 Quick Check

1. Explain the relationship between XPath 2.0 and XQuery 1.0.
2. Provide a path expression to retrieve a sequence of all clothing products from the gjc_products.xml file.
3. Provide a path expression to retrieve data on customers from the city of Bellevue from the gjc_customers.xml file. Enclose the path expression within an element named `report` with an attribute named `customerTotal` and an element value equal to the number of customers in Bellevue.
4. Provide code to declare a global variable named *custCity* using the data type xs:string and storing the value 'Bellevue'.
5. Provide code to declare a global variable named *custCity* using the data type xs:string but whose value is set by the XQuery processor when the query is run.
6. What are some reasons to use a FLWOR query in place of a path expression?
7. Provide a FLWOR query to return the list of customers from the city of Bellevue using data from the gjc_customers.xml file. Order the query result by the customer's last name, and return information on each customer.
8. Provide the query code to report the number of customers from the city of Bellevue listed in the gjc_customers.xml file. Use the FLWOR structure in your query.

Session 9.2 Visual Overview:

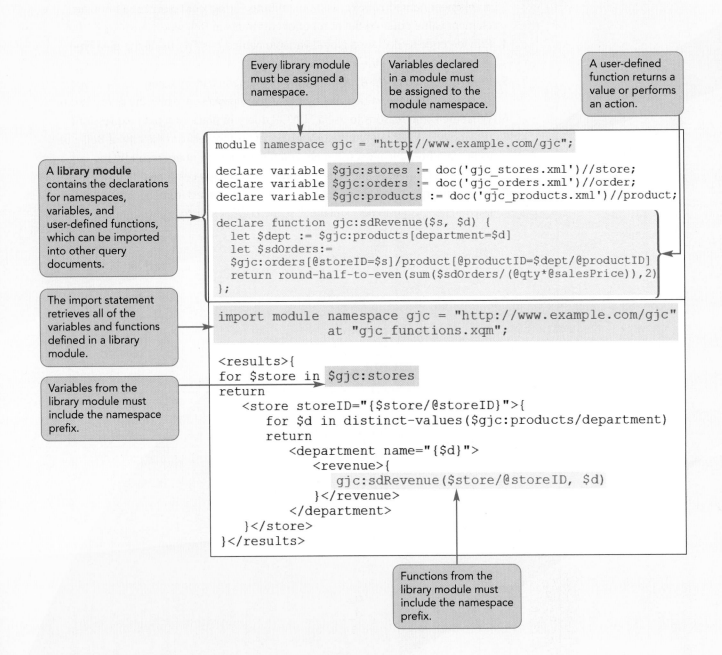

Every library module must be assigned a namespace.

Variables declared in a module must be assigned to the module namespace.

A user-defined function returns a value or performs an action.

A library module contains the declarations for namespaces, variables, and user-defined functions, which can be imported into other query documents.

The import statement retrieves all of the variables and functions defined in a library module.

Variables from the library module must include the namespace prefix.

```
module namespace gjc = "http://www.example.com/gjc";

declare variable $gjc:stores := doc('gjc_stores.xml')//store;
declare variable $gjc:orders := doc('gjc_orders.xml')//order;
declare variable $gjc:products := doc('gjc_products.xml')//product;

declare function gjc:sdRevenue($s, $d) {
  let $dept := $gjc:products[department=$d]
  let $sdOrders:=
  $gjc:orders[@storeID=$s]/product[@productID=$dept/@productID]
  return round-half-to-even(sum($sdOrders/(@qty*@salesPrice)),2)
};
```

```
import module namespace gjc = "http://www.example.com/gjc"
               at "gjc_functions.xqm";

<results>{
for $store in $gjc:stores
return
    <store storeID="{$store/@storeID}">{
        for $d in distinct-values($gjc:products/department)
        return
          <department name="{$d}">
              <revenue>{
                gjc:sdRevenue($store/@storeID, $d)
              }</revenue>
          </department>
    }</store>
}</results>
```

Functions from the library module must include the namespace prefix.

Functions and Modules

This shows the total revenue broken down by store and department.

```xml
<?xml version="1.0" encoding="UTF-8"?>
<results>
    <store storeID="Store001">
        <department name="Clothing">
            <revenue>902.6</revenue>
        </department>
        <department name="Gear">
            <revenue>1154.2</revenue>
        </department>
        <department name="Parts">
            <revenue>467.2</revenue>
        </department>
        <department name="Nutrition">
            <revenue>211.95</revenue>
        </department>
    </store>
    <store storeID="Store002">
        <department name="Clothing">
            <revenue>4381.85</revenue>
        </department>
        <department name="Gear">
            <revenue>1916.8</revenue>
        </department>
        <department name="Parts">
            <revenue>1092.35</revenue>
        </department>
        <department name="Nutrition">
            <revenue>517.65</revenue>
        </department>
    </store>
```

This shows the query result.

Joining Data from Multiple Files

In the last session, you limited your FLWOR queries to single source documents; however, a query can also draw information from multiple sources. One way to query data from several sources is to apply a `for` clause to each document source as in the following code in which one `for` clause iterates over the list of customer orders and a second `for` clause iterates over a list of stores:

```
for $o in doc('gjc_orders.xml')//order
for $s in doc('gjc_stores.xml')//store
```

The two variables are then joined using the following `where` clause, which matches each order to the store in which the order was placed:

```
where $o/@storeID=$s/@storeID
```

You can also use a predicate in the second `for` clause to match the ID from the first `for` clause as follows:

```
for $o in doc('gjc_orders.xml')//order
for $s in doc('gjc_stores.xml')//store[@storeID=$o/storeID]
```

Which approach you use is a matter of personal preference, but many programmers prefer using the `where` clause because it results in a less complicated query expression that is easy to manage and modify. Once you join the two source documents, you can include information from both sources in the `return` clause of the FLWOR query.

Querying Two Source Documents

Jessica wants you to revise the query you created in the last session that displayed orders of $500 or more to include data on the store in which the order was placed. You'll revise the query by adding a second `for` clause that adds the store data to the `return` clause.

To join two source documents:

▶ **1.** If you took a break after the previous session, make sure the **gjc_query2.xq** file is open in your editor.

▶ **2.** Below the initial `for` clause in the gjc_query2.xq document, insert the following `for` clause to iterate through the list of stores:

```
for $s in doc('gjc_stores.xml')//store
```

▶ **3.** Add the following condition to the `where` clause:

```
and $o/@storeID=$s/@storeID
```

▶ **4.** Go to the `return` clause and add the following expression after the revenue element to display data on each individual store:

```
{$s}
```

Figure 9-19 highlights the newly added code in the query that displays information from the GJC stores.

Figure 9-19   **FLWOR query using two source documents**

iterates over every store in the gjc_stores.xml file

matches each order to the corresponding store data

returns the contents of the store data

```
for $o in doc('gjc_orders.xml')//order
for $s in doc('gjc_stores.xml')//store
let $total := sum($o/product/(@qty*@salesPrice))
where $total >= 500
        and $o/@storeID=$s/@storeID
order by $total descending

return
  <order
    orderID="{$o/@orderID}"
    orderDate="{$o/@orderDate}">

    <revenue>{
      concat("$",round-half-to-even($total,2))
    }</revenue>

    {$s}
    {$o/product}
  </order>
```

▶ **5.** Save your changes to the file and then rerun the query, using gjc_query2.xq and saving the result to the gjc_results2.xml file. Figure 9-20 shows the contents of the first order returned from that query.

Figure 9-20   **Store information included in the query result**

store data from the selected order

```
<?xml version="1.0" encoding="UTF-8"?>
<results>
   <order orderID="Ord3013" orderDate="2017-07-25">
      <revenue>$692.75</revenue>
      <store storeID="Store001" market="C" region="Southwest">
         <street>85 East Landing Avenue</street>
         <city>Albuquerque</city>
         <state>NM</state>
         <ZIP>87121</ZIP>
         <phone>(505) 555-6614</phone>
         <manager>Wanda Holden</manager>
      </store>
      <product productID="CL262M" qty="1" salesPrice="69.95"/>
      <product productID="BC195U" qty="3" salesPrice="195.95"/>
      <product productID="BH060U" qty="1" salesPrice="34.95"/>
   </order>
```

Based on the query results, Jessica now knows that the sample order with the highest revenue to the company was placed at the Albuquerque store.

Querying Three Source Documents

You can continue to add other source documents to the query by including them in the for clause and then linking them to the other documents using the where clause. Jessica wants her query to also include data on the customer making the order. You'll add the contents of the gjc_customers.xml to her query and rerun the query using your XQuery processor.

To include the customer information:

1. Return to the **gjc_query2.xq** file in your editor and add the following `for` clause to iterate through the list of customers:

```
for $c in doc('gjc_customers.xml')//customer
```

2. Add the following condition to the `where` clause:

```
and $o/@custID=$c/@custID
```

3. Add the following expression to the `return` clause directly after the statement `{$s}`:

```
{$c}
```

Figure 9-21 highlights the code to add customer information to the query.

Figure 9-21   **FLWOR query using three source documents**

iterates over every customer in the gjc_customers.xml file

matches each order to the corresponding customer data

returns the contents of the customer data

```
for $o in doc('gjc_orders.xml')//order
for $s in doc('gjc_stores.xml')//store
for $c in doc('gjc_customers.xml')//customer
let $total := sum($o/product/(@qty*@salesPrice))
where $total >= 500
      and $o/@storeID=$s/@storeID
      and $o/@custID=$c/@custID
order by $total descending

return
  <order
   orderID="{$o/@orderID}"
   orderDate="{$o/@orderDate}">

    <revenue>{
      concat("$",round-half-to-even($total,2))
     }</revenue>

    {$s}
    {$c}
    {$o/product}
  </order>
```

4. Save your changes and then rerun the query, using gjc_query2.xq and saving the result to the gjc_results2.xml file. Figure 9-22 shows the contents from the first order in the document.

Figure 9-22 Customer data shown in the query result

```xml
<?xml version="1.0" encoding="UTF-8"?>
<results>
    <order orderID="Ord3013" orderDate="2017-07-25">
        <revenue>$692.75</revenue>
        <store storeID="Store001" market="C" region="Southwest">
            <street>85 East Landing Avenue</street>
            <city>Albuquerque</city>
            <state>NM</state>
            <ZIP>87121</ZIP>
            <phone>(505) 555-6614</phone>
            <manager>Wanda Holden</manager>
        </store>
        <customer custID="Cust071136">
            <firstName>Tom</firstName>
            <lastName>Caskey</lastName>
            <street>987 7th Street</street>
            <city>Albuquerque</city>
            <state>NM</state>
            <ZIP>87112</ZIP>
        </customer>
        <product productID="CL262M" qty="1" salesPrice="69.95"/>
        <product productID="BC195U" qty="3" salesPrice="195.95"/>
        <product productID="BH060U" qty="1" salesPrice="34.95"/>
    </order>
```

customer data on the selected order

The revised query provides Jessica with information on the customer and the store associated with each order. Next, Jessica would like to summarize the orders by store so that she can determine which stores showed the largest sales over the sample data period.

INSIGHT

Understanding Joins

A **join** is a database operation used to combine two or more database tables based on fields or columns that are common to the tables. The default join type is the **inner join**, in which only those records that contain matching values between the tables are included in the query result. For example, in the previous queries, only those orders that had matching store IDs and matching customer IDs from the gjc_stores.xml and gjc_customers.xml files were included. If an order had a store ID or a customer ID that was not matched by an entry in those two files, it would not be included in the result.

An **outer join** takes all of the records from one table and then matches those records to values in the other tables if possible. If no matching value is present, the record from the first table is still part of the query result but displays missing values for any data from the other tables.

The default in XQuery is to create inner joins, but you can create an outer join by nesting one FLWOR structure within another. The outer FLWOR structure iterates through all of the records in the first table, displaying all of the records, while the inner FLWOR structure iterates through all of the records in the other tables, returning missing values if no matching record is found.

Grouping the Query Results

Data from one source document can be used to group outcome values from another source document. In Jessica's database, every store has a storeID attribute and every order is marked by the same storeID attribute. To calculate the total revenue from each store you create a `for` clause to iterate through each store in Jessica's database and then use a predicate to select only those orders matching the current store in the `for` loop. The query code to select lists of orders from each store is

```
let $stores := doc('gjc_stores.xml')//store
let $orders := doc('gjc_orders.xml')//order
for $s in $stores
let $storeOrders := $orders[@storeID=$s/@storeID]
```

Jessica wants the query to display the most profitable stores first; so, for each store, the query will calculate the total revenue from all orders and then sort the query results by store revenue in descending order, as shown in the code that follows:

```
let $storeTotal := sum($storeOrders/product/(@qty*@salesPrice))
order by $storeTotal descending
```

Finally, the query will display the store address and the total revenue (formatted as currency). The code for the `return` clause is

```
return
<store id="{$s/@storeID}">
  {$s/street}
  {$s/city}
  {$s/state}
  <revenue>{
    concat("$",round-half-to-even($storeTotal,2))
  }</revenue>
 </store>
```

You'll add the complete code of this query to an XQuery file and then run the query to summarize the orders by store.

To group the results of a query:

1. Open the **gjc_query4txt.xq** file from the xml09 ▸ tutorial folder. Enter **your name** and the **date** in the comment section at the top of the file. Save the file as **gjc_query4.xq**.

2. Enter the following code within the results element in the query file:

```
let $stores := doc('gjc_stores.xml')//store
let $orders := doc('gjc_orders.xml')//order
for $s in $stores
let $storeOrders := $orders[@storeID=$s/@storeID]
let $storeTotal := sum($storeOrders/product/(@qty*@salesPrice))
order by $storeTotal descending

return
<store id="{$s/@storeID}">
  {$s/street}
  {$s/city}
  {$s/state}
  <revenue>{
    concat("$",round-half-to-even($storeTotal,2))
  }</revenue>
</store>
```

Figure 9-23 shows the query code to calculate the total revenue from each store.

Figure 9-23   **Query to calculate total revenue from each store**

```
<results>{
  let $stores := doc('gjc_stores.xml')//store
  let $orders := doc('gjc_orders.xml')//order
  for $s in $stores
  let $storeOrders := $orders[@storeID=$s/@storeID]
  let $storeTotal := sum($storeOrders/product/(@qty*@salesPrice))
  order by $storeTotal descending

  return
  <store id="{$s/@storeID}">
    {$s/street}
    {$s/city}
    {$s/state}
    <revenue>{
      concat("$",round-half-to-even($storeTotal,2))
    }</revenue>
  </store>
}</results>
```

displays the store address

displays the total revenue formatted as currency

sums up the total revenue from all orders at a specified store

▶ **3.** Save your changes and run the query from gjc_query4.xq, using your XQuery processor and saving the result to the **gjc_results4.xml** file. Figure 9-24 shows the content from the first two stores, out of 20, listed in the document.

Figure 9-24   **Top two best-selling stores**

```
<?xml version="1.0" encoding="UTF-8"?>
<results>
    <store id="Store014">
        <street>7662 Faulk Street</street>
        <city>Portland</city>
        <state>OR</state>
        <revenue>$13036.75</revenue>
    </store>
    <store id="Store016">
        <street>672 East Topeka Lane</street>
        <city>San Antonio</city>
        <state>TX</state>
        <revenue>$10082.2</revenue>
    </store>
```

Trouble? The revenue value for the San Antonio store is displayed as $10082.2 for a revenue value of $10,082.20. The missing ending 0 is a limitation of XQuery in presenting formatted values and is not an error in your code.

▶ **4.** Close the file.

Based on the query, Jessica has learned that the store with the most sales is located in Portland, with a total revenue of $13,036.75. The store with the second most sales is the San Antonio franchise, with $10,082.20. While this query tells Jessica where the most sales are located, it doesn't tell her what customers are buying. She wants you to write another query that displays sales grouped by product department.

Grouping by Distinct Values

When you grouped the query results by store, you worked with a unique set of store IDs from the gjc_stores.xml file. However, sometimes queries are based on elements in which there is no predefined set of unique values. In those situations, you can construct a list of unique values using the following XPath 2.0 `distinct-values()` function:

```
distinct-values(expression)
```

where *expression* references a list of values from which the unique values are extracted. For example, products sold by Green Jersey Cycling are organized by department. You can construct a list of the department names by applying the following `distinct-values()` function:

```
distinct-values(doc('gjc_products.xml')//department)
```

The function will then return a sequence of string values that, in this data set, is the sequence containing the names of the four departments at Green Jersey Cycling: Clothing, Gear, Parts, and Nutrition.

Summary Statistics by Group

To retrieve the sales for each department, you first create a FLWOR query, like the one that follows, that iterates through each unique department name, storing the list of products from each department in the *deptProducts* variable:

```
let $products := doc('gjc_products.xml')//product
for $d in distinct-values($products/department)
let $deptProducts := $products[department=$d]
```

To retrieve the list of orders made for each product in the orders variable and then to create a second list in the *deptOrders* variable containing the list of orders made for each product by department, you use `let` clauses like the ones that follow:

```
let $orders := doc('gjc_orders.xml')//product
let $deptOrders := $orders[@productID=$deptProducts/@productID]
```

The total revenue from the product orders within each department is stored in the *deptTotal* variable as

```
let $deptTotal := sum($deptOrders/(@qty*@salesPrice))
```

The last part of the query returns the total revenue per department. The `return` clause follows:

```
return
<department name="{$d}">{
  <revenue>{
   concat("$",round-half-to-even($deptTotal,2))
  }</revenue>
}</department>
```

You'll create this query now and then run it using your XQuery processor.

To display sales by department:

▶ 1. Open the **gjc_query5txt.xq** file from the xml09 ▶ tutorial folder. Enter **your name** and the **date** in the comment section at the top of the file. Save the file as **gjc_query5.xq**.

2. Enter the following FLWOR query within the results element in the query:

```
let $products := doc('gjc_products.xml')//product
for $d in distinct-values($products/department)
let $deptProducts := $products[department=$d]

let $orders := doc('gjc_orders.xml')//product
let $deptOrders := $orders[@productID=$deptProducts/@productID]

let $deptTotal := sum($deptOrders/(@qty*@salesPrice))

return
<department name="{$d}">{
  <revenue>{
   concat("$",round-half-to-even($deptTotal,2))
  }</revenue>
}</department>
```

Figure 9-25 highlights the code to return the total revenue from each department.

Figure 9-25   Query to calculate total revenue from each department

iterates through the list of department names

retrieves orders for products within each department

returns department name and total revenue formatted as currency

calculates total revenue from product orders within each department

```
<results>{
 let $products := doc('gjc_products.xml')//product
 for $d in distinct-values($products/department)
 let $deptProducts := $products[department=$d]

 let $orders := doc('gjc_orders.xml')//product
 let $deptOrders := $orders[@productID=$deptProducts/@productID]

  let $deptTotal := sum($deptOrders/(@qty*@salesPrice))

  return
 <department name="{$d}">{
   <revenue>{
    concat("$",round-half-to-even($deptTotal,2))
   }</revenue>
 }</department>
}</results>
```

3. Save your changes and run the query from gjc_query5.xq, using the XQuery processor and saving the result to the **gjc_results5.xml** file. Figure 9-26 shows the sales from every department at Green Jersey Cycling.

Figure 9-26   Total revenue from each department

```
<?xml version="1.0" encoding="UTF-8"?>
<results>
    <department name="Clothing">
        <revenue>$56140.5</revenue>
    </department>
    <department name="Gear">
        <revenue>$28640.3</revenue>
    </department>
    <department name="Parts">
        <revenue>$18014.2</revenue>
    </department>
    <department name="Nutrition">
        <revenue>$6523.55</revenue>
    </department>
</results>
```

There are four departments recorded in Jessica's sample database. The Clothing department recorded the largest total revenue, with $56,140.50 in total sales; Gear was next, with $28,640.30 in sales; Parts was third in sales, with $18,014.20; and the department selling nutritional food recorded $6,523.55 in sales over the past 2 months.

INSIGHT

Defining Position with the at Keyword

In a FLWOR query you might want to track the number of iterations. You can't use the `position()` function because that function only has meaning within a predicate in an XPath expression. Instead, you can include the **at keyword** within the `for` clause as follows:

```
for $variable at $position in expression
```

where `$position` stores the iteration number in the `for` clause. For example, the FLWOR query

```
for $d at $count in distinct-values(doc('gjc_products.xml')//
department)
return
<dept num="{$count}">{$d}</dept>
```

results in the following XML fragment:

```
<dept num="1">Clothing</dept>
<dept num="2">Gear</dept>
<dept num="3">Parts</dept>
<dept num="4">Nutrition</dept>
```

Note that the position numbers are based on the `for` clause only. If you were to sort the results of the query using the `order by` clause, it would not affect the value of the position numbers. For example, if you sort the query by department by adding the following `order by` clause to the query:

```
order by $d
```

the processor will return the following result:

```
<dept num="1">Clothing</dept>
<dept num="2">Gear</dept>
<dept num="4">Parts</dept>
<dept num="3">Nutrition</dept>
```

with the position numbers matching the order of the items in the initial sequence and not matching the order in which they are written to the result document.

Declaring a Function

The query you've just written is complicated to interpret due to the different variables required to group the sales results. One way to simplify your query code is through the use of functions.

A query function contains a collection of statements that can be referenced throughout the query document. Functions can be declared either within the query prolog or within an external file. The general syntax of a function declaration is

```
declare function prefix:name(params) as type
{
   query expression
};
```

where *prefix* is the namespace prefix of the function, *name* is the name of the function, *params* is a comma-separated list of parameters used in the function, *type* is the data type returned by the function, and *query expression* is an XQuery expression that performs an action or returns a value. User-defined functions are often declared with the namespace prefix `local`, which is a built-in XQuery namespace; thus, it doesn't have to be defined in the query prolog.

The list of parameters used in the function follows the syntax

```
$param1 as type, $param2 as type, …
```

where *param1*, *param2*, etc., are the names of the parameters and *type* is the parameter's data type. Declaring the data type is optional, but it does act as a check against incorrect data values being sent to a function.

For example, the following revenue() function calculates and formats the total revenue for a list of product orders using code that should now be familiar to you:

```
declare function local:revenue($products as element()*)
  as xs:string
{
concat("$",
  round-half-to-even(sum($products/(@qty*@salesPrice))
  ,2))
};
```

The function has a single parameter, products, which contains a sequence of product orders. It uses the `sum()` function to calculate the total revenue from every order and applies the `concat()` function and the `round-half-to-even()` function to format the results as a currency string.

REFERENCE

Declaring a Query Function

- To declare a query function, insert the following code into the query prolog:

```
declare function prefix:name(params) as type
{
    query expression
};
```

where *prefix* is the namespace prefix of the function, *name* is the name of the function, *params* is a comma-separated list of parameters used in the function, *type* is the data type returned by the function, and *query expression* is an XQuery expression that performs an action or returns a value.

- To call a query function, use the expression

```
prefix:name(values)
```

where *prefix* is the namespace of the function, *name* is the function name, and *values* is a comma-separated list of values assigned to each parameter in the function.

To explore how to create and use your own user-defined functions, you'll rewrite the query to calculate total revenue by department using two user-defined functions: the deptOrders() function to return a list of orders for a specified department and the revenue() function described earlier to calculate the total revenue from a list of orders.

To create a user-defined function:

1. Open the **gjc_query6txt.xq** file from the xml09 ▸ tutorial folder. Enter **your name** and the **date** in the comment section at the top of the file. Save the file as **gjc_query6.xq**.

User-defined functions need to be placed within the local namespace or namespace of the programmer's choosing.

2. Directly after the comment section but before the results element, insert the following deptOrders() function to return all of the orders belonging to a department specified by the d parameter:

```
declare function local:deptOrders($d as xs:string)
  as element()*
{
  let $deptProducts :=
  doc('gjc_products.xml')//product[department=$d]
  let $orders := doc('gjc_orders.xml')//product

  return $orders[@productID=$deptProducts/@productID]
};
```

3. Next, directly after the deptOrders() function and before the opening results tag, enter the following revenue() function to calculate the total revenue from a list of product orders:

```
declare function local:revenue($products)
  as xs:string
{
  concat("$",
    round-half-to-even(
      sum($products/(@qty*@salesPrice))
  ,2)
  )
};
```

Figure 9-27 shows the function code in the XQuery document.

Figure 9-27	**Declaring two user-defined functions**

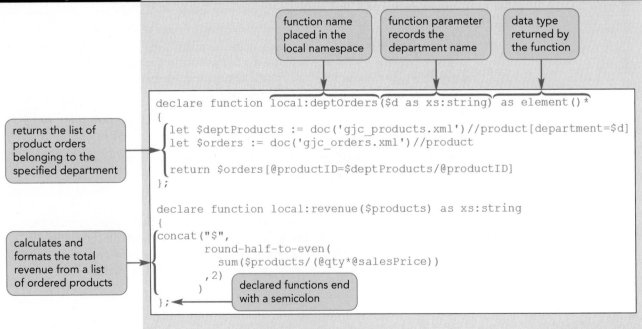

4. Save your changes to the file.

Note that the variable and parameter names used in a function have local scope. Thus, you can use the same variable names within a function and within the query without creating a conflict between the names.

Calling a User-Defined Function

To call a user-defined function, you enter the function name with its namespace prefix along with the parameter values (if any). Thus, to call the revenue() function using all of the product orders in the gjc_orders.xml file, you could enter the following statement:

```
local:revenue(doc('gjc_orders.xml')//product)
```

where `doc('gjc_orders.xml')//product` is the value of the *$products* parameter specified in the function.

You'll simplify the query code you used in the gjc_query5.xq file now by calling the deptOrders() and revenue() functions to accomplish the same task in gjc_query6.xq of calculating total revenue by department.

To call a user-defined function:

▶ **1.** Within the **gjc_query6.xq** file, insert the following within the results element to calculate the total revenue for each department listed in the gjc_products.xml file:

```
for $d in distinct-values(doc('gjc_products.xml')//department)
return
<department name="{$d}">
  <revenue>
    {local:revenue(local:deptOrders($d))}
  </revenue>
</department>
```

Figure 9-28 highlights the code to calculate the total revenue for each department.

Figure 9-28	Calling user-defined functions

calls the revenue() function to calculate and display the total revenue from the list of customer orders

calls the deptOrders() function to return the list of customer orders made in the specified department

```
<results>{
  for $d in distinct-values(doc('gjc_products.xml')//department)
  return
  <department name="{$d}">
    <revenue>
      {local:revenue(local:deptOrders($d))}
    </revenue>
  </department>
}</results>
```

iterates through all of the unique department names in the gjc_products.xml file

▶ **2.** Save your changes to the file.

▶ **3.** Use your XQuery processor to apply the gjc_query6.xq file, storing the query result in the **gjc_results6.xml** file.

▶ **4.** Verify that the contents of the gjc_results6.xml match the total revenue by department values from the results5.xml file shown earlier in Figure 9-26.

▶ **5.** Close the files.

By moving the statements that set up and format the customer order data into user-defined functions, you've reduced the number of lines in the FLWOR query, making it much easier to read and interpret. Often in your data analysis you will want to use the same functions in several different queries. You can make your functions available to other XQuery documents through the use of modules.

INSIGHT

Using Recursive Functions in XQuery

As with XSLT, many calculations and operations in XQuery can be performed using recursion, in which the XQuery function calls itself repeatedly until a stopping condition is met. The general structure of a recursive function in XQuery is

```
declare function prefix:name(params)
{
    query expression
    return prefix:name(param values)
};
```

where *prefix* is the namespace prefix of the function, *name* is the function name, *params* are the function parameters, and *query expression* is the query that ends with a `return` statement that calls the recursive function.

For example, the following recursive function calculates the sum of a sequence of integers:

```
declare function local:nsum($x as xs:integer*) as xs:integer
{
    if (empty($x)) then 0
    else $
        let $first := $x[1]
        return $first + local:nsum($x[position() gt 1])
};
```

The `nsum()` function stores the sequence of integers in the *x* parameter. If the sequence is empty, the function does nothing; otherwise, the function keeps calling itself, adding the first item in the sequence to the sum of the items in the sequence after the first item (indicated by the value of the `position()` function being greater than 1). When the sequence is empty, the recursion ends and the last calculated value is returned by the function, providing the sum of all of the variables in the sequence. For example, the expression

```
local:nsum((3, 5, 11, 2, 4))
```

returns a value of 25.

Creating a Query Library Module

XQuery identifies two types of modules. The **main module** is the XQuery file that contains the query to be executed and any variables or functions declared in the query prolog. All of the query files you've worked with so far have been main module files. The global variables and functions you've created in the main module can be stored in external files known as library modules. A library module is an external XQuery file that contains only the declarations for namespaces, variables, and user-defined functions. Because it supports the query found in the main module, it does not contain any query of its own. In effect, a library module acts as a query prolog stored in an external file.

Exploring Library Modules

All library modules begin with the statement

```
module namespace prefix = uri;
```

where *prefix* is the prefix that is assigned to the module and *uri* is the URI of the module namespace. For example, the following statement assigns a library module with the gjc prefix to the http://www.example.com/gjc namespace URI:

```
module namespace gjc = "http://www.example.com/gjc";
```

All of the variables and functions declared in the library module have to be assigned to that namespace. This distinguishes library variables and functions from variables and functions assigned to other namespaces. For example, the variable declaration

```
declare variable $gjc:stores := doc('gjc_stores.xml')//store;
```

creates the *stores* variable and places it within the namespace assigned to the library module by inserting the gjc namespace prefix before the variable name.

Jessica wants you to create a library module for use in her queries. You'll start creating the module by defining the namespace and declaring all of the module variables.

TIP

Module library files are often saved with the file extension .xqm.

To create a library module:

1. Use your editor to open the **gjc_functxt.xqm** file from the xml09 ▸ tutorial folder. Enter **your name** and the **date** in the comment section near the top of the file. Save the file as **gjc_functions.xqm**.

2. Insert the following statement at the top of the file above the comment section:

```
module namespace gjc = "http://www.example.com/gjc";
```

3. Below the module statement, add the following variable declarations to reference the list of store, order, and product elements, placing the variables within the namespace for the library module:

```
declare variable $gjc:stores := doc('gjc_stores.xml')//store;
declare variable $gjc:orders := doc('gjc_orders.xml')//order;
declare variable $gjc:products := doc('gjc_products.xml')//
product;
```

Figure 9-29 highlights the code for the declaration of the module namespace and the variables defined with the module.

Figure 9-29   **Declaring variables in a library module**

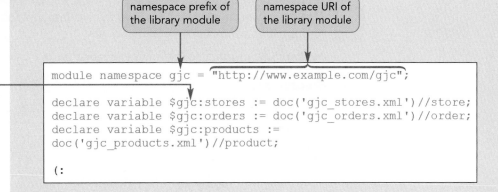

4. Save your changes to the file.

In addition to creating variable declarations, a library module also contains user-defined functions that can be shared by other XQuery files. User-defined functions are declared with the general syntax

```
declare function prefix:name(params) {
    query expression
};
```

where *prefix* is the namespace prefix of the library module, *name* is the function name, *params* is a comma-separated list of parameters required by the function, and *query expression* is the query code used in the function.

Jessica wants you to create a query that displays the revenue for each department within each store. For her query, Jessica will need to create a function in the library module that returns all of the product orders from a specified store and department. The code to declare the function is

```
declare function gjc:storeDeptOrders($sID as xs:string, $dept as
xs:string) as element()*
{
  let $deptProducts := $gjc:products[department=$dept]
  return $gjc:orders[@storeID=$sID]/product
   [@productID=$deptProducts/@productID]
};
```

The function has two parameters: the *sID* parameter identifies the store through its store ID and the *dept* parameter contains the department name. The *deptProducts* variable contains the sequence of all products that belong to the specified department. The function then returns a sequence of all of the orders that were placed in the specified store within the specified department.

You'll add this function and the revenue() function to the gjc_functions.xqm library module now.

To add a user-defined function to a library module:

▶ 1. Within the gjc_functions.xqm file, add the following storeDeptOrders() function below the comment section of the file:

```
declare function gjc:storeDeptOrders($sID as xs:string, $dept
as xs:string) as element()*
{
  let $deptProducts := $gjc:products[department=$dept]
  return $gjc:orders[@storeID=$sID]/product
   [@productID=$deptProducts/@productID]
};
```

▶ 2. Add the following revenue() function to calculate and format the total revenue from a list of purchased products:

```
declare function gjc:revenue($products) as xs:string
{
concat("$",
  round-half-to-even(
    sum($products/(@qty*@salesPrice))
    ,2)
  )
};
```

Figure 9-30 shows the function code in the module to calculate the orders within a department and the total revenue from a sequence of product orders.

Figure 9-30	Declaring functions in a library module

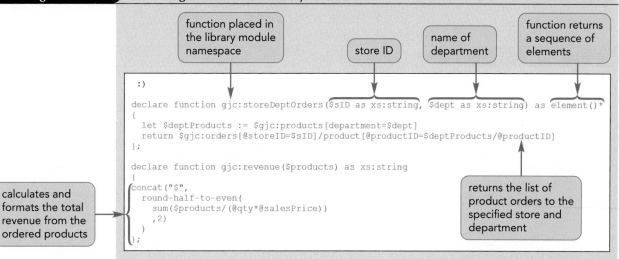

3. Save your changes to the module.

4. Close the file.

Next, you'll use this library module to simplify the code used in a query that displays the total revenue by store and department.

Importing a Module

To reference a library module within a query document, the following import statement must be added to the query prolog:

```
import module namespace prefix = uri at file;
```

where **prefix** is the namespace prefix of the module, **uri** is the namespace URI of the library module, and **file** is the name of the library module file. For example, to reference the gjc_functions.xqm module file just shown, the following import statement must be added to the query prolog:

```
import module namespace gjc = "http://www.example.com/gjc"
  at "gjc_functions.xqm:;
```

When you import a library module, the module URI in the import statement must match the URI in the library module file; however, the namespace prefix used in the import statement and the prefix used in the library module file do not need to match as long as they point to the same namespace URI.

You'll import the gjc_functions.xqm library module into a new query file that Jessica has started for you.

To import a library module:

1. Use your editor to open the **gjc_query7txt.xq** file from the xml09 ▸ tutorial folder. Enter **your name** and the **date** in the comment section near the top of the file. Save the file as **gjc_query7.xq**.

▶ **2.** Below the comment section, insert the following import statement:

```
import module namespace gjc = "http://www.example.com/gjc" at
"gjc_functions.xqm";
```

Figure 9-31 highlights the code to import the library module stored in the gjc_functions.xqm file.

Figure 9-31   **Importing a library module**

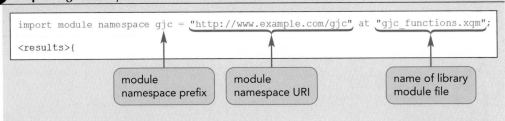

```
import module namespace gjc = "http://www.example.com/gjc" at "gjc_functions.xqm";

<results>{
```

module namespace prefix   module namespace URI   name of library module file

▶ **3.** Save your changes to the file.

Next, you'll use the variables and functions defined in the library module in a query that displays the total revenue broken down by store and by department within each store. Because you are using variables and functions from the library module, those variables and functions need to include the module namespace prefix used in the library module file.

To reference variables and functions from a library module:

▶ **1.** Within the results element, insert the following FLWOR query to iterate through the list of stores, returning a store element for each Green Jersey Cycling store:

```
for $s in $gjc:stores
let $sID := $s/@storeID
return
  <store storeID="{$sID}" location="{$s/city}, {$s/state}">
    {
    }
  </store>
```

▶ **2.** Within the store element, insert the following nested FLWOR query, which displays the total revenue for each department within the current store:

```
for $d in distinct-values($gjc:products/department)
return
  <department name="{$d}">
    <revenue>
      {gjc:revenue(gjc:storeDeptOrders($sID, $d))}
    </revenue>
  </department>
```

Figure 9-32 highlights the query code in the file.

Figure 9-32   **Query to retrieve total revenue by store and department**

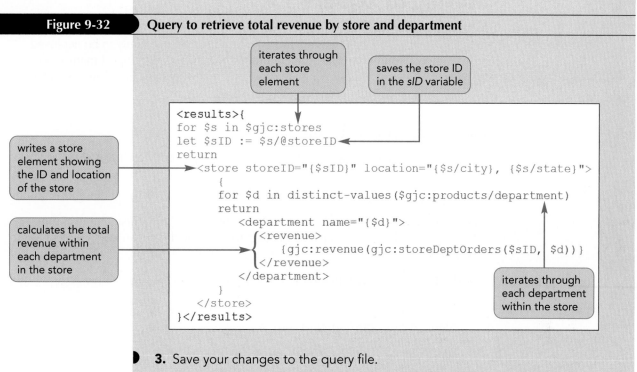

iterates through each store element

saves the store ID in the *sID* variable

writes a store element showing the ID and location of the store

calculates the total revenue within each department in the store

iterates through each department within the store

```
<results>{
for $s in $gjc:stores
let $sID := $s/@storeID
return
  <store storeID="{$sID}" location="{$s/city}, {$s/state}">
    {
    for $d in distinct-values($gjc:products/department)
    return
      <department name="{$d}">
        <revenue>
          {gjc:revenue(gjc:storeDeptOrders($sID, $d))}
        </revenue>
      </department>
    }
  </store>
}</results>
```

▶ **3.** Save your changes to the query file.

▶ **4.** Use your XQuery processor and the gjc_query7.xq file to run the query, storing the results in a file named **gjc_results7.xml**.

▶ **5.** View the contents of the query results in your editor or browser. Figure 9-33 shows the total revenue for the first store broken down by department.

Figure 9-33   **Total revenue for the first store by department**

```
<?xml version="1.0" encoding="UTF-8"?>
<results>
  <store storeID="Store001" location="Albuquerque, NM">
    <department name="Clothing">
      <revenue>$902.6</revenue>
    </department>
    <department name="Gear">
      <revenue>$1154.2</revenue>
    </department>
    <department name="Parts">
      <revenue>$467.2</revenue>
    </department>
    <department name="Nutrition">
      <revenue>$211.95</revenue>
    </department>
  </store>
```

Jessica is pleased with the results of the query and notes that by placing the variable definitions and functions within a library module, the code for the query is cleaner and easier to interpret. The library module can also be used with other queries or combined with other library modules for future projects.

Moving to XQuery 3.0

In April 2014, the W3C gave the XQuery 3.0 specifications Recommendation status, indicating that XQuery 3.0 was a mature and stable language ready to be deployed in working environments. Your XQuery processor may already support many of the features of XQuery 3.0. Following are some of the new features in XQuery 3.0 that you might use in your future query projects.

Grouping Query Results

XQuery 3.0 adds the following **group by** clause to the already established FLWOR structure:

```
group by key
```

where *key* is a value by which you want to group the FLWOR query. For example, the following FLWOR query groups the product totals using the department element as the grouping key:

```
let $p := doc('gjc_products.xml')//product
group by $p/department
return
   <dept name="{$p/department}">
       {count($p)}
   </dept>
```

The result is the following XML fragment showing the number of products within each department:

```
<dept name="Clothing">40</dept>
<dept name="Gear">42</dept>
<dept name="Parts">25</dept>
<dept name="Nutrition">22</dept>
```

The `group by` clause supports multiple levels of grouping. Thus, to group by both department and gender within department you would enter the following FLWOR query:

```
let $p := doc('gjc_products.xml')//product
group by department, gender
return
   <dept name="{$p/department}">
       {count($p)}
   </dept>
```

The `group by` clause is often used in conjunction with the **order by** clause to both group the query result and to sort those groups in ascending or descending order.

The count Clause

The **count clause** was added to the FLWOR structure in XQuery 3.0 to provide a way of counting each iteration in the query result. The syntax of the `count` clause is

```
count variable
```

where *variable* is a variable that will store the count of each iteration. The following FLWOR structure employs the `count` clause to count each department name:

```
for $d in distinct-values('gjc_products.xml')//department
count $n
return
<dept num="{$n}">{$d}</dept>
```

resulting in the following XML fragment:

```
<dept num="1">Clothing</dept>
<dept num="2">Gear</dept>
<dept num="3">Parts</dept>
<dept num="4">Nutrition</dept>
```

Unlike the `at` keyword used in XQuery 1.0 to determine the position of an item in the for loop iteration, the count clause will reflect the ordering of the query in the result document and will be modified by both the `where` and `order by` clauses. For example, the following FLWOR query

```
for $p in $products
order by $p/sales descending
count $rank
where $rank <= 10
return $p
```

will sort the query results by sales in descending order and return only the top-ten-selling products.

Try and Catch Errors

A common technique in other programming languages is to evaluate code for possible errors and, if the code produces an error, substituting a different code set to be executed instead of running the original code. XQuery 3.0 provides this debugging technique using the following **try ... catch** structure:

```
try
   {expression1}
catch *
   {expression2}
```

where *expression1* is an expression that the XQuery processor should test for errors; if any errors result, the processor runs *expression2*. For example, the following code tests whether the expression `$i div $j` returns an error:

```
try
   {$i div $j}
catch *
   {"invalid division"}
```

but, if it doesn't, the processor performs the division and continues with the query. However, if it does catch an error (such as will happen if the program tries to divide by zero), the processor returns the value "invalid division", but then continues the query code without halting execution of the program. The asterisk * symbol next to the `catch` keyword indicates that any type of error will trigger the catch expression. However, you can replace the asterisk with a specific error code to trap only particular types of errors. For example, the following code

```
try
   {$i div $j}
catch FOAR0001
   {"invalid division"}
```

only traps errors that result in the error code FOAR0001 (an error code for some XQuery processors that represents division by zero).

Written Communication: Creating Effective Queries

A well-designed query is efficient, runs quickly, and is less prone to error. You should design your queries to be clear and concise, easy to maintain, and easy for others to interpret and edit if necessary. Here are some principles of query design you should follow:

- **Format the Query**. Use indentation, white space, and appropriately placed parentheses to make your code easier to read and understand.
- **Use Meaningful Names**. Give your variables and functions meaningful names that convey their purpose to the reader.
- **Comment Your Code**. Use XQuery comments to explain your query and its goals. Use XSLT comments to display your comments in the query result document.
- **Apply Modularity**. Put often-used variables and functions in library modules to make your queries easier to read and develop.
- **Avoid Repeating Expressions**. Storing location paths in variables will speed up the query processing because the processor will not have to re-evaluate the path each time it is encountered.
- **Avoid Unnecessary Sorting**. Sorting a query result takes up valuable processor time. Unless sort order is important to your results, speed up your queries by avoiding unnecessary sorting.
- **Use Predicates in Place of where Clauses**. In general, a processor can run a predicate expression faster than it can run a where clause.
- **Use Explicit Paths**. Location paths that use the general descendant step pattern (//) take longer to process than explicit paths because the processor must check every part of the node tree.

The benefits of good query design become most noticeable as the size of your data set increases. A data set that contains hundreds of thousands of records can only be effectively managed when the query code is written to be clear, concise, and efficient.

At this point, you're finished writing queries for Jessica. She can apply the queries you've written to other data sets, providing more detailed information about sales at Green Jersey Cycling, as well as the performance of specific stores and departments. She will get back to you if she needs your help in designing additional queries using XQuery.

Session 9.2 Quick Check

REVIEW

1. Provide a FLWOR query to display the contact information of customers whose total order exceeded $600 using data from the gjc_orders.xml and gjc_customers.xml files.
2. Provide a FLWOR query using the `distinct-values()` function to calculate the total revenue by state using the gjc_orders.xml and gjc_stores.xml files.
3. Prove the code to declare a user-defined function named calcRange() that returns the range (the maximum value minus the minimum value) from a sequence of values specified in a parameter named *sampleValues*.
4. Provide code to call the calcRange() function using the values of the price attribute from the gjc_products.xml file.
5. How does a library module differ from a main module?
6. Provide the code for the initial statement in a library module, setting the module in namespace URI "http://www.example.com/greenjersey" with the namespace prefix "cycling".
7. Within the library module defined in the last question, provide code to declare a variable named *customers* containing all of the customer elements in the gjc_customers.xml file.
8. Provide code to import the library module from Question 6 into the main module using the same namespace URI and prefix.

Review Assignments

Data Files needed for the Review Assignments: cycle_functxt.xqm, cycle_query1txt.xq - cycle_query4txt.xq, +2 XML files

Jessica received another data set containing a customer survey. The structure of the cycle_survey.xml file is shown in Figure 9-34. She is also working with the same XML documents that you examined in the tutorial that describe the company's stores and products, although she renamed the files.

Figure 9-34 **Structure of the cycle_survey.xml document**

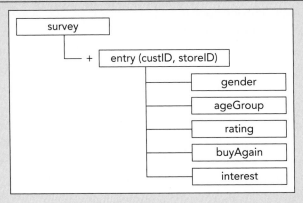

The survey file contains information on each customer's gender and age group, a customer satisfaction rating of Green Jersey Cycling (1 = poor to 4 = excellent), whether or not the customer intends to buy again from the store (yes, no), and his or her general interest in outdoor sports (1 = low to 5 = high).

Jessica wants you to use XQuery to analyze customer opinions and their ratings of Green Jersey Cycling products, as well as the service provided by the company. Jessica wants to know which stores received the highest ratings for customer satisfaction, and she wants to know whether there is a difference in the ratings based on customer demographics, such as age.

Complete the following:

1. Using your editor, open the **cycle_functxt.xqm**, **cycle_query1txt.xq**, **cycle_query2txt.xq**, **cycle_query3txt.xq**, and **cycle_query4txt.xq** files from the xml09 ▸ review folder. Enter *your name* and the *date* in the comment section of each file, and save them as **cycle_functions.xqm**, **cycle_query1.xq**, **cycle_query2.xq**, **cycle_query3.xq**, and **cycle_query4.xq**, respectively.

2. The first query Jessica wants you to create is to display the average rating at the GJC store specified by the user. Go to the **cycle_query1.xq** file in your editor and do the following:

   a. Declare an external variable named **store** with the `xs:string` data type. This variable will be used to save the store ID specified by the user.

   b. Declare a variable named **rating** that will return all of the rating elements from the cycle_survey.xml file for the specified store ID.

   c. Within the results element, insert an element named **avgRating** with an ID attribute equal to the value of the *store* variable. Within this element enter an expression to display the average value of the *rating* variable to two decimal places.

3. Save your changes to the cycle_query1.xq file and then, using your XQuery processor, use the cycle_query1.xq file to run the query for a store with a store value of **Store005**. Save the results of the query to the **cycle_results1.xml** file.

4. Review the cycle_results1.xml file in your XQuery processor, and then close both files. (*Note*: The average rating for Store 005 is 3.11.) Close the files when you're finished.

5. Jessica wants to report on stores that average less than a 3 rating on the customer satisfaction survey. Go to the **cycle_query2.xq** file in your editor and create the following query:

   a. Within the results element, insert a FLWOR query that iterates through every store in the cycle_stores.xml file.

   b. For each store, save the ratings from the cycle_survey.xml file in the **ratings** variable.

   c. Use the `let` clause to create the **avgRating** variable equal to the average of the *ratings* variable, rounded to two-decimal-place accuracy.

   d. Use the `order by` clause to order the query by the descending values of the *avgRating* variable.

   e. Use the `where` clause to include only those stores whose average rating is less than 3.

   f. For each store that matches the query, use the `return` clause to return a store element containing the complete store information and the store's average rating.

6. Save your changes to the cycle_query2.xq file and then, using your XQuery processor, use cycle_query2.xq to run the query, saving the results to the **cycle_results2.xml** file.

7. Review cycle_results2.xml in your XQuery processor, and then close both files. (*Note*: Eight stores are listed in descending order, starting with Store 017, which has an average rating of 2.88, and ending with Store 013, which has an average rating of 2.06.)

8. Jessica wants to compare ratings across age groups. Go to the **cycle_query3.xq** file in your editor and create the following query:

   a. Within the avgRating element, create a FLWOR query iterating through each unique *ageGroup* value from the cycle_survey.xml file.

   b. For each age group, calculate the average rating within that group, rounded to two decimal places.

   c. Sort the query by the average rating in descending order.

   d. Return the following XML fragment for each age group:

   ```
   <age group="ageGroup">
   rating
   </age>
   ```

   where *ageGroup* is the value of the current age group and `rating` is the average rating within that group.

9. Save your changes to the cycle_query3.xq file and then, using your XQuery processor, use the cycle_query3.xq file to run the query, saving the results to the **cycle_results3.xml** file.

10. Review cycle_results3.xml in your XQuery processor, and then close both files. (*Note*: For the age group 0–20, the average rating is 3.32.)

11. The average ratings summarize the results, but Jessica would like to create a table breaking down the ratings by the number of 1s, 2s, 3s, and 4s each store received. First, go to the **cycle_functions.xqm** library module file in your editor and complete the following:

   a. Place the module in the **http://www.example.com/cycling** namespace with the prefix **bike**.

   b. Declare the **stores** variable in the bike namespace pointing to the store elements within the cycle_stores.xml file.

   c. Declare the **survey** variable in the bike namespace pointing to the entry elements within the cycle_survey.xml file.

   d. Declare a function named **ratingTable** in the bike namespace. The function has a single parameter named **ratings** with the data type `element()*`. The *ratings* parameter will be used to store a sequence of customer ratings. Have the function run a FLWOR query by iterating through the unique values of the *ratings* parameter, sorted in ascending order. For each item in the `for` clause return the following XML fragment:

   ```
   <rating score="rating">
      count
   </rating>
   ```

   where `rating` is the current rating value in the iteration and `count` is the number of items in ratings equal to rating.

   e. Save your changes to library module.

12. Go to the **cycle_query4.xq** file in your editor. Complete the query by doing the following:

    a. Import the cycle_functions.xqm module using the same namespace prefix and URI.

    b. Within the results element, insert the FLWOR query that iterates through every store listed in the *bike:stores* variable.

    c. For each store, store the sequence of ratings for that store from the survey document using the storeID attribute to match each survey entry with the corresponding store. Save the ratings to the **storeRatings** variable.

    d. Return the following XML fragment for each store:

    ```
    <store id="storeID">
      <city>city</city>
      <state>state</state>
      ratings table
    </store>
    ```

    where *storeID* is the ID of the store, *city* and *state* provide the location of the store, and *ratings table* is the list of ratings for the store using the ratingTable() function from the library module and the *storeRatings* variable as the parameter value.

13. Save your changes to the cycle_query4.xq file and then, using your XQuery processor, run the query, saving the results to the **cycle_results4.xml** file.

14. Review cycle_results4.xml in your XQuery processor, and then close both files. (*Note:* The results for Store 001 are as follows: 6 ones, 20 twos, 12 threes, and 3 fours.)

Case Problem 1

Data Files needed for this Case Problem: dc_query1txt.xq - dc_query3txt.xq, +1 XML file

CrimeStats Alain Johnson is a researcher at CrimeStats, a non-profit organization that tracks crime statistics in major U.S. cities. He has received an XML file containing a list of crimes reported in Washington, D.C., during the months of June, July, and August. The structure of the document is shown in Figure 9-35.

Figure 9-35 **Structure of the dc_crime.xml document**

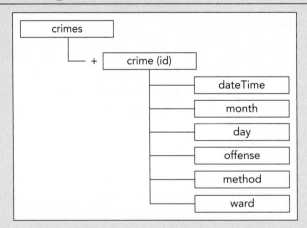

Alain has asked your help in using XQuery to create summary statistics from his document. Complete the following:

1. Using your editor, open the **dc_query1txt.xq**, **dc_query2txt.xq**, and **dc_query3txt.xq** files from the xml09 ▶ case1 folder. Enter *your name* and the *date* in the comment section of each file, and save them as **dc_query1.xq**, **dc_query2.xq**, and **dc_query3.xq**, respectively.

2. Take some time to view the contents and structure of the **dc_crime.xml** file. Note that the type of crime has been stored in the offense element and the crime method is stored in the method element.

3. Go to the **dc_query1.xq** file in your editor. Alain wants to know the total number of robberies in Washington, D.C. Complete the query as follows:

   a. Declare an external variable named **crimeType** with data type `xs:string`.

   b. Declare a variable named **crimes** returning the list of all crime elements in the dc_crime.xml file.

   c. Within the results element, have the query write the following XML fragment:

   ```
   <incidents type="crimeType">
      count
   </incidents>
   ```

   where *crimeType* is the value of the *crimeType* variable and *count* is the number of crime elements of that offense.

4. Save your changes to the query file and then run the query using your XQuery processor and dc_query1.xq to calculate the number of ROBBERY offenses that have occurred in Washington, D.C. Write the results of the query to the **dc_results1.xml** file. Confirm that there were 1030 robberies committed in Washington, D.C., over the time period recorded in the sample database.

5. Next, Alain wants to break down the total number of crimes based on the day of the week to discover whether some days experience more crimes than others. Go to the **dc_query2.xq** file in your editor and create the following query:

   a. Declare a global variable named **crimes** that points to all of the crime elements in the dc_crime.xml file.

   b. Within the results element create a FLWOR query that iterates through each unique value of the day element.

   c. Order the query by the number of crimes that occur on each day in descending order.

   d. Return the following XML fragment from the query:

   ```
   <crime day="day">
      count
   </crime>
   ```

   where *day* is the current day of the week in the iteration and *count* is the number of crimes that occurred on that day.

6. Save your query and then use your XQuery processor and the dc_query2.xq file to generate the query result into the **dc_results2.xml** file.

7. Open the file and note which days of the week appear to have the most crime and which days have the least. Confirm that Saturday has the most crimes followed by Monday and then Sunday.

8. Finally, Alain is interested in the number of crimes committed with a gun and wants to see which wards appear to have the most gun-related crimes. Go to the **dc_query3.xml** file in your editor and complete the following query:

   a. Declare a global variable named **crimes** that points to all of the crime elements in the dc_crime.xml file.

   b. Within the gunCrimes element insert a FLWOR query that iterates through all of the distinct values of the ward element.

   c. Include only those ward elements in which the crime method was "GUN".

   d. Sort the query by the count of gun-related crimes in each ward in descending order.

   e. Return the following XML fragment from each iteration in the query:

   ```
   <count ward="ward">
      count
   </count>
   ```

   where *ward* is the current ward in the iteration and *count* is the count of gun-related crimes in that ward.

9. Save your changes to the query and then run the query using your XQuery processor and dc_query3.xq, saving the result to the **dc_results3.xml** file.

10. Open the query result file and determine which wards had the most gun-related crimes and which wards had the least. Confirm that the 7th ward has the most crimes; the 3rd ward the least.

APPLY

Case Problem 2

Data Files needed for this Case Problem: cd_query1txt.xq - cd_query3txt.xq, +1 XML file

CinemaDat   Matt Vaughn manages an online film information service called CinemaDat. In his site's database, Matt has collected information on thousands of movies including moviegoers' ratings of those films on a scale of 1 star to 5 stars. He has recently compiled an XML document containing data on films created from 2001 to 2005. The structure of his document, cinemadat.xml, is shown in Figure 9-36.

Figure 9-36   **Structure of the cinemadat.xml document**

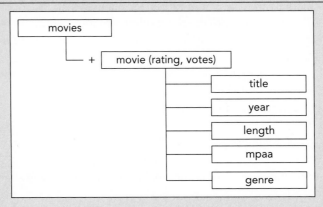

Matt wants you to write a series of queries to retrieve data from his document. He wants listings that show the most popular movies in terms of user ratings for every genre and within genres. Complete the following:

1. Using your editor, open the **cd_query1txt.xq**, **cd_query2txt.xq**, and **cd_query3txt.xq** files from the xml09 ▸ case2 folder. Enter *your name* and the *date* in the comment section of each file, and save them as **cd_query1.xq**, **cd_query2.xq**, and **cd_query3.xq**, respectively.

2. Take some time to view the contents and structure of the **cinemadat.xml** file. Notice that the genre values are entered as a comma-separated list because a movie may fall into more than one genre.

3. Your first query will list all of the movies that received a 4-star rating or better based on a sample of at least 5000 votes. Go to the **cd_query1.xq** file in your editor and complete the query as follows:

   a. Within the results element create a FLWOR query that iterates through every movie element in the cinemadat.xml file.

   b. Limit the query to movies for which the value of the votes attribute is greater than or equal to 5000 and the rating attribute is greater than or equal to 4.

   c. Sort the selected movies by rating and then by votes in descending order.

   d. Return each movie element that matches the criteria.

4. Save the query file and run it using your XQuery processor and the cd_query1.xq file, saving the results to the **cd_results1.xml** file. Confirm that the highest-rated film in the survey is *Lord of the Rings: Return of the King* with an average rating of 4.22 based on 103,664 votes, followed by *Sin City* with an average rating of 4.14 based on 23,650 votes.

5. Next, Matt wants a query in which he can specify the genre of the movie. Go to the **cd_query2.xq** file in your editor and complete the following:

   a. Declare an external variable named **genreType** with the data type `xs:string`.

   b. Within the results element insert a FLWOR query that iterates through every movie element in the cinemadat.xml file.

Function	Description	Version
min(*item*)	Returns the minimum value from the *item* sequence or node set	2.0
minutes-from-dateTime(*dateTime*)	Calculates the minutes component from the *dateTime* value	2.0
minutes-from-duration (*dayTimeDuration*)	Calculates the minutes component from the *dayTimeDuration* value	2.0
minutes-from-time(*time*)	Calculates the minutes component from the *time* value	2.0
month-from-date(*date*)	Calculates the month component from the *date* value	2.0
month-from-dateTime(*dateTime*)	Calculates the month component from the *dateTime* value	2.0
month-from-duration(*dayTimeDuration*)	Calculates the month component from the *dayTimeDuration* value	2.0
name([*node-set*])	Returns the full name of *node-set*; if no node set is specified, returns the full name of the context node	1.0
namespace-uri([*node*])	Returns the URI of *node*; if no node is specified, returns the URI of the context node	1.0
namespace-uri-for-prefix (*string*, *element*)	Returns the namespace URI for the prefix *string* in the element *element*	2.0
namespace-uri-from-QName(*QName*)	Returns the namespace URI from the qualified name *QName*	2.0
nilled(*node*)	Returns true if *node* is an element node that is nilled	2.0
node-name(*node*)	Returns the name of *node* as a qualified name	2.0
normalize-space([*string*])	Normalizes *string* by removing leading and trailing white space; if no *string* is specified, normalizes the content of the context node	1.0
normalize-unicode([*string*])	Normalizes *string* using Unicode normalization; if no *string* is specified, normalizes the content of the context node	2.0
not([*Boolean*])	Changes the logical value of *Boolean* from false to true or true to false; if no *Boolean* value is specified, returns the value false	1.0
number([*item*])	Converts *item* to a number where *item* is a text string or a node set; if no *item* value is specified, converts the value of the context node	1.0
one-or-more(*items*)	Returns *items* only if it contains one or more items	2.0
position()	Returns the position of the context node within the node set being processed	1.0
prefix-fromQName(*QName*)	Returns the namespace prefix from the qualified name *QName*	2.0
QName(*uri*, *string*)	Returns a qualified name with the namespace URI *uri* and the local name *string*	2.0
remove(*item*, *int*)	Returns the sequence from *item* after removing the object at the *int* position	2.0
replace(*string1*, *string2*, *string3*)	Replaces in *string1* each occurrence of characters that match *string2* with *string3*	2.0
resolve-QName(*string*, *element*)	Returns a qualified name from a text string *string* using the in-scope namespace for *element*	2.0
resolve-uri(*uri1*, *uri2*)	Resolves *uri1* based on the base URI specified in *uri2*	2.0
reverse(*items*)	Reverses the sequence of items in *items*	2.0
root([*node*])	Returns the root node of *node*; if no *node* is specified, returns the root of the context node	2.0
round(*number*)	Rounds *number* to the nearest integer	1.0
round-half-to-even(*number*, *int*)	Rounds *number* to int decimal places	2.0
seconds-from-dateTime(*dateTime*)	Calculates the seconds component from the *dateTime* value	2.0
seconds-from-duration (*dayTimeDuration*)	Calculates the seconds component from the *dayTimeDuration* value	2.0
seconds-from-time(*time*)	Calculates the seconds component from the *time* value	2.0
starts-with(*string1*, *string2*)	Returns true if *string1* starts with *string2*	1.0

Function	Description	Version
static-base-uri()	Returns the base URI of the element in which the function is called	2.0
string([item])	Converts item to a text string; if no item is specified, converts the value of the context node	1.0
string-join(string1, string2, ..., string)	Concatenates string1, string2, and so on into a single text string using string as the separator	2.0
string-length(string)	Returns the number of characters in string	1.0
string-to-codepoints(string)	Returns a sequence of Unicode code points based on the content of string	2.0
subsequence(item, int1, [int2])	Returns a subsequence from item where int1 is the position of the first object to be returned and int2 indicates the number of objects; if no int2 value is specified, returns all items from int1 to the end of the sequence	2.0
substring(string, int1, [int2])	Returns a substring from string where int1 is the position of the first character to be returned and int2 indicates the number of remaining characters; if no int2 value is specified, returns all characters from int1 to the end of the string	1.0
substring-after(string1, string2)	Returns a substring from string1 that occurs after the first occurrence of string2	1.0
substring-before(string1, string2)	Returns a substring from string1 that occurs before the first occurrence of string2	1.0
sum(items)	Calculate the sum of the numeric values in items	1.0
system-property(string)	Returns information about the system property string	1.0
timezone-from-date(date)	Calculates the time zone component from the date value	2.0
timezone-from-dateTime(dateTime)	Calculates the time zone component from the dateTime value	2.0
timezone-from-time(time)	Calculates the time zone component from the time value	2.0
tokenize(string, regex)	Splits string into a collection of substrings at each location in string that matches the regular expression regex	2.0
trace(item, string)	Debugs the processing of item, returning the error message string if an error is discovered	2.0
translate(string1, string2, string3)	Substitutes string3 characters into string1 at every occurrence of string2	1.0
true()	Returns the Boolean value true	1.0
unordered(items)	Returns the items in items in implementation-dependent order	2.0
unparsed-entity-public-id(string)	Returns the public ID of the unparsed entity string	2.0
unparsed-entity-uri(string)	Returns the URI of the unparsed entity string	1.0
unparsed-text(uri, [encoding])	Returns the content of the text file held at uri, using the encoding encoding	2.0
unparsed-text-available(uri, [encoding])	Returns true if there exists text content at uri, using the encoding encoding	2.0
uppercase(string)	Converts string to uppercase characters	2.0
year-from-date(date)	Calculates the year component from the date value	2.0
year-from-dateTime(dateTime)	Calculates the year component from the dateTime value	2.0
year-from-duration(yearMonthDuration)	Calculates the year component from the yearMonthDuration value	2.0
zero-or-one(items)	Returns items only if it contains zero or one item	2.0

Using Saxon for XSLT and XQuery

There are many different processors for XSLT. If you are working with XSLT 1.0 and do not need to use external parameters, you can view your result document using a Web browser for transformations that result in a well-formed XML or HTML document. For other tasks or for working with XQuery, you will need a separate processor. One of the more popular processors is Saxon, which is available in pay and free versions. In this appendix, we'll examine how to install and work with Saxon.

Getting Started with Saxon

Saxon is available in several different versions. The commercial version supports XSLT 1.0, 2.0, and 3.0 as well as XQuery 1.0 and 3.0. If you need to work with these versions or have to validate your work against a user-defined schema, you will have to purchase the commercial version. At the time of this writing, the free version of Saxon supports XSLT 1.0 and 2.0, as well as XQuery 1.0, but not schemas.

The Saxon processor is accessed either within an XML editor or through a command-line interface. In the steps that follow, we'll assume that a standalone command-line interface is being used. To use Saxon within another XML editor, see that editor's documentation and help file for instructions. Additional information about using Saxon in other programming environments is available at *http://www.saxonica.com*.

Installing Java

Running Saxon within a command-line window requires the user to first install either Java or the .NET framework. Let's examine how to install Java.

To download and install Java:

▶ **1.** Go to the Java download page at *http://www.oracle.com/technetwork/java/javase/downloads*

▶ **2.** Locate the link for the Java JDK (Java Development Kit) for your operating system.

▶ **3.** Download the installation file to your computer.

The installation file will be stored in an archive file. At the time of this writing the Java JDK for Windows x64 is stored in the self-extracting archive file jdk-8u20-windows-x64.exe; the file for Windowx x86 is jdk-8u20-windows-i586.exe, and for the Mac OS X x64 operating system the file is jdk-8u20-macosx-x64.dmg.

▶ **4.** Run the installation file and install the Java JDK to the folder location of your choice.

Once you've completed the installation, you should verify that Java has been installed on your computer.

To verify the Java installation:

▶ **1.** Open a Command Prompt window on your PC or a Terminal window on your Macintosh.

▶ **2.** Type **java –version** on the command line and press **Enter**.

Trouble? Be sure to type the space after java.

If Java is installed, the Java version will be displayed as shown in Figure E-1 (note that your version number may differ).

Figure E-1 | **Validating Java is installed**

```
C:\>java -version
java version "1.8.0_05"
Java(TM) SE Runtime Environment (build 1.8.0_05-b13)
Java HotSpot(TM) 64-Bit Server VM (build 25.5-b02, mixed mode)

C:\>
```

Once you have verified that Java has been installed, you can download and install Saxon.

Installing Saxon

At the time of this writing the free version of Saxon is the Home Edition version, Saxon-HE 9.5. If you wish to purchase and install a commercial version, modify the steps that follow to download the commercial version of your choice.

To download Saxon-HE:

1. Go to the Saxon download page at *http://sourceforge.net/projects/saxon/files/*
2. Click the link for the **Saxon-HE** download page.
3. Click the link for the latest version of Saxon-HE.
4. Download the archive file for the latest version of Saxon-HE.

   At the time of this writing the archive file for the latest version is SaxonHE9-5-1-5j.zip.
5. Open the archive file and extract all of the files to a folder of your choice (for example, c:/saxon).

Before proceeding, you need to test whether you have correctly extracted the Saxon files to your folder. Do the following test to verify the Saxon files.

To test the Saxon files:

1. Open a Command Prompt window or a Terminal window in the folder containing the Saxon files.
2. Type **java net.sf.saxon.Query -t -qs:current-date()** on the command line and press **Enter**.

   Saxon returns the current date and time and the amount of execution time required to run the query. See Figure E-2.

| Figure E-2 | Result of testing for Saxon files |

```
C:\saxon>java net.sf.saxon.Query -t -qs:current-date()
Saxon-HE 9.5.1.5J from Saxonica
Java version 1.8.0_05
Analyzing query from {current-date()}
Analysis time: 163.071282 milliseconds
<?xml version="1.0" encoding="UTF-8"?>2017-07-09-06:00Execution time: 42.430584ms
Memory used: 6380976

C:\saxon>
```

Next, you'll set up Saxon so that it can be run from within any folder.

Setting the CLASSPATH Variable

If you want to run Saxon from different folders, you have to add the Saxon folder to the CLASSPATH environmental variable so that your operating system knows where to find the Saxon .jar file. One way to specify this information is to include the following parameter in any Saxon query or transformation run from the command line:

```
-cp path
```

where *path* is the absolute path to the Saxon folder on your computer. For example, the statement

```
java -cp c:\saxon\saxon9he.jar net.sf.saxon.Query -t
-qs:current-date()
```

returns the current date and time using the Saxon processor no matter what folder is active in the Command Prompt window, assuming the Saxon .jar file is saxon9he.jar located in the c:\saxon folder.

If you don't want to add the **-cp** *path* parameter to every Saxon command, you can modify the CLASSPATH environment variable to the operating system.

To add the CLASSPATH environment variable to Windows:

▶ **1.** Open the Windows Control Panel.

▶ **2.** Click **System and Security** and then **System** to open the System dialog box containing properties for your Windows operating system.

▶ **3.** Click **Advanced system settings** to open the System Properties dialog box.

▶ **4.** Click the **Environment Variables** button to open the Environment Variables dialog box.

▶ **5.** In the System Variables list, select the **CLASSPATH** variable if it exists and select **Edit**. If it does not already exist in the list, then select **New**.

▶ **6.** In the New System Variable dialog box, enter **CLASSPATH** in the Variable name box.

▶ **7.** In the Edit System Variable dialog box, verify that CLASSPATH has already been entered for the variable name.

▶ **8.** In the Variable value box, enter the path and filename of the .jar file used by Saxon. For example, if you are running Saxon-HE9 installed in the c:\saxon folder you will want to enter the value **c:\saxon\saxon9he.jar**. If there is a different path and .jar file already listed in the Variable value box, type a semicolon followed by the path and filename of your Saxon .jar file.

▶ **9.** Click the **OK** button several times to exit the System dialog box and then close the Control Panel.

Another solution that does not involve modifying the CLASSPATH environment variable is to move the Saxon .jar file to the library subfolder of the folder containing your Java files.

- On the Windows operating system, add the Saxon .jar files to the lib subfolder of the folder where you installed Java.
- On the Mac OSX system, add the Saxon .jar files to the /System/Library/Java/ Extensions folder.

Once you have modified the CLASSPATH environment variable or you have moved the Saxon .jar file to your Java library subfolder, you should test Saxon to verify that it can be run from any folder.

To test Saxon within any folder:

▶ **1.** Open a Command Prompt window or a Terminal window in any folder other than a folder containing your Saxon .jar file.

▶ **2.** Enter **java net.sf.saxon.Query –t –qs:current-date()** on the command line and press **Enter**.

Verify that Saxon returns the current date and time.

Running Transformations from the Command Line

Once you have Java and Saxon installed and available from the command line, you can run your XSLT transformations on your style sheets and source documents. For simple transformations, run the command

```
java net.sf.saxon.Transform -s:source -xsl:stylesheet -o:output
```

where *source, stylesheet*, and *output* are the source XML file, the XSLT style sheet, and the output file, respectively.

For the .NET platform, the command is simply

```
Transform -s:source -xsl:stylesheet -o:output
```

As long as you list the source and the style sheet files before the output document, you can leave out parameter flags and simply enter

```
java net.sf.saxon.Transform source stylesheet -o:output
```

or, for the .NET platform

```
Transform source stylesheet -o:output
```

The following table lists the Saxon options that can be applied to Saxon transformation command line:

Option	Description
`-a[:(on|off)]`	Uses the xml-stylesheet processing instruction in the source document to identify the stylesheet to be used. The stylesheet argument must not be present on the command line
`-catalog:filenames`	Defines the catalogs to define how public identifiers and system identifiers (URIs) used in a source document, stylesheet, or schema are to be redirected, typically to resources available locally, where `filenames` is either a filename or a list of filenames separated by semicolons
`-config:filename`	Indicates that configuration information should be taken from the supplied configuration file. Any options supplied on the command line override options specified in the configuration file
`-cr:classname`	Uses the specified CollectionURIResolver in `classname` to process collection URIs passed to the `collection()` function
`-dtd:(on|off|recover)`	Sets DTD validation where `off` (the default) suppresses DTD validation, `recover` performs DTD validation but treats the error as non-fatal if it fails, and on performs DTD validation and rejects the document if it fails
`-expand:(on|off)`	Determines whether to expand default values defined in the DTD or schema to the transformation

Option	Description
-explain[:*filename*]	Displays an execution plan for the stylesheet stored in *filename*
-ext:(on|off)	Determines whether to suppress calls on dynamically loaded external Java functions
-im:*modename*	Selects the initial mode for the transformation
-init:*initializer*	Provides the value of a user-supplied class that implements the interface net.sf.saxon
-it:*template*	Selects the initial named template to be executed
-l[:(on|off)]	Causes line and column numbers to be maintained for source documents; these are accessible using the extension functions saxon:line-number() and saxon:column-number()
-m:*classname*	Uses the specified Receiver *classname* to process the output from xsl:message, where the class must implement the net.sf.saxon.event.Receiver class
-now:*yyyy-mm-ddThh:mm:ss+hh:mm*	Sets the value of current-dateTime() (and implicit-timezone()) for the transformation
-o:*filename*	Sends output from the transformation to *filename*
-opt:0...10	Sets optimization level of the transformation from 0 (no optimization) to 10 (full optimization)
-or:*classname*	Uses the specified OutputURIResolver to process output URIs appearing in the href attribute of xsl:result-document. The OutputURIResolver is a user-defined class that implements the net.sf.saxon.OutputURIResolver interface
-outval:(recover|fatal)	Specifies whether a validation error is fatal or treated as a warning
-p[:(on|off)]	Uses the PTreeURIResolver. This option is available in Saxon-PE and Saxon-EE only. It cannot be used in conjunction with the -r option, and it automatically switches on the -u and -sa options. The effect is twofold. Firstly, Saxon-specific file extensions are recognized in URIs (including the URI of the source document on the command line). Currently, the only Saxon-specific file extension is .ptree, which indicates that the source document is supplied in the form of a Saxon PTree. This is a binary representation of an XML document, designed for speed of loading. Secondly, Saxon-specific query parameters are recognized in a URI. Currently, the only query parameter that is recognized is val, which may take the values strict, lax, or strip. For example, source.xml?val=strict loads a document with strict schema validation
-quit:(on|off)	Specifies whether or not to quit the Java virtual machine and returns an exit code if a failure occurs
-r:*classname*	Uses the specified URIResolver in *classname* to process all URIs
-repeat:*integer*	Performs the transformation n times, where n is the specified *integer*
-s:*filename*	Identifies the source file or directory (mandatory unless the -it option is used)
-sa	Invokes a schema-aware transformation (when supported by the Saxon version)
-strip:(all|none|ignorable)	Specifies what white space is to be stripped from source documents (applies both to the principal source document and to any documents loaded, for example, using the document() function)
-t	Displays version and timing information
-T[:*classname*]	Displays stylesheet tracing information and switches line numbering on for the source document; if *classname* is specified, it is a user-defined class, which must implement net.sf.saxon.trace.TraceListener; if *classname* is omitted, a system-supplied trace listener is used

Option	Description
`-threads:n`	Controls the number of threads (*n*) used to process the files in the directory (used only when the -s option specifies a directory)
`-TJ`	Switches on tracing of the binding of calls to external Java methods
`-TP:filename`	Causes trace profile information to be set to the specified `filename`
`-traceout:filename`	Indicates that the output of the `trace()` function should be directed to a specified `filename`
`-tree:` `(tiny|linked|tinyc)`	Selects the implementation of the internal tree model where `tiny` selects the "tiny tree" model (the default), `linked` selects the linked tree model, and `tinyc` selects the "condensed tiny tree" model
`-u`	Indicates that the names of the source document and the stylesheet document are URLs; otherwise, they are taken as file-names, unless they start with "http:" or "file:", in which case they are taken as URLs
`-val[:(strict|lax)]`	Requests schema-based validation of the source file and of any files read using the `document()` or similar functions; validation is available only with Saxon-EE, and this flag automatically switches on the -sa option (specify `-val` or `-val:strict` to request strict validation, or `-val:lax` for lax validation)
`-versionmsg:(on|off)`	Specifies whether or not to suppress version warnings
`-warnings:` `(silent|recover|fatal)`	Indicates the policy for handling recoverable errors in the stylesheet where `silent` means recover silently, `recover` means recover after writing a warning message to the system error output, and `fatal` means signal the error and do not attempt recovery
`-x:classname`	Uses specified SAX parser for source file and any files loaded using the `document()` function using `classname`
`-xi:(on|off)`	Specifies whether or not to apply XInclude processing to all input XML documents (including schema and stylesheet modules as well as source documents)
`-xmlversion:(1.0|1.1)`	Specifies the XML version of the source document
`-xsd:file1;file2;file3..`	Loads additional schema documents as specified by `file1`, `file2, file3`, …
`-xsdversion:(1.0|1.1)`	Specifies the XML Schema version
`-xsiloc:(on|off)`	Specifies whether or not to load any schema documents referenced in xsi:schemaLocation and xsi:noNamespaceSchemaLocation attributes in the instance document
`-xsl:filename`	Specifies the file containing the principal stylesheet module
`-xsltversion:(2.0|3.0)`	Determines whether an XSLT 2.0 processor or XSLT 3.0 processor is to be used. By default the value is taken from the version attribute of the xsl:stylesheet element
`-y:classname`	Uses the SAX parser specified by `classname` for stylesheet file, including any loaded using xsl:include or xsl:import
`-feature:value`	Sets a feature defined in the Configuration interface where the names of features are defined in the Javadoc for class FeatureKeys
`-?`	Displays the Saxon command syntax

In addition to the listed built-in parameters, user-defined parameters can be added using the name/value pair

`name=value`

where `name` is the name of the parameter from the style sheet and `value` is the value to be passed to the parameter.

Running Queries from the Command Line

XQuery queries are run using the command line

```
java net.sf.saxon.Query [options] -q:queryfile [params...]
```

where *options* are the query options, *queryfile* is the name of the XQuery file, and *params* are user-defined query parameters.

On the .NET platform, the command is simply

```
Query [options] -q:queryfile [params...]
```

If a source file and an output document is specified, the general form is

```
java net.sf.saxon.Query [options] -s:source -o:output -q:queryfile
[params...]
```

where source is the XML source file and output contains the output from the query. On the .NET platform the equivalent command is

```
Query [options] -s:source -o:output -q:queryfile [params...]
```

The options must come first, and then the user-defined parameters. If the last option before *params* has no leading hyphen and option letter, then it is recognized as the -q option.

The following table lists the XQuery options supported by Saxon in the command line mode:

Option	Description
-backup:(on|off)	Specifies whether or not to enable a backup; when backup is enabled, any file that is updated by the query will be preserved in its original state by renaming it, adding ".bak" to the original filename; if backup is disabled, updated files will be silently overwritten
-catalog:*filenames*	Lists the files that are OASIS XML catalogs and are used to define how public identifiers and system identifiers (URIs) are used in a source document
-config:*filename*	Indicates that configuration information should be taken from the supplied *filename*
-cr:*classname*	Uses the specified CollectionURIResolver in *classname* to process collection URIs passed to the collection() function
-dtd:(off|recover|on)	Sets DTD validation where off (the default) suppresses DTD validation, recover performs DTD validation but treats the error as non-fatal if it fails, and on performs DTD validation and rejects the document if it fails
-expand:(on|off)	Determines whether to expand default values defined in the DTD or schema to the transformation
-explain[:*filename*]	Displays an execution plan for the stylesheet stored in *filename*
-ext:(on|off)	Determines whether to suppress calls on dynamically loaded external Java functions
-im:*modename*	Selects the initial mode for the transformation
-init:*initializer*	Provides the value of a user-supplied class that implements the interface net.sf.saxon
-it:*template*	Selects the initial named template to be executed
-l[:(on|off)]	Causes line and column numbers to be maintained for source documents; these are accessible using the extension functions saxon:line-number() and saxon:column-number()

Option	Description
`-mr:classname`	Uses the specified ModuleURIReceiver `classname` to process the output from xsl:message, where the class must implement the net. sf.saxon.event.Receiver class
`-o:filename`	Sends output from the transformation to `filename`
`-opt:0...10`	Sets optimization level of the transformation from 0 (no optimization) to 10 (full optimization)
`-outval:(recover|fatal)`	Specifies whether a validation error is fatal or treated as a warning
`-p[:(on|off)]`	Uses the PTreeURIResolver. This option is available in Saxon-PE and Saxon-EE only. It cannot be used in conjunction with the -r option, and it automatically switches on the -u and -sa options. The effect is twofold. Firstly, Saxon-specific file extensions are recognized in URIs (including the URI of the source document on the command line). Currently, the only Saxon-specific file extension is .ptree, which indicates that the source document is supplied in the form of a Saxon PTree. This is a binary representation of an XML document, designed for speed of loading. Secondly, Saxon-specific query parameters are recognized in a URI. Currently, the only query parameter that is recognized is val, which may take the values strict, lax, or strip. For example, source.xml?val=strict loads a document with strict schema validation
`-pipe:(push|pull)`	Executes query internally in `push` (default) or `pull` mode
`-projection:(on|off)`	Specifies whether or not to use document projection to analyze a query to determine what parts of a document it can potentially access and to leave out those parts of the tree that cannot make any difference to the result of the query
`-q:queryfile`	Identifies the file containing the query
`-qs:querystring`	Provides the `querystring` to allow the query to be specified on the command line
`-quit:(on|off)`	Specifies whether or not to quit the Java virtual machine and returns an exit code if a failure occurs
`-qversion:(1.0|3.0)`	Specifies the version of the XQuery language to be applied to the query
`-r:classname`	Uses the specified URIResolver in `classname` to process all URIs
`-repeat:integer`	Performs the transformation n times, where n is the specified `integer`
`-s:filename`	Identifies the source file or directory (mandatory unless the -it option is used)
`-sa`	Invokes a schema-aware transformation (when supported by the Saxon version)
`-strip:(all|none|ignorable)`	Specifies what white space is to be stripped from source documents (applies both to the principal source document and to any documents loaded, for example, using the `document()` function)
`-t`	Displays version and timing information
`-T[:classname]`	Displays stylesheet tracing information and switches line numbering on for the source document; if `classname` is specified, it is a user-defined class, which must implement net.sf.saxon.trace. TraceListener; if `classname` is omitted, a system-supplied trace listener is used
`-TJ`	Switches on tracing of the binding of calls to external Java methods

Option	Description
`-traceout:filename`	Indicates that the output of the `trace()` function should be directed to a specified `filename`
`-tree:(tiny|linked|tinyc)`	Selects the implementation of the internal tree model where `tiny` selects the "tiny tree" model (the default), `linked` selects the linked tree model, and `tinyc` selects the "condensed tiny tree" model
`-u`	Indicates that the names of the source document and the stylesheet document are URLs; otherwise, they are taken as file-names, unless they start with "http:" or "file:", in which case they are taken as URLs
`-update:(on|off|discard)`	Indicates whether XQuery Update syntax is accepted
`-val[:(strict|lax)]`	Requests schema-based validation of the source file and of any files read using the `document()` or similar functions; validation is available only with Saxon-EE, and this flag automatically switches on the -sa option (specify `-val` or `-val:strict` to request strict validation, or `-val:lax` for lax validation)
`-wrap`	Wraps the result sequence in an XML element structure that indicates the type of each node or atomic value in the query result
`-x:classname`	Uses specified SAX parser for source file and any files loaded using the `document()` function using `classname`
`-xi:(on|off)`	Specifies whether or not to apply XInclude processing to all input XML documents (including schema and stylesheet modules as well as source documents)
`-xmlversion:(1.0|1.1)`	Specifies the XML version of the source document
`-xsd:file1;file2;file3..`	Loads additional schema documents as specified by `file1`, `file2`, `file3`, ...
`-xsdversion:(1.0|1.1)`	Specifies the XML Schema version
`-xsiloc:(on|off)`	Specifies whether or not to load any schema documents referenced in xsi:schemaLocation and xsi:noNamespaceSchemaLocation attributes in the instance document
`-feature:value`	Sets a feature defined in the Configuration interface where the names of features are defined in the Javadoc for class FeatureKeys
`-?`	Displays the Saxon command syntax

User-defined parameters are added to the query using the general form

`name=value`

where `name` is the name of the parameter from the style sheet and `value` is the value to be passed to the parameter.

APPENDIX **F**

Understanding Regular Expressions

A regular expression is a text string that defines a character pattern. One use of regular expressions is **pattern matching**, in which a text string is tested to see whether it matches the pattern defined by a regular expression. For example, with extended postal codes or zip codes, you might create a regular expression that describes the pattern of five digits followed by a hyphen and another four digits. Pattern matching is just one use of regular expressions. They can also be used to extract substrings, insert new text, or replace old text. The greatest advantage of regular expressions is that the code is compact and powerful, so that what might take several lines of code using other text string methods can be done in a single line with a regular expression. However, with this power comes complexity: the syntax of regular expressions can be intimidating to new programmers, especially because they take time and practice to master.

Writing a Regular Expression

Regular expressions have the general syntax

`/pattern/modifiers`

where `pattern` is the text string of the regular expression and `modifiers` defines how the regular expression pattern should be applied. For example, the following expression contains the regular expression pattern \b\w+\b followed by the g modifier:

`/\b\w+\b/g`

You'll explore what each of these characters means in the sections that follow.

Matching a Substring

The most basic regular expression consists of a string of characters specified as

`/chars/`

where `chars` is the text of the substring. For example, the regular expression

`/Audio/`

matches any text string containing the sequence of characters "Audio". Thus, the text string "Audio Studio" would be matched by this regular expression; however, because regular expressions are case sensitive, the text string "audio studio" would not be matched.

Regular Expression Modifiers

To change a regular expression so that it matches patterns regardless of case, you add a modifier to the regular expression. The modifier to make the expression insensitive to case (so that upper- and lowercase letters are treated the same) is the i character, added to the regular expression as

`/pattern/i`

Thus, the regular expression

`/Audio/i`

would match the text string "audio studio". By default, a regular expression returns only the first occurrence of a specified pattern. To allow a global search for all pattern matches, you append the regular expression with the g modifier as follows:

`/pattern/g`

Finally, to apply both modifiers at the same time, you append both the i and g modifiers to the regular expression as follows:

`/pattern/ig`

Therefore, the expression

`/Audio/ig`

would return two matches from the text "Audio Studio for audiophiles".

Defining Character Positions

The examples you've seen so far are very basic because they involve matching only specified characters found anywhere within a text string. The true power—and complexity— of regular expressions comes with the introduction of special characters that allow you to match text strings based on the type, content, and placement of those characters. The first such characters you will consider are positioning characters. The four positioning characters are described in Figure F-1.

Figure F-1	Character positions

Character	Description	Regular Expression	Matches
^	start of text string	/^audio/	Any text string starting with "audio"
$	end of text string	/audio$/	Any text string ending with "audio"
\b	word boundary	/\baudio/	Any word beginning with "audio"
\B	no word boundary	/\Baudio\B/	Any word containing "audio" but not at the beginning or end of the word

Regular expressions recognize the beginning and end of a text string, indicated by the ^ and $ characters, respectively. The following pattern uses the ^ character to mark the start of the text string:

```
/^audio/
```

Any text string that starts with the characters "audio" is matched by this regular expression; however, a text string such as "great audio", in which the characters "audio" are not at the start of the text string, would not be matched. In the same way, the end of the text string is indicated by the $ character; thus, the following regular expression matches only text strings that end with "audio":

```
/audio$/
```

The ^ and $ characters are often used together to define a pattern for a complete text string. For example, the following pattern matches only the text string "audio" and nothing else:

```
/^audio$/
```

The other positioning characters are used to locate words within a text string. The term *word* has a special meaning in regular expressions. **Words** are composed of word characters, where a **word character** is any letter, number, or underscore. Symbols such as *, &, and – are not considered word characters, nor are spaces, periods, or tabs. Thus, "R2D2" is considered a single word, but "R2D2&C3PO" is considered two words, with the & symbol acting as a boundary between the words. In a regular expression, the presence of a word boundary is indicated with the \b symbol. Thus, the following pattern matches any word that starts with the characters "art", but does not match words that do not start with these characters, such as "dart":

```
/\bart/
```

The \b symbol can also indicate a word boundary at the end of a word. Thus, the following regular expression matches words such as "dart" and "heart", but not "artist":

```
/art\b/
```

If you place the \b symbol at both the beginning and the end of a pattern, you define a complete word. The following expression matches only the word "art" but no other word:

```
/\bart\b/
```

In some cases, you want to match substrings only within words. In these situations, you use the \B symbol, which indicates the absence of a word boundary. The following regular expression:

```
/\Bart\B/
```

matches the substring "art" only when it occurs inside of a word such as "hearts" or "darts", but not next to a word boundary, as in "artist" or "smart".

Defining Character Types and Character Classes

Another class of regular expression characters indicates the type of character. The three general types of characters are word characters, digits (numbers 0 to 9), and white space characters (blank spaces, tabs, and new lines). Figure F-2 describes the regular expression symbols for these character types.

| Figure F-2 | Character types | | |

Character	Description	Regular Expression	Matches
\d	a digit (from 0 to 9)	/\dth/	Any digit followed by "th"
\D	a non-digit	/\Dth/	Any non-digit character followed by "th"
\w	a word character (an upper- or lowercase letter, a digit, or an underscore)	/\w\w/	Any two consecutive word characters
\W	a non-word character	/\W\W/	Any two consecutive non-word characters
\s	a white space character (a blank space, tab, new line, carriage return, or form feed)	/\d\s\s\d/	A digit followed by two spaces and then another digit
\S	a non-whitespace character	/\d\S\S\d/	A digit followed by two non-whitespace characters and then another digit
.	any character	/.../	Any three characters

For example, a digit is represented by the \d symbol. To match any occurrence of a single digit, you use the regular expression

    /\d/

This expression would find matches in such text strings as "105", "6", or "U2" because they all contain an instance of at least one single digit. If you want to match several consecutive digits, you can simply repeat the \d symbol. The following regular expression matches three consecutive digits:

    /\d\d\d/

and thus would match text strings such as "105" or "EX1250", but not "27" or "E2". If you wanted to limit matches only to words consisting of three-digit numbers, you could use the \b symbol to mark the boundaries around the digits. Thus, the following pattern matches words consisting of five-digit numbers such as "52145" or "91573":

    /\b\d\d\d\d\d\b/

Similarly, the following pattern matches only an entire text string that consists of a five-digit number and no other characters, as you would see in a five-digit postal code:

    /^\d\d\d\d\d$/

For more general character matching, use the \w symbol, which matches any word character, or the \s symbol, which matches any white space character such as a blank space, tab, or line return.

Using Character Classes

No character type matches only letters. However, you can specify a collection of characters known as a character class to limit a regular expression to a select group of characters. The syntax to define a character class is

```
[chars]
```

where *chars* is characters in the class. For example, the following regular expression matches the occurrence of any vowel found within a text string:

```
/[aeiou]/g
```

Character classes can also be created for characters that don't match a class description using the following expression:

```
[^chars]
```

> **TIP**
>
> The ^ symbol used to indicate the negative of a character set is the same symbol used to mark the beginning of a text string.

Thus, the following regular expression matches all of the characters in a text string that are not vowels:

```
/[^aeiou]/g
```

Character sets have a sequential order. You can take advantage of this fact to create character classes that cover ranges of characters. For example, the following expression defines a class for all lowercase letters:

```
[a-z]
```

For uppercase letters, you would use

```
[A-Z]
```

and for both uppercase and lowercase letters, you would use

```
[a-zA-Z]
```

You can continue to add ranges of characters to a character class. The following character class matches only uppercase and lowercase letters and digits:

```
[0-9a-zA-Z]
```

Figure F-3 summarizes the syntax for creating regular expression character classes.

Figure F-3	Character classes

Class	Description	Regular Expression	Matches
[chars]	class based on the characters listed in chars	/[tap]/	t, a, or p
[^chars]	class based on the characters not listed in chars	/[tap]/	any character that is not t, a, or p
[char1-charN]	class based on characters from char1 up through charN	/[a-m]/	any letter from a up through m
[^char1-charN]	class based on character not listed from char1 up through charN	/[^a-m]/	any character that is not a letter up through m
[a-z]	all lowercase letters	/[a-z][a-z]/	two consecutive lowercase letters
[A-Z]	all uppercase letters	/[A-Z][A-Z]/	two consecutive uppercase letters
[a-zA-Z]	all letters	/[a-zA-Z][a-zA-Z]/	two consecutive letters
[0-9]	all digits	/[1][0-9]/	the numbers 10 through 19
[0-9a-zA-Z]	all digits and letters	/[0-9a-zA-Z][0-9a-zA-Z]/	any two consecutive letters or numbers

Specifying Character Repetition

The regular expression symbols you've seen so far have all applied to single characters. Regular expressions can also include symbols that indicate the number of times to repeat a particular character. To specify the exact number of times to repeat a character, you append the character with the symbol

$\{n\}$

where n is the number of times to repeat the character. For example, to specify that a text string should contain only five digits—as in a postal code—you could use either

/^\d\d\d\d\d$/

or the more compact form

/^\d{5}$/

For more general repetitions, you can use the symbol * for 0 or more repetitions, + for 1 or more repetitions, or ? for 0 repetitions or 1 repetition. Figure F-4 describes these and other repetition characters supported by regular expressions.

Figure F-4	Repetition characters

Character	Description	Regular Expression	Matches
*	repeat 0 or more times	/\s*/	0 or more consecutive white space characters
+	repeat 1 or more times	/\s+/	1 or more consecutive white space characters
?	repeat 0 or 1 time	/colou?r/	color or colour
{n}	repeat exactly n times	/\d{9}/	a 9-digit number
{n,}	repeat at least n times	/\d{9,}/	a number with at least 9 digits
{n,m}	repeat at least n times but no more than m times	/\d{5,9}/	a number with 5 to 9 digits

Using Escape Sequences

Many commonly used characters are reserved by the regular expression language. The forward slash character (/) is reserved to mark the literal beginning and end of a regular expression. The ?, +, and * characters are used to specify the number of times a character can be repeated. But what if you need to use one of these characters in a regular expression? For example, how would you create a regular expression matching the date pattern *mm/dd/yyyy* when the / character is already used to mark the boundaries of the regular expression?

In these cases, you use an escape sequence. An **escape sequence** is a special command inside a regular expression that tells the JavaScript interpreter not to interpret what follows as a character. In the regular expression language, escape sequences are marked by the backslash character (\\). You have been learning about escape sequences for several pages now—for example, you saw that the characters \\d represent a numeric digit, while d alone simply represents the letter d. The \\ character can also be applied to reserved characters to indicate their use in a regular expression. For example, the escape sequence \\$ represents the $ character, while the escape sequence \\\\ represents a single \\ character. Figure F-5 provides a list of escape sequences for other special characters.

Figure F-5	Escape sequences

Escape Sequence	Represents	Regular Expression	Matches
\/	the / character	/\d\/\d/	A digit followed by "/" followed by another digit
\\	the \ character	/\d\\\d/	A digit followed by "\" followed by another digit
\.	the . character	/\d\.\d\d/	A digit followed by "." followed by two more digits
*	the * character	/[a-z]{4}*/	Four lowercase letters followed by "*"
\+	the + character	/\d\+\d/	A digit followed by "+" followed by another digit
\?	the ? character	/[a-z]{5}\?/	Five lowercase letters followed by "?"
|	the | character	/a\\|b/	The letter "a" followed by "|" and then "b"
\(\)	the (and) characters	/\(\d{3}\)/	Three digits enclosed within a set of parentheses
\{ \}	the { and } characters	/\{[a-z]{4}\}/	Four lowercase letters enclosed within curly braces
\^	the ^ character	/\d+\^\d/	One or more digits followed by "^" followed by a digit
\$	the $ character	/\$\d{2}\.\d{2}/	Currency value starting with a "$" followed by two digits, a decimal point, and then two more digits
\n	a new line	/\n/	An occurrence of a new line
\r	a carriage return	/\r/	An occurrence of a carriage return
\t	a tab	/\t/	An occurrence of a tab

Specifying Alternate Patterns and Grouping

In some regular expressions, you may want to define two possible patterns for the same text string. You can do this by joining different patterns using the | character. The general form is

    pattern1|pattern2

where `pattern1` and `pattern2` are two distinct patterns. For example, the expression

    /^\d{5}$|^$/

matches a text string that either contains only five digits or is empty. The regular expression pattern

    /Mr\.|Mrs\.|Miss/

matches "Mr.", "Mrs.", or "Miss".

Another useful technique in regular expressions is to group character symbols. Once you create a group, the symbols within that group can be treated as a single unit. The syntax to create a group is

    (pattern)

where `pattern` is a regular expression pattern. For example, a phone number might be entered with or without an area code. The pattern for a phone number without an area code, matching such numbers as 555-1234, is

    /^\d{3}-\d{4}$/

If an area code is included in the format 800-555-1234, the pattern is

    /^\d{3}-\d{3}-\d{4}$/

To allow the area code to be added, you place it within a group and use the ? repetition character applied to the entire area code group, resulting in the following regular expression:

    /^(\d{3}-)?\d{3}-\d{4}$/

which matches either 555-1234 or 800-555-1234.

GLOSSARY/INDEX